Veterinary Forensic Medicine and Forensic Sciences

Veterinary Forensic Medicine and Forensic Sciences

Edited by
Jason H. Byrd
Patricia Norris
Nancy Bradley-Siemens

CRC Press
Taylor & Francis Group
Boca Raton London New York

CRC Press is an imprint of the
Taylor & Francis Group, an **informa** business

First edition published 2020
by CRC Press
6000 Broken Sound Parkway NW, Suite 300, Boca Raton, FL 33487-2742

and by CRC Press
2 Park Square, Milton Park, Abingdon, Oxon, OX14 4RN

CRC Press is an imprint of Taylor & Francis Group, LLC

ISBN: 978-1-138-56372-8 (hbk)
ISBN: 978-1-315-12191-8 (ebk)

CONTENTS

FOREWORD

Veterinary forensic medicine can be defined as "the application of veterinary knowledge to the purpose of the law" and is a discipline that has expanded greatly in recent years. The speciality bears some similarities to routine diagnosis and treatment of diseases of animals, but veterinary *forensic* medicine is often very different in practice—a point often not fully appreciated by those with a training and background focused on animal health.

"Forensic sciences" is the second part of the title of this book. The term has been used for many decades and refers to the application of various scientific disciplines to criminal and civil legal investigation. Increasingly, however, the practice of forensic science and specific aspects of veterinary forensic medicine are being used in respect of non-legal activities such as insurance claims, appearances at tribunals, inquiries, environmental impact assessments, and allegations of professional misconduct. It is the forensic *method* that is important rather than the reason why it is being employed.

The origins of what we would now consider to be veterinary forensic medicine are very difficult to unearth. The subject was associated in part with the evolution of human forensic medicine and in some measure with the growth and maturation of the veterinary profession. As far as the former is concerned, some of the earliest records of a medical input into legal investigations came from China, where those with knowledge of health and disease, whether in humans or animals, were often involved in claims for compensation for infirmity or death. The Egyptian Papyrus of Kahun (1900 BCE) and Vedic literature in ancient India are generally accepted as providing some of the first written records of the practice of veterinary medicine. There is little evidence that early "forensic" investigations were used to investigate cruelty to animals, as opposed to damage caused to them, and yet concern about living things and how they are treated goes back many centuries. The world's great religions provided teaching on this topic: thus, both the Bible and the Sayings of the Prophet Mohammed instruct believers not to take young birds from the wild but, instead, to leave them with their mother—possibly one of the earliest examples of species protection!

A dark period as far as respecting the welfare of animals was concerned occurred during thirteenth to sixteenth centuries when it was the practice in many European countries to put animals on trial and, often, to punish them for their perceived misdemenours. E.P. Evans' book on this subject *The Criminal Prosecution and Capital Punishment of Animals* (1906) recounts that distressing period, as have more recent papers. The procedure was not just a mediaeval aberration. In 1916, an elephant named Mary murdered her trainer and was hanged in Tennessee, in the United States, using a crane, and reports appear periodically of similar incidents elsewhere.

Much of the history of forensic medicine, whether relating to humans or animals, is buried in records and writings other than those in English. Such linguistic disparity means that there are still gaps in our deeply-Westernised knowledge of what has been advanced—and is sometimes still used—in other parts of the world. The language employed in legal proceedings is very relevant. In the fifteenth century, in Europe, Latin was used almost exclusively in legislation; in some countries, in order to assist the court, "Masters of Grammar" were called to interpret this when clarification was needed. Six centuries later, the most commonly used languages in the world are, in order, Mandarin (955 million native speakers), Spanish (405 million), English (360 million), Hindi (310 million), and Arabic (295 million native speakers). Many other tongues are spoken by smaller numbers of people—and understood by few outsiders—and yet each of these is used to conduct legal proceedings in that particular country or region. Some jurisdictions have their own rules as to what is acceptable in court. In Hungary, for example, forensic expert work, including the investigation of wildlife crime, may only be performed by a person who meets all the criteria specifically set for the given field of expertise. This is not dissimilar to the Daubert standard in the United States regarding the admissibility of expert witness testimony in federal cases.

It was not until the Middle Ages that the first attempts to organise and regulate the practice of treating animals took place in Europe. The focus was generally on horses because of their economic significance. Prior to the establishment of veterinary schools in Europe, farriers (blacksmiths) combined the shoeing of horses with "horse doctoring." In 1356, the Lord Mayor of London, concerned at the poor standard of care given to horses, asked all farriers operating within a 7-mile radius of the city of London to form a "fellowship" to regulate and improve their practices.

The first veterinary college in Europe was founded in Lyon, France, in 1762 by Claude Bourgelat. In Britain, the physician James Clark (1737–1819) argued for the training of persons specifically for the treatment of livestock, a move that was strongly endorsed by John Hunter (1728–1793)—see later. In 1790, through the campaigning of Granville Penn (grandson of William Penn, founder of the colony of Pennsylvania in the United States), Benoit Vial de St. Bel travelled from France to become head of the newly established London Veterinary School, now the Royal Veterinary College. The first veterinary schools were established in the early nineteenth century in Boston, New York, and Philadelphia.

Returning to human forensic medicine, *postmortem* examinations (autopsies) for legal purposes were performed in Italy and Germany from about the thirteenth century. The use of scientific knowledge in legal proceedings in Europe gradually found favour in the late Middle Ages because of the prevalence then of poisoning. Diagnosis was not easy because the symptoms and clinical signs were often similar to those of many infectious diseases. It was not until the beginning of the nineteenth century that the first steps were made to demonstrate the use of poison by analysing the cadaver for toxic substances.

Medical evidence from physicians and surgeons began to be admitted at trials in England in the seventeenth and eighteenth centuries, but standards were poor and there was no specific regulation. In the late 1800s, deficiencies in the British system began to be rectified. An important role was played by the famous Hunter brothers, William and John, each of whom contributed to the discipline by means of medical research, writing, and lecturing. For instance, William Hunter (1783) wrote an important paper about the signs of murder in "bastard" children—that is, children born out of wedlock. John Hunter (see earlier) had an absorbing interest in what would now be called "comparative medicine" or "One Health." He produced lecture notes and essays describing improved methods for dissection of humans and for the diagnosis of disease. He also gave evidence in legal cases, notably in the trial for murder of Captain John Donellan in March 1781, where he appeared as the medical witness for the defence. Hunter's caution in respect to his views were ridiculed and essentially overridden by the judge and, instead, "more emphatic, dogmatic, and unscientifically-based evidence of the other doctors"* held sway. As a result, John Donellan was executed. Hunter was badly shaken by this ordeal; he told his students "A poor devil was lately hanged at Warwick upon no other testimony than that of physical men [physicians] whose first experiments were made on this occasion." The "experiments" referred to by Hunter were poorly-performed toxicological studies and necropsies carried out on dogs by the doctors called by the prosecution.

It was George Edward Male who wrote the first reliable text, *Epitome of Juridical or Forensic Medicine: for the Use of Medical Men, Coroners and Barristers*, in 1816. The accolade of "the father of modern forensic science" is, however, often given to Alexandre Lacassagne, a French physician and criminologist. His better-known assistant, Edmond Locard, was born in Lyon, France in 1877. Locard was awarded a doctorate in medicine and, having an interest in law, sat and passed his bar examination. In 1907, Locard embarked on a journey throughout Europe and the United States in order to meet scientists and to visit crime departments. He returned to Lyon in 1910 and opened the world's first crime investigation laboratory. Locard's most famous published work is undoubtedly the seven-volume *Traité de criminalistique* (Treaty of Criminalistics), in which he explained his

* Davis, B.T. 1974. George Edward Male MD—The father of English Medical Jurisprudence. *Proc. Roy. Soc. Med.* Volume 67.

famous exchange principle: "It is impossible for a criminal to act, especially considering the intensity of a crime, without leaving traces of this presence." That axiom is the basis of forensic science today.

Forensic investigations began to be popularised by authors such as Sir Arthur Conan Doyle (1859–1930), through his portrayal of Sherlock Holmes. Interestingly, Sir Arthur's first published story depicts Holmes in the chemical laboratory of a hospital, projected as one who trusts the power of scientific reasoning and deduction.

The summarised history given above is a reminder that the forensic sciences—and branches of them, such as veterinary forensic medicine—have undergone a long and sometimes tortuous evolution and continue to develop and change.

Terms such as "veterinary forensic medicine" are sometimes seen to be synonymous with animal cruelty investigations, but this is not the case. As we pointed out earlier—and stressed in our book *An Introduction to Veterinary and Comparative Forensic Medicine* (Blackwell, 2007) over a decade ago, the discipline is increasingly concerned with a spectrum of legal and non-legal matters relating to living creatures—amongst them, of course, conservation issues and "wildlife crime." An important landmark in this respect was the establishment by the United States Fish and Wildlife Service (USFWS) in 1989 of a wildlife forensic laboratory in order to provide a service to wildlife law enforcement bodies and others. Similar institutions now exist in many parts of the world.

This book, edited by Jason Byrd, PhD, Patricia Norris, MS, DVM, and Nancy Bradley, DVM, and the contributors to its 20 chapters, reflect the multidisciplinary and interdisciplinary nature of the subject matter. With a strong leaning toward animal welfare law enforcement, it is a new contribution within the context of the United States to the international canon of literature on veterinary forensic science.

Two of the editors are veterinarians; the senior editor, Jason Byrd, is an experienced and internationally recognised entomologist. This is most appropriate. Insects and other invertebrates can provide important evidence in the investigation of crime. Understanding this concept is not new; the ability of maggots to transform and ultimately to destroy a carcass was recognized in the eighteenth century, notably by Linnaeus (1757), but the mechanisms and the genesis of the insects were not then understood.

What might be broadly termed "animal forensics" is a rapidly evolving subject. It will progressively influence not only veterinarians but also specialists from other disciplines who are concerned with the care or management of captive and free-living species. New fields requiring their disparate skills are emerging as a result of concern over climate change, global pollution, and declines in biodiversity. The public are increasingly insistent that action should be taken regarding illegal and irresponsible damage to our planet.

In Book III, Part III of his *De Legibus*, drafted during the last years of the Roman Republic, Marcus Tullius Cicero wrote "*Salus populi suprema lex esto*" (The greatest law is the people's welfare). This is probably correct, and proper, and indeed is reflected in the legislation of many nations. However, litigation relating to animals is also important, and this requires the application of proficient procedures and protocols exercised by suitably trained and qualified persons. We are in no doubt that *Veterinary Forensic Medicine and Forensic Sciences* will help to provide the necessary skills.

John E. Cooper, DTVM, FRCPath, FRSB, Hon FFFLM, FRCVS
RCVS Specialist in Veterinary Pathology
Diplomate, European College of Veterinary Pathologists
Diplomate, European College of Zoological Medicine

Margaret E. Cooper, LLB, FLS, Hon FFFLM, Hon FRCPath
Solicitor (not in private practice)
Wildlife Health, Forensic and Comparative Pathology Services (UK)
Honorary Research Fellow, DICE
The University of Kent
Canterbury, England, United Kingdom

PREFACE

The goals of this book are to provide guidance from a wide breadth of experience from our contributors, to provide reference material for professionals working in the field of veterinary forensic sciences, and to open dialogue between human and animal forensic science professionals. Both areas of forensic science will benefit from enhanced training and collaboration. Veterinary forensic science extends beyond animal abuse cases. It involves the concept of One Health, addresses the human–animal bond, and recognizes and affirms the link between interpersonal violence and animal cruelty. This book also describes and accentuates the importance of veterinarians with training in forensic sciences in situations where the animal is the aggressor, that is, in civil cases. It also stresses the importance of animals and their management as physical evidence in a wide range of criminal cases, not just those involving animal abuse. A veterinarian with training in the forensic sciences should be involved in every criminal or civil case involving an animal because they are the veterinary medical science professional. This book provides a resource for these veterinarians as they seek to assist both the humans and animals involved in these cases.

EDITORS

Jason H. Byrd, PhD, D-ABFE, is a board certified forensic entomologist and Diplomate of the American Board of Forensic Entomology. He is the first person to be elected president of both professional North American forensic entomology associations. Dr. Byrd serves as the associate director of the William R. Maples Center for Forensic Medicine, University of Florida College of Medicine, Gainesville.

Outside of academics, Dr. Byrd serves as an administrative officer within the National Disaster Medical System, Disaster Mortuary Operational Response Team, Region IV. He also serves as the logistics chief for the Florida Emergency Mortuary Operations Response System. He is currently a subject editor for the *Journal of Medical Entomology*, and has published numerous scientific articles on the use and application of entomological evidence in legal investigations. Dr. Byrd has combined his formal academic training in entomology and forensic science to serve as a consultant and educator in both criminal and civil legal investigations throughout the United States and internationally. Dr. Byrd specializes in the education of law enforcement officials, medical examiners, coroners, attorneys, and other death investigators on the use and applicability of arthropods in legal investigations. His research efforts have focused on the development and behavior of insects that have forensic importance, and he has over 15 years' experience in the collection and analysis of entomological evidence. Dr. Byrd is a fellow of the American Academy of Forensic Sciences.

Patricia Norris, DVM, is director of the Veterinary Division Animal Welfare Section of the NC Department of Agriculture and Consumer Services in North Carolina. The Animal Welfare Section licenses public and private animal shelters, boarding kennels, and pet shops and oversees the state's Spay and Neuter Fund. She was previously the staff veterinarian for the Doña Ana County Sheriff's Office (DASO), Las Cruces, New Mexico, the only position of its kind in the country. She provided veterinary forensic services for their cases of animal cruelty and animal crime and was frequently asked to assist other law enforcement agencies throughout New Mexico. She has served as veterinarian for the New Mexico Animal Sheltering Board since its inception in 2007 and was a member of the DASO Mounted Patrol Horseback Search and Rescue Team. Dr. Norris earned her Doctor of Veterinary Medicine from the Virginia Tech College of Veterinary Medicine in 1986 and has a graduate certificate in veterinary forensic science from the University of Florida College of Veterinary Medicine. Dr. Norris was in private veterinary practice for 25 years in Virginia, North Carolina, and New Mexico. She served as veterinarian at the Duke University Lemur Center (Durham County, North Carolina) to provide care for their colony of endangered lemurs. She also served as veterinarian for the Pitt County Board of Health and on the County Animal Response Teams for Pitt and Madison counties (North Carolina).

Nancy Bradley-Siemens, DVM, has been a veterinarian for 27 years. She started out in private practice and ultimately moved on to emergency medicine. The majority of her career has been in shelter medicine, working for both an animal control agency and a nonprofit humane society. Dr. Bradley-Siemens was the chief veterinarian at Maricopa County Animal Care & Control (Phoenix, Arizona) for 2 years, and the chief veterinarian and eventually medical director for the Arizona Humane Society. During her years in shelter medicine, Dr. Bradley-Siemens has been heavily involved in investigation and expert witness testimony in animal abuse cases. She served as a reserve police officer for over 12 years; 3 of those years as a detective with the Maricopa County Sheriff's Office Animal Crimes Unit in the Phoenix area. She was an adjunct assistant clinical professor at Midwestern University (MWU) College of Veterinary Medicine in

Glendale, Arizona for one year. Since 2016, she has been a full-time assistant clinical professor of Shelter Medicine at MWU, teaching multiple classes but primarily third-year electives in shelter medicine and veterinary forensics and fourth-year shelter medicine rotations. She has earned a master's degree in nonprofit management and a master's degree in veterinary forensics. Her next major goal is to become boarded in Shelter Medicine.

CONTRIBUTORS

Nancy Bradley-Siemens
Department of Pathology and Population Medicine
Midwestern University
Glendale, Arizona, USA

Jason W. Brooks
Animal Diagnostic Laboratory
The Pennsylvania State University
University Park, Pennsylvania, USA

Adrienne Brundage
Department of Entomology
Texas A&M University
College Station, Texas, USA

Jason H. Byrd
W.R. Maples Center for Forensic Medicine
University of Florida College of Medicine
Gainesville, Florida, USA

Ann Cavender
W.R. Maples Center for Forensic Medicine
University of Florida College of Medicine
Gainesville, Florida, USA

and

Salem Veterinary Services
Salem, Michigan, USA

AnnMarie Clark
W.R. Maples Center for Forensic Medicine
University of Florida College of Medicine
Gainesville, Florida, USA

Adriana de Siqueira
School of Veterinary Medicine and Animal Science
University of Sao Paulo
Butanta, Sao Paulo, Brazil

Sharon Gwaltney-Brant
W.R. Maples Center for Forensic Medicine
University of Florida College of Medicine
Gainesville, Florida, USA

Maranda Kles
W.R. Maples Center for Forensic Medicine
University of Florida College of Medicine
Gainesville, Florida, USA

Mary Manspeaker
Humane Society of Memphis and Shelby County
Memphis, Tennessee, USA

Patricia Norris
Animal Welfare Section
North Carolina Department of Agriculture and Consumer Services
Raleigh, North Carolina, USA

Barbara Sheppard
Department of Infectious Diseases and Pathology
College of Veterinary Medicine
University of Florida
Gainesville, Florida, USA

Martha Smith-Blackmore
Forensic Veterinary Investigations LLC
Boston, Massachusetts, USA

Lerah Sutton
W.R. Maples Center for Forensic Medicine
University of Florida College of Medicine
Gainesville, Florida, USA

Scott Sylvia
Investigations and Major Case Management Team
Ontario SPCA and Humane Society
Stouffville, Ontario, Canada

Susan Underkoffler
Wildlife Forensic Sciences and Conservation
W.R. Maples Center for Forensic Medicine
University of Florida College of Medicine
Gainesville, Florida, USA

Elizabeth Watson
W.R. Maples Center for Forensic Medicine
University of Florida College of Medicine
Gainesville, Florida, USA

Michelle Welch
Animal Law Unit
Virginia Attorney General's Office
Richmond, Virginia, USA

INTRODUCTION

> As a member of the veterinary medical profession, I solemnly swear that I will use my scientific knowledge and skills for the benefit of society. I will strive to promote animal health and welfare, relieve animal suffering, protect the health of the public and environment, and advance comparative medical knowledge.
>
> **The Veterinarian's Oath (rev. 2010)**

> Whilst Man, however well-behaved,
> At best is but a monkey shaved!
>
> **Charles Darwin**
> *The Origin of Species*

Animals have always been first. Out of the primordial ooze came structure and cells that eventually coalesced into animal form. Around 650 million years ago, an animal made its world debut, and those first, low, creeping animals eventually evolved into the fish, amphibians, reptiles, birds, and mammals with which we cohabit this Earth. The relative newcomers of the *Homo* species only arrived at the party 6.8 million years ago. Though we are a late arrival to this evolutionary tree, today's *Homo sapiens* have all along learned from the creatures that walked, flew, and swam before our time, observing and utilizing them to increase our own knowledge.

Goats and sheep were likely the first domesticated animals. By mutual consent or unilateral exploitation, the wolf transformed into the modern-day domesticated dog. These domesticated animals were the first to be probed, cut open, and explored by humans seeking to understand what makes a body function. Through dissection, these animals revealed to us the circulatory system, digestive processes, and neural networks. Though these animals were the first to tell us about ourselves, early medical colleges established in twelfth-century Europe focused on human health and medicine. Similarly, the earliest organized medical group, the American Medical Association, predated by 16 years the foundation of the American Veterinary Medical Association in 1863.

Even in forensic medicine and pathology, animals continue to help us understand physical processes, such as decomposition and the way bones break in response to external forces. Though animals have taught us about ourselves, our application of that knowledge back to our teachers has lagged. Only relatively recently have forensic scientists and veterinarians been asked to assess animals in the light of anthropogenic traumas. The types of animals most commonly involved in these cases vary somewhat depending on the locality, for example, domestic dogs have been reported to be the most common subjects of veterinary forensic casework in Canada, and cats are most commonly assessed in Brazil. In wildlife forensic cases, avian species—especially raptors—are heavily represented. Correspondingly, the most common cause of death in these cases may also differ. Nonaccidental injury or poisoning is more common in domestic species (McEwen, 2012; Salvagni et al., 2012; Ottinger et al., 2014; Listos et al., 2015), while trauma is the most common cause of death in wild animals (Millins et al., 2014).

Why the recent heightened interest in veterinary forensics? In many places in the world, animals are being raised from the status of property and renewable resource to the level of companion, health asset, and finite resource. Domestic animals are increasingly being considered members of the human family, and their legal protections have followed a commensurate course (Animal Legal Defense Fund 2017 U.S. Animal Protection Laws Rankings, https://aldf.org/wp-content/uploads/2018/06/Rankings-Report-2017_FINAL.pdf). Litigation to address anthropogenic acts against animals has also increased (Listos et al., 2015). The elevation of animal rights in human consciousness has led to increased communication between animal welfare groups and law enforcement entities. These partnerships have allowed law enforcement officials to recognize links between violent crimes among humans and the interspecific crime of animal abuse. For non-domestic species, links have similarly been found between international wildlife trafficking and organized crime (National Intelligence Council [U.S.], 2013).

With the increased attention on forensic activities and results comes increased scrutiny of forensic methodology. Early in this century, news media illumination of the dishonest practices of some forensic practitioners prompted a comprehensive review of forensic science in the United States by the National Research Council (2009). The resulting report found that standardization and validation were lacking in many areas of forensic science and offered suggestions on how to improve the sensitivity and specificity of many forensic disciplines. From this hard analysis grew discipline-specific scientific working groups and, eventually, the Organization of Scientific Area Committees (OSAC) for Forensic Science to address the discrepancies found and follow the paths suggested by the 2009 report.

At the time of the report, veterinary forensics was largely a side practice performed by few willing veterinarians or practitioners of human forensics. In fact, the word "veterinary" exists nowhere in the entire 328 pages of the report. In this respect, perhaps, it is better that the humans were first! The new and ongoing efforts to strengthen the forensic sciences in general affords the veterinary forensic field the opportunity to establish itself as a sound, comprehensive, and sustainable facet of forensic science.

Challenges within the veterinary forensic medicine field include a lack of formal training, a dearth of published research, and difficulties associated with engaging law enforcement in the pursuit of cases (Ottinger et al., 2014; McEwen, 2016). However, an increased demand for forensic training opportunities has led some veterinary schools to offer courses in veterinary ethics and animal welfare training, and precipitated the formation of the International Veterinary Forensic Sciences Association (IVFSA.org), bringing together veterinarians, law enforcement, and legal professionals to collaborate on ways to move the field forward. Information and knowledge gained through these collaborations is increasingly being disseminated through the general forensic science literature as well as animal-focused periodicals, such as the *Journal of Veterinary Forensic Sciences* (JVFS.net).

The pages of this text, too, will help to fill some of the gaps in the veterinary forensic literature. Those familiar with forensic science only as depicted on television will find true and accurate instruction on the basics of animal crime scene investigation and forensic physical examination by experienced field practitioners in Chapters 1 through 3. The basics of trauma evaluation, wound assessment, and appropriate sampling are addressed in Chapters 6 through 10. Chapter 11, describing in detail how to perform a forensic necropsy and the procedures and documentation needed to build a robust case, will help to increase the confidence of veterinarians asked to assist with a forensic investigation. Analytical techniques utilizing DNA (Chapter 4), entomology (Chapter 5), toxicology (Chapter 15), and forensic radiology (Chapter 19) help to round out the basic understanding of facets of veterinary forensic casework. Finally, specific and (unfortunately) common animal crimes, such as hoarding, fighting, and abuse are described in order to help the veterinarian recognize the physical and behavioral changes associated with these entities. Veterinarians who are new to forensics as well as those looking for more in-depth information will find the material contained herein useful.

Animals continue to be our instructors, showing us how our bodies work and how our behavior can be affected by the world around us. They remain our first resource for scientific exploration and, often, companionship. When they are unable to stand and speak for themselves, it behooves us as animal lovers and scientists to take their cue, use the forensic knowledge and skills available to us, and be the first to speak for them.

References

Committee on Identifying the Needs of the Forensic Sciences Community, National Research Council. 2009. Strengthening Forensic Science in the United States: A Path Forward. 352 pages. https://www.ncjrs.gov/pdffiles1/nij/grants/228091.pdf (accessed 28 August 2018)

Listos, P., Gryzinska, M., Kowalczyk, M. 2015. Analysis of cases of forensic veterinary opinions produced in a research and teaching unit. *Journal of Forensic and Legal Medicine*, 36, 84–89.

McEwen, B.J. 2012. Trends in domestic animal medico-legal pathology cases submitted to a veterinary diagnostic laboratory 1998–2010. *Journal of Forensic Science*, 57(5), 1231–1233.

McEwen, B. J. 2016. A survey of attitudes of board-certified veterinary pathologists to forensic veterinary pathology. *Veterinary Pathology*, 53(5), 1099–1102.

National Intelligence Council (U.S.). 2013. *Wildlife Poaching Threatens Economic, Security Priorities in Africa*. Office of the Director of National Intelligence. Washington, DC.

Millins, C., Howie, F., Everitt, C., Shand, M., Lamm, C. 2014. Analysis of suspected wildlife crimes submitted for forensic examinations in Scotland. *Forensic Science, Medicine and Pathology*, 10, 357–362.

Ottinger, T., Ottinger, T., Rasmusson, B., Segerstad, C.H.A. 2014. Forensic veterinary pathology, today's situation and perspectives. *Veterinary Record*, 175(18), 459.

Salvagni, F.A., de Siqueira, A., Maria, A.C.B.E. 2012. Forensic veterinary pathology: Old dog learns a trick. *Brazilian Journal of Veterinary Pathology*, 5(2), 37–38.

CHAPTER 1

CRIME SCENE INVESTIGATION

Patricia Norris

OVERVIEW

On February 27, 2018, a man was sentenced to 12 years for stomping on and throwing a small boxer-type puppy against a wall. Despite veterinary care, the puppy was euthanized due to its injuries. In a news interview about the case, Collin County District Attorney Greg Willis was quoted as saying "We have to make sure we have an evidence-based prosecution. Sometimes things happen, and we don't have the evidence for a strong case. In this case, we did have the evidence and it helped" (Miles, 2018). The need for evidence-based investigation and prosecution of animal crime cases is one of the driving forces behind the development of the field of veterinary forensic science.

Veterinary forensic science has been defined as: "the application of a broad spectrum of sciences, including veterinary medicine to answer questions of interest to a court of law" (Touroo, 2012). Inherent in this definition is the inclusion of veterinary medicine. The practice of veterinary medicine is defined by the American Veterinary Medical Association (AVMA) as "to diagnose, prognose, treat, correct, change, alleviate, or prevent animal disease, illness, pain, deformity, defect, injury, or other physical, dental, or mental conditions by any method or mode" (American Veterinary Medical Association, 2017). The AVMA defines veterinarian to mean "a person who has received a professional veterinary medical degree from a college of veterinary medicine" (American Veterinary Medical Association, 2017).

The field of veterinary forensic science has recently expanded with the establishment of the International Veterinary Forensic Science Association (IVFSA) in 2008. One of the stated purposes of this organization is to "educate the animal welfare community, law enforcement, crime scene analysts, forensic scientists, veterinarians, attorneys, judges, and pathologists on the application of forensic science techniques and crime scene processing methods to cases of animal abuse, neglect, cruelty, fighting, and death" (International Veterinary Forensic Science Association, 2018).

Inherent in the need for an investigation utilizing veterinary forensic science is that some act, or failure to act, has occurred affecting the well-being of an animal(s). (For the purposes of this chapter and for the sake of brevity, the term "act" will automatically include "failure to act" even when not stated.) Law enforcement and/or judicial agencies are the ones tasked with deciding whether an act or failure to act rises to the level of a "crime." In addition, depending on the case, the location where the act occurred warrants investigation as well. Therefore, "crime scene" investigation procedures and protocols can play a very large part in the investigation of an animal crime. For the purposes of this chapter, animal crime refers to any act, or failure to act, which has a negative impact on the health and welfare of an animal(s), or an act by an animal that has a negative impact on the health and welfare of another animal or human.

One of the purposes of crime scene investigation is the collection of physical evidence, which Dr. Edmond Locard deemed "the silent witness" (Fisher et al., 2009). Locard's Exchange Principle essentially states that every time someone enters an environment, something is added and removed from it (Fisher et al., 2009). The "something" may be a primary transfer, meaning a direct transfer such as from the suspect to the victim, or vice versa. Secondary transfer involves multiple transfers of the evidence such as from the victim to the scene and then from the scene to the suspect. Documentation of these transfers may tell the story of the link(s) between the elements of the crime: the suspect(s), the victim(s), and the scene(s).

A corollary to Locard's Exchange Principle is that "every contact leaves a trace" (Fish et al., 2011). As it pertains to animal crimes, the crime scene may be an entire property, dwelling, room, kennel, or the animal itself. One justification for the collection of evidence and processing of a crime scene is to reveal the presence any link of the suspect to the victim, the suspect to the scene, and/or the victim to the scene, and to objectively document this link.

An additional reason to conduct a thorough crime scene investigation is that, for many animal crimes, the totality of circumstance of the scene has a direct impact on the decision as to whether or not the act reaches the level of a crime. In order for an act to be considered a crime, the elements of the crime contained in the statutory language must be present. For example, in the instance of hoarding, a judgment has to be reached that the conditions of the environment and the owner's failure to provide adequate housing and care had such a negative impact on the animal that this neglect constitutes a crime, versus the situation in which the care, housing, and environment was less than ideal but not criminal. The only way this judgment can be reached in a fair and unbiased manner is by thorough, objective investigation of the scene (Fish et al., 2011).

CRIME SCENE INVESTIGATION

Initial questions to be answered are: (1) What is the crime scene? (2) Where is the crime scene? and (3) What techniques will be needed to thoroughly investigate and document this scene?

Crime scenes are as varied as the acts investigated. It may be that the only scene to be processed is the animal itself, or the scene may involve multiple premises that extend for acres. Obviously, investigative protocols must take into account the uniqueness of a specific scene while abiding by the general procedures common to scene investigations. Each investigation has its own set of variables requiring documentation. Case documentation may only require examination of a single animal or may involve extensive documentation of hundreds of housing units spread over acres of land. The following information, describing possible evidence documentation, is not meant to imply that all techniques or procedures are required for every case. What is required is thorough documentation of the evidence relevant to the act, which is relayed to the judicial system in an accurate, unbiased manner so the judicial body can make a fair and just decision.

Although each crime scene may not require every forensic technique, agencies investigating animal crime scenes can adopt the FBI's 12-step process as a guideline for investigation of the scene (Fish et al., 2011; U.S. Department of Justice, 2013). These 12 steps include: "(1) prepare, (2) approach scene, (3) secure and protect scene, (4) initiate preliminary survey, (5) evaluate physical evidence possibilities, (6) prepare narrative descriptions, (7) depict scene photographically, (8) prepare diagrams and sketches of scene, (9) conduct a detailed search, (10) record and collect physical evidence, (11) conduct a final survey, and (12) release scene" (Fish et al., 2011).

With animal crime scenes, the number of personnel may vary from a single animal control officer to a full response with law enforcement officers, animal control officers, prosecutors, veterinarians, regulatory officers (U.S. and/or State Department of Agriculture, or other state and/or federal government agencies such as the Drug Enforcement Agency [DEA]), crime scene investigators, forensic specialists, nongovernmental animal welfare agencies, and so on. Therefore, the number of personnel in the response can have a direct effect on the extent of the crime scene investigation and documentation.

Subsequent sections of this chapter will discuss some of the investigative tools available for documenting the crime scene in general. These sections will use the FBI's 12-step process as a guideline, and notes where certain adaptations or techniques may be useful for the challenges of evidence collection and documentation unique to animal crimes. Subsequent chapters of this book will address evidence collection and documentation specific to a particular act, if specialized evidence collection is appropriate.

PLANNING STAGE OF AN ANIMAL CASE

The development of animal cases typically follows one of two courses: (1) the case that is stumbled upon during the routine performance of duties by a law enforcement agency or (2) the case in which agencies are allowed the opportunity to plan out the steps of the investigation. If the course of events of an animal case allows for a planning stage, seeking input from all of the resources available for the case can be invaluable.

One of the first discussions that must occur during the planning stage of a case is a frank discussion of the expectations of the law enforcement agency for the roles and responsibilities of all of the personnel that will be involved in the case. The personnel and resources must be willing and able to provide what the law enforcement agency requests for the duration of the case. If the personnel or resource has restrictions or limitations, these must be discussed during the planning stage, rather than emerging as a surprise mid-course. Open discussion at the beginning of the case allows for adjustments or development of alternative courses of action, which minimize the impact on the case. In complex cases, multiple briefings may be advantageous in the long run.

Although some larger cases may involve the prosecutor in the planning stages and on scene, typically, the law enforcement agency is the lead agency and all other personnel are assistants. As many of these cases involve an animal(s), alive or deceased, on scene, having a veterinarian to assist with the case is imperative. In most cases, the veterinarian is an assistant to law enforcement during a case, as has been the author's personal experience. Even in the role as an assistant, the veterinarian must be allowed and able to maintain independence and objectivity in their professional opinion and actions.

Examples of how frank discussions may result in an alternate course of action include:

1. If the species involved are not animals typically treated by the veterinarian or are animals that require specialized veterinary assessment and/or care, then the initial consulting veterinarian can advise the law enforcement agency of other resources such as specialized veterinarians or veterinary colleges that may better suit the needs of the case.
2. If the species involved are to be transported but governmental regulations require special handling, communicable disease testing, identification, or documentation, the veterinarian can advise law enforcement of the proper procedures. This may mean involving state or other government regulatory agencies in the planning stages.
3. If one of the resources involved in the planning of the case has a specific time conflict or limitation, the timing of the execution of the search warrant may be modified.

A crucial aspect of the planning briefing is the discussion on animal handling and management on scene. Not all law enforcement agencies have animal control resources to aid in the handling of animals. The veterinarian may be the only person with significant animal experience present at the planning briefing. The challenges of animal handling and management are often magnified and can quickly become problematic in large-scale cases (Touroo & Fitch, 2016). In addition, certain cases may involve species of animals which require specialized equipment for handling.

The veterinarian, animal control, or other animal welfare resources can advise law enforcement of a logical flow of animal procedures and movement at the crime scene to meet the needs of law enforcement and the judicial agencies. During the initial case planning briefing, the law enforcement agency (and prosecutors, if present) should detail their expectations of these resources. Responsibility for procedures such as scene triage, environmental impact assessment, animal triage and assessment, loading for transport, transport, scene and animal evidence identification, collection and preservation, security and sheltering of the animal evidence, monitoring and care of the animal evidence, and final disposition of the animal evidence must be detailed during the planning briefing.

APPROACH TO THE CRIME SCENE AND SECURING OF THE SCENE

Depending on the presentation of the case, one of two scenarios is most common:

1. The spontaneous case occurs when, during the normal course of their duties, law enforcement or animal control officers find evidence of a possible animal crime. In these

cases, there is no planning briefing for the case; rather the officer relies on their routine training and agency procedures to initiate the investigation. The officer may observe a crime in progress or discover what appears to be the scene of a crime. In either case, the officer will secure the scene and proceed with the investigation.
2. The planned case occurs when information is received prior to the initiation of the investigative action and the stages of the case are planned out and scheduled.

While there may be a few very narrow, specific exemptions in exigent circumstances, one of the initial steps of crime scene investigation involves obtaining permission to search the scene. The Fourth Amendment of the U.S. Constitution protects citizens from unreasonable search and seizure (Fish et al., 2011). This means that in order for the agency to search an area, it must obtain permission. This permission can come either two sources: (1) a person legally able to give voluntary consent, or (2) from the court system in the form of a search warrant. There are advantages and disadvantages of each type of permission. The discussion of the pros and cons of voluntary consent versus search warrant, as well as the procedures for writing and executing each, is beyond the scope of this text.

One rule to keep in mind is that evidence removed from a scene must conform to the Fourth Amendment and to the confines of the search warrant (Fish et al., 2011). If the scene reveals unexpected evidence which is beyond the scope of the search warrant, one option to consider is to secure an additional warrant using this new information. Opposing attorneys commonly challenge the search warrant and the collection of evidence, so the agency will often consult with the prosecutors on the drafting of the search warrant. Strict attention to the details of the warrant while collecting evidence is essential. Evidence taken in violation of the Fourth Amendment and/or beyond the scope of the search warrant as well as information gleaned from such evidence may be ruled inadmissible in court if argued by the opposing side that it was "fruit of the poisonous tree" (Fish et al., 2011; Touroo & Fitch, 2016).

The next step is often the securing of the scene. This step is common to most types of criminal investigations. Given the intensity of emotion of animal crime scenes, it is safest to have the premises secured before civilians enter. Incidents have occurred in which an animal control officer was killed while on the premises of an animal crime (National Animal Control Association, 2018).

In the spontaneous case, the initial officer will secure the scene and request assistance if appropriate. This officer is to keep the scene as untouched and unchanged as possible until it can be processed.

For safety reasons, typically, the scene of a planned investigation is secured by the law enforcement agency prior to the entry of civilian assistants. The methods used to secure the scene are typically detailed by the agency's procedures and protocols.

One step that may be necessary for an animal crime scene is securing any loose animals, especially those that are aggressive. Sometimes dogs that have been used as protection or alert systems may be roaming the crime scene. These animals should be documented then secured before the civilian team members enter.

CRIME SCENE TRIAGE

Step 4 of the FBI 12-step process is the preliminary survey or triage of the crime scene. The purpose of this step is to "look, but don't touch" (Fish et al., 2011; U.S. Department of Justice, 2013). The scene is documented photographically and videographically prior to any intervention or modification of the scene. The person assigned to this task will often start at the entrance to the premises and then walk through the scene, area by area, documenting the overall scene and close-ups of particular areas of interest. The overall scene documentation should be done from as many vantage points as practical. For instance, pictures and videos of a room should be taken from as many sides and corners of the room as possible, while not disturbing any evidence in the process. If video is being taken, the operator should consider the advantages and disadvantages of a narrated versus silent recording. If the audio is left on, all personnel in the area should be made aware of when the recording starts and stops.

During this initial walkthrough and documentation, the number of additional personnel should be minimal; a few well-trained personnel can take notes and assess the situation to triage and develop a plan of action. It is often advantageous for the veterinarian to participate in the initial walkthrough of the crime scene to start the animal triage planning. Some animals may be in severe distress, while others are not. Having the veterinarian on the initial walkthrough allows the veterinarian the opportunity to plan out the sequence of animal assessment and emergency treatment if needed. Another advantage to having the veterinarian on the initial walkthrough is it gives the opportunity for the veterinarian to assess the overall environment's effect on the animals. Transient, volatile environmental evidence such as ammonia levels and fecal waste odors, amount of sunlight or darkness the animals are housed in, and the animals' response to these factors while still in the original housing situation can be documented. The veterinarian, with permission from the officer in charge of the scene, may video or photograph environmental conditions and/or animals in situ as documentation of the environmental stress the animals endured as part of the veterinary medical record. This overall environmental assessment may become an important aspect in relaying to the judge or jury the condition in which the animals were housed in and its effects on the health and welfare of the animals.

Although it is often difficult for personnel to restrain themselves and not intervene immediately, evidence, including the animals, should not be moved or modified during this initial documentation. The veterinarian can, however, note which animals are in severe distress and direct that the first intervention will be assessment and relief for those animals prior to assessment and movement of less distressed animals. If the veterinarian has participated in the initial scene assessment and triage, they can better explain to the judicial system why, in their professional judgment, these animals required immediate assistance and relief.

The other immediate need to assess during the triage of the scene is the presence of transient evidence. Transient evidence can be defined as physical evidence that is likely to be altered, damaged, or destroyed if not immediately preserved (Fish et al., 2011). In animal cases, a classic example of transient evidence is the ammonia level of the atmosphere of the housing area. In hoarding, puppy mill situations, or other high-density housing scenarios, the ammonia level can be extremely high, so much so as to pose a significant health hazard to the crime scene personnel. In addition, the measurement of this level can be very telling as to the chronic, hazardous conditions under which the animals were housed. The ammonia level can drop very quickly with the opening of doors and movement which ventilates the area; therefore, it is best to measure this level immediately upon accessing the housing area.

Once the overall photographs, video, and initial notes are taken, personnel should reconvene in an area in which there is little risk of damaging evidence. At this time the action plan can be discussed, adjusted, or fine-tuned as to the order in which the areas are to be documented and tasks completed. Overall photographs, videos, and notes can be used to identify areas and plan out the collection of evidence.

One of the challenges of large-scale animal cases is maintaining and documenting the methodical processing of each unit or area within the scene. During the fine tuning of the action plan, agreement on the identification and labeling of each area is essential. For example, each section of a puppy mill's kennels or room of a hoarding scene may be given a designation, such as a letter, and every animal or piece of evidence is numbered sequentially (Touroo & Fitch, 2016) For example, an animal assigned the identification of "A-12" is the 12th dog from Room A. Once the identification system is agreed upon, then it is incumbent upon all scene personnel to adhere to it. This allows for ease and consistency of identification further along in the process of documenting the evidence of the case.

SCENE DOCUMENTATION WITH PHOTOGRAPHY AND VIDEO

Although few, if any, crime scene investigations have access to all of the sophisticated tools shown on popular television crime shows, equipment for photography and videography are essential for crime scene investigations.

Prior to arrival on the crime scene, the investigator should be familiar with the operation of the equipment. If the equipment uses a digital date and time stamp, this should be checked for accuracy before being used on scene. Backup batteries, SD cards, and cameras are integral to proper preparation. The equipment should be checked for operation and cleanliness, especially the lenses.

One general principle of scene documentation is that the photographs and video should progress from general to specific. Both photographs and videos should start with an overview that covers the entire area. Once the overview is complete, mid-range photographs or videos should be taken. These photographs and videos must be done in such a manner that the location or relevance of the object documented is clear. Close-up documentation of the object should proceed upon conclusion of the mid-range documentation. Again, this needs to be done so that it is clear where and why the photograph or video was taken (Figure 1.1).

Each area or piece of evidence should be photographed and videoed prior to modification. The next set of documentation should show the area or evidence with its identification marker. For clarity, fully document that area, animal, or evidence before moving on to the next. If you realize that additional photographs or videos would be beneficial to the case, start again with the full identification of the object and then take the additional photographs or videos as appropriate.

Figure 1.1 (a–d) Series of scene photographs showing progression from overview to macro-photograph for proper evidence documentation.

DIAGRAMMING AND SKETCHING OF THE CRIME SCENE

Step 8 of the FBI's 12-step process is the preparation of the diagrams and sketches of the scene. Sketches and diagrams can show the overall layout of a scene and detail the relationship between pieces of evidence in a way not possible by photographs or videos. Depending on the type of scene and the preference of the person, the sketches can be drawn on plain, lined, or graph paper.

Although particulars of the sketch will depend on the scene, most sketches should indicate the north direction and depict the major unmovable landmarks. Several sketches may be required to fully capture the elements of the scene. Just as with photographs, overall sketches should be drawn for orientation and the mid-level sketches give the details of the evidence. Bird's-eye or plan view show objects on a horizontal level. An elevation sketch shows objects in a vertical plane so that the differences location in height can be clarified. The cross-projection sketch combines elements of the plan and elevation views.

Sketches are not typically drawn to scale but measurements between landmarks and evidence are noted on the sketches. At least two measurements for each point should be noted. To keep the sketch from becoming overly cluttered, the measurements may be numbered or otherwise labeled. If the measurements are numbered or labeled, then somewhere on the sketch the actual measurements should be recorded (Fish et al., 2011; Merck, 2013; U.S. Department of Justice, 2013; Fitch, 2015).

A legend should be included for each sketch. The legend should include at least: type of plan/sketch, location depicted in the sketch, name and identification of the sketcher, date the sketch was made, North arrow, scale of sketch or disclaimer that the sketch is not drawn to scale (Fish et al., 2011; Merck, 2013; U.S. Department of Justice, 2013; Fitch, 2015) (Figure 1.2).

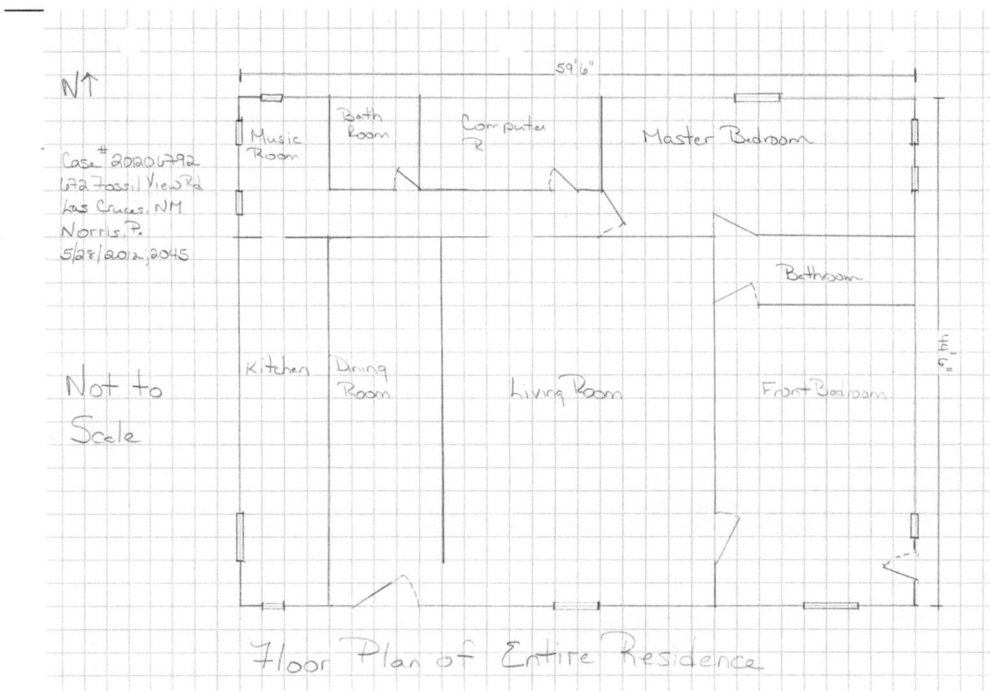

Figure 1.2 Rough, not-to-scale sketches should be done at the scene. This example shows a plan view, or bird's-eye, sketch with a legend, a north indicator, and the disclaimer "not to scale."

SEARCH FOR EVIDENCE AT THE CRIME SCENE

The search for evidence must be thorough and detailed. Remembering that seized evidence must conform to the constraints of the Fourth Amendment, it is imperative that all relevant evidence is recognized as such. Henry Lee stated: "The foundation of all forensic investigations is based on the ability of the crime scene investigator to recognize the potential and importance of physical evidence, large and small, at the crime scene" (Lee et al., 2007). Once the scene has been released, the opportunity to recognize and collect evidence in pristine condition and circumstance may be lost.

Crucial to this ninth step is the training and experience of the personnel on scene. The highly trained personnel will be able to recognize otherwise mundane-appearing objects as critical evidence. For instance, those trained on cockfighting paraphernalia will understand the significance of waxed string and hacksaw blades in kits at fight scenes. Although treadmills can be found in many homes and garages, they can have special significance when found at a scene where dogfighting is suspected, as this item is often associated with the training of fight dogs.

Evidence that is not recognized as such cannot be collected and documented in the next step.

Fish noted, "if it catches your attention, document it" (Fish et al., 2011). By the same token, excessive collection of irrelevant objects will just bog down and hinder the efficient processing of the scene. Particularly on the large scene or the scene subject to impending modification (e.g., tide changing on a beach, snow melting, approaching rain), implementation of an efficient, systematic method of searching is essential. The lead agency may decide to conduct a particular pattern of searching, such as strip search, grid search, link search, zone search, wheel search, or spiral search (Fish et al., 2011; Merck, 2013; Fitch, 2015).

The same methodical approach is required for smaller areas of a crime scene. For example, a kennel full of animal housing units requires the same detailed approach. Each unit must be meticulously searched as well as the areas around the unit (above, beneath, and around all sides). The area to be searched may be a single animal. Again, starting at one point the investigator then moves down and across the animal until all parts of the animal have been examined, as well as the areas adjacent to the animal, if it is still in situ.

When planning out a search of an area, whether it be a large property or a single room, there are four general search patterns. They are:

1. *Spiral*: This pattern is often used for crime scenes within a facility or structure. Typically, a person starts on the perimeter of the area to be searched and slowly spirals inward searching for evidence. This pattern is not typically utilized.
2. *Line*: This type of search is commonly used in large outdoor scenes in which a line of personnel walk with equidistant spacing, usually at arm's length, over a defined area together. The boundaries of the area should be marked out and the integrity of the line has to be maintained in order not to skip areas.
3. *Grid*: The grid search is essentially a line search that has a second line search perpendicular to the initial line search. Again, this is typically used in scenes that cover a large amount of territory.
4. *Zone*: Zone searches are for small, usually confined areas or larger areas that can be subdivided into distinct regions (Fish et al., 2011; Fitch, A., 2015). This pattern can be utilized in lieu of a spiral search in interior locations.

As animal crime scenes are as varied as the crimes investigated, a combination of these types of searches may be used on a particular scene.

DOCUMENTATION AND COLLECTION OF EVIDENCE

This step can be time consuming and tedious, but mistakes made in this step can severely impact the progression and prosecution of the case. According to Lee et al. (2007), physical evidence is best described as "any evidence that can provide useful information for investigators in solving cases." This description leaves the field wide open.

Physical evidence, in general terms, is any tangible object that relates to a crime or that can assist in establishing that a crime occurred. Physical evidence can also be an item that links a crime to its victim or suspect. Evidence adds information to the case. Evidence can provide facts of the case, including the timeline, demonstrate links between the elements of the crime, such as the scene, the victim, potential suspects, and items used during or relevant to the crime, substantiating or refuting witness accounts, elucidating the role of other evidence, identifying unknown items or substances, and reconstructing the crime and the crime scene (Gianelli, 2009; Fish et al., 2011; Fitch, 2015).

For animal cases, in the author's experience, three general types of physical evidence are typically documented and collected: stable, biological, and live. Each of these types of evidence can require specialized handling. Obviously, stable evidence usually requires the least amount of initial processing. These objects, depending on the size, are often collected into evidence bags, sealed with evidence tape, signed by the collector, and secured in an evidence lockup area prior to any appropriate testing. The evidence tape and signature should be oriented so that opening of the package is easily visible. The package should be labeled with all information required by the agency in charge of evidence collection. This information may include case number, item number, agency, brief description, date and time of collection, and identification of the person collecting the evidence. It is often easier to label the container prior to packaging the evidence (U.S. Department of Justice, 2013).

Some additional general guidelines for the collection and storage of evidence include:

1. Fragile evidence or evidence that would be lost easily lost should be packaged first. Rigid cardboard containers can be used to prevent crushing of the evidence.
2. Evidence is usually placed in paper evidence bags, as plastic bags may be conducive to moisture condensation and mold growth.
3. If there is not sufficient time to allow wet items to air-dry while on scene, wet evidence can be temporarily packaged. As soon as the evidence has been moved to a secure area, the package can be opened and the evidence allowed to dry and then be repackaged. This evidence handling, opening, and resealing of the evidence packages should occur as soon as possible to minimize any deterioration due to the moisture. In addition, the handling procedures should be fully documented to maintain the chain of custody.
4. Liquid evidence can be collected and stored in vials with proper lids.
5. Small items of trace evidence, such as hairs or powder, can be collected into envelopes (manila or glassine) or contained in a druggist-folded paper.
6. In most circumstances, each piece of evidence is collected and packaged individually (Fish et al., 2011; Fitch, 2015; Merck, 2013).

Biological evidence is evidence that comes from a human or animal body. Examples include bodily fluids such as blood, semen, saliva, and other bodily secretions. Skin cells, hair, and hair follicles are also biological evidence but are not often collected as stains or smears. Proper collection techniques for biological evidence are essential to avoid the natural degradation that occurs with time and exposure to the environment (Merck, 2013; U.S. Department of Justice, 2013; Fitch, 2015).

Collection techniques for biological evidence commonly used are sterile (moistened with sterile or distilled water if the stain is dry) cotton swabs or gauze to collect the stain, or a sterile tool such as a scalpel or razor blade to scrape up the material (Fish et al., 2011; Merck, 2013; U.S. Department of Justice, 2013). One of the most inclusive techniques to collect and preserve biological evidence is to collect the entire material where the evidence is found. This can be done by cutting out the relevant section of material. Consideration should also be given to collection of control samples of materials not stained by the biological evidence (Merck, 2013; U.S. Department of Justice, 2013). If the biological samples are wet, they should be allowed to dry in areas free of contamination before they are sealed into evidence bags, when possible.

Another fairly common example of biological evidence found at the scene of an animal crime is the body of a deceased animal. The animal's body can provide crucial information for the case and should be handled carefully during collection. At the scene, the paws are often covered with paper bags and the body wrapped in a clean sheet prior to being placed in a bag so that trace evidence is not lost during transit (DiMaio & DiMaio, 2001; Touroo & Fitch, 2016). The handling and collection of evidence from deceased animals, as well as necropsy protocols, will be discussed in Chapter 10.

A later section will address personnel safety during crime scene investigations, but it bears repeating that when handling biological samples, the investigator must take reasonable caution against contaminating the samples with their DNA or cross-contaminating samples. In addition, the investigator must be very careful not to expose themselves to any pathogens contained in the biological samples. The use of disposable gloves that are changed between the collections of samples is standard ,and many investigators use the double-glove technique to minimize exposure to pathogens.

The International Association of Property and Evidence, Inc. published an online manual for detailing the professional standards of managing and storing evidence. Many of generalities that apply to evidence collection and storage for human crime scenes will also be applicable to animal crime scenes (International Association for Property and Evidence Inc., 2016).

Unique to animal cases is the presence, collection and preservation of live evidence—the animals themselves. Because of the unique challenges of live evidence, the collection, documentation, and preservation (housing) of live evidence will be discussed in detail in the following sections.

Live Evidence

Akin to transient evidence such as a tire track in melting snow, animals are changing even as they are being collected. The very presence of investigators on a scene can influence the animal. Animals are subject to injury, which is an altered state, by the process of handling them for identification and transportation to a safe shelter. Therefore, it is imperative that documentation of the animal(s) upon presentation is thorough and complete. Depending on the case, the animal may be the only crime scene available to the investigator.

Identification of Live Evidence

Each section of a crime scene is uniquely identified, as are the animals that come from those areas. Obviously, the identification of a single or a few animals is not nearly as problematic as when the animal numbers reach into the dozens to hundreds and occasionally thousands. Each animal is typically identified as to where the animal was housed or found and then its sequential number for processing. For example, an animal may be labeled as B-32, meaning it came from the kennel labeled as "B" on the crime scene documentation and is the 32nd animal processed from that area. The common need is that whatever identification is assigned to the animal at the crime scene is carried through the entire course of the case until the final disposition of that animal has occurred. If there is a need to modify the identification, there needs to be written documentation containing the old identifier and the new one with an explanation for the change. The most common example of this is when evidence animals are implanted with a microchip. The microchip has now become an unchangeable, permanent (usually) identification for that animal (Figure 1.3).

Figure 1.3 A typical alphanumeric animal numbering system for use on crime scenes to keep the animal and physical evidence associated with the recovery location at the scene. The location receives the letter designation. The animal receives a numeric designation.

Physical Examination of Live Evidence

When conditions and resources are available, it is prudent to conduct at least a triage examination with photographic documentation of each animal immediately upon contact with that animal and before its transport to the housing location. This is just one of the reasons why having a veterinarian on the crime scene as part of the investigative team is invaluable. The veterinarian can conduct a physical examination, either triage or complete, on scene and document any lesions present at the time of collection as well as normal findings.

The animal should receive a physical examination (PE) by a licensed veterinarian if time allows on scene, or as soon as reasonable upon arrival at the housing area. The examination should be conducted in a manner as to meet the standards expected/accepted by the regulatory agency such as the Veterinary Medical Board over that jurisdiction. The PE should follow a standardized format for all of the animals in the case, with small variations as appropriate to accommodate different findings. In addition, the PE should be repeated in the same format as needed throughout the progress of the case. If the decision is made to do full temperature, pulse, respirations (TPRs) for an animal, it should be done for every animal for that case unless there are extenuating circumstances. For instance, if during the planning briefing for the case, it is noted that all of the animals will be unsocialized or feral cats, serious consideration should be taken as to the advisability and safety of trying to obtain a rectal temperature from a feral cat. Any extenuating circumstances should be documented as any reason for deviating from the standard protocol in place for that case.

The examination should also include photographic or videographic documentation of all findings, both normal and abnormal. Photographs and/or video should be taken to show left and right sides, a frontal view and a dorsal view of the animal, if possible, for identification purposes. The same principles apply here as for the crime scene. The photographs/video should start with a view of the animal with no identification, a view with identification, then overall views followed by mid-range views and then close-ups. The overall views should include left side, right side, frontal, and rear views. When appropriate, views showing the dorsum (the back) and ventrum (the belly) should be taken. The identification shown in the documentation and on the written documentation should be consistent with the identification assigned at the crime scene (Figure 1.4).

Other considerations with physical examination of live evidence are thoroughness and documentation. It is an axiom of this field that "if it is not documented, it did not happen." This also applies to PEs as any procedure. If the documentation does not denote all of the parts of

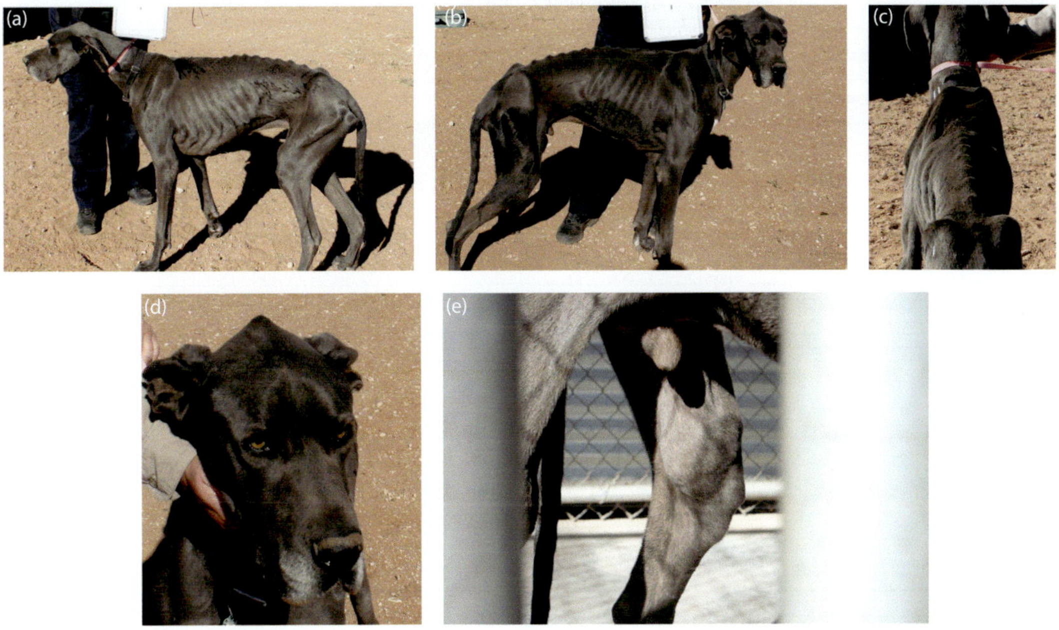

Figures 1.4 (a–e) Each animal should have a series of initial photographs made to document the condition found. These photographs should show both the left and right sides of the animal, and head, as well as dorsal and ventral views. The initial intake photos should also include macro (close-up) views of any lesions or injuries.

the examination or all of the parts examined, then in the view of the court, it did not happen. The veterinarian may have their credibility challenged by the opposing attorney based on the routine parts of the examination which, although they may have been conducted and judged to show normal findings, were not documented. The author recommends the use of standardized examination forms that allow for quick acknowledgement of examination of all body systems. The same forms should be used throughout a case for every animal. The examination forms can be customized to species or specific needs of a situation if appropriate (Figure 1.5).

Although their inclusion is increasing in routine veterinary medical examinations (personal experience), body condition scores are commonly included in veterinary forensic examinations. There are numerous species-specific body condition scoring systems. The scoring systems are specific to species and sometimes to type of species. For example, there is a body condition score (BCS) chart for dairy cattle and a different one for beef cattle. The BCS charts for donkeys are different from those for horses. This subject, as it pertains to equine and livestock, will be addressed in Chapter 17.

To date, there is no independent research showing a significant advantage of one system over another. Consistent use of a specific system for each species throughout the course of the case is recommended. Documenting the scorer's training in the use of the scoring system could be beneficial.

One common BCS system for dogs is the Tufts Animal Care and Condition Scale (TACC) (Patronek, 1997). The TACC is based on a five-level scale for the condition of the animal, with "5" being emaciated and "1" being ideal. This scale does not allow for assessment of the overweight or morbidly obese dog. This scoring system does have the advantage of a second part which evaluates the conditions under which the dog was kept. The TACC environment scale allows for evaluation of (1) weather safety scale, (2) environmental health scale, and (3) physical care scale. This system allows for evaluation of the "totality of circumstance" in the assessment of the animal in relation to its care (Patronek, 1997).

(a)

Agency ____ Case # ____
Address ____ Case Agent ____ Animal # ____
____ Date ____ Time ____

Veterinary Medical Evaluation

History: ____

Description of the Animal ____

Temp: ____ **Pulse:** ____ **Resp:** ____ **Weight:** ____ **BCS:** ____
Behavior/Attitude: ____

Mental: N Abn	**Skin:** N Abn NE	**Ears:** N Abn NE
Muc. Mem: N Abn	**Heart:** N Abn NE	**MuscSkel:** N Abn NE
Hydration: N Abn	**L Nodes:** N Abn NE	**Nose:** N Abn NE
Lungs: N Abn NE	**Neuro:** N Abn NE	**Eyes:** N Abn NE
Mouth: N Abn NE	**Abdomen:** N Abn NE	**Urogen:** N Abn NE
Discomfort: Yes No	**Distress:** Yes No	**Pain:** Yes No

Paws/Feet/Hooves/Nails: ____
Hair/Feathers: ____
Abnormal Findings: ____

Examiner: ____ **Page** ____ **of** ____

(b)

Agency ____ Case # ____
Address ____ Case Agent ____ Animal # ____
____ Date ____ Time ____

Additional Findings (continued) ____

Examiner: ____ **Page** ____ **of** ____

Figure 1.5 (a–b) A standard intake examination form used by the author.

Another common BCS system which has charts for dogs and cats is the LaFlamme scale, commonly known as the Purina scale (LaFlamme, 1997; Nestle Purina Pet Care Center, 2002a,b). This scale has 9 levels, with 5 being considered "ideal"; level 1 is "emaciated" and 9 is "grossly obese." The charts contain both sample pictures and descriptions of animal body conditions.

The comfort level, or lack thereof, for the animal should also be noted during the initial and subsequent examinations. Documentation of this level should be included in the examination notes. Labels and descriptions of these comfort levels should be documented and standardized for the duration of the case. For example, these levels could be noted as comfortable, in discomfort, in distress, painful, or suffering (Touroo, 2012).

One tool that has been used to assess the comfort level, or conversely the suffering, of animals is Patronek's chart of the quality of life (Cummings School of Veterinary Medicine, Tufts University, 2020) which is based on the Five Freedoms established by the Farm Animal Welfare Council in the UK (Farm Animal Welfare Council, 2009, Brewster & Reyes, 2013).

The Five Freedoms include:

1. Freedom from hunger and thirst
2. Freedom from discomfort
3. Freedom from pain, injury, or disease
4. Freedom to express normal behavior
5. Freedom from fear and distress

If an animal is found to be in pain, then this observation is to be documented in the examination notes. Objective documentation using pain scores is often valuable to the judicial system in assessing the extent of the criminal act. A list of easily available references for the assessment and management of a pain in animals is included at the end of Chapter 16. Pain scoring systems with charts and pictures such as the Colorado State Acute Pain Scales for dogs (Hellyer et al., 2006a), cats (Hellyer et al., 2006b), and horses (Blossom et al., 2007) and the Short Form of the Glasgow Composite Measure are also available (Reid et al., 2007). These forms can be incorporated as part of the veterinary medical record. Additional information on the assessment of pain is discussed in Chapter 16. Pain scoring assessment should continue throughout all reassessment examinations for the animals.

Reassessment of Live Evidence

Inherent in the handling of live evidence is the fact that this evidence is subject to constant change. Animals age, become ill or injured, improve or decline in health and body condition, and so on, throughout the duration of the case. Whether an agency has custody of live evidence only at the scene or seizes and holds the animal for the duration of the case, that animal is constantly changing. The very act of handling the animal can alter the findings of the examination. Therefore, it is prudent to document the animal in situ prior to handling. Some of the alterations may be minimal or transient, but others may be permanent.

If the animal is held in protective custody for the duration of the case, this evidence needs to be periodically reassessed, preferably by the same examiner. The intervals of reassessment will depend on the species, the circumstances of the case, the age and condition of the animal, and any unanticipated medical developments. The intervals themselves should be decided in the planning stage of the case when practical and adjusted throughout the case as appropriate.

BIOSECURITY REQUIREMENTS OF A CRIME SCENE

Animal crime scenes, like any other crime scene, can pose several hazards to the health and safety of crime scene personnel. A safety and health hazard discussion should be part of every planning briefing. Most law enforcement agencies have protocols detailing the required personal protection equipment (PPE) for a crime scene to be in compliance with Occupational Safety and Health Administration (OSHA) requirements. All required PPE protocols should be followed by all personnel on a crime scene. If personnel encounter unique situations for which they are uncertain of the appropriate safety protocols, then the scene should be secured and the local HAZMAT resource consulted.

The following potential hazards and appropriate PPE along with options for mitigation should be detailed:

1. Ammonia levels
2. Bioaerosols
3. Bloodborne and other human pathogens
4. Zoonotic diseases
5. Sharp instruments such as cock-fighting blades
6. Needles and syringes
7. Aggressive animals
8. Poisonous or biting insects and snakes
9. Poisonous plants, such as: poison ivy, poison oak, poison sumac (Fish et al., 2011; Merck, 2013; Cummings School of Veterinary Medicine, Tufts University, 2018a,b)

As previously mentioned, elevated ammonia levels are common findings in housing situations with poor sanitation and ventilation. The Centers for Disease Control/National Occupational Safety and Health (CDC/NIOSH) website notes that the current OSHA permissible exposure limit (PEL) for pure ammonia is 35 ppm as a 15-minute short-term exposure limit (STEL). A STEL is a 15-minute time-weighted average (TWA) exposure which should not be exceeded at any time during the workday. NIOSH established a recommended exposure limit (REL) of 25 ppm as an 8-hr TWA and 35 ppm as a STEL limit (Center for Disease Control/National Safety and Occupational Health, 2018). NIOSH has designated 300 ppm of ammonia as the concentration that is "immediately dangerous to life and health" (Center for Disease Control/National Safety and Occupational Health, 2018; Cummings School of Veterinary Medicine, Tufts University, 2018a). Keep in mind the ammonia that develops in unsanitary animal housing is often mixed with other chemicals from decaying urine, feces, and carcasses. Therefore, it is likely in housing situations with high ammonia levels that there will be additional noxious and toxic chemicals.

While the specific bioaerosols found in unsanitary animal housing facilities have not been identified or quantified, research has shown that exposures to these chemicals can be associated with a wide range of health effects (Douwes et al., 2003). Therefore, it would be prudent, until further research clarifies the specific bioaerosols in this environment, to use appropriate PPE while working this type of crime scene.

Bloodborne pathogens are a crime scene concern regardless of the type of crime. Pathogens are microorganisms such as viruses, bacteria, prions, and fungi that can cause disease. The crime scene investigator should always bear in mind that these pathogens are often found in any of the biological samples that are collected as fluids. Any bodily fluid such as blood, urine, feces, saliva, semen, sweat, vomitus, and other bodily secretion may harbor pathogens. Common pathogens of concern include human immunodeficiency virus (HIV), hepatitis B and C, and sexually transmitted diseases (STDs) (Fish et al., 2011). Although true of any unsanitary crime scene, fecal pathogens such as *Salmonella* and *Escherichia coli* may be present, as quite often in hoarding situations the septic/sewage systems of the house or facility are nonfunctional. In kennel areas with poor sanitation, these fecal pathogens and others may be in high concentration in the feces-contaminated environment. Concern for pathogen contamination extends to collecting and processing evidence from these scenes as well as physical presence on scene.

Zoonotic disease is also of concern when working the scene of an animal crime. In the author's experience, common diseases of concern are rabies, leptospirosis, giardiasis, ringworm, and sarcoptic mange (Figure 1.6).

Figure 1.6 Early lesions consistent with sarcoptic mange.

Sharp instruments are also a hazard at animal crime scene. If the crime scene involves disruption of a cockfight in progress or preparation, the gaffs and knives may already be attached to some of the birds. Use extreme caution and visually observe both legs of the rooster before capturing and handling the bird. Also, be aware that the box or container of knives/gaffs may have been placed within easy reach of the fighter, so always look before placing your hand or foot on any surface. Fighters, both dog and cock, may have scalpel blades and/or razor blades on site (Figure 1.7).

Often on scene of organized animal activities such as fighting, training, housing, and breeding, new and used needles and syringes are often present. The used needles and syringes may be contaminated with blood, vaccines, anabolic steroids, or other illicit substances. Use caution while searching for evidence and when collecting these items as evidence. Most law enforcement agencies have SOPs for needlestick incidents. Follow these protocols in the event of exposure. Be sure to inform the medical officer that the needle may have been contaminated with animal pathogens as well as human ones.

Aggressive animals and/or unsocialized animals are extremely common in large-scale cases and smaller cases in which there has been neglect or minimal human interaction with the subject animal(s). Inherent in large-scale cases is the fact that there are large numbers of animals and usually very few caregivers, and therefore the animals are not used to being handled or have had negative interactions with humans in the past. As noted in the earlier section, part of the initial securing of the scene involves containing or restraining any loose aggressive animals such as dogs. Be very cautious when entering a building or section of a premises for the first time, as undetected aggressive animals may be present.

Although professional level dog fighters often will not tolerate aggression toward humans, many street level fighters also train their dogs to be "protective." As a result, these animals can be very aggressive toward strangers. Animal hoarders rarely are able to socialize the animals in their house or facility. Oftentimes, cats from these situations are essentially feral cats contained inside a structure. Leather or fabric gloves do not protect against bloodborne pathogens (Fish et al., 2011) but they may be needed to handle aggressive animals. If this is the case, then wearing nitrile gloves as a first layer and leather gloves as a second layer may be an option.

Insects can present a hazard to crime scene investigators. Animals who are suffering from poor or negligent veterinary medical care may be infested with fleas, ticks, and/or lice. These parasites may also be found free in the environment so even personnel on scene who are not handling the animals should be alert to this danger. Personnel experience of the author has been that homes of animal hoarders may also have large numbers of poisonous insects such as black widow spiders and/or scorpions. Brushy areas may be hiding snakes both venomous and non-venomous. Occasionally,

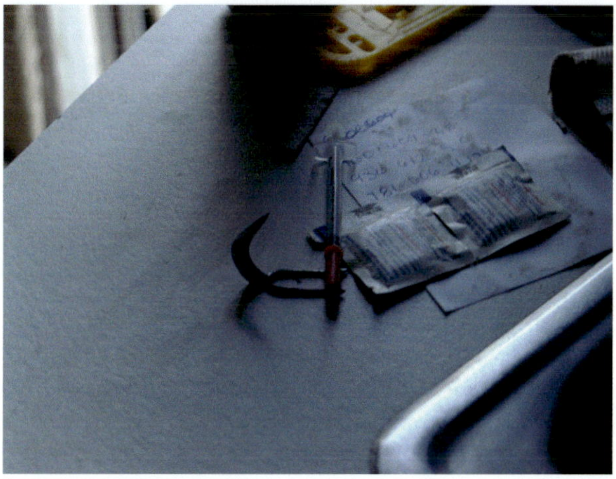

Figure 1.7 Sharps found in the bird preparation area at the scene of a cockfight.

the animals being hoarded may themselves be problematic, such as with exotic reptile collections housing vipers and large dangerous animals such as alligators and Komodo dragons.

Depending on the geographic location, participating in grid or line searches in brushy or woody areas may result in exposure to poisonous plants such as poison ivy or poison oak, or thorny plants such as mesquite. Proper apparel is mandatory to avoid injury.

Although not all types of PPE are required for every scene, keeping all of the hazards listed above in mind, certain PPE should be available for most scenes. These include but are not limited to nitrile gloves, animal handling gloves, Tyvek™ or similar protective outerwear, boots, boot and shoe covers, eye protection, respirators appropriate for the situation/environment, and so on (Fish et al., 2011). There should be ample supplies of PPE as they may need to be changed multiple times during the course of the crime scene processing. They may also need to be changed and disposed of in the event of collecting different pieces of evidence to avoid cross-contamination, or in the event of a tear or gross contamination. All PPE must be disposed of in accordance with biohazard material protocols.

Another consideration with the use of PPE is the physical toll it imparts on the personnel. Wearing respirators and Tyvek-type coveralls can cause heat stress, especially in high heat and high humidity environments with poor ventilation, typical of unsanitary conditions of animal crime scenes. Although timely processing of the scene is important, the risk and potential harm to the scene personnel must be taken into consideration during the planning stage. This concern should also be reassessed throughout the scene processing period, and adjustments made accordingly.

References

American Veterinary Medical Association. 2017. Model Veterinary Practice Act. https://www.avma.org/KB/Policies/Pages/Model-Veterinary-Practice-Act.aspx.

Blossom, J.E., P.W. Hellyer, P.M. Mich, N.G. Robinson, and B.D. Wright. 2007. *Equine Comfort Assessment Scale.* Colorado State University Veterinary Medical Center. http://csu-cvmbs.colostate.edu/Documents/anesthesia-pain-management-pain-score-equine.pdf.

Brewster, M. P. and C. L. Reyes. 2013. *Animal Cruelty: A Multidisciplinary Approach to Understanding.* Durham, NC: Carolina Academic Press, p. 207.

Centers for Disease Control/National Safety and Occupational Health. 1994. *Ammonia. Immediately Dangerous to Life or Health (IDLH) Values.* (https://www.cdc.gov/niosh/idlh/7664417.html).

Center for Disease Control/National Safety and Occupational Health. 2018. Occupational Health Guidelines for Chemical Hazards. https://www.cdc.gov/niosh/ docs/81-123/pdfs/0028-rev.pdf.

Cummings School of Veterinary Medicine. 2018a. Tufts University. Animal Welfare for Hoarding of Animals Research Consortium. http://vet.tufts.edu/wp-content/uploads/fivefreedoms.jpg

Cummings School of Veterinary Medicine. 2018b. Tufts University. Public Health for Hoarding of Animals Research Consortium. http://vet.tufts.edu/hoarding/public-health/.

Cummings School of Veterinary Medicine. 2020. Tufts University. Animal Welfare for Hoarding of Animals Research Consortium. http://vet.tufts.edu/hoarding/animal-welfare/.

DiMaio, V., and D. DiMaio. 2001. *Forensic Pathology,* 2nd ed. Washington, DC: CRC Press.

Douwes, J., P. Thorne, N. Pearce, and D. Heederik. 2003. Bioaerosol health effects and exposure assessment: Progress and prospects. *Annals of Occupational Hygiene,* 47(3): 187–200.

Farm Animal Welfare Council. 2009. Five Freedoms. http://www.fawc.org.uk/freedoms.htm.

Fish, J.T., L.S. Miller, and M.C. Braswell. 2011. *Crime Scene Investigation.* Boston MA: Elsevier – Anderson Publishing, p. 2, 16, 18,19, 33, 36, 37, 65–69, 79-80, 110, 150–151.

Fisher, B.A., W.J. Tilstone, and C. Woytowicz. 2009. *Criminalistics: The Foundation of Forensic Science.* Boston, MA: Elsevier Academic Press, p. 4.

Fitch, A. (Lectures) *Animal Crime Scene Processing, Summer 2015, Course 6052.* University of Florida: ASPCA.

Gianelli, P.C. 2009. *Understanding Evidence,* 3rd ed. New Providence, NJ: LexisNexis.

Hellyer, P.W., S.R. Uhring, and N.G. Robinson. 2006a. *Canine Acute Pain Scale.* Colorado State University Veterinary Medical Center. http://www.vasg.org/pdfs/CSU_Acute_Pain_Scale_Canine.pdf

Hellyer, P.W., S.R. Uhring, and N.G. Robinson. 2006b. *Feline Acute Pain Scale.* Colorado State University Veterinary Medical Center. http://www.vasg.org/pdfs/CSU_Acute_Pain_Scale_Kitten.pdf.

International Association for Property and Evidence Inc. 2016. Professional Standards. http://home.iape.org/evidence-resources/iape-documents.html as viewed on 3/4/2018.

International Veterinary Forensic Sciences Association. 2018. 3/4/2018. www.ivfsa.org

Laflamme, D.P. 1997. Development and validation of a body condition score system for dogs. *Canine Practice*. July/August. 22: 10–15.

Lee, H.C., T. Palmbach, and M.T. Miller. 2007. *Henry Lee's Crime Scene Handbook*. Boston MA: Elsevier Academic Press, p. 1, 6.

Merck, M. 2013. *Veterinary Forensics*, 2nd ed. Ames, Iowa: Wiley-Blackwell Publishing, pp. 21–22, 24, 29–30.

Miles, J.D. 2018. CBS News Dallas-Fort Worth Affiliate. Man Sentenced to 12 Years for Stomping On, Throwing Puppy (https://dfw.cbslocal.com/2018/02/27/man-sentenced-stomping-throwing-puppy/).

National Animal Control Association. 2018. *Animal Control Officer Memorial. Wall of Hero's.* http://www.nacanet.org/page/WallofHeroes.

Nestle Purina Pet Care Center. 2002a. *Body Condition System for Dogs*. Version 3.13. https://oregonvma.org/files/Purina-Dog-Condition-Chart.pdf.

Nestle Purina Pet Care Center. 2002b. Body *Condition System for Cats*. https://oregonvma.org/files/Purina-Cat-Condition-Chart.pdf.

Patronek, G.J. 1997. Tufts Animal Care and Condition (TACC) scales for assessing body condition, weather and environmental safety, and physical care in dogs. In: Olson, P. *Recognizing and Reporting Animal Abuse: a Veterinarian's Guide*. American Humane Association, Denver, CO. Tufts University, Tufts Animal Care and Condition Scale. http://vet.tufts.edu/wp-content/uploads/tacc.pdf.

Reid, P., J. Nolan, A. Nolan, and L. Hughes. 2007. Development of the short-form glasgow composite measure pain scale (CMPS-SF) and derivation of an analgesic intervention score. *Animal Welfare Supplement*. 1.

Touroo, R. 2012. *VME 6575 - Veterinary Forensic Medicine*. Distance education course. University of Florida, Gainesville, FL: Spring.

Touroo, R., and A. Fitch. 2016. Identification, collection, and preservation of veterinary forensic evidence: On scene and during the postmortem examination. *Veterinary Pathology*, 53(5): 880–887.

U.S. Department of Justice. 2013. *Crime Scene Investigation: A Guide for Law Enforcement*. https://www.nist.gov/sites/default/files/documents/forensics/Crime-Scene-Investigation.pdf.

CHAPTER 2

GENERAL PRINCIPLES OF VETERINARY FORENSIC SCIENCES AND MEDICINE

Nancy Bradley-Siemens

INTRODUCTION

Some of the recognized pioneers in veterinary forensic sciences are Dr. Melinda Merck, Dr. Ranald Munro, Dr. Helen M.C. Munro, Dr. John Cooper, Dr. Randall Lockwood, and Dr. M.V. Thrushfield. These pioneering authors have been thought leaders on the subject since at least the late1990s. Through their work, the initial foundations of veterinary forensic sciences have been established. Today, when one thinks of veterinary forensic medicine, the first thought that comes to mind is dealing with animal abuse cases, with both living and deceased animals. There are diverse terms such as forensic veterinarian or forensic veterinary pathologist. Terms like human–animal bond and "the link" arise in discussing the relationship of animal cruelty to all forms of human violence.

Forensic medicine, whether applied to humans or animals, is becoming more important in our modern and litigious society, which is captivated by crime-based television. Medical and legal issues are increasingly coalescing in both civil and criminal matters, increasing the challenge to provide forensic expertise in a myriad of areas. It is therefore imperative that veterinary practitioners providing expert witness testimony to the courts possess essential knowledge and experience to perform examinations and evaluations in a manner that will enable the courts to reach a verdict (Cooper & Cooper, 2007).

DEFINING VETERINARY FORENSICS

Currently, there is no single definition for veterinary forensic sciences. When people think about veterinary forensic sciences, they envision animal abuse cases and mandatory reporting of such cases. Within veterinary forensic medicine, there is already an established expectation that veterinary forensic sciences involve pathology, prosecution of animal abusers, or wildlife crime (Bailey, 2016). In reality, veterinary forensic sciences often involve many more independent sciences that have a forensic application in a court of law. Veterinary forensic sciences, in the realm of animal abuse cases, may involve prosecution and defense testimony. A forensic veterinarian in many instances is the conduit for information across multiple veterinary specialties, as well as professions. A forensic veterinarian will know or be familiar with the veterinary communities: boarded specialists; experts in specific areas such as reptiles, birds, and wildlife; and zoo veterinarians. These veterinarians, although experts in the specific areas, may be unfamiliar with legal or regulatory issues.

Forensic techniques applied to the understanding and resolution of crimes has been well documented for well over a century. Even with this longstanding history, forensic medicine is still evolving (Cooper & Cooper, 2007). The specialty of veterinary forensic medicine is now an established, but novel, specialist area (Cooper & Cooper, 2007).

Just as human forensic medicine covers many diverse areas, so does forensic veterinary practice. These diverse areas of practice include animal welfare, abuse, biodiversity, and regulatory issues (Cooper & Cooper, 2007).

Defining veterinary forensic sciences is difficult. The word forensic, defined in the Merriam-Webster Dictionary is defined as means "belonging to, used in, or suitable to courts of judicature or to public discussion and debate." A secondary definition of "relating to or dealing with the application of scientific knowledge to legal problems" also exists (Merriam-Webster 2018). The dictionary then defines forensic medicine as "a science that deals with the relation and application of medical facts to legal problems." Therefore, it encompasses much more than just animal abuse cases. Veterinary forensic science is the application of a broad spectrum of sciences, including veterinary medicine, to answer questions of interest to a court of law (Touroo, 2015). An even broader definition of veterinary forensics is "the application of science in the resolution of legal disputes involving animals and animal derivatives" (Bailey, 2016).

Today forensic science is a multidisciplinary science with contributions from differing areas of science and technology. In addition, the term "forensic" addresses multiple non-legal issues. Issues outside the courts include insurance claims, environmental impact assessments, public service commissions, or addressing allegations of professional misconduct or other disciplinary concerns considered by state veterinary examining boards (Cooper & Cooper, 2007).

FORENSIC SCIENCE HISTORY

Human forensic medicine history goes back well over 1000 years, with some of the earliest records originating from China (Cooper & Cooper, 2007). Islamic medicine applied forensic approaches to investigate disease and causes of death going back hundreds of years (Bradley, 1927). Forensic medicine essentially evolved in Europe and has led medicolegal investigations there throughout the last millennium (Cooper & Cooper, 2007). One of the more eminent forensic pathologists in the recent past was Sir Bernard Spilsbury (1877–1947) in developing the forensic field (Cooper & Cooper, 2007). He was involved in most of the publicized murder cases in the United Kingdom at the turn of the century. At that time the medical forensic expert, usually the pathologist, would have had immense authority in all medical matters but would have also been the conduit to other people from other forensic disciplines (Cooper & Cooper, 2007).

THE FORENSIC VETERINARIAN TODAY

A forensic veterinary practitioner today is much like the pathologist in Spilsbury's time, or at least it seems so in the author's experience. No one forensic veterinarian or forensic veterinary pathologist can know everything, however they are the veterinary professionals usually in tune with surrounding needs and events in animal forensic matters. The forensic veterinarian may be asked to consult on state veterinary examining board matters involving malpractice or misconduct. Regarding endangered or wildlife resources, if wildlife is injured or killed in a questionable manner a forensic veterinarian may be sought. In civil matters, the author has been involved in multiple cases. The forensic veterinarian is a conduit (facilitator of contacts and information) in many legal matters involving animals. The author has been contacted by different law enforcement agencies to consult on various cases involving diverse types of species. The forensic veterinarian is usually involved in their community/state at multiple levels. They may be contacted by fellow veterinarians, humane investigators, law enforcement agencies, or lawyers. The forensic veterinarian may become directly involved in a case as a sole expert witness, work with veterinary boarded specialists, and may work with a forensic veterinary pathologist or forensic experts from other disciplines. The forensic veterinarian will have a solid knowledge of local, state, and federal laws regarding animal legal issues. An experienced forensic veterinarian will have a plethora of contacts within veterinary medicine including pathologists, species experts, and board certified veterinarians. On the other side, they will also have contacts within law enforcement and in the human forensic arena in areas including forensic odontology, blood spatter analysis, ballistics, tool mark experts, and so on (Figure 2.1).

An example of this was a case of burglary where the family dog was missing and only a large amount of blood remained (Bradley & Zannin, 2015). The author was contacted by a police detective. A blood analyst was contacted and recruited via the author for the case. Based on blood volume and patterns at the scene and a review of current veterinary medical records (dog weight), the dog may have been alive when it was taken from the scene and had sustained multiple stab wounds. Additional felony animal abuse charges were pursued against the suspect in the absence of an animal body.

In Italy in 2011, a man and his dog were struck and killed by a vehicle. The driver stated that the man and his dog were illegally crossing the road in front of him when he struck them. A medical

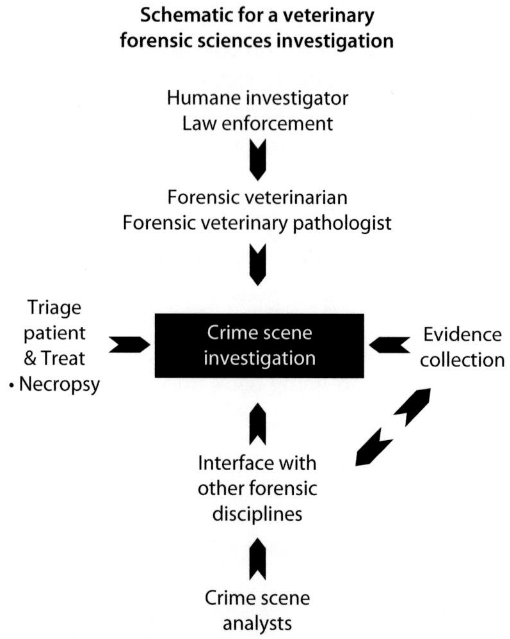

Figure 2.1 Diagram of the process of a typical veterinary forensic sciences investigation. (Courtesy of L. Siemens.)

examiner and a veterinary pathologist were jointly consulted in this case. In both postmortem examinations the driver's story was not adding up. Both the man and the dog had sustained injuries from behind, not from the side. A more detailed examination of the crime scene demonstrated that the car had actually left the roadway and drove over the sidewalk path on which the man and the dog were walking when they were struck from behind. The driver had moved the bodies into the street further down the roadway, altering the crime scene. The joint forensic efforts of both professions were instrumental in solving this crime (Aquila et al., 2014). The author receives calls and questions on a regular monthly basis that involve putting the correct veterinarians and human forensic experts in contact with one another. This may be simply suggesting a forensic necropsy be performed, involve a visit to a crime scene, or court testimony.

COMPARING VETERINARY FORENSIC SCIENCES TO HUMAN FORENSIC SCIENCES

Forensic science as applied to human crime investigation is very specialized, and the related sciences extend well beyond the pathologist. This includes crime scene analysis to analytical and laboratory disciplines (Bailey, 2016). Forensic science is still a novelty in the veterinary world and is dependent on human forensic disciplines as it becomes an established discipline itself. The most significant difference between human and veterinary forensic sciences is the former is physical but inanimate and may consist of any form of physical evidence such as fingerprint imaging or metal fragments, while in veterinary forensic science the evidence can be "living." This characteristic of veterinary forensic science cannot be replicated or learned from human forensic studies. Veterinary evidence can become sick, die, may be dead, or has been killed. Animal evidence may improve or decline in health. Living evidence is a foreign concept in human forensic sciences (Bailey, 2016). Forensic evidence can be bagged, labeled, and stored for long durations prior to trial, but not animals. Animals are sentient beings needing to eat, drink, relieve themselves, and live. In this area, veterinary forensic sciences cannot use the human forensic field for guidance (Bailey, 2016). A forensic veterinarian may need to act as a veterinarian triaging and treating animals at a crime scene as well as being a forensic expert. In human forensics, each professional has their specific role, even though they are part of a larger team of investigators. A forensic veterinarian is also part of a forensic team; however, their roles are more diverse.

APPLICATION OF VETERINARY FORENSIC SCIENCES TO LEGAL INVESTIGATIONS

Animals may be involved in legal issues in two distinct ways: they may be the victim (i.e., object) of the animal abuse, or the instigator (i.e., the subject) where the animal causes the incident (Cooper & Cooper, 2007). In veterinary forensic sciences, the veterinarian needs powers of observation (detective) and the ability to assess clinical findings with history and background information to establish a whole picture of an animal's involvement (Cooper & Cooper, 2007). Basic principles of forensic investigation regarding meticulous record-keeping, systematic examination, and correct treatment of material are identical, regardless of whether the victim is a human or an animal.

THE ANIMAL VICTIM

Animal injuries may be accidental or malicious and may involve attacks (predation), unnatural acts, and mutilations. There are a multitude of injuries and/or insults that can be inflicted on animals by humans. These are forms of physical, sexual, and psychological abuse (Arkow & Munro, 2008; Cooper & Cooper, 2007). Physical injuries may result from trauma, heat, cold, placement in water, and so on; usually these are unintentional but may include "nonaccidental injury" (NAI) (Cooper & Cooper, 2007). Injuries resulting from a sexual insult may be from attempted animal sexual abuse, or surgical or malicious destruction of urogenital regions. These may be true sexual abuse or veterinary husbandry/surgical practices (Cooper & Cooper, 2007). A third insult, not recognized legally in most instances, is psychological in nature. This may result from threatening or teasing an animal or depriving an animal of companionship, or unsuitable social groupings (Cooper & Cooper, 2007). There are now behavioral studies being conducted by forensic animal behaviorists regarding animal hoarding situations documenting these types of psychological effects (McMillan et al., 2011). In addition, forensic animal behaviorists have performed work with fighting pit bulls, establishing behaviors specific to animals that have been trained to fight. This area is wide open, and there is potential for future laws involving emotional (psychological) abuse. Any of the above abusive activities may result in injury, health concerns, pain/distress, or even death. These implications vary depending on the species and the surrounding circumstances (Cooper & Cooper, 2007).

ANIMAL AS THE CAUSE

Injuries caused by animals can include bites from domestic and wild species, trauma, stings, and hypersensitivity (Cooper & Cooper, 2007). Animals can infect humans with pathogenic organisms leading to a variety of zoonotic diseases. Animals may cause damage or disrupt human activity in many ways. These may include:

- Damage to property, i.e., livestock knocking down fences or damaging a vehicle while escaping confinement, birds destroying crops
- Noise, i.e., dogs barking, roosters crowing

- Smell, i.e., dairy or feedlots in close proximity to a residential neighborhood
- Allergens, i.e., sensitivity to fur or feathers
- Fear; general fear of animals, i.e., cats (ailurophobia) (Cooper & Cooper, 2007)

Bites

Bites involve the discovery and investigation of wounds. Bites can occur within a species with unsupervised contact and directed at humans. Animals bite one another when they fight. This may be grounds for criminal or civil action if the animal victim is someone's property. Bites from domestic dogs and cats are the most common and arguably the most litigious form (Cooper & Cooper, 2007). Bites, scratches, and injuries are always a consideration when working with domesticated, free living, or wild species (Cooper & Cooper, 2007). Animal bites inflicted on humans provide an excellent example of when medical and veterinary professionals work together (Cooper & Cooper, 2007).

Zoonosis

Zoonoses are diseases transmitted between animals and humans (Green, 2011). Zoonotic diseases are highly important in forensic medicine. The occurrence or dissemination of a zoonotic disease can constitute a crime, especially if risk assessments have been disregarded, and can be cause for civil action, insurance claims, or allegations of veterinary negligence (Cooper & Cooper, 2007).

Zoonosis can be categorized in various ways, but a practical approach suggested by Cooper and Cooper (2007) for court purposes is divided into three groups:

1. Diseases hazardous to both humans and animals, i.e., rabies, anthrax, avian influenza.
2. Disease that rarely affects animal health overall, but may result in serious disease in humans, i.e., brucellosis, salmonella.
3. Diseases responsible for severe epizootics (epidemics) in domestic or wild animals but rarely impairing humans, i.e., foot-and-mouth disease, Newcastle disease.

Another zoonotic concern is the possible spread of methicillin-resistant *Staphylococcus aureus* (MRSA) from domestic animals to humans and vice versa. MRSA has been observed in dogs, cats, and horses (Cooper & Cooper, 2007; Green, 2011). This has been observed by the author in animal hoarding situations and can become a legal issue in regard to public health.

TYPES OF FORENSIC MEDICINE

Requirements of Veterinary Forensic Medicine

Veterinary forensic work is subject to open discussion and scrutiny, specifically in public venues such as court and other legal proceedings. These are rarely private (Cooper & Cooper, 2007). Veterinary forensic medical work is very different from routine case workups, diagnosis, and treatment. A forensic veterinarian will have knowledge of criminal and regulatory statutes, including animal abuse, orders of protection for animals, animal seizure, and animal attacks. Veterinary forensic medicine is subject to open debate (Cooper & Cooper, 2007). The veterinarian giving evidence (even if considered an expert by the court) will be exposed to interrogation and/or cross-examination, scrutiny, criticism, and attempts to discredit them professionally (Cooper & Cooper, 2007). Therefore, veterinary forensic medicine needs a specific approach and experience base that not all private practice or emergency practitioners, surgeons, or pathologists within veterinary medicine are comfortable with. A forensic veterinarian, given the transparent nature of modern forensic science, specifically involving required court appearances, must be fully prepared, both professionally and psychologically (Cooper & Cooper, 2007).

Veterinary Forensic Medicine

Human forensic medicine is an established and highly developed specialty. For decades, members of the human medical profession have been able to undertake training, pursue postgraduate recognition and credentialing, and obtain full-time employment. Veterinary medicine has not had the equivalent level of professional development and its comparable advantages (Cooper & Cooper, 2007). Veterinarians are only now beginning to be recognized in primary roles in forensic investigations, with ready access to forensic training, and postgraduate credentials. In the past veterinarians interested in forensic studies had to pursue training within the human medical forensic professions without benefit of continuing education credits.

"As legislation relating to animal welfare, conservation and allied subjects increases and society becomes more litigious, especially in Western countries, the demand for specialists in animal forensic sciences is likely to grow and the gaps in education and training are likely to be gradually filled" (Cooper & Cooper, 2007).

Although beginning to be more sought after and utilized, veterinary forensic medicine has not been formally recognized as a discipline in its own right (Cooper & Cooper, 2007). Currently, the only recognition as a specialty is offered within the board certification offered in the Shelter Medicine specialty. The increased prestige of veterinary medicine within the courts and elsewhere has been linked with the expansion of "wildlife crime" (Cooper & Cooper, 2007). In the United States, the establishment by the United States Fish and Wildlife Service (USFWS) of its wildlife forensic laboratory in Ashland, Oregon, resulted in the development of service to wildlife law enforcement agencies and others (Cooper & Cooper, 2007). During this same time period, in the late 1990s Wobeser (1996) published information on medicolegal necropsy of wildlife in Canada.

The perceived and potential value of the veterinarian in conservation cases and subsequent recognition has created a stronger role for the veterinary profession in legal cases relating to other disciplines concerning animals, including welfare and abuse (Cooper & Cooper, 2007). Veterinary forensic medicine is similar to human forensic medicine; however, the focus may differ: welfare and conservation usually occupy animal cases, and issues of death or drug abuse may be more common in human forensic medicine (Cooper & Cooper, 2007).

Comparative Forensic Medicine

Dr. John Cooper defines comparative forensic medicine (CFM) as "the discipline concerned with forensic studies on different vertebrae and invertebrate species of animals, including humans, and the application of such work to the provisions of scientific information to assist in judicial and other processes" (Cooper & Cooper, 2007). Dr. Cooper argues that veterinary forensic medicine and comparative forensic medicine are distinct entities, with overlapping qualities (Cooper & Cooper, 2007). Veterinary medicine in the historical sense relates to the health of domesticated animals. Veterinary forensic medicine involves many species beyond those that are domesticated. Comparative forensic medicine is a discipline in its own right. This branch of comparative medicine bridges the gap between studies of humans and animals. This approach means that one can learn from studies of different species and then apply the findings to species where specific information may be limited (Cooper & Cooper, 2007). This truly emulates the relationship in many ways with human and veterinary forensic applications.

Comparative medicine has been recognized as a discipline in the United States (Cooper & Cooper, 2007), as demonstrated by published contributions by human medical professionals in animal pathology and oncology and by the recognition of veterinarians and others working with varying species by professional bodies like the American Academy of Forensic Science and the Centers for Disease Control in the United States. Comparative forensic medicine involves areas of both human and veterinary medicine where investigative methods are similar. It includes topics such as zoonosis, where there is cooperation among professionals working with both humans and animals. It also incorporates a broad approach to all animal species, not limiting it to domesticated species (Bradley, 1927; Cooper & Cooper, 2007).

Veterinary forensic medicine is a form of comparative medicine in that we continue to learn from human forensic disciplines as veterinary medicine begins to create its own areas of expertise while still being an important component of a forensic investigative team. In the United States this is referred to as the One Health system. One Health is a collaborative professional effort by multiple disciplines at local, state, national, and international levels to sustain optimal health for people, animals, and the environment (American Veterinary Medical Association, 2008).

Current Trends

There is no board certification for veterinary forensic medicine. However, it is incorporated into the board certification for Shelter Medicine under the American Board of Veterinary Practitioners (ABVP Shelter Medicine Practice Board). The veterinary forensic science components required for the shelter board credentialing process are to:

- Participate in the investigation of at least two single animal cases involving alleged criminal animal abuse or neglect including live animal examination for documentation (ABVP Shelter Medicine Practice Board)
- Participate in the investigation of at least one multi-animal case involving alleged criminal animal abuse or neglect (ABVP Shelter Medicine Practice Board)
- Perform at least one forensic necropsy (ABVP Shelter Medicine Practice Board)

FUTURE OF VETERINARY FORENSICS

The future of veterinary forensic sciences will depend on several factors (Cooper & Cooper, 2007):

- Awareness among veterinarians
- Education
- Access to current and reliable information
- Research and development of relevant techniques
- Collaboration among forensic professionals

Awareness

Many veterinarians are not aware of the need to be prepared for legal cases (Cooper & Cooper, 2007). These may be professional board complaints, civil matters, or criminal matters. Most veterinarians are unaware of their state veterinary examining board process when a case is filed against them, let alone mandatory reporting for animal abuse cases and the potential testimonial commitments (requirements) in court that will inevitably follow.

Education

Many veterinary schools in the United States are taught jurisprudence classes; however, testifying in court or the role of an expert witness are sorely lacking in the curriculum (Cooper & Cooper, 2007). Less than 13% of veterinary colleges in the United States (4/30) offer any form of veterinary forensic science training in their curriculums.* However, over 35 states in the United States require some form of mandatory reporting for animal abuse (welfare)-related issues (Lockwood & Arkow, 2016). This needs to be rectified by incorporating in veterinary coursework specific lectures and

* A survey of each veterinary school in the United States was conducted via phone regarding forensic training within course curriculums.

practical demonstrations as part of the curriculum, available electives, and as adjunct to other subjects such as clinical medicine and pathology (Cooper & Cooper, 2007).

At present, postgraduate training in veterinary forensic medicine is becoming more available. There are a few programs in the United States. Graduate certificates and master's degree in veterinary forensics are available at the University of Florida and VetFolio Program through the North American Veterinary Community (NAVC) and American Animal Hospital Association (AAHA), offering continuing education certificates in veterinary forensic science and medicine and animal crime scene investigation. In addition, as of 2008 the International Veterinary Forensic Science Association (IVFSA) offers an annual conference with continuing education credits for veterinarians in the forensic sciences. More veterinary conferences in the United States such as the NAVC and American Veterinary Medical Association (AVMA) annual conferences are offering tracks in veterinary forensics as well. There is a postgraduate forensic internship offered at the American Society for Prevention of Cruelty to Animals (ASPCA) in New York and at the University of Florida in Gainesville.

As veterinary forensics is gaining more momentum and recognition from national organizations such as the American Academy of Forensic Sciences (AAFS), crossover training with human forensic medicine professionals and law enforcement agencies is becoming more accessible. It can be sought out from local resources in the veterinarian's community. Additional resources are accessible at state, regional, and national levels. These types of training venues exist with medical professions such as medical examiners and forensic nurses and include additional training with law enforcement professionals and crime scene analysts in areas such as shooting reconstruction, blood spatter, and so on. It has been the author's experience with her state veterinary medical examining board that attendance and petition for full or partial continuing education credits for these types of trainings has been well received, especially if the veterinarian attains a reputation in their community for addressing veterinary forensic issues.

Even with all these advances, the number of veterinarians specializing in this area is still small. Those who are actively involved in forensic investigations rely on experience and advice from others, rather than obtaining specific training as part of a veterinary curriculum or coursework leading to recognition as a specialist.

Other educational opportunities consist of enrollment in postgraduate degree and certificates primarily targeted at the medical profession or forensic science, in a subject area veterinarians or other professionals concerned with animals can gain knowledge when appropriate (Cooper & Cooper, 2007). Those veterinarians interested in forensic studies and investigation should strive for membership in appropriate forensic societies in addition to specialist qualifications (Cooper & Cooper, 2007). A prime example would be the AAFS and IVFSA. These types of associations keep experts from multiple disciplines in touch with one another. In addition, this increases an expert witness's standing in the court due to their affiliation with recognized forensic organizations (Cooper & Cooper, 2007).

Accreditation of veterinary professionals involved in forensic work is likely to become an issue in the future, especially in countries where such systems are in place for human forensic medicine (Cooper & Cooper, 2007). In the United Kingdom, the Council for the Registration of Forensic Practitioners (CRFP) is in place, and many forensic veterinarians there are listed in the CRFP Register (Cooper & Cooper, 2007). In the absence of such a body in the United States, additional training and professional forensic society affiliations are extremely beneficial for credibility as an expert witness in veterinary forensic medicine.

Access to Information

Improved teaching and specialized training for veterinarians interested in forensic medicine is becoming more available. There is currently an abundance of relevant information. Articles, papers, and books relating to veterinary forensic work with domestic animals and wildlife (Cooper &

Cooper, 2007) are becoming more prevalent; for example, the *Journal of Veterinary Forensic Sciences* was published in the spring of 2020 in conjunction with IVFSA, and the *Veterinary Pathology* September 2016 issue was exclusively dedicated to veterinary forensic pathology. In addition, the recent two-volume book *Veterinary Forensic Pathology*, edited by Dr. Jason Brooks, Springer International, Cham, Switzerland, 2018. Books and papers primarily involving human forensic work can also be invaluable (Cooper & Cooper, 2007), such as the *Journal of Forensic Science*, published by the AAFS.

As discussed in the previous section it is useful for veterinarians to join human forensic societies and organizations. These organizations have membership consisting of medical and biomedical disciplines (Cooper & Cooper, 2007) as well as law enforcement crime analysts. These organizations hold conferences that provide professional or technical contacts and offer access to publications and guidelines that can be valuable to veterinary forensic work. Again, a prime example in the United States is the AAFS.

These professional organizations and societies provide professional status, with a code of practice and disciplinary systems (Cooper & Cooper, 2007). A forensic expert can gain much from participating in the functions of societies where there is the opportunity to exchange views with others, especially those from differing forensic disciplines, and present and share information at these conferences (Cooper & Cooper, 2007). Topics such as preparation of reports, compensation (fees), and current state and federal forensic legislation are also discussed (Cooper & Cooper, 2007).

ESTABLISHMENT: STANDARDIZATION OF SYSTEMS AND PROTOCOLS

One of the main factors hindering the development of veterinary forensic medicine is the wide diversity or absence of standard systems and protocols (Cooper & Cooper, 2007). Systematic and strictly followed protocols are needed when dealing with live or deceased animals (Cooper & Cooper, 2007). To the author's knowledge, there are no proven guidelines about how or which samples should be obtained from animal material for legal cases or techniques for labeling, transportation, or storage. In addition, veterinarians or animal humane investigators unfamiliar with forensic work may be unaware of maintaining a chain of custody and not aware of the necessity of tamper-proof evidentiary containers in transporting evidence (Cooper & Cooper, 2007).

The forensic expert's system of collecting and processing evidence, not their opinion, is often the vulnerable area in a court case (Cooper & Cooper, 2007). It is easier for an attorney to find issue with technical work (i.e., procedures, record keeping) than to challenge an expert's opinion (Cooper & Cooper, 2007). Veterinary forensics is a developing discipline, and it is imperative that those who use or develop protocols share the information and receive feedback to facilitate continued alterations and improvements (Cooper & Cooper, 2007).

Since January 2016, the Federal Bureau of Investigation (FBI) National Incident-Based Reporting System (NIBRS) has been collecting data from law enforcement agencies on acts of animal abuse including gross neglect, torture, organized abuse (animal fighting), and sexual abuse. Acts of animal cruelty are now counted alongside felony crimes such as arson, burglary, assault, and homicide in the FBI's expansive criminal information database (Desousa, 2016). This may provide a venue to establish databases involving animal abuse cases. Dr. Cooper in his book stresses the importance of establishing animal forensic archives for the diverse veterinary forensic issues. These might be maintained at veterinary schools or research institutes, and the material would be available for both research and evidentiary purposes (Cooper & Cooper, 2007).

Research and Development: Investigative Techniques

Since Dr. Cooper's book in 2007, there has been minimal research in the field of animal forensic sciences. Mirroring human forensic work is helpful but not always ideal. Comparative forensic medicine should be utilized, permitting lessons to be learned and applied from diverse species and disciplines. Postmortem changes and their interpretation, specifically regarding time of death, is an important example of where specific study and evaluation are required (Cooper & Cooper, 2007; Merck, 2017). Another area of interest is ballistics in animals that have been shot, especially those at distance (Cooper & Cooper, 2007). An animal shot at close range where gunshot residue (GSR) may be present is difficult to access or document due to fur. A great deal of information still needs to be researched in veterinary forensic medicine.

Collaboration

Veterinary forensic medicine does not exist in a vacuum (Figure 2.2). It overlaps with many other forensic fields and professions. Veterinary forensic medicine may require information from both medical and dental professions in the investigation of bite wounds or animal abuse cases (Aquila et al., 2014; Cooper & Cooper, 2007). This is also plausible in a reverse sense. There have been issues of human medical examiners (MEs) performing necropsies on companion animals. Human MEs are not veterinarians, and evidence may be discarded if it is not obtained by a qualified veterinary professional (McEwen & McDonough, 2016). Advances in veterinary forensic medicine will be enhanced if scientists and professionals from varied disciplines collaborate their efforts. The medical and dental professions exemplify how techniques used in humans can be applied to veterinary work or when humans and other creatures suffer similar abuse (Cooper & Cooper, 2007). Collaborative efforts with non-medical groups (i.e., law enforcement crime analysts) can also be beneficial. An example, discussed earlier in this chapter, is the cooperation between the author and a blood spatter pattern expert. The demand for interdisciplinary collaboration is increasing.

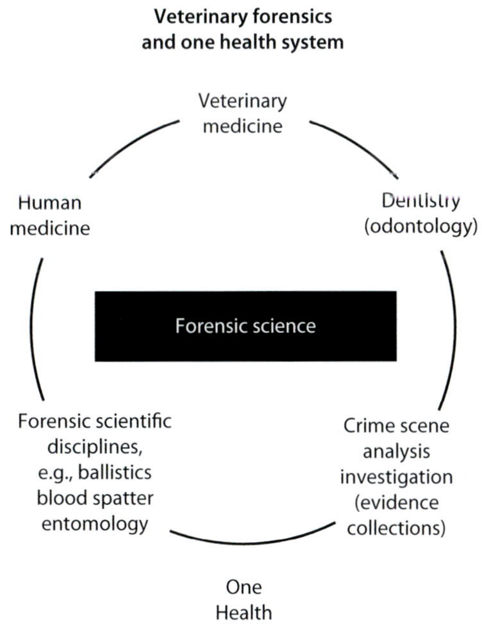

Figure 2.2 Diagram of the integration of veterinary forensic sciences and the One Health concept. (Courtesy of L. Siemens.)

Developments in science and multidisciplinary applications will cause ethical dilemmas that will necessitate legislation, codes of practice, or both (Cooper & Cooper, 2007).

Networking

Networking is communication with individuals who have similar interests, where sharing information may be beneficial to both parties. Networking encompasses communication via e-mail, exchanging literature, collaborative effort in authoring literature (Bradley & Rasile, 2014), and meeting in person. Conferences both nationally and internationally are excellent opportunities for networking. The exchange of literature can refer to published and unpublished information but may also include data that has not appeared in print but is available to individuals for reference (Cooper & Cooper, 2007).

CONCLUSION

Veterinary forensic science goes well beyond animal cruelty issues. Increasing demands are being placed on veterinarians in the United States for mandatory reporting and increasing involvement in animal welfare, wildlife, and regulatory, criminal, and civil-related issues. Education in these areas needs to be addressed in veterinary university curriculums. Research regarding veterinary forensics needs to be addressed through ongoing studies at veterinary universities and collaborative efforts with human forensic science disciplines. Veterinary forensic science is a form of comparative medicine linking human and veterinary medicine and is an important factor in the future One Health system proposed in the United States, benefiting both humans and animals (American Veterinary Medical Association, 2008).

References

American Veterinary Medical Association. 2008. One Health Initiative Task Force: Final Report July 15, 2008. One Health: A New Professional Imperative, One Health: World Health through Collaboration.

American Board Veterinary Practitioners (ABVP). 2018. Shelter Medicine Practice Board Certification. www.abvp.com.

Aquila, I. C., Di Nunzio O., Paciello D., Britti F., Pepe E., De Luca, and P. Ricci. 2014. Case report: An unusual pedestrian road trauma: From forensic pathology to forensic veterinary medicine. *Forensic Sci International* 234: e1–e4.

Arkow, P. and H. Munro. 2008. The veterinary profession's roles in recognizing and preventing family violence: The experiences of the human medicine field and the development of diagnostic indicators of non-accidental injury. In: Ascione F., ed. *The International Handbook of Animal Abuse and Cruelty: Theory, Research, and Application*. West Lafayette, IN: Purdue University Press, pp. 31–58.

Bailey, D. 2016. *Practical Veterinary Forensics*. CAB International, Oxfordshire, UK, 201p.

Bradley, O. C. Nov 1927. What is comparative medicine? *Proc R Soc Med*. 21(1):129–134.

Bradley, N. and K. Rasile. April 2014. Recognition and management of animal sexual abuse. *Clinician's Brief*. 73–75.

Bradley, N. and A. Zannin. 2015. Bloodstain Pattern Analysis. Presented at *8th Annual Veterinary Forensic Sciences Conference of the International Veterinary Forensic Science Association*, May 13–15, Orlando, Florida.

Cooper, J. and M. E. Cooper. 2007. *Introduction to Veterinary and Comparative Forensic Medicine*. Oxford, UK: Blackwell Publishing Ltd.

Desousa, D. 2016. NIBRS User Manual for Animal Control Officers and Humane Law Enforcement. National Council on Violence Against Animals. Animal Welfare Institute. 31p.

Green, C. E. 2011. *Infectious Diseases of the Dog and Cat*. 4th ed. St. Louis: MI: Elsevier Saunders, 1376p.

International Veterinary Forensic Science Association (IVFSA). 2018. www.ivfsa.org.

Lockwood, R. and P. Arkow. 2016. Animal Abuse and Interpersonal Violence: The cruelty connection and its implications for veterinary pathology. *Vet Pathol.* 53(5):910–918.
McEwen, B., S. P. McDonough. 2016. Domestic dogs (*Canis lupus familiaris*) and forensic practice. *Forensic Sci Med Pathol.* Letter to the Editor. Published online, September 12.
McEwen, B. 2017. Personal Interview. September 7.
McMillan, F. D., Duffy, D. L., and J. A. Serpell. 2011. Mental health of dogs formerly used as "breeding stock" in commercial breeding establishments. *Applied Animal Behavior Sci.* 135:86–94.
Merck, M. 2017. Personal Interview. September 5.
Touroo, R. 2015. *VME 6575–Veterinary Forensic Medicine.* Spring Semester, University of Florida, Gainesville, Florida.
Vetfolio Program NAVC/AAHA. Graduate Certificate Program. http://www.vetfolio.com/
Wobeser, G. 1996. Forensic (medicolegal) necropsy of wildlife. *J WIldl Dis.* 32(2):240–249.

CHAPTER 3

HUMANE LAW ENFORCEMENT

From Initial Report to Final Appeal

Susan Underkoffler and Scott Sylvia

OVERVIEW

When one hears the term "humane law enforcement," often the first thoughts that come to mind are of the overdramatized, media-hyped sagas of the animal cops seen on reality television. While the stories may be superficially true, what is most often not acknowledged are the mundane but vital intricacies of the profession, along with the constant emotional roller-coaster ride stemming from days spent mired in what can often be some of the most egregious acts of abuse humans can inflict. The field of animal cruelty investigation is nebulous and confusing, due in large part to little understood legalities and regulations that fluctuate between states and counties, boroughs and municipalities (Figure 3.1). Laws are little understood by both enforcement officers and lawyers, and judges are often so unfamiliar with them that cases can be dismissed out of ignorance. This can result in not only lack of justice but continuation of the disheartening spiral of negative emotions a humane law enforcement (HLE) officer can feel. Investigating crimes against animals can seem bleak and hopeless, especially when one considers the fate of the animal victims; often they are left to decline physically and mentally in a shelter for months, if not years, while the case drags on, or forced to heal from wounds in the frenetic, noisy setting of a busy veterinary facility or shelter hospital with little individual attention.

However, being on the front lines fighting animal abuse can be in equal measure undeniably rewarding. The satisfaction that comes from removing an animal from a harmful or neglectful situation can mitigate the sadness. And an airtight, efficient case that results in a suitable outcome serves as an incentive to continue the fight. Knowing that the investigation was conducted properly, that all necessary facts were gathered, and that the case was succinct and well prepared can ease the uncertainty of the courtroom appearance. While not always possible, ensuring a positive outcome for an animal can help future cases in that they often build upon themselves and serve as examples for future cases.

This chapter is written in the form of a testimonial rather than a how-to guide. Plenty of sources are already in existence which detail step-by-step animal cruelty forensic techniques (Sinclair et al., 2009; Merck, 2007) and explain the various forms of animal abuse and neglect, including other chapters in this book. This chapter will mention some useful methodologies and some of the types of cases which may be encountered and will also detail aspects of HLE that are seldom described in print, including procedures that may be utilized during the investigative process, the ambiguous nature of the profession and the lack of respect it often garners, and the emotional toll this line of work exacts.

Figure 3.1 Pennsylvania Humane Law Enforcement officer badge.

INITIAL NOTIFICATION AND REPORTING

Depending on state or municipality, a report of animal cruelty may come in many different forms. Citizens are often unaware of how to report such cases, and very few organizations have cruelty hotlines. This is often where the first problems arise, as an untold number of cruelty cases go unreported due to a lack of knowledge of how to report them. A neighborhood resident may see dogs chained in a backyard with no food, water, or shelter, but may not know which agency, if any, to notify of the issue. Confusion surrounding to whom to report the incidents can result in delayed action and in worst-case scenarios, an animal's death.

There may be any number of groups with the ability to intervene in cases of animal abuse or neglect depending upon location, but their roles may vary. In some areas, animal cruelty cases may be handled by local, city, or state police, many of whom are often too overburdened to take on what may be seen as a less important crime. These officers may be instructed to filter these issues on to other groups. In some large metropolitan locations, there may be a city-run animal control facility that utilizes animal control officers tasked with performing rudimentary investigations, but who have little to no formal law enforcement training and whose main job it is to remove stray or nuisance animals. In many rural areas, there may be no one specific person or group assigned to animal cases, and the terms "animal abuse" or "animal cruelty" may not carry the same importance or even a sense of obligation. Yet in other towns and cities some private, nonprofit animal rescue or sheltering groups may have the capacity to not only take in and house unwanted or abused animals but may also employ investigators or specific humane law enforcement officers to respond to complaints or incidents of animal cruelty. Indeed, many societies for the prevention of cruelty to animals (SPCAs) or humane societies, which are so named by their board of directors or governing bodies (the terms are ubiquitous and can be used by any private organization that so chooses), are recognized for their focused missions to combat animal cruelty. Their officers may be sworn law enforcement personnel whose job it is to enforce that state or municipality's animal cruelty statutes, and they may have been given the authority to arrest those who violate the law. They may have police academy or weapons training. Their agencies may have use of force policies and they may be licensed to carry firearms. Washington, DC, Pennsylvania, California, and Massachusetts are all examples of states that have recognized HLE officers.

Whatever the agency, group, or facility, investigators or officers may be notified of a possible cruelty incident when a direct call from a citizen is made to their organization, or the police may reroute calls and complaints they receive but are unequipped to handle. Sometimes tips may come from passersby when officers in uniform are on the street investigating other reports. Marked animal emergency response or law enforcement vehicles can attract a good deal of attention and will often prompt community members to approach to ask questions or mention something they have seen. If by phone, the calls may be disseminated to officers by dispatchers based on the officers' assigned territories. Some agencies in large urban areas have a ranking system for cruelty complaints that prioritize the calls based on an assessment of the animal's welfare provided by the complainant, with "danger of death" being of the highest importance. Dispatchers may be trained to ask specific questions of callers to gauge the animal's condition. Danger of death calls are typically investigated within less than 24 hours, and often require an on-call response. These types of reports can indicate an animal in distress due to weather extremes, visible suffering in the form of emaciation, active visible physical abuse or torture, animal fighting, or any other form of cruelty or neglect that places the animal's well-being in immediate danger. These situations often necessitate the prompt removal of the animal from the situation and emergency medical care. While all reports should be investigated, it is important to have a system of some type in place to process the often overwhelming number of complaints needing to be handled by organizations with extremely limited resources and personnel in order to save the most lives. Unfortunately, many organizations do not have such a system for determining priority calls, and the calls are simply investigated as time or staffing allows.

Lower-priority reports may include those regarding hoarding situations, abandonment, or unsanitary conditions. While serious in nature, these forms of cruelty are sometimes able to be resolved without extensive investigation or court involvement. Notification of these possible cases could appear from community members who hear a dog barking inside a property that appears vacant on their block, or from neighbors who notice a foul odor of ammonia emanating from a home nearby. It is the officer's responsibility and duty to investigate each possible case, but as is true in most aspects of law enforcement, an officer must use their own discretion and experience in deciding what actions to take to remedy the situation. The initial notification of a possible animal cruelty or neglect case may come from someone the officer routinely deals with or has dealt with in the past. This may be a repeat "alarmist" caller, or a disgruntled neighbor who is simply acting on a grudge. It may come from an offender themselves, who, having been assisted by the officer in the past, recognizes that they have a problem with keeping too many animals and receives no help from anyone but the officer—the "system" has failed them. The myriad of situations that the HLE officer can be involved in calls for extreme prudence and diplomacy (Arluke, 2004).

HLE officers can also be notified to potential abusive situations through the observations made by police or child and social welfare workers (Figure 3.2). These workers will often encounter possible animal neglect or ill-treatment in the course of investigations into other crimes. It is common for animal abuse and spousal or child abuse to occur in the same household (Lockwood & Ascione, 1998). Recognizing the signs of both are critical to stemming the cycle of escalating violence. The National Link Coalition and the National Coalition Against Domestic Violence report that "13% of intentional animal abuse cases involve domestic violence, and 71% of pet owners entering domestic violence shelters report that their batterer had threatened, injured, or killed family pets" (nationallinkcoalition.org; www.ncadv.org, 2006). Programs are now in existence to train officers on deciphering perceptions and diagnosing potential problems. One such program, offered by the National Children's Advocacy Center, purports to teach intervention strategies such as "addressing when maltreated children turn to abusing animals and successful multidisciplinary team responses including cross-training and cross-reporting abuse" (NCAC, 2013).

Reports of animal cruelty may be nothing more than an anonymous caller disclosing an address but who refuses to give their name or personal information. This request for anonymity stems from the fact that witnesses to cruelty incidents are often reluctant to communicate what they've seen for

Figure 3.2 HLE officers need to recognize that domestic abuse and animal abuse often occur together. (Marine Corps photo by Sgt. Valerie Eppler.)

a number of reasons, including fear of being identified for retribution. Animal cruelty is commonly associated with other crimes such as drug trafficking or gambling. Being labeled as a "snitch" could prove dangerous where witness intimidation is commonplace. In some large cities the problem of speaking up is so pervasive that finding witnesses willing to speak to police, let alone testify in court, is next to impossible. The "stop snitching" culture is palpable without being communicated verbally (USDOJ, 2009).

Even veterinarians may hesitate to report possible occurrences. Afraid of disclosing private client information or of violating the trust between practitioner and client, they may remain silent. In addition, some feel that asking questions or interrogating the person bringing the animal for treatment alienates or targets that person, who may be the one person operating as an advocate for the animal. Many veterinarians are also reluctant to provide testimony in animal cruelty cases for several reasons, including fear of retribution, negative press, or a misunderstanding of immunity from liability. However, that attitude is changing, and veterinarians are increasingly realizing that they are an integral link to breaking the cycle of violence and that their expertise is vital to saving the lives of animals and humans alike. Many states have enacted laws requiring veterinarians to report suspected abuse. Other states provide immunity for those veterinarians who report cruelty.

A veterinarian's testimony can without question make or break a case—when a veterinarian describes the feeling of hundreds of tiny parasites crawling around in an ear canal, feeding on ear wax and leaving thick, black, crusty material behind to block the ear canal and cause extreme itching, discomfort, depression, frustration, and in some cases constant head shaking and tilting—a judge or jury has a much clearer (albeit more repugnant) picture of an ear mite malady and why failure to treat the condition could be serious enough to merit "lack of veterinary care" or neglect charges. A statement from an officer regarding the same condition but phrased as "black discharge in an animal's ears" most likely would not elicit the same visceral response.

INVESTIGATION, PROBABLE CAUSE, AND SEARCH WARRANTS

Investigation

If a report of suspected cruelty is submitted by a witness who chooses to leave contact information, the officer should first speak with that witness. Obtaining as much information as possible can sometimes help determine the best initial course of action. But once again, discretion should be used when communicating with a complainant in order to remain objective. It is common for an HLE officer to speak with a complainant who is willing to provide their name and phone number but refuses to testify in court. Officers need to communicate to the complainant that often the only thing that will bring justice is an eyewitness account. When those who file reports understand that animal cruelty can be difficult to prosecute, that the cases are typically not given much validity in courtrooms, and that judges or juries demand irrefutable proof before enforcing penalties, they can sometimes be persuaded that their testimony is vital.

Filtering nuisance complaints is a prevalent task among those investigating animal maltreatment. It is imperative in a field where hundreds of reports are received daily. Officers frequently find that a call about animal cruelty stems from spousal conflicts of a vindictive nature, neighbors frustrated by a continually barking dog, or landlords or tenants irritated by an unresolved argument. In some instances, an officer who speaks directly with the person reporting suspected abuse will find that there were other circumstances that prompted the call. Neighbor disputes are frequently the cause of falsified or inflated reports, and in certain circumstances, by the time the officer is able to contact the complainant, they will have had time to "cool off." If the report seems baseless, an officer can

Figure 3.3 Actual scene photograph of dilapidated stables—an example of inadequate shelter.

often flush out the true reason for it by asking the right questions. HLE policing is often rewarded by using excellent communication skills (Arluke, 2004).

HLE officers are responsible for determining which reports are investigated as cruelty and which are unfounded. They use their personal judgment and experience to decide whether actual laws have been broken or whether a report of cruelty is merely a moral or ethical offense. They must interpret the law themselves due to its nebulous and arbitrary nature. In many states the statutes do not define terms such as "cruelty" or "torture," and they do not elaborate on their meaning, leaving plenty of room for misinterpretation or for clarification as an officer sees fit. Anticruelty statutes are often explained and applied on a case-by-case basis due to how loosely they are detailed. The phrase "proper food, water, and shelter" can be defined in many ways; is proper shelter a leaky, wooden structure with broken slats and a partial roof; is it a large, heavy plastic drum turned on its side? Is proper water considered fresh at all times, or is water that may have dirt or insects or a thin film of algae or that has not been changed in many days sufficient? Officers often must make recommendations to respondents based on opinions or a veterinarian's suggestions rather than hard facts. One person's definition of "beating" or "overworking" may be completely different than someone else's. It is this very ambiguity that both frustrates officers and allows them a bit of flexibility when enforcing the laws (Figure 3.3).

Flexibility can also take the form of making decisions on which cases officers will pursue as criminal based in part on the age or condition of the respondents, coupled with the nature of the violation. Infractions of a nonviolent or non-malicious nature could be handled with coaching, instruction, or aid versus criminal penalties. Cases involving elderly or mentally handicapped respondents can be treated as educational pursuits or opportunities to compromise. This is common with repeat hoarding offenders who have the ability to recognize their problem and frequently call officers who had been understanding with them in the past. To most officers it is more important to help both the people and the animals than to pursue an 82 year old through the court system for possessing more animals than the law allows. It also builds stronger community relationships and gives people safe options. In these cases, the officers' help could come in the form of an agreement not to press charges if the respondent voluntarily surrenders some of the animals, or in the form of free veterinary treatment if needed.

Visiting the location where a cruelty incident is said to have occurred is often where the most information will be obtained (Arluke, 2004). Often, an officer may have little to go on before

Figure 3.4 Investigative photograph—a property where it was reported that animals were abandoned inside a home.

conducting an inspection of the property. An HLE officer's judgments can start forming the moment they receive an address; experience and knowledge of the location can tell them something of the ethnicity, economic level, and common law infractions or crimes, if any, generally encountered there. Certain areas may be prone to certain types of crime; for instance, in Philadelphia, Pennsylvania, dogfighting is often encountered in the southern sections of the city. Cockfighting is often associated with certain ethnic groups, as is ritualistic or religious animal crime. An awareness of locale is important not only to prepare an officer for what may be occurring there but also to inform them of possible safety threats. A seasoned officer knows the territory and which areas are the most dangerous and prone to crime or violence. But since reports of animal cruelty can come from anywhere, all calls must be investigated with caution. It is never a given what might happen when an officer knocks on a door. HLE officers may work with local police to investigate residents' backgrounds or past crimes at a particular property, either before visiting the location or after the initial visit or contact. If it is found that a resident of that property has had prior arrests, the humane officer may request police accompaniment (Figure 3.4).

If no one is at home or if no one answers the door when the officer knocks, they may do a brief property inspection to determine if anything can be seen or heard. An officer may be walking a fine line when doing this, as they must be aware of trespassing laws and privacy rights. But if an animal can be seen and briefly visually inspected from a safe distance it can inform the officer of the necessary next steps. Humane officers become trained to use all their senses when investigating, noting sounds of dogs or cats crying, the smell of urine or feces, or the sight of an overturned bucket and a heavy chain. All of this is important to their case.

If no one answers their initial knock, the officer may leave their business card or a written notice which is taped to the door and photographed as evidence, giving the property owner a certain amount of time to respond (frequently 24–48 hours). If no one responds within that given time period and a violation of the animal cruelty law exists or is thought to exist, the officer may choose to obtain a search warrant. This is characteristic of abandonment cases (Figure 3.5).

Communicating with respondents directly is always the goal; however, speaking with respondents can be tricky. Officers must approach every situation with a critical, and in some cases, cynical outlook because of the unpredictable nature of the investigations. Officers must anticipate the possibility of not only an undesirable response from the respondents themselves, but they must also

Figure 3.5 Photograph obtained during an investigation without entering the property; photo taken from an alleyway behind the property.

assume that the animal or animals they've been dispatched to check on could attack them. Danger presents itself from every angle. Experienced officers have learned to "read" animal behavior, and sometimes can make a determination of whether the animal is in serious pain or suffering, although this is preferably determined by a veterinarian. Veterinary accompaniment to scenes of potential animal crime when possible is extremely helpful.

Respondents can react differently in each situation. They may be receptive and cooperative, but in many instances they can become hostile and belligerent. Seeing someone in uniform approach their door can cause immediate suspicion and defensiveness. The respondent may have had unfavorable dealings with police in the past and may not take the time to notice an officer's badge identifying them as HLE. Even after becoming aware of an HLE officer's professional association, a respondent may still exhibit hostility due to feeling threatened or cornered. They may be afraid of the officer seizing their animals, even if the officer has only come to do a brief investigation. It is common for HLE officers to encounter respondents who react in an adverse manner when told that a witness reported an incident on their property—respondents commonly demand to know who reported the problem and often become so agitated that they don't focus on the problem needing to be addressed. It is imperative that an HLE officer retain control of the situation. This may be accomplished by redirecting the heated conversation back to the matter at hand or by calmly listening and diffusing the situation by compromise. Much of an officer's job is education—respondents often have little knowledge of the law, leaving the officer to try to communicate it to the best of their ability. Because the laws themselves are vague, the officers can make recommendations knowing full well that the law doesn't require specifics. This is a commonly frustrating aspect of the profession, as officers can find themselves faced with what they know is inadequate care for the animal, but since no law has been broken, all they can do is try to communicate what is proper and hope for the best. If calm explanations and suggestions do not achieve results, officers may then escalate to warnings or threats of legal action. But this tactic too could have mixed outcomes. It may cause the respondent to become even more combative. They may refuse to let the officer inside, slam the door in the officer's face, or hurl obscenities. They may threaten the officer in some way. A refusal to cooperate may require an officer to obtain a search warrant to further the investigation.

Probable Cause

If the situation merits a search warrant, it is important to ensure that probable cause exists. The fourth amendment guarantees a person's right to remain free from unreasonable searches and seizures. However, where probable cause exists, and circumstances justify it, some searches can be conducted without a search warrant where there is little to no expectation of privacy, such as in an open field or a car. But since many cases of animal cruelty require searches of buildings, homes, and property, obtaining a search warrant is often the safest course of action. Probable cause can be defined as having sufficient facts and circumstances that would warrant a person of reasonable care and caution to believe that an offense is being or has been committed (Ingram, 2009). An officer typically obtains probable cause when someone gives it to them, but there is a determination of reliability that must be made when procuring probable cause that requires both a basis of knowledge and veracity of information, along with a consideration of the totality of the circumstances. If this is not ensured, the warrant request may be denied, and evidence may be suppressed. A bad reputation, mere suspicion, or unfounded information is not sufficient for probable cause. An officer needs to do all they can to obtain the facts. On abandonment calls, often an officer can hear barking through a locked door, see a cat in an upstairs window, or observe an injured, neglected puppy through a broken basement hatch. These firsthand observations can constitute proper, justified probable cause.

Search Warrants

Warrants should ideally be approved by an attorney to ensure correctness, but in all cases, they should specify the location and all buildings or structures to be searched including curtilage, or the area immediately surrounding the home or structure, which still counts as part of that home; it is important to be as specific and inclusive as possible. If it is believed that there may be sufficient reason to search outbuildings, sheds, barns, garages, and so on, these should all be included in the warrant.

When executing a search warrant, it is advisable to utilize the help of local or state police, and to be accompanied by other HLE officers. These situations are inherently dangerous, can escalate quickly and without warning, and may require a great deal of time to properly process a scene, should one exist. Having backup for protection and additional help to gather evidence, seize animals when necessary, and assist with paperwork is invaluable.

Warrants also require that they be executed within a strict time frame. Even executing a warrant at the scene of an abandonment should include at least one additional officer, since there is always the possibility of hidden danger, and if there are multiple animals to be removed from a property, extra people can alleviate the burden and help process the scene. Having additional personnel can secure multiple property entrances and exits as well. If a property needs to be secured from the outside or watched while pursuing procurement of a search warrant is obtained, it is advisable to have multiple officers stationed near all entries and exits. When the warrant is in hand and if no one answers repeated vocal commands announcing the officers' presence and possession of a warrant or their knocks on the door, officers may enter the property. Extreme caution must be exercised in this case for the obvious reason that the respondent, suspect, or homeowner may still be inside, possibly with a weapon, and there is also the threat of a potential attack by animals.

Once inside and after the scene has been secured, photographs of the property and of the animal(s) in situ (accompanied by proper identification and case numbers) need to be taken before anything is altered or removed. Documentation of the scene as it is found is of extreme importance and holds true whether the scene is indoors or out. As with any crime scene, the safety of personnel is paramount, followed by help for the victims. Animals should be removed and transported immediately for veterinary evaluation and treatment. Mail or papers with names, addresses or other identifying information should be confiscated in order to help track down the property owner, and these should be photographed where they are found prior to removal and logged on an evidence recovery sheet, along with any other evidentiary materials recovered. Evidence can be defined as "anything that tends to prove or disprove a fact in contention" (Gardner, 2005). For each case, the evidentiary materials may be different. In a dogfighting case, there may be medications, fighting and training paraphernalia, or quantities of illegal drugs or weapons on the premises. In an abandonment case, there may be empty food and water containers or soiled crates or cages that should be considered evidence. Heavy chains, items used to hit or beat animals, overflowing, unsanitary litter boxes, or ropes or tethers used to improperly constrain animals are just some of the items that may be seized as having evidentiary value to the case (Figure 3.6).

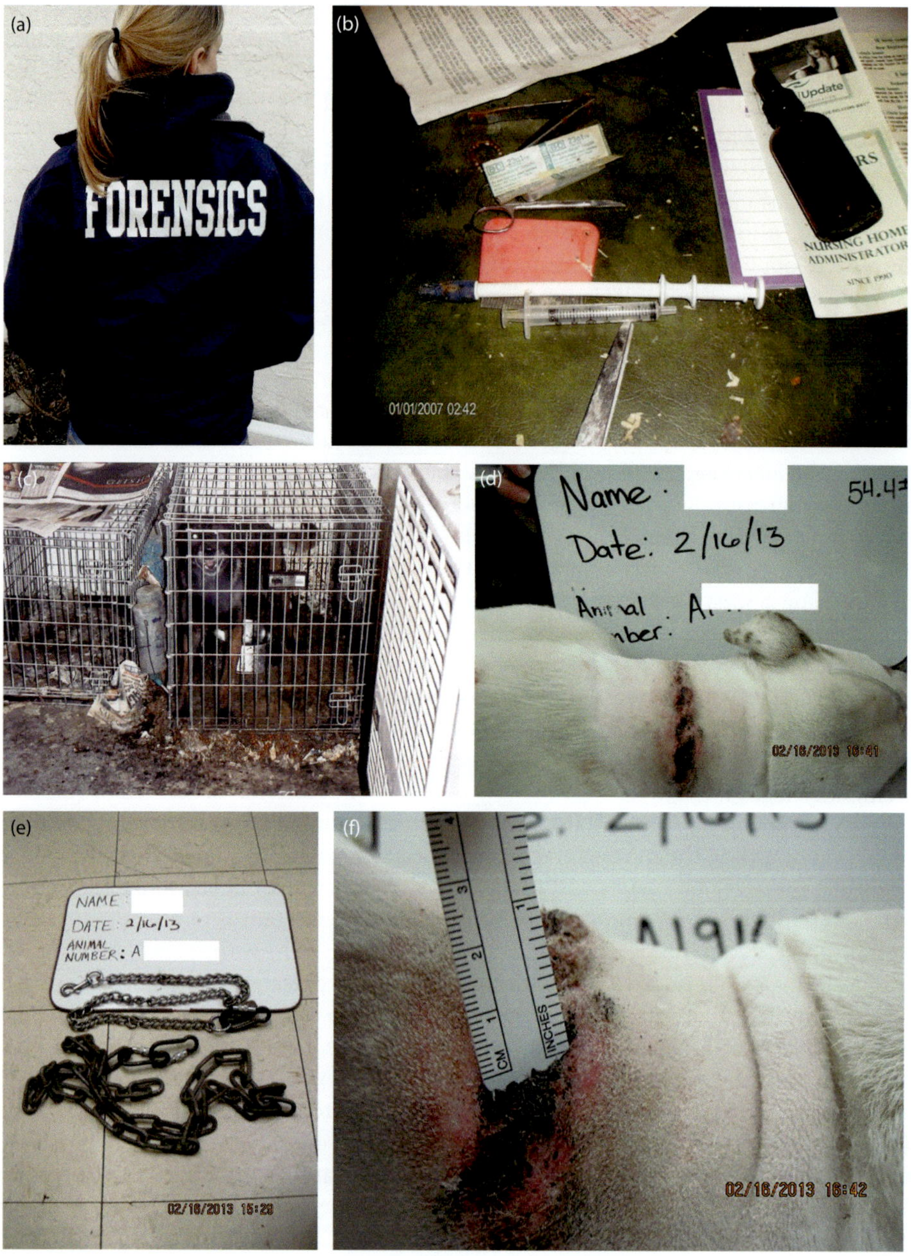

Figure 3.6 (a) Utilizing in-house forensics personnel or outside agencies is a necessity for proper scene documentation of large or high-profile cases. (b) In situ scene photograph of evidence (veterinary supplies) found on the premises. (c) In situ photographs of animals prior to removal from the scene. (d) Evidentiary photo of embedded chain after removal. (e) Evidentiary photo of embedded chain. (f) Evidentiary photo of depth of embedded chain wound.

JOINT-AGENCY INVESTIGATIONS AND OPERATIONAL PLANNING

HLE may not always be the only agents involved in an animal cruelty investigation. In matters where the investigation may be complex, or where the investigating agency is not equipped to manage the scale or requirements of the investigation, that is, a large number of compromised animals, hoarding, animal fighting (dogfighting or cockfighting), bestiality, and so on, the investigating officer may request support from an outside agency with more comprehensive resources. Authorities, duties, and responsibilities differ from state to state and country to country. Regardless of which service, department, or agency is primary, the humane response body should be as organized and prepared as the lead agency.

In most law enforcement agencies, the most common operational planning system that is followed and recognized worldwide is known as SMEAC (situation, mission, execution, administration and logistics, and command and control). This system of operational planning began with the military and goes back several generations. The SMEAC operational plan allows for team leaders, regardless of agency, to bring together all departments and persons that will be involved and prepare for all possible contingencies. It sets out the Who/What/Where/When/Why/How for every person involved, from the police to the veterinarian to the animal handling team. Even if something goes awry (and it always does), such operational planning allows for personnel to remain on task, and should the unexpected happen, the delay can be minimized.

HLE, animal rescue services, or animal emergency response teams are the experts when it comes to animal cruelty and are well-versed in animal care, triage, transport, shelter setup, veterinary care, and veterinary forensic needs. When working with another agency as the lead, or even with multiple agencies, having an operational plan that uses the same format as the assisting agencies allows for clear communication between all levels and departments with regard to roles and responsibilities.

One example of an HLE agency that has developed an effective team approach is the Ontario Society for the Prevention of Cruelty to Animals (OSPCA), which functions as the primary HLE service in Ontario. Agents and inspectors of the OSPCA are appointed under provincial law as peace officers and are granted all the authorities and privileges of police officers for the purpose of enforcing any legislation in Ontario for the protection of animals. In 2009, the Provincial Government of Ontario (Canada) made significant changes to provincial animal protection laws, establishing new offenses and penalties for persons who commit acts of cruelty. In 2014, the Ontario government mandated that a specialized team of animal cruelty investigators be established for the investigation and management of large-scale and complex animal cruelty investigations in Ontario. This resulted in the formation of the OSPCA Major Case Management (MCM) team. The MCM team is made up of a number of highly trained peace officers who receive specialized training in crime scene management, investigative techniques, crime scene photography and videography, search warrants and alternate search authorities, evidence collection, and animal handling and triage. The team responds to large-scale emergencies and natural disasters as part of the protocol for response with Emergency Management Ontario, and as such must be prepared to be deployed at the earliest notice. The team members are also provided with numerous resources and equipment to aid in accomplishing their goals, and all members are cross-trained on every person's role, which can be interchangeable at any time.

In Ontario, in any investigation where the MCM team is required, prior to being deployed the team creates the operational plan. Several steps in planning and preparation are carried out, including review or preparation of search warrants and details of the investigation to date, logistical support, equipment inspection and preparation, personnel support, and assistance from other policing agencies and local veterinary resources. The team will then prepare a written operational plan and hold a briefing with all personnel involved, allowing for an open forum of clear communication.

When arriving on scene, the MCM team first begins with scene control and biosecurity. All steps are taken to minimize the risk of cross-contamination of evidence and disease transfer, and the safety of the officers is given high priority. In all cases, a certified veterinarian will accompany the MCM team to the locations; usually this is a veterinarian who is trained in veterinary forensic procedures. Working together, the team and the veterinarian plan the initial assessment of the scene, the priority of animal care, and the triage and subsequent removal of the animals from the location.

Following the first scene assessment, the priority then moves to the triage and care of the animals. Those in need of immediate care will be transported to veterinarians that have been identified as being located within a few minutes of the scene. The remaining animals, after triage, are then loaded and moved to secondary care locations which had been established during the operational planning stages prior to attending the scene. If possible, any evidence associated with the animals will be collected before removing them from their original locations, and photographs and video will be taken of the evidence and the animals in situ. After animals are removed from the location, the collection and processing of evidence continues. Officers, police, and forensic veterinarians work hand in hand, implementing government-established guidelines and best practices throughout the execution and processing of the scene.

Following completion of the operation, a debriefing must be held as soon as practicably possible to discuss what worked and what did not, to identify problems or breakdowns, and to implement best practices for future operations.

Case Examples: Veterinary Forensics with Singular Officer and Joint-Agency Operations

CASE 1: "The Groomer"

In this case, the OSPCA was contacted by a private citizen whose small Lhasa Apso–type dog died shortly after it had been taken to a groomer.

The owners had dropped off their dog at the groomer at 10:00 AM. The groomer was familiar with the dog, as its owner was a regular customer. About one and a half hours after the dog had been dropped off, the groomer contacted the owners telling them that there was an "incident" and their dog had died. When the owners arrived, the groomer told them that their dog had "choked on his collar." The owners were taken to their dog, which was lying on a table in the back of store wrapped in a towel. When they picked it up the owners noted that the dog was wet, to which the groomer explained that he tried putting water on the dog to revive him. The owners took the dog to their veterinary clinic, at which time the dog was pronounced dead on arrival. An OSPCA agent was assigned and the owners signed over the body of the dog for further examination. The dog was immediately transported to the Animal Health Laboratory in Guelph, Ontario and submitted for necropsy.

When the groomer was interviewed, he stated that the dog had a history of being aggressive during nail trimmings. On this occasion, the groomer used a muzzle and had the dog tethered to the grooming table using a single tether strap around the neck. The groomer claimed that the dog became aggressive and jumped off the table, and while he tried to release the tether and muzzle the dog became unresponsive.

The preliminary necropsy findings stated that there was a 5 mm focal acute hemorrhage of the conjunctiva of the right eye. There was a vertical linear hemorrhage in the subcutaneous tissue 5 cm long by 1 cm wide on the left flank just behind the ribs on the hind end. Internal examination revealed that the lungs were congested and edematous.

Histopathology confirmed that there was swelling in the brain; diseases that might have caused this, such as rabies, equine encephalitis, and West Nile virus, were ruled out. The cause of death was determined to be from traumatic brain injury. The veterinary pathologist stated that the manner of death was inconclusive, but based on the postmortem examination, accidental or nonaccidental blunt force trauma and possible asphyxia should be considered. Following the results of the investigation, these two possibilities could then either be ruled in or ruled out.

Further investigation based on the veterinary forensic report led to the conclusion that the dog had not choked on its collar as originally stated by the groomer. During further interviews, it was revealed that the groomer was alone at the time of the grooming. At some point the groomer had stepped away from the dog and left it in the muzzle and restraint. When he returned, the dog was found unresponsive.

It was determined through the findings of the veterinary pathologist and the interviews with the groomer that the dog had become agitated while being restrained and struggled to get free, causing it to fall from the table. Unable to regain footing, the dog had asphyxiated. The markings found on the body during the preliminary postmortem were consistent with the size and position of the wire restraints used on the grooming table—one around the neck, the other around the hind end—and not the dog's collar, as originally stated at the time of the incident.

As a result, the groomer was charged and convicted under provincial law for causing distress to an animal. While the court ruled that the incident was not intentional, it was deemed neglectful and therefore preventable. The penalty was 12 months of probation, restitution to the owners in the amount of $2500, and payment of costs to the OSPCA in the amount of $1500. In addition, the court ordered that the groomer be given 6 months to modify the grooming facility to ensure that safe handling practices and equipment were put in place to prevent such incidents from occurring in the future. A later inspection by the OSPCA confirmed that the groomer created an employee policy that stated a minimum of two persons would be with each animal to ensure its safety, and the equipment was positioned in the facility to limit the movement of the animal during grooming in order to prevent accidental falls.

CASE 2: "The Rabbit Hoarder"

In early 2014, members of the OSPCA MCM Team were deployed to assist on an OSPCA Section 12 (1) warrant (animal in distress), at a residential home in Eastern Ontario. The OSPCA were contacted after a solicitor attended the property and became concerned about the foul odor emanating from inside the home. This was reported to 911, and fire services arrived in response. On arrival, firefighters reported that there was no one in the home, but found that the home was filled with rabbits of different breeds. There were feces, garbage, and decomposing carcasses of animals throughout the home. The homeowner was a local resident who was not able to be located at the time. A local OSPCA agent assisted fire service in providing water to the live animals that could be accessed, and a request was made for the OSPCA MCM team to be deployed.

Within 24 hours, members of the OSPCA MCM team had prepared an operational plan, which included drafting a search warrant and organizing the participation and coordination of numerous agencies: police, fire services, public health officials, local veterinarians and animal shelters, and a forensic veterinarian to accompany the team to the scene. Police were to be responsible for scene security and officer safety; fire services were to be on standby at the site to help with safety inspections and to provide assistance with negative pressure fans used to move poor air out of the residence; public health officials were to be permitted to inspect the location after the initial assessment and would make decisions regarding not only the residence itself, but the impact on the adjoining properties and people. The forensic veterinarian was to assist team members responsible for evidence collection, and to provide instructions on how and what would be taken as samples for further examination. OSPCA MCM team members were assigned respective duties as well: scribe, first aid, and team safety officer, photography, evidence collection, assistance to the forensic veterinarian, and animal handling in triage. One team member was designated as officer in charge and was responsible for overseeing the team actions and duties.

At approximately 2:00 PM the following afternoon, members of the OSPCA MCM team arrived at the location. The location was secured for preparation of inspection. Upon exiting their vehicles, they were immediately aware of a foul odor emanating from the residence; the odor was pungent and was recognized as that of rotting or decomposing meat. There was no response from inside the residence and the owner was not present.

The OSPCA MCM team members established biosecurity as a priority and donned personal protective equipment including coveralls, safety boots, full-face respirators, and latex gloves. At 2:20 PM, the first wave of OSPCA members—the assessment team—accompanied by the forensic veterinarian, entered the residence to ascertain whether animals were in distress and to what extent, and to photograph and document the location as it appeared.

Upon opening the front door of the residence, it was noted the odor became much stronger, and it was apparent that it was indeed emanating from inside the residence. At 2:23 PM, the veterinarian had ordered all live animals be removed from the property due to unsafe and unsanitary conditions.

Following the initial inspection, at 2:40 PM the second wave of team members entered the residence through the front door to assist in the systematic removal of the live animals from inside the residence. Upon entering, one team member noted that the interior of the residence was almost impassible; piles of trash and debris, old clothes, and feces were observed everywhere. As they proceeded further into the residence through the living room, they observed several live rabbits in cages, some on their own and others in cages with dead and decomposing animals.

Team members also observed several guinea pigs running loose in the living room and kitchen. They noted the water that had been provided to the live animals in cages on the previous evening by the local agent and fire services.

In the living room, team members observed several large garbage bags that were torn. After documenting these with photography, they found decomposing rabbit carcasses; other bags contained animal feces. The number of carcasses in bags was undetermined at the time because the level of decomposition was in various stages, with some in a partial state of decay and others that had become liquefied. Debris, trash, and dead and decomposing animals were found throughout the residence, in the kitchen, bedrooms, and basement. In the basement, there were several large rabbit carcasses, some of which were very bloated and beginning to decompose. Several large live rabbits were seen moving about as well.

In the bathroom on the main floor, the partially decomposed body of a small breed dog (possible terrier type) was observed. This body was later taken as evidence, as directed by the forensic veterinarian.

At 3:00 PM, the team members assigned to animal handling and triage began with the removal of the live animals. The animals were removed to the outside, photographed and logged, and preliminary medical assessment was conducted on each animal by the veterinarian; animals in need of immediate care were separated and transported to a local veterinary hospital. Following the removal of the live animals, several carcasses were seized for postmortem at the direction of the forensic veterinarian. An Ontario SPCA Certificate of a Veterinarian was executed and fourteen live rabbits, four guinea pigs, one deceased dog, and four deceased rabbits were removed from the property. It was later determined that there were approximately 300 animal carcasses in the home.

Following the removal of animals, public health officials not only condemned the home as a public health hazard, but also directed the families on either side of the home to be evacuated until the home could be cleaned and inspected by the health department and deemed safe for them to return.

The forensic veterinarian assisted the investigating officers with properly packaging the animals seized for postmortem for transport to a veterinary pathologist. The veterinarian also assisted with clearly articulating the necessary details and expectations required by the pathologist and providing details of the scene and the conditions.

The final report from the pathologist who examined the deceased animals clearly demonstrated that the cause of death was emaciation due to starvation. In addition, trauma was clearly ruled in as a potential factor. In one rabbit, cause of death was determined to be from an untreated kidney disorder. The conclusion was that the animals in this situation suffered needlessly because of neglect to provide even the basic standards of care.

The owner was eventually located and charged with several counts under provincial law. The owner was sentenced and received 2 years probation and a lifetime ban on owning, caring for, or living with any animals. She was fined $6000 and was also ordered to pay $4969.20 in restitution to the Ontario SPCA.

It can be seen from these case examples that while most situations handled by HLE are small enough that a single agency can fulfill all the duties, some require additional assistance from outside groups. Regardless of which agencies join the investigation, it is important that they are notified as early in the process as possible, and that all roles and responsibilities are clearly distributed.

PREPARING THE CASE

It is imperative that an officer be extremely meticulous when gathering information and solidifying the case. All animals seized during the course of an investigation must be evaluated by a veterinarian, preferably one with some (however meager) forensic experience, and who is willing to testify in court. Veterinarians can be considered expert witnesses based on their training and experience, and are often the only ones who can not only provide important information as to the extent of injury or neglect but whose testimony regarding their observations can be the difference between a petty offense, misdemeanor, or felony charge (Sinclair et al., 2006).

While an HLE officer may have little or no veterinary training, they must ensure that all possible testing and evaluation has been completed for the animal(s) in question. Working closely with the veterinarian will ensure that nothing is missed. The officer should review the veterinarian's notes and reports along with any photographic or radiographic evidence that has been collected so that proper charges are filed. The HLE officer can provide their own expertise when the veterinarian examines the animal by communicating to the treating vet the case background and conditions the animal was removed from, along with possible evidence to look for. Might there be clues such as fiber or botanical traces in the animal's fur? Are the animal's nails worn down or broken, or are they severely overgrown? Did the owner say the animal "fell" on its left side, but the radiographs show trauma to its right side as well? When an embedded collar is removed, can measurements of the deepness of the wound be made? An officer can also provide assistance during a necropsy (should one be needed) by photographing or scribing (taking notes). It is very difficult and impractical for a vet to stop in the middle of a necropsy to take pictures, but pictures lend credibility, and in a

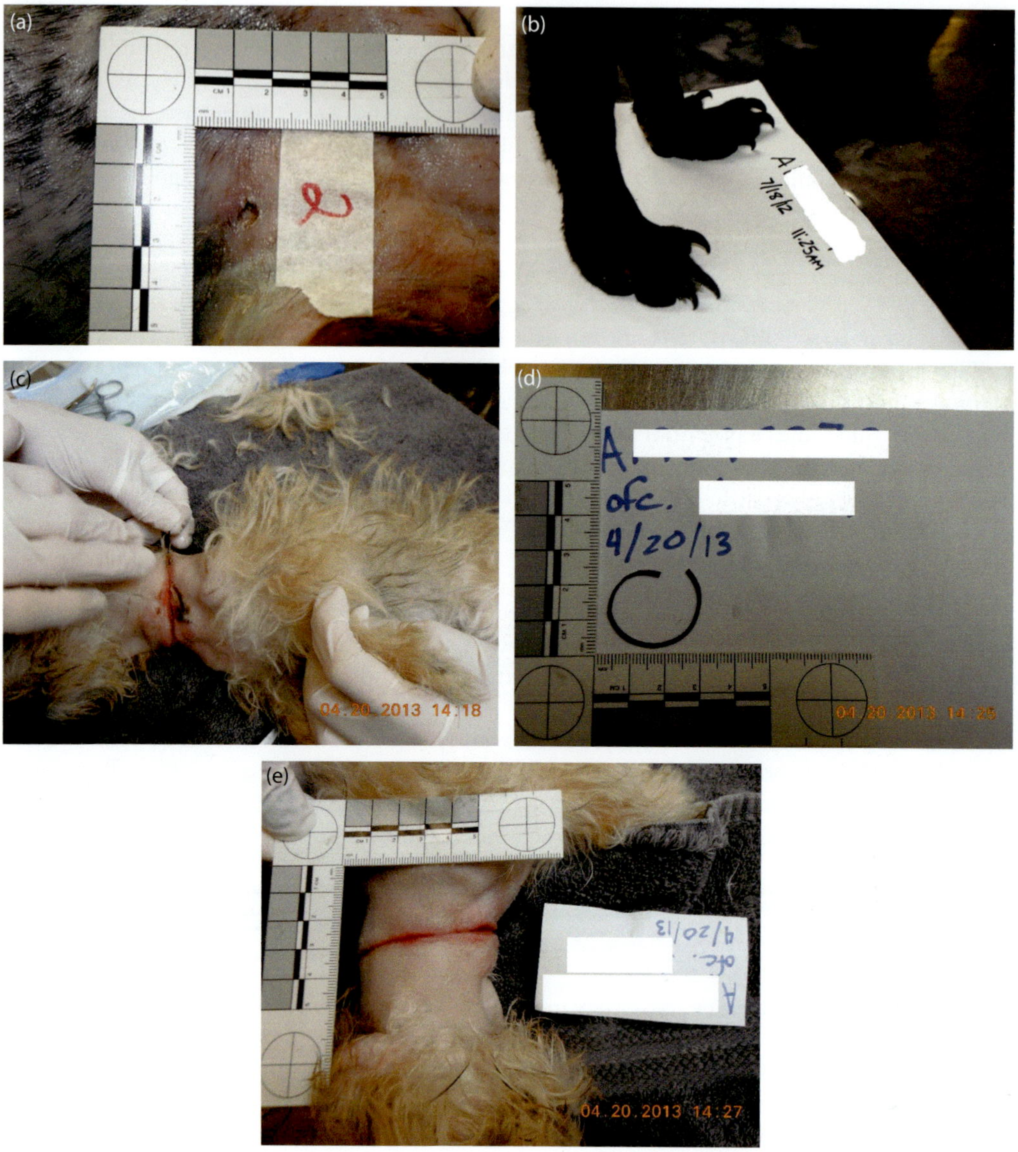

Figure 3.7 (a) Example of a close-up necropsy photo of a bullet wound with scale. (b) Example of a live examination photo with identifier card. (c) Photo of embedded rubber band at the time of removal. (d) Photo of rubber band after removal with proper identifier. (e) Photo of wound from rubber band after removal.

court of law when trying to explain complicated subjects to lay people, photos can speak volumes. Pictures of the animal should be taken before examination, at each stage of the examination, whenever a significant discovery or piece of evidence is found, and at each stage of the necropsy. Close-up, mid-range, and overview shots should be taken, both with and without a scale or ruler and including some type of identifier card listing date, officer, animal number, case number, and agency (Figure 3.7a–e).

Whenever possible, a veterinarian should accompany an officer to the scene of the incident in order to assess the conditions firsthand and from a medical perspective. A veterinarian will be able to identify medications that may be onsite and that are used to treat animal conditions; these may be missed by an officer unfamiliar with them (Sinclair et al., 2006). In the case of animal

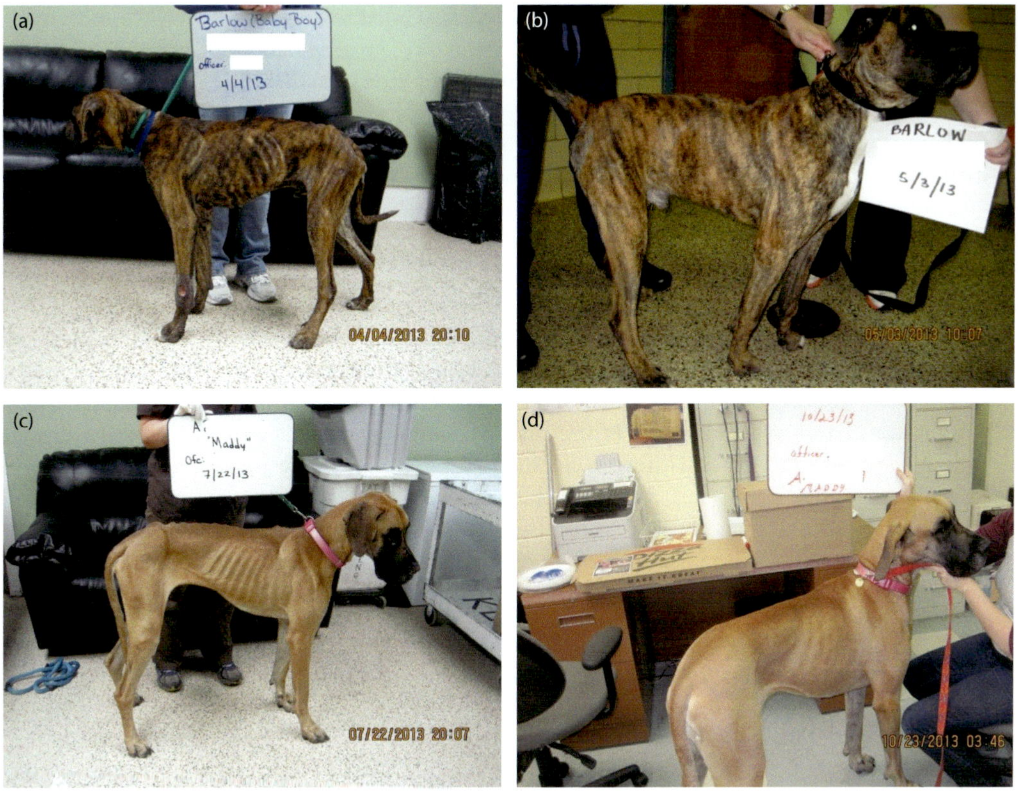

Figure 3.8 (a) Photograph of "Barlow" taken on the date of intake. (b) Photograph of "Barlow" following refeeding treatment. (c) Photograph of "Maddy" taken on the date of intake. (d) Photograph of "Maddy" following refeeding treatment. Photos taken upon intake and again following treatment, when combined with detailed veterinarian treatment records including test results, are necessary to demonstrate that an animal was deliberately neglected or maltreated.

fighting, breeding, or even hoarding, medications and supplements are frequently encountered. A veterinarian will also be able to determine which animals are in the most immediate need of treatment in cases of neglect, hoarding, and physical abuse. Forensic evaluations need to occur as soon as possible. In cases of cruelty, the animal is considered evidence. As previously mentioned, recording the animal in its in situ condition by way of photographs or video is proper evidence handling and will help the animal not only receive prompt treatment, but will allow the judge or jury to see the animal as it lived in what were most likely deplorable conditions. Video is an excellent means of documenting neurologic trauma, orthopedic injuries, or other conditions that may not be captured with still photography, or for depicting the perhaps countless animals at a hoarding or puppy mill scene. It is also good for recording an animal's behavior on the scene or after initial seizure by officers, and this video footage can then be compared to footage taken following treatment or rehabilitation, as a type of "before-and-after" montage. This is an especially poignant way of documenting starvation: photographs of the animal emaciated when seized on scene or when first arriving at the hospital or care facility, at specific times throughout the refeeding treatment, and then once treatment has been completed, can help dispute claims from a defendant that the animal "just refused to eat" or, when accompanied by bloodwork and test results, that the animal "suffered from an underlying medical condition" (Figure 3.8a–d).

An HLE officer should treat all scenes as potential crime scenes. The same techniques a police officer uses to process a scene can and should be used in animal cases. Some HLE officers have little or no training in these techniques, but it doesn't take a specialist to know some of the basics that can help ensure a solid case—wearing gloves to handle evidence, logging, labeling, and properly storing and processing evidence, making sure enough photographs are taken, limiting the amount of people on a scene, making appropriate statements to the press, and so on. Cases have been lost because of innocent "mistakes" such as logging all animals into a database at a certain time after seizure, but on a different day than (1) the day the warrant was executed, and (2) written statements regarding the date/time of the animals' seizures. Above all, working with others is necessary and essential, especially police officers, veterinarians, and prosecuting attorneys. Meeting with attorneys on a regular basis following an on-scene investigation is crucial since the burden of proof is very high in cases of animal cruelty, as is determining the offender's intent.

Whatever way an officer and attorney choose to handle a case from a legal standpoint, the animals should figure prominently in their minds from beginning to end. As mentioned, they should be documented, photographed and videotaped as they were when found, at regular increments following removal and treatment, and at the end of treatment, regardless of the severity of injury. Photographs are mandatory, and there is no such thing as too many photographs. Each animal must be photographed on scene, with each having a unique, identifying number. This can be accomplished by assigning the animal a number which then gets transcribed onto a card or dry erase board along with the date, time, and the officer's name, case number, and address. This card or board should be photographed alongside the animal. This step is essential in cases of hoarding when there may be dozens of animals in one location.

Hoarding

Hoarding cases are difficult and time consuming. It may take hours, days, or even weeks to document everything on the property. It is especially important to have a veterinarian present on-scene to evaluate, photograph, and record each animal as it is captured or removed from its enclosure. The cages and enclosures themselves are evidence, and each animal needs to be associated via photographs and written records with its specific cage. Scene sketches and maps are valuable in this instance in order to obtain a more logical layout of the property than mere photographs can show, but if the animals are free roaming, it may not help (Figure 3.9a,b).

Puppy Mills

Similar in nature in some respects to hoarding cases, puppy mills have their own unique sets of circumstances. These cases often occur in relatively closed, close-knit communities where

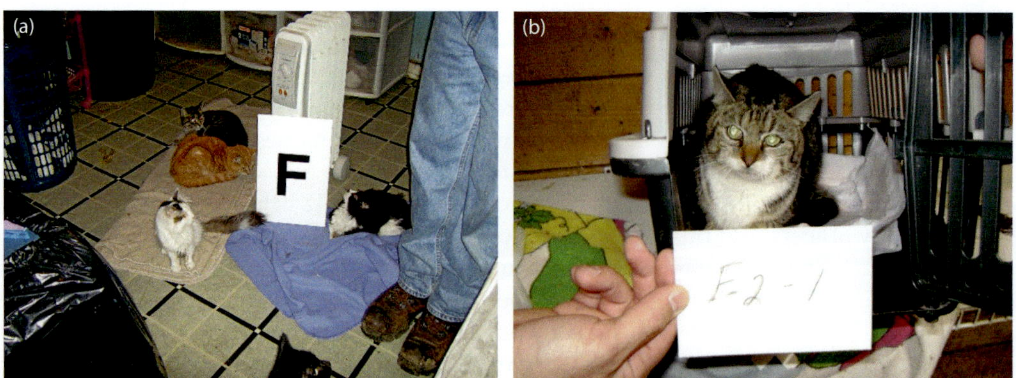

Figure 3.9 (a) All animals in a hoarding situation need to be photographed in situ with some type of identifying number or letter. (b) All animals in a hoarding situation need to be photographed again individually with an identifier that ties them to the in situ photo.

"outsiders" are not welcome and law enforcement is scorned. Amish or Mennonite communities, where puppy mills are frequently encountered, typically frown on photography or are generally removed from popular culture, and it can take a great deal of skill on the officer's part to be both respectful and courteous of a different way of life while still trying to obtain the facts and enforce the law.

THE COURTROOM, POSSIBLE OUTCOMES, AND THE EMOTIONAL TOLL

The Courtroom

HLE officers typically face a court system that simply doesn't place much emphasis on animal cruelty cases. Incidents of cruelty may result in mere summary or petty offense charge and may be treated as little more than a parking violation. At this level the case will most likely never see a jury trial, and the judges handling bench trials in some cities have such a heavy load that they cannot stop to familiarize themselves with the state animal laws. In some rural areas a judge may be completely naïve of them, having scarcely seen cases of animal cruelty, if at all. Occasionally, judges and attorneys will trivialize the matter even further, mocking a medical condition they are ignorant of, or poking fun at "Fluffy's" silly expression in a photo, further destroying any validity that the case may have had. This not only demeans the law but also an officer's self-respect and peace of mind. They may have worked the case for weeks or months, only to have it be made fun of or laughed at in an apathetic or indifferent manner. In addition, at the petty offense level the defendant often chooses to plea bargain, resulting in the officer having no opportunity to present the facts they may have worked hard to obtain, and having a small fine be the only punishment. Judges may refuse to even look at the photographs or video, or some judges may find a defendant guilty but still award custody of the animals back to the defendant for any number of reasons; the officers can see this as defeating the entire purpose and may feel as if they failed the animals they were trying to save (Arluke, 2004).

Possible Outcomes

Petty offenses can rise to the level of misdemeanors depending on many aggravating factors, which differ from state to state. For example, in Pennsylvania an offender can be charged with a misdemeanor if they maim or disfigure an animal; in a case of hoarding, for example, the charges can rise from a summary offense to a misdemeanor if one of the hoarded animals has a broken leg. In contrast, in Colorado, an offender's first conviction of animal cruelty is a misdemeanor. But frequently built into the statute are the terms "knowingly" or "intentionally," and proving this awareness or intent can be difficult. Misdemeanor cases will sometimes be tried before a jury, but typically in many large cities they are heard by a judge. Convictions usually do not result in jail time, however, no matter where the case is tried.

Although all 50 states now have felony provisions for animal cruelty, what constitutes a felony charge differs from state to state. A second animal cruelty offense in a state where the first conviction was a misdemeanor would result in a felony charge; such as in Colorado. Dogfighting is a felony in all states. In Florida, a felony charge can result from an intentional act that results in excessive or repeated unnecessary pain or suffering or cruel death (www.leg.state.fl.us).

What of the Animals?

As surprising as it may seem, the animals that were the recipients of such inhumane treatment are often either forgotten or pushed to the backburner as soon as they arrive at the facility tasked with caring for them, or they are simply viewed as a burden. If a defendant is found guilty, appeals can continue the case for years. Some appeals have reached state supreme courts. Unless voluntary surrender has been obtained or a court order relinquishes custody of the animals involved to the agency providing care, they must remain on hold for the duration of the appeal. This can, in some ways, be seen as just as cruel as the initial act.

An animal from a cruelty case may be considered evidence for the entire duration of its case. Animal cruelty law varies from state to state but most states do not have provisions for the disposition of the animals while the case is still active. This may mean that any animals seized must remain at an animal shelter or animal welfare facility for months to even years until their case is adjudicated. The cost of treating, feeding, and caring for these animals can be exorbitant. The animals often cannot be spayed or neutered or given any treatment that is not lifesaving in nature (such as dental work or lipoma removal) due to the fact that "evidence," even in the form of a live animal, cannot be altered or changed in any way. If special treatment is needed, the HLE officer or prosecuting attorney can petition the judge in the case to obtain approval or can speak with the defendant's attorney, who can then communicate the request to the defendant for permission, but this can be a burdensome process. The possibility of these difficulties and of the enormous financial burden can deter many agencies from pursuing legal action in these cases, creating yet another disincentive for enforcing the animal cruelty statutes. One case handled in part by the Humane Society of the United States (HSUS) resulted in the seizure of over 200 dogs which were held for more than 13 months and required over $600,000 in care (Sinclair et al., 2013).

Some animal welfare facilities have foster care programs in place that allow an animal to be placed in a home until the case is resolved, but many do not. Still, for the agencies fortunate enough to have these programs, it can be difficult to locate willing participants. Foster "parents" must be made to understand and are required to sign a contract agreeing that the animal does not legally belong to them and that they cannot alter the animal, have it spayed or neutered, or post photographs of the animal on social media. If an animal accidentally becomes pregnant while in protective custody foster, the offspring immediately become part of the case as well. It can be difficult to find individuals or families willing to make a commitment to care for and bond with an animal that may be returned to its original owner per court order, even after spending a significant amount of time in the foster home.

Cost of Care

There are several ways to try to alleviate the prohibitive financial encumbrance and lengthy detriment to the wellbeing of the animals. One is for an HLE officer to obtain a voluntary surrender of the animals in question from the owner at the beginning of an investigation or as soon as possible thereafter. This is quite possibly the best option as it allows for the animals to receive all necessary treatment and be placed up for adoption quickly. Many HLE officers will offer this as an option to pet owners who do not have the means or the willingness to provide veterinary care or who refuse to comply with the animal cruelty code. Doing so allows them to present an alternative to pet owners; that is, they can either surrender the animal to a humane society or animal shelter or face charges if proper actions are not taken—such as, providing adequate food, water, or shelter, or veterinary treatment. Often, the threat of a court case is enough to cause a respondent to concede that they cannot care for the animal properly. In more serious cases the option to surrender ownership will not completely void the need for charges to be filed, but it can certainly allow for reduced stress to the animal and reduced financial obligations for the humane society (Bond Posting for Animal Cruelty State Statutes).

Another way that cost of care can be mitigated is by means of bond posting and forfeiture provisions. Some states like Colorado, Washington, Vermont, and Indiana have passed legislation that requires the offender to post a pre-conviction bond that will cover the costs associated with caring for the animals for the duration of the case. Should the offender choose not to pay, they must forfeit the animals, allowing them to be placed up for adoption. The costs associated with housing, feeding, and medical care are typically established by the agencies tasked with caring for the animal, in conjunction with the employed or consulting veterinarians who are providing the medical treatment. Meticulous records need to be kept regarding all treatment and expenses.

Seeking restitution is another way to recoup some of the costs associated with housing and care of the animals, but the officer needs to make this request to the attorney handling the case at the outset. Courts can include restitution as part of an offender's sentence. As with cost of care documentation, the costs associated with caring for the animal for the duration of the case should be meticulous and accurate. The court can order restitution payments be made to the facility that provided the care, and any violations can result in the placement of liens on the offender's property until the debt is settled.

Abandonment

Abandonment cases are handled differently depending on state and municipality. In some areas animals who have been left for a certain amount of time with no care, food, water, or shelter can be considered abandoned property, without owner, and can be seized by humane law enforcement. With regard to property that may be abandoned, one must consider the totality of the circumstances surrounding it: "there must be proof that the owner or possessor intended to give up all title, interest, claim, and/or right to possess; abandonment is not determined exclusively by a property rights analysis, but the intention to abandon may be inferred from word, acts, and deeds that indicate the person has given up sufficient interest in the property" (Ingram, 2009). Because they are considered abandoned the former owner cannot lay claim to them. However, some agencies choose to seize the animal and hold it until a property disposition can be completed, in which the officer must, by all means necessary, track down the property owner and if one cannot be located, request that ownership be transferred to the animal welfare agency by a judge. However, this process can be time consuming and laborious.

Emotional Toll

The refusal or unwillingness of the court system to take animal cruelty seriously or place emphasis on its unacceptability can make an officer wonder why they bothered at all. Over time this discouragement can result in an attitude of apathy and lassitude. HLE officers not only have to perform a job that exacts enormous emotional damage, but they also have to perform it while facing possible danger from people and animals. They must have policing skills and knowledge of the law, an excellent ability to communicate and "read" situations, a general knowledge of animal behavior, and the ability to walk a fine line between maintaining a sensitivity to the plight of animal suffering and succumbing to the defense mechanism of complete emotional shut down. They must do all this while occasionally enduring ridicule, disrespect, passivity, and indifference. They are frequently dismissed as "dog catchers," confused with animal control, discredited as law enforcers, and wrongly labeled as activists. Many HLE officers felt drawn to the work in part because of their love for animals, and to witness some of the most atrocious acts of violence committed on animals while still maintaining professionalism is no easy task. But despite all of the negativity, most HLE officers are proud of their roles. They know that while they cannot win every case or save every life, the lives they do save are worth any amount of hardship. Being the voice of those who cannot speak for themselves makes up for the difficulties. No matter the cost, they will keep fighting in the hope that one day there will be no need to fight anymore.

References

Arluke, A. 2004. *Brute Force; Animal Police and the Challenge of Cruelty.* West Lafayette, IN: Purdue University Press.

Bond Posting for Animal Cruelty State Statutes. http://www.tufts.edu/vet/hoarding/Bondlaws.htm.

Florida Legislature. 1995–2015. http://www.leg.state.fl.us.
Gardner, R. M. 2005. *Practical Crime Scene Processing and Investigation*. Boca Raton, FL: CRC Press.
Ingram, J. 2009. *Criminal Procedure: Theory and Practice*, 2nd ed. Upper Saddle River, NJ: Prentice Hall.
Lockwood, R., and F. R. Ascione. 1998. *Cruelty to Animals and Interpersonal Violence: Readings in Research and Application*. W. Lafayette, IN: Purdue University Press.
Merck, M. 2007. *Veterinary Forensics: Animal Cruelty Investigations*. Ames, IA: Blackwell Publishing.
National Children's Advocacy Center (NCAC) Training and Conferences. 2013. http://www.nationalcac.org/online-training/web-caught-in-the-crossfire-how-the-abuse-of-animals-co-occurs-with-family-violence.html.
National Coalition Against Domestic Violence. 2006. http://www.ncadv.org.
National Link Coalition. nationallinkcoalition.org; Fact Sheet: Nationallinkcoalition. http://org/wp-content/.../DV-FactSheetNCADV-AHA.pdf.
Sinclair, L., M. Merck, and R. Lockwood. 2006. *Forensic Investigation of Animal Cruelty: A Guide for Veterinary and Law Enforcement Professionals*. Washington, DC: Humane Society Press.
Sinclair, L., M. Merck, and R. Lockwood. 2009. *The Stop Snitching Phenomenon: Breaking the Code of Silence*. Washington, DC: U.S. Department of Justice.
Sinclair, L., M. Merck, and R. Lockwood. 2013. The cost of care. *All Animals Magazine*. Humane Society of the United States.
U.S. Department of Justice (USDOJ). 2009. The Stop Snitching Phenomenon: Breaking the Code of Silence. https://www.policeforum.org/assets/docs/Free_Online_Documents/Crime/the%20stop%20snitching%20phenomenon%20-%20breaking%20the%20code%20of%20silence%202009.pdf.

CHAPTER 4

ANIMAL GENETIC EVIDENCE AND DNA ANALYSIS

AnnMarie Clark

INTRODUCTION

DNA is the gold standard for human forensics. The information obtained is reliable, repeatable, and readily accessible. It is also becoming the gold standard for animal forensics. DNA can tell us what species we are dealing with, what gender that animal is, who that individual animal is (genetic profile), and can match the profile of an individual animal to the profile generated from evidence at a crime scene. This information can place an individual in a specific place and is of great assistance to law enforcement in prosecuting crimes.

It has been documented that there is a strong association between people who abuse animals and those who abuse women and children (Becker & French, 2004; Gullone & Robertson, 2008; Lockwood & Hodge, 1986). Along with this, it has been shown that abusive behavior escalates while the perpetrator is free and not within the confines of law enforcement (Johnson, 2000). The ability to identify and document animal abuse through DNA is a powerful tool for law enforcement.

In many cases, DNA may be the primary connection between perpetrators and the crime where animals are involved. In cases of dog fighting, it is the DNA that can associate a dog or group of dogs to a specific fighting venue and therefore to specific people. The same is true of cock fighting. When dealing with wildlife, DNA can link the meat in a freezer with the blood on a truck or knife and the animal on the ground. DNA from elephant tusks and rhino horns is being used to identify the population and geographic origin of a confiscated item and, in some cases, with the specific animal that was found, killed, and mutilated (Comstock et al., 2003).

Forensic DNA investigations in animals is more difficult than human investigations. Humans are a single species. The questions asked of human DNA involve the sex of the individual and the genetic profile of individuals to be compared to the genetic profiles generated from the evidence of a crime scene. In the case of animals, the species needs to first be identified. Then the sex of the animal can usually be determined if it is relevant. However, the markers used to generate a genetic profile are unique to each species and must be developed for each species. This means that for each species, appropriate markers must be identified from the genome, tested for reliability and information, and then a database designed and built that can generate appropriate statistics. The database then needs to meet legal challenges for use in a court of law. This must be done for *each* species of interest.

DNA is a powerful tool for criminal investigators who understand how to use it. They understand what questions can be answered, how to collect at a crime scene so evidence is not compromised, and should have a basic understanding of how DNA evidence is processed. This chapter will explore these questions and provide a better understanding of how and why to use DNA for forensic investigations.

DNA is present in all living individuals and, with the exception of identical twins, the genetic makeup of an individual is unique. No two individuals have the same genetic structure. While about 98% of human DNA, or DNA within a species, is identical, that 2% that is different is significantly different and allows identification of an individual with a unique genetic signature. DNA is present in two forms in the cells of the body: in the nucleus and the mitochondria. Mammal blood has nucleated white blood cells, but the red blood cells lack a nucleus. Avian, reptiles, and amphibians have nucleated red blood cells, which essentially doubles the amount of available DNA, a trait that helps with forensic analysis. The different DNAs have different properties that can answer different forensic questions.

Within a cell, DNA is present in two specific, well-defined areas: the nucleus (nDNA) and the mitochondria (mtDNA) of the cell. The nucleus contains the double-stranded helical DNA that most people are aware of. The nuclear DNA is organized into chromosomes. Humans have 23 pairs of chromosomes (46 individual chromosomes), dogs have 39 pairs, elephants have 56, and turkeys have 80 sets of chromosomes! Half of the chromosomes come from the mother and the homologous other half comes from the father. When cells replicate the chromosomes are duplicated, so the two daughter cells have identical sets of chromosomes (Figure 4.1). However, during the

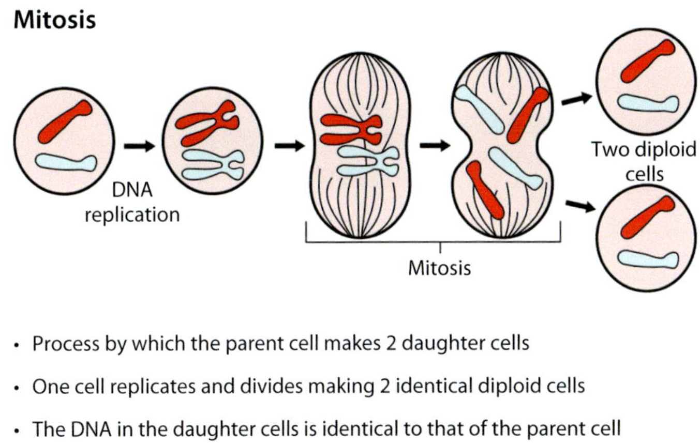

Figure 4.1 Mitosis is the somatic replication of daughter cells. One cell replicates and divides, producing two identical cells. (Courtesy of NIH.)

production of gametes, the chromosome pairs separate and during the replication process, there is a swapping of homologous sections of chromosomes. This results in four chromosomes that are not the exact copies of the original chromosomes (Figure 4.2). When a zygote is formed, joining of one paternal chromosome and one maternal chromosome, there are differences due to the swapping of homologous genetic material so that no zygote has the identical genetic profile of either the mother or the father, or of any siblings.

The nucleus in a cell is surrounded by a membrane that contains the nuclear structures and keeps the chromosomes safe. The rest of a cell is filled with cytoplasm which contains a variety of organelles and extranuclear bodies that are associated with energy, RNA production, and maintain the health of the cell. One of the sets of organelles consists of small oval structures called mitochondria (Figure 4.3). The mitochondria are responsible for cellular function including respiration and repair of the cell. They were once referred to as the powerhouse of the cell before

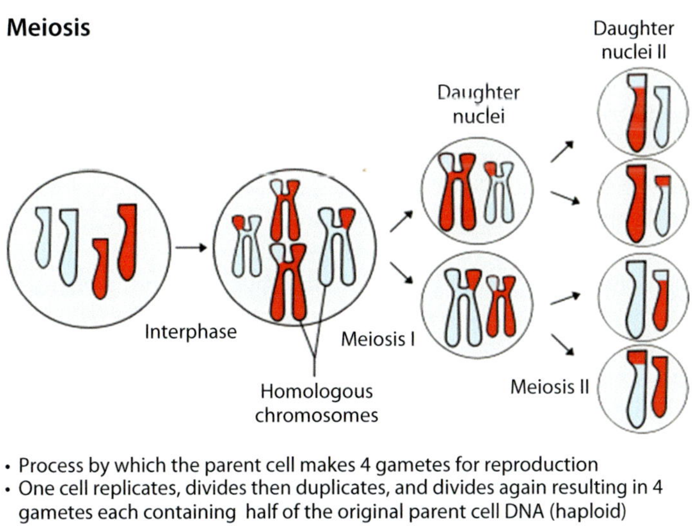

Figure 4.2 Meiosis is the production of gametes. One cell replicates, with some homologous areas swapping. This is then replicated and the two cells separate into four cells, each with one-half of the DNA complement. At fertilization, one cell with half the parent DNA will combine with one cell from the other parent with a half complement of DNA resulting in a zygote with a full complement of DNA. (Courtesy of NIH.)

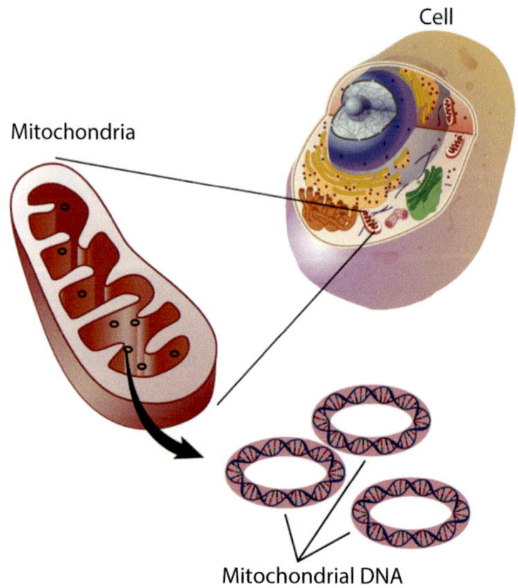

Figure 4.3 Mitochondria are extranuclear bodies in the cytoplasm of the cell. They are important for cellular respiration and function. There may be a few to several hundred mitochondria in each cell, and within each mitochondrion there is a small circular bit of DNA that is used for its function. The mtDNA is small (about 15,000 bases long), circular, non-recombining, and maternally inherited. The DNA in the mitochondria is used to identify species. (From: Wikipedia.)

scientists really understood all the biological functions the mitochondria participate in. The number of mitochondria within a cell varies from a few organelles to thousands of identical organelles. One of the unique and interesting features of mitochondria is that they have their own DNA. It is a small circular double-stranded structure. It is non-recombining, meaning that it does not swap bits of homologous DNA during replication, and is maternally inherited, meaning that an individual has their mother's mtDNA. Almost all of the mtDNA codes for a biological function with little or no duplications or filler DNA. mtDNA has a bump, referred to as the D-loop because of its shape, where replication of the molecule begins and ends. Because this portion of the mtDNA is noncoding, there is little evolutionary pressure on it so it can mutate more readily without consequence to the organism. This is the portion of the mtDNA that is traditionally used to identify species.

In general, mtDNA is maternally inherited and non-recombining. Because it is non-recombining and because cellular function is driven by the gene codes it contains, the mutation rate is lower than in nuclear DNA, since misplaced mutations are lethal. The D-loop, however, is not under evolutionary pressure so it is freer to accumulate non-lethal mutations. Other areas of the mtDNA drive vital gene functions and therefore cannot change much without a change of function. Since species tend to become species because similar animals breed among themselves, the mutations accumulated within the D-loop become associated with different species and become fixed for that species. Population genetics involves identifying species, then defining the populations they form and documenting the interactions of populations with each other and their surroundings.

INFORMATION AVAILABLE FROM mtDNA

What forensic questions can be asked of the mitochondrial DNA that will help to resolve legal cases? If a domestic crime has been committed and blood or hairs are present on the perpetrator, the species, or source, of the blood or hair can be identified. If blood or hairs are identified as belonging a dog or cat, then they can potentially be tested further to identify if they belong to the family dog or cat. This can put the perpetrator at the crime scene. If a deer has been killed out of season and a suspect has unidentified meat in his freezer, the meat in the freezer can be identified to species, the gender of the animal can be determined, and then genetic profiles generated for the meat in the freezer and the animal on the ground and those profiles can be compared to determine if they are sourced from the same animal. If chickens are being killed during the night, the perpetrator could be a loose dog, feral cat, coyote, fox, opossum, raccoon, or other animal. mtDNA can be used to determine the species of animal killing the chickens, and the owner can target the correct perpetrator. The common wildlife questions from law enforcement is first what species, then the sex of the individual, and finally comparisons of nuclear genetic profiles for matches of evidence that can be presented in court.

mtDNA can also be used to eliminate individuals from a suspect pool. If the blood evidence is tested for species and an individual is also tested with the same marker for their mtDNA profile and the profiles are different, then the individual is essentially eliminated from the pool of suspects. However, since mtDNA is maternally inherited and all the offspring of a female have the same profile, an individual cannot be eliminated if those profiles match. The perpetrator could theoretically be anyone in the maternal lineage.

Species identification is accomplished by reviewing the sequencing data from a sample, exporting it as a text file, and then using the text file to query databases. The primary database often used is GenBank, which is a public database managed by the National Institutes of Health.* It contains millions of sequences from most species at most areas of their genomes. While it is not a failsafe database, it is an ideal way of beginning the determination of species when the source of the sample is unknown. The basic local alignment search tool (BLAST) algorithm is used to begin a query. BLAST will do a comparison of all the sequences in its database or a selection of sequences depending on the parameters indicated at the beginning of the search. The results are a list of first 100 closest potential matches. If one gets a "hit" for *Gallus gallus* and all 100 hits are for *Gallus gallus*, then in all likelihood that is the source of the sample. If, however, there are other genuses or species, then the result is not as solid. The issue could be a poor sequence, a contaminated sample where the contaminate dominated the polymerase chain reaction (PCR), or few examples of sequence for the suspected genus and species in the database. This is true of forensically important insects. There is an across-the-board representation of the different species, but not a large enough database to reliably select the correct species.

INFORMATION AVAILABLE FROM nDNA

Nuclear DNA (nDNA) is used to generate individual genetic profiles. A genetic profile is the result of gametes that have undergone random recombination. Each gamete has a unique selection of DNA from each parent, has an equal opportunity to be selected, and will produce a zygote that is unique. Only identical twins have identical DNA. The same is true of animals. The sex of an animal is determined by identifying the XY chromosomes in mammals (females are XX and males are XY) or the WZ chromosomes in avians (females are WZ and males are WW). Some species such as crocodilians, turtles, and tortoises have temperature-dependent sex determination, which means they must have a full complement of both sets of sex chromosomes so they cannot be genetically sexed. However, individual identification is still possible.

nDNA is the gold standard for identifying individuals. In a criminal case, the evidence needs to be processed for DNA residue before the exemplars, the known DNA contributors, are processed. Evidence may be blood stains or saliva collected from a fighting pit, bites, blood in the back of a

* National Center for Biotechnology Information, U.S. National Library of Medicine 8600 Rockville Pike, Bethesda MD, 20894.

truck, on the ground, hairs from kennels or crates, teeth, bones, or clothing. After the species has been established using mtDNA, the gender of the donor (X/Y chromosomes from nDNA) and the unique profile are determined from nDNA. A genetic profile can only be generated if the markers are available. If markers and a database are available, then the genetic profile can be compared to the profiles generated from the exemplars, such as buccal swabs taken from dogs, tissue samples from dead deer or other livestock, or perhaps hair samples taken from a captured bear. The information obtained will help to determine if the dogs were in a specific fighting pit, which dogs were involved in a biting or mauling incident, which bear was involved in a home invasion, or if a doe was taken out of season. DNA evidence can immeasurably strengthen a case.

A genetic profile is generated by using multiple markers that take advantage of a particular class of repetitive DNA, referred to as short tandem repeats (STRs). These microsatellites repeats are 2 to 6 nucleotides that are repeated usually 8 to 20 or more times, like a stutter. The number of repeats at a homologous site often differ between the mother and the father. This is nDNA, so one strand of DNA comes from the mother and the other strand from the father. They may, by chance, have the same number of repeats or a different number of repeats. The combination of differences at multiple sites becomes a genetic profile that is unique for each individual. The process used to assay the loci, PCR, allows for the lengths of both alleles (one from each parent) at each locus to be identified and visualized (Figure 4.4).

Processing a crime scene and collecting evidence is dealt with in detail in Chapter 1. It is important to remember that when evidence is being collected for DNA analysis, gloves must be worn, wet samples allowed to dry if at all possible, and items must be properly packaged to prevent contact contamination or contamination from investigators. All samples must be properly labeled with date, location, case number, collector, an individual identifier, and a brief description. The laboratory technician was not at the scene and will not have any reference for a sample except for the identifier and description on the container.

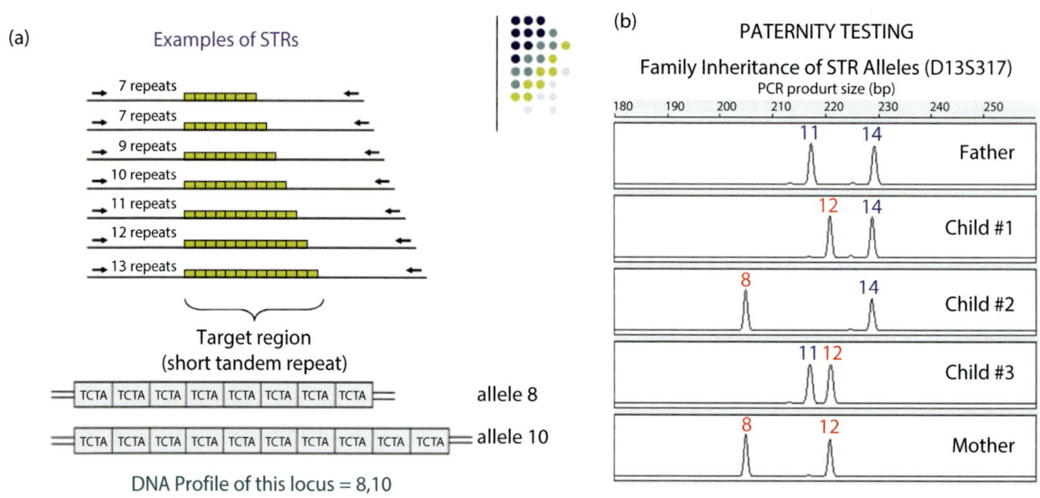

Figure 4.4 Visualization of STRs (short tandem repeats) (a) STRs are made up of short repeats of DNA. One strand (allele) is from the mother and the other strand from the father. They may be the same number or a different number of repeats. (b) This is an illustration of peaks at one locus used for analysis. The father and mother are heterozygous (two different-sized peaks: 11/14 and 8/12, respectively) at this one locus. Child 1 (12/14) is also heterozygous, getting the 12 allele from the mother and the 14 allele from the father. Child 2 (8/14) received the 8 allele from the mother and the 14 allele from the father. Child 3 (11/12) received the 11 allele from the father and 12 allele from the mother. This is one locus. Many loci added together result in a profile that is unique to the individual. ([a] From: https://www.slideshare.net/RanaMuhammadAsif/forensic-dna-typingm-asif-59208013. [b] https://slideplayer.com/slide/4798394/.)

It is good to over-collect evidence samples. The scene is secure only once and it is difficult to go back for more evidence collection. Not all samples need to be processed, only those necessary to address the questions of the case. Also, if a sample fails, then there is more material to go back to for analysis.

Evidence needs to be stored appropriately, and the conditions when collected should be relayed to the laboratory technician, such as if there has been exposure to the elements, sun, or chemical compounds. All of these conditions accelerate the degradation of DNA, as does time. If evidence has been exposed to negative conditions, the technician will want to process the evidence in a timely manner to avoid more degradation and to capture the most information possible. mtDNA is hardier and less susceptible to degradation because it is circular and there is much more of it in each cell (10–1000 copies in each cell as compared to a single structure in the nucleus). nDNA begins to degrade as soon as there is cell death and the nucleus walls begin to break down. The sooner the DNA can be captured and the degrading process halted, the better the information that can potentially be extracted. To slow the degradation process once the DNA evidence has been collected, the evidence should be dried if collected wet. If it cannot be dried at the collection site, it should be frozen as soon as possible. These actions stop the enzyme and bacterial activity that initiate DNA breakdown. Samples that are collected in a warm, humid environment should be stored at the collection site in a cooler with ice packs until transportation to the final storage facility. This will protect the DNA evidence from further damage due to heat, exposure to sun, and sweating within its collection container. It is best to store evidence in paper or cardboard to prevent sweating. Plastic should be used only if there is risk of contact contamination or when the item is thoroughly dry, such as bones.

METHODOLOGY

There are several ways that DNA can be extracted. One of the more common methods involves using a kit that contains a column. The sample is placed into a small tube and kit reagents are added to the sample, as per manufacturer's protocols. The reagents are designed to stop any protein activity, lyse open the cells, and release the DNA into the solution. The reagents have compounds in them to maintain the DNA so it does not oxidize or degrade rapidly. The solution is introduced to a column. The column has a disc which acts as a physical barrier to capture cell particles and has a static charge which allows the DNA to stick to the surface when the pH is correct. After washing the DNA to remove debris, a buffer with a different pH is introduced to the column which has the effect of altering the static charge, allowing the DNA to wash off the column. In the end, only clean, genomic DNA (mtDNA and nDNA) is in the tube with the buffer (Figure 4.5).

After the DNA extraction has been quantified, PCR is conducted to target a specific area of the genome, depending on the question asked. PCR is a way of chemically replicating a locus millions of times so that the product of the PCR is visible with special instrumentation (Figure 4.6). If the question is species, then a portion of the mtDNA is targeted, amplified, and sequenced. In this case, the actual order of the nucleotides is what is important. That sequence is then queried in GenBank or another database to determine the species. If the question is who and/or does the evidence match an individual, then multiple areas of the nDNA will be targeted by the PCR, amplified, and visualized on the same instrument. In this case the size of the PCR products for each allele at each locus is the important information that is used. The order of the nucleotides is unimportant (Figure 4.4).

The reliability of the results is a direct consequence of the database that the information is being compared to. Databases applied to animal forensic applications were originally extensions of databases designed for population and conservation genetic studies. Once a species was identified as a species, samples were collected to answer the question of what constitutes a population for

1. Sub-sample is removed from the evidence and placed in a tube
2. Reagents are added to lyse the cells and release the DNA
3. The lysed solution is introduced to a column to bind the DNA
4. The bound DNA is washed to remove impurities
5. The DNA is eluted into a fresh tube

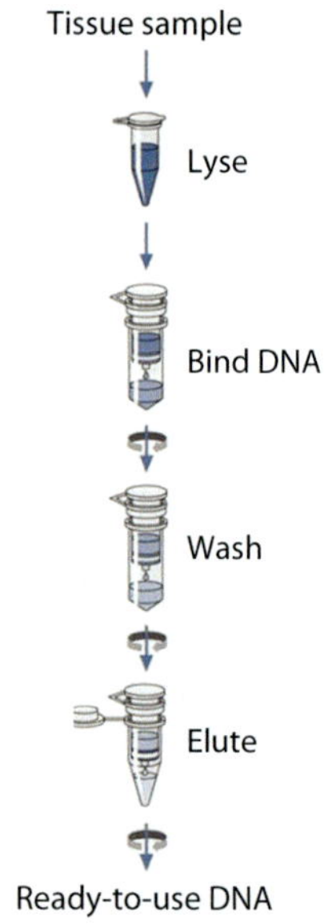

Figure 4.5 DNA extraction using a column-based kit. (From: Qiagen Dneasy Blood and Tissue Kit.)

this specific species. Samples were collected to determine the relationships of individuals within a population and between populations. The ability to identify a species is based on databases that have enough samples in them to take into account variability within species. Since every individual cannot be sampled, whether or not an individual belongs to a specific group is based on statistical analyses. If enough individuals have been sampled to establish a trend, then it is possible to say with confidence what group (species or population) an unknown sample belongs to.

This is an important aspect of a "good" database. *People v Axell*, 1991 (235 Cal.App.3d 836, 866–867) demonstrated how important it is for a database to take into account variability within and between populations. In this case, the statistics used against the defendant were called into question. Axell was Hispanic, and the defense asked if the potential for sub-structuring based on ethnicity had been taken into account. The ensuing legal wrangling generated a paper published in *Science* (Cohen et al., 1991; Devlin et al., 1993) which called into question all databases used for

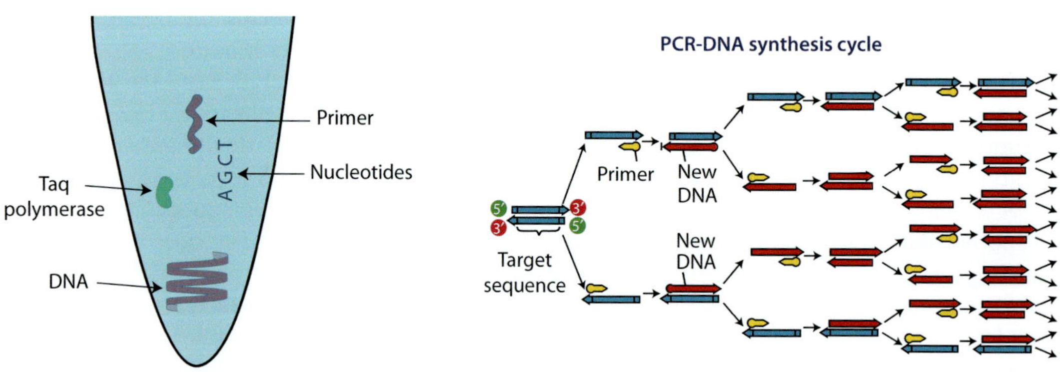

Figure 4.6 The process of polymerase chain reaction (PCR) involves adding all the necessary reagents and DNA to a small tube. The tube is subjected to rigidly defined heating and cooling cycles to make copies of the target DNA so that enough target is produced to visualize. ([a] From: https://www.biologyexams4u.com/2014/04/pcr-polymerase-chain-reaction.html#.XVRtd-NKjcs. [b] https://www.slideshare.net/biotechvictor1950/technique-of-polymerase-chain-reaction-pcr-experimental-biotechnology.)

forensic purposes. Was the database properly built to capture variability, and were there enough samples, enough data, in the database for reliable statistical analyses?

A database that has been created to answer population structure questions is a good starting point. Samples are initially collected to represent the individual populations and/or across a geographic distribution. To make a population database more applicable to a forensic question, sufficient samples need to be collected and added to capture within and between variability within populations, and samples collected across a geographic range need to be added in to make the database less biased to a specific area or population. This applies to databases that are used to address species identification as well as individual identification.

For example, a tissue sample submitted for species identification will have the DNA extracted, be PCR amplified, the PCR product cleaned, and sequenced. Once the technician has reviewed the data from the sequencer and determined it is good, the exported text of that sequence will be compared to databases to determine the source species. The sequence can be submitted to GenBank for a BLAST search and it may be found to belong to one of the species of sea turtles. GenBank may not have a very large bank of sea turtle sequences, maybe several hundred from several specific studies. However, if that sequence is now compared to an internal database consisting of many thousands of sequences of all species of sea turtles and it is found to belong to the group of Kemps Ridleys, the technician can be statistically certain that the sample is from that particular species. In addition, the beach of origin can generally be identified because sea turtles have natal homing and return to nest on the same beach their nest was.

GenBank results should be viewed with caution. Care is taken to identify and verify all sequences that are submitted to GenBank but it is not foolproof, and errors are present. It is a good place to start, as with the sea turtle example. There are enough sea turtle sequences present to make the technician confident that it is indeed a sea turtle. Further investigation will confirm the species of sea turtle. However, if the technician is looking for the genus and species of an insect that has been found associated with remains, it can be problematic. GenBank has very few sequences of certain insects. There is limited representation of within species variability, and there may be many genera and species present but only one or two representatives of each in the database. Ideally, an extensive internal database for each species a laboratory deals with should be designed and maintained; however, this is not always feasible, so GenBank remains a good place to start.

Databases for genetic profiles, nDNA, are quite different. These databases must be species specific and should be as unbiased as possible. There is not a repository of species-specific genetic profiles. These are databases that are built in-house by the laboratories assaying the specific species. Human profiles are generated using kits that have the same loci, so all human profiles can, in theory, be compared anywhere in the country or the world. Genetic profiles for nonhuman species, with a few exceptions, are not available as kits. There are some kits for horses, cattle, and dogs, but the kits among the different manufacturers do not have the same loci represented so there is no continuity. In general, species-specific loci are either developed in the laboratory using them or they are pulled from the literature. A laboratory using 10 loci for dog identification may not be, and probably is not, using the same loci as another laboratory, so there cannot be shared databases. The statistics generated from these databases are only as good as the size of the database and the representation of individuals within the database. For instance, a database of dogs should have about 50% "mutts" and 50% purebreds. The mix of mutts and purebreds should represent not only the local dogs, but dogs across a geographic range to show that there is no substructure or other event that skews the data. Databases for nonhuman assays are expensive and take a long time to populate.

Databases need to be large enough and properly representative to be able to generate reliable and consistent statistics. If too small or too biased, the statistics may not be able to support the DNA evidence in a case and the evidence may be thrown out and not considered. A well-designed database with many loci will generate a statistic that can be safely used in testimony and will be acceptable to the judge and jury.

CONCLUSION

DNA data is vital to criminal investigations whether for humans or animals. It may be the only way of linking individuals to crime scenes. DNA is used to identify species that have been involved in or used in various criminal activities. It is used to identify species of forensically important insects during early development when they are indistinguishable from one another.

DNA is used to identify individual dogs, deer, or other species. It is used to link the meat in a freezer with the blood in the back of a truck or on someone's clothing and the tissue of a dead deer taken out of season.

The evidence is collected with all the same precautions and requirements as human evidence collection. It is processed using many of the same protocols and kits. Unlike human forensics, the species is often not known and must be determined before individual identification can be done. Individual identification is based on databases that have been designed and built for the species involved. Courtrooms around the world are recognizing that DNA evidence from animals needs to be treated in essentially the same way as human DNA evidence. Animal DNA used for forensic investigations is becoming the gold standard and is more and more often looked for in a court of law. It is a very exciting time for animal forensic DNA evidence.

References

Becker, F and French, L 2004. Making the links: Child abuse, animal cruelty and domestic violence. *Child Abuse Review* 13 (6):399–414.

Cohen, JE., Lynch, M, Taylor, CE, Green, P, Lander, ES, Devlin, B, Risch, N, and Roeder, K 1991. Forensic DNA Tests and Hardy-Weinberg Equilibrium. *Science*. 253:1037–1041.

Comstock, KE et al. 2003. Amplifying nuclear and mitochondrial DNA from African elephant ivory: A tool for monitoring the ivory trade. *Conservation Biology* 17 (6):1840–1843.

Devlin, B, Risch, N, and Roeder, K 1993. Statistical Evaluation of DNA Fingerprinting: A Critique of the NCR's Report. *Science*. 259:748–749.

Gullone, E and Robertson, N 2008. The relationship between bullying and animal abuse behaviors in adolescents: The importance of witnessing animal abuse. *Journal of Applied Developmental Psychology* 29 (5):371–379.

Johnson CP 2000. Crime Mapping and Analysis Using GIS. *Geomatics 2000: Conference on Geomatics in Electronic Governance*. Paper 4.

Lockwood, R and Hodge, GR 1986. Tangled Web of Animal Abuse; The Links Between Cruelty to Animals and Human Violence. *Humane Society News* (Summer). http://www.ncjrs.gov/App/publications/abstract.aspx?ID=155688

People v Axell 1991. 235 Cal.App.3d 836, 866–867. https://caselaw.findlaw.com/ca-court-of-appeal/1769953.html

CHAPTER 5

FORENSIC ENTOMOLOGY

Jason H. Byrd and Adrienne Brundage

INTRODUCTION

Forensic entomology has been utilized in various aspects of human medicolegal death investigation since thirteenth-century China. However, the use of entomological evidence in wildlife and animal investigations has not been widely adopted by the forensic science or wildlife conservation communities. Nevertheless, with increased awareness and training for wildlife conservation officers, the use of forensic entomology in the investigation of wildlife crimes is increasing. A recent example of the application of wildlife forensic entomology is from Canada. At the peak of summer in Winnipeg, Manitoba, witnesses discovered three dead black bears near a garbage dump. The animals had been shot, disemboweled with gallbladders removed, and covered in garbage. The removal of the gallbladders suggested a profit motive. Authorities apprehended suspects in the area, but none possessed any animal tissue at the time of the arrest. Officers on scene understood the use insects in death investigations and were able to collect insect eggs from the abdominal wounds. Part of the collected samples were preserved for examination, while the remainder were placed alive on bear liver for observation. The consulting forensic entomologist, Dr. Gail Anderson, identified three species of blowflies (Diptera: Calliphoridae) on the remains: *Phormia regina*, the black blowfly; *Lucilia sericata*, the common green bottle fly; and *L. illustris*, the green bottle fly. These flies are well known in the forensic entomological community, develop at a predictable rate dependent upon ambient temperature, and primarily oviposit on freshly dead animals. Dr. Anderson was able to use this information to estimate the age of the insects when collected from the bear carcasses. Since colonization of the carcasses with fly eggs would likely not have occurred until after the bears had been killed, the estimated time of colonization was used to estimate the animal time of death. This work positively linked the apprehended suspects to the bears and resolved with each poacher serving jail time (Anderson, 1999).

BACKGROUND

Forensic entomology is the intersection between arthropod science and the judicial system (Amendt et al., 2007; Benecke, 2008; Smith, 1986; Byrd & Castner, 2010). Entomology is the study of arthropods, particularly insects and their close relatives. The word is derived from the Greek *entomo*, meaning insect, and *logus*, meaning study. The field involves a range of biological disciplines and applied fields, one of which is forensics (Gullan & Cranston, 2009). The common denominator of these disciplines is that they all involve insects as the focus of study.

All arthropods have several basic characteristics in common: bilateral symmetry, segmented external appendages, an exoskeleton formed from chitin (or long-chain polymer of N-acetylglucosamine, a derivative of glucose), and external segmentation. Arthropods are broken up into several groups based on their external characteristics. One can differentiate insects from all other arthropods based on the presence of three major body regions (head, thorax, and abdomen), a single pair of antennae, often modified for specialized functions, and three pairs of segmented legs (Foottit & Adler, 2009; Gullan & Cranston, 2009).

Insects are the most diverse group of organisms on earth. They constitute approximately half of the global species diversity and represent 50% of all described species of living organisms (Foottit & Adler, 2009). Members of this group are found in all ecosystems and have the ability to exploit vacant niches through adaptation. Their small size, highly organized neuromotor system, and rapid developmental cycles allow these organisms to cope with variable environments (Gullan & Cranston, 2009). It is this coping ability that makes insects such a valuable tool in forensics.

While forensic entomology is any intersection between entomology and the judicial system (Catts & Haskell, 2008; Byrd & Castner, 2010), wildlife forensic entomology is a specific subset of that science (Anderson, 1999). Wildlife forensic entomology is a branch of forensic entomology dealing specifically with animals other than humans. This branch tends to focus on domestic animals, although, as illustrated in the introductory case, has been successfully used in poaching and other cases involving wild animals. It is uniquely simple to use our knowledge of forensic entomology in a case involving wildlife; the bulk of forensic entomological research has been carried out not on human cadavers, but on animal carcasses (Table 5.1). This leads to a large amount of knowledge associating insects with various animals. Often, whatever animal is present in a wildlife forensic entomology case has an associated decomposition and succession study, which leads to a direct application of forensic entomological research to this particular discipline.

BASIC INSECT ANATOMY

The foundation of entomology is the anatomy of an insect. Arthropods in general have evolved strategies to live successfully under a variety of conditions, and a strong understanding of external and internal anatomy of the insects involved in decomposition will give an investigator a place to start.

The overall body form of an insect is basically cylindrical and elongate and as noted previously, is broken up into three major body regions: the head, the thorax, and the abdomen. The head is made of sclerotized, or hardened, segments fused to form a capsule. It is rigid to protect the brain and give strength to the mouthparts, and houses the sensory center of the organism. The sensory center consists of visual input, through the simple and compound eyes, and olfactory input, through the antennae (Gullan & Cranston, 2009).

Visual input allows the insect to see movement, potential oviposition site, potential food, and find mates. Most insects have two types of eyes: the simple eyes and the compound eyes. The compound eyes, when present, take up the bulk of the insect head, and consist of many individual units or lenses working together to form a single image. This image is supported by individual lenses, called the simple eyes, which give the insect information about light and dark. Working together, the compound and simple eyes allow flies and other insects find carrion (Nation, 2011).

The insect mouthparts come in a variety of forms. Some insects have chewing type mouthparts, which allow that insect to feed on a variety of substrates and chew that food. Other insects have piercing and sucking mouthparts, which allow the insect to pierce through the skin of an animal or the surface of a plant and feed on the internal fluids. Still others have sponging mouthparts, which enable the insect to produce digestive juices into the environment and soak up the resulting digested substance (Nation, 2011). Some insects have siphoning mouthparts which act like a straw and allow the insect to feed on freely available liquids like water and nectar. Some immature insects have specialized mouth hooks in place of the mouth parts, which can scrape food in the environment for eating. The types of mouthparts found in forensically important insects varies based on the type of tissue each insect is feeding upon. Those insects that feed during the early stages of decomposition tend to have sponging mouthparts as adults and mouth hooks as larvae. Those that feed during the later stages of decomposition, when tissue tends to be tougher, tend to have chewing mouthparts (Mullen & Durden, 2002).

The thoracic region of the adult insect has three pairs of legs, and often has wings. The legs are five-segmented, and adapted for walking, running, digging, grasping, jumping, or a myriad of other behaviors common to the individual insect. There are usually two pairs of wings, and the wings tend to be slender with veins throughout for strength. These veins and the open areas between the veins (the cells) are used to identify many insect species. While wings are common, there are a few groups of insects that evolved without wings, such as silverfish, and those that lost their wings as they specialized to feed on living animals, such as fleas. Other insects have modified wings for protection or flight. Beetles have two pairs of wings, but the first pair is hardened into a protective covering for the hind wings. Flies have one pair of well-developed wings, while the hind wings are reduced into knob-like organs that are used for balance during flight (Gullan & Cranston, 2009).

Table 5.1 Selection of insect succession studies on nonhuman animals by region

Region	Animal Subject	Reference
North America	Alligator	Nelder et al. (2009), Watson Carlton (2003), Watson (2005)
	Bear	Swiger et al. (2014), Watson & Carlton (2003), Watson (2005)
	Bird	Brand et al. (2003), De Jong (1994), Lord and Burger (1984), Sanford (2015), Tessmer et al. (1995)
	Cat	De Jong (1994), Early and Goff (1986), Johnson (1975), Sanford (2015)
	Deer	De Jong (1994), Watson and Carlton (2003), Watson (2005)
	Dog	De Jong (1994), Reed (1958), Sanford (2015)
	Fox	Smith (1975)
	Mouse	De Jong (1994)
	Opossum	Johnson (1975)
	Moose	Samuel (1988)
	Pig	Anderson and Vanlaerhoven (1996), Avila and Goff (1998), Benbow et al. (2013), Caballero and León-Cortés (2014), Davis (2000), Gill (2005), Hewadikaram and Goff (1991), Macaulay et al. (2009), Michaud et al. (2010), Pastula and Merritt (2013), Payne (1965), Payne (1968), Richards and Goff (1997), Sharanowski et al. (2008), Tabor (2004), Tenorio et al. (2003), Vanlaerhoven and Anderson (1999), Watson and Carlton (2003), Watson (2005)
	Rabbit	Johnson (1975), De Jong and Chadwick (1999), Mckinnerney (1978)
	Raccoon	De Jong (1994), Joy et al. (2002)
	Rat	De Jong and Hoback (2006), Keiper (1997), Patrican and Vaidyanathan (1995), Parmenter and Macmahon (2009), Tomberlin and Adler (1998)
	Salamander	De Jong and Hoback (2006), Regester and Whiles (2006)
	Skunk	De Jong (1994)
	Squirrel	De Jong (1994), Johnson (1975)
	Turtle	De Jong (1994), Abell et al. (1982)
Central and South America	Dog	Jiron (1981)
	Fish	Moretti et al. (2008)
	Lizard	Cornaby (1974)
	Mouse	Moretti et al. (2008)
	Pig	Barrios and Wolff (2011), Battan Horenstein (2010), Martinez (2007), Mayer and Vasconcelos (2013), Ortloff et al. (2012), Rosa et al. (2011)
	Rabbit	Mise et al. (2013), Vasconcelos et al. (2013)
	Rat	Moretti et al. (2008), Moura et al. (1997), Mauricio Osvaldo (2005), Vasconcelos et al. (2013)
	Snake	Moretti et al. (2009), Vanin (2012)
	Toad	Cornaby (1974)
Europe	Bird	Arnaldos et al. (2001), Arnaldos et al. (2004), Blackith and Blackith (1990), Kuusela and Hanski (1982)
	Fish	Kuusela and Hanski (1982)
	Mice	Blackith and Blackith (1990), Putman (1977), Lane (1975)
	Pig	Bajerlein et al. (2011), Bonacci et al. (2011), Grassberger and Frank (2004), Matuszewski et al. (2010), Turner and Howard (1992), Malgorn (2001), Prado E Castro (2012)
	Rabbit	Bourel et al. (1999)
	Rat	Kocarek (2003)

(*Continued*)

Table 5.1 (*Continued*) Selection of insect succession studies on nonhuman animals by region

Region	Animal Subject	Reference
	Vole	Lane (1975)
Africa	Dog	Boulkenafet Sélima Berchi et al. (2015)
	Elephant	Coe (1978)
	Fish	Kyerematen et al. (2012)
	Impala	Braack (1986), Braack (1987), Ellison (1990)
	Rabbit	Tantawi et al. (1996), Mabika et al. (2014)
	Pig	Kyerematen et al. (2012), Kelly et al. (2009)
Asia	Bird	Azwandi et al. (2013)
	Goat	Zaidi and Chen (2011)
	Monkey	Ahmad et al. (2011)
	Pig	Chin (2007), Wang et al. (2008)
	Rabbit	Azwandi et al. (2013), Shi (2009), Shi (2010), Mahat et al. (2008), Abouzied (2014)
	Rat	Azwandi et al. (2013)
Austraila	Brushtail possum	Lang et al. (2006)
	Dog	O'Flynn (1983)
	Fish	Schlacher et al. (2013)
	Fox	O'Flynn and Moorhouse (1979)
	Guinea pigs	Bornemissza (1957), Voss et al. (2009)
	Kangaroo	O'Flynn and Moorhouse (1979)
	Sheep	O'Flynn (1983)
	Pig	O'Flynn and Moorhouse (1979), Eberhardt and Elliot (2008), Voss (2008), Archer and Elgar (2003)

The abdomen is generally cylindrical and varies from 9 to 11 obvious segments. Each segment bears a pair of holes on the lateral surfaces called the spiracles, which allow for oxygen to diffuse into the internal trachea. The abdomen does not usually have any appendages, and primarily serves to house the internal organs. The terminal end of the abdomen houses the genitalia and other specialized structures. Some female genitalia are heavily sclerotized and are used for defense as stingers (Gullan & Cranston, 2009).

These internal organs of the insect are housed within the body cavity, or the haemocoel. The haemocoel contains all the organs, including the modified heart, the brain, and the digestive, reproductive, nervous, and respiratory systems. The organs are bathed in a nutrient-rich fluid which fills the haemocoel, called hemolymph. The hemolymph combines some of the functions of vertebrate blood and lymph, delivering nutrients, removing metabolites, and carrying out basic immune functions.

Circulation of hemolymph is maintained mostly by a system of muscular pumps moving the hemolymph through compartments separated by membranes. Insects have an open circulatory system: hemolymph is not confined to vessels. Instead, it sloshes around the haemocoel and bathes the organs with nutrients and hormones while removing wastes and assisting in immune functions (Nation, 2011). Most insect hemolymph does not carry oxygen, and therefore does not have the characteristic red color that mammalian blood has. The only conducing tube is not a true vessel, but a simple dorsal tube, closed at the posterior end and dotted with openings called ostia. The ostia allow hemolymph to enter the dorsal vessel (or "heart") and the vessel pumps the hemolymph forward toward the brain. It then flows backward in the haemocoel, assisted by muscle contractions in the ventral diaphragm (Mullen & Durden, 2002).

Oxygen is provided to the tissues via the respiratory system. Insects must obtain oxygen from the environment and eliminate carbon dioxide from the cells. Air usually enters the insect via the openings found on the lateral or posterior surfaces of the body. These openings are called spiracles and attach to a network of tracheal tubes. These tubes branch throughout the body, with the finest branches, or tracheoles, contacting all the internal organs and tissues (Mullen & Durden, 2002).

The digestive system is responsible for the breakdown of foods and the excretion of waste products. It is broken up into several sections, as follows.

The foregut receives the ingested food and is responsible for the initial digestion through muscular grinding. Chemical digestion primarily takes place in the midgut, where enzymes break down carbohydrates and proteins into absorbable units. These digestive products pass through a protective sieve that lines the midgut, the peritrophic membrane, and are absorbed through the midgut lining. Whatever is left over after absorption moves into the hindgut, which absorbs excess water and ions and excretes the waste products. Hanging off the hindgut is a variable number of tubes known as Malpighian tubules. The tubules float free in the hemolymph and filter out waste products. The waste is sent to the rectum and eliminated from the insect body (Nation, 2011).

The insect nervous system is in charge of conveying and integrating information about the internal and external environments. It consists primarily of the brain, found along the dorsal region of the head capsule, and a ventral nerve cord, which travels ventrally from the brain along the thorax and abdomen. The nerve cord is studded with ganglia, thickened regions of tissue that contain nerve cells. Each ganglion is the nerve center for its associated segment and sends information from that segment back to the brain for processing (Nation, 2011).

THE INSECT LIFE CYCLE

Reproduction in most insects involves two sexes. The female reproductive system is responsible for producing and storing eggs, providing eggs with nutrition, receiving and storing the sperm, fertilizing the eggs, and depositing the eggs into the environment. The male reproductive system is responsible for producing sperm and presenting it to the female for egg fertilization (Nation, 2011).

The primary forensically important insects are the Diptera, or the true flies. Since Diptera are generally the first insect to colonize animal remains, it is the dipteran life cycle that is most commonly used in forensic cases. The dipteran life cycle is therefore considered the most important life cycle to understand (Smith, 1986; Catts & Haskell, 2008; Nation, 2011). All flies start out as eggs that are usually laid in the environment, although some eggs remain in the body of the female and are placed in the environment as larvae (Mullen & Durden, 2002). The adult flies arrive at a dead animal and lay their eggs or larvae onto the natural bodily openings and wounds of that animal (Nation, 2011). The resulting larvae feed on the body until they are ready to pupate. Flies have what is called a complete life cycle, or metamorphosis: they begin as eggs, hatch into larvae, pupate, and eclose from the pupae into the adult stage. The larvae go through three stages, or instars, before they finish feeding on the body and move into the dispersal or wandering stage (Mullen & Durden, 2002). This dispersal stage takes the larvae 15–20 feet away from the carrion and to a protected place in which to pupate (Catts & Haskell, 2008). The dispersing larvae will crawl under things in the environment, or dig a few centimeters down into the soil, where the outer cuticle of the larva hardens into a protective shell, or pupal case. Inside this pupal casing enzymes transform the larvae into an adult (Gullan & Cranston, 2009).

USE OF ENTOMOLOGICAL EVIDENCE

The evaluation of entomological evidence at a scene has the potential to lend invaluable information about the scene and surrounding circumstances (Anderson et al., 1984; Braack & Retlef, 1986;

Benecke, 2001; Watson & Carlton, 2005; Velasquez, 2008). The interpretation of entomological evidence can inform an investigator about many different aspects of the scene, including time of colonization (and by extension, time of death), season of colonization, location of colonization and potential movement or storage of the remains after death, evidence of neglect, sites of trauma on the remains, and presence of chemicals in the remains (Smith, 1986; Catts & Haskell, 2008; Byrd & Castner, 2010; Barnes & Gennard, 2011). This information may then inform several stages of the investigation.

Time of Colonization

On the morning of July 2, 2014, a family went into their backyard and noted their 6-month-old Labrador retriever puppy missing. The puppy had spent the night in a doghouse within the fenced yard. There was not apparent damage to the fencing, and no obvious means of escape. The body of the animal was found 2 days later, on July 4, 2014 at approximately 5:00 PM, located in a vacant lot near the home. The dog had been dismembered postmortem. A large number of fly larvae were present on the remains and were observed to be traversing the entire body. Fly larvae were identified as third instar *Lucilia sericata*. This species is common in the area where the animal was found and is expected during the summer months. The age of the collected larvae was estimated at 2 days, indicating that the larvae had colonized the body of the animal sometime on July 2, 2014. Since the puppy was observed as healthy the night before it disappeared, the flies likely colonized the dog just after death, putting the animal's time of death sometime on July 2, the day it disappeared.

Insects reveal a great deal about a scene to a knowledgeable investigator. First and most sought after is the time of colonization (TOC) estimation, which is often associated with the postmortem interval (PMI), or time of death (Byrd & Castner, 2010). Many insects important in forensics are in the ecological group of decomposers—those organisms that utilize the nutrients bound up in dead matter (Price, 1997). Decomposers efficiently find and exploit dead matter, and those that rely upon ephemeral resources such as animal carcasses excel at resource location (Price, 1997; Cain et al., 2008). Insects may arrive at a newly dead animal within minutes after death (Hall, 1995; Catts & Haskell, 2008), and either feed upon the carcass directly or colonize the carcass through egg oviposition (Price, 1997; Byrd & Castner, 2010). Because of the efficiency of resource location, it may be assumed that an insect with unfettered access to a carcass arrived and colonized that carcass within minutes of animal death. Therefore, estimation of the age of the insects colonizing the animal body (TOC estimation) may be used as an indicator of how long that carcass has been available for insect colonization, and, by extension, how long that animal has been dead (PMI) (Byrd & Castner, 2010; Tomberlin et al., 2011).

Insect age estimation relies on their basic physiology. Insects are poikilothermic, meaning their growth and development is affected by ambient temperature (115). Lower ambient temperatures lead to slower insect growth, while higher ambient temperatures lead to faster insect growth. Each insect species has an upper and lower threshold, above or below which the insect no longer grows (Yang et al., 1995; Price, 1997). We can describe and predict this growth based on ambient temperature by using a mathematical formula (see section Calculating Time of Colonization) (Higley et al., 1986; Byrd & Castner, 2010; Michaud & Moreau, 2011).

Investigators are able to use the ability of insects to quickly locate and colonize carrion, and the entomologist's ability to mathematically estimate insect age given ambient temperature, to estimate a PMI. However, there are some assumptions that must be made. If we assume that the insects arrived very soon after death and that their growth was dictated by ambient temperature, then we can calculate how long it would take an observed insect to reach an observed developmental stage at a given ambient temperature. This calculated time is the minimum PMI (Smith, 1986; Catts & Haskell, 2008; Byrd & Castner, 2010). If the exact arrival time of insects at carrion is unknown, however (i.e., before or after death the animal was blocked from insect activity, etc.), this calculated time is the time of colonization interval (Byrd & Castner, 2010; Tomberlin et al., 2011).

Extended Time of Colonization

The desiccated and decomposed remains of a canine were discovered indoors on a January morning in 2012 (Figure 5.1). The canine was wedged behind a partially open door leading into a room packed with refuse. The owner of the house was a known hoarder and had recently been removed from the premises. The body of the canine was found surrounded by empty pupal casings and uneclosed pupae. A total of 28 eclosed pupal casings and 3 uneclosed pupal casings were identified. Four of the eclosed pupal casings were identified to the family Calliphoridae (blowflies) but were unable to be identified to species. Seven of the eclosed pupal casings and one of the uneclosed pupae were identified as *Fannia scalaris*. Fifteen of the eclosed pupal casings and one of the uneclosed pupae were identified as *F. canicularis*. The presence of *Fannia* species in this situation indicated an extended PMI, and the life cycle time associated with all the species found on and around remains were used to extend the PMI and TOC estimation.

This case illustrates a method by which TOC may be extended beyond the length of time it takes the first fly to arrive, colonize remains, and complete the larval stage. This method is known as insect succession and relies upon the fact that decomposing insects arrive in a particular order and last a particular amount of time on remains (Price, 1997; Michaud et al., 2015). Knowledge of the order in which insects arrive at carrion and the time they take utilizing that carrion as a resource allows investigators to estimate TOC (and, by extension, minimum postmortem interval [mPMI]) to include the life of several successive waves of insects.

Cause and Manner of Death

Sites of trauma can alter the typical pattern of insect arrival found on deceased animals with no external trauma. In animal cruelty cases, most common trauma which alters insect colonization patterns is either gunshot or sharp force injury. Trauma to the head may not significantly alter the overall pattern, as insects would normally colonize the natural orifices on the head (Figure 5.2). Trauma provides insects with an additional avenue of access to the tissue underlying the dermal layers. The blood produced externally as a result of trauma provides adult flies with a food source of sugars and proteins. The site of trauma will often be the first area colonized by early-arriving flies. The additional access to the interior of the carcass allows for slightly accelerated decomposition due to larval feeding. Due to the nature of the cranial structure, head trauma is generally easily recognized, and often first reported by the forensic pathologist or anthropologist. Wounds of this

Figure 5.1 Insect succession can be utilized to assist in estimating the mPMI in cases of extended postmortem intervals.

Figure 5.2 Trauma to the head will not alter the overall pattern of anterior to posterior insect-driven decomposition. However, trauma to other areas of the body are likely to alter this pattern. During the early postmortem interval, insect distribution on the body should not occur in seemingly random patches. Insect distribution on the body that is seemingly randomly distributed could indicate areas of trauma.

nature in other regions of the body would change the typical head-down decomposition pattern, however, and result in maggot masses in unexpected places.

Animals found hanged to death will attract insects in the same pattern as those killed in other ways. Even in the instance when the animal is fully suspended and not touching the ground, insects will colonize natural bodily openings and wounds. In some instances, external tissue damage may be present in the areas associated with ligatures, in which case flies will lay eggs on these damaged areas and larvae will begin to feed at the margins of the damaged tissues. This tissue damage is not universal, however, with only internal tissue damage showing indication of hanging. Flies are attracted to natural bodily openings in these cases, and can be found along the mouth, eyes, nose, and ears (Figure 5.3). This will result in the common head-down decomposition pattern. Unfortunately, advanced decomposition may make it impossible for pathologists to determine cause or manner of death in instances without obvious wounds or abnormal insect colonization.

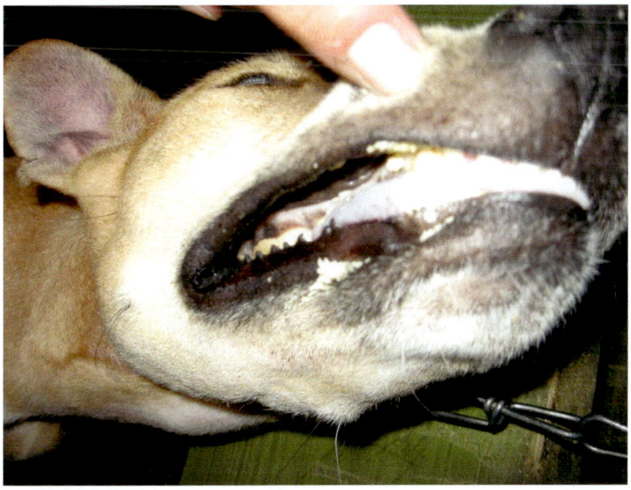

Figure 5.3 In the absence of trauma, insects will frequently colonize the eyes, nose, mouth, and ears before any other areas of the body. Anal and genital areas will also be colonized, but typically some time after the natural openings of the head.

These examples illustrate just some of information that may be gleaned from the insects colonizing an animal carcass. However, the potential cause and mechanism of death may be critical to the investigation (Smith, 1986; Byrd & Castner, 2010; Roberts & Márquez-Grant, 2012). This information may be derived from knowledge of the general behavior of a colonizing insect. Most decomposers, regardless of their arrival time, will colonize tissue that is easily accessible, and in a state ready for consumption. This means that insects that arrive very quickly after death will colonize an animal in areas of the body that provide easy access, protected from the elements and predators, and allow for easy feeding for the offspring. These areas include natural body openings and wounds (Catts & Haskell, 2008; Byrd & Castner, 2010). In addition to colonizing the eyes, ears, mouth, nose, and anal and genital openings, adult flies also tend to lay their eggs in the folds of skin (Smith, 1986; Campobasso, 2001). The resulting larvae will feed on the tissues in the general vicinity of the egg mass and then move into new areas. Early maggot masses can therefore be frequently expected in the head and neck regions, and in the anal and genital regions. If maggot masses are found in any other area, especially the legs, back, or center chest, then there was likely a wound of some sort in that area that allowed for larval access. The presence of wounds may indicate a death from something other than natural causes (Smith, 1986).

Season of Colonization and Postmortem Movement

All arthropods have a distribution range based on a variety of factors, including food availability, ability to disperse, and preferred climate. This results in different species of decomposers living in different areas at different times of the year. Knowledge of the range and distribution of various insects is important when it comes to forensic science analysis, since it can speak to the potential location of death. Many scientific studies indicate the known range and ecological differences of various forensically important species (see Baumgartner, 1985; Mariluis & Mulieri, 2003; Baz et al., 2007; Honda et al., 2008; Brundage et al., 2011), and these same studies show distinct preferences of insect habitats. For example, Brundage et al. (2011) showed that forensically important flies showed significant habitat differences within a single county, with different communities maintained in urban, rural, and riparian habitats. This suggests that animals killed and colonized in urban areas will have different species of flies feeding on the remains than those killed and colonized just a few miles away in rural habitats. Similarly, Gruner et al. (2007) showed significantly different species composition of flies colonizing animal remains in winter, spring, summer, and fall. This indicates that animal remains found in the same area at different times of year will be associated with different insect species (Figure 5.4a,b). Knowledge of the types of forensically important insects common to different regions and different seasons can allow an investigator to determine potential location of death and colonization, differentiate the place of death from a potential dump site, and narrow down the season during which the animal remains decomposed.

A second way that insects may indicate the movement of an animal after death has to do with the basic life cycle of the fly. Diptera larvae exploit carrion for a relatively short time. After they have completed feeding upon the carcass, they leave that carcass and find a protected place to undergo pupation. This area may be directly underneath the carrion, or in the vicinity of the carcass. The presence of numerous pupal casings or pupating flies indicate that at one time a carcass was in that location and may give evidence that a dead animal was once in the area, even if the carcass is no longer present.

Similarly, fly larvae may continue to feed on purged fluids from a decomposing animal long after the majority of the tissue has been removed through scavenger feeding or movement of the body to conceal a crime (Haglund & Sorg, 1996). Maggots that were once associated with the carrion proper may remain in fluids that have seeped into the ground, soaked bedding (Catts & Goff, 1992; Kelly et al., 2009), or other material, or dropped from a suspended carcass (Haglund & Sorg, 1996; Fisher et al., 2006). These larvae may be analyzed in the same way as those removed directly from

Figure 5.4 (a) Swine carcass, 6 days postmortem showing extensive insect colonization and advanced decomposition stage during July in northern Florida. (b) Swine carcass, 6 days postmortem showing minimal insect colonization and fresh decay stage during January in northern Florida.

the carrion and used to construct a time of colonization estimation of the purged fluids. This could give investigators information about when the carrion was removed.

Evidence of Neglect

A dog was found in a moderate state of neglect, with obvious matting of the coat. The animal was incapacitated and unable to groom itself properly. As a result, the hair became feted with urine and fecal material. The feted hair attracted adult flies, which began oviposition on the decomposing material in the air coat, and the resulting larvae began to feed within the feted fur (Figure 5.5). Maggots generally feed by partially liquefying tissues, and the feeding mechanisms of maggots often produce ulcerous sores on the skin of living animals. In turn, as these ulcerous sores produce necrotic tissue, new and different fly species are attracted and begin to feed directly on the tissues of the animal (Figure 5.6). This is a common occurrence in cases of animal neglect. A careful analysis of the species infesting the coat and differentiating between those feeding directly on the tissues helped determine how long the period of neglect was before onset of tissue feeding or death.

This case illustrates an important distinction in wildlife forensic entomology, which is the need to quantify neglect. While insects colonizing an animal are most commonly used to determine time of death (Byrd & Castner, 2010), their ability to colonize festering wounds of still-living animals should not be overlooked (Mullen & Durden, 2002). An investigator can use the same techniques as discerning time of colonization or PMI to calculate a time of neglect: the primary difference is the former describes insects that colonized an animal after death, while the latter describes insects that colonized an animal before death. The science is the same. An investigator can use the ambient temperature and knowledge of the insect life cycle to estimate the age of the larvae collected from the animal. Assuming that the insects colonized an open wound, the age of the insect indicates how long that insect has been feeding on the animal. If the insect is large enough to see or is feeding on apparent areas (rather than internally or in areas that are not easily visible) then it can be inferred

Figure 5.5 Larval mass in a fetid fur coat. The hair of an animal may become soiled with urine or excrement. This will attract fly species that will feed on the excrement and not just the tissues of the animal. The larval feeding behavior results in a liquefaction of the food source, and this liquid can produce ulcers or lesions on underlying tissue. Keeping the insects recovered from only the hair coat separate from those collected directly from the underlying tissues can help the entomologist in determining how long the period of neglect or lack of care may have occurred before the tissues were colonized.

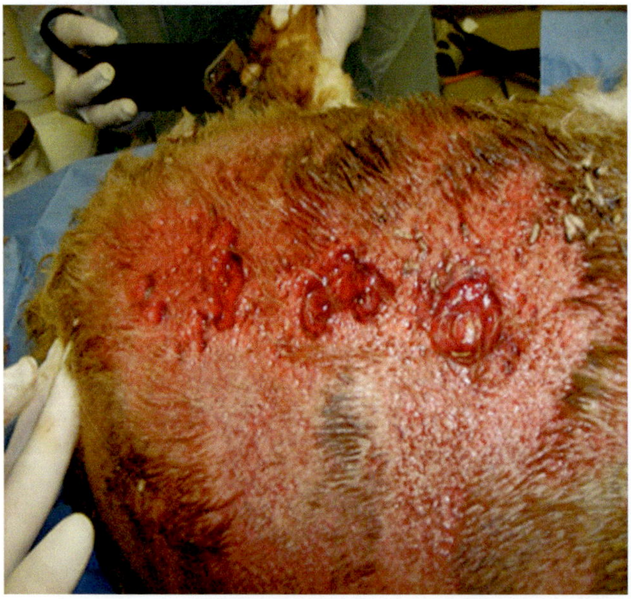

Figure 5.6 Analysis of the larvae collected directly from the tissue can be utilized to establish the time of colonization. Both time periods together could be utilized to establish the period of neglect, or the minimum postmortem interval if death occurred.

that the animal was neglected for as long as the insect was feeding. This gives the investigator an estimated time of neglect.

Time of neglect may cause some problems when trying to determine time of colonization for PMI estimation, however. It is important to keep in mind that many of the same species that colonize dead animals have the ability to colonize open wounds and may be present *before* the animal was dead (Mullen & Durden, 2002). If these insects did colonize the animal before death, then using the full insect age will lead to an incorrect PMI estimation. Caution should be used when attempting these estimations unless it is known for certain that the insects colonized after death, and not before.

Presence of Wounds

The typical pattern of insect-driven decomposition in the absence of trauma is head-down, with the areas of most tissue loss being anterior (Figure 5.7). Insects are attracted to the natural bodily openings in the head region, and the maggot mass typically starts in the head and moves posterior as the tissues are consumed. The resulting tissue loss is usually prevalent anteriorly and becomes less pronounced posteriorly.

Large animals such as cattle and other species with very thick skin show a slightly different decomposition pattern. With many livestock species, there is a normal colonization pattern with the first areas of egg or larvae deposition being in the natural openings of the head. However, the thickness of the skin impedes maggot feeding, and the larval activity is concentrated on the tissue that is more moist and somewhat pliable, as well as the underlying tissues. The result is skeletal material that remains covered in a layer of dried hide, which in some environments can persist for several months, or years.

Animal skin, fur, and hair can prevent easy access to tissue by some insect species. The colonizing decomposers will seek areas on the animal that are easy to access and provide a ready feeding site for developing larvae. In most cases, these sites consist of natural bodily openings (eyes, ears, mouth, anus, etc.). Wounds are also attractive colonization sites. Wounds that penetrate soft tissue but do not damage hard tissue are disguised during the decomposition process and may be overlooked by investigators. Insect activity may also be prominent around areas of vertebrate scavenging, such as the ears, abdomen, and external genitalia. The presence of insect colonization in body parts that would not normally support colonization (e.g., chest, back, flanks, and extremities) indicates the presence of wounds in that region.

Presence of Drugs

One important but lesser-used bit of information that may be gleaned from insect colonizers is the presence of drugs, poisons, or other chemicals in the animal body (Introna et al., 2001). Since insects

Figure 5.7 Canine remains illustrating the typical head-down skeletonization pattern of insect-driven decomposition. In the absence of trauma, fly larvae colonize the area of the head first, and move posteriorly as the tissues are consumed. These fly larvae either enter the wandering and prepupal stage away from the body, or the remaining tissue becomes dry and unsuitable as a food resource for the early arriving fly larvae. This tissue may be consumed by later-arriving beetle species, or by fly species if it becomes wet from rainfall.

are feeding directly on animal tissue, the saying "you are what you eat" applies. Any substances present in animal tissues are ingested, and the decomposers lack the physiology to excrete many of these substances (Pounder, 1991; Gosselin et al., 2011). The chemicals end up being stored in the insect body and can be extracted through common toxicological methods. It is therefore possible to test for the presence of chemicals in a decomposed or mummified animal by testing the insect colonizers rather than the animal tissue itself (Gosselin et al., 2011).

One important limitation to this technique is it is unable to determine an exact amount of substance presence in animal tissues (Tracqui et al., 2004). As the colonizers feed, they will intake varying amounts of the substance, and store that substance within their tissues. This leads to bioaccumulation of the chemical. There is no known correlation between the amount of chemical present in the living animal and the amount of chemical stored in insect tissues (Tracqui et al., 2004). Therefore, we cannot quantify the chemical using this method. We can, however, answer the yes-or-no question "was this chemical present in this animal?" with certainty.

As with all forensic sciences, forensic entomology is simply the application of a science to a practical situation. These cases and scenarios illustrate the most common use of insects in casework, although the applications are truly endless. Any practical application simply takes advantage of the knowledge we have gained about insects through general study.

CALCULATING TIME OF COLONIZATION

Dipteran larvae are poikilothermic, and therefore do not produce their own heat (Beck, 1983; Nation, 2011). Instead, they are affected by the ambient temperature, which determines how quickly or slowly they grow (Davidson, 1944; Beck, 1983; Nation, 2011). The warmer the ambient temperature, the faster they go through their instars and pupal stage. The slower the ambient temperature, the slower they go through their instars and pupal stage. It is this property that allows forensic entomologists to apply insect development data to determine a time of colonization estimation on animal remains. This also makes temperature the most important density independent factor for insects (Beck, 1983; Byrd & Castner, 2010).

Temperature has a profound effect on dipteran metabolic and developmental rate (Nation, 2011). Generally, within certain temperature ranges, larval development is accelerated as ambient temperature increases. This does not hold true at temperature extremes, however. Every insect has thermal activity and death thresholds—both lower and upper limits, below or above which they can no longer function (Block, 1982; Beck, 1983; Nation, 2011). These thermal thresholds are naturally different for different species. Those species that evolved in tropical or warmer areas will have higher upper limits than those that evolved in temperate or colder areas (Addo-Bediako et al., 2000). Therefore, there is a huge variation among species when it comes to temperature thresholds. The lower limits are better known than the upper limits and become important when mathematically calculating a time of colonization estimation (Block, 1982; Nation, 2011). Developmental thresholds for forensically important flies are usually between 6°C and 10°C and are experimentally determined. If a specific fly species developmental threshold is not available, a general rule of thumb is to use 6°C for winter species or flies in cold areas, and 10°C for warm weather species or flies in warmer areas (Davies & Ratcliffe, 1994; Anderson, 2000; Ames & Turner, 2003; Catts & Haskell, 2008).

Each stage of insect growth, from egg to adult, requires a certain amount of heat above a minimum temperature and below a maximum temperature (Davidson, 1944; Hagstrum & Milliken, 1988). This growth rate can be represented with a linear model that represents the amount of heat necessary for a given fly to go through each of its developmental stages. These linear models are called degree day or degree hour models, because development is recorded as the temperature above the minimum developmental threshold multiplied by time (days or hours) (Pruess, 1983; Yang et al., 1995; Megyesi et al., 2005; Michaud & Moreau, 2011).

This model allows us to calculate the time it takes a fly to develop using ambient temperature and this formula:

$$(\text{Average Ambient Temperature} - \text{Minimum Threshold}) \times \text{Unit of Time}$$

This formula takes the average ambient temperature over a given time period, subtracts the minimum threshold for the insect species, and multiplies the result by a unit of time. The result is called a "degree day" (if the unit of time used was a day) or a "degree hour" (if the unit of time used was an hour). These are the two most common units of time seen in this type of model, because weather stations often record ambient temperature in daily or hourly intervals.

The formula may be used to calculate how many degree days (DD) or degree hours (DH) are necessary for an insect to get through various stages in its life cycle, as well as how many degree days have accumulated over time. The DD/DH necessary for an insect to get through its life cycle is determined by experiment. The data are recorded as hours needed for a species to develop at a given temperature, and these data may be converted into DD or DH by using the formula.

Table 5.2 shows several forensically important insects and the time it takes each insect to develop at various temperatures. Take, for example, the hours necessary for the black blowfly, *Phormia regina*, to develop at 27°C. According to research, it takes *P. regina* eggs 16 hours to go from freshly laid to hatching, 18 hours to go through the first larval instar, 11 hours to go through the second larval instar, and 36 hours to go through the third larval instar. To turn this information into degree hours, simply plug the data into the equation:

Egg DH:

$$(27°\text{C} - 10°\text{C}) \times 16 \text{ hours}$$

$$(17°\text{C}) \times 16 \text{ hours}$$

$$272 \text{ DH}$$

In this case, it takes *P. regina* 272 DH to go through its entire egg stage. This same calculation may be used to determine DD.

Egg DD:

$$(27°\text{C} - 10°\text{C}) \times 0.67 \text{ days}$$

$$(17°\text{C}) \times 0.67 \text{ days}$$

$$11.39 \text{ DD}$$

Table 5.2 Example of average ambient temperatures and calculated DD/ADD from a weather station

Date	Average Temp °C	DD	ADD
May 15	21	11	11
May 14	25	15	26
May 13	22	12	38
May 12	18	8	46
May 11	22	12	58
May 10	20	10	68
May 9	15	5	73

The number of DD or DH necessary for each stage of *P. regina* development may be calculated in this same way.

First instar DH/DD:

$$(27°C - 10°C) \times 18 \text{ hours}$$

$$(17°C) \times 18 \text{ hours}$$

$$306 \text{ DH or } 12.75 \text{ DD}$$

Second instar DH/DD:

$$(27°C - 10°C) \times 11 \text{ hours}$$

$$(17°C) \times 11 \text{ hours}$$

$$180 \text{ DH or } 7.5 \text{ DD}$$

Third instar DH/DD:

$$(27°C - 10°C) \times 36 \text{ hours}$$

$$(17°C) \times 36 \text{ hours}$$

$$612 \text{ DH or } 25.5 \text{ DD}$$

The results may be summed up to determine the accumulated degree days (ADD) or accumulated degree hours (ADH necessary for *P. regina* to develop from freshly oviposited egg through the end of the third instar):

$$11.39 \text{ DD} + 12.75 \text{ DD} + 7.5 \text{ DD} + 25.5 \text{ DD} = 57.14 \text{ DD}$$

This may be calculated for any range of developmental stages in an insect's life cycle.

Once the ADD or ADH necessary for insect development is known, it is possible to calculate the time necessary for the DD to accumulate at recorded ambient temperatures. The species threshold temperature is used in the same DD formula, but the average temperature is a weather station recording over a given period of time.

If, for example, a weather station recorded an average temperature of 15°C over one day, then the DD accumulated over that one day may be calculated:

$$(15°C - 10°C) \times 1 \text{ day}$$

$$(5°C) \times 1 \text{ day}$$

$$5 \text{ DD}$$

This calculation shows that five DDs accumulated over that one day. Each passing day may be calculated in the same way, and the results added up to produce the accumulated degree days over any given period of time:

Average temperature (°C) on 4 separate days: 15°C, 20°C, 21°C, 18°C

DD for each day: 5 DD, 10 DD, 11 DD, 8 DD

ADD over the 4 days: 5 DD + 10 DD + 11 DD + 8 DD = 34 DD

Once all this information is calculated, the DD necessary for an insect species to develop is applied to the total DD accumulated over a period of time to determine how long it would take an insect to develop to an observed life stage given the recorded ambient temperature. This information is easiest when visualized in Table 5.2.

Notice that the dates in the table are listed in descending order; this method allows an entomologist to start with the date on which insect evidence was collected, and work backward in time to determine the minimum insect colonization interval. In Table 5.2, 11 DD were accumulated on May 15, 15 DD on May 14, 12 DD on May 13, etc., so 57.14 DD to get from egg through the end of the third instar.

If maggots at the very end of the third instar were found on an animal at the end of the day on May 15, the ADD necessary for those maggots to develop through the third instar may be used to determine when the eggs were laid. In this case, *P. regina* needs 57.14 DD to develop through the third instar. There were not enough DD accumulated on May 15 to reach that number, so the eggs could not have been laid on May 15 and had time to reach the observed life stage. Since only 25 DD accumulated between May 14 and 15, there still wasn't enough time for the fly to reach its third instar. Enough DD accumulated between May 11 and May 15, however, for the insect to reach its observed life stage. In this instance, we can say the eggs had to have been laid sometime on May 11 or earlier to reach the third instar by May 15. This gives a minimum time of colonization estimation based on the life history of the flies colonizing an animal.

The efficacy of this method of the DD model of time of colonization estimation is dependent upon the availability of growth rate data for particular necrophagous species. These data are experimentally obtained and tend to be published as a life table or developmental rate of particular insect species. Table 5.3 represents a selection of published developmental data for commonly encountered forensically important flies.

INSECT SUCCESSION AND EXTENDED TIME OF COLONIZATION

Arthropods associated with carrion are associated with ecological groups: necrophagous species, which feed upon the animal remains; omnivorous species, which feed upon both the animal remains and other organisms colonizing those remains; predators and parasites of the necrophagous or omnivorous species; adventive species, which use the remains as an extension of the environment; and incidental species which are associated with animal remains due to happenstance (Smith, 1986; Roberts & Márquez-Grant, 2012).

Necrophagous insects arrive on and in a corpse in a somewhat predictable sequence and are arguably the most useful for forensic entomology. This is the ecological succession of insects, and is influenced by the environment, season, and the decompositional state of the carrion. The insects arrive in blending waves, called seres, of organisms, each comprised of different species attracted to a particular state of decay (Smith, 1986; Goff, 1993).

Early research in entomology indicated that the number of seres varies according to the placement of the carrion. Mégnin (1894) showed that animals exposed to the environment yielded eight distinct insect seres, while those that were buried attracted only three distinct insect seres. This difference speaks to the availability of the tissue to colonizing insects, along with the ability of those insects to reach tissue that is blocked from easy access. Different insects are attracted to different stages of generalized decomposition. While stages of decomposition are not discrete and can sometimes be difficult to characterize with precision, historically scientists have broken up decomposition of animal remains into five major stages: fresh, putrefaction, active decay, butyric fermentation, and dry decay (Haglund & Sorg, 1996). Each of these stages attracts one or more seres of insects and other arthropods in a predictable sequence.

Table 5.3 Developmental data by species, observed temperature, and author

Species	°C	Egg (h)	1st Instar (h)	2nd Instar (h)	3rd Instar (h)	Post-Feeding Larvae (h)	Pupa (h)	Adult Emergence (Egg-Adult) (d)	Reference
Calliphora latifrons	23	–	19	42	74	130	170	15.56	Anderson (2000)
Calliphora vicina	23	–	25	49	81	160	250	19.87	Anderson (2000)
C. vicina	27	24	24	20	48	128	264	18	Kamal (1958)
C. vicina	26	17	18	22	54	–	–	–	Ratcliffe (1984)
Calliphora vomitoria	27	26	24	48	60	360	336	23	Kamal (1958)
C. vomitoria	26	18	25	29	64	–	–	–	Ratcliffe (1984)
Chrysomya albiceps	25	–	6	42	84	24	120	11.5	Thyssen et al. (2014)
Chrysomya megacephala	25	17	16	26	40	81	119	12.40	Bharti et al. (2007)
Ch. megacephala	26	–	6	24	68	–	121	9.63	Rabêlo et al. (2011)
Ch. megacephala	27	21	50	50	84	–	84	16.05	Sukhapanth et al. (1988)
Ch. megacephala	25	–	6	42	48	24	96	9.00	Thyssen et al. (2014)
Chrysomya putoria	26	–	6	31	90	–	180	13.29	Rabêlo et al. (2011)
Ch. putoria	25	–	6	42	60	12	108	9.50	Thyssen *et al.* (2014)
Chrysomya rufifacies	25	12	18	34	106	–	119	12.04	Byrd and Butler (1997)
Ch. rufifacies	28	16	36	32	92	–	84	–	Flores et al. (2014)
Cochliomyia macellaria	25	12	18	24	62	–	124	10.00	Byrd and Butler (1996)
Cynomyopsis cadaverina	27	19	20	16	72	96	216	18.00	Kamal (1958)
Fannia canicularis	24	67	38	67	166	–	247	24.4	Meyer and Mullens (1988)
F. femoralis	24	67	38	69	86	–	201	19.3	Meyer and Mullens (1988)

(Continued)

Table 5.3 (*Continued*) Developmental data by species, observed temperature, and author

Species	°C	Egg (h)	1st Instar (h)	2nd Instar (h)	3rd Instar (h)	Post-Feeding Larvae (h)	Pupa (h)	Adult Emergence (Egg-Adult) (d)	Reference
L. cuprina	27	13.37	–	–	–	–	–	13.31	Ash and Greenberg (1974)
L. illustris	21	–	26	59	93	162	258	21.49	Anderson (2000)
L. sericata	27	14.38	–	–	–	–	–	13.52	Ash and Greenberg (1974)
L. sericata	25	14	16	19	36	87	125	12.38	Grassberger and Reiter (2001)
L. sericata	26	12	24	22	316	–	189	23.45	Kim et al. (2007)
L. sericata	23	–	21	45	77	152	264	22.77	Anderson (2000)
L. sericata	27	18	20	12	40	90	168	12	Kamal (1958)
L. sericata	26	15	19	22	35	–	–	–	Ratcliffe (1984)
L. sericata	22	19	26	47	84	–	157	33.5	Rueda et al. (2010)
Musca domestica	27	18	37	42	60	–	102	15.07	Sukhapanth et al. (1988)
Phormia regina	25	18.9	25	44	95	156	209	14.25	Byrd and Allen (2001)
P. regina	23	–	22	82	135	202	243	16.75	Anderson (2000)
P. regina	27	16	18	11	36	84	144	11.00	Kamal (1958)
Protophormia terraenovae	20	–	26.25	67.92	127.92	–	251	19.35	Clarkson et al. (2005)
P. terraenovae	25	–	44	70	148	192	232	15.83	Warren and Anderson (2013)
P. terraenovae	27	15	17	11	34	80	243	11.00	Kamal (1958)
P. terraenovae	26	19	39	20	54	–	–	–	Ratcliffe (1984)
Ophyra aenescens	24	20	46	40	124	–	168	16.58	Lefebvre (2004)
Sarcophaga haemorrhoidalis	25	–[a]	12	32	112	–	300	19.00	Byrd and Butler (1998)

Note: Data recorded in mean hours (h) or days (d) of developmental time necessary to complete individual life stage at the given standard temperature. "–" indicates no data for a particular life stage given in publication.

[a] *Sarcophaga haemorrhoidalis* is larviporous and therefore does not have an egg stage.

From the moment of death, the insect fauna of an animal body begins to change. Any ectoparasites associated with the body leave relatively quickly as the body cools and the blood ceases to circulate (Mullen & Durden, 2002). Myiasis causing flies may or may not die; it is dependent upon if they are obligate parasites of living tissue, or facultative parasites that can feed on both living and dead animals. Bot flies, for example, are dependent upon a living host, and if the host dies, the bot fly dies. *Cochliomyia* species, on the other hand, can feed on living or dead hosts, and may just continue to feed after the animal dies (Mullen & Durden, 2002; Byrd & Castner, 2010).

Necrophagous insects, or those attracted to dead tissue, are attracted to the body within minutes of death, and are associated with the fresh stage of decay. In general, the first adults are observed on a newly dead animal within an hour after death, as long as there is adequate access to the body (Byrd & Castner, 2010). Some investigators report female flies arriving within 15 seconds of death (Catts & Haskell, 2008). Eggs and early instar maggots tend to appear with the onset of autolysis. In general, the animal will be characterized in this early sere by the presence of adult flies and fly eggs. Eggs will be found near natural bodily opening, on wounds, and sometimes in protected folds of skin or coverings. Those eggs will hatch to first instars quickly in warm environments, but there will not be a large maggot mass on the body; the tissue will still look fresh. The most common groups of insects found during this fresh stage include species from the fly families of Calliphoridae, Muscidae, and Sarcophagidae (Schoenly & Reid, 1987; Smith, 1989).

As the carrion begins to putrefy, the young maggots will move throughout the body, spreading bacteria, secreting digestive enzymes, and feeding on tissue. They move as a maggot mass, benefitting from communal heat and shared digestive secretions. Larvae first feed between muscles, then on the muscle fibers themselves as the maggots grow and the digestive juices get to work. The rate of decay increases, and the odors emitted from the body attract more blowflies, flesh flies, beetles, and mites. They are joined by parasitic wasps that lay their eggs inside maggots and later inside pupae. The most common insects associated with this putrefaction stage, however, are species in the fly families of Calliphoridae and Sarcophagidae (Smith, 1986).

Once the carrion enters active decay, there will be several generations of maggots present on the body. Some of the maggots will be large, well into the third instar. The oldest maggots will begin to disperse from the carrion to find pupation sites. These maggots will crawl under objects in the environment, or burrow into the soil to become pupae. The early seres or pioneer flies cease to be attracted to the corpse, making way for those insects that prefer later stages of decay. Predatory maggots are much more abundant at this stage and may be feeding upon other species in the maggot mass (Nelder et al., 2009). Predatory beetles lay their eggs in the corpse and their larvae then hatch to feed on the dead animal and other insects colonizing that animal. Parasitic wasps are even more common, attacking the huge maggot masses and developing pupae. Active decay attracts a new sere characterized by beetles in Dermestidae, and grease moths. As active decay moves into butyric fermentation, two additional seres are attracted: first, a sere consisting of cheese skippers, *Fannia* species, spesid beetles, and beetles in the family Cleridae arrives at the body. The second sere consists of dump flies, flies in the family Phoridae, beetles in the family Silphidae, and clown beetles (Smith, 1986).

As the carrion is stripped of most of its soft tissue, the remaining tissue begins to dry out (Figure 5.8). The reduction in soft food makes the body less palatable to the mouth hooks of maggots, and more suitable for the chewing mouthparts of beetles. Beetle adults and larvae feed on skin and ligaments, while certain late stage flies, such as the cheese fly, arrive to feed on whatever moist flesh remains. Predators and parasites are still prevalent at this stage, feeding on the straggling maggots or other soft bodied insects in the vicinity (Smith, 1986; Schoenly, 1992).

Once the carrion has completely dried out, the body attracts insects that can feed on hair and dried skin (Figure 5.9). This dry stage of decomposition is highly attractive to a new sere consisting of mites, followed by a sere of beetles in Dermestidiae and Tinidae, and finally a sere of primarily Ptinidae and Tenerionidae. This stage tends to last for a long while, since the business of feeding on

Figure 5.8 (a) This bovine carcass shows the typical tissue loss around the mouth from maggot feeding. (b) Insect will colonize the anal and genital area of animals and the insect feeding may leave postmortem artefacts visible for week or months after the insects have departed the remains.

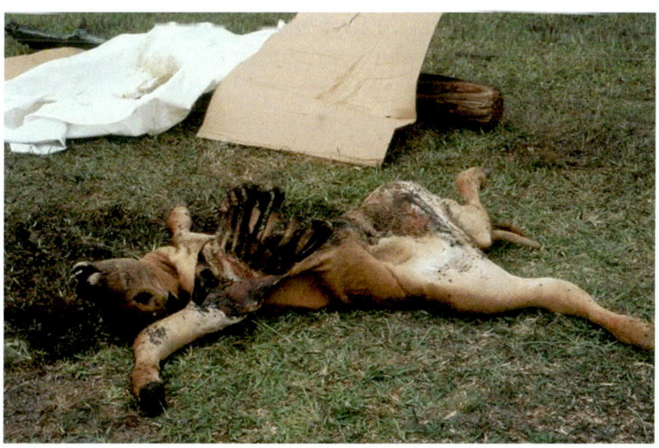

Figure 5.9 This calf shows marked decomposition in the thoracic region, a much different pattern than the cow shown in Figure 5.8. This pattern of decomposition is indicative of vertebrate scavenging. Notice the near-intact tissue along the limb and head, yet the skeletonization of the ribs. The insects had access to the thoracic cavity, which does not happen in intact carcasses. The maggot feeding was therefore concentrated around the ribs and abdominal organs, resulting in the unusual decomposition pattern shown.

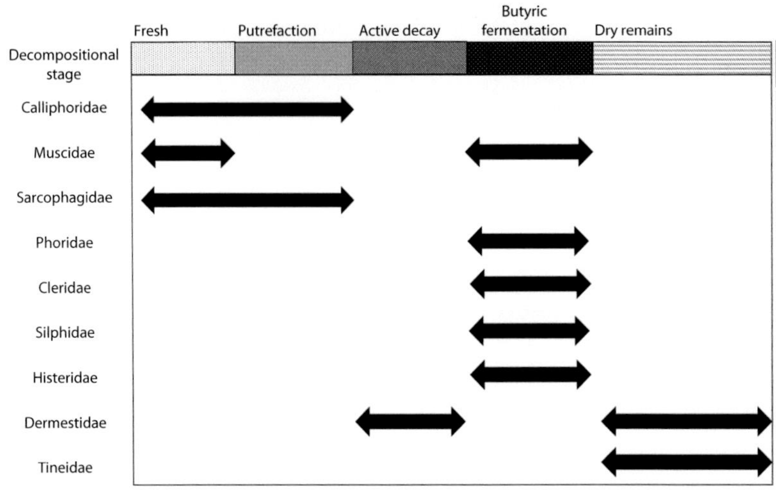

Sere #	Decomp. stage	Families
1	Fresh	Calliphoridae, Muscidae, Sarcophagidae
2	Putrefaction	Calliphoridae, Sarcophagidae
3	Active decay	Dermestidae, Pyralidae
4	Butyric fermentation	Muscidae, Phoridae
5	Butyric fermentation	Silphidae, Histeridae
6	Dry remains	Acari (Mites)
7	Dry remains	Dermestidae Tineidae
8	Dry remains	Ptinidae, Tinebrionidae

Figure 5.10 General arrival of forensically important insect families by phase of decomposition. In addition to insect development, insect succession can be utilized to estimate the postmortem interval. Insect succession is the presence or absence of insect species and the sequence in which they arrive and depart. Knowledge of insect succession in a geographic location can assist the forensic entomologist with postmortem interval estimations.

dried-out tissue takes a great deal of time and digestive enzymes. The beetles will remain on the bones as long as the carrion is undisturbed and has dried tissue (Smith, 1989).

After the dried tissue has been cleaned by the beetles, moths, and mites, only the bones remain along with empty pupal casings. There is no longer any major insect activity, and any further decomposition is accomplished by bacteria and physical factors (Haglund & Sorg, 1996).

By way of comparison, a buried animal has fewer seres with lower species diversity (Payne, 1968). Fresh buried animals tend to attract flies in Calliphoridae, Muscidae, Sarcophagidae, and Phoridae. Buried animals in active decay may attract root-eating beetles, and those in dry decay are populated by rove beetles.

Since Mégnin's original experiments, there have been numerous attempts to characterize the number of seres that show up on animals of different sizes. The consensus is that these successional waves range from 8 to 10, and any attempts to discreetly define the arthropod community associated with the seres is confounded by the continual nature of decomposition. There is a broad general agreement of orders and families that show up on a decomposing body (Smith, 1986; Catts & Haskell, 2008; Byrd & Castner, 2010). There is also a general agreement of sequence, and the idea that the first sere is primarily composed of *Dipteran* species. Succession is affected by the location of the carrion, any covering, animal type, local insect species, time of year, and a myriad of other factors. At the family level, succession looks like Figure 5.10. Knowing the general succession of insects on a corpse in a particular area enables the entomologist to extend the time of colonization estimation even if the primary colonizers of the first sere have come and gone.

ADVENTIVE AND INCIDENTAL SPECIES

In addition to those insects listed above, a myriad of other insect and arthropod species may be associated with decomposing carrion. These organisms are using the carrion for shade, shelter, or as a vantage point for predation. These arthropods could just as easily use any object in the environment, and do not have any intrinsic forensic significance. However, their presence may indicate an extended PMI (e.g., the presence of a spider web on animal carrion indicates an extended

PMI). As a group, the organisms that may be found on carrion but do not have any direct forensic application are called adventive species (Braack, 1986; Smith, 1986).

Any mobile terrestrial or airborne arthropod may accidentally land on or in the vicinity of carrion. These specimens may be collected along with the forensically important organisms, but do not have any forensic value due to their unpredictable arrival and accidental nature. These organisms are called incidental species as a group and are often identified and ignored during a forensic case (Smith, 1986; Byrd & Castner, 2010).

IMPORTANT INSECTS IN DECOMPOSITION

Diptera are commonly known as the true flies and are one of the largest and most diverse orders. The order name literally means "two-winged," and refers to the fact that the hind pair of wings is greatly modified and reduced. There are approximately 120,000 species worldwide, with around 20,000 found in North America. Diptera are considered the most important order to human and animal health, due to their vector capabilities, and are the most important in forensics, since they often compose the bulk of the first sere.

The Diptera exhibit a complete metamorphosis, meaning they start out as eggs, hatch into the first of several larval instars, pupate, and eclose into adults. Most dipteran females lay eggs and are termed oviparous. Others retain the eggs internal until they hatch, and deposit early instar larvae into the environment. This is called ovoviviparous or larviparous. A very few groups retain the developing larvae in their bodies until the larvae are ready to pupate. These are called pupiparous flies.

The larvae tend to inhabit aquatic or semiaquatic environments during these immature stages. The number of larval stages, termed instars, varies with species. In general, flies have three or four larval instars before pupation. Once the larval stage has finished feeding, the immature fly will change in form and turn into the pupae. The pupal stage can last for a long while, and eventually the fully mature adult will emerge.

There are several families within the true flies that may lend important information to a case. These include Oestridae, Calliphoridae, Sarcophagidae, Muscidae, and Phoridae.

Oestridae

The Oestridae are commonly known as bot flies. They are obligate parasites of mammals, and show a high degree of host specificity, parasitizing only one species or a small group of related hosts. They also show a marked level of site specificity in a normal host, and the site of invasion by the first instar bot maggot generally is not the site of maggot development. Members of this family may be grouped based on their preferred feeding site, and fall into the New World skin bot flies, the Old World skin bot flies, the nose bot flies, and the stomach bot flies.

The larval stage, or the maggot, of Oestridae is the invasive form, and is a thick, grub-like organism covered with moderate to heavy spines (Figure 5.11). These larvae are obligate parasites and need a living animal to survive. They cannot complete their life cycle in a dead host; if the host dies, so does the bot fly. The exact time it takes a bot fly to die after host death has yet to be quantified, however. When exploiting the skin of a host, the bot fly produces an inflamed and painful swelling of the flesh called a furuncle. This furuncle is generally sterile, does not attract myiasis-producing flies, and is not usually a site for maggot development.

Calliphoridae

This family is commonly known as the blowflies, bottle flies, and screwworms, and includes the most important and common species to inhabit carrion. The Calliphoridae are members of the first

Figure 5.11 The larvae of *Dermatobia hominis*, the human bot fly. This species is parasitic to humans, primates, and many other animals. Unlike most other species of maggot, bot flies require a living host.

sere of decomposing insects, and therefore tend to arrive at a body very quickly after death. Some species may exploit open wounds in living animals and continue feeding after the animal dies.

The adult calliphorid ranges from 6 to 14 mm in length, although the final adult size is dependent upon species and food availability in the larval stages. Most of the species are metallic in appearance, ranging from bright green or blue to bronze or shiny black. Some adults have a covering of fine hairs or powder that may mask the metallic coloration, giving them a dull or dusty look.

Blowflies are among the first insects to detect and colonize animal remains. In experimental studies, calliphorid adults have been recorded to arrive at carcasses within minutes of carcass exposure, making this family the preferred group for use in time of colonization estimation. Blowflies locate remains in a two-step process that begins with chemical detection, followed by a visual assessment of the carcass. Adults prefer to lay their eggs in natural body openings and wounds, which allow for protection of the eggs and newly hatched larvae.

Eggs are laid in large bunches called clutches. The individual eggs are glued to each other and to the substrate with a thin, sticky coating placed on each egg during oviposition. This bunch of eggs leads to a large mass of maggots hatching at the same time in the same area and leads to a patchy maggot mass effect on large carrion. Female flies lay clutches of about 200 eggs at once, which take around 24 to 48 hours to hatch, depending on species and temperature.

The eggs hatch into the first of three larval instars. The larval body is tapered with a head and mouth hooks at the pointed anterior end, and a pair of spiracles, or breathing tubes, at the blunt posterior end. The head is greatly reduced, lacks eyes, and is supported internally by a sclerotized cephalopharyngeal skeleton. The complex structure of the cephalopharyngeal skeleton is partially visible through the integument of live larvae, but the larva must be cleared of excess protein to see the entire structure. The shape of this cephalopharyngeal skeleton is very useful in identification of the larvae.

The first instar is the smallest in size and the shortest in duration. The maggots are tiny and feed near where the egg mass was originally oviposited. As they grow, they move into less putrid material further away from the original oviposition site. The mature or third instar larvae range from 8 to 23 mm in length and are white or cream colored. The terminal segment contains the posterior spiracles, which are the primary breath apparatus of the larvae.

The posterior spiracles are important morphological indicators for species identification and larval stage. The slits that form the opening to each spiracle slant toward the midline in Calliphoridae. Other families have very different spiracular opening slits. The number of slits in each spiracle is indicative of the larval stage. First instar larvae have one u-shaped slit, second instar larvae have two slits, and third instar larvae have three slits.

It takes between 4 and 21 days to go through all three larval stages, dependent upon species and temperature. Naturally, the warmer the temperature, the faster the larvae develop. The third instar larvae is the longest stage and features the most voracious feeding.

Once the maggots have finished feeding, they disperse from the body and find a protected area in which to pupate. They tend to do this en masse, and large numbers of maggots can be seen dispersing or wandering from the carrion at once. This stage is often called the pre-pupal stage and is characterized by maggots discontinuing feeding and dispersing from feeding sites. The stage can last anywhere from 3 days to 2 weeks, depending on if the maggots are able to find a suitable pupation site. The larvae usually wander 15 to 20 feet away from the carrion and dig down into the soil or crawl under protected areas in the environment, such as leaves, rocks, furniture, or carpet. On exceptionally smooth surfaces, like tile or linoleum, the maggots can wander upward of 100 feet away from a feeding source. It is important to remember that this stage is a non-feeding stage, and the larvae are simply looking for a suitable pupation site. In some cases, such as animals that may possess a thick and matted fur coat, the pupae may be found in the fur of the animal. In many such animal cases, the typical wandering stage of the larvae is truncated and the pupal stage is formed within the fur coat of the animal.

Once in a protected area, the pre-pupae will shorten, and the outer cuticle will harden into the pupal casing. This pupal stage can last from 3 to over 20 days, and adults have been known to eclose from pupae months old. As the pupal ages, the pupal casing changes color. Young pupae start out creamy white, the same color as the larval stage, and then morph into a dark brown. This is a good way to approximate the age of a pupa, although it is more of a qualifiable than quantifiable method.

When adults are ready to eclose, or emerge, from the pupal casing, they inflate a special bladder and break the end of the pupal casing off at weakened sutures. Newly emerged adults are light in color and do not have the characteristic metallic bodies. Their wings are collapsed so they are unable to fly right away. It takes them about 45 minutes to extend their wings and harden their bodies, during which time they are very vulnerable to predation and parasitization.

It is easy to tell the difference between male and female Calliphoridae. Both sexes have internal genitalia that is only exposed during mating or oviposition, but both also have an external characteristic that is indicative of sexual dimorphism: the eyes. In females, the compound eyes are widely spread apart, leaving a gap of several millimeters between the medial edges of the eyes. In males, the eyes are touching at the vertex of the head, leaving no space in between.

There are several species of Calliphoridae that are forensically important in the United States. Each species can be found in a specific range, and generally prefers a specific set of temperatures.

Phormia regina (Meigen)

Phormia regina is commonly known as the black blowfly. It is found throughout the United States, with the exception of southern Florida. The adult ranges from 7 to 9 mm in length and is a dark green to olive color on both the thorax and abdomen. The legs and head are both a deep black. The anterior thoracic spiracle is surrounded by bright orange hairs, giving it a bright orange appearance. *Phormia regina* is typically a cold weather fly and tends to be most abundant in southern regions during the spring and the fall. In northern latitudes, it is common in summer. The larvae of this species develop mainly on carrion but are known to produce myiasis. It appears to prefer larger carcasses and tends to arrive on those carcasses later in succession.

Cochliomyia macellaria (Fabricius)

Cochliomyia macellaria is commonly called the secondary screwworm and is the most common *Cochliomyia* species in North America. It is found primarily in the southwestern United States, from California through Texas, and good specimens are easily identified even without the use of a microscope. The adults have an obvious greenish-blue coloration, with three pronounced dark green longitudinal stripes called vittae on the dorsal surface of the thorax. The head has an orange coloration, and the legs are a reddish brown. The larvae have readily visible respiratory trachea on their posterior end, which appear as swirling black lines easily visible against the maggot's body. They prefer warm, humid weather, and are most abundant during rainy periods in the southern United States. Species frequent carrion in both sunny and shaded locations and are only rarely recovered from indoor habitats. They are not cold tolerant and are not common during winter months.

Compsomyiopes callipes (Bigot)

Compsomyipes callipes closely resembles *Cochliomyia macellaria*. It has the same dark metallic coloring, along with three dorsal vittae and bright orange coloration on the head. It tends to be slightly bigger, though, and has clavate palps on the mouth parts, long dark setae on the hind coxa, and dark calypters. It is currently found exclusively in the southwestern United States and prefers rural areas and large carrion.

Chrysomya rufifacies (Macquart)

Chrysomya rufifacies is commonly known as the hairy maggot blowfly. It is indigenous to the Australian and Oriental regions of the world and was introduced into the United States in the early 1980s. It is now well established throughout the southern U.S. regions. It is rapidly expanding its range and has most recently been found up through southern Canada during the warmest months of the year. The adults have stout, brilliant blue-green bodies with dark blue–tinged abdominal segments. The adults prefer outdoor settings, and rarely enter dwellings. The larvae are readily distinguished from other species by the presence of prominent flesh protrusions along their body, giving them their common name of the hairy maggot. The larvae will not only feed on carrion, but are predacious and cannibalistic, often totally eliminating other species on a carcass (Smith, 1986; Baumgartner, 1993; Whitworth, 2006).

Chrysomya megacephala (Fabricius)

Chrysomya megacephala is commonly known as the oriental latrine fly, and is widely distributed throughout Oriental regions, South Africa, and South America. It is now well established in the southern United States, particularly in Florida, Georgia, Alabama, Mississippi, Louisiana, and southern Texas. The adults have short, stout bodies similar in appearance to C. *rufifacies* but with a noticeably larger head. The eyes are unusually large and a very prominent shade of red, making this species easy to recognize in the field. Both male and female adults are attracted to carrion, fruits, sweet foods, and fecal material, hence the common name. Once the adults have settled on a food source, they are not easily disturbed, and therefore may often be collected off of carrion even if they are present in relatively low numbers. This species readily enters dwellings to find food and oviposition sites. The larvae are primarily carrion feeders and the adults show preference for fresh remains (Smith, 1986; Whitworth, 2006).

Calliphora vicina (Meigen)

Calliphora vicina is commonly known as the European blue bottle fly. Several species share the common name "blue bottle fly," but C. *vicina* is the most widespread, with worldwide distribution. It is most abundant in the northern half of the United States and is common on large carrion. It is a large fly, ranging from 10 to 14 mm long. The head is black, with the lower part of the cheeks appearing red to yellow. The thorax is dark blue but covered with fine hairs and a grayish powder which gives it an overall dusty or silvery appearance. The thorax has faint vittae of dark blue or black, and the abdomen is a pronounced metallic blue with patterns of silver. Overall, the body appears very bristly. This is a common urban species, and adults are attracted to most types of decaying matter and frequent rotting fruit, decaying meat, and feces. Larvae are found primarily on carrion and are often the dominant *Calliphora* species on carrion in temperate urban areas (Hall, 1948; Whitworth, 2006).

Calliphora vomitoria (Linnaeus)

Calliphora vomitoria is commonly known as the Holarctic blue blowfly. This species is common in the United States from Virginia to California, and north through Canada to Alaska. It is 7–13 mm in length and has a dark blue thorax with four dark longitudinal stripes and a very stocky and bristly body. It is covered with fine hairs and gray dust, giving it a silver coloration. The abdomen is bright metallic blue and patterned with silver-gray powder. It is similar in appearance to C. *vicina*, except the head is entirely black; it lacks the orange cheek area characteristic of C. *vicina*. This species is common in wooded rural and suburban areas, where it prefers shaded locations. In Canada, it is chiefly a forest species which can be found at higher altitudes and is especially common around refuse in human settlements. It is a slow-flying fly and makes a loud buzzing sound during flight. The larvae are carrion feeders, and the most common *Calliphora* species on carrion in rural settings.

Calliphora (Eucalliphora) latifrons (Hough)

Calliphora latifrons is commonly known as the blue bottle fly and is a species that is common from Mexico to Canada, and into Wisconsin and Ontario. It is most common in the Rocky Mountain region from Colorado onward, and has been reported up through Alaska. The thorax of this species is dark blue and marked with dark stripes. It is not as common as other *Calliphora* species and is most often collected from excrement and decomposing tissues (Hall, 1948; Smith, 1986; Whitworth, 2006).

Calliphora livida (Hall)

Calliphora livida is commonly known as the blue bottle fly and is generally 8–10 mm in length. It is overall dark, shiny blue in coloration, with a dulled thorax due to a gray dust-like substance. The abdomen has abundant setae that give it some white markings on the dorsal and ventral surfaces. Its head is fully black in color, and this species can be easily confused with other *Calliphora* species. C. *livida* is widespread across the North American continent.

Calliphora alaskensis (Shannon)

Calliphora alaskensis is a widespread but relatively rare species, found only at high elevations in the southern portions of its range. It is found from Alaska throughout Canada, and into the United States through Tennessee and North Carolina. Adults are approximately 7–13 mm long with a metallic blue abdomen and thorax, possibly dulled with grayish coloration. The head is overall black (Whitworth, 2006).

Cynomya cadaverina (Robineau-Desvoidy)

Cynomya cadaverina is a species that is common on the North American continent, with its greatest abundances along the Canadian–U.S. border. It is present only rarely in the warmest, southern most regions of the United States, but has been found as far south as Texas. It is a fairly large species, approximately 9–14 mm in length, with a dark blue abdomen. The head beneath the eyes is reddish brown to black, and often covered with small, yellow hairs. C. *cadaverina* has peaks of abundance in the spring and fall, although adults may appear in midwinter in the southern most regions of its range. Adults are attracted to excrement and carrion in the later stages of decay. The larvae may generally be found on carrion after *Lucilia* and *Cochliomyia* species (Whitworth, 2006).

Cynomya mortuorum (Linnaeus)

Cynomya mortuorum is closely related to *Cy. cadaverina* but has a much more limited range. It is found only in the far north in Alaska near the Arctic Circle, indicating it is a cold-adapted blowfly. The adults can be found on woodland edges and meadows, often near flowering plants. The adult body ranges from 8 to 15 mm in length, with metallic blue coloration on the thorax and abdomen. It can be easily distinguished from *Cy. cadaverina* due to its bright orange head. Due to its range, the larval stage of this species is longer than most other blowflies, taking upward of 38 days to complete all three instars. The larvae are most commonly found colonizing the small mammals common to the region but can survive on excrement in the absence of carrion (Smith, 1986; Whitworth, 2006).

Protophormia terraenovae (Robineau-Desvoidy)

Protophormia terraenovae is commonly known as the northern blowfly or the blue bottle fly. It has a deep blue to purple coloration and is a large fly, measuring 7–12 mm in length. It is characterized by a black to brown anterior thoracic spiracle, a black head, and black legs. This species is common throughout the northern regions of the United States up through Canada and Alaska. It is known as a cold weather fly and may rarely be found in the southern United States during the winter months. It becomes more common at high elevations during the summer, and is abundant in the Arctic, having been found within 550 miles of the North Pole. In these regions, it is most abundant during July (Hall, 1948; Whitworth, 2006).

Lucilia illustris (Meigen)

Lucilia illustris is commonly known as the green bottle fly and is one of several species given this common name. It may be one of the most common *Lucilia* species throughout the Western hemisphere and is widespread throughout in the northern regions of the United States and throughout Canada. Adults are approximately 6–8 mm long with a bright green thorax and abdomen, and black legs. It is considered a warm weather species and is most abundant in open woodlands during summer months. Adults are primarily attracted to fresh carrion, although they may sometimes be collected from excrement. Females are most active and commonly oviposit on remains in bright or sunlit locations. The larvae can feed and develop on excrement, but seem to prefer carrion (Stevens & Wall, 1996; Whitworth, 2006).

Lucilia sericata (Meigen)

Lucilia sericata is commonly known as the sheep blowfly and may be placed in the genus *Phaenicia* in some texts. *L. sericata* may be the most common species of Calliphoridae worldwide. In North America, it can be collected throughout the United States and Canada and is most commonly found in the western regions. The adults are 6–9 mm in length with a brilliant blue-green, yellow-green, or green-bronze thorax and abdomen. The thorax has three prominent transverse grooves on the dorsal surface, and the front femora are black or deep blue. The larvae can successfully develop on a wide variety of food substrates but are best suited to carrion. This is one of the earliest species to arrive on carrion and will oviposit within a few hours after death. The adults prefer carcasses located in bright sunshine and open habitats but will seek shaded areas of the body to deposit eggs, although this species is known to cause myiasis in many animals. This is one of two species commonly used in maggot debridement therapy for the removal of necrotic tissues in wounds (Smith, 1986; Stevens & Wall, 1996; Whitworth, 2006).

Lucilia cuprina (Wiedemann)

Lucilia cuprina is commonly known as the Australian sheep maggot or the bronze bottle fly. It is closely related to *L. sericata*, but *L. sericata* is more cold tolerant and found most abundantly in the northern portions of its range. *L. cuprina* is most common in the southern regions of North America, particularly in the southeastern United States It is most common from Virginia, west through Missouri to California. This fly is 6–8 mm long, and usually with metallic yellow-green or dull copper tinted with green coloration and green metallic femora. The adults seem to prefer excrement to carrion, but are commonly attracted to both, as well as decaying fruit. They often alight on the ground or on vegetation in close proximity to a food source and will take flight readily when disturbed. This makes the adults very difficult to collect at a scene. The larvae are most frequently found on carrion, although they are a causative agent of sheep strike and myiasis in some animals. This species is abundant from spring though fall and is collected year-round in Florida. They are often found near dwellings and will readily enter homes. This is the second of two common species used in maggot debridement therapy.

Lucilia coeruleiviridis (Macquart)

Lucilia coeruleiviridis is primarily located in the southeastern United States but may be rarely found in the northeast and midwest. It is most commonly found from Maryland south to Florida, and north to Michigan and Wisconsin. It is much less abundant west of the Mississippi River. Adults are generally 8.0–9.5 mm in length, with a shining green thorax and abdomen. The fifth abdominal segment is often tinged with red or purple along the dorsal surface and tends to be highly polished and shining.

Lucilia cluvia (Walker)

Lucilia cluvia highly resembles *L. coeruleiviridis*, but tends to be slightly smaller, ranging from 7.5 to 8.0 mm on average. Other minor differences between *L. cluvia* and *L. coeruleiviridis* include the color of the hairs on the head and the relative shininess of the fifth abdominal segment. Identification of this species is best left to experts due to its similarity with *L. coeruleiviridis*. The adults of *L. cluvia* are limited to the southeastern United States from Florida north to North Carolina and west to southern Mississippi (Whitworth, 2006).

Lucilia mexicana (Macquart)

Lucilia mexicana is primarily a southwestern U.S. fly, common from California through Texas, and ranging from southern Utah south through Mexico. The adults are 6–9 mm long with a bright metallic green coloration on both the thorax and abdomen. The legs are usually black, as is the head. This species can be found in both wooded areas and urban habitats due to its attraction to animal and human feces, garbage, and fresh carrion (Stevens & Wall, 1996; Whitworth, 2006).

Lucilia elongate (Shannon)

Lucilia elongate is a relatively rare species, found in the western regions of the United States, throughout California, Colorado, Oregon, and Washington, and up through British Columbia. It typically has a shining blue-green thorax and abdomen, with a black head and black legs (Smith, 1986; Whitworth, 2006).

Muscidae

The family Muscidae has worldwide distribution and includes many species that are common on carrion, excrement, and the products of decomposition. Muscidae have a close relationship with humans and are therefore considered synanthropic flies. This association has led to the inadvertent distribution of this family across the world, where it thrives in association with humans (McAlpine, 1981). In general, muscid flies tend to arrive after blowflies when colonizing a carcass and are therefore considered secondary colonizers (Byrd & Castner, 2010). Many of the species are associated with refuse and fecal matter and are common in rural areas, especially near large numbers of confined animals, such as poultry farms (Hewitt, 1912; McAlpine, 1981).

Musca domestica (Linnaeus)

Musca domestica is commonly known as the housefly and is a synanthropic species that has followed humans around the world. The adult is 6–9 mm in length, with an overall gray coloration. It is easily distinguished from other Muscidae by the sharp angle in its fourth long wing vein, and the presence of four black stripes on the dorsal thorax. It is commonly found indoors where it will search out food, refuse, feces, or carrion. The adult feeds on most anything with moisture and is particularly attracted to the products of decomposition. Larvae are often found in fecal matter in pastures or agricultural buildings, although they have the ability to develop on carrion. It is distributed throughout North America from Alaska and the northern regions of Canada down through the southern regions of the United States (James, 1947).

Musca autumnalis (DeGeer)

Musca autumnalis is commonly called the face-fly and is most often identified as a pest of cattle. The fly adults will feed on the body secretions of large animals, especially around the eyes and muzzle, and will cause irritation to animals and humans in large numbers. It is native to the Old World and was introduced into North America during the 1940s. It is currently found through the mid- to northern United States and up into southern Canada, in areas with moderate summer temperatures. It is currently not found in Arizona, New Mexico, Louisiana, or Florida. The body resembles *M. domestica* but may be distinguished by a bright orange-yellow abdomen with a black median stripe in the males. The adults may be found aggregating indoors or under cover, and the larvae develop readily on cattle droppings. It will rarely infest carrion in the larval stage, but when present is attracted to fresh carrion and found in the first wave of decomposers (Huckett, 1975; McAlpine, 1981).

Hydrotaea (Ophyra) leucostoma (Wiedemann)

Hydrotaea leucostoma is a shining, blue-black species that is common around lavatories, slaughterhouses, and confined animals. It is widely distributed in North America and can be found north of Mexico up through the southern regions of Canada. The males have a characteristic hover behavior that is associated with the hoverflies. The larvae develop primarily in excrement but have been found exploiting carcasses in the late stages of decay. In the second and third instars the larvae are predaceous and will attack other larvae exploiting the same resources. The larvae will pupate deep in the soil and have been found burrowed three feet beneath the surface. Adults are abundant during warmer times of the year and are most common from June through October (Huckett, 1975; Smith, 1986).

Hydrotaea dentipes (Meade)

Hydrotaea dentipes is widely distributed in North America, ranging from the Gulf Coast north through southern Alaska and east into Newfoundland. Adults are of similar size and description to the housefly, approximately 8 mm long, but do not have the sharp vein in the fourth wing vein. The male is much darker than the female and has translucent dark wings. The female is lighter in coloration with clear wings. Adults are found on fecal matter and decaying fruit and are associated with latrines and offal. The larvae are found in compact and drying feces, carrion, and rotting fruit. The third instar larvae are predatory, feeding on other larvae within the same resource (Huckett, 1975).

Hydrotaea (Ophyra) aenescens (Wiedemann)

Hydrotaea aenescens, commonly known as the black dump fly or the American black dump fly, is common to warm areas of the New World. It is found throughout Canada, south through the United States, and into Mexico. It is a eusynanthropic species, frequenting dump sites and animal filth throughout the North American continent. In colder regions, it is able to withstand freezing temperatures by remaining on fermenting garbage. The adults are small, shiny black, and compact (Huckett, 1975).

Muscina stabulans (Fallen)

Muscina stabulans is a cosmopolitan species, widely distributed and especially common throughout the temperate regions of North America. It has been recorded in the north from Alaska to Newfoundland, and in the south from California to Georgia. It resembles *Musca domestica*, except without the sharply bent wing vein. The body is overall gray, and the hind tibia have a yellow coloration. Adults are found near human habitation and agricultural areas, especially poultry houses and stables. Adults will often move indoors and will feed on decaying matter of all types. The larvae become predaceous in the second and third instar and have been known to attack nestling birds. *M. stabulans* is often associated with buried carrion and has the ability to exploit decomposing matter below the soil surface (Huckett, 1975).

Fannia scalaris (Fabricius)

Fannia scalaris is primarily an outdoor species with cosmopolitan distribution. It has been recorded as far north as central Alaska, and as far south as Mexico (Huckett, 1975). If found indoors, it is associated with primitive conditions such as lavatories and cesspits and is therefore commonly known as the latrine fly. The larvae develop in semi-liquid masses of decomposing material and are associated with liquid in the abdominal cavity and the later stages of decay (Hewitt, 1912).

Fannia canicularis (Linnaeus)

Fannia canicularis is commonly known as the lesser housefly, and resembles *Muscia domestica*, except for the lack of a sharp bend in the long veins of the wings. The adults have an overall yellow coloration with a gray facial region, and an elongate brown-gray abdomen. The legs are dark brown with yellow joints. The adults appear to prefer cooler conditions than most *Musca* species, but is found all over the North American continent. The adults are common in rural areas near large accumulations of feces and are attracted to urine and other excrement-associated volatiles. It is common in the later stages of decay, and often associated with the second wave of decomposing insects (Grisales et al., 2012).

Sarcophagidae

The Sarcophagidae are commonly known as the flesh flies. Members are found throughout North America, although most species occur in the warmer regions of the continent. Adults are medium to large flies, with usually three black longitudinal strips on the dorsal thorax and a checkerboard (or tessellated) pattern on the abdomen (McAlpine, 1981). The larvae are large and inhabit decomposing flesh. Species in this family are very difficult to identify and are often simply referred to by the family name (Smith, 1986; Nation, 2011). Adults are attracted to carrion under most conditions and are often found on animals that are decomposing indoors (Sanford, 2015). Females will primarily larviposit rather than oviposit, causing the larvae to appear as the oldest on carrion. Common species will arrive concurrently with or slightly after Calliphoridae (Mullen & Durden, 2002).

Sarcophaga haemorrhoidalis (Fallen)

Sarcophaga haemorrhoidalis is commonly known as the red-tailed flesh fly, due the obvious red terminal end of the adult abdomen. It is associated with humans and human environments, and is distributed throughout most of North America, north of Mexico. This is a large species, with black coloration and a dusting of white powder that gives the adults an overall gray appearance. Adults have three obvious dorsal stripes on the thorax and a distinct checkerboard pattern on the abdomen (McAlpine, 1981). The adults are known to feed on fecal matter and carrion and have been known to cause myiasis in animals (James, 1947; Smith, 1975).

Sarcophaga bullata (Parker)

Sarcophaga bullata, the gray flesh fly, is closely related to *S. haemorrhoidalis*, and has approximately the same distribution, although it is most common in the southern United States The adults are nearly identical to other Sarcophagidae, and positive identification relies upon the use of specialized keys for the male genitalia (McAlpine, 1981; Vairo et al., 2011).

Phoridae

The Phoridae is a large family of flies that occur worldwide. The adults are small to medium sized, with dull black, yellow, or brown coloration and an expanded thorax which gives them a "hump-backed" appearance. The pupae are dorsoventrally flattened with a pair of distinctive respiratory horns on the anterior end. They are collectively called the scuttle flies due to their propensity to run about on the substrate in an erratic manner, or humpbacked flies due to their appearance. Larvae are found in decaying organic matter, and many species are associated with animal carrion. Several species have the ability to reproduce underground, and are associated with burials (McAlpine, 1981; Smith, 1986).

Megaselia abdita (Schmitz)

Megaselia abdita, the scuttle fly, is often found in association with other *Megaselia* species. The adults are well known from subterranean carrion and have the characteristic hump-backed appearance and scuttling movement that characterizes many of the Phoridae. The adults are attracted to decomposing materials and have the ability to colonize buried bodies. As a forensic indicator, *M. abdita* has been associated with carrion in colder months (Greenberg & Wells, 1998; Manlove & Disney, 2008), but has yet to be researched in depth.

Megaselia scalaris (Loew)

Megaselia scalaris is commonly known as the humpback fly or the coffin fly. The adults are 2–3 mm in length with a yellow or yellow-brown thorax and abdomen. This species is primarily found in warm climates but extends into the northern regions of North America. It is associated with humans and has been transported to new regions as humans have moved around the globe. The females are attracted to foul-smelling fluids and will lay eggs on most organic matter. The larvae consume a wide range of organic materials and will infest everything from living plants to decomposing matter. Some larvae may become facultative parasites of other invertebrates under the correct circumstances, and many have been found to cause myiasis (James, 1947; Disney, 2008). This species ranges from the southern regions of the United States up through southern Canada (James, 1947).

Megaselia rufipes (Meigen)

Megaselia rufipes, the scuttle fly, is closely related to *M. scalaris*, and often found in association with the latter. The adults are 2–3 mm long with a dark brown thorax and abdomen, and light yellow legs. The ventral surface of the fly presents as light yellow. This species is found from the southern most regions of Florida up through Alaska. Preliminary observations indicate *M. rufipes* may oviposit on animal carrion within a few days of exposure and have the ability to access decomposing matter that is buried or concealed indoors (Manlove & Disney, 2008).

Piophilidae

The Piophilidae are collectively known as the skipper flies and exhibit their greatest diversity in temperate regions (McAlpine, 1981). The adults are small, and overall metallic blue or black. They colonize a large number of decomposing habitats and are commonly found during the later stages of animal decay. They earn their common name due to a characteristic behavior exhibited by the larvae. The larvae have protrusions located on the last abdominal segment, and they will grasp these protrusions with their mouth hooks. The sudden release of the mouth hooks causes the maggot to "leap" into the air over a distance of several inches. Infestation by Piophilidae maggots often results in a description of "jumping worms" on animal carrion (Huckett, 1975; McAlpine, 1981; Nation, 2011).

Phiophila casei (Linneaus)

Piophila casei, commonly known as the cheese skipper, cheese fly, or bacon fly, is a small species, approximately 2.5–4.0 mm in length. It has an overall black body and a distinctly round head, and the lower part of the head, the antennae, and parts of the legs yellow. It is a cosmopolitan and synanthropic species, commonly associated with carrion and considered a pest species in the food industry. The larvae tend to arrive in the later stages of succession, and the larvae have been known to cause myiasis in living animals. It is widespread in the United States and Canada, ranging from southern Louisiana and the Gulf Coast north through Alaska and the Canadian Arctic (Martin-Vega, 2011; Rochefort et al., 2015).

Stearibia nigriceps (Meigen)

Stearibia nigriceps adults range from 2.5 to 4.1 mm in length and are glossy black with a metallic blue tinge. The legs vary in coloration from entirely yellow to partially yellow and black. This species is a synanthropic fly that frequents carrion in both the adult and larval stages and is also a known pest of the food industry. It is most commonly associated with the advanced stages of decomposition and can be of forensic importance in buried carrion. It is widespread in the United States and Canada, ranging from the Yukon Territory and British Columbia to Nova Scotia, and south through Louisiana (Martin-Vega, 2011; Rochefort et al., 2015).

References

Abell D., S. Wasti, and G. Hartmann, Saprophagous Arthropod Fauna Associated with Turtle Carrion, *Applied Entomology and Zoology*. 17, 1982, 301–307.

Abouzied E. M., Insect Colonization and Succession on Rabbit Carcasses in Southwestern Mountains of the Kingdom of Saudi Arabia, *Journal of Medical Entomology*. 51, 2014, 1168–1174.

Addo-Bediako A., S. L. Chown, and K. J. Gaston, Thermal Tolerance, Climatic Variability and Latitude, *Proceedings of the Royal Society of London. Series B: Biological Sciences*. 267, 2000, 739–745.

Ahmad N. W., L. H. Lim, C. C. Dhang, C. W. Kian, R. Hashim, S. M. Azirun, H. C. Chin, A. G. Abdullah, W. N. W. Mustaffa, and J. Jeffery, Comparative Insect Fauna Succession on Indoor and Outdoor Monkey: Carrions in a Semi-Forested Area in Malaysia, *Asian Pacific Journal of Tropical Biomedicine*. 1, 2011, S232–S238.

Amendt J., C. P. Campobasso, E. Gaudry, C. Reiter, H. N. Leblanc, and M. J. R. Hall, Best Practice in Forensic Entomology—Standards and Guidelines, *International Journal of Legal Medicine*. 121, 2007, 90–104.

Ames C. and B. Turner, Low Temperature Episodes in Development of Blowflies: Implications for Postmortem Interval Estimation, *Medical & Veterinary Entomology*. 17, 2003, 178–186.

Anderson G. S., Wildlife Forensic Entomology: Determining Time of Death in Two Illegally Killed Black Bear Cubs, *Journal of Forensic Sciences*. 44, 1999, 856–9.

Anderson G. S., Minimum and Maximum Development Rates of Some Forensically Important Calliphoridae (Diptera), *Journal of Forensic Sciences*. 45, 2000, 824–832.

Anderson G. S. and S. L. Vanlaerhoven, Initial Studies on Insect Succession on Carrion in Southwestern British Columbia, *Journal of Forensic Sciences*. 41, 1996, 617–625.

Anderson J. M. E., E. Shipp, and P. J. Anderson, Distribution of Calliphoridae in an Arid Zone Habitat Using Baited Sticky Traps, *General & Applied Entomology*. 16, 1984, 3–8.

Archer M. and M. Elgar, Yearly Activity Patterns in Southern Victoria (Australia) of Seasonally Active Carrion Insects, *Forensic Science International*. 132, 2003, 173–176.

Arnaldos I., E. Romera, M. D. García, and A. Luna, An Initial Study on the Succession of Sarcosaprophagous Diptera (Insecta) on Carrion in the Southeastern Iberian Peninsula, *International Journal of Legal Medicine*. 114, 2001, 156–162.

Arnaldos M., E. Romera, J. Presa, A. Luna, and M. García, Studies on Seasonal Arthropod Succession on Carrion in the Southeastern Iberian Peninsula, *International Journal of Legal Medicine*. 118, 2004, 197–205.

Ash N. and B. Greenberg, Developmental Temperature Responses of the Sibling Species Phaenicia Sericata and Phaenicia Pallescens, *Annals of the Entomological Society of America*. 68, 1974, 197–200.

Avila F. W. and M. L. Goff, Arthropod Succession Patterns onto Burnt Carrion in Two Contrasting Habitats in the Hawaiian Islands, *Journal of Forensic Sciences*. 43, 1998, 581–586.

Azwandi A., H. Nina Keterina, L. C. Owen, M. D. Nurizzati, and B. Omar, Adult Carrion Arthropod Community in a Tropical Rainforest of Malaysia: Analysis on Three Common Forensic Entomology Animal Models, *Tropical Biomedicine*. 30, 2013, 481–494.

Bajerlein D., S. Matuszewski, and S. Konwerski, Insect Succesion on Carrion: Seasonality, Habitat Preference and Residency of Histerid Beetles (Coleoptera: Histeridae) Visiting Pig Carrion Exposed in Various Forests (Western Poland), *Polish Journal of Ecology*. 59, 2011, 787–797.

Barnes K. M. and D. E. Gennard, The Effect of Bacterially Dense Environments on the Development and Immune Defences of the Blowfly *Lucilia sericata. Physiological Entomology*. 36, 2011, 96–100.

Barrios M. and M. Wolff, Initial Study of Arthropods Succession and Pig Carrion Decomposition in Two Freshwater Ecosystems in the Colombian Andes, *Forensic Science International*. 212, 2011, 164–172.

Battan Horenstein M., A. Xavier Linhares, B. Rosso De Ferradas, and D. Garcia, Decomposition and Dipteran Succession in Pig Carrion in Central Argentina: Ecological Aspects and Their Importance in Forensic Science, *Medical and Veterinary Entomology*. 24, 2010, 16–25.

Baumgartner D. L., Distribution and Medical Ecology of the Blow Flies (Diptera: Calliphoridae) of Peru, *Annals of the Entomological Society of America*. 78, 1985, 565–587.

Baumgartner D. L., Review of *Chrysomya rufifacies* (Diptera: Calliphoridae), *Journal of Medical Entomology*. 30, 1993, 338–352.

Baz A., B. Cifrian, L. M. D. Aranda, and D. Martin-Vega, The Distribution of Adult Blow-Flies (Diptera: Calliphoridae) Along an Altiudinal Gradient in Central Spain, *Annales-Societe Entomologique de France*. 43, 2007, 289–296.

Beck S. D., Insect Thermoperiodism, *Annual Review of Entomology*. 28, 1983, 91–108.

Benbow M., A. Lewis, J. Tomberlin, and J. Pechal, Seasonal Necrophagous Insect Community Assembly During Vertebrate Carrion Decomposition, *Journal of Medical Entomology*. 50, 2013, 440–450.

Benecke M., A Brief History of Forensic Entomology, *Forensic Science International*. 120, 2001, 2–14.

Benecke M., A brief survey of the history of forensic entomology, *Acta. Biologica Benrodis*. 14, 2008, 15–38.

Bharti M., D. Singh, and Y. P. Sharma, Effect of Temperature on the Development of Forensically Important Blowfly, *Chrysomya megacephala* (Fabricius) (Diptera: Calliphoridae), *Entomon*. 32, 2007, 149–151.

Blackith R. and R. Blackith, Insect Infestations of Small Corpses, *Journal of Natural History*. 24, 1990, 699–709.

Block W., Cold Hardiness in Invertebrate Poikilotherms, *Comparative Biochemistry and Physiology Part A: Physiology*. 73, 1982, 581–593.

Bonacci T., T. Zetto Brandmayr, P. Brandmayr, V. Vercillo, and F. Porcelli, Successional Patterns of the Insect Fauna on a Pig Carcass in Southern Italy and the Role of *Crematogaster scutellaris* (Hymenoptera, Formicidae) as a Carrion Invader, *Entomological Science*. 14, 2011, 125–132.

Bornemissza G. F., An Analysis of Arthropod Succession in Carrion and the Effect of Its Decomposition on the Soil Fauna, *Australian Journal of Zoology*. 5, 1957, 1–12.

Boulkenafet Sélima Berchi F, S. Lambiase, F. Boulkenafet, S. Berchi, and S. Lambiase, Preliminary Study of Necrophagous Diptera Succession on a Dog Carrion in Skikda, North-East of Algeria. *Journal of Entomology and Zoology Studies*. 3, 2015, 364–369.

Bourel B., L. Martin-Bouyer, J. C. Cailliez, V. Hedouin, D. Gosset, and D. Derout, Necrophilous Insect Succession on Rabbit Carrion in Sand Dune Habitats in Northern France, *Journal of Medical Entomology*. 36, 1999, 420–425.

Braack L., Arthropods Associated with Carcasses in the Northern Kruger National Park, *South African Journal of Wildlife Research*. 16, 1986, 91–98.

Braack L., Community Dynamics of Carrion-Attendant Arthropods in Tropical African Woodland, *Oecologia*. 72, 1987, 402–409.

Braack L. E. and P. F. Retlef, Dispersal, Density and Habitat Preference of the Blow-Flies *Chrysomyia albiceps* (Wd.) and *Chrysomyia marginalis* (Wd.) (Diptera: Calliphoridae), *Journal of Veterinary Research*. 53, 1986, 13–18.

Brand L. R. M. Hussey, and J. Taylor, Decay and Disarticulation of Small Vertebrates in Controlled Experiments, *Journal of Taphonomy*. 1, 2003, 233–245.

Brundage A., S. Bros, and J. Y. Honda, Seasonal and Habitat Abundance and Distribution of Some Forensically Important Blow Flies (Diptera: Calliphoridae) in Central California, *Forensic Science International*. 212, 2011, 115–120.

Byrd J. H. and J. C. Allen, The Development of the Black Blow Fly, Phormia Regina (Meigen), *Forensic Science International*. 120, 2001, 79–88.

Byrd J. H. and J. F. Butler, Effects of Temperature on *Cochliomyia macellaria* (Diptera: Calliphoridae) Development, *Journal of Medical Entomology*. 33, 1996, 901–905.

Byrd J. H. and J. F. Butler, Effects of Temperature on *Chrysomya rufifacies* (Diptera: Calliphoridae) Development, *Journal of Medical Entomology*. 34, 1997, 353–358.

Byrd J. H. and J. F. Butler, Effects of Temperature on *Sarcophaga haemorrhoidalis* (Diptera: Sarcophagidae) Development, *Journal of Medical Entomology*. 35, 1998, 694–698.

Byrd J. H. and J. L. Castner, *Forensic Entomology the Utility of Arthropods in Legal Investigations*, 2nd ed., Boca Raton, 2010

Caballero U. and J. L. J. E. M. León-Cortés, Beetle Succession and Diversity between Clothed Sun-Exposed and Shaded Pig Carrion in a Tropical Dry Forest Landscape in Southern Mexico, *Forensic Science International*. 245, 2014, 143–150.

Cain M. L., W. D. Bowman, and S. D. Hacker, *Ecology*, Sunderland, 2008.

Campobasso C. P., Factors Affecting Decomposition and Diptera Colonization, *Forensic Science International*. 120, 2001, 18–27.

Catts E. P. and M. L. Goff, Forensic Entomology in Criminal Investigations, *Annual Review of Entomology*. 37, 1992, 253–272.

Catts E. P. and N. H. Haskell, *Entomology and Death: A Procedural Guide*, 2nd ed., Clemson, SC, 2008.

Chin H. C., A Preliminary Study of Insect Succession on a Pig Carcass in a Palm Oil Plantation in Malaysia, *Tropical Biomedicine*. 24, 2007, 23–27.

Clarkson C. A., N. R. Hobischak,, and G. Anderson, Developmental Rate of *Protophormia terraenovae* (RD) Raised under Constant and Fluctuating Temperatures, for Use in Determining Time Since Death in Natural Outdoor Conditions, in the Early Postmortem Interval, *Canadian Police Research Centre*, 2005.

Coe M., The Decomposition of Elephant Carcasses in the Tsavo (East) National Park, Kenya, *Journal of Arid Environment*. 1, 1978, 71–86.

Cornaby B. W., Carrion Reduction by Animals in Contrasting Tropical Habitats, *BioTropica*. 6, 1974, 51–63.

Davidson J., On the Relationship between Temperature and Rate of Development of Insects at Constant Temperatures, *Journal of Animal Ecology*. 13, 1944, 26–38.

Davies L. and G. G. Ratcliffe, Development Rates of Some Pre-Adult Stages in Blowflies with Reference to Low Temperatures, *Medical and Veterinary Entomology*. 8, 1994, 245–254.

Davis J. B., Decomposition Patterns in Terrestrial and Intertidal Habitats on Oahu Island and Coconut Island, Hawaii, *Journal of Forensic Sciences*. 45, 2000, 836–42.

De Jong G. D., An Annotated Checklist of the Calliphoridae (Diptera) of Colorado, with Notes on Carrion Associations and Forensic Importance, *Journal of the Kansas Entomological Society*. 67, 1994, 378–385.

De Jong G. D. and J. W. Chadwick, Decomposition and Arthropod Succession on Exposed Rabbit Carrion During Summer at High Altitudes in Colorado, USA, *Journal of Medical Entomology*. 36, 1999, 833–845.

De Jong G. D. and W. W. Hoback, Effect of Investigator Disturbance in Experimental Forensic Entomology: Succession and Community Composition, *Medical and Veterinary Entomology*. 20, 2006, 248–258.

Disney R. H. L., Natural History of the Scuttle Fly, *Megaselia scalaris, Annual Review of Entomology*. 53, 2008, 39–60.

Early M. and M. L. Goff, Arthorpod Succession Patterns in Exposed Carrion on the Island of Oahu, Hawaiian-Islands, USA, *Journal of Medical Entomology*. 23, 1986, 520–531.

Eberhardt T. L. and D. A. Elliot, A Preliminary Investigation of Insect Colonisation and Succession on Remains in New Zealand, *Forensic Science International*. 176, 2008, 217–223.

Ellison G., The Effect of Scavenger Mutilation on Insect Succession at Impala Carcasses in Southern Africa, *Journal of Zoology*. 220, 1990, 679–688.

Fisher R. S., W. U. Spitz, and D. J. Spitz, Chapter 2, part 3. In William C. Rodriguez and Wayne D. Lord (eds.), *Spitz and Fisher's Medicolegal Investigation of Death: Guidelines for the Application of Pathology to Crime Investigation*. Charles C Thomas Publisher, 2006.

Flores, M. M. Longnecker, and J. K. Tomberlin, Effects of Temperature and Tissue Type on *Chrysomya rufifacies* (Diptera: Calliphoridae)(Macquart) Development, *Forensic Science International*. 245, 2014, 24–29.

Foottit R. G. and P. H. Adler, *Insect Biodiversity: Science and Society*, 2009.

Gill G. J., Decomposition and Arthropod Succession on above Ground Pig Carrion in Rural Manitoba, 2005, 1–180.

Goff M. L., Estimation of Post-Mortem Interval Using Arthropods' Development and Successional Patterns, *Forensic Science Reivew*. 5, 1993, 81–94.

Gosselin M., S. M. Wille, M. D. M. R. Fernandez, V. Di Fazio, N. Samyn, G. De Boeck, and B. Bourel, Entomotoxicology, Experimental Set-Up and Interpretation for Forensic Toxicologists, *Forensic Science International*. 208, 2011, 1–9.

Grassberger M. and C. Frank, Initial Study of Arthropod Succession on Pig Carrion in a Central European Urban Habitat, *Journal of Medical Entomology*. 41, 2004, 511–523.

Grassberger M. and C. Reiter, Effect of Temperature on *Lucilia sericata* (Diptera: Calliphoridae) Development with Special Reference to the Isomegalen- and Isomorphen-Diagram, *Forensic Science International*. 120, 2001, 32–36.

Greenberg B. and J. D. Wells, Forensic Use of *Megaselia abdita* and *M. scalaris* (Phoridae: Diptera): Case Studies, Development Rates, and Egg Structure, *Journal of Clinical Forensic Medicine*. 5, 1998, 215–215.

Grisales D., M. Wolff, and C. J. B. De Carvalho, Neotropical Fanniidae (Insecta, Diptera): New Species of Fannia from Colombia, *ZOOTAXA*. 3591, 2012, 1–46.

Gruner S. V., D. H. Slone, and J. L. Capinera, Forensically Important Calliphoridae (Diptera) Associated with Pig Carrion in Rural North-Central Florida, *Journal of Medical Entomology*. 44, 2007, 509–515.

Gullan P. J. and P. S. Cranston, *The Insects: An Outline of Entomology*, 3rd Edition, Wiley-Blackwell, 2009. 528p.

Haglund W. D. and M. H. Sorg, *Forensic Taphonomy: The Postmortem Fate of Human Remains*, CRC Press, 1996. 668p.

Hagstrum D. W. and G. A. Milliken, Quantitative Analysis of Temperature, Moisture, and Diet Factors Affecting Insect Development, *Annals of the Entomological Society of America*. 81, 1988, 539–546.

Hall D. G., *The Blowflies of North America*, Baltimore: Thomas Say Foundation, 1948.

Hall M. J. M., Trapping the Flies That Cause Myiasis: Their Responses to Host-Stimuli, *Annals of Tropical Medicine and Parasitology*. 89, 1995, 333–357.

Hewadikaram K. A. and M. L. Goff, Effect of Carcass Size on Rate of Decompostion and Arthropod Succession Patterns, *American Journal of Forensic Medicine and Pathology*. 12, 1991, 235–240.

Hewitt C. G., *Fannia* (Homalomyia) *canicularis* Linn, and *F. scalaris* Fab. An Account of the Bionomics and the Larvae of the Flies and Their Relation to Myiasis of the Intestinal and Urinary Tracts, *Parasitology*. 5, 1912, 161–174.

Higley L. G., L. P. Pedigo, and K. R. Ostlie, Degday: A Program for Calculating Degree-Days, and Assumptions Behind the Degree-Day Approach, *Environmental Entomology*. 15, 1986, 999–1016.

Honda J. Y., A. Brundage, C. Happy, S. C. Kelly, and J. Melinek, New Records of Carrion Feeding Insects Collected on Human Remains, *Pan-Pacific Entomologist*. 84, 2008, 29–32.

Huckett H. C., *Muscidae of California: Exclusive of Subfamilies Muscinae and Stomoxyinae*, 1975.

Introna F., C. P. Campobasso, and M. L. Goff, Entomotoxicology, *Forensic Science International*. 120, 2001, 42–47.

James M. T., *The Flies That Cause Myiasis in Man*, Washington, DC, 1947.

Jiron L. F., Insect Succession in the Decomposition of a Mammal in Costa Rica. *Journal of the New York Entomological Society*. 89, 1981, 158–165.

Johnson M. D., Seasonal and Microseral Variations in the Insect Populations on Carrion, *American Midland Naturalist*. 93(1), 1975, 79–90.

Joy J. E., M. L. Herrell, and P. C. Rogers, Larval Fly Activity on Sunlit Versus Shaded Racoon Carrion in Southwestern West Virginia with Special Reference to the Black Blowfly (Diptera: Calliphoridae), *J. Med. Entomol*. 39, 2002, 392–397.

Kamal A. S., Comparative study of thirteen species of sarcosaprophagous Calliphoridae and Sarcophagidae (Diptera) I. Bionomics. *Annals of the Entomological Society of America*. 51.3, 1958, 261–271.

Keiper J. B., Midge Larvae (Diptera: Chironomidae) as Indicators of Postmortem Submersion Interval of Carcasses in a Woodland Stream: A Preliminary Report, *Journal of Forensic Sciences*. 42, 1997, 1074–1079.

Kelly J. A., T. C. V. D. Linde, and G. S. Anderson, The Influence of Clothing and Wrapping on Carcass Decomposition and Arthropod Succession During the Warmer Seasons in Central South Africa, *Journal of Forensic Sciences*. 54, 2009, 1105–1112.

Kim H. C., S. J. Kim, J. E. Yun, T.-H. Jo, B. R. Choi, and C. G. Park, Development of the Greenbottle Blowfly, *Lucilia sericata*, under Different Temperatures, *Korean Journal of Applied Entomology*. 46, 2007, 141–145.

Kocarek P., Decomposition and Coleoptera Succession on Exposed Carrion of Small Mammal in Opava, the Czech Republic, *European Journal of Soil Biology*. 39, 2003, 31–45.

Kuusela S. and I. Hanski, The Structure of Carrion Fly Communities: The Size and the Type of Carrion, *Ecography*. 5, 1982, 337–348.

Kyerematen R., B. A. Boateng, and E. Twumasi, Insect Diversity and Succession Pattern on Different Carrion Types, *Journal of Research in Biology*. 2, 2012, 1–8.

Lane R. P., Investigation into Blowfly (Diptera: Calliphoridae) Succession on Corpses, *Journal of Natural History*. 9, 1975, 581–588.

Lang M. D., G. R. Allen, and B. J. Horton, Blowfly Succession from Possum (*Trichosurus vulpecula*) Carrion in a Sheep-Farming Zone, *Medical & Veterinary Entomology*. 20, 2006, 445–452.

Lefebvre F. and T. Pasquerault, Temperature-Dependent Development of *Ophyra aenescens* (Wiedemann, 1830) and *Ophyra capensis* (Wiedemann, 1818)(Diptera, Muscidae), *Forensic Science International*. 139, 2004, 75–79.

Lord W. D. and J. F. Burger, Arthropods Associated with Herring Gull (*Larus argentatus*) and Great Black-Backed Gull (*Larus marinus*) Carrion on Islands in the Gulf of Maine, *Environmental Entomology*. 13, 1984, 1261–1268.

Mabika N., G. Mawera, and R. Masendu, An Initial Study of Insect Succession on Decomposing Rabbit Carrions in Harare, Zimbabwe, *Asian Pacific Journal of Tropical Biomedicine*. 4, 2014, 561–565.

Macaulay L. E., D. G. Barr, and D. B. Strongman, Effects of Decomposition on Gunshot Wound Characteristics: Under Moderate Temperatures with Insect Activity, *Journal of Forensic Sciences (Blackwell Publishing Limited)*. 54, 2009, 443–447.

Mahat N. A., P. T. Jayaprakash, and Z. Zafarina, *Necrophagous Infestation in Rabbit Carcasses Decomposing in Kubang Kerian Kelatan. Malaysian Journal of Medical Sciences*. 15, 2008, 124–124.

Malgorn Y., Forensic Entomology or How to Use Informative Cadaver Inhabitant, *Problems of Forensic Sciences*. XLVI, 2001, 76–82.

Manlove J. D. and R. H. L. Disney, The Use of *Megaselia abdita* (Diptera: Phoridae) in Forensic Entomology, *Forensic Science International*. 175, 2008, 83–84.

Mariluis J. C. and P. R. Mulieri, The Distribution of the Calliphoridae in Argentina (Diptera), *Revista de la Sociedad Entomologica Argentina*. 62, 2003, 85–97.

Martinez E., Succession Pattern of Carrion-Feeding Insects in Paramo, Colombia, *Forensic Science International*. 166, 2007, 182–189.

Martin-Vega D., Skipping Clues: Forensic Importance of the Family Piophilidae (Diptera), *Forensic Science International*. 212, 2011, 1-5.

Matuszewski S., D. Bajerlein, S. Konwerski, and K. Szpila, Insect Succession and Carrion Decomposition in Selected Forests of Central Europe. Part 1: Pattern and Rate of Decomposition, *Forensic Science International*. 194, 2010, 85–3.

Mauricio Osvaldo M., M.-F. Emygdio Leite De Araújo, and C. Claudio José Barros De, Heterotrophic Succession in Carrion Arthropod Assemblages, *Brazilian Archives of Biology and Technology*. 2005, 477.

Mayer A. C. G. and S. D. Vasconcelos, Necrophagous Beetles Associated with Carcasses in a Semi-Arid Environment in Northeastern Brazil: Implications for Forensic Entomology, *Forensic Science International*. 226, 2013, 41–45.

Mcalpine J. F., *Manual of Nearctic Diptera*. Ottawa, 1981.

Mckinnerney M., Carrion Communities in the Northern Chihuahuan Desert, *The Southwestern Naturalist*. 23(4), 1978, 563–576.

Mégnin, P. *La Faune Des Cadavres: Application De L'entomologie À La Médicine Légale*, 1894.

Megyesi M. S., S. P. Nawrocki, and N. H. Haskell, Using Accumulated Degree-Days to Estimate the Postmortem Interval from Decomposed Human Remains, *Journal of Forensic Sciences*. 50, 2005, 618–626.

Meyer J. A. and B. A. Mullens, Development of Immature *Fannia* Spp. (Diptera: Muscidae) at Constant Laboratory Temperatures, *Journal of Medical Entomology*. 25, 1988, 165–171.

Michaud J.-P., C. G. Majka, J.-P. Privè, and G. Moreau, Natural and Anthropogenic Changes in the Insect Fauna Associated with Carcasses in the North American Maritime Lowlands, *Forensic Science International*. 202(1–3), 2010, 64–70.

Michaud J.-P. and G. Moreau, A Statistical Approach Based on Accumulated Degree-Days to Predict Decomposition-Related Processes in Forensic Studies, *Journal of Forensic Sciences (Blackwell Publishing Limited)*. 56, 2011, 229–232.

Michaud J.-P., K. G. Schoenly, and G. Moreau, Rewriting Ecological Succession History: Did Carrion Ecologists Get There First? *Quarterly Review of Biology*. 90, 2015, 45–66.

Mise K. M., R. C. Correa, and L. M. Almeida, Coleopterofauna Found on Fresh and Frozen Rabbit Carcasses in Curitiba, Parana, Brazil. *Brazilian Journal Biology*. 73(3), 2013, 543–548.

Moretti T. D. C., O. B. Ribeiro, P. J. Thyssen, and D. R. Solis, Insects on Decomposing Carcasses of Small Rodents in a Secondary Forest in Southeastern Brazil, *European Journal of Entomology*. 105, 2008, 691–696.

Moretti T. D. C., S. M. Allegretti, C. A. Mello-Patiu, A. M. Tognolo, O. B. Ribeiro, and D. R. Solis, Occurrence of *Microcerella halli* (Engel)(Diptera, Sarcophagidae) in Snake Carrion in Southeastern Brazil, *Revista Brasileira de Entomologia*. 53, 2009, 318–320.

Moura M. O., C. J. D. Carvalho, and E. L. Monteiro-Filho, A Preliminary Analysis of Insects of Medico-Legal Importance in Curitiba, State of Paraná, *Memórias do Instituto Oswaldo Cruz*. 92, 1997, 269–274.

Mullen G. R. and L. A. Durden, *Medical and Veterinary Entomology*, 2002.

Nation J. L., *Insect Physiology and Biochemistry*, 2011 (Nation 2011).

Nelder M. P., J. W. Mccreadie, and C. S. Major, Blow Flies Visiting Decaying Alligators: Is Succession Synchronous or Asynchronous? *Psyche*. 2009(0033–2615), 2009, 1–7.

O'Flynn M. A., The Succession and Rate of Development of Blowflies in Carrion in Southern Queensland and the Application of These Data to Forensic Entomology, *Journal Austrailian Entomological Society*. 22, 1983, 137–148.

O'Flynn M. A. and D. E. Moorhouse, Species of *Chrysomya* as Primary Flies in Carrion. *Australian Journal of Entomology*. 18, 1979, 31–32.

Ortloff A., P. Peña, and M. Riquelme, Preliminary Study of the Succession Pattern of Necrobiont Insects, Colonising Species and Larvae on Pig Carcasses in Temuco (Chile) for Forensic Applications, *Forensic Science International*. 222, 2012, e36–e41.

Parmenter R. R. and J. A. Macmahon, Carrion Decomposition and Nutrient Cycling in a Semiarid Shrub-Steppe Ecosystem, *Ecological Monographs*. 79, 2009, 637–662.

Pastula E. C. and R. W. Merritt, Insect Arrival Pattern and Succession on Buried Carrion in Michigan, *Journal of Medical Entomology*. 50, 2013, 432–439.
Patrican L. A. and R. Vaidyanathan, Arthropod Succession in Rats Euthanized with Carbon Dioxide and Sodium Pentobarbital, *Journal of the New York Entomological Society*. 103, 1995, 197–207.
Payne J. A., A Summer Carrion Study of the Baby Pig Sus Scrofa Linnaeus, *Ecology*. 46, 1965, 592–602.
Payne J. A., Arthropod Succession and Decomposition of Burried Pigs, *Nature*. 219, 1968, 1180–1968.
Pounder D. J., Forensic Entomo-Toxicology, *Journal of the Forensic Science Society*. 31, 1991, 469–472.
Prado E Castro C., A. Serrano, P. Martins Da Silva, and M. D. García, Carrion Flies of Forensic Interest: A Study of Seasonal Community Composition and Succession in Lisbon, Portugal, *Medical & Veterinary Entomology*. 26, 2012, 417–431.
Price P. W., *Insect Ecology*, 1997. New York: John Wiley & Sons.
Pruess K. P., Day-Degree Methods for Pest Management, *Environmental Entomology*. 12, 1983, 613–619.
Putman R. J., Dynamics of Blowfly, *Calliphora Erythrocepha*, within Carrion. *Journal of Animal Ecology*. 46, 1977, 853–866.
Rabêlo K. C., P. J. Thyssen, R. L. Salgado, M. S. Araújo, and S. D. Vasconcelos, Bionomics of Two Forensically Important Blowfly Species *Chrysomya megacephala* and *Chrysomya putoria* (Diptera: Calliphoridae) Reared on Four Types of Diet, *Forensic Science International*. 210, 2011, 257–262.
Ratcliffe, G. G. Comparative studies on the developmental rates of the larvae of certain blowflies (diptera: calliphoridae) at constant and alternating temperatures. *Diss*. Durham University, 1984.
Reed H. Jr, A Study of Dog Carcass Communities in Tennessee, with Special Reference to the Insects, *American Midland Naturalist*. 59, 1958, 213–245.
Regester K. J. and M. R. Whiles, Decomposition Rates of Salamander (*Ambystoma maculatum*) Life Stages and Associated Energy and Nutrient Fluxes in Ponds and Adjacent Forest in Southern Illinois, *Copeia*. 2006, 2006, 640–649.
Richards E. N. and M. L. Goff, Arthropod Succession on Exposed Carrion in Three Contrasting Tropical Habitats on Hawaii Island, Hawaii, *Journal of Medical Entomology* 34, 1997, 328–339.
Roberts J. and N. Márquez-Grant, *Forensic Ecology Handbook: From Crime Scene to Court*, Wiley-Blackwell, 2012.
Rochefort S., M. Giroux, J. Savage, and T. A. Wheeler, Key to Forensically Important Piophilidae (Diptera) in the Nearctic Region Cjai 27—January 22, 2015, *Canadian Journal of Arthropod Identification*. 27, 2015, 1–37.
Rosa T. A., M. L. Y. Babata, C. M. De Souza, D. De Sousa, J. Mendes, C. A. De Mello-Patiu, and F. Z. Vaz-De-Mello, Arthropods Associated with Pig Carrion in Two Vegetation Profiles of Cerrado in the State of Minas Gerais, Brazil, *Revista Brasileira de Entomologia*. 55, 2011, 424–434.
Rueda L. C., L. G. Ortega, N. A. Segura, V. M. Acero, and F. Bello, Lucilia Sericata Strain from Colombia: Experimental Colonization, Life Tables and Evaluation of Two Artifcial Diets of the Blowfly *Lucilia sericata* (Meigen)(Diptera: Calliphoridae), Bogotá, Colombia Strain, *Biological Research*. 43, 2010, 197–203.
Samuel W., The Use of Age Classes of Winter Ticks on Moose to Determine Time of Death, *Canadian Society of Forensic Science Journal*. 21, 1988, 54–59.
Sanford M. R., Forensic Entomology of Decomposing Humans and Their Decomposing Pets, *Forensic Science International*. 247, 2015, e11–e17.
Schlacher T. A., S. Strydom, and R. M. Connolly, Multiple Scavengers Respond Rapidly to Pulsed Carrion Resources at the Land–Ocean Interface, *Acta Oecologica*. 48, 2013, 7–12.
Schoenly K., A Statistical Analysis of Successional Patterns in Carrion-Arthropod Assemblages: Implications for Forensic Entomology and Determination of the Postmortem Interval, *Journal of Forensic Sciences*. 37, 1992, 1489–1513. (172)
Schoenly K. and W. Reid, Dynamics of Heterotrophic Succession in Carrion Arthropod Assemblages: Discrete Seres or a Continuum of Change? *Oecologia*. 73, 1987, 192–202.
Sharanowski B. J., E. G. Walker, and G. S. Anderson, Insect Succession and Decomposition Patterns on Shaded and Sunlit Carrion in Saskatchewan in Three Different Seasons, *Forensic Science International*. 179, 2008, 219–240.
Shi Y. W., Effects of Malathion on the Insect Succession and the Development of *Chrysomya megacephala* (Diptera: Calliphoridae) in the Field and Implications for Estimating Postmortem Interval, *American Journal of Forensic Medicine and Pathology*. 31, 2010, 46–51.
Shi Y. W., Seasonality of Insect Succession on Exposed Rabbit Carrion in Guangzhou, China, *Insect Science*. 16, 2009, 425–439.

Smith K. G., *A Manual of Forensic Entomology*, 1986.
Smith K. G., The Faunal Succession of Insects and Other Invertebrates on a Dead Fox, *Entomological Gazette*. 26, 1975, 277.
Smith P. H., Causes and Correlates of Loss and Recovery of Sexual Receptivity in *Lucilia cuprina* Females after Their 1st Mating, *Journal of Insect Behavior*. 2, 1989, 325–337.
Stevens J. and R. Wall, Classification of the *Genus lucilia* (Diptera: Calliphoridae): A Preliminary Parsimony Analysis, *Journal of Natural History*. 30, 1996, 1087–1094.
Sukhapanth N., E. Upatham, and C. Ketavan, Effects of Feed and Media on Egg Production, Growth and Survivorship of Flies (Diptera: Calliphoridae, Muscidae and Sarcophagidae), *Journal of the Science Society Thailand*. 14, 1988, 41–50.
Swiger S. L., J. A. Hogsette, and J. F. Butler, Larval Distribution and Behavior of *Chrysomya rufifacies* (Macquart) (Diptera: Calliphoridae) Relative to Other Species on Florida Black Bear (Carnivora: Ursidae) Decomposing Carcasses, 2014.
Tabor K. L., Analysis of the Successional Patterns of Insects on Carrion in Southwest Virginia, *Journal of Medical Entomology*. 41, 2004, 785–795.
Tantawi T. I., E. M. El-Kady, B. Greenberg, and H. A. El-Ghaffar, Arthropod Succession on Exposed Rabbit Carrion in Alexandria, Egypt, *Journal of Medical Entomology*. 33, 1996, 566–580.
Tenorio F. M., J. K. Olson, and C. J. Coates, Decomposition Studies, with a Catalog and Descriptions of Forensically Important Blow Flies (Diptera: Calliphoridae) in Central Texas, *Southwestern Entomologist*. 28, 2003, 37–45.
Tessmer J. C., Meek, and V. Wright, Circadian Patterns of Oviposition by Necrophilous Flies (Diptera: Calliphoridae) in Southern Louisiana, *Southwestern Entomologist (USA)*. 20(4), 1995, 439–445.
Thyssen P. J., C. M. De Souza, P. M. Shimamoto, T. De Britto Salewski and T. C. Moretti, Rates of Development of Immatures of Three Species of *Chrysomya* (Diptera: Calliphoridae) Reared in Different Types of Animal Tissues: Implications for Estimating the Postmortem Interval, *Parasitology Research*. 113, 2014, 3373–3380.
Tomberlin J. K. and P. H. Adler, Seasonal Colonization and Decomposition of Rat Carrion in Water and on Land in an Open Field in South Carolina, *Journal of Medical Entomology*. 35, 1998, 704–9.
Tomberlin J. K., R. Mohr, M. E. Benbow, A. M. Tarone, and S. Van Laerhoven, A Roadmap for Bridging Basic and Applied Research in Forensic Entomology, *Annual Review of Entomology*. 56, 2011, 401–421.
Tracqui A., C. Keyser-Tracqui, P. Kintz, and B. Ludes, Entomotoxicology for the Forensic Toxicologist: Much Ado About Nothing? *International Journal of Legal Medicine*. 118, 2004, 194–196.
Turner B. and T. Howard, Metabolic Heat Generation in Dipteran Larval Aggregations: A Consideration for Forensic Entomology, *Medical & Veterinary Entomology*. 6, 1992, 179–181.
Vairo K. P., C. A. D. Mello-Patiu, and C. J. De Carvalho, Pictorial Identification Key for Species of *Sarcophagidae* (Diptera) of Potential Forensic Importance in Southern Brazil, *Revista Brasileira de Entomologia*. 55, 2011, 333–347.
Vanin S., Carrion Breeding Fauna from a Grass Snake (*Natrix natrix*) Found in an Artificial Nest, *Lavoro Societa Veneziana di Scienze Naturali*. 37, 2012, 73–76.
Vanlaerhoven S. L. and G. S. Anderson, Insect Succession on Buried Carrion in Two Biogeoclimatic Zones of British Columbia, *Journal of Forensic Sciences*. 44, 1999, 32–43.
Vasconcelos S. D., T. M. Cruz, R. L. Salgado, and P. J. Thyssen, Dipterans Associated with a Decomposing Animal Carcass in a Rainforest Fragment in Brazil: Notes on the Early Arrival and Colonization by Necrophagous Species, 2013.
Velasquez Y., A Checklist of Arthropods Associated with Rat Carrion in a Montane Locality of Northern Venezuela, *Forensic Science International*. 174, 2008, 67–69.
Voss S. C., Decomposition and Insect Succession on Cadavers inside a Vehicle Environment, Forensic Science, *Medicine & Pathology*. 4, 2008, 22–32.
Voss S. C., H. Spafford, and I. R. Dadour, Annual and Seasonal Patterns of Insect Succession on Decomposing Remains at Two Locations in Western Australia, *Forensic Science International*. 193, 2009, 26–3.
Wang J., Z. Li, Y. Chen, Q. Chen, and X. Yin, The Succession and Development of Insects on Pig Carcasses and Their Significances in Estimating Pmi in South China, *Forensic Science International*. 179, 2008, 11–18.

Warren J. A. and G. S. Anderson, The Development of *Protophormia terraenovae* (Robineau-Desvoidy) at Constant Temperatures and Its Minimum Temperature Threshold, *Forensic Science International*. 233, 2013, 374–379.

Watson E. J., Insect Succession and Decomposition of Wildlife Carcasses During Fall and Winter in Louisiana, *Journal of Medical Entomology*. 42, 2005, 193–203.

Watson E. J. and C. E. Carlton, Spring Succession of Necrophilous Insects on Wildlife Carcasses in Louisiana, *Journal of Medical Entomology*. 40, 2003, 338–347.

Watson E. and C. Carlton, Succession of Forensically Significant Carrion Beetle Larvae on Large Carcasses (Coleoptera: Silphidae), *Southeastern Naturalist*. 4, 2005, 335–346.

Whitworth T., Keys to the Genera and Species of Blow Flies (Diptera: Calliphoridae) of America North of Mexico, *Proceedings of the Entomological Society of Washington*. 108, 2006, 689–725.

Yang S., J. Logan, and D. L. Coffey, Mathematical Formulae for Calculating the Base Temperature for Growing Degree Days, *Agricultural and Forest Meteorology*. 74, 1995, 61–74.

Zaidi F. and X.-X. Chen, A Preliminary Survey of Carrion Breeding Insects Associated with the Eid Ul Azha Festival in Remote Pakistan, *Forensic Science International*. 209, 2011, 186–194.

CHAPTER 6

ANIMAL SEXUAL ABUSE

Martha Smith-Blackmore and Nancy Bradley-Siemens

Animal sexual abuse (ASA) is also known by terms such as bestiality, zoophilia, or animal sexual assault. Bestiality is typically defined in human psychology as relating to recurrent intense sexual fantasies, urges, and sexual activities with nonhuman animals or any kind of sexual contact with an animal from which one experiences sexual excitement or pleasure. Zoophilia refers to sexual preference for or sexual attraction to an animal or animals; the term zoophilia is one that suggests "love" or "attraction" rather than abuse.

Animal sexual abuse is derived from "child sexual abuse," a term more precise and complete than bestiality or zoophilia (Munro & Munro, 2008). While recurrent intense fantasies and urges are not illegal activities, most states classify actual sexual contact with animals as a felony and/or misdemeanor. In some states animal sexual contact is technically legal (e.g., Hawaii, Kentucky, New Mexico, West Virginia, and Wyoming).

There is ongoing interest in specifically banning ASA because, like minors and impaired adults, animals cannot give legal consent; in effect animals are wards under our control, and human–animal sexual relations almost always involve coercion (Beirne et al., 2017). Additionally, and significantly, there is overlap between the worlds of animal and child sexual abuse.

Where ASA is not specifically illegal, sexual contact with animals that inflicts pain and/or suffering, or where physical or chemical restraint for the purposes of ASA causes pain and/or suffering, is still well within the paradigm for designation as animal cruelty. The size of the animal, implements or body parts used, and the type of sexual contact will influence the resulting injuries.

Where no detectible physical harm has been inflicted and animal sexual interaction is illegal, forensic science may be relied upon to prove penetration or contact, depending on the prevailing legal standard. The types of sexual interaction between a human and an animal include masturbating the animal, receiving or performing oral sex, performing vaginal intercourse, performing anal intercourse, sodomy with objects, and the animal as a surrogate for a behavioral fetish, such as sadomasochistic practices or sexual killing (Merck, 2013). Nonaccidental trauma may be classified as ASA based on any action involving the genitalia or anorectal area (Merck, 2013). Trauma applied specifically to the nipples may also be sexually motivated animal abuse.

HISTORICAL CONTEXT

The earliest known illustrations of human interest in sexual contact with animals date back at least 25,000 years to cave paintings depicting sexual intercourse between humans and animals. Human–animal sexual relations are also portrayed through the ages and in a variety of cultures in art and mythology. There is no certain knowledge about the context of early artistic or literary representations of human sexual intercourse with animals and what, in fact, has taken place or whether these are intended as interpretations of mythology (Figure 6.1).

In some historical and cultural contexts, sex with animals has been promoted or condoned as a means of increasing virility, fertility, as a way to gain sexual experience before marriage, as a treatment against nymphomania, as a manhood test, as part of the cultivation of black magic and witchcraft, or as a way to gain the strengths of an animal, or has been condemned as an unnatural sexual act or as a crime. Depending on the societal context in time and place, sexual contact with animals has ranged from acceptance or tolerance to social banishment, imprisonment, torture, or execution.

DEFINING CRIME IN THE CONTEXT OF ANIMAL SEXUAL ABUSE

Laws against human–animal sexual contact vary across the United States and around the world; however, the legality of sex with animals has been decreasing over the past 20 years. Historical "sodomy laws" prohibited "crimes against nature"; they outlawed homosexual acts along with bestiality. An effort to eradicate sodomy laws banning acts between consenting adults meant that bestiality was inadvertently made legal in many states. As of 2018, 45 states and 2 territories ban sex with animals, while 5 states and the District of Columbia have decriminalized it due to repeal of sodomy laws.

To correct this unintended consequence, anti-bestiality laws have been instated using language similar to: "A person commits an offense who knowingly engages in any sexual activity with an

Figure 6.1 Cabra y Pan Papiri. (From Wikimedia.)

animal; causes, aids, or abets another person to engage in any sexual activity with an animal; permits any sexual activity with an animal to be conducted on any premises under his or her charge or control; engages in, organizes, promotes, conducts, advertises, aids, abets, participates in as an observer, or performs any service in the furtherance of an act involving any sexual activity with an animal for a commercial or recreational purpose; or photographs or films, for purposes of sexual gratification, a person engaged in a sexual activity with an animal. Sexual activity with an animal can be defined as physical sexual contact between the person and the animal.

IS ANIMAL SEXUAL ABUSE A PSYCHOPATHY IN HUMANS?

Findings from inmate research suggests that bestiality may represent a risk factor for future interpersonal violence (Holoyda, 2016), and zoophilia has been cited as an early marker for psychosis (Lesandrić et al., 2017). Animal sexual abuse, particularly when experienced as a child, has been shown to be the single largest risk factor and strongest predictor of increased risk for committing child sexual abuse (Abel, 2008). Thirty-five percent of arrests for bestiality also involve child sexual abuse or exploitation. In addition, nearly 40% of offenders have prior criminal records for bestiality, child sexual abuse, domestic violence, battery, adult rape, substance abuse, trespass, public indecency, and even murder (Edwards, 2018).

Motivations for sexual abuse may include opportunistic (experimental), fixated, or domineering sadistic traits. Opportunists are individuals who seek out animals because they are accessible, vulnerable, and nonthreatening. Fixation involves the type of abuser who has a sexual preference for or attraction to animals. The domineering (sadistic) abuser may derive gratification from forcing a vulnerable individual, like a child, into having sex with an animal to humiliate, dominate, control, or exploit their human animal victims. This type of person derives sexual gratification from the pain and suffering inflicted while sexually abusing others, including animals. This type of abuser is likely to injure or kill an animal in the course of their abuse (Sinclair et al., 2006).

In the 1970s, the belief was that bestiality behaviors were transitory, occurring when there is no other sexual outlet available. More recent studies report that most self-identified zoophiles do not have sex with animals because there is no other sexual outlet but do so because it is their sexual preference. The most common reasons for engaging in zoophilic relationships were attraction to animals out of a desire for affection, and a sexual attraction toward and/or a love for animals (Holoyda and Newman, 2016).

Until the advent of the internet, most scientific or clinical reports on ASA were case reports of individuals who sought treatment for their sexual predilection. Since the advent of the internet, there are dozens of social websites for zoophiles. Beast Forum is the largest online zoophile community in the world with over a million users and approximately ten thousand members online at a given time. The increasing availability of animal pornographic imagery and supportive communities may contribute to a growing incidence of ASA.

Sexual assault on animals is not limited to domesticated species or any particular animal size. Any animal species can be an animal victim. However, sexual activity has been found to be prevalent in dogs and horses (Williams & Weinberg, 2003). Dogs and horses were also the most common victims according to a 2002 survey of 93 zoophiles by Dr. Hani Miletski (Miletski, 2005a,b) For females, the main stated reasons for having sex with animals was because they were sexually attracted to the animal (100%), claimed love and affection for the animal (67%), and/or because they said the animal wanted sex with them (67%). Only 12% of her sample said they engaged in sex with animals because there were no human partners available, and only 7% said it was because they were too shy to have sex with humans. Most of Miletski's sample preferred sex with dogs (87% males; 100% females) and/or horses (81% males; 73% females).

ANIMAL SEXUAL ABUSE INCIDENCE

Drs. Helen Munro and Michael Thrusfeld's foundational study "Battered Pets: Sexual Abuse" was published in 2001 and was the outcome of a survey of nonaccidental injury in small animals in the UK, based on responses from a random sample of small animal practitioners (Munro and Thrusfield, 2001). Of the 448 reported cases, 6% were identified as being sexual in nature. Of the sexual abuse cases, 21 cases occurred in dogs, 5 in cats, and 2 in unspecified species. Reasons for veterinarians suspecting sexual abuse included the type of injury, behavior of the owner, statements from witnesses, and admission by the perpetrator. Types of injury included vaginal and anorectal penetrative (penile and non-penile) injury, perianal damage, and trauma to the genitals. Some injuries (such as castration) were extreme, and some were fatal. In contrast, other cases revealed no obvious damage. The type and severity of injuries were similar to those described in texts on child abuse and human forensic pathology.

The incidence of ASA is higher among child sexual abusers. English et al. (2003) studied 180 adults who committed sex offenses against children. Although case records indicated that only 4.4% had engaged in animal sexual assault, when polygraphed, 36.1% admitted such activities.

Because of the variation of legality and definition in ASA and the limitations with law enforcement data collection, there is not a clear picture of how much ASA occurs. In the FBI's release of 2016 National Incident-Based Reporting System (NIBRS) data, the first year ASA data was collected as a discrete data point, just 9 incidents were reported of 1126 total reported incident of animal cruelty. That represents less than 1% of the total cases reported (Figure 6.2 and Table 6.1).

Charging a defendant with ASA requires prosecutorial courage; some cases will instead be charged as indecency crimes, breach of the peace, or other lesser charges. Offenders may negotiate the opportunity to plead guilty to lesser charges or to charges which obscure the sexual nature of the offense. These defense tactics may cloud statistics related to prosecutorial outcomes, but they should not obscure *incident* reporting.

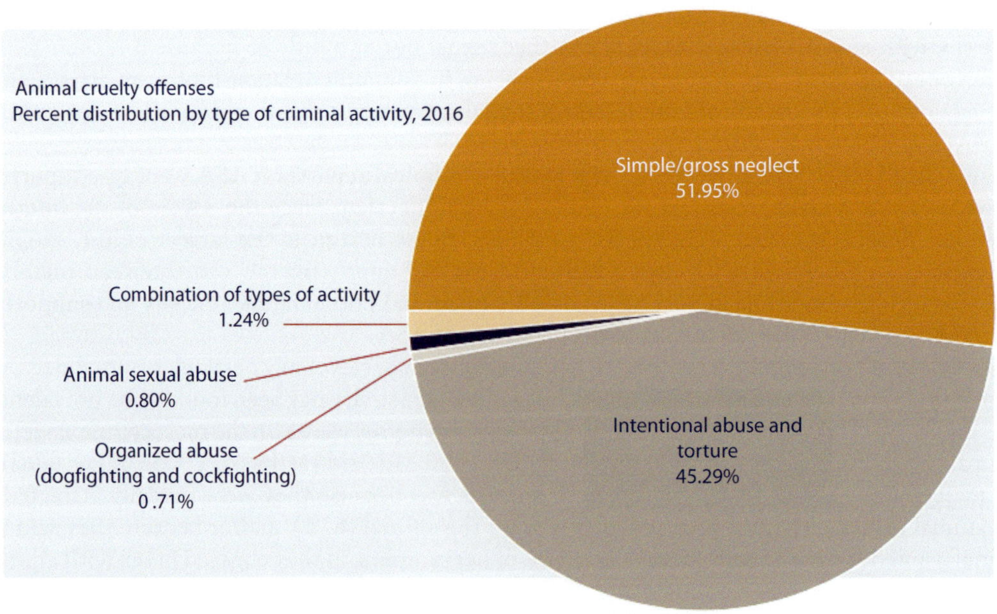

Figure 6.2 Animal cruelty offenses: percent distribution by type of criminal activity.

Table 6.1 Open data repositories that were quality checked by *scientific data*

Animal Cruelty Offenses: Distribution by Type of Criminal Activity, 2016*					
State	**Total Offenses**	**Simple/Gross Neglect**	**Intentional Abuse and Torture**	**Organized Abuse**	**Animal Sexual Abuse**
TOTAL	1126	599	523	12	9
Colorado	8	7	1	0	0
Delaware	494	214	289	3	0
Massachusetts	2	1	1	0	0
Michigan	130	91	38	1	1
Minnesota	1	0	1	0	0
Missouri	15	8	6	1	0
North Dakota	7	5	3	0	0
Oregon	105	45	58	1	1
South Dakota	10	5	5	0	0
Tennessee	219	143	69	4	5
Washington	85	50	34	0	2
West Virginia	13	8	4	1	0
Wisconsin	37	22	14	1	0

* Agencies can submit up to three types of criminal activity per offense. See the data declaration for more information.

CASE 1

History: This case was brought to the attention of law enforcement via routine screening of digital photograph submissions for development. Multiple photos of a person inserting a mallet handle into the vagina of what appeared to be a dog and additional photographs of human male genitalia penetrating the vulva/vaginal area of what appeared to be a dog.

Physical Exam: A search warrant was obtained to seize two female Labrador Retrievers approximately 3–5 years of age from the home of the suspect. Both dogs exhibited evidence of sustained vaginal trauma. Both had 360° linear lesions to a depth of over 10 cm into the vagina.

Outcome: Law enforcement was able to show in court that the dogs' owner was the individual in the photographs. Testimony hinged on the amount of "perceived torture," pain, and suffering the dogs endured, not the actual sexual abuse. Due to the diligence of a dedicated prosecutor, a felony conviction was eventually obtained. In addition, there was a motion to have the suspect listed as a registered sex offender; however, this never came to fruition.

Note: This case occurred in a state prior to implementing a bestiality statute. There were existing animal cruelty laws, but prosecution was made more complex due to vagueness of the existing animal cruelty statutes.

EXAMINATION OF THE SUSPECTED ANIMAL SEXUAL ABUSE VICTIM

All animals can potentially be victims of ASA. It is imperative that veterinarians recognize conditions or behaviors that may signal animal abuse and include them on their list of differentials. Animal sexual abuse victims may be identified by law enforcement or others upon presentation to a veterinarian for examination or because of witness accounts. Any reported history of ASA must be approached with gravity and an open clinical mind.

When a veterinarian is reporting ASA to law enforcement, it is important to be thorough in communications. The veterinarian is the animal expert but may not be as familiar with legal proceedings in sexual abuse cases as medical doctors may be. Law enforcement officers may need to be reminded that the veterinarian requires guidance or input.

The nature of an ASA incident may range from contact without physical harm to death as a sequela of penetration, strangulation, other accompanying trauma, or overdose of an administered sedative agent. After the physical exam with trace collection and lesion documentation, baseline blood work, urine for urinalysis, and fecal sample should be collected and submitted to a reference laboratory.

If sedative agents are suspected to have been used in a drug-facilitated animal sexual assault, sufficient samples should be collected to provide for toxin screens before any sedatives are given for the purposes of the veterinary exam. The first voided urine sample of a female dog should be handled very carefully to preserve any spermatozoa that may be present.

Veterinarians in private, shelter, and emergency practices are the front line in the response to animal cruelty cases. The manner in which the initial examination and treatment of a patient is handled can directly impact the ability of law enforcement and forensic professionals to collect and document critical evidence needed for a successful prosecution. This is especially true in cases of sexual assault.

Conditions That Can Mimic Animal Sexual Abuse

When examining a patient with suspicious conditions, veterinarians must consider the question: Is this in fact an ASA case?

Animal sexual abuse should be an included differential in any form of abnormal urogenital or perineal presentation. However, differentials for abnormal genitals may include neoplastic, inflammatory, or hormonal causes. Abrasions, swellings, or other abnormalities in these areas may require further diagnostics to differentiate from acquired or natural conditions using laboratory tests, biopsy, or ultrasound.

When ASA is suspected, adequate examination and testing should rule out natural or acquired conditions that mimic ASA. The examining veterinarian must exhibit scientific impartiality when examining an animal alleged to have been the victim of ASA. Conditions that can mimic injury to the anus, vulva, and perineum must be considered and ruled in or out when appropriate. The presence of a disease condition does not exclude ASA as a possibility, but this raises the bar for finding trace evidence to corroborate allegations. Sexual abuse should be a differential in any case of genital or anorectal injury or trauma.

The Anus and Perineum

The anus is normally thick and prominent in intact males due to testosterone-dependent hypertrophy of the apocrine glands. This secondary sex characteristic does not cause the abrasions or broken hairs that can be seen with anal penetration.

Dogs may self-traumatize or have ulcerations on or near the anus due to anal sac impaction or gastrointestinal parasites. Animals may traumatize their own perineum due to irritation from

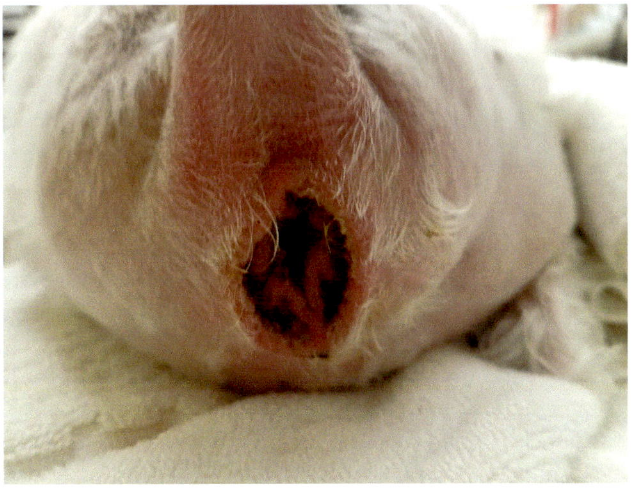

Figure 6.3 Pseudocoprastasis trauma post-removal of a fecal dam in a 6-year-old spayed female Bichon Frisé. (Author's photograph.)

allergies. Perianal fistulas and fissures are an immune mediated lesion of the anus and perianal region of dogs. Perineal hernias are seen in intact older male dogs with prostate gland enlargement and obstipation. Rectal prolapse may occur secondary to tenesmus or excessive postpartum straining.

A long-haired dog or cat that has experienced pseudocoprostasis (a hair mat with feces entanglement obstructing the anal opening, also known as a fecal dam) may have a dilated anus and a rim of reddened swollen tissue ringing the anus after the mat is removed (Figure 6.3)

The Vulva and Vagina

Swelling of the vulva is normal during estrus. Excessive or persistent swelling is abnormal but occurs commonly in dogs. This can happen with hyperestrogenism of ovarian tumors or with exposure to estrogenic substances. The vaginal mucosa swells with edema and this tissue can protrude through the vulva exposing the mucosa.

Vaginal hyperplasia, hypertrophy, and/or prolapse of bitches are common conditions seen during proestrus of the first few estrus periods of young dogs, and this is seen more often in brachiocephalic breeds. It is thought that there is an increased sensitivity to estrogen and there is excessive edema of the submucosal tissues of the vagina. Severe swelling can cause protruding vaginal tissue that can become excoriated and ulcerated. This condition will spontaneously regress during diestrus or after spaying.

Vaginal polyps occur in most species and they are particularly common in dogs. They may protrude through the vaginal opening and ulcerate. Stricture or stenosis of the vagina or vestibule may occur as a congenital anomaly or following traumatic injury at parturition. Mycotoxins can cause hyperestrogenism and subsequent vaginal hypertrophy in some species, especially pigs.

The most common neoplasm of the vagina and vulva is a squamous cell neoplasm. They occur in all species but are most common in the cow, ewe, and mare. These are more common with exposure to sunlight on less pigmented tissue. Canine transmissible venereal tumors may be present in dogs of both sexes. Female dogs may develop leiomas of the vaginal wall.

Most species have a species-specific herpes virus which can cause genital lesions. Genital herpes can cause multifocal epithelial necrosis, apoptosis, and erosion. In some species the ulcers will coalesce to form large ulcers up to several centimeters in diameter. These lesions may leave depigmented marks after healing.

Post-parturient vulvitis and vaginitis occur when they are lacerated during dystocia and become infected. Granular vulvitis is the descriptive term for the appearance of the vulva and vagina in inflammatory diseases and can be the result of hyperplasia of lymphoid follicles.

The Penis, Scrotum, and Testes

Diseases of, or accidental trauma to the scrotum and testes (orchitis or epididymitis) can cause swelling and discoloration; torsion of the testicle and scrotal hernias can cause spontaneous acute swelling and discoloration. Hematogenous or ascending spread of *Escherichia coli* or other gram-negative bacteria can cause orchitis with marked swelling and ulceration of the scrotum. Intact dogs may experience scrotal burns from sitting on caustic substances such as kennel disinfectants that have been inadequately rinsed from the primary enclosure. Dogs may lick and chew at the affected scrotum and cause a fistula to the scrotal contents.

Male horses may have habronemiasis, which is aberrant migration of fly larvae deposited on the penis or prepuce. Equine sarcoids may also present with ulcerated, proliferative lesions on the penis and prepuce.

Many of the above-listed conditions require histologic evaluation to properly diagnose them. Biopsies may help to support the absence of a disease condition and confirm a diagnosis of ASA. A fecal analysis for gastrointestinal parasites and a careful and documented exam of the anal glands can help to discern whether any perineal trauma is likely related to those conditions.

As a veterinarian, depending on your jurisdiction, you may be a mandatory reporter. If an injury does not fit with the history given, it is your duty to question it and report it. Veterinarians are advocates not only for their animal patient, but for societal health and safety as well.

STEPS FOR THE VETERINARY EXAMINER TO TAKE IN CASES OF SUSPECTED ANIMAL SEXUAL ABUSE

1. Ensure there is appropriate law enforcement seizure paperwork in place, or consent form/permission of animal owner to perform an exam.
2. Review any witness statements or written accounts of the ASA. The affidavit for a search warrant should have a detailed history and explanation of the theory of the offense.
3. Obtain a verbal history of the alleged assault from law enforcement, family, or available witnesses. Write down any statements verbatim and quote it in the history.
4. Review a detailed health history if available.
5. If the owner is present, explain what the exam will entail, and the extent of the injuries discovered.
6. Physical exam to assess the animal's condition, to include general overall health and specific potential injuries related to any potential animal sexual assault or nonaccidental injury. Overall exam should include whole-body alternate light source (ALS) examination, whole-body radiography, and infrared photography when possible.
7. Perform objective documentation of injuries with notes, sketches, and photography where possible.
8. Collect and preserve potential trace evidence. Collect blood and samples for complete blood counts, chemistry, and toxicology screening. In a female patient who may have been penetrated vaginally, the first urine passed should be caught and preserved by refrigeration. This urine sample should not be spun in the centrifuge.
9. Provide treatment for any conditions found.
10. Observe body language/mannerisms of the family members who are present. If unusual or suspicious, include in law enforcement notification.
11. Refer to resources available to assess follow-up needs, regular DVM as appropriate (Bradley and Rasile, 2014a,b).

THE PHYSICAL EXAM

A complete nose-to-tail exam should be conducted with the examining veterinarian and assistants wearing powder-free gloves, with the animal contained on a clean white sheet or butcher paper to catch any trace evidence that may be shed during the exam. The examining veterinarian must bear in mind that coercion must be used to allow the perpetrator to abuse an animal sexually, and such restraint may be physical (stunning blows to the head, binding restraints of head, muzzle, and/or limbs, forceful gripping), chemical (sedative agents), or through behavioral training for a conditioned response. Any observed signs of such coercion should be noted in the medical record, diagrammed, photographed, or videotaped as might be appropriate.

If sedative or anxiolytic drugs are going to be used to aid in the physical exam, radiography, and evidence collection, and pharmacology may have been used to perform the animal sexual assault, bloodwork should be collected prior to the administration of sedative, anesthesia, or analgesia.

A careful, deliberate, systemic, and complete head-to-tail exam should be performed looking for injuries such as abrasions, bruises, pattern injuries, lacerations, bite marks, burns, head trauma, blunt force injuries, injuries to the ears (chronic changes to the ear canals may be seen with repeated restraint by the ears), evidence of ligatures and/or bindings (around muzzle or limbs), toenail injuries, petechia in the sclera or fundus related to strangulation or attempted strangulation injuries around neck, and tail injuries, especially at the base.

The examination should include considerations for detection and collection of trace evidence, and detection and documentation of suspected injuries differentiated from accidental or natural causes of injury or disease which may mimic nonaccidental ASA injury. Trauma or trace evidence of ASA may be found because of human oral contact or penetration by a penis or a foreign object to the genitalia, perineum, oral cavity, or elsewhere on the animal, or evidence of animal oral contact or penetration of a person.

Crescent-shaped or ovoid fingertip bruises may be present on the caudal abdomen or medial thighs. These bruises are consistent with a strong manual grip hold for restraint. In deceased animals, a careful dissection with reflection of the skin should be performed to asses any bruises that are not evident on external exam of the shaved skin.

In smaller animals, where orifices are too small to allow penile, digital, or object penetration, the perineum or cloacal region may be invaginated through the pelvic opening. In these cases, there may be a large "target lesion" where the fur or feathers are wet, clumped, or missing in a large circle around the center of the target. This type of abuse is almost always fatal.

For the genital examination of a female dog, begin with the external genitalia and work inward. Sedation will facilitate the internal speculum exam for females. This should be performed without the use of lubricants, so the introduction of a speculum must be done with great care. A sterile human plastic vaginal speculum can be used for this exam (these can be equipped with light source). An otoscope with sterile cone can be used for exam and light source.

Observe for internal injuries of the vaginal opening, vaginal wall, and cervix opening, noting any injury to the fossa clitoris, left and right labium, vaginal opening, vestibule, urethral opening, perineum, and anus. With vaginal penetration the vulva may protrude inward. Vaginal prolapse may be present in the spayed female. Once swabbing has been performed, lubricants may be used if it will facilitate photography of internal lesions.

For the male external genitalia, examine the urethral opening, prepuce, sheath, scrotum, perineum, and anus. (Radiograph or palpate the penis do diagnose fracture of the os penis.) Rectal prolapse and prostatitis may be present. Look for bite marks or bruising to the penis and scrotum and lacerations in the folds of the anal opening. Assess circumferentially so all surfaces of the penile shaft are examined.

The rectal opening may be penetrated in animals of either sex, and rectal prolapse may result. A perineal and rectal examination should be completed along with photos of the external anal tissue, documenting any tissue tears. During all internal examinations, be alert for any possible retained foreign bodies.

Alternate Light Source Examination

A blacklight (UV or Wood's lamp) or other ALS should be used to examine the entire body for the presence of any proteinaceous substance (i.e., semen, saliva, vomit, or blood) which is more likely to be visible when illuminated. Any evidence found with the blacklight or ALS should be swabbed or collected (snipping clumps of fur) and documented.

The preferred ALS to detect human semen is a wavelength of 420–450 nm, viewed through orange lenses. Most veterinary hospitals have a Wood's lamp on hand, and this light emits a wavelength of 300–400 nm. The Bluemaxx BM500 (Sirchie; Medford, NJ) is recommended as a more specific light source to detect human semen (Stern and Smith-Blackmore, 2016).

The entire animal should be examined with an ALS to detect proteinaceous deposits (semen, saliva, or blood), scanning the entire body in a systematic pattern. The location on the body where the evidence was collected should be recorded in notes and sketches. An ALS may also identify an injury that is not yet visible.

Infrared thermal imaging may assist in the detection of areas of trauma and inflammation in the living patient. Thermal imaging can be used to map blood flow and areas of increased blood flow. There are a variety of thermal imaging cameras available on the market, including a cell phone adaptor.

Trace Evidence

When ASA is suspected, measures should be taken to collect and preserve trace evidence such as body fluids, lubricants, fibers, and foreign hairs. The principle in forensic science related to trace evidence is known as the Locard exchange principle.

Edmund Locard was a French criminalist known as the "Sherlock Holmes of France." He is best known for formulating the basic principle of forensic science which became the cornerstone of forensic science: "Human contact with any person, place or thing, will result in an exchange of physical materials or evidence" (Bader and Gabriel, 2010). This pertains to all crime scenes, living and inanimate.

All first responders and examiners should be aware of the Locard exchange principle and allow for this when handling, transporting, and performing a medical-forensic exam on animal victims. It is imperative that first responders note contact and activities that have occurred from the time of the suspected assault until the animal is in the forensic examiner's possession.

Contact with the animal should be minimized, and everyone who has contact with the animal needs to understand that the animal is the crime scene and treat them as such. This means not grooming an animal until after the forensic exam is conducted, separating animals into individual primary enclosures, and placing an e-collar on the animal until the exam is conducted to prevent self-grooming. Whenever possible, animals should be transported in clean airline transportation crates lined with a clean white sheet or clean cage liners.

DNA Evidence

A buccal swab collection brush should be used to collect a reference DNA profile on the victim animal (the "biological standard"). The profile generated may be used to match with an injured perpetrator (bites or scratches) or to match with any foreign objects that may have been used to restrain, penetrate, or injure the animal. Any materials collected that are presumed to have animal DNA present should be analyzed by an ANSI National Accreditation Board–accredited veterinary genetics diagnostic laboratory. Materials requiring analysis for the presence of human DNA should be submitted to the crime lab.

Sterile cotton-tipped swabs should be used to swab any suspect areas as well as the oral cavity. External perineal, perianal, or perivulvar swabs should be taken before swabbing deeper into orifices. The preputial opening should be swabbed before swabbing the penis. Dry areas to be swabbed should be swabbed with a sterile swab moistened with sterile water, and the cotton tip of the swab should not contact any areas other than the sample collection area. The swabs should be placed in individual, labeled swab boxes or individual paper envelopes. Internal vaginal and rectal exams may be aided by the use of a vaginal speculum or otoscopic cone.

Labels should indicate the time and date of collection, the area collected, and the collector's name. These samples should be sealed, recorded, and tracked by a chain-of-custody procedure as described elsewhere in this text. Toenail scrapings, clippings, and clumps of fur snipped with dried material may be submitted in a paper evidence fold. Biological material must never be stored at room temperature in plastic, as this will cause mildew to develop and denature the DNA evidence. Obtain swabs of the mouth under the tongue and between the cheek and gum, tongue, and the roof of the mouth. Buccal swabs taken to be used as a biological standard should be kept separate from swabs obtained from the mouth looking for evidence of human contact. Penile and scrotal swabs should be performed on males and vaginal and cervical swabs should be collected from female patients, and anal swabs should be obtained from all suspected ASA victims. If the animal defecated after the sexual assault, the stools should be collected. After thorough internal examination and swabbing for forensic evidence, vaginal or rectal washes with sterile water can be performed to extract any remaining forensic evidence if present.

Toenail scrapings, swabs, and clippings should be collected, as the animal may have scratched the suspect during the assault. Hair combing should be performed of urogenital regions; trace evidence may be present in the combings. Package the comb used, as evidence may be found on the teeth of the comb. Control hair samples should be submitted from the surrounding area. Pre-packaged sexual assault kits are commercially available and may be preferred as they are a familiar format for crime labs to process.

Sexual assault examinations are performed routinely by sexual assault nurse examiners on human victims of sexual assault, also known as medical-forensic exams. However, many people, even in law enforcement, do not realize that medical-forensic examinations should be done on animal victims of actual or suspected sexual assault (Table 6.2). Fortunately, recent years have seen a dramatic increase in the justice system's response to animal cruelty cases as well as developments in veterinary forensics. Locard's exchange principle should be applied to any victim of animal cruelty, especially in cases of ASA; a veterinarian being aware of the principle and reminding law enforcement professionals of the principle may go a long way toward preserving evidence.

Swabbing

1. All areas on the body where contact was possible should be swabbed.
2. Body surfaces should be swabbed using a swab moistened with a drop of sterile water and followed by a dry swab.
3. The swab is held at a 45-degree angle, concentrating the area in contact with skin to top of the swab.
4. When swabbing mucous membranes or moist materials, it is not necessary to moisten the first swab.
5. After the swabs are obtained, they should be dried. Using a swab dryer is an option.
6. If using a swab dryer, swabs dry for 1 hour before being packaged.
7. If a swab dryer is not available, swabs should be placed in a cardboard swab box and kept at room temperature for 24 hours. All samples should be transferred to law enforcement custody as soon as possible.
8. Label each box with the location the swabs are from. Check with your crime lab for specific packaging guidelines (Bradley and Rasile, 2014a,b).

Table 6.2 Animal cruelty offenses: distribution by type of criminal activity

Medical-Forensic Examination	
Preservation of evidence: time constraints	If a person is responsible for presenting the animal for exam, explain that as time passes, the potential for collecting evidence is lost. If an animal sexual abuse victim is examined more than 120 hours post-contact, the possibility of gathering DNA evidence is doubtful; however, a report should still be filed with law enforcement. Discuss the case with police officer/investigator, find out what has been alleged to have transpired and whether some evidence may still be present on or in the animal. Discuss evidence that may be present on the suspect or at the crime scene if known.
If unable to perform medical-forensic exam immediately	Take care not to damage any potential forensic evidence; do not feed, do not wash or take rectal temperature. Stress urgency for forensic exam. Place in a clean kennel with clean removable bedding, e-collar, keep animal NPO. Notify law enforcement if not already done, contact forensic veterinarian if available ASAP. Recommend that law enforcement examine, photograph, and swab the suspect.
Sexual assault kit/sampling equipment	Consent form if owner is known, or law enforcement seizure paperwork. Maintain chain of custody of all evidence. Anticipate other evidence: saliva, semen, blood, vomit, insects. Collect and preserve evidence; each in a separate envelope/container that is labeled not only with contents, but with date, time, and location where it was obtained. Use sterile water and sterile cotton applicators, swab bite marks and surrounding area as well as any substances that fluoresce with ultraviolet light or identified with other alternate light source. How evidence is preserved will be dictated by the crime lab facility used (contact via law enforcement ahead of time).

Record Keeping

Injuries should be notated in the medical record along with measurements. The description of the injuries found should be sufficiently described that the reader will understand the appearance of the lesions. In addition, the injuries should be drawn on a body map or diagram of the animal's outline, noted by size, appearance, and location. If there are multiple injuries, it may be useful to also maintain a separate log to describe injuries.

Documentation of perineal injuries may be done by using the face of a clock for reference points. The anus is located at the 12 o'clock position and in females the vulva is at the 6 o'clock position; everything else is in between. In the male, the scrotum is the 6 o'clock position.

A forensic ruler should be used to measure lesions, and the ruler should be included in photographs of the lesions. Measurements should be taken of each injury using width, length, and depth if applicable, and then documented. If multiple injuries are clustered in one area, measure and notate the largest to the smallest. The ASPCA maintains useful example forms for forensic documentation of animal cruelty cases at their ASPCAPro.com website.

Photography

General overall photos of the animal should be taken before photographing the individual injuries. All photographs should be taken in a series of three: overall, regional, and close-up of the lesion, one set with a ruler for scale, and another without the ruler. This helps to maintain the context of the photos. Photos should be taken of injuries before and after any cleaning, shaving, or wound treatment. In cases of alleged or suspected ASA, all genitals should be photographed, whether or not injury is noted. If using a speculum, also photograph using the speculum or a scope to record internal injuries noted. All photographs should be maintained in a computer file, with discs or portable drives of the images burned and shared for use by law enforcement or the prosecutor's office as appropriate.

Radiography

Full-body radiography should be performed and the internal reproductive organs, the abdominal cavity, and the tail-base should be examined closely for evidence of trauma. Foreign objects may be inserted into the vagina or rectum of animal sexual assault victims and retained in those locations. In the case of objects inserted into the vagina of a spayed female, the object may penetrate the end of the uterine stump and be found free in the abdomen. In some patients, the only presenting sign for ASA is peritonitis of unknown etiology. This is thought to be due to translocation of bacteria across traumatized colon wall, through micro-tears.

CASE 2

History: A young male juvenile presented to an emergency room for bite wound injuries to his genitalia. When asked how he received such wounds he openly admitted, even bragged, about having sex with the family dog. Police were contacted by hospital staff and he was arrested.

Physical Exam: The family surrendered the dog for examination. The dog was a female Australian Shepherd approximately 3 years of age. There was external bruising noted in the perineal area. A vaginal exam under sedation reveled erythema and contusions of the vaginal lining consistent with some form of object penetration. A sexual assault kit was performed and submitted to law enforcement.

Outcome: Police took custody of the forensic evidence obtained from the dog. No charges were pursued against the suspect.

CASE 3

History: Two 3-month-old, 4-pound, female Shih Tzu puppies were presented to different veterinary clinics on different days with severe rectal trauma. One puppy presented to a private practice and died immediately. The second puppy presented to another clinic in lateral recumbency. The second puppy immediately had a rectal temperature taken and the rectal area was lavaged with dilute chlorhexidine solution. The dog was placed on IV fluids and later died.

Physical Exam/Postmortem: Both puppies were transferred to a local shelter for further investigation. The outer rectal lining of both puppies was significantly dilated and lacerated, with contusions to the perineal and ventral abdominal regions. A forensic exam was performed on the first puppy only and a sample obtained. A necropsy was performed on both dogs.

Outcome: Both puppies had originated from the same home, even though they were presented to different practices. Necropsy findings in both animals were consistent with sexual abuse. There was extensive dilation of the anal tissue with lacerations and contusions to the perineum and ventral abdomen. There were proximal and distal rectal tears with concurrent peritonitis. No charges were ever filed.

CHAIN OF CUSTODY

Proper chain-of-custody practices should be followed when collecting and submitting trace evidence. Seal each envelope or bindle with packing tape. Write the time and date sealed and your initials across the tape and the envelope. Many agencies prefer that a copy of the police report be included with all submitted evidence. The detective or animal control officer working the case should be consulted for specifics of procedure. Seal the entire "kit" the same way you sealed the envelopes.

Keep a copy of the chain of custody and list of contents outside the sealed kit. The person taking possession of the kit must sign the chain of custody, thereby preserving the chain of custody.

Provide a copy of the entire veterinary report (including the chain of custody) to the investigator. Some agencies may request a copy of clinical or postmortem photos. Refer to your agency policy for direction as to whether a subpoena is required or if there is a position statement guiding making all clinical photos available to law enforcement. Be sure to keep all originals of the report and the photos.

CONDITIONING

Animals may be conditioned or trained to accept sexual abuse or to perform sexual acts. Any conditioned behaviors exhibited, such as assuming a posture of lordosis during the exam, thrusting, or spontaneous ejaculation should be noted, and videotaped if possible.

CASE 4

History: A stray 3-year-old female, small in stature, German shepherd mix was admitted to a veterinary facility. The dog appeared to have severe trauma to the outer vulva area with bleeding, scabbing, and what appeared to be ulcerative tissue.

Physical Exam: It was immediately assumed that the dog was sexually abused. Other than the external lesions described above, there were no internal lesions or indication of trauma. No perineal bruising was observed. Forensic evidence was incorrectly obtained using unsterile swabs and collection equipment. The lesions were immediately lavaged with chlorhexidine solution so no further forensic testing could be attempted.

Outcome: Impression smears of the outer vulvar lesions were eventually performed. Cytology indicated transmissible venereal tumors.

Note: It is always correct if in doubt to perform a forensic exam and collect evidence prior to doing any form of rectal temperature or treatment of the affected perineal area, but it is better to do nothing than contaminate forensic evidence if you are not equipped or able to perform it correctly. Prepare ahead or contact a forensic veterinarian to talk you through or assist with the examination.

CONCLUSION

All cases of animal cruelty, including suspected or actual ASA, are serious crimes. Any form of animal abuse can potentially be a precursor to crimes against humans. Many veterinarians are unaware of the impact their exam can have on a case. It is imperative that the veterinarian adheres to best forensic practices when caring for an animal that is a suspected victim of ASA.

References

Abel, G. G. 2008. What can 44,000 men and 12,000 boys with sexual behavior problems teach us about preventing sexual abuse? *Paper presented at the California Coalition on Sexual Offending 11th AnnualTraining Conference, Emerging Perspectives on Sexual Abuse Management*, San Francisco, CA.

Bader, D. M. G. and Gabriel S. 2010. *Forensic Nursing: A Concise Manual.* CRC Press, Boca Raton, FL.

Beirne, P., Maher, J., and Pierpoint, H. 2017. Animal sexual assault. In J. Maher, H. Pierpoint, and P. Beirne (Eds.). *The Palgrave International Handbook of Animal Abuse Studies.* London: Palgrave Macmillan, pp. 59–85.

Bradley, N. and Rasile, K. K. 2014a. Recognition and management of animal sexual abuse. *Clinician's Brief*, 4:73–75.

Bradley, N. and Rasile, K. K. 2014b. Addressing animal sexual abuse. *Clinician's Brief*, 4, 77.

Edwards, J. 2018. Arrest and prosecution of animal sex abuse (bestiality) offenders in the USA, 1975–2015. In Press. From http://www.mjennyedwards.com/laws.html and https://www.researchgate.net/project/Variance-in-Adjudicated-Cases-of-Animal-Sexual-Abuse-and-Exploitation-in-the-US/update/5b1141fe4cde260d15e25b17

English, K., Jones, L., Patrick, D., and Pasini-Hill, D. 2003. Sexual offender containment: Use of the postconviction polygraph. *Annual New York Academy of Sciences*, 989, 411–427.

Holoyda, B. 2016. Bestiality in Forensically Committed Sexual Offenders: A Case Series. *Journal of Forensic Sciences*, 62(2), 541–544.

Holoyda, B. J. and Newman, W. J. 2016. Childhood animal cruelty, bestiality, and the link to adult interpersonal violence. *International Journal of Law and Psychiatry*, 47, 129–135.

Lesandrić, V., Orlović, I., and Vjekoslav, P. 2017. Zoophilia as an Early Sign of Psychosis. *Alcoholism and Psychiatry Research: Journal on Psychiatric Research and Addictions*, 53(1), 27–32.

Merck, M. 2013. *Veterinary Forensics: Animal Cruelty Investigations*, 2nd ed. Wiley Blackwell, Ames, Iowa.

Miletski, H. 2005a. A history of bestiality. In A. M. Beetz, and A. L. Podberscek (Eds.). *Bestiality and Zoophilia: Sexual Relations with Animals.* West Lafayette, IN: Purdue University Press, pp. 1–22.

Miletski, H. 2005b. Is zoophilia a sexual orientation? A study. In A. M. Beetz, and A. L. Podberscek (Eds.). *Bestiality and Zoophilia: Sexual Relations with Animals.* West Lafayette, IN: Purdue University Press, pp. 82–97.

Munro, H. and Thrusfield, M. V. 2001. Battered pets: Sexual abuse. *Journal of Small Animal Practice*, 42, 333–337.

Munro, R. and Munro, H. M. C. 2008. *Animal Abuse and Unlawful Killing: Forensic Veterinary Pathology.* Saunders Elsevier, Edinburgh, UK.

Sinclair, L., Merck, M., and Lockwood, R. 2006. *Forensic Investigation of Animal Cruelty: A Guide for Veterinary and Law Enforcement Professionals.* Humane Society Press, United States.

Stern, A. W. and Smith Blackmore, M. 2016. Veterinary forensic pathology of animal sexual abuse. *Veterinary Pathology*, 53(5), 1057–1066.

Williams, C. and Weinberg, M. 2003. Zoophilia in men: A study of sexual interest in animals. *Archives of Sexual Behavior*, 32, 523–535.

CHAPTER 7

BLUNT FORCE TRAUMA

Patricia Norris

TYPES OF TRAUMA

An outside force can be applied with sufficient impact to cause injury to an animal. In veterinary forensic science, two common types of forces and resulting traumas are blunt force trauma (BFT) and sharp force trauma (SFT). Sharp force trauma is addressed in Chapter 8.

In agreement with Munro and Munro, the author recommends dividing the discussion and description of BFT into two successive stages: (1) the description of the wound(s) and lesions as to their nature, extent and location, and then (2) any opinion and/or conclusions that can be drawn about these injuries as their cause, and whether the cause was accidental, nonaccidental, or undetermined (Munro & Munro, 2008).

BFT is the application of an outside or external force to an animal by a non-sharp object. Ressel, Hetzel, and Ricci put forth the argument that there is a gray area between blunt and sharp force trauma but also make the very practical statement that "we apply the term *blunt force* trauma to all lesions caused by clearly non-sharp objects" (Ressel et al., 2016). The injuries from that result from BFT come from the transference of the kinetic energy from the moving object onto the body or from a moving body impacting a blunt object or a combination of the two (Gerdin, 2014). The classic equations are:

$$\text{Force} = \text{Mass} \times \text{Acceleration} \qquad \text{Kinetic Energy} = \tfrac{1}{2}\,\text{Mass} \times \text{Velocity}^2$$

This transfer of energy can cause damage to the body at a macroscopic level (abrasion, contusion/bruising, lacerations, and fractures) and at a microscopic level (cell injury and/or death). Therefore, a complete description of the effects of the trauma would include both levels.

The forces may act on the body through compression, tension, shearing, torsion, bending, or a combination of these (Gerdin, 2014). Compression pushes the tissues together, while tension pulls them apart. Bending is compression of tissue along one side, which tends to result in tension along the opposite side. Shear is a force that slides along the tissue at an angle, while torsion twists the tissue along its axis.

Although the amount of force certainly influences the extent of injuries, other factors may also be involved. These factors can include the time and surface area over which the impact occurs and the particular area of the body where the impact occurs.

The time over which the impact occurs can be a factor in at least two ways. The first is the time in which the impact is delivered to the body (i.e., the rate of impact) for a discrete incidence (Gerdin, 2014). For example, if the impact occurs over a sufficient length of time, the body may have sufficient time to stretch or otherwise adapt to the impact. In this scenario, the body may be able to absorb and dissipate the force (to a limited extent). These adaptations could minimize or at least lessen the effect of the impact to the animal's body. An impact delivered at a faster rate would not allow the body to absorb/dissipate the force and would be more likely to result in failure of the tissue (laceration, fracture, etc.). The other consideration of time would be relevant in the case of an impact that is chronically applied to an area of the body. Common examples of this chronic impact are pressure sores seen over bony prominences of emaciated animals (Figure 7.1a,b). The amount of time the bony prominence is in contact with the hard, blunt surface (concrete floor, metal cage) may affect the depth and degree of severity of the lesions of the tissues in these regions.

The surface area over which the impact is delivered can also significantly affect the damage done to the tissue. If a strong force is applied over a relatively small surface area, the amount of transferred energy is concentrated onto fewer tissues with the potential for more catastrophic effects to those tissues than if the transferred energy is spread out to more tissues. By spreading out the energy transfer over a larger surface area, the energy transfer can be better absorbed or dissipated by the increased volume of tissues.

The area of the body impacted can vary tremendously in its ability to absorb the force from the impact. Impact to skin covering soft tissues such as muscles may not cause as extensive lesions as

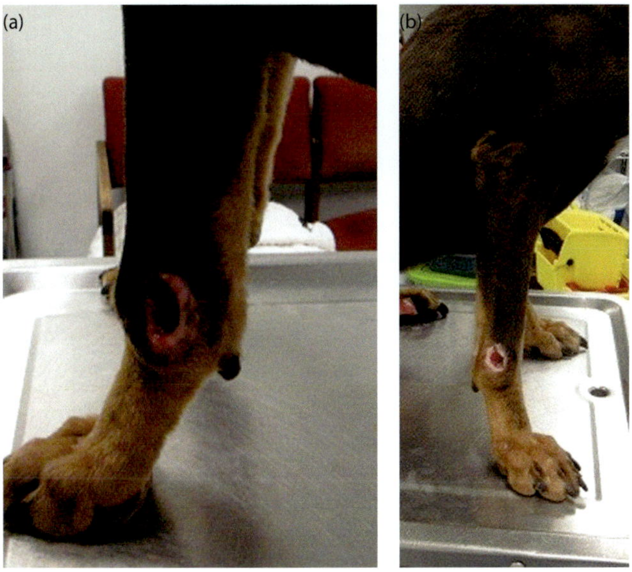

Figure 7.1 (a) This emaciated dog, housed in an animal shelter for several months with little to no bedding, developed pressure sores. (b) Pressure sores also developed on the right front leg of the same dog.

the impact of the same force, duration, and surface area to skin covering bone such as the skull. In addition, some medical conditions of the animal such as brittle bone disease or connective tissue defects such as Ehlers–Danlos (Ettinger & Feldman, 2000) may affect the final outcome of the impact to the animal.

Other factors can also influence the final outcome to the animal of BFT. The site of the impact may mean the difference between the life and death of the animal. A force sufficient to fracture a femur may cause an abrasion to the skin, bruising, and hemorrhage to the subcutaneous and overlying muscles and fragmentation of the femur. Should the force impact the femur in such a way that the femoral artery is ruptured, then the impact may be fatal. The same can be said about BFT to the abdomen; the final outcome in these cases may depend not so much on the amount of force but rather on the location of the injuries caused by the force.

Studies have shown that blunt force trauma can have an effect on the coagulation abilities and processes of animals (Abelson et al., 2013; Gottlieb et al., 2017). The effect appears to be rare in animals suffering mild to minor BFT but may be significant with severe trauma (Abelson et al., 2013; Gottlieb et al., 2017). Assessment of activated partial thromboplastin time (aPTT) should be considered in the evaluation of animals suffering severe traumatic injuries, as it may be altered in animals suffering from severe BFT (Holowaychuk et al., 2014).

In the author's training during and after veterinary school, any tear in the skin of an animal was referred to as a laceration and the term "incised wound" was rarely, if ever, used. For the sake of consistency here, the descriptions for typical lesions seen from BFT will be taken from the human medical forensic field. The most common lesions that are associated with BFT—abrasions, contusions, lacerations and fractures—are described in the following sections.

Abrasions

An abrasion can be defined as an injury to the skin in which the epidermis has been partially or completely removed by friction against a rough surface or has been destroyed by compression (DiMaio & DiMaio, 2001; Ressel et al., 2016) (Figure 7.2). In some cases, the damage extends into the superficial dermal layer as well. Abrasions can be caused by blows, falls, dragging, scratching,

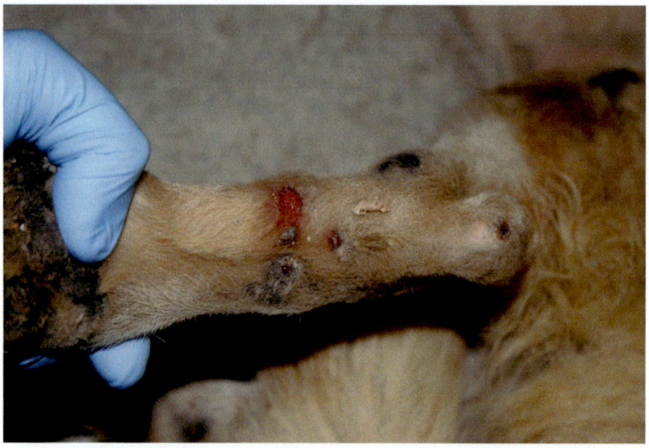

Figure 7.2 During a hoarding investigation, this abrasion was documented on the caudal surface of the leg of a dog.

rubbing, chafing, and/or indentation of the skin at the entry of a puncture wound (Figure 7.3a,b). Abrasions can be found in conjunction with other lesions such as contusions and lacerations.

Antemortem abrasions tend to be reddish brown, moist or scabbed, with blurred or indistinct margins, and may show evidence of an inflammatory reaction on histopathological examination. Healed abrasions do not show scarring (DiMaio & DiMaio, 2001). Postmortem abrasions tend to be yellow, translucent, dry surface without a scab, with sharp or well-demarcated edges and no evidence of inflammatory reaction on microscopic examination.

Depending on the angle of impact of the object with the body, abrasions can be subdivided into three categories: scrape, imprint, or contact and pattern (Ressel et al., 2016).

Scrape (or Brush) Abrasions

A scrape abrasion occurs when the object contacts the body at an angle other than 90 degrees (Ressel et al., 2016). One type of scrape abrasion, called a scratch, is caused by a pointed object moving across the skin at an angle. A typical example in veterinary medicine is a scratch by a toenail or tooth from another animal. In non-haired or lightly haired skin, if the object strikes the skin at an acute angle, it may tend to push and pile up skin cells. In these cases, the direction of the scratch can be determined as the starting point is denuded of cells, but the end point has the pile of cells where the object stopped contacting the skin (Munro & Munro, 2008). DiMaio contends that this directionality is more theoretical than practical (DiMaio & DiMaio, 2001).

As animals are often covered in hair, the hair coat of animals may diffuse the force of the scratch. Examination of the hair coat may show broken hair shafts. Because the object is moving across the hair and skin at an angle, the shape and size of the lesion may not necessarily correlate with the size and shape of the object (Gerdin, 2014).

A wide scratch abrasion may be called a graze. This type of abrasion can be associated with sliding and friction when the body tends to slide across a surface or an object slides across a large section of skin. One of the most common grazes in veterinary medicine is road rash from an animal being hit by a vehicle and sliding across the pavement. Another type of graze from friction would be the lesion caused by a collar, harness, or ligature rubbing with force and friction against the skin. These lesions should be examined closely for associated debris from the ground or pavement, or fibers from the object. Depending on the force of the friction, these pieces may be found embedded into the dermis (DiMaio & DiMaio, 2001; Gerdin, 2014; Merck, 2013).

If a scrape abrasion extends into the dermis, bleeding or fluid seepage may occur. When the fluid dries, it leaves a reddish-brown scab (DiMaio & DiMaio, 2001; Gerdin, 2014).

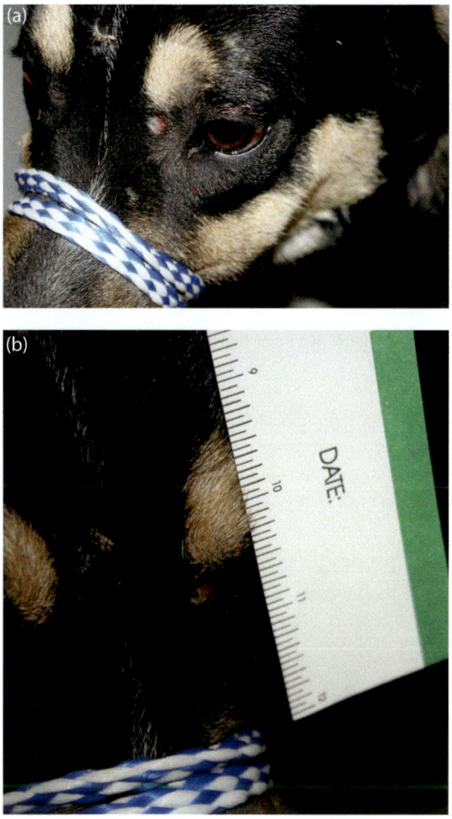

Figure 7.3 (a) Abrasion documented on the face of a dog. (b) All photographs should be made with and without a scale.

Impact (Contact) Abrasions

Impact abrasions occur when the blunt object impacts the animal perpendicularly (DiMaio & DiMaio, 2001; Ressel et al., 2016). The force impacts the body such that the tissue underneath the object is crushed. The location of the impact dictates the injury from this type of force. A dense hair coat may dissipate the force such that there is no visible lesion to the skin. If the site of impact is over a bony prominence such as the zygomatic arch or skull, an abrasion may be visible. If the site is over an area with underlying tissue such as muscle or bone, then the impact may produce a mixed trauma such as abrasion, contusion, and/or fracture of underlying bone.

Pattern Abrasions

A pattern abrasion is one in which the shape of the object can be determined by the impression it leaves on the body. The hair coat of animals tends to dissipate the impact of the object, although a distinct pattern might be visible in areas of bare skin or sparse hair coat. Depending on the object impacting the body, shaving the hair coat may reveal the pattern abrasion. A pattern abrasion can also be a scrape or impact type of abrasion. Ressel and Ricci (2016) describe how nail abrasions are the most common pattern abrasion in animals: circular nail marks from primates, crescent marks from human nails, and narrow elongated mark from canids. Their case material suggests that felids and birds of prey leave abrasions with lacerations or puncture wounds.

Contusions (Bruises)

A contusion (also called a bruise) can be defined as injury or discoloration due to hemorrhage into tissue from a ruptured blood vessel(s) beneath the skin surface without disruption of the skin itself

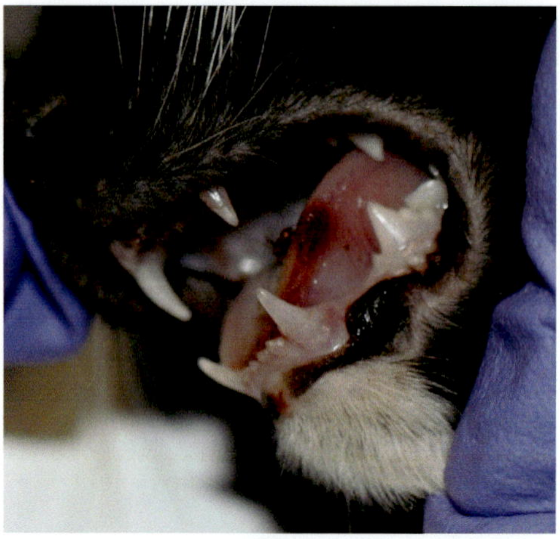

Figure 7.4 Documentation of a contusion on the tongue of a deceased cat.

(*Dorland's Illustrated Medical Dictionary*, 1988). A contusion has also been defined as a visible lesion from extravasation of red blood cells into subcutaneous and surrounding tissues due to trauma from a blunt instrument (Barington & Jensen, 2013). Contusions can also occur within the internal organs and the brain.

Contusions occur when BFT, while leaving the skin intact, ruptures blood vessels resulting in hemorrhage of the tissue underneath (Figure 7.4). The hemorrhage, under the influence of gravity, will travel along the tissue planes following the path of least resistance. Because of this, the pattern of the contusion may not accurately reflect the size and shape of the object causing the trauma. The size, shape, and development of the bruise can be affected by the thickness of the skin, location, size and type of blood vessel damaged (artery, vein, capillary), the depth and extent of the injury, the dispensability of the tissue, the type of tissue damaged, the activity of the animal, and the blood pressure of the animal at the time of the trauma. Contusions may be difficult to observe on an animal, depending on its hair coat and skin pigmentation.

Depending on the object causing the trauma and the factors described above, a contusion may retain the pattern of the object. Although patterned bruises are relatively rare in animals, in part due to the dissipation of the force from the hair coat, the patterned bruise called a "tramline" caused by impacts from narrow objects onto thinly-haired skin have been seen in animals (Munro & Munro, 2008). Tramlines are parallel lines of bruising separated by skin that appears normal. This occurs when the object compresses but does not rupture the underlying blood vessels, while shearing forces tear the peripheral vessels resulting in hemorrhage. In pigs, due to the light pigmentation and thin hair coat, the pattern of the object causing the trauma may be distinctive, especially after the removal of the epidermis (Barington, & Jensen, 2013).

Contusions go through color changes as well. Initially, the red blood cells appear bright to dull red depending on their oxygenation saturation. As the oxygen levels fall, the bruise turns from red to blue-purple. The red blood cells deteriorate and leak hemoglobin. As the hemoglobin is metabolized to different byproducts, the color changes to green (biliverdin), yellow (hematoidin), and brown (hemosiderin) (DiMaio & DiMaio, 2001; Gerdin, 2014; McCausland & Dougherty, 1978; Munro & Munro, 2008).

Hemorrhage can occur as a result of BFT or natural causes. A bruise is typically considered to be a hemorrhage of 1 cm or larger in diameter (Gerdin, 2014). Hemorrhage measuring <3 mm is called petechiae and may be caused by thrombocytopenia (low platelet counts) or diseases causing platelet dysfunction. Purpura is hemorrhage measuring 3 mm–1 cm and is often a result of a disease-causing vasculitis (Gerdin, 2014). Ecchymosis, hemorrhage of >1 cm, can be caused by a disease such as von Willebrand disease (Côtė 2007) or ingestion of a toxic substance such as rodenticides

(Miller & Zawistowski, 2013). Ecchymosis and bruising may be difficult to distinguish clinically. Large amounts of hemorrhage containing blood clots are often called hematomas (Gerdin, 2014).

Clinically, bruising must be differentiated from disease conditions and/or toxin ingestion. If the opportunity exists, the clinician should take an exhaustive history from the owner, officer, or reporting party. Since the size, pattern of distribution, and location of the lesions may be the deciding factors, the veterinarian should conduct a thorough physical examination with mapping and detailed description of each lesion. Depending on the situation, the clinician should consider clipping or shaving the animal to locate all of the lesions (Munro & Munro, 2008). BFT to the skin may cause concurrent abrasions and/or lacerations. These lesions would not be associated with disease or toxin ingestion (Gerdin, 2014). On live animals, the lesions should be photographed as soon as possible and again during the subsequent evaluations of the animal to chart the progress, development, and resolution of the contusion(s). On deceased animals, the skin should be reflected from the body to document all of the contusions. Forensic necropsy techniques and documentation of blunt force trauma are further explained in Chapter 10.

Lacerations

A medical dictionary defines a laceration as "a torn, mangled wound" (*Dorland's Illustrated Medical Dictionary*, 2008). In the author's experience in veterinary medicine practice, the word "laceration" is typically used to mean any cut or tear in the animal's skin or underlying tissue regardless of cause. In the veterinary forensic field, a laceration is an injury caused by BFT in which the tissue is torn, split, sheared, stretched, or crushed (Gerdin, 2014; Tong, 2014) (Figure 7.5). Like contusions, lacerations can be found in internal organs without visible wounds to the overlying tissues. Lacerations may or may not reflect the shape of the object which caused the injury. DiMaio suggests that long thin objects tend to produce linear lacerations, while objects with flatter surfaces tend to produce irregular or Y-shaped lesions (DiMaio & DiMaio, 2001).

The margins of lacerations may also show abrasions and/or contusions. In addition, there is often bridging present within the laceration. This bridging is made up of tissue strands that were not completely torn at the time of the trauma. Bridging is typically not found in sharp force wounds (Gerdin, 2014; Gerdin & McDonough, 2013). Sharp force wounds are generally called incised, chop, or stab wounds. Keep in mind that a gray area may exist between BFT and SFT: a dull knife may cause abrasions on the skin margins, and a large, heavy object with a sharp edge may produce a lesion mimicking an incised wound. In these cases, terms such as "penetrating blunt trauma" or "puncture wound" may be appropriate (DiMaio & DiMaio, 2001; Recknagel & Stefan et al., 2011).

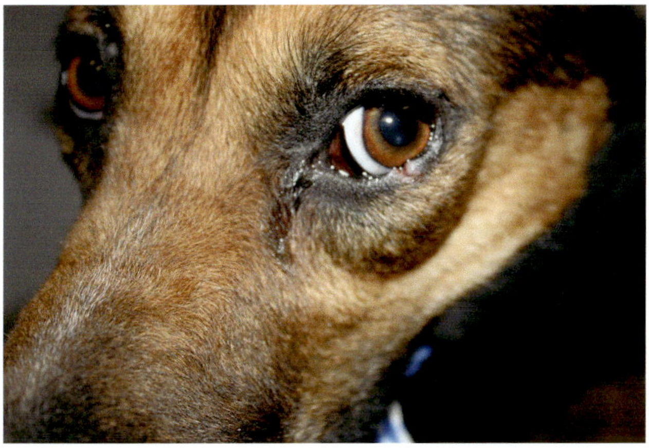

Figure 7.5 Documentation of an eyelid laceration with swelling (edema).

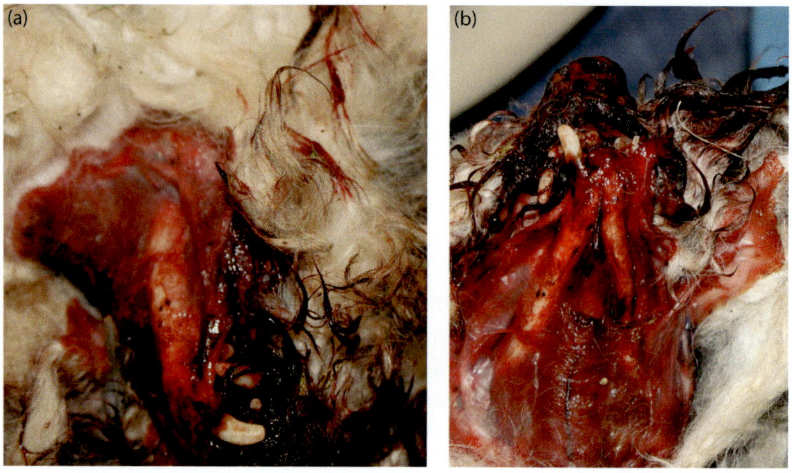

Figure 7.6 (a) Example of a degloving injury to mandible of a dog. (b) Additional view of the same degloving injury.

Exploration of the depths of a laceration may show debris or trace evidence from the impacting object (DiMaio & DiMaio, 2001). In addition, if the BFT occurs tangentially to the skin, the side from which the blow came may be beveled and abraded while the skin on the receiving side may be undermined (DiMaio & DiMaio, 2001).

A special class of laceration is an avulsion. Avulsions are seen when the shearing force impacts the body at an angle such that the tissues are twisted. These avulsions may cause the creation of pockets between and within tissue in which hemorrhage may occur. If severe enough, an avulsion may result in the "twisting off" of the skin from the underlying tissue or of the organ from the pedicle attaching it to the body (avulsion of a kidney). A typical avulsion injury is the degloving of an extremity (Figure 7.6a,b). An injury resulting in the skin being peeled away from the paw/leg is often from a vehicular accident or may be secondary to a ligature (Merck, 2013). In the author's experience, some cases in which the skin has been peeled back from the rib cage were the result of coyote attacks on small dogs and cats.

Fractures

A fracture is caused by a force that exceeds the cohesive strength of a bone. The fracture is directly related to the type, direction, and energy of the force causing the injury (Fossum, 2007; Gerdin, 2014; Touroo, 2012) (Table 7.1). Except possibly with the greenstick fracture, soft tissue injuries occur concurrently with fractures. Lacerations, contusions, puncture, and/or penetrating wounds and hemorrhage which can sometimes be extensive will also be seen with fractures. Fractures in live animals are typically diagnosed by physical examination followed by an orthopedic examination supported with diagnostic imaging such as radiography and possibly computed tomography (CT) (Fossum, 2007). In

Table 7.1 Forces and types of fractures

Type of Fracture	Type of Force
Transverse	Bending
Oblique	Compression (axial)
Oblique, comminuted	Bending with compression
Spiral	Torsion
Comminuted	High energy
Simple	Low energy

Source: Adapted from Fossum, T. 2007. *Small Animal Surgery*. 3rd ed. St. Louis MO: Mosby Elsevier.

general, a minimum of two views (e.g., lateral and cranial/caudal views of limbs) of an area should be radiographed and whole-body radiographs should be taken when BFT is suspected (Gerdin, 2014). On occasion, advanced modalities such as magnetic resonance imaging (MRI) and bone scintigraphy may be beneficial for difficult diagnoses and/or documenting recovery (Fossum, 2007).

Fractures can be caused by falling or jumping, animal fighting, sports injuries, motor vehicle accidents (MVAs), and nonaccidental injuries (NAIs), such as blunt force trauma and gunshots (Fossum, 2007; Gerdin, 2014; Harvey et al., 1990; Intarapanich et al., 2016; Tong, 2014) (Figure 7.7a,b). Tong noted six characteristics associated with fractures that may raise the index of suspicion that a fracture or fractures may be the result of NAI. These include (1) multiple fractures; (2) fractures in more than one area of the body; (3) transverse fractures; (4) delayed seeking of veterinary care for a fracture; and (5) multiple fractures found to be in different stages of healing (Lockwood & Arkow, 2016; Tong, 2014). A retrospective study of injuries noted that in MVA the injuries tended to be abrasions, degloving wounds of limbs, sacroiliac luxations, fractures of the pelvis and/or sacrum, and thoracic injuries (pneumothorax and pulmonary contusions). The study found the injuries associated more with NAI included skull fractures, scleral hemorrhage, broken teeth, fractured vertebrae, rib fractures that could be on either or both sides of the body,

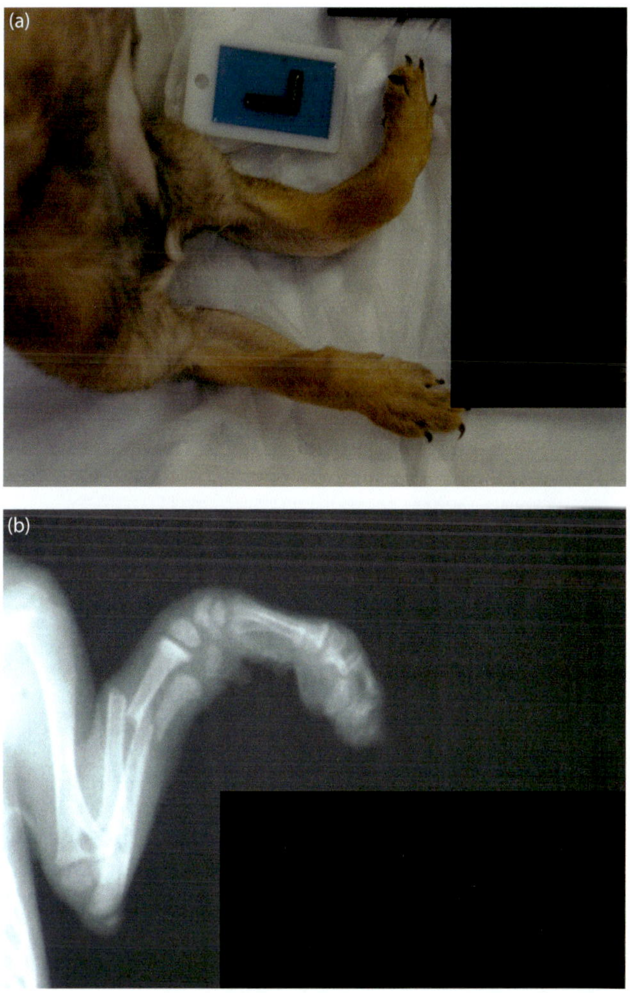

Figure 7.7 (a) The left front leg of this dog was fractured during a domestic violence incident. (b) This is the radiograph of fractured radius and ulna of the same dog.

torn fractures of the skull, teeth, vertebrae, and ribs, scleral hemorrhage, and damage to the nail beds. This study also found, like the Tong study, that the fractures often appeared to be in a more advanced stage of healing (Intarapanich et al, 2016; Tong, 2014).

Pathologic Fractures

Pathologic fractures are fractures that occur with or without the application of an outside force. Pathologic fractures occur because the bone has been severely weakened or destroyed by a disease process. The three most common disease processes include infectious disease, metabolic disease, and neoplastic disease (Fossum, 2007). An additional possibility, in the case of small thin-boned dogs confined to a small cage for a long time, is that the bones are more fragile than normal from disuse. The evaluation of the animal and the fracture should include diagnostic assessments to rule out these possibilities.

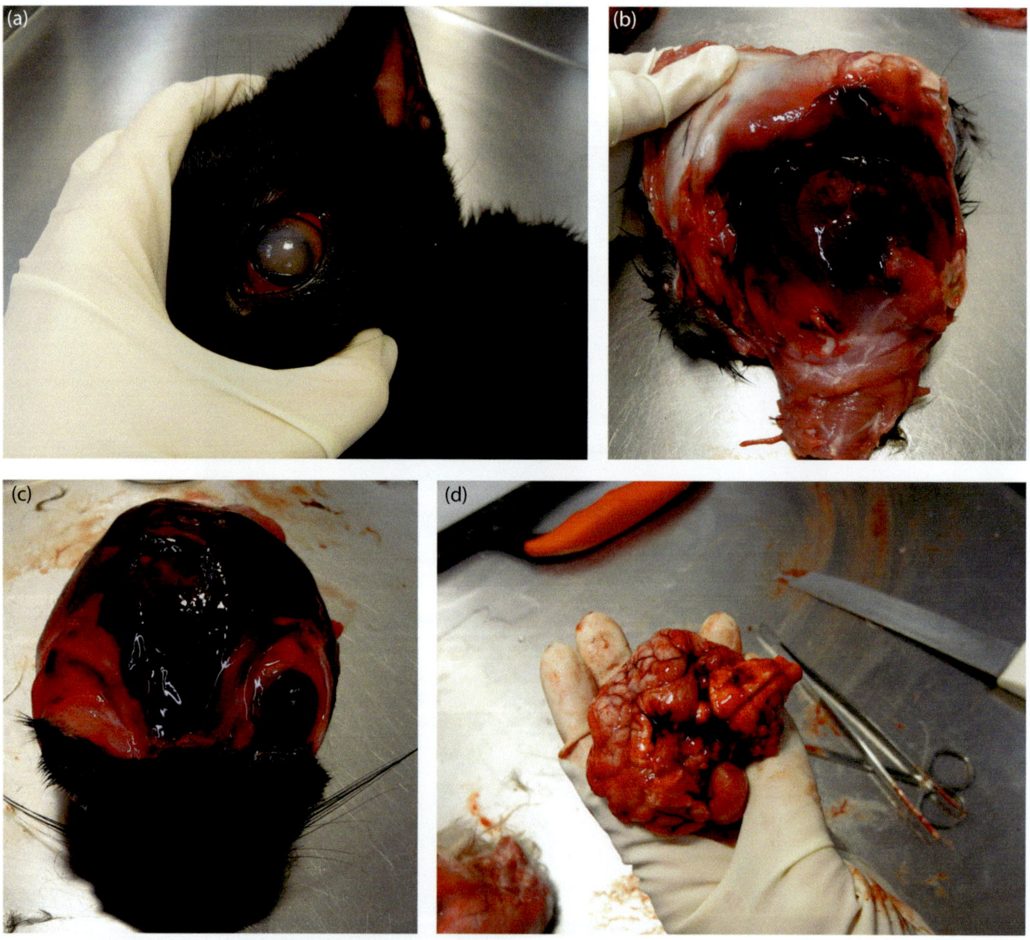

Figure 7.8 (a) This scleral hemorrhage reportedly occurred due to BFT to head of kitten. (b) The skin of the skull has been reflected back to demonstrate the hemorrhage due to the reported BFT inflicted on this kitten. (c) Additional documentation of the hemorrhage on the surface of the skull of this kitten reportedly due to BFT. (d) Examination of the brain documents the extend of the hemorrhage associated with the reported BFT. (Photographs courtesy of Mahogany Wade-Caesar, MS, DVM.)

Skull Fractures and Blunt Force Trauma to the Head

With most fractures, the associated hemorrhage is not necessarily problematic for the surrounding tissues. This is not the case for skull fractures and BFT to the head. The initial force impacting the skull damages the tissues in the immediate area (coup lesion). Given the confined nature of the skull and the consistency of the brain, the force is transmitted to the brain and the brain will impact the opposite side of the skull also resulting in tissue damage (contrecoup lesions) (Ressel & Ricci, 2016; Touroo, 2012). The hemorrhage is most severe at the area of impact (Figure 7.8a–d). The hemorrhage may be in the form of an epidural hematoma (bleeding in the space between the medial surface of the skull and the dura), a subdural hematoma (bleeding in the space between the brain and the dura, which may also occur without a skull fracture), and/or a cerebral contusion (bleeding within the brain) (Gerdin, 2014; Ressel & Ricci, 2016; Touroo, 2012).

AGING OF LESIONS

Abrasions

Histologic examination of abrasions may be used to roughly estimate their age, based on the general sequence of events of wound healing (hemorrhage, infiltration of leukocytes, and regeneration and fibrosis), and bolstered by species-specific knowledge of infiltrates and processes, where applicable (Gerdin, 2014; Gerdin & McDonough, 2013).

Generally there are considered to be four stages of healing: scab formation, epithelial regeneration, subepidermal granulation, and regression (Ressel & Ricci, 2016; Roberston & Hodge, 1972; Touroo, 2012). A guideline for time intervals for each stage is: scab formation, 0–12 hours; epithelial regeneration, 30–72 hours; subepidermal granulation, 5–12 days; and regression, more than 12 days (Ressel & Ricci, 2016; Roberston & Hodge, 1972; Touroo, 2012). Caution is advised in using this general guideline to assess the age of a lesion, as the effects of variables such as species variability, incidence of self-trauma, malnutrition, protein deprivation, and disease are not fully known and may be challenged in a court setting.

Contusions

In both medical and veterinary forensics, there has been longstanding interest in the aging of contusions. As discussed above, contusions go through stages of development from the initial BFT, through the migration of the red blood cells (RBCs) of the hemorrhage via the path of least resistance and gravity, to appearance near or within the skin layer where the contusion may or may not be visible. The change in oxygenation levels of the RBCs and then the metabolism and subsequent production of byproducts of the RBCs result in the color changes in bruises.

Controversy exists as to the reliability and accuracy of aging contusions based on their visual appearance. Langlois extensively reviewed the range of colors often attributed to bruises along with the physiologic processes that may account for these changes in humans. He discussed the use of spectrophotometry to assess contusions and detailed the limitations of relying on visual assessments (Langlois & Gresham, 1991; Langlois, 2007).

Observations of the visual appearance of contusions in specific animal species have been made. Munro references a study in which bruises in cattle and sheep were documented to be red and hemorrhagic between 0–10 hours, becoming dark colored by 24 hours, having a watery consistency by 24–38 hours, and then appearing to be rusty orange in color with a soapy texture when more than 3 days old (Gracey et al., 1999; Merck, 2013; Munro & Munro 2008, 2013). Other authors state that visual assessment of bruises as a method to determine the age of a bruise has been shown to be unreliable (Barington & Jensen, 2013; Grossman et al. 2011; Pilling et al., 2010).

Histology may assist in the general evaluation of a contusion to estimate whether the lesion is very recent (less than 24 hours), recent (12–24 hours), or more than a few days old (more than 48 hours) (Gerdin, 2014; Gerdin & McDonough, 2013). Evaluation of the histologic appearance, progression, and healing associated with contusions in some animals has been published. Research on the estimation of the age of bruises in pigs is generally based on studies of wound healing (Barington & Jensen, 2013). Studies show it is possible to estimate the age of bruises in pigs to be more or less than 4 hours. For bruises more than 4 hours old in pigs, an age of the contusion can be estimated based on the pattern of cell infiltration and by comparing the reaction to wound healing (Oehmichen, 2004; Raekallio, 1980). The average number of neutrophils in the subcutis and the average number of macrophages in the muscle tissue correlated with the age of the bruises. In addition, the localization of leukocytes in muscle tissue was also time dependent. Using this information, bruises could be determined as being either less than 4 hours or between 4 and 10 hours of age in pigs (Barington & Jensen, 2013).

Similar studies have been done using lamb and calf carcasses sent for slaughter. McCausland and Dougherty (1978) established histologic criteria for aging contusions for up to 48 hours. The criteria considered the presence and relative numbers of polymorphonuclear leucocytes, macrophages, fusiform cells, and new capillaries. This study found that the microscopic criteria were the same in the two species and concluded that the yellow color present in contusions that were approximately 48 hours old was useful in the aging of these lesions in calves and lambs.

In addition to the age of the lesion, the force of the impact may also affect the histologic findings. One study found that the impact force significantly influenced the severity of hemorrhage and amount of necrotic muscle tissue. The number of neutrophils in the subcutaneous tissues was increased with increasing age of bruises and impact force. The author of that study argues that in the case of BFT, whenever possible, the underlying muscle as well as the subcutis should be evaluated. The study also found that the number of macrophages in the muscle tissue was relevant for age determination only in contusions resulting from the highest forces. Therefore, forensic histologic evaluation of contusions should consider the impact force as well as timing of the blunt force trauma incident (Barington et al., 2016).

Fractures

Fracture healing has three phases: inflammatory, reparative, and remodeling phase (Harvey et al., 1990). The inflammatory phase begins at the time of injury and includes hematoma formation and necrosis of damaged osteocytes and other cells leading to an influx of inflammatory cells and the secretion of cytokines, growth factors, and inflammatory mediators (Fossum, 2007; Harvey et al., 1990; Ressel et al., 2016). The reparative phase begins with organization of the hematoma, the beginning of neovascularization, and appearance of mesenchymal cells (Carlson & Weisbrode 2012, Harvey et al., 1990, Ressel & Ricci, 2016). The vascularization of mature animals differs from that of immature animals in that immature animals have arteries that perforate the bone (Fossum, 2007). This difference may affect the extent of the hemorrhage and hematoma formation. The reparative stage generally starts within 24–48 hours of the injury (Carlson et al. 2012; Ressel et al., 2016). The reparative stage progresses with the appearance of woven bone (approximately 36 hours post injury), then proceeds with the generation of a bone callous and formation of hyaline cartilage (4–6 weeks) (Carlson & Weisbrode, 2012; Harvey et al., 1990; Ressel et al. 2016). The final stage of remodeling occurs within months to years as the form takes the shape to best adapt to the stresses and pressures applied to it (Fossum, 2007; Harvey et al., 1990; Ressel et al. 2016).

A unique characteristic of fracture healing is the occurrence of delayed healing, or nonunion healing of fractures. Delayed healing is diagnosed when a fracture has not healed in the expected time frame. Factors that may cause delayed healing include excessive movement of the bone fragments, lack of or inadequate immobilization of the fracture site, inadequate blood supply to damaged tissue, misalignment of the fracture pieces, bone loss leading to insufficient scaffolding, infection of the surrounding tissues, infection of the bone fragments (osteomyelitis), administration of certain medications (e.g., corticosteroids), starvation, age (usually geriatric patients), and/or metabolic disease (Fossum, 2007; Harvey et al., 1990). A study has also shown that thoracic trauma may delay healing of fractures in rats (Raekallio, 1980). This may be a consideration in an animal with multiple, severe injuries.

A nonunion healing occurs when the bone no longer continues to heal. This is noted radiographically as an unhealed bone, typically with sclerotic edges that may appear smooth. Nonunions occur when there is failure to treat a fracture or inadequate immobilization of the fracture during the healing phase (Fossum, 2007; Harvey et al., 1990). Consideration of the possibility of a delayed union or a nonunion fracture should be included in the assessment of the animal and the estimated time of injury.

Challenges to Aging Abrasions, Contusions, Lacerations, and Fractures

While there has been extensive research into lesions and the aging of such associated with BFT, less research has been done in animals. There are over 40,000 vertebrate species and millions of invertebrates (Cooper & Cooper, 2008). One of the most basic questions is: Can the criteria for assessing these lesions and their age be extrapolated across all species, or even just the warm-blooded species? If not, then which, if any, are valid and for which species? Clinical veterinary forensic medicine may be called into play for an animal of any species that is found neglected, ill, injured, or deceased.

Research shows that cats heal more slowly than dogs, with granulation tissue formation being faster in dogs than cats. Other studies show that wounds in ponies heal quicker than in horses due to a more intense initial inflammatory response (Munro & Munro, 2013).

Other challenges involve the animals themselves. Animals are notorious for licking, chewing, scratching, and even self-mutilating lesions that they can reach with their mouths and paws/claws/hooves. Although the initial injury may have been from BFT, the animal itself may cause secondary lesions that obscure or complicate the evaluation of the initiating trauma. Their actions may cause secondary infections which may profoundly affect the clinical and histologic findings. Healing times and processes can be confounded and delayed significantly.

Other factors that may affect the appearance of lesion(s) and healing are malnutrition, severe protein deficiency, parasite infestation(s), poor or excessive body condition, age, concurrent disease, additional injury(ies), and so on. To what degree these factors would affect an individual would need to be considered in the evaluation of that animal and the estimation of the age of the lesion. Therefore, the clinician may want to determine if the visual appearance and/or histologic finding(s) is/are consistent with the time frame of the reported trauma, rather than attempting to specify a precise age of a lesion (Gerdin, 2014; Gerdin & McDonough, 2013).

ASSESSMENT OF BFT VICTIMS

Clinical veterinary forensic medicine applies the science to the clinical patient. Given the science and information above concerning BFT and the injuries it may cause to animals, the following aspects should be considered when assessing an animal suspected of having suffered such an incident:

1. *Physical examination:* As described in Chapter 1, the animal should receive a full physical examination with documentation of both normal and abnormal findings. Injuries should be examined closely for trace evidence, particularly the depths of lacerations and the area beneath the nails/claws.

2. *Blood work:* Consideration should be given to evaluating a complete blood cell count and serum chemistry. In animals showing contusions, a full clotting profile, including an activated partial thromboplastin time, should be considered. Other blood work tests necessary to eliminate or confirm other rule-outs should be completed, as well. It may be appropriate, with some lesions, to biopsy the area, including the juncture between the normal and abnormal areas.
3. *Radiographs:* Full-body radiographs should be considered for both live and deceased animals. Full-body radiographs may detect injuries not visually detectable and may aid in establishing a pattern of injury. Advanced imaging such as MRI, CT, ultrasonography, and scintigraphy can be utilized in select cases.
4. *Documentation of the injuries:* Documentation of all injuries is critical. The external injuries should be located and described in relation to distinctive anatomical landmarks (preferably two landmarks per injury). The injuries should be described as to type (abrasion, contusion, laceration, fracture), size (length, width, depth), shape (regular, irregular, indistinct, patterned), color, and any associated findings (edema, foreign bodies, debris, etc.). Descriptions of fractures should include whether they are open or closed, greenstick or complete, degree of comminution, location, and whether articular surfaces are included along with the amount of displacement. Evidence of healing, secondary infections/injuries, and related findings should also be documented. Any evidence of internal injuries should be noted. Results of all ancillary tests should be documented as well.
5. *Photography:* The entire animal, including all injuries, should be photographed. The photographs should include overall, mid-range, and close-up views of the animal and each injury.
6. *Reevaluations:* As some recent lesions, such as bruises, may develop over time, the animal and its injuries should be reevaluated and photographed as appropriate for the case.
7. *Deceased animal:* Deceased animals should be documented and photographed in situ and then submitted for a forensic necropsy and appropriate diagnostic testing.

References

Abelson, A. L., T. E. O'Toole, A. Johnston, M. Respess and A. M. de Laforcade. 2013. Hypoperfusion and acute traumatic coagulopathy in severely traumatized canine patients. *Journal of Veterinary Emergency and Critical Care.* 23(4): 395–401.

Barington, K. and H. E. Jensen. 2013. Forensic cases of bruises in pigs. *Veterinary Record.* 173(21): 526–531.

Barington, K. and H. E. Jensen. 2016. The impact of force on the timing of bruises evaluated in a porcine model. *Journal of Forensic and Legal Medicine.* 40: 61–66.

Carlson, C.S. and S. E. Weisbrode. 2012. Bones, joints, tendons and ligament. In: James F. Z. and M. Donald McGavin (eds)*Pathologic Basis of Veterinary Disease.* 5th ed. St. Louis: MO: Mosby Elsevier.

Cooper, J. E. and M. E. Cooper. 2008. Forensic veterinary medicine: A rapidly evolving discipline. *Forensic Science, Medicine and Pathology.* 4: 75–82.

Côté, E. 2007. *Clinical Veterinary Advisor: Dogs and Cats.* St. Louis: MO: Mosby Elsevier.

DiMaio, V. and D. DiMaio. 2001. *Forensic Pathology.* 2nd ed. Washington, DC: CRC Press.

Dorland's Illustrated Medical Dictionary. 27th ed. 1988. Philadelphia, PA: W.B. Saunders Company.

Ettinger, S. and E. C. Feldman. eds. 2000. *Textbook of Veterinary Internal Medicine.* 5th ed. Philadelphia, PA: W.B. Saunders Company.

Fossum, T. 2007. *Small Animal Surgery.* 3rd ed. St. Louis MO: Mosby Elsevier.

Gerdin, J.A. and S. P. McDonough. 2013. Forensic pathology of companion animal abuse and neglect. *Veterinary Pathology.* 50(6): 994–1006.

Gerdin, J. A. 2014. (Lectures) Veterinary Forensic Pathology. Summer 2014, Course 6576, University of Florida: ASPCA.

Gottlieb, D., J. Prittie, Y. Buriko, and K. E. Lamb. 2017. Evaluation of acute traumatic coagulopathy in dogs and cats following blunt force trauma. *Journal of Veterinary Emergency and Critical Care.* 27(1): 35–43.

Gracey, J. F., D. S. Collins, and R. J. Huey. (eds) 1999. From Farm to Slaughter. In *Meat Hygiene*. 10th ed. London: Saunders, 163–196.

Grossman, S. E., A. Johnston, P. Vanezis, and D. Perrett. 2011. Can we assess the age of bruises? An attempt to develop an objective technique. *Medicine Science and the Law*. 51: 170–176.

Harvey, C. E., C. D. Newton, and A. Schwartz. 1990. *Small Animal Surgery*. Philadelphia, PA: J.B. Lippincott.

Holowaychuk, M. K., R. M. Hanel, R. D. Wood, L. Rogers, K. O'Keefe, and G. Monteith. 2014. Prospective multicenter evaluation of coagulation abnormalities in dogs following severe acute trauma. *Journal of Veterinary Emergency and Critical Care*. 24(1): 93–104.

Intarapanich, N. P., E. C. McCobb, R. W. Reisman, E. A. Rozanski, and P. P. Intarapanich. 2016. Characterization and comparison of injuries caused by accidental and non-accidental blunt force trauma in dogs and cats. *Journal of Forensic Sciences*. 61(4): 993–999.

Langlois, N. E. and G. A. Gresham. 1991. The ageing of bruises: A review and study of the colour changes with time. *Forensic Science International*. 50(2): 227–238.

Langlois, N. E. I. 2007. The science behind the quest to determine the age of bruises–a review of the English language literature. *Forensic Science. Medicine and Pathology*. 3(4): 241–251.

Lockwood, R. and P. Arkow. 2016. Animal abuse and interpersonal violence: The cruelty connections and its implications for veterinary pathology. *Veterinary Pathology*. 53(5): 910–918.

Maguire, S., M. Mann, J. Sibert, and A. Kemp. 2005. Can you age bruises accurately in children? A systematic review. *Archives of Disease in Childhood*. 90: 187–189.

McCausland, I. P. and R. Dougherty. 1978. Histological ageing of bruises in lambs and calves. *Australian Veterinary Journal*. 54: 525–527.

Merck, M. 2013. *Veterinary Forensics*. 2nd ed. Ames, IA: Wiley-Blackwell Publishing.

Miller, L. and S. Zawistowski. 2013. *Shelter Medicine for Veterinarians and Staff*. 2nd ed. Ames, IA: Wiley-Blackwell.

Munro, R. and H. M. C. Munro. 2008. *Animal Abuse and Unlawful Killing: Forensic Veterinary Pathology*. Philadelphia, PA: Saunders Elsevier.

Munro, R. and H. M. C. Munro. 2013. Some challenges in forensic veterinary pathology: A review. *Journal of Comparative Pathology*. 149(1): 57–73.

Oehmichen, M. 2004. Vitality and time course of wounds. *Forensic Science International*. 144: 221–231.

Pilling, M. L., P. Vanezis, D. Perrett, and A. Johnston. 2010. Visual assessment of the timing of bruising by forensic experts. *Journal of Forensic and Legal Medicine*. 17: 143–149.

Raekallio, J. 1980. Histological estimation of the age of injury and histochemical and biochemical estimation of the age of injuries. In *Microscopic Diagnosis in Forensic Pathology*. Eds J. A. Perper & C. H. Wecht. Illinois, USA: Thomas Books, pp. 3–35.

Recknagel, S., R. Bindl, J. Kurz, T. Wehner, C. Ehrnthaller, M. W. Knoferl, F. Gebhard, M. Huber-Lang, L. Claes, and A. Ignatius. 2011. Experimental blunt chest trauma impairs fracture healing in rats. *Journal of Orthopedic Research*. 29(5): 734–739.

Ressel, L., U. Hetzel, and E. Ricci. 2016. Blunt force trauma in veterinary forensic pathology. *Veterinary Pathology*. 53(5): 941–961.

Roberston, I. and P. R. Hodge. 1972. Histopathology of healing abrasions. *Forensic Science*. 1(1): 17–25

Tong, L. J. 2014. Fracture characteristics to distinguish between accidental injury and non-accidental injury in dogs. *Veterinary Journal*. 199: 392–398.

Touroo, R. 2012. *Introduction Veterinary Forensic Sciences*. Spring course 6575. Gainesville, FL: University of Florida.

CHAPTER 8

SHARP FORCE TRAUMA

Adriana de Siqueira and Patricia Norris

INTRODUCTION

Sharp force trauma consists of lesions caused by sharp objects, such as knives, scissors, screwdrivers, needles, or machetes (Pounder, 2000; Humphrey & Hutchinson, 2001; Bury et al., 2012; Parmar et al., 2012), and each object may leave a unique mark on the skin that may lead to their identification. In some cases, lesions caused by sharp objects may be misinterpreted as blunt force lesions, thus a histopathological analysis may be helpful to differentiate them (Ressel et al., 2016). Postmortem identification of lesions is crucial to the investigation of possible crimes against animals. For this purpose, veterinary pathologists play an important role by identifying the nature of the lesions, describing, measuring, and photographing them, giving a clue of the type of objects that might have caused them (Gerdin & McDonough, 2013; Salvagni et al., 2014). Wound patterns, such as position, shape, depth, and path may provide a lead as to whether the act that provoked them was intentional or accidental (Knight, 1975; Dettmeyer et al., 2014)—in this case, this information should be analyzed together with other crime scene findings, such as bloodstain pattern analysis (Attinger et al., 2013).

Lesions are not always easily identified in animals due to their physical aspects, such as the covering of hair and/or the color and the depth of their skin (Campbell-Malone et al., 2008; Munro & Munro, 2008; Merck, 2012). Thus, dry blood on the fur/feather and/or skin may indicate an underlying sharp lesion. Postmortem interval, the action of microorganisms and local entomofauna (Brundage & Byrd, 2016), environmental aspects, and crime scene elements (e.g., weather—humidity, dryness, or other climate conditions, or the place where the carcass was found—lake, river, indoor or outdoor) may interfere with the actual morphology of the lesions (Byard et al., 2005). Sharp lesions may or may not be lethal. Therefore, the necropsy may clarify the cause with the complete external and internal examination, which may give cause, manner, and mechanism of death.

Animals may present with sharp injuries that result from a variety of causes, such as social violence. They are considered as family members and they may be victimized by abusive acts as well as hunting, traffic accidents, or those involving vessels in the case of marine animals, therapeutic procedures, and religious practices (Arkow, 1994; Ascione et al., 2007; Aquila et al., 2014; Melo et al., 2014).

DEFINING SHARP TRAUMA LESIONS AND SHARP OBJECTS

Sharp trauma lesions can be divided into four categories: (1) stab wounds, (2) incised wounds, (3) chop wounds, and (4) therapeutic/diagnostic wounds (Jones et al., 1994; Di Maio & Di Maio, 2001; Hainsworth et al., 2008; Dettmeyer et al., 2014). In some cases, it is important to hypothesize the positioning between the perpetrator and the victim, and the type of sharp object that caused the lesion (Spitz, 1993). Some characteristics of sharp objects and the stabbed area may provide some leads about it. Table 8.1 depicts their definitions and corresponding sharp objects.

Stab and Incised Wounds

Stab and incised wounds are the most common sharp force trauma and are often caused by a knife. The parts of the knife are ricasso, handle, guard, edge, and tip or point (Figure 8.1). Depending on the force and the angle of the thrust, characteristic marks will be left in the skin and subcutaneous tissue.

Each part of the knife may leave a different skin mark, and the pattern of the lesion should be analyzed to determine which part of the knife was involved in the stab (Di Maio & Di Maio, 2001; De Siqueira et al., 2016). The ricasso leaves a square-like appearance on skin. When the force of the stab is greater, it is possible to see the mark of the guard. It should be considered that

Table 8.1 Sharp lesions: Type, definition, and instruments

Type of Sharp Lesion	Definition	Corresponding Sharp Object
Stab wounds	Depth of the wound exceeds its length and results from the movement of the long axis of the blade in the plane approximately perpendicular to the surface of the body	Knives,[a] scissors, screwdrivers, barbecue forks, broken glass,[c] arrows
Incised wounds	Slashes and cuts where the length exceeds the depth	The same that cause stab wounds
Chop wounds	Produced by heavy instruments, with an incised wound on the skin and bony fractures and/or a deep groove in the bone	Axes, cleavers, and machetes
Therapeutic/diagnostic wounds[b]	Result from veterinary intervention[b]	Needles, scalpels

[a] Most common.
[b] These occur when animals involved in criminal cases have been provided veterinary care (Salvagni et al., 2016).
[c] Depends on the regularity of shape and sharpness.

the animal may move while the perpetrator is trying to stab it or hesitates to stab. Therefore, the knife may leave superficial incised marks on skin, similar to wounds left by attempted suicide in humans (Spitz, 1993; Di Maio & Di Maio, 2001; Merck, 2012). In cases of hunting or killing to provide meat, incised wounds on the neck are performed to cause exsanguination. In the former, the hunter may try to remove the projectile from the tissue or to hide the wound caused by it (Stroud & Adrian, 1996).

In some cases, it is difficult to distinguish between the patterns created by common straight-edged and serrated knives. Such differentiation will only be possible in cases where the latter leave linear or parallel scratches around the wound (Pounder et al., 2011; Crowder et al., 2013). In animals, fur and feathers may obscure the identification of these lesions on gross examination, and the histopathological analysis may help only in cases where there were marks of striations in bones or cartilage. However, the angle of the impact was found to be the most influential factor for the distance between striations left by blade teeth.

In incised wounds, the angle of the blade in contact with the skin will determine the type of margin of the wound. For example, an extreme angle may produce a skin flap, whereas an oblique angle will produce an undermined margin on one side and a beveled margin on the other side. Another characteristic of incised wounds is the direction of the cut of the knife because the cut may be more superficial at the terminal segment of the wound. However, when analyzing a sharp wound, the pathologist should consider: (1) that the movement between perpetrator and victim

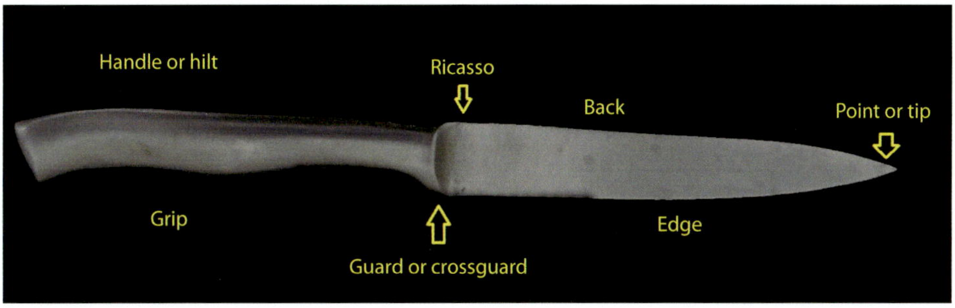

Figure 8.1 Major components of a typical knife.

is dynamic; (2) the topography of the stabbed area; and (3) the characteristics of the underlying tissue, for example, if there is bone, cartilage, or soft tissue and viscera (Di Maio & Di Maio, 2001; Dettmeyer et al., 2014).

Other factors that determine the pattern of wound edges are the force and the angle of the thrust (Mazzolo & Desinan, 2005). If the bone or cartilage is hit by the stab, the impact of the sharp object will leave marks. The greater the force employed by the perpetrator on the stab, the greater the chance of internal organs being hit, depending on the positioning between the perpetrator and the victim (Munro & Munro, 2008). The positioning or the angle of entry of stab wounds will determine the type of skin mark: a perpendicular angle of entry will leave the mark of the guard and it will be symmetrical; in other angles, the skin mark will be above or below the wound. In animals, such differentiation may be difficult to determine because of the depth and pigmentation of their skin, or their type of hair coat. Some attackers immobilize the head of the animal to stab the ventral aspect of the neck; in these cases, if the affected structures are on the left side of the neck, it is possible that the attacker was right-handed, and vice versa if they were left-handed (Campbell-Malone et al., 2008; Munro & Munro, 2008).

Another problem occurs when the guard is not symmetrical, because the lesion may be misinterpreted as blunt force trauma (BFT) (Hainsworth et al., 2008; Ressel et al., 2016). BFT leaves lacerations or bridges of soft tissue between the edges of the lesion that presents irregular edges and tearing, with contusion. The edges of sharp wound are angular or linear and usually without contusion. A contusion may be present if parts of the knife are dull, and depending on the angle and force used during the stabbing (Spitz, 1993; Di Maio & Di Maio, 2001). In addition, the characteristics of the affected area may affect these findings. With BFT, it is common to find lacerations, contusions, abrasions, and bony fractures depending on the force utilized and anatomical localization of the wound. Histopathological analysis and crime scene findings should be analyzed together to make this assessment (Byard et al., 2006).

Screwdrivers and scissors are sharp objects that leave distinctive marks on skin, mainly scrape marks left by the dull surfaces of these objects. A Phillips screwdriver produces X-shaped lesions, if it is superficial, with four edges and a circular pattern, similar to a bayonet. A flathead screwdriver produces slit-like lesions with abraded margins, with regular and small squared ends. Sharp lesions caused by scissors may cause two stab wounds; however, the morphology of the lesion will depend on the force used to produce sharp wounds, and/or if they were held by the handle or the finger holes (Parmar et al., 2012).

Chop Wounds

These wounds are caused by heavy objects, such as machetes, axes, and meat cleavers and may produce characteristic lesions mainly in bones. They may present striations that lead to the identification of the chop object. For example, machetes produce small bony fragments in wider and irregular wounds, and axes cause crushing of the bones (Lynn & Fairgrieve, 2009). Due to the pattern of lesions left on the bones, the detailed, accurate examination of the wound may help to differentiate chop wounds from BFT.

Animal dismemberment occurs in cases of meat consumption and it may occur for ritualistic purposes. In some cases, in addition to the utilization of axes or machetes, a saw may be used for dismemberment. Upon examination, the edges of such postmortem injuries are dry and lack evidence of bleeding (Spitz, 1993). Some religions practice animal sacrifice in rituals in which animals are offered to the devotees' gods based on their beliefs. Different animal species are utilized for such purposes, such as pigeons, poultry, bovine, and ovine and caprine species. In cases of Satanistic rituals, cats and dogs are often seen with signs of mutilation and torture (Gill et al., 2009).

Boat propellers may cause chop-like wounds in marine animals, whose lesions may be a combination of sharp and blunt trauma (Lightsey et al., 2006). Boat propellers may cut the skin, but

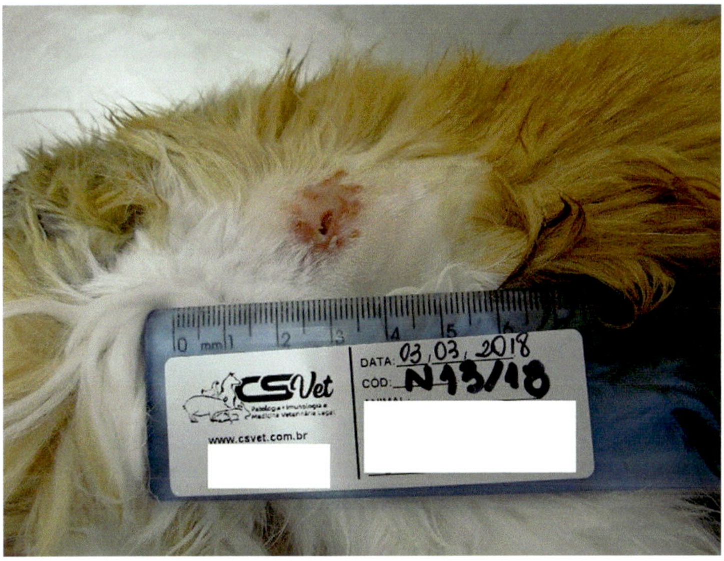

Figure 8.2 Feline neck, left aspect. Therapeutic wound due to ozone therapy. Note the clean and circular border of the lesion.

they can also amputate a limb. A detailed, accurate examination is necessary because these lesions may not be readily seen. Depending on the anatomical site, these injuries may lead to death or, in the case of survival, the animal may present with complications due to post-injury infections. High-speed boats may leave parallel lesions, with patterns consistent with both chop and incised wounds. A high-speed boat propeller may leave closely parallel lesions that may present characteristics of both incised and chop wounds, or even blunt and incised ones, since propellers may not have sharp edges (Byard et al., 2012).

Therapeutic/Diagnostic Wounds

Therapeutic or diagnostic sharp injuries are mainly caused by health care procedures, including incisions, venipuncture, and catheter placement (Dettmeyer et al., 2014). These lesions are produced by needles and scalpels (Figure 8.2). Such injuries may vary from spots of blood to large hematomas in skin and subcutaneous tissue, depending on the force utilized to produce them or coagulative disorders of the animal (Fogh & Fogh, 1988). Incisions may result from a surgical procedure or be a part of therapeutic procedures to treat lesions caused by lacerations, that need to be cleaned and sutured or to remove bullets. However, in a report of a serial killing of dogs and cats, death resulted from hypovolemic shock caused by multiple sharp injuries from needles, which lacerated large blood vessels and thoracic viscera (Salvagni et al., 2016).

MISCELLANEOUS OBJECTS

Barbecue forks with two or three prongs can cause sharp injuries, that can be identified as groups of two or three wounds, with regular or irregular distances between the wounds caused by each prong depending on the angle and force of the stabbing (Spitz, 1993; Di Maio & Di Maio, 2001). Broken glass produces incised wounds with jagged and sharp edges. In cases of multiple wounds, they may exhibit distinctive shapes, depths, and sizes. In these cases, the wounds should be inspected for glass fragments (Spitz, 1993; Di Maio & Di Maio, 2001).

Hunting activities that utilize arrows and crossbow bolts may produce sharp force wounds. However, even domestic animals may suffer penetrating wounds from arrows or other non-identified sharp objects, as revealed in a study of cats (De Siqueira et al., 2012). Wounds will vary from circular to X-shaped lesions and in varying sizes and shapes. Because of the force used to produce them, wounds may have bony fractures, hemorrhage, and damage to internal organs. They may be difficult to differentiate from bullet wounds. The track of the wound may assist with differentiation, because a bullet may leave an abrasion ring and an arrow will slice the underlying tissue and may cut a line in the adjacent hair. In both cases, radiographic examination is crucial. Bullets may leave lead pathway or fragments that may reach the bone, and other sharp objects may leave metal fragments only seen by radiographic examination. Ice picks may cause lesions that mimic shotgun pellets because they result in small, slit-shaped or round wounds (Spitz, 1993; Di Maio & Di Maio, 2001).

The veterinary pathologist may be summoned as an expert witness (Frederickson, 2016), and may be asked about positioning, type of object/weapon, and force utilized by the perpetrator. Biomechanical factors to consider include the properties of the knife (weight, shape, and sharpness), velocity and type of thrust and the movement of the knife within the body, skin and organ resistance (viscera, bone), movement of the victim, movement of the knife from the skin to its termination within the body, and the speed and direction of delivery of the blow (Knight, 1975; Annaidh et al., 2012). However, the exact quantification of forces can be difficult to determine, even with all these elements present.

IDENTIFYING AND EXAMINING SHARP TRAUMA LESIONS

The identification and examination of sharp trauma lesions requires a protocol, as depicted in Figure 8.3.

Considering all types of sharp injuries that may be encountered in a criminal investigation, the following procedures are recommended (Byard et al., 2006; Cooper & Cooper, 2008; Merck, 2012; Salvagni et al., 2014; Brownlie and Munro, 2016):

1. *Radiographic examination*: Before performing the necropsy in cases of suspicious death, radiographic examination will aid in discovering bone fractures and/or blade fragments. Another use is to differentiate tool marks, which may indicate the type of weapon used to produce the stab wound.
2. *Inspection of fur/feathers and skin*: Sharp lesions in humans are readily seen and are obvious. This is not always the case in animals, due to hair coat or feathers, pigmentation of the skin, and unique characteristics of the skin depending on the species. A careful external examination should be performed to look for crusted or dry blood. The wound should be palpated. In cases of multiple wounds, they should be individually numbered and documented using a diagram of the animal body and indicating the anatomical location.
3. *Photographic documentation*: Photograph the animal with and without identification. As each wound is found, photograph it with a scale and animal identification before and after washing with water and shaving. Whenever possible, compare the photographs with those taken at the crime scene. In some cases, the morphology of the wound may be changed by the movement of the carcass or due to postmortem phenomena. Modifications of the positioning of the carcass, in addition to postmortem phenomena, may modify the shape of the lesions, leading to misinterpretations. Thus, it is recommended that photographs should be taken both at the crime scene and in the necropsy room. These photographs should be compared, and differences should be noted and analyzed.

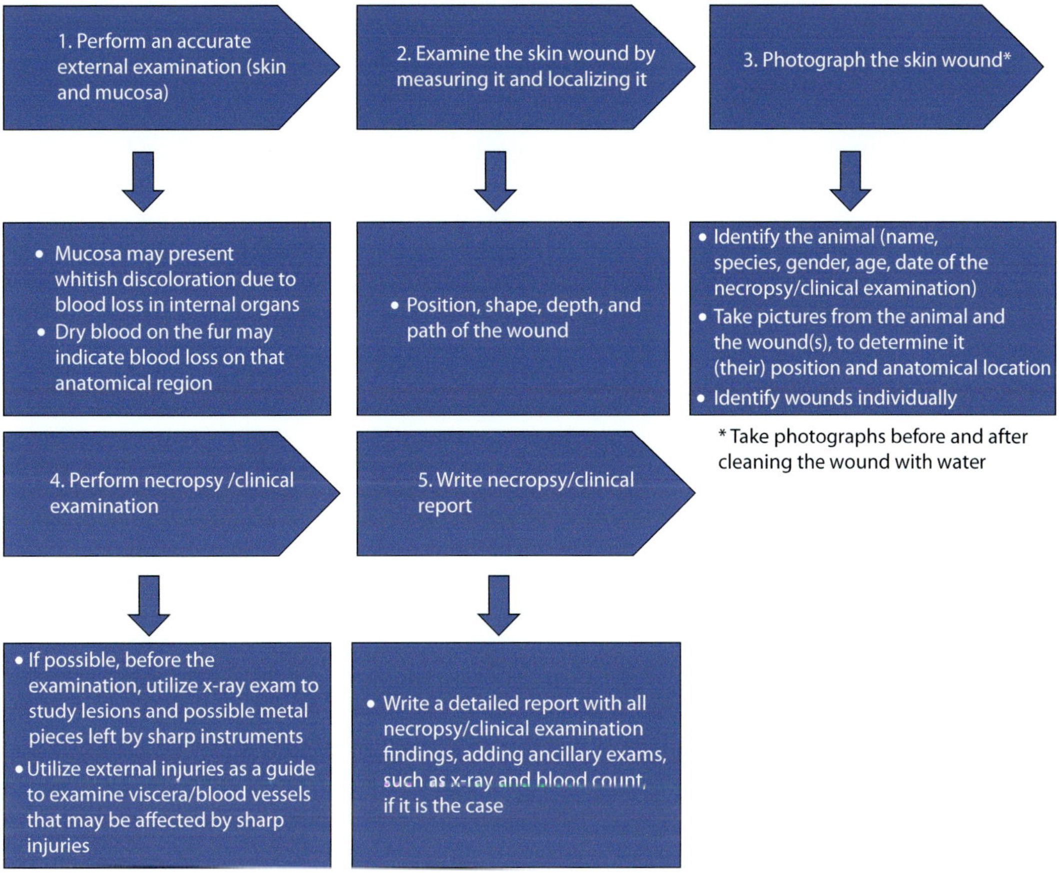

Figure 8.3 Stepwise flowchart for the examination of sharp force injury.

4. *Accurate description of lesions*: This should include marks around the wound, color, edges, and shape. Reflect the skin to reveal and document possible lesions in subcutaneous tissue. The shape of the lesion may be affected by the sharpness of the instrument, the movement of the victim, the force of the thrust and the underlying tissue (bone, cartilage, soft tissue, viscera). A typical sharp force wound may occur when the victim moves or the knife twists. In such cases, lesions may present a V-shaped pattern that is produced by a slight movement of the victim or the knife, and/or a Y- or L-shaped pattern that can be produced by a secondary path produced by the removal of the knife.
5. *Obtain an estimation of blade width and length*: To obtain an estimation of blade width and length, reconnect and measure the edges of the lesion. The length of the stab wound is equal to or greater than the width of the blade. In cases of multiple lesions, each one should be measured, and the average measurement may give an estimate of the blade width and length. Consider the contraction of the skin due to its elasticity. Other consideration should be given to the cleavage or Langer's lines. They are patterns of collagen and elastic fibers that produce elasticity to the skin, and the shape of the wound should be correlated to the angle formed with these lines. It should be noted that a particular knife can be ruled out, but not conclusively ruled in without metal fragments matching it from a wound.
   - Stab parallel to Langer's lines: A *narrow slit-like wound* is produced.
   - Stab perpendicular to Langer's lines: These fibers pull the edges of the wound apart, creating a *gaping wound*.

- Stab oblique to Langer's line may produce an asymmetrical or semicircular patten depending on the fibers.

6. *Trace the track of the stab*: Examine underlying tissue and viscera that may be affected in deeper wounds due to the force and the angle of the thrust.
7. *Histopathological analysis*: Collect fragments of both sides of the wound to look for evidence of hemorrhage. Chop wounds and stab wounds made with dull objects, or with uneven edges should be differentiated from blunt force trauma lesions. In cases that involve bone and cartilage, the detailed and accurate observation of the specimens may help to find marks of sharp objects, which may lead to their identification.

DETERMINING MANNER, MECHANISM, AND CAUSE OF DEATH

For forensic purposes, it may be important to determine if the lesions were inflicted postmortem or antemortem, if they were lethal or not, and the age of lesions. This information may be determined at necropsy and histopathological exam. If the lesion was inflicted antemortem, hemorrhage will occur and be detected by gross and/or microscopic examination and will extend through several tissue planes. Postmortem hemorrhage is generally distinguished microscopically by confinement of the blood to a single fascial plane; however, if the body is putrefied, such determination is difficult (Betz & Eisenmenger, 1996; Sauvageau & Racette, 2008).

The cause of death should be defined as sharp injury with an indication of the topographical region(s) affected, and it depends on the site and vessels/organs involved. The most frequent cause of death is hypovolemic shock resulting from hemorrhage, which occurs when major blood vessels are affected (see Table 8.2). Stabbing in the thorax or abdomen may cause internal bleeding (Dettmeyer et al., 2014). When the limbs, head, or neck are affected, there may be a large amount of blood at the crime scene. The mechanism of death depends on the site and vessels/organs involved, but the most frequent cause of death is hypovolemic shock resulting from hemorrhage, which occurs when major blood vessels are severed (Di Maio & Di Maio, 2001; Dettmeyer et al., 2014). Lesions in the thorax and neck are most likely to be fatal; when the trachea is affected, the mechanism of death may be asphyxiation due to the aspiration of blood. The manner of death should be determined in conjunction with crime scene data, that is, bloodstain patterns. Histopathological analysis may be useful in cases of multiple wounds, because it may be difficult to determine the timing of wounds relative to death based only on their gross appearance. The amount of hemorrhage may not be a reliable indicator because unless the circulation has ceased for some time, some bleeding is likely to occur from injuries that are inflicted near death or shortly thereafter (Illinois Coroners and Medical Examiners Association, 2007).

Table 8.2 Sharp force trauma: Cause, mechanism, and manner of death considerations

Cause of Death[a]	Mechanism of Death	Manner of Death
• Sharp injury with an indication of the topographical region(s) affected	• Hypovolemic shock resulting from hemorrhage • Hemothorax; hemoperitoneum	• Should be determined in conjunction with crime scene data, as blood stain analysis, and possible weapon found
Consider the vessels and viscera affected by the thrust and multiple lesions		It is not common to find the weapon inserted in the wound, or even at crime scene

[a] Munro & Munro (2008); Schlesinger et al. (2014).

In cases of sharp force trauma to the lung, liver, spleen, or kidney, bleeding in the internal cavities is also likely to occur for several hours after death until all of the blood from the area has drained (Di Maio & Di Maio, 2001; Dettmeyer et al., 2014).

Late complications due to sharp force trauma include undetected bleeding in internal viscera, including lung, liver, spleen, or kidney, that may occur for several hours after death. Infections may also occur in days or weeks after sharp injuries have occurred in cases of non-lethal lesions. Sharp force injuries in intestines may cause peritonitis. Other causes may be from intentional wounds, such as torture or aggression and undiagnosed accidental stab wounds, such as in vehicular accidents (Byard et al., 2012).

CRIME SCENE FINDINGS

Whenever possible, in cases of violent or suspicious deaths of animals, crime scene investigation is highly recommended. In cases of sharp force injuries, bloodstain pattern analysis (BPA) may give information about angle and distance of the blood spatter (de Bruin et al., 2011; Attinger et al., 2013). Its shape and pattern may indicate its source or point of origin. Blood spatter indicates the direction of the origin of the bleeding. All length and width spatter measures should be taken, in addition to the distance of the drops from their point of origin. BPA may provide information about the type of weapon used, the position of the weapon(s), the objects, the victim and the perpetrator, the movement of the individuals present at the crime scene, and an estimation of the number of stabs, blows, or shots. A castoff pattern may be found in cases of sharp force trauma, where the blood is projected from an object or other bloody source. The information provided by these parameters may assist in the reconstruction of the events that culminated in death. BPA should be paired with necropsy findings and molecular biology. The DNA of the blood may be considered to determine whether the blood is from the animal or from the perpetrator, who may have received injuries during the stabbing or shooting. The reconstruction of events may be interpreted based on this information. The examination of the crime scene may contribute to the elucidation of the cause and manner of death, as well as the interpretation of particular postmortem findings (Peschel et al., 2011; Osborne et al., 2016).

CONCLUSION

Sharp force trauma injuries present diagnostic challenges to the veterinary pathologist and clinician, partly because of fur/feathers and skin characteristics of the animal. A detailed, accurate examination is required. The differentiation between sharp and blunt injuries is necessary because in some cases their patterns may be similar. Utilization of radiographic examination and histopathological analysis may be helpful in such cases to detect bony fractures and metal fragments. It is important to remember that the interaction between the perpetrator/sharp object and the victim is dynamic, thus some lesions may present with different patterns from those expected in regular sharp force injuries.

References

Annaidh, A.N., Cassidy, M., and Curtis, M. 2012. A combined experimental and numerical study of stab-penetration forces. *Forensic Science International*. 233(1–3):7–13.

Aquila, I., Di Nunzio, C., and Paciello, O. 2014. An unusual pedestrian road trauma: From forensic pathology to forensic veterinary medicine. *Forensic Science International*. 234:e1–e4.

Arkow, P. 1994. Child abuse, animal abuse, and the veterinarian. *Journal of the American Veterinary Medical Association*. 204(7):1004–1007.

Ascione, F.R., Weber, C.V., and Thompson, T.M. 2007. Battered pets and domestic violence: Animal abuse reported by women experiencing intimate violence and by nonabused women. *Violence Against Women*. 13(4):354–373.
Attinger, D., Moore, C., and Donaldson, A. 2013. Fluid dynamics topics in bloodstain pattern analysis: Comparative review and research opportunities. *Forensic Science International*. 231(1–3):375–396.
Betz, P. and Eisenmenger, W. 1996. Morphometrical analysis of hemosiderin deposits in relation to wound age. *International Journal of Legal Medicine*. 108(5):262–264.
Brownlie, H.W. and Munro, R. 2016. The veterinary forensic necropsy: A review of procedures and protocols. *Veterinary Pathology*. 53(5):919–928.
Brundage, A. and Byrd, J.H. 2016. Forensic entomology in animal cruelty cases. *Veterinary Pathology*. 53(5):898–909.
Bury, D., Langlois, N. and Byard, R.W. 2012. Animal-related fatalities—Part I: Characteristic autopsy findings and variable causes of death associated with blunt and sharp trauma. *Journal of Forensic Sciences*. 57(2):370–374.
Byard, R.W., Gehl, A. and Tsokos, M. 2005. Skin tension and cleavage lines (Langer's lines) causing distortion of ante- and postmortem wound morphology. *International Journal of Legal Medicine*. 119(4):226–230.
Byard, R.W., Kemper, C.M. and Bossley, M. 2006. Veterinary forensic pathology: The assessment of injuries to dolphins at postmortem. In: Tsokos, M., ed. *Forensic Pathology Reviews*. Vol 4. Totowa, NJ: Humana. 415–436.
Byard, R.W., Machado, A. and Woolford, L. 2012. Symmetry: The key to diagnosing propeller strike injuries in sea mammals. *Forensic Science, Medicine, and Pathology*. 9(1):103–105.
Campbell-Malone, R., Barco, S.G. and Doust, P.Y. 2008. Gross and histologic evidence of sharp and blunt trauma in North Atlantic right whales (Eubalaena glacialis) killed by vessels. *Journal of Zoo and Wildlife Medicine*. 39(1):37–55.
Cooper, J.E. and Cooper, M.E. 2008. Forensic veterinary medicine: A rapidly evolving discipline. *Forensic Science, Medicine, and Pathology*. 4(2):75–82.
Crowder, C., Rainwater, C.W. and Fridie, J.S. 2013. Microscopic analysis of sharp force trauma in bone and cartilage: A validation study. *Journal of Forensic Sciences*. 58(5):1119–1126.
de Bruin, K.G., Stoel, R.D. and Limborgh, J.C. 2011. Improving the point of origin determination in bloodstain pattern analysis. *Journal of Forensic Sciences*. 56(6):1476–1482.
de Siqueira, A., Cassiano, F.C., Landi, M.F.D.A., Marlet, E.F. and Maiorka, P.C. 2012. Non-accidental injuries found in necropsies of domestic cats: A review of 191 cases. *Journal of Feline Medicine and Surgery*. 14(10):723–728.
de Siqueira, A., Cuevas, S.C., Salvagni, F.A. and Maiorka, P.C. 2016. Forensic veterinary pathology: Sharp injuries in animals. *Veterinary Pathology*. 53(5):979–987.
Dettmeyer, R.B., Verhoff, M.A. and Schütz, H.F. 2014. Pointed, sharp, and semi-sharp force trauma. In: Dettmeyer, R.B., Verhoff, M.A. and Schütz, H.F., eds. *Forensic Medicine: Fundamentals and Perspectives*. Berlin, Germany: Springer. 135–154.
Di Maio, V.J. and Di Maio, D. 2001. Wounds caused by pointed and sharp-edged weapons. In: Di Maio, V.J. and Di Maio, D., eds. *Forensic Pathology*. 2nd ed. New York, NY: CRC Press.
Fogh, J.M. and Fogh, I.T. 1988. Inherited coagulation disorders. *Veterinary Clinics of North America: Small Animal Practice*. 18(1):231–243.
Frederickson, R. 2016. Demystifying the courtroom: Everything the veterinary pathologist needs to know about testifying in an animal cruelty case. *Veterinary Pathology*. 53(5):888–893.
Gerdin, J.A. and McDonough, S.P. 2013. Forensic pathology of companion animal abuse and neglect. *Veterinary Pathology*. 50(6):994–1006.
Gill, J.R., Rainwater, C.W. and Adams, B.J. 2009. Santeria and Palo Mayombe: Skulls, mercury, and artifacts. *Journal of Forensic Sciences*. 54(6):1458–1462.
Hainsworth, S.V., Delaney, R.J. and Rutty, G.N. 2008. How sharp is sharp? Towards quantification of the sharpness and penetration ability of kitchen knives used in stabbings. *International Journal of Legal Medicine*. 122(4):281–291.
Humphrey, J.H. and Hutchinson, D.L. 2001. Macroscopic characteristics of hacking trauma. *Journal of Forensic Sciences*. 46(2):228–233.
Illinois Coroners and Medical Examiners Association. 2007. Guidelines for the determination of manner of death. http://www.coronersillinois.org/images/20151116085155.pdf

Jones, S., Nokes, L. and Leadbeatter, S. 1994. The mechanics of stab wounding. *Forensic Science International.* 67(1):59–63.

Knight, B. 1975. The dynamics of stab wounds. *Forensic Science.* 6(3):249–255.

Lightsey, J.D., Rommel, S.A. and Costidis, A.M. 2006. Methods used during gross necropsy to determine watercraft-related mortality in the Florida manatee (*Trichechus manatus latirostris*). *Journal of Zoo and Wildlife Medicine.* 37(3):262–275.

Lynn, K.S. and Fairgrieve, S.I. 2009. Macroscopic analysis of axe and hatchet trauma in fleshed and defleshed mammalian long bones. *Journal of Forensic Sciences.* 54(4):786–792.

Mazzolo, G.M. and Desinan, L. 2005. Sharp force fatalities: Suicide, homicide or accident? A series of 21 cases. *Forensic Science International.* 147(suppl):S33–S35.

Melo, R.S., Silva, O.C. and Souto, A. 2014. The role of mammals in local communities living in conservation areas in the northeast of Brazil: An ethnozoological approach. *Tropical Conservation Science.* 7(3):423–439.

Merck, M.D. 2012. Patterns of non-accidental injury: Penetrating injuries. In: Merck, M.D., ed. *Veterinary Forensics: Animal Cruelty Investigations.* Ames, IA: Wiley-Blackwell. 101–114.

Munro, R. and Munro, H.M.C. 2008. Introduction. In: Munro, R. and Munro, H.M.C., eds. *Animal Abuse and Unlawful Killing: Forensic Veterinary Pathology.* London, UK: Elsevier. 1–2.

Osborne, N.K., Taylor, M.C. and Zajac, R. 2016. Exploring the role of contextual information in bloodstain pattern analysis: A qualitative approach. *Forensic Science International.* 260:1–8.

Parmar, K., Hainsworth, S.V. and Rutty, G.N. 2012. Quantification of forces required for stabbing with screwdrivers and other blunter instruments. *International Journal of Legal Medicine.* 126(1):43–53.

Peschel, O., Kunz, S.N. and Rothschild, M.A. 2011. Blood stain pattern analysis. *Forensic Science, Medicine, and Pathology.* 7(3):257–270.

Pounder, D.J. 2000. Sharp injury. In: Siegel, J.A., Saukko, P.J., and Knupfer, G., eds. *Encyclopedia of Forensic Sciences.* London, UK: Academic Press. 340–342.

Pounder, D.J., Bhatt S., and Cormack, L. 2011. Tool mark striations in pig skin produced by stabs from a serrated blade. *American Journal of Forensic Medicine and Pathology.* 32(1):93–95.

Ressel, L., Hetzel, U., and Ricci, E. 2016. Veterinary forensic pathology: Gross and histological features of blunt force trauma. *Veterinary Patholology.* 53(5):941–961.

Salvagni, F.A., de Siqueira, A., Fukushima, A.R., de Albuquerque Landi, M.F., Ponge-Ferreira, H., and Maiorka, P.C. 2016. Animal serial killing: The first criminal conviction for animal cruelty in Brazil. *Forensic Science International.* 267:e1–e5.

Salvagni, F.A., de Siqueira, A., and Maria, A.C.B.E. 2014. Patologia veterinária forense: Aplicação, aspectos técnicos e relevância em casos com potencial jurídico de óbitos de animais. *Clinica Veterinaria.* 112:58–73.

Sauvageau, A. and Racette, S. 2008. Postmortem changes mistaken for traumatic lesions: A highly prevalent reason for coroner's autopsy request. *American Journal of Forensic Medicine and Pathology.* 29(2):145–147.

Schlesinger, L.B., Gardenier, A., and Jarvis, J. 2014. Crime scene staging in homicide. *Journal of Police and Criminal Psychology.* 29(1):44–51.

Spitz, W.U. 1993. Sharp force injury. In: Spitz, W.U., and Spitz, D.J., eds. *Spitz and Fisher's Medicolegal Investigation of Death: Guidelines for the Application of Pathology to Crime Investigation.* 3rd ed. Springfield, IL: Charles C Thomas. 252–310.

Stroud, R.K. and Adrian, W.J. 1996. Forensic investigational techniques of wildlife law enforcement investigations. In: Fairbrother, A., Locke, L.N., and Hoff, G.L., eds. *Noninfectious Diseases of Wildlife.* Ames, IA: Iowa State University Press. 3–18.

CHAPTER 9

GUNSHOT WOUNDS AND WOUND BALLISTICS

Nancy Bradley-Siemens

INTRODUCTION

Veterinary forensics is a novel discipline within the forensic sciences. The importance of forensic veterinarians and veterinary pathologists within this discipline are particularly important in cases involving projectile injuries. Projectile injuries can present in the live animal patient, may result in euthanasia, or are often lethal and tend to result in litigation. This chapter will describe projectile injuries encountered within the United States and the types of weapons and ammunition associated with these types of injuries. Stages of ballistics including internal, external, and terminal as well as wounding capacity are discussed. A forensic examination is described including gunshot wound examination, establishing projectile trajectories, range and direction determination, imaging procedures, collection and containment of projectile evidence, and gunpowder analysis. This chapter illustrates aspects of projectile injury investigation that need to be considered in combination with standard forensic practices and procedures to ensure reliable conclusions are reached for medicolegal and diagnostic purposes.

CONSIDERATIONS IN ANIMAL BALLISTIC CASES

Projectile injuries may present as a seemingly uncomplicated problem to diagnose in medical terms; however, these cases can involve live or deceased animals, can be extremely complex, and should not be initiated without full knowledge of the case circumstances and expectations of the applicant (case submitter) (Bradley-Siemens & Brower, 2016). As of this writing, there is currently no minimum standard of documentation to be completed if the legal status of a case is unknown. Throughout this chapter, the author recommends steps similar to human forensic protocols and suggests these be performed for every case involving a projectile injury (Bradley-Siemens & Brower, 2016).

Not all animal shootings are illegal. The shooting has to be determined to have been done without an owner's consent, out of hunting season, without statutory protection, or have caused unnecessary suffering before being investigated as a crime (Munro & Munro, 2008; Bradley-Siemens & Brower, 2016). Gunshot wound injuries to animals can be accidental or intentional and can involve complex crime scenes and investigations. The accused suspects range from juveniles to adults. These types of cases may incorporate public endangerment or property damage and can involve legal or illegal firearms (Munro & Munro, 2008; Merck, 2013; Bradley-Siemens & Brower, 2016).

In order to understand and interpret gunshot injuries, forensic veterinarians and forensic veterinary pathologists need to understand wound ballistics and be aware that these types of cases require investigation and documentation of large quantities of evidence. The veterinarian must be able to distinguish entrance and exit wounds and interpret factors that may affect or disturb their appearance. The veterinarian may need to assist in the approximation of the distance from which a projectile was fired based on wound examination and "wound path" trajectory into and/or through the animal body. Collection and preservation of ballistic evidence and assistance with other facets of an investigation may be required. Finally, accurate documentation and preparation of a forensic medical report involve knowledge of medicolegal needs and requirements (Merck, 2013; Bradley-Siemens & Brower, 2016).

TYPES OF PROJECTILE INJURY CASES ENCOUNTERED

There is limited information on the number of animal abuse cases investigated or prosecuted annually involving projectile injuries. Currently, there is no national database for these types of crimes or profile information on suspects committing animal abuse using firearms (Merck, 2013; Bradley-Siemens & Brower, 2016).

Projectile-injury profile characteristics that have been reported illustrate that shooting incidents predominantly involve male suspects and that the type of firearm used may reflect the age of the suspect (Lockwood, 2011, 2013; Tedeschi, 2015; Bradley-Siemens & Brower, 2016). As an example, juvenile shooters are more likely to use air- or gas-powered firearms that fire BB or pellet projectiles, and adults are more likely to use high-powered firearms and shotguns (Merck, 2013; Bradley-Siemens & Brower, 2016). Weapon type usage has been reported, with handgun injury most prevalent in urban areas, rifles and shotguns in rural areas, and air- or gas-powered firearms in suburban areas (Pavletic, 1985; Merck, 2013; Bradley-Siemens & Brower, 2016). The majority of dogs with projectile injuries are young and sexually intact (Jason, 2004; Bradley-Siemens & Brower, 2016). The majority of companion animals shot with a weapon tend to be "outside and unsupervised," with many of the animals roaming at large (Pavletic, 1985; Merck, 2013; Bradley-Siemens & Brower, 2016).

An online resource, Pet-abuse.com (http://pet-abuse.com), gathers data on animal abuse investigations in the United States. According to this source, in 2017 projectile injuries accounted for over 11% of the recorded animal abuse cases, and from 1998 to 2010, 10.3% involved projectile injuries to companion animals (dogs, cats, and horses), with the most common animal victim being dogs (Bradley-Siemens & Brower, 2016).

TYPES OF FIREARM WEAPONS

A general knowledge of firearms and ammunition is required to determine the extent of damage caused by gunshot wounds. The five categories of small arms are handguns, rifles, shotguns, submachine guns, and machine guns (DiMaio, 1999; Merck, 2013). Projectile wounds encountered in veterinary medicine are most commonly caused by handguns, rifles, shotguns, and air guns (Bradley-Siemens & Brower, 2016; Bradley-Siemens et al., 2018). Low-velocity weapons can include handguns and air-powered guns with a projectile velocity around 1000 feet/second. High-velocity weapons can include handguns and rifles with a projectile velocity of 2500 feet/second or higher (Merck, 2013).

The caliber of a weapon is based on the diameter of the bore of the gun measured from land to land. It is the diameter of a barrel before the rifling is created. Caliber designations are given in inches or as metric units. An example of the former using inches includes the 0.38 Special, 0.45 ACP, or a 0.357 Magnum, and the latter metric units include 9 × 18 mm Makarov or 5.56 × 45 mm (Bradley-Siemens & Brower, 2016; Bradley-Siemens et al., 2018). An example of both the American system in inches and metric system used in Europe is the famous James Bond gun, the Walther PPK, referred to as a 0.32 ACP or 7.65 mm.

Handguns

The most common types of handguns in the United States are revolvers and auto-loading pistols (semi-automatics and rarely automatics) (DiMaio, 1999; Bradley-Siemens & Brower, 2016; Bradley-Siemens et al., 2018). Handguns have rifled barrels. A revolver has a revolving cylinder with multiple chambers, and each chamber will contain an individual cartridge. The cylinder rotates mechanically to line up each chamber with the firing pin and the barrel. A pistol has a magazine holding multiple cartridges. The magazine is usually seated in the hand grip of the pistol. Handguns may be considered high- or low-velocity weapons depending on caliber and load (DiMaio, 1999; Merck, 2013; Bradley-Siemens & Brower, 2016; Bradley-Siemens et al., 2018).

Air, Gas, or Spring Guns

Air-, gas-, or spring-powered weapons range from toys to highly powerful pistols and rifles. Air rifles use the expanding force of compressed air or gas to propel a projectile down a rifled barrel. An air gun is differentiated from and air rifle by its smooth-bored (non-rifled) barrel. In a spring-powered gun, a cocking action is used to put a firing pin under spring pressure which strikes the projectile upon pulling the trigger. The same type of projectiles can be used in these types of weapons (Bradley-Siemens & Brower, 2016; Bradley-Siemens et al., 2018). Air, gas, or spring guns, like handguns, are usually considered low-velocity weapons (DiMaio, 1999).

Rifles

A rifle is a weapon designed to be fired from the shoulder. Rifles are used for greater distances and have more precision and accuracy than handguns. In the United States rifles have a minimum legal barrel length of 16 inches. There are multiple types of rifles including hinged or single shot, lever action, bolt action, pump action, and auto loading (DiMaio, 1999; Bradley-Siemens & Brower, 2016; Bradley-Siemens et al., 2018). An auto-loading rifle can either be semi-automatic or automatic. In a semi-automatic rifle, the weapon fires one round each time the trigger is depressed. In an automatic, the weapon will continue to fire rounds as long as the trigger is depressed or until the weapon runs out of ammunition (DiMaio, 1999; Bradley-Siemens & Brower, 2016; Bradley-Siemens et al., 2018). Rifles have rifled barrels and are generally considered high-velocity weapons (DiMaio, 1999; Bradley-Siemens & Brower, 2016).

Shotguns

A shotgun is fired from the shoulder. The barrel of a shotgun is generally smooth bored; no rifling is present. Rifled barrels are available for use with slugs. A shotgun barrel diameter is called a gauge, most commonly either 10, 12, 16, 20, or 28 gauge, although other sizes do exist. Gauge more appropriately refers to the weight of a solid metal sphere that fits into the barrel of a gun, and this weight is determined as a fraction of a pound. An example is a one-twelfth pound ball fits a 12-gauge bore. Shotguns are used for dispersal of shots on a moving target at short distances. A shotgun can fire multiple types of ammunition (shells), including pellets, buckshot, and slugs. In the United States, federal law mandates a barrel length of no less than 18 inches for shotguns. Shotgun barrels are available in several choke sizes: cylinder bore (no choke), improved cylinder choke, modified choke, and full choke, that influence the dispersal pattern of shotgun pellets. A shotgun may also have a device known as a variable or adjustable choke or interchangeable choke tubes attached to the barrel that can switch between different chokes without switching barrels. This may affect the interpretation of the range of discharge in a shotgun wound (DiMaio, 1999; Merck, 2013; Bradley-Siemens & Brower, 2016; Bradley-Siemens et al., 2018).

Miscellaneous Types of Weapons

These are types of weapons or instruments that utilize firearm characteristics and can be used outside their scope of purpose to commit acts of animal abuse.

Nail (Stud) Gun

A nail gun, also referred to as a stud gun, is a construction tool that utilizes blank cartridges or compressed air to propel a metal nail into an object such as wood, concrete, or steel. The caliber range of the blank cartridges is 0.22–0.38. The cartridges contain a quick-burning propellant that can reach pressures higher than a firearm. The nail is intended to penetrate a surface into which it is being discharged, but it can ricochet off a hard surface. Injuries acquired are usually accidental; however, nail guns have been used to cause intentional injuries to victims (Merck, 2013; Bradley-Siemens et al., 2018).

Bang Stick

A bang stick is cylindrically shaped device used to kill sharks, large fish, and alligators. The weapon is designed to fire when in direct contact with the target or subject. The bang stick is a single metal

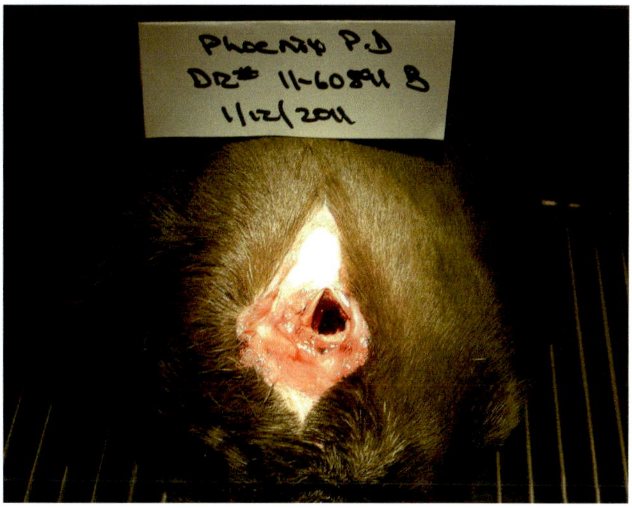

Figure 9.1 Captive bolt device used to kill dog, circular penetration through skull. (Photo courtesy C. West.)

cylinder acting in the capacity of a cartridge chamber, with a firing pin device. Bang sticks use standard handgun ammunition such as 0.357 Magnum or 0.44 Magnum cartridges. The resulting force of the bang stick is not from a projectile, but from the high-pressure gas that is forced into the targeted animal (Merck, 2013; Bradley-Siemens et al., 2018).

Captive Bolt Gun

A captive bolt gun utilizes compressed air, or a blank cartridge ignited by a firing pin. The metal bolt device is a 7 to 12 cm rod, which is driven down the barrel of the captive bolt gun and then recoils back into the barrel using spring tension. The end of the bolt is circular, 7–12 mm in diameter, with sharp edges, resulting in a sharp-edged, circular hole penetration in the skin and the bone. The device is designed for slaughtering livestock or other large animals. There have been reported cases of captive bolt gun use in companion animals (DiMaio, 1999; Merck, 2013; Bradley-Siemens et al., 2018). The author had a case with two dogs killed and dumped in a dumpster with what appeared to be a gunshot wound to the head of each animal. There was a circular hole in each skull with sharp margins. No gunshot residue was present and there was no exit wound in either animal. Radiographs of the skull revealed a small circular piece of the skull bone in the frontal brain region (Figure 9.1).

AMMUNITION

Ammunition is a combination of a primer, a propellant, and a projectile developed to accomplish specific parameters of distance, target penetration, and wounding capacity. To realize this, ammunition construction must take into consideration the caliber of the weapon in which it will be used, projectile composition, and the quantity and burn rate of the propellant (DiMaio, 1999; Bradley-Siemens & Brower, 2016; Bradley-Siemens et al., 2018).

A cartridge will consist of a cartridge case, a primer, propellant (gunpowder), and a bullet (projectile) (Figure 9.2). The cartridge case is composed of metal, commonly brass or steel. The cartridge case is designed to expand and isolate the chamber of the gun against a backward escape of gases when the cartridge is fired. The primer is the ignition component of the cartridge, igniting the propellant (gunpowder) in the cartridge when it is struck by the firing pin of the weapon. Primer

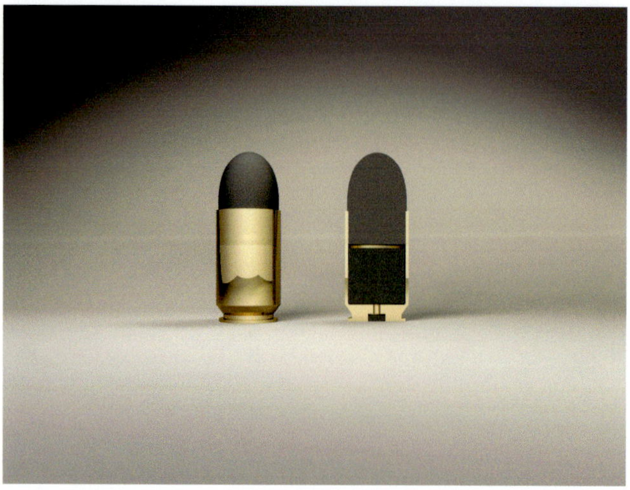

Figure 9.2 Bullet cartridge with cutaway view; bottom is the primer, middle is the propellant, top is the projectile. (Photo courtesy L. Siemens.)

compounds in the United States usually consist of lead styphnate, barium nitrate, and antimony sulfide. Primers are classified as a rimfire or a center-fire, with the primer in the rim or the center of the cartridge base. Propellant is the gunpowder in the cartridge that is ignited to move the projectile forward. The bullet (projectile) is the portion of the cartridge that exits the barrel of the gun when it discharges (DiMaio, 1999).

Bullets consist of two categories: jacketed and unjacketed. The former category is further subdivided into full-jacketed and semi-jacketed projectiles. There are multiple projectile shapes, including round nose, wadcutter, semi-wadcutter, and hollow point. Round-nose projectiles have a blunt, conical shape, with a flat or beveled base. A wadcutter projectile is cylindrical with a base that is beveled or hollow. A semi-wadcutter projectile has a truncated cone with a flat surface at the tip, and at the base of the cone there is a shoulder lip the diameter of the base. A hollow-point projectile has a cavity in the nose portion of the projectile to enhance expansion (mushrooming) of the projectile when it contacts the target (DiMaio, 1999; Bradley-Siemens & Brower, 2016) (Figure 9.3).

Figure 9.3 Different types of projectiles (left to right): jacketed hollow point, semi-jacketed flat nose, semi-jacketed hollow point, semi-wadcutter, lead round nose. (Photo courtesy L. Siemens.)

Figure 9.4 Lead projectile (mushroomed out) (right) and jacketed portion (left). These may become separated in the animal's body. The jacketed portion will have rifling present. Both need to be collected for evidence. (Photo courtesy L. Siemens.)

Lead projectiles at high velocities may melt or fragment; jacketing provides a shielding metal casing around the projectile. As a result, jacketed rounds are more frequently used in higher velocity weapons. The metal jacketing can separate from the lead projectile after entry into the body of an animal. The jacketed portion is important for ballistics. This segment of the bullet can retain rifling marks which can be used to identify a specific gun (DiMaio, 1999; Bradley-Siemens & Brower, 2016; Bradley-Siemens et al., 2018) (Figure 9.4).

Shotgun shells consist of a primer in the base, powder, wadding, and shot encased in a cardboard or plastic casing (Figure 9.5). Verbiage to describe shells will vary throughout the world. In the United States there are three sizes of shells based on length: 2 3/4, inches, 3 inches, and 3 1/2 inches, with the most noted caliber sizes of 12 (18.5 mm bore diameter), 16 (16.8 mm bore), and 20 (15.7 mm bore). The length of the shell will define the amount of gunpowder, and the volume of shot varies depending on the size and number of shot pellets. The pellets are metallic spherical projectiles ranging in diameter from 1 to 9 mm. Shotgun pellets in the smallest range are called birdshot pellets

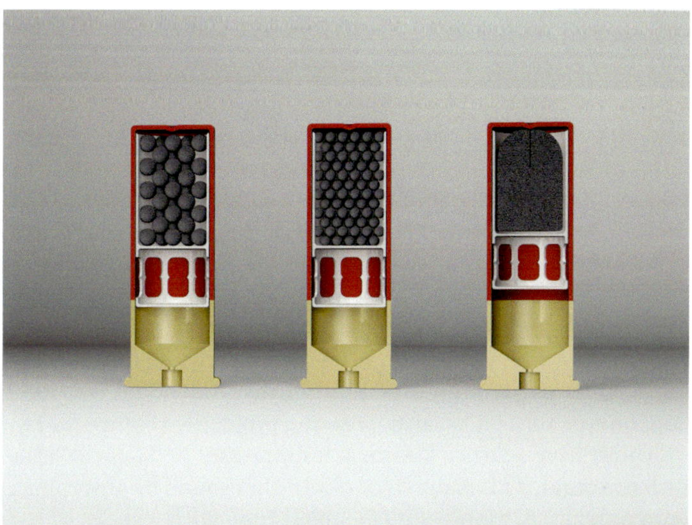

Figure 9.5 Shotgun shells: Buckshot, birdshot, and a slug. (Photo courtesy L. Siemens.)

and range in size from 0.05 to 0.16 inches (1.3 to 4 mm), also known as 12 to 1 shot using the U.S. shot size standards. The larger shotgun pellets, 0.24 to 0.36 inches (6.1 to 9.1 mm), or #4 to #000 shot, are known as buckshot. Shotgun shells can also contain a slug, a solid piece of metal similar to a bullet (DiMaio, 1999; Haag & Haag, 2011; Bradley-Siemens et al., 2018). Shotgun shells can contain more than one size and/or shape, dependent on the manufacturer. Home-loaded shells may contain any combination of materials (DiMaio, 1999).

Air-, gas-, and spring-powered weapons fire pellets or BBs. Pellets consist of various shapes, including round nose, pointed, wadcutter, or flat. The most prevalent pellet has a "wasp waist," also referred to as a diablo style. BBs are spherical in shape and resemble large shot pellets. BBs and pellets are made of various materials depending on the brand. These materials include, but are not limited to, copper, lead, steel, and zinc (DiMaio, 1999; Bradley-Siemens & Brower, 2016; Bradley-Siemens et al., 2018).

FIRING A GUN

The discharge of a firearm is commenced when the trigger of the weapon is pulled, initiating the release of the firing pin within the gun. The firing pin strikes the primer of the cartridge case, and it ignites, causing a flame. The flame enters the cartridge case chamber, igniting the powder and producing large quantities of gas and heat. One gram of propellant can produce 1 liter of gas under high temperature and pressure. The heat generated by the gas exerts pressure on the projectile and the sides of the cartridge. The gas pressure at the base of the projectile drives it down the barrel of the gun (Clasper, 2001). When the bullet exits the barrel, an eruption of flame, gas, and unburnt powder, soot, primer residue, and vaporized metal from the projectile and cartridge all follow the projectile. This material is referred to as gunshot residue (GSR). In revolvers, this type of material may also escape from both the cylinder-barrel gap and the barrel (DiMaio, 1999; Bradley-Siemens & Brower, 2016; Bradley-Siemens et al., 2018). The GSR may also travel backward from the weapon to the shooter.

The speed at which projectile leaves the barrel of a gun is called the muzzle velocity. The velocity is based on the type and the caliber of the ammunition, barrel length, the propellant (gunpowder) burn rate, and the gas production after the ignition of the primer.

RIFLING

Handguns, rifles, and air- or gas-powered guns have rifled barrels. The process of rifling a barrel involves cutting spiral grooves the length of the inside or bore of the gun barrel (Figure 9.6). The remaining metal left between the grooves is referred to as the lands (DiMaio, 1999; Merck, 2013; Bradley-Siemens & Brower, 2016). The purpose of the rifling is to create a rotational spin to the projectile along its longitudinal axis, stabilizing the projectile's flight through the air. Rifling stabilizes the bullet and increases accuracy; however, it also slows it down. The diminished velocity is caused by the projectile energy being deviated from a forward direction (Clasper, 2001; Bradley-Siemens & Brower, 2016) and thus rifling decreases the velocity. Rifling acts as a fingerprint of an individual weapon placed on the ammunition used in that individual weapon by imprinting the internal barrel rifling, unique to each firearm, onto the projectile (Figure 9.7).

A handgun or a rifle may have a device known as a suppressor or "silencer" attached to the end of the barrel to diminish its sound. This suppressor diminishes sound by absorbing gases and particles emitted from the gun muzzle. A suppressor is a metal tube with a series of baffles within it that divert the gases and particles expelled from the gun barrel. This can alter the dispersal of gunshot residue affecting distance determination (Bruzeka-Mucha, 2017). The suppressor can also have

Figure 9.6 Rifling within a gun barrel. (Photo courtesy L. Siemens.)

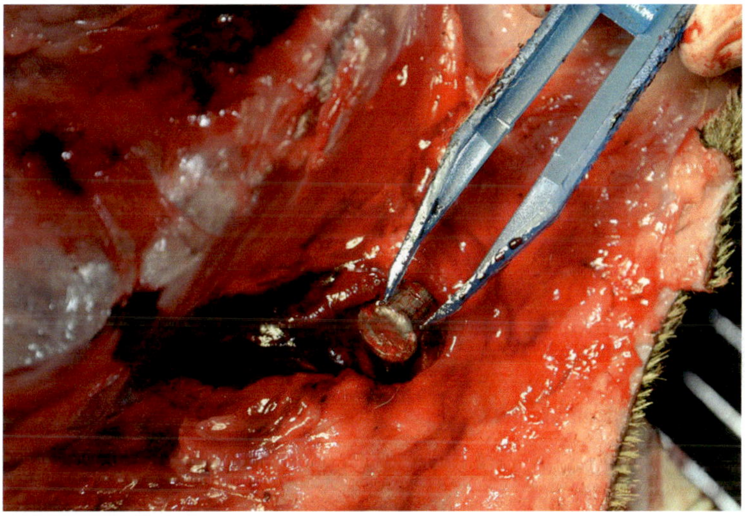

Figure 9.7 Removal of projectiles must be done with gloved fingers or instruments such as shown here, that will not alter rifling on the projectile.

effects on ammunition fired through the weapon if it is placed incorrectly on the muzzle or a homemade suppressor is used. These can alter the projectile as it leaves the barrel, causing nicks or indentations. These defects to the projectile are referred to as a "baffle strike" (Haag & Haag, 2011).

BALLISTICS

Ballistics is the science of projectile travel. A flight path of a projectile can be described in three stages, consisting of internal, external, and terminal ballistics. Internal ballistics describes the path of the projectile inside the firearm. External ballistics describes the projectile's flight through the air. Terminal ballistics is the projectile's pathway within an object (animal). When a projectile enters the body of an animal, this type of ballistics may be referred to as "wound ballistics"

(Bradley-Siemens & Brower, 2016; Bradley-Siemens et al., 2018). This concept is expressed in the equation:

$$\text{Kinetic Energy (KE)} = \tfrac{1}{2}\,\text{Mass} \times \text{Velocity}^2$$

The equation relates the effects of mass and velocity on the amount of kinetic energy potentially delivered to animal tissues by a projectile. The equation demonstrates that if the mass of a projectile is doubled the KE is doubled, but if the velocity is doubled, the KE is quadrupled (DiMaio, 1999; Merck, 2013; Bradley-Siemens & Brower, 2016; Bradley-Siemens et al., 2018).

The distances a projectile travels and changes in the media it transgresses on its pathway will affect the capacity of a projectile to elicit tissue damage. The velocity of a projectile alters with the distance it travels before contact, affecting the amount of kinetic energy transferred to the tissue. The resistance of tissues to a projectile will also affect the amount of energy released into the tissue. Skin maintains enough resistance that a minimum projectile velocity of 50–60 m/s is necessary for penetration. Ballistics impact the KE transferred to the tissue; the KE in combination with the type of weapon used is what best anticipates the wounding capacity of a projectile (DiMaio, 1999; Santucci & Chang, 2004; Bradley-Siemens & Brower, 2016; Bradley-Siemens et al., 2018).

The type of ammunition used will have effects on wounding capacity, but the ability or tendency of a projectile to fragment or to partially or completely flatten (mushroom) on impact, in conjunction with the caliber of the projectile and any jacketing, will also significantly affect wounding capacity (Clasper, 2001; Felsmann et al., 2012; Bradley-Siemens & Brower, 2016).

WOUNDING CAPACITY

The resulting tissue damage from a projectile injury can occur in three ways: from laceration or crushing, by cavitation, and through shock waves. Tissue damage occurs along the path of the projectile or the path its fragments travel through the animal's body. A temporary wound cavity is created by outward expansion, stretching, and tearing of tissue along the projectile pathway. The pulsating collapse of the temporary cavity can result in the development of a permanent cavity.

During the formation of a wound cavity, both crush and stretch forces affect tissue, and a multiphase medium is created around the projectile as it travels through the tissue. The phases involve fluid composed of blood, lymph, and cellular fluids, surrounded by a radially disseminated phase of solid tissue. The radially accelerated tissue may cause an abrasion ring in the entry wound and can cause back-spatter if tissue is removed from the wound cavity. There can be a gas phase, formed by air within the tissue and/or gas generated by the projectile. The creation of the wound cavity also creates a vacuum that may pull hair or debris into an entry wound (Merck, 2013; Bradley-Siemens & Brower, 2016).

The type of tissue along the projectile trajectory will influence the degree of damage produced. Elastic tissues that give on impact, including lung or muscle, are more resistant to injury, especially from cavitation (DiMaio, 1999; Santucci & Chang, 2004; Bradley-Siemens & Brower, 2016; Bradley-Siemens et al., 2018). Soft tissue of thicker consistency such as liver and brain and dense rigid tissue like bone have greater resistance, increasing the level of energy transfer (Clasper, 2001; Santucci & Chang, 2004; Bradley-Siemens & Brower, 2016). Projectile-caused bone fractures are dependent on the type of bone and the angle of impact. For instance, cancellous bone is softer, increasing its ability to absorb energy, causing less fragmentation. Cortical bone, with its greater density, may fracture and fragment. When a projectile strikes the skull, increased intracranial pressure can contribute to concentric fractures forming target-shaped fracture lines. When a projectile has contact with bone, there is a deceleration, deformation, and possibly fragmentation or tumbling effect on the bullet and/or bone itself. Bone fragments may act as additional projectiles and may affect the range and direction of the primary projectile (DiMaio, 1999; Clasper, 2001; Bradley-Siemens & Brower, 2016). Tissue consistency may also affect drag on a projectile's terminal ballistics, changing the velocity it travels through the tissue (Bradley-Siemens & Brower, 2016).

WOUND ANALYSIS

Whether the animal gunshot victim is alive or deceased will have to be considered in wound analysis. Findings may be relatively straightforward, as in the case of a single gunshot wound with a retained projectile, or more complex with multiple gunshot wounds. In the event the animal is alive you may be able to access the projectile. Multiple gunshot wounds and/or projectiles (such as shotgun pellets), through-and-through wounds with little or no projectile fragmentation, and the generation of secondary projectiles from bone fragments can all complicate analysis and interpretation (Jason, 2004; Merck, 2013; Bradley-Siemens et al., 2018).

Projectile injuries must be differentiated from other injuries, including wounds from motor vehicles, animal bites, and lacerations. In the absence of an accurate history of the injuries, whole-body radiographs prior to the examination need to be obtained. Examination findings consistent with trauma, including projectile-caused injuries, encompass hemorrhage, fractured organs (liver and spleen), bone fractures, and emboli (Bradley-Siemens et al., 2018). Projectile injuries are indicated by the presence of entry, exit, and intermediary wounds. It is essential that these lesions are identified and documented during the external examination of the live or deceased animal victim. Determination of entry versus exit wounds and establishing whether an intermediary wound exists is critical when conducting a complete projectile injury forensic physical or postmortem external examination (Bradley-Siemens & Brower, 2016).

Projectile wounds can be penetrating or perforating. A penetrating wound occurs when the projectile enters the animal's body and does not exit. A perforating wound occurs when a projectile passes completely through the body of the animal. Projectile wounds can be further classified as graze or tangential. Graze wounds involve the projectile striking the skin at a shallow angle, causing an abrasion. A tangential wound causes the skin to be torn to the level of the subcutaneous tissue (DiMaio, 1999; Merck, 2013; Bradley-Siemens & Brower, 2016).

Entrance Wounds

An entrance wound usually has sharp margins. Entry wounds appear as a punched-out circular hole, usually of a small diameter. The diameter of the wound may be similar to the projectile. There may be an abrasion ring (collar) around the periphery of the wound and an inward indentation of the skin or fur (Bradley-Siemens & Brower, 2016) (Figure 9.8).

Entrance wounds can have soot marks, also referred to stippling or tattooing, or an abrasion ring from the discharge of the projectile if it was shot at close to intermediate range. When a firearm is discharged, in addition to the powder, soot from the ignition of the gunpowder emerges from the muzzle. Soot is carbon and contains vaporized metals from the primer, projectile, and cartridge case. If the muzzle of the firearm is held close to the animal's body, soot may be deposited on the animal. These marks may be found on exposed skin; however, long or dense fur can alter these findings. The "flame" or muzzle flash may cause searing of the skin or fur around contact and near-contact gunshot entrance wounds (DiMaio, 1999; Bradley-Siemens & Brower, 2016). Soot or burned fur may still be present and thus it is important to obtain samples of fur over projectile wounds before further examination of the entrance wound. The size, intensity, and appearance of the soot pattern and range at which it occurs will depend on multiple factors, consisting of range of fire, type of gunpowder, angle of the weapon muzzle to the animal body, barrel length of the firearm, firearm caliber, type of gun, and the type of target. Most regions on an animal victim to

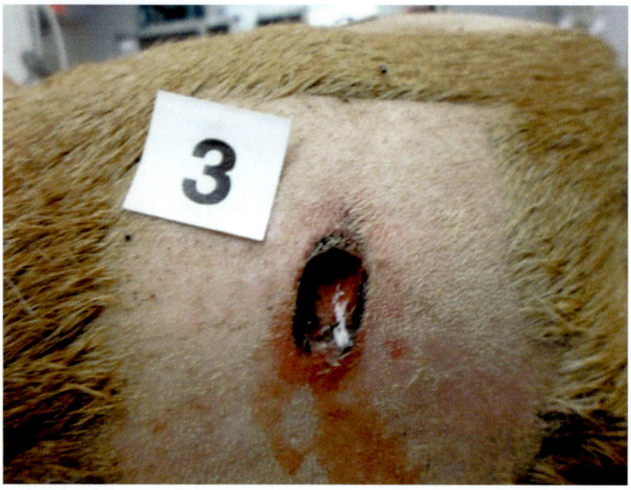

Figure 9.8 Entrance wound with abrasion ring.

be examined will have hair and it will be necessary to sample fur for gunpowder or soot. It will also be required to shave the area around the gunshot wound to discover any evidence on the skin beneath the fur (DiMaio, 1999; Merck, 2013; Bradley-Siemens & Brower, 2016; Bradley-Siemens et al., 2018).

Intermediary Wounds

This type of wound occurs when a projectile passes through one part of the body and enters another part, causing a reentry wound. This reentry wound will not normally have an abrasion ring. This can help differentiate it from an entrance wound. An intermediary wound can develop when a projectile passes through an intermediary object, including a door, wall, or window before entering the animal's body. Either situation can alter the appearance and number of entry wounds and will make wound interpretation more difficult (Merck, 2013; Bradley-Siemens & Brower, 2016; Bradley-Siemens et al., 2018).

Exit Wounds

An exit wound usually has jagged margins and a larger diameter than an entrance wound. The jagged margins can consist of slit-shaped, stellate, or irregular patterns. There usually is no abrasion ring with gunshot residue. There may be protruding underlying tissue or bone (Merck, 2013; Bradley-Siemens & Brower, 2016; Bradley-Siemens et al., 2018) (Figure 9.9).

RANGE DETERMINATION

As the firing distance moves from the contact to varying distances away from the animal, the deposition of soot or gunpowder residue will alter. Accurate interpretation of these differences requires additional diagnostics with a scanning electron microscope or spectrometer. Morphology of skin defects, margins, or abrasions may remain the same. A ballistic expert will evaluate the appearance of an entry wound, considering the weapon and type of ammunition, and may also need to test fire a specific weapon and ammunition to determine the distance the weapon was fired (DiMaio, 1999; Bradley-Siemens & Brower, 2016).

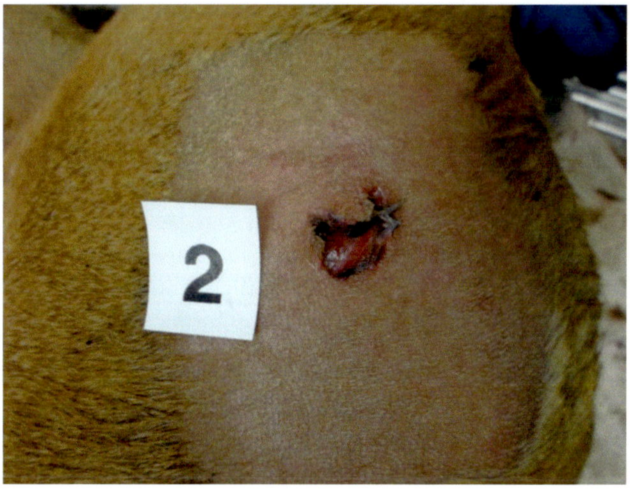

Figure 9.9 Exit wound; notice outward protruding of the tissue flap.

Contact

A contact wound is caused by placing the end of the gun barrel in direct contact with the animal's skin when the weapon is fired. There are hard-, loose-, angled-, or incomplete-contact wounds (DiMaio, 1999; Bradley-Siemens & Brower, 2016). In a hard-contact wound, the muzzle of the firearm is pushed against the skin, causing the skin to rise up around the barrel periphery (pushing outward). The borders of the wound are seared by the hot gasses exiting the muzzle. This type of wound is caused by soot and gas being forced into the skin (DiMaio, 1999; Bradley-Siemens & Brower, 2016). In skin regions elevated by bone, the skin may separate from the subcutis, causing a "soot cavity." A loose-contact wound occurs when the barrel of the gun is held lightly against the animal's skin. Any gas exiting prior to the projectile pushes the skin inward, causing a gap between the skin and the end of the muzzle, allowing the gas to exit. Soot is discharged in a zone surrounding the entrance wound (DiMaio, 1999; Bradley-Siemens & Brower, 2016). Angled contact wounds result when a gun barrel is at an acute angle to the animal's skin; the circumference of the end of the muzzle is not in total contact with the skin. The gas and soot emanate outward from the end of the barrel where contact was not complete. An eccentric pattern of soot with two zones will develop. The inner zone, most evident, is a blackened seared area of skin or fur with a pear, circular, or oval shape. The larger outer zone is shaped like a fan of light gray soot. The majority of the inside zone will be on the opposite side of the wound from the muzzle, signifying the direction the gun was fired (DiMaio, 1999; Bradley-Siemens & Brower, 2016). Incomplete-contact wounds resemble angle-contact wounds. The barrel of the gun is in contact with the animal's skin, but the body surface may not be completely flat, resulting in a space between the end of the barrel and the skin. Soot and gas escape from the space, causing an area of seared skin or fur (DiMaio, 1999; Bradley-Siemens & Brower, 2016).

Near (Close) Contact

This type of wound is created when a weapon is not in contact with the animal's skin but held a short distance away. The distance is so small many of the particles exiting cannot disperse and mark the skin. In close-contact wounds, the entry wound is surrounded by a zone of powder soot over seared and blackened skin or fur. This zone of searing is larger than loose-contact wounds. The soot is buried in the skin and seared zone (DiMaio, 1999; Bradley-Siemens & Brower, 2016). In close-contact angled wounds, soot will radiate outward from the end of the muzzle, causing two zones like an angled-contact wound. However, the majority of the blackened seared zone is on the same side of the muzzle pointing toward the firearm. The actual direction of fire is in the opposite direction (DiMaio, 1999; Bradley-Siemens & Brower, 2016).

Intermediate Distance

These wounds occur when the end of the barrel is held at a distance away from the animal's body when fired yet close enough for powder grains discharged with the bullet to cause "powder tattooing" of the skin. This involves embedding of gun powder particles in the skin and resulting hemorrhage. This hemorrhage is caused by the tattooing and appears as reddish-brown to orange-red punctate lesions around an entry wound. The dissemination around the wound may be symmetrical or eccentric dependent on the angle the gun was fired. Powder tattooing is an antemortem event and its presence indicates the animal was alive when it was shot (DiMaio, 1999; Bradley-Siemens & Brower, 2016).

The distance for intermediate wounds may be over 1.0 M dependent on the weapon fired; however, an intermediate range from a handgun is generally 10.0 mm (DiMaio, 1999; Bradley-Siemens & Brower, 2016). In addition, these wounds can help determine direction of fire based on tissue beveling and the angle of an abrasion ring or soot marks (Bradley-Siemens & Brower, 2016).

Indeterminate Distance

Beyond intermediate ranges, soot or powder tattooing is not evident near an entrance wound. The only marks may be those produced by the projectile perforating the animal's skin. At greater distances abrasion rings may not be present (DiMaio, 1999; Bradley-Siemens & Brower, 2016).

Shotgun Wounds

As the muzzle-to-animal distance increases, the diameter of the shotgun shell pellet pattern will increase and the margins of the entrance wound will be more indented. As distance increases, pellets disperse, creating single injuries or striking surrounding objects (Figure 9.10a–c). If the shotgun is fired at an angle perpendicular to the animal's body, the pellet pattern will usually be circular. An angled discharge will cause an eccentric pattern. In both situations, the diameter of the pattern is range dependent. A projectile pattern spread will vary based on shot size and velocity. The wad from a shotgun shell may often present as a secondary projectile at close range. It may look like a second shot with bruising (sometimes in a petal formation) with or without penetration (DiMaio, 1999; Haag & Haag, 2011; Bradley-Siemens & Brower, 2016) (Figure 9.11).

EXAMINATION OF ALIVE OR DECEASED ANIMAL GUNSHOT VICTIMS

Projectile injuries must be differentiated from puncture wounds, bite wounds, or lacerations. An animal with unexplained wounds should receive whole-body radiographs. Additional findings indicative of projectile injury may include pneumothorax, pneumomediastinum, cardiac tamponade, dyspnea, fractures, peritonitis, hemoabdomen, or hemothorax (Merck, 2013).

If possible, it is beneficial to have all the investigatory information and crime scene findings, specifically with regard to the type of firearm and ammunition, before the animal victim is examined. All confirmed gunshot wound victims must have whole-body radiographs. Consideration needs to be given that other injuries may be present such as those sustained from blunt force trauma. The skin may be reflected in deceased animals to define evidence of injury (Merck, 2013).

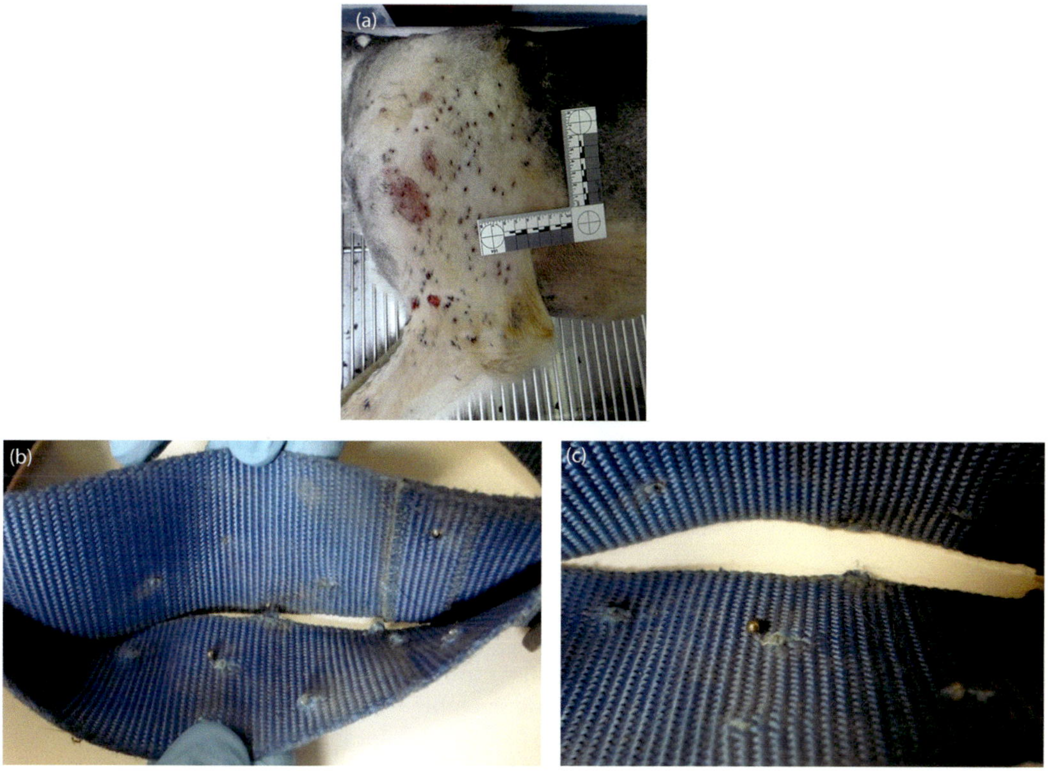

Figure 9.10 (a) Dog shot with shotgun (birdshot) from the left side. (b and c) Collar from dog shot with shotgun containing pellets from a shotgun round.

Figure 9.11 Wadding from a shotgun shell found near a dog's body.

In addition to a standard physical examination or necropsy procedures and reporting, the forensic veterinarian or pathologist must provide information regarding entry and exit wounds, projectile trajectory, and associated forms of tissue injury. The veterinarian must be aware of external evidence that needs to be collected as the animal is being examined (live animal) or prior to a postmortem examination to properly identify and retrieve ballistic evidence. Before initiating treatment or manipulation of the carcass (if deceased) a plan should be created taking into account the best sequence of gathering evidence (Bradley-Siemens & Brower, 2016; Bradley-Siemens et al., 2018).

Before a gunshot case is encountered, a forensic veterinarian will need to communicate with local law enforcement agencies, crime scene analysts, or state crime laboratories, and be familiar with the types of evidence they can process and how evidence should be collected and submitted. These entities can offer expertise in evidence handling and collection and can direct trained personnel (ballistic experts) in obtaining and analyzing evidence such as gunshot residue and projectiles (Merck, 2013; Bradley-Siemens et al., 2018).

Photographs

Any wound surface or wound tract evidence should be collected only after photo documentation (Merck, 2013; Bradley-Siemens et al., 2018). The animal's entire body will be photographed. Standard photographs will consist of front and back, left and right sides, and above (dorsal) and below (ventral). Each projectile wound should be photographed as it is found, then the fur shaved to identify wound characteristics or skin surface evidence and again photographed. All photographs will be taken with and without measurement (Merck, 2013).

Radiology

In any suspected gunshot injury, whole-body radiographs should be taken prior to a necropsy and at the earliest possible time frame, if the animal victim is alive. If a veterinarian will be actively participating in a forensic projectile casework, radiographic equipment must be available onsite or accessible through a working relationship with a facility that does. A minimum of two views with standard markers and identification needs to be obtained (Figure 9.12a,b). A radiograph will illustrate the shape and density traits of the projectile and the location of the projectile within the animal's body (Figure 9.13a,b). Radiographs may define the pathway of the projectile within the body. Wound tracts may be defined based on the presence of gas, hemorrhage, bone, or metal opacities (Lockwood, 2013; Bradley-Siemens & Brower, 2016; Bradley-Siemens et al., 2018). The direction of fragments or beveling of bone in radiographs can assist with the direction determination of the projectile and define entry or exit wound identification (Figure 9.14). When a projectile strikes a bone, bone fragments will usually be found behind the damaged bone, showing the direction of the projectile (Bradley-Siemens & Brower, 2016).

Computed axial tomography (CAT) scans can be immensely beneficial in a forensic workup of either a deceased or live animal and, if available, is strongly advised by the author.

EXTERNAL EVIDENCE COLLECTION

Gunshot residue (GSR) is the result of the discharge of a weapon through gases and particles leaving the muzzle or through other openings in a firearm. GSR is the primer, powder, and/or projectile material and products of their combustion (DiMaio, 1999; Merck, 2013). GSR may be deposited around a projectile wound (as discussed in distance determination section) or on the hands of a shooter. This is a common type of external evidence found in projectile injuries.

Again, as protocols may differ between forensic laboratories, collection of external evidence should be discussed with these organizations prior to initiating this type of case. Depending if the animal victim is alive or deceased, tissue surrounding an entry wound may be excised. The skin and adjacent underlying soft tissues may be placed on a piece of cork or Styrofoam to maintain shape, size, and anatomical orientation for further analysis. A sample such as this can be analyzed using a scanning electron microscope and/or x-ray spectrometer to establish the quality and quantity of soot particles, information that can assist in range of discharge determination. There are several

(a)

(b)

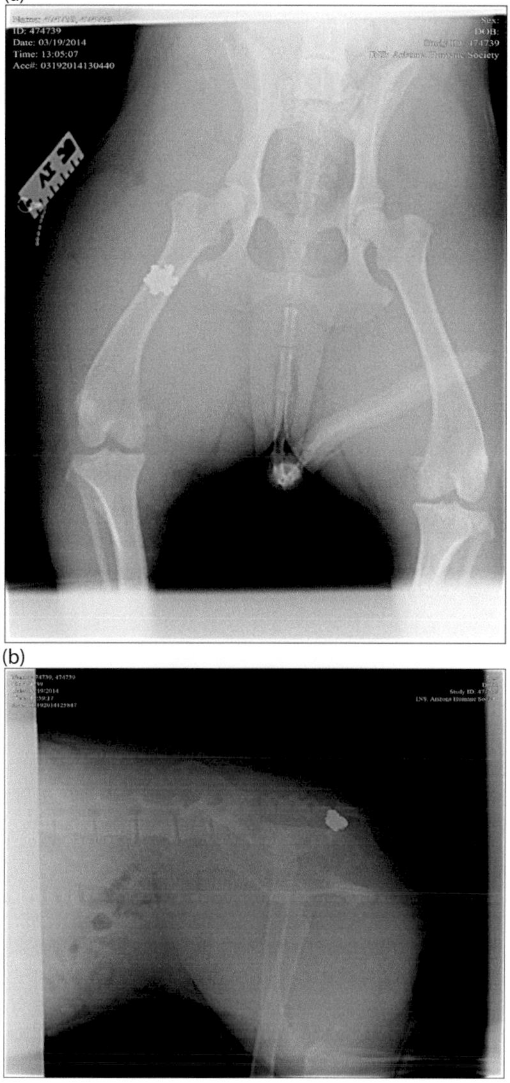

Figure 9.12 (a,b) V/D and lateral radiographs of gunshot wound to the thigh.

techniques used to collect evidence during an examination of projectile wounds. If powder particles associated with projectile wounds are found, they can be scraped into a Post-it note and placed in a sealed paper envelope. Entry and exit wounds can be shaved and the hair placed in a cellophane or waxed paper envelope. Clear tape can be utilized to obtain stippling from tissue and then placed on a glass slide. Areas of skin with contact wounds with soot or stippling can be taken at necropsy and either forwarded to a ballistic expert or photographed, sampled for residue, and fixed in formalin (DiMaio, 1999; Pavletic, 2010; Bradley-Siemens & Brower, 2016).

Although fired cartridge cases are usually observed at a crime scene surrounding or near an animal victim's body, they may be accidentally collected when the animal's remains are placed in a body bag and/or on the animal victim. A fired cartridge case can exhibit individual and class characteristics that can be used to identify a type of weapon or even a specific firearm. If a cartridge case is discovered on a killed or injured animal, it is important to save it as evidence (Haag & Haag, 2011) (Figure 9.15).

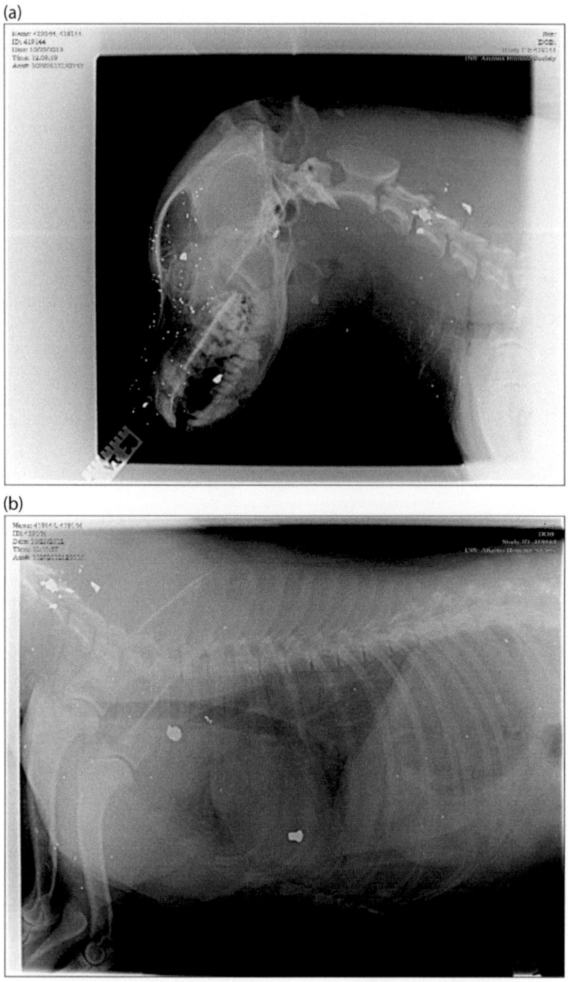

Figure 9.13 (a,b) Same dog shot multiple times with different types of ammunition. (a) 0.22 snake shot (pelleted rounds) to the face. (b) 0.22 rounds to the thoracic region.

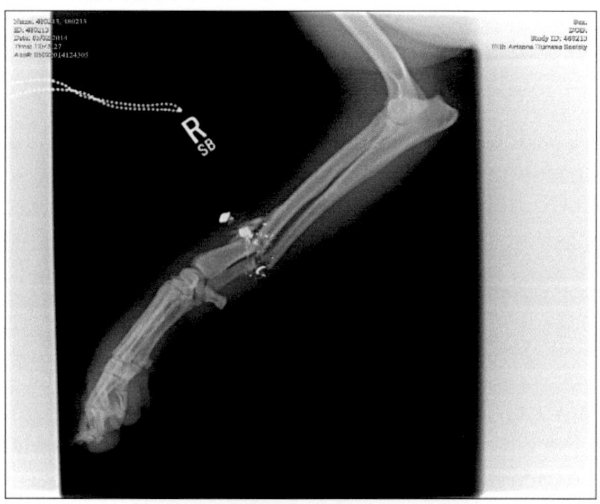

Figure 9.14 Gunshot wound to front of right leg, causing a radial-ulnar fracture and fragmentation of the projectile.

Figure 9.15 This is a cartridge casing found at the scene where a dog was shot, it is important that these be recovered for evidentiary purposes. Casings may be found in an animal's fur or in a body bag when remains are collected for necropsy. (Photo courtesy Phoenix Police Department.)

Gunpowder Analysis Techniques

Modern gunpowder contains nitrated cellulose. During the firing of a gun, particles of burnt, unburnt, and partially burnt gunpowder containing nitrite and nitrate compounds are emitted. Ballistic experts can utilize chemical analysis called a Modified Griess Test to detect organic nitrite residue on hair or skin (Jason, 2004; Haag & Haag, 2011; Bradley-Siemens & Brower, 2016). A ballistic expert can also use microscopy of fur or skin from entrance wounds to define particles of burnt or unburnt GSR (Jason, 2004; Haag & Haag, 2011; Bradley-Siemens & Brower, 2016). Infrared photography can be beneficial in demonstrating nitric acid presence in ammunition on the fur of an animal (Bradley-Siemens & Brower, 2016; Weiss et al., 2016). This can illustrate a residue pattern that can assist in determining a distance from which a projectile was fired. In addition, alternate light sources (ALS) and other tests such as sodium rhodizonate may be utilized in GSR detection and potential range determination (Weiss et al., 2016).

The ability to estimate firing distance to a target can be improved via various tests for GSR. The ability to conduct these types of tests will be on a case-by-case basis dependent on necessity and resources. It is advised that photography and visual enhancement be attempted prior to chemical tests that may alter or destroy a GSR pattern (Weiss et al., 2016).

Trajectory

The ability to define a projectile path or trajectory is important in the reconstruction of a crime scene or to corroborate or refute evidence provided by a witness or suspect. A trajectory can provide information about the location of a shooter, distance from an animal victim, and help determine the type of weapon and ammunition used.

To establish a trajectory, the veterinarian must first identify the entrance wound or wounds. Measurements of the length and width of a projectile entrance wound are obtained to establish the degree of angle of the wound. In addition, if GSR patterns exist these may further assist with directionality of the weapon discharge (DiMaio, 1999; Bradley-Siemens & Brower, 2016).

If the animal is deceased, trajectory rods help visualize and characterize a projectile's trajectory in some cases. Rods must be straight, and may be made of fiberglass, plastic, or wood. The rods are meant to simulate the path of the bullet into and through an animal's body. Rods must be placed with caution as to not create artificial tracts (Figure 9.16a,b). Once placed (animal in sternal

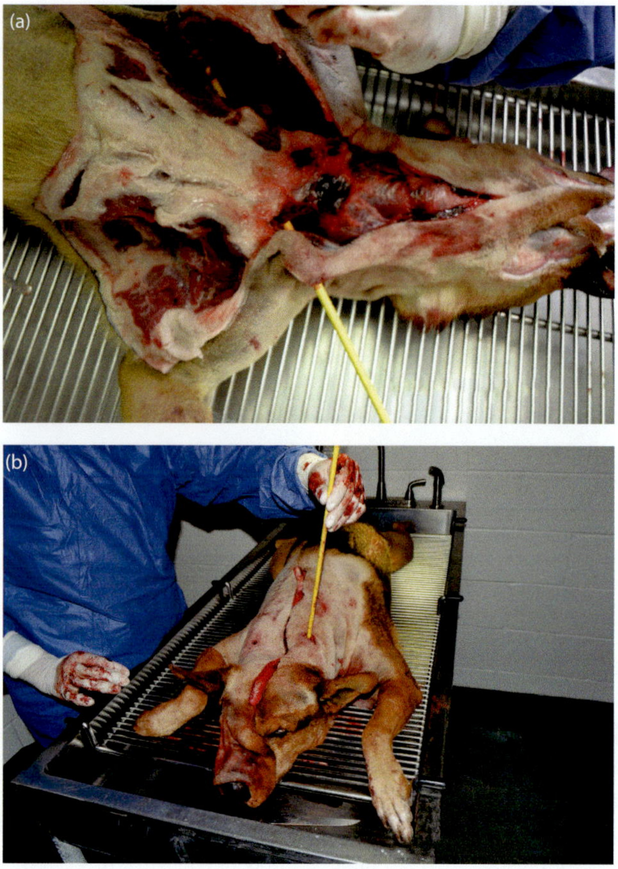

Figure 9.16 (a,b) Using a trajectory rod to assist in documenting projectile pathways through the animal.

recumbency), photographs should be taken from the front, back, both sides, bottom, and above the body. These photographs can assist in the development of theories based on investigation findings (Bradley-Siemens & Brower, 2016).

DOCUMENTATION

All ballistic injuries and evidence should be photographed and documented with written and diagram information. An identification system corresponding to associated wounds needs to be used (Merck, 2013). Numbers may be used to identify other lesions or wounds on the animal's body. Dr. Melinda Merck suggests a letter-number system where letters designate the gunshot wound and numbers designate entrance versus exit wounds; the number one (1) is used for entrance and the number two (2) is used for exit wounds. For example; A1 = entrance wound A, A2 = an exit wound associated with A1 (Merck, 2013).

Projectile wounds that are identified with a letter or a number does not designate the sequence in which the gunshot wounds occurred. It is a common practice among medical examiners, according to Dr. Mary Dudley (boarded in Anatomic and Forensic Pathology, former Chief Medical Examiner, Jackson County Medical Examiner's Office, Kansas City, Missouri) to start number or lettering sequences of projectile wounds from the head working caudally (personal communication, Dudley, 2018).

The gunshot wound location should be identified using location direction references (e.g., ventral, cranial) and measurements of nearby anatomical landmarks. The wound and surrounding characteristics need to be described (Merck, 2013). In the case of a shotgun wound, where multiple wounds are present, they should be grouped (Merck, 2013). Surrounding characteristics must be referred to like the hands of a clock, making the midline of the body 12:00.

Injuries will be described involving all tissues and/or organs penetrated or perforated. The pathway of the projectile through the animal's body will be documented. A suggested method for directionality of a projectile is to keep it simple, using terms *front/back, side to side,* and *up/down* (personal communication, Dudley, 2018). The appearance and weight of any recovered ballistic evidence needs to be described and its location documented (Merck, 2013; Bradley-Siemens & Brower, 2016; Bradley-Siemens et al., 2018).

CONCLUSION

Deciding to accept any form of veterinary forensic case, projectile injury, or any other type of case can be challenging for veterinarians and veterinary pathologists. Understanding what additional tasks a forensic examination may require and what expectations exist beyond traditional diagnostic reports is a crucial part of the decision-making process. This chapter provides background information on the types of projectile injury and describes examination techniques. In addition, it is the author's hope that the necessity for establishing relationships with an extended team of forensic experts and forensic laboratories required for these types of forensic cases has been clearly conveyed.

References

Bradley-Siemens N, Brower AI. 2016. Veterinary forensics: Firearms and investigation of projectile injury. *Vet Pathol.* 53(5):988–1000.

Bradley-Siemens N, Brower AI, Kagan R. 2018. Firearm injuries. Ch. 7. In: Brooks JW, ed. *Veterinary Forensic Pathology Volumes 1&2.* Springer.

Bruzeka-Mucha Z. 2017. A study of gunshot residue distribution for close range shots with a silenced gun using optical and scanning electron microscopy, xray microanalysis, and infrared spectroscopy. *Sci Justice.* 57:87–94.

Clasper J. 2001. The interaction of projectiles with tissues and the management of ballistic fractures. *JR Army Med Corps.* 147:52–61.

DiMaio VJ. 1999. *Gunshot Wounds: Practical Aspects of Firearms, Ballistics, and Forensic Techniques,* 2nd ed. Boca Raton, FL: CRC Press.

Felsmann MZ, Szarek J, Felsmann M, Babinska I. 2012. Factors affecting temporary cavity generation during gunshot wound formation in animals-new aspects in the light of flow mechanics: A review. *Veterinarni Med.* 57(11):569–574.

Haag MG, Haag LC. 2011. *Shooting Incident Reconstruction,* 2nd ed. Amsterdam, Netherlands: Elsevier.

Jason A. 2004. Effect of hair on the deposition of gunshot residue. *Forensic Sci Commun.* 6(2):1–12.

Lockwood R. 2011. When animal and humans attack: Veterinary and behavior forensic issues in investigating animal attacks and shootings [abstract]. Paper presented at *joint ASPCA/NAVC Conference,* January 15–19, 2011, Orlando, FL.

Lockwood R. 2013. Factors in the assessment of the dangerousness of perpetrators of animal cruelty. http://coloradolinkproject.com/dangerousness-factors-2/.

Merck M. 2013. *Veterinary Forensics: Animal Cruelty Investigations,* 2nd ed. Ames, IA: Wiley-Blackwell.

Munro R, Munro H. 2008. *Animal Abuse and Unlawful Killing: Forensic Veterinary Pathology.* Edinburg, UK: Saunders Elsevier.

Pavletic M. 1985. A review of 121 gunshot wounds in the dog and cat. *Vet Surg.* 14:61–62.

Pavletic M. 2010. *Atlas of Small Animal Wound Management and Reconstructive Surgery,* 3rd ed. Ames, IA: Wiley-Blackwell.

Pet-abuse.com (http://pet-abuse.com).

Santucci RA, Chang YJ. 2004. Ballistics for physicians: Myths about wound ballistics and gunshot injuries. *J Urol*. 171:1408–1414.

Tedeschi P. 2015. Methods of forensic animal maltreatment evaluations. In: Levitt L, Patronek G, Grisso T, eds. *Animal Maltreatment: Forensic Mental Health Issues and Evaluations*. Oxford, UK: Oxford University Press, 309–331.

Weiss CA, Ristenbatt RR, Brooks JW. 2016. Shooting Distance Estimation Using Gunshot Residue on Mammalian Pelts. Poster Presentation. Penn State Eberly College of Science.

CHAPTER 10

THE FORENSIC NECROPSY

Jason W. Brooks

INTRODUCTION TO THE MEDICOLEGAL NECROPSY

A forensic necropsy is a postmortem examination of a body performed at the request of a law enforcement agency for the purpose of generating a written report to be used in legal proceedings. The forensic necropsy differs in some respects from a standard diagnostic necropsy as will be described subsequently; however, the dissection and examination of the body is nearly identical in either case (Brownlie & Munro, 2016; Kagan & Brooks, 2018). The primary differences between the forensic necropsy and the diagnostic necropsy are: (1) the purpose of the examination, (2) the documentation of the examination, and (3) the collection of evidence generated during the examination. It is critical for the veterinary pathologist to consider that, in the course of conducting a forensic necropsy, it is not the responsibility of the pathologist to determine whether or not a crime was committed, but rather to simply and objectively describe and interpret the pathologic anatomic findings on the body (Gerdin & McDonough, 2013; McDonough et al., 2015). Any determination of criminal or civil wrongdoing will be determined by the court, possibly using the necropsy report and/or the pathologist's testimony as evidence.

A diagnostic necropsy is typically performed on an animal carcass following death due to a perceived natural cause and/or when there is no expectation of criminal activity. This is somewhat comparable to a hospital autopsy of a human patient who has died from perceived progression of a natural disease process or in any other circumstance in which there is no suspicion of criminal action. The diagnostic necropsy, as a general rule, should consist of a thorough gross and microscopic examination of all major organ systems of the body including the cardiovascular, respiratory, gastrointestinal, nervous, musculoskeletal, urogenital, endocrine, lymphatic, and integumentary systems. The purpose of the diagnostic necropsy is to determine the cause of death; thus diagnostic assays for the detection of microorganisms, trace nutrients, and toxins often prevail (McDonough & Southard, 2017). The intended audience of the diagnostic necropsy report is typically the owner or veterinarian of the animal examined, and the examination is deemed successful if the results generated by the examination and communicated in the report are practical and useful to the owner or veterinarian. In this case, brevity, clarity, and rapidity are among the most highly valued traits of a successful examination and report. This differs substantially from a forensic necropsy, in which thoroughness and extensively detailed documentation of findings, both positive and negative, are paramount. The actual examination of the body does not differ significantly, if at all, from that of a standard diagnostic exam. The forensic necropsy should consist of a thorough gross and microscopic examination of all major organ systems of the body including the cardiovascular, respiratory, gastrointestinal, nervous, musculoskeletal, urogenital, endocrine, lymphatic, and integumentary systems, as was previously described for a diagnostic exam. The purpose of the forensic exam, however, is dependent upon the investigation and is typically to determine the cause of death, perhaps specifically to include or exclude the possibility of a certain cause; however, other questions may be asked such as the time of death or the manner of death (Merck et al., 2013). The intended audience of the forensic necropsy report is the court, and the report should be written with this audience in mind.

The need for the forensic autopsy of a human decedent is dictated by law, and typically is required in any of the following conditions (Peterson & Clark, 2006):

1. A human death due to violence or suspected to be due to a non-natural cause or any other unusual or suspicious circumstances
2. Unexpected or unexplained death in an infant or child or person in apparent good health
3. Death of a person in custody
4. Death known or suspected to be due to a disease threatening public health
5. Death of persons not under the care of a physician

Human deaths due to unusual or suspicious circumstances are further defined as (Peterson & Clark, 2006):

1. Death associated with police action
2. Death associated with acute workplace injury
3. Death caused by apparent electrocution
4. Death caused by apparent intoxication by alcohol, drugs, or poison
5. Death caused by apparent drowning
6. A human body is unidentified
7. A human body is charred or skeletonized
8. A forensic pathologist deems it necessary

The need for the forensic necropsy of an animal is not currently regulated by any such law, thus it is entirely at the discretion of a law enforcement officer to open an investigation and submit the animal carcass for examination. This author suggests that the following be considered as justification for the forensic necropsy of an animal:

1. An animal death is due to suspected violence or other non-natural cause or any other unusual or suspicious circumstances
2. Death of an animal occurs while in the custody of a veterinarian, boarding facility, groomer, or other temporary custodian
3. Death of an animal is associated with police action
4. A law enforcement officer or veterinary examiner deems it necessary

TRAINING AND AUTHORITY

In most jurisdictions, the investigation of a human death is required by law, in certain circumstances, to include an autopsy of the decedent's body with oversight of the medical investigation by a coroner or medical examiner (ME) who issues a death certificate (CDC, 2015; Touroo et al., 2018). Depending on the jurisdiction, this medical examiner may be a pathologist or forensic pathologist or, in the case of a coroner, an elected official who may have very little medical training (Institute of Medicine (U.S.). Committee for the Workshop on the Medicolegal Death Investigation System, 2003). If the ME/coroner is not a pathologist, the autopsy is typically performed by a pathologist, preferably one with extensive advanced training in performing forensic autopsies for the court. In that case, the pathologist produces an autopsy report that serves as the foundation of the medical investigation by the ME or coroner who issues the death certificate. Animal crime investigations, however, are not typically held to any statutory requirement for the postmortem examination of the body or the issuance of any sort of death certificate. Therefore, there exists no veterinary equivalent of the coroner or medical examiner. However, as societal expectations develop and the legal landscape surrounding animal crimes changes, the need for the forensic necropsy of animal carcasses continues to increase. It will become increasingly difficult for law enforcement agencies to locate a veterinary professional who is qualified, competent, and willing to offer this service.

At the current time there exists no formally recognized forensic pathology training or certification program for the veterinary pathologist; thus there can be no legal requirement or guideline to request that a forensic necropsy be performed by a veterinary forensic pathologist, as this subspecialty is not formally recognized (McDonough et al., 2015). Similarly, there exists no formally recognized training or certification program for a forensic veterinarian. However, a board certified veterinary pathologist with extensive experience in forensic pathology (informally referred to as a veterinary forensic pathologist) or a clinical veterinarian with extensive experience in forensic medicine (informally referred to a forensic veterinarian) should be sought to perform the forensic necropsy (Munro & Munro, 2011; Ottinger et al., 2014). If no such expert is available, then a clinical veterinarian with necropsy experience may be considered to conduct the examination; however, this should be considered only as an alternative solution and must be justified to the court. The individual requested by law enforcement to perform the forensic necropsy of an animal will hereafter be referred to as the veterinary examiner. The veterinary examiner, consistent with the use of the term medical examiner, does not define a specific professional background, but rather defines the role of the individual in the investigation. The professional training required for eligibility to serve as a veterinary examiner should be established by professional standards in the coming years. At this time, however, no such standards exist, and the following shall serve as a guideline for future development. Thus, the veterinary examiner, by virtue of professional qualifications, should be, in order of preference:

1. A board certified veterinary pathologist with training and experience in forensic pathology, or a resident training under such expert
2. A clinical veterinarian with training and experience in forensic medicine, or a resident training under such expert
3. A board certified veterinary pathologist without forensic training
4. A clinical veterinarian without forensic training, but with sufficient necropsy experience

If a decision is made by a law enforcement officer or veterinary examiner to conduct a forensic necropsy, then, following receipt of the body, the veterinary examiner assumes the responsibility of completing and documenting the entire forensic necropsy and maintaining the integrity of the chain of custody of all evidentiary items submitted by law enforcement or generated during postmortem examination. The investigating officer is responsible for providing the veterinary examiner with any relevant police reports, photographs, medical records, or witness statements that may assist in the interpretation of the necropsy results. The remains of the carcass after necropsy and all items of evidence must be secured and eventually either returned to law enforcement or destroyed at the discretion of the investigating agency. Documentation of storage and movement of any items must be strictly maintained. The veterinary examiner is expected to summarize the findings of the examination into a complete written report using common language for use by the court; this report should contain a complete description of the necropsy findings, the cause of death, and possibly the manner of death. The necropsy report will be described in detail later in this chapter.

TECHNIQUES

History and Death Scene Investigation

Before accepting any body for examination, it is imperative that the veterinary examiner obtains a detailed history from the investigating officer or other party (Gerdin & McDonough, 2013). This history should include as much relevant information as known such as, but not limited to, the species, breed, age, and sex of the animal to be examined; the number of animals to be examined; the geographic location in which the body was found; the circumstances of the death; a description of the scene; the date and time the animal was found dead; the last known time the animal was alive; how the body was stored since it was found; whether the owner is known and whether the owner is suspected to have been involved in the animal's death; specific questions to be answered by the necropsy. Any communications including telephone conversations, personal conversations, emails, text messages, or any others should be documented by the veterinary examiner with date and time in the case file. The consideration of the case history by the pathologist prior to conducting the necropsy is a topic of occasional debate; however, its merits far outweigh any theoretical drawbacks in the hands of an unbiased professional. Only by understanding the facts surrounding the death as they are known can the pathologist consider the death in the proper context and answer the questions asked by law enforcement. For example, the body of a wet dog presented for necropsy may have resulted from drowning, or from immersion in water after death from another cause, or from hypothermia and exposure during a rainstorm. If witnesses describe the latter, and there is no body of water nearby in which the body could have been immersed, then the veterinary examiner can tailor the necropsy report to emphasize the likelihood of this scenario as the cause of death. Critics of this approach suggest that the veterinary examiner may be biased to believe that witness accounts are naturally factual and thereby be misled to an incorrect cause of death. In fact, any veterinary examiner must consider all of the evidence presented (including witness accounts which may or may not be truthful) and synthesize this into the postmortem examination of the body. Only in this way can the pathologist answer the question when asked by the court "are these necropsy findings consistent with the events described by the defense or with those described by the prosecution?"

Although it is common for medical examiners or coroners in some jurisdictions to begin a death investigation by visiting the death scene, this is not common practice in veterinary death investigations. Visiting the death scene can provide the pathologist with invaluable information that may be overlooked or not completely captured by the scene reports provided by law enforcement (Lew & Matshes, 2005; Touroo & Fitch, 2018). Valuable evidence may be collected from the scene at this time during which the scene is secured by law enforcement. After the scene is released by police, it may be difficult or impossible to regain lawful access to the scene to collect evidence, therefore it is essential that an investigator familiar with animal crimes is present to guide the collection of evidence relevant to the prosecution of the case. This individual may be the veterinary examiner when possible, or more commonly it may be a law enforcement officer. If the veterinary examiner does not visit the death scene, it is essential that the veterinary examiner be provided a copy of the police report with a written description of the scene and, preferably, photographs of the scene and the body in the position in which it was found.

Submission of the Body and Other Evidence

Prior to accepting and logging a case, it is advised that the submitter provide several documents to the receiving laboratory. The submitter should complete a submission form or, in the case of a clinical practice, a patient admission form. This form should include the names and addresses of any parties associated with the case, a description of the animal(s) to be examined, a description of the services requested by the examiner, and the complete history as known to the investigator with accompanying documentation as appropriate. The submitter should also sign a release form agreeing to the terms of the exam, testing, fees, subsequent communication of results, and disposition of the body and evidence after the exam. Also, both the receiving laboratory and the submitter should sign a chain of custody to document the transfer of custody of the animal(s) from the submitter to the examiner's facility.

Preliminary Imaging Techniques

Radiographic examination of the body is an invaluable tool for the postmortem assessment of orthopedic injuries and identification of foreign bodies and projectiles (Gerdin & McDonough, 2013). Radiographs are encouraged for all forensic cases; however, they should be considered compulsory for cases in which the body is incinerated or if skeletal injury, foreign body, or projectile injury is suspected.

If radiographic imaging is performed, it should be done prior to examination of the body. Specifically, radiography is ideally performed as the first stage of the examination, prior to removal of the body from any packaging in which it was submitted (Figure 10.1). If this is not possible or reasonable, radiography may be delayed until after external examination but prior to internal examination. Attempting radiography after the body has been opened will almost certainly create artifacts, precluding evaluation of some features. This technique should only be used if pre-necropsy radiography was not possible. Radiographic examination is frequently declined by the submitter due

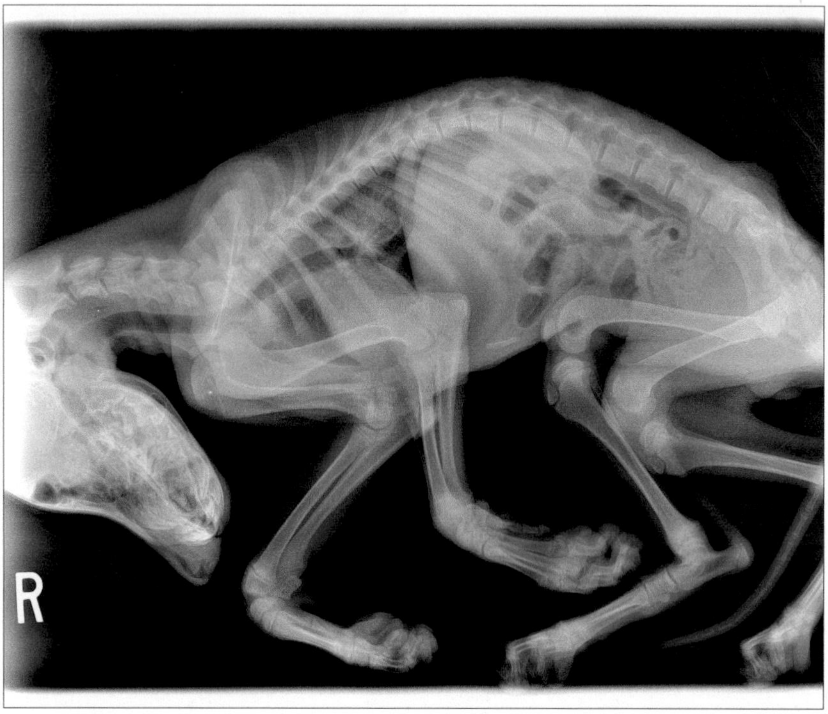

Figure 10.1 Radiograph of a dog submitted within two layers of plastic bags. Positioning and reduction of artifacts from bagging material can present a challenge, but good quality images can be obtained.

to cost. If declined, this should be documented in the case record, preferably with the signature of the submitter. A radiography release form, explaining the costs and benefits of pre-necropsy radiography, may aid the examiner in obtaining permission or documenting refusal.

Radiographs should consist of two orthogonal views of each body region, and all body regions should be imaged. All radiographs should include the date, case number, clinic or laboratory name, animal ID, and positional markers.

Establishing the Identity of the Body

The examination of the body begins with a thorough description of the evidence as submitted with emphasis on the external characteristics of the body so as to establish the identity of the victim. The examiner should record, either by written or dictated record, all examination findings. By using a standardized form, the examiner can ensure that all aspects of the examination are completed and there is no omission. Additionally, a photo log may be used to record a description of each photograph taken if resources permit. An initial photo should be taken of a laboratory or clinical document that contains identifying information such as the case number, animal or submitter name, and exam date. This is useful in establishing the identity of all subsequent photographs.

Documentation of identity should begin with a description of the manner in which the animal was received by the submitter. This should state, for example, whether the animal was delivered by the submitter or shipped by a courier. The description should further describe the packaging materials and cooling devices used, if any, to contain and preserve the body. These items should be sequentially photographed throughout the unpacking and unwrapping process; the packing materials should then be properly preserved. The examiner then photographs the carcass including case numbers in the photos. All surfaces of the body should be photographed as originally submitted, and additional emphasis should be placed on any identifying features such as unique markings, tattoos, or identification tags (Kagan & Brooks, 2018). These photos will also serve to document general features for the confirmation of animal species and breed, including color and length of hair coat or feathers. Documentation of sex and body measurements are critical to the identity of the animal and will be described in the next section. The examiner scans the carcass for the presence of an implanted microchip. Prior to scanning it is advised to run a positive control using a known microchip to confirm the proper functioning of the scanner. If a chip is detected, the information (such as microchip number and/or manufacturer) displayed by the scanner should be recorded; if no chip is detected, this should be recorded. The scanner result should be photographed.

Following this written description and photographic documentation of the identifying features of the victim, the veterinary examiner is then compelled to collect and properly preserve any items that will serve to maintain the identity of the animal. Such items may include identification tags or devices found on the body as well as biologic samples for DNA analysis. Each item collected is recorded in a written evidence log. Samples to be collected for DNA include hair (preferably with intact roots), buccal mucosal swabs, and scrapings of dried fluids. Hair samples should be stored in paper or glassine evidence envelopes, while wet fluids should be swabbed, allowed to dry in a drying rack, and placed in a swab holder box or paper envelope (Figure 10.2). Dry fluids may be swabbed with a moistened swab and then stored as previously described for wet fluid swabs. Any other tissue samples should be frozen at –20°C to –80°C.

External Examination

The external examination is perhaps the most critical and time-consuming aspect of the forensic autopsy. In order to evaluate the autopsy findings in context and form professional interpretations, the veterinary examiner should ideally review the circumstances of death or clinical history prior to initiating this portion of the examination. If not already done, all surfaces of the body should be photographed as submitted without any cleaning or other alteration. Special attention and documentation should be given to areas in which wounds, medical or surgical intervention, or other abnormal findings are identified. If any relevant foreign materials are present that may be considered as trace evidence, these should be collected and documented.

The examiner should record the body measurements including weight, crown–rump length, overall nose–tail length, chest girth, and shoulder height. The examiner should record the sex and neuter status as well as the apparent age. The nutritional condition of the animal should be described, preferably in accordance with an accepted species-specific body condition scoring system if one exists. It is prudent to specify the scale used by both name and by the range of possible scores so as to avoid uncertainty in interpretation. The veterinary examiner should then describe the state of hygiene and grooming using a standardized scale or descriptive objective language to characterize the condition and cleanliness of the hair coat, nails, ears, and teeth, and the presence or absence of any external parasites. Any dental anomalies, such as broken, loose, or missing teeth, should be noted using a standard species-specific dental chart.

Consideration should be given to the removal of nails or claws if they may contain trace evidence to be preserved. In this case, the keratin portion of the claw in its entirety can be severed with a sharp instrument and preserved in a paper evidence bag or envelope. Alternate light sources may assist with the evaluation the carcass and packaging materials when searching for trace evidence. After the initial external examination and collection of evidence, the body may be washed if necessary, to permit more complete evaluation, and then further examined and photographed.

When the examination of the superficial external body surfaces is complete, the examiner must consider the most appropriate strategy for evaluating the skin surface beneath the hair coat or feathers. Depending on the condition of the hair or feathers it may be preferable to clip the hair or pull the feathers to expose the skin surface. This may not be possible if the hair coat is wet or severely matted or if decomposition is advanced. In the case of wet or matted hair, it may be necessary to limit the clipping of hair to small suspect areas, to shave the hair over suspect areas using a razor or scalpel,

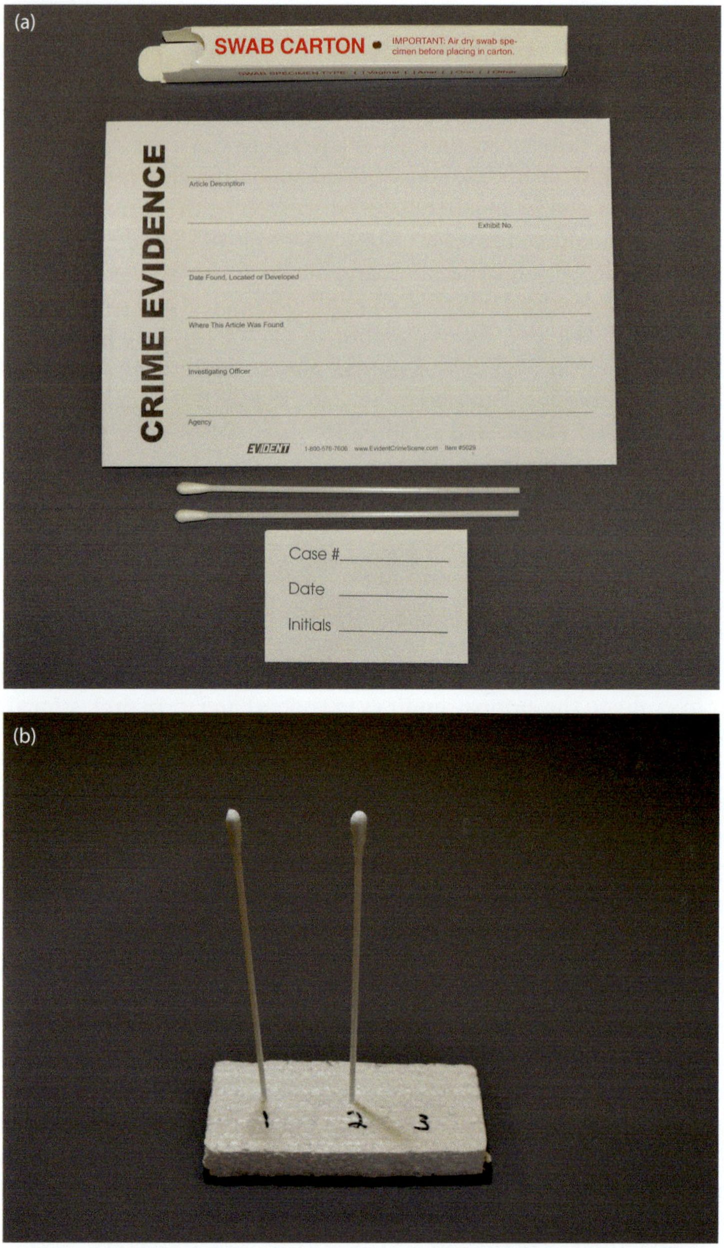

Figure 10.2 Samples to be collected to establish the identity of the body. Samples should minimally include swabs of the oral mucosa and hair with intact roots.

or to forgo the examination of the external skin surface and instead rely on the subcutaneous exam as described in the next section. In the case of advanced decomposition resulting in skin sloughing, the mechanical removal of the epidermis is often easily achieved by gentle hydraulic pressure from a water hose. This method results in diffuse removal of the epidermis from the body surface and loss of superficial detail, but changes to the subjacent dermis are made clearly visible.

The examiner should describe the state of postmortem preservation, documenting any postmortem changes including lividity, rigor, decomposition, and insect development (Brooks & Sutton, 2018). If appropriate, the body temperature should also be measured and recorded with notation of the site at which the temperature was measured, and the temperature range of

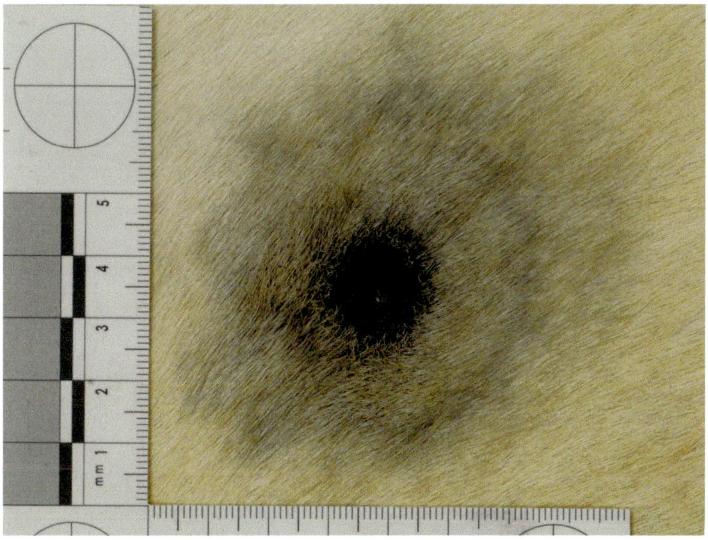

Figure 10.3 Photograph of gunshot wound on the skin of a cow. Note the camera angle is perpendicular to the surface of the skin and the scale is in the same plane of focus as the lesion.

the thermometer used. Many clinical thermometers do not record below 35°C (95°F), however hypothermia thermometers will read to much lower temperatures, thus a reading below the limit of the thermometer must be further defined.

To complete the external examination, any external wounds or injuries should be thoroughly described noting the injury type, location, size, shape, and pattern; such lesions should be photographed with a scale (Figure 10.3). Similarly, any evidence of medical or surgical intervention should be documented. All body orifices should be evaluated for exudate, hemorrhage, or foreign materials; special attention should be paid to the genitalia and anus for indication of sexual abuse. All extremities such as limbs, wings, and tail, must be palpated or otherwise examined for indication of internal injuries such as crepitus, deformity, etc. Any abnormalities detected on external examination should be photographed and should be documented on a pictorial diagram to indicate the location on the body using measurements from major body landmarks (Figure 10.4).

Internal Examination

Following completion of the external examination, a complete evaluation of all body cavities and systems should be conducted. This begins with an examination of the subcutis by reflecting the skin, preferably over the entire body, but at least over the major body areas including the head, chest, and abdomen, and over any area of the body with grossly visible external injury. The subcutaneous tissues should be evaluated for evidence of injury, most likely visible as hemorrhage (Figure 10.5). If any external evidence of injury is detected, in addition to reflecting the skin, the musculoskeletal structures and other internal tissues subjacent to the affected area should also be examined. Any skeletal lesions are to be recorded in the case record, preferably in diagrammatic form using a standardized skeletal examination form (Figure 10.6).

The veterinary examiner opens the body and examines the body cavities and organs in situ. Special attention and documentation should be given to areas in which wounds, medical or surgical intervention, or other abnormal findings are identified. The organs from the cranial, thoracic, abdominal, and pelvic cavities must be removed and examined individually. The examiner should open or dissect and describe each organ, and measure and describe its content if any. The absence of any content should also be noted for any hollow organs. Organs may be individually weighed if appropriate, although well-defined reference values do not exist for many tissues across species

Figure 10.4 Examples of pictorial diagrams of the external surface of the body. Diagrams can be easily found or created for various animal species.

and breeds. The examiner should describe any internal postmortem changes including lividity, rigor, decomposition, insect development, and so on. An assessment should be made of the stores of internal adipose tissue and the quantity and quality of bone marrow. Collection of bone marrow will be described in the next section. Any internal wounds or injuries should be described and photographed with a scale. When practical, an attempt may be made to correlate internal injuries to external injuries by showing the spatial relationship between the affected body areas; trajectory rods may be helpful for demonstrating wound tracts extending through multiple body surfaces (Figure 10.7).

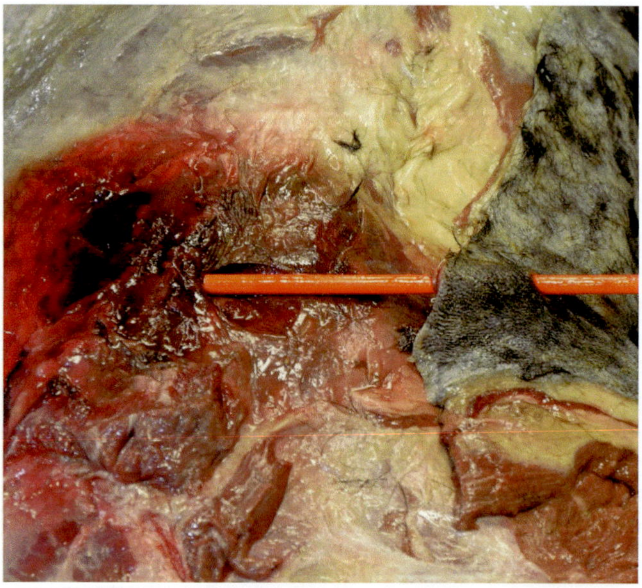

Figure 10.5 Subcutaneous hemorrhage on the abdomen of a dog at the site of a gunshot wound. In this image, a trajectory rod is being used to demonstrate the spatial relationship between wounds in various body planes.

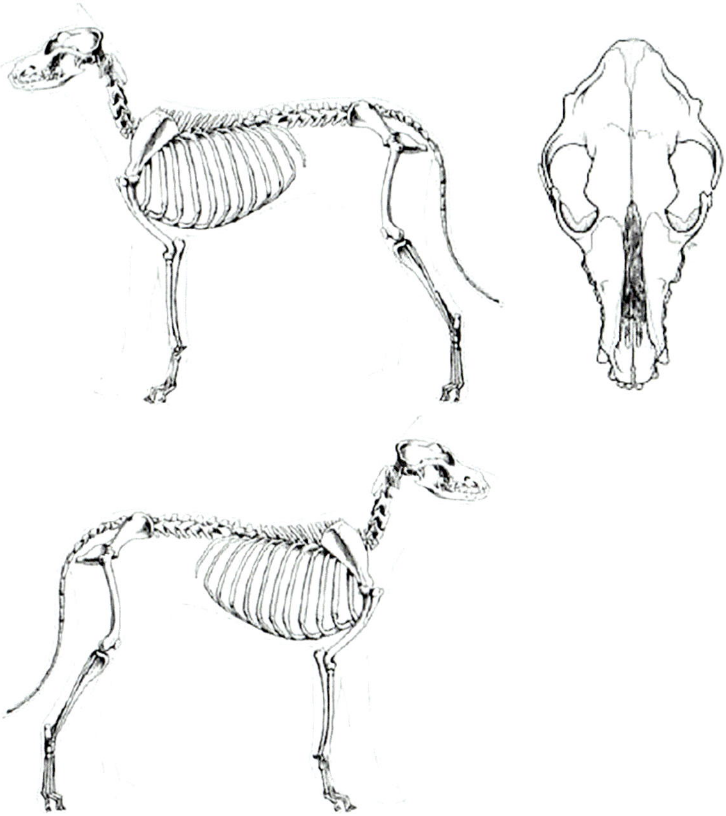

Figure 10.6 Examples of pictorial diagrams of the skeleton. Diagrams can be easily found or created for various animal species.

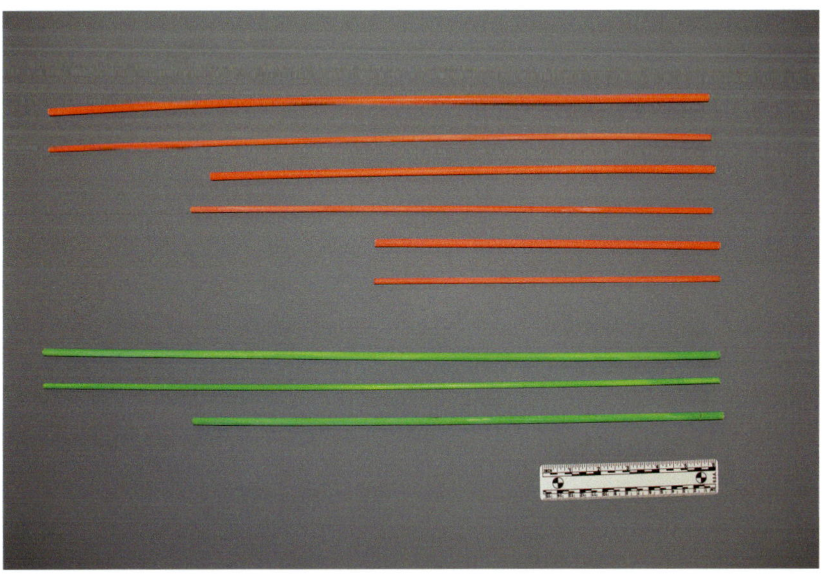

Figure 10.7 Trajectory rods made of wooden dowels painted in different colors. Rods of various lengths and diameters can be useful depending on the size of the wound tract.

Upon completion of the examination, the examiner should collect and document appropriate trace evidence from within the body and collect tissues to be preserved for ancillary testing. Any abnormalities detected on internal examination should be photographed and documented.

Microscopic Examination

After completion of the gross examination, it is considered compulsory that a microscopic examination is performed on all major organs and any additional relevant tissues based on gross exam findings (Peterson & Clark, 2006; Gerdin & McDonough, 2013). This may include both cytological evaluation of biological fluids or impression smears as well as histologic evaluation of tissues. Cytological examination should be performed by a veterinarian with training in cytology, preferably by a clinical veterinary pathologist. It is highly recommended that the histologic evaluation is performed by an anatomic veterinary pathologist. If the examiner is not a veterinary pathologist, then tissues should be sent to a veterinary pathologist for evaluation and consultation. Tissues in this set should include at a minimum: representative samples of brain, heart, lung, liver, spleen, kidney, intestine, pancreas, and margins of any gross lesions such as abscesses, tumors, burns, bruises, or other wounds. Depending on history and gross findings, additional tissues to consider for evaluation are skeletal muscle, spinal cord, peripheral nerve, lymph node, adrenal gland, thyroid gland, pituitary gland, thymus, stomach, esophagus, trachea, mammary gland, urinary bladder, testis, ovary, eye, skin, bone, bone marrow, or any other tissue containing gross change or of particular relevance (McDonough & Southard, 2017).

The interpretation of microscopic changes due to natural causes is readily performed by a veterinary pathologist; however, interpreting changes due to trauma, neglect, or other nonaccidental injury is best performed by an individual with training in forensic pathology. Many references are available to assist the forensic pathologist with the interpretation of such lesions; however, most are dedicated to human death investigation (Dettmeyer, 2011). In addition to individual case reports, a small number of references dedicated to veterinary forensic pathology have recently been published. The reader is directed to these resources for assistance in interpretation of microscopic changes (Brooks, 2018a, 2018b; Rogers & Stern, 2018).

Ancillary Diagnostic Techniques

In addition to the gross and microscopic examination, there are numerous diagnostic analyses that may be applied to the biological samples and other evidence collected at necropsy. The need for any further analysis must be determined by the investigating officer and the veterinary examiner giving careful consideration to cost, turnaround time, interpretation of results, and the legal implication of positive or negative results. The examiner and investigator must consider that well-defined reference ranges for many infrequently performed analyses do not currently exist for many animal species, making the interpretation of results problematic. Furthermore, failure to detect an agent by an available assay may be easily considered by the court to represent a true negative without consideration of the constraints that could result in a false negative.

Radiography

Radiography has already been discussed earlier in this chapter. Briefly, radiographs are strongly recommended for all forensic cases, but should be considered mandatory for cases in which the body is incinerated or if skeletal injury, foreign body, or projectile injury is suspected. Radiographs should consist of two perpendicular views of each body region, and all body regions should be imaged. All radiographs should include the date, case number, clinic or laboratory name, animal ID, and positional markers.

Alternate Light Source Examination

As an aid to enhance the visualization of various types of trace evidence such as biological fluids, fibers, bruising, and so on, alternate light source (ALS) devices may be utilized by properly trained personnel

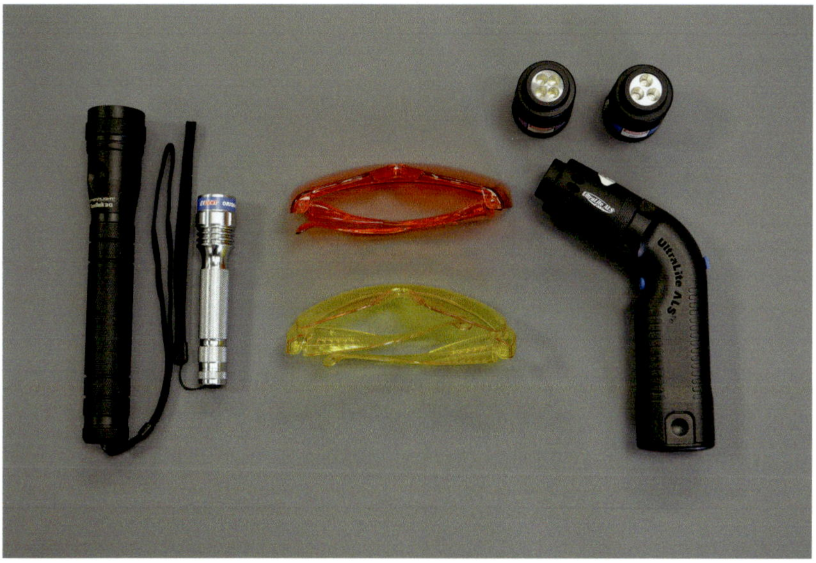

Figure 10.8 Examples of hand-held alternate light sources (ALS) showing devices capable of projecting light of various wavelengths and eyeglass filters.

(Figure 10.8). The body should be located in a darkened room and all external body surfaces examined using an ultraviolet (UV) light source (375–390 nm) with clear or yellow filter goggles. Alternatively, a blue (455 nm) light source with orange filter goggles may be used in addition to or in place of the UV light source. Other light sources and filters may be useful in other specific applications; however, these are the most generally useful combinations for most necropsy conditions. The reader is directed to other resources for further information on ALS (Maloney & Housman, 2014).

Toxicology

If indicated by history or gross or microscopic changes, tissues may be submitted for toxicological analysis. Even if no analysis is initially requested, the examiner is advised to properly collect and store samples for possible future analysis. Samples of the greatest value for toxicology include blood (anticoagulated whole blood and serum), urine, ocular fluid, stomach content, liver, kidney, brain, and fat. Other tissues may be of possible value for specific toxins. In general, tissues should be collected into leakproof containers or bags, and liquids should be collected into leakproof shatter-resistant tubes. Samples should be refrigerated if immediately submitted for analysis, otherwise they should be frozen unless otherwise directed by a toxicologist. The reader is referred to other resources for further information on veterinary toxicology (Murphy & Kagan, 2018).

Parasitology

A quantitative or semi-quantitative fecal egg exam is an inexpensive and easily run assay that is often considered a key indicator of the general quality of animal husbandry and hygiene. The examiner should consider submitting a sample of feces for parasite egg count assay, if indicated, to evaluate the gastrointestinal parasite load. Because numerous fecal egg count methods exist, if an egg count is performed, the necropsy report should specify the method used. Similarly, the examiner or the laboratory that performs the assay should interpret the results of the egg count, as results will vary across methods.

Bone Marrow Fat Analysis

Law enforcement officers frequently ask the examiner to evaluate the nutritional status of the victim. A useful tool, and one of the only quantitative postmortem measures of nutritional status,

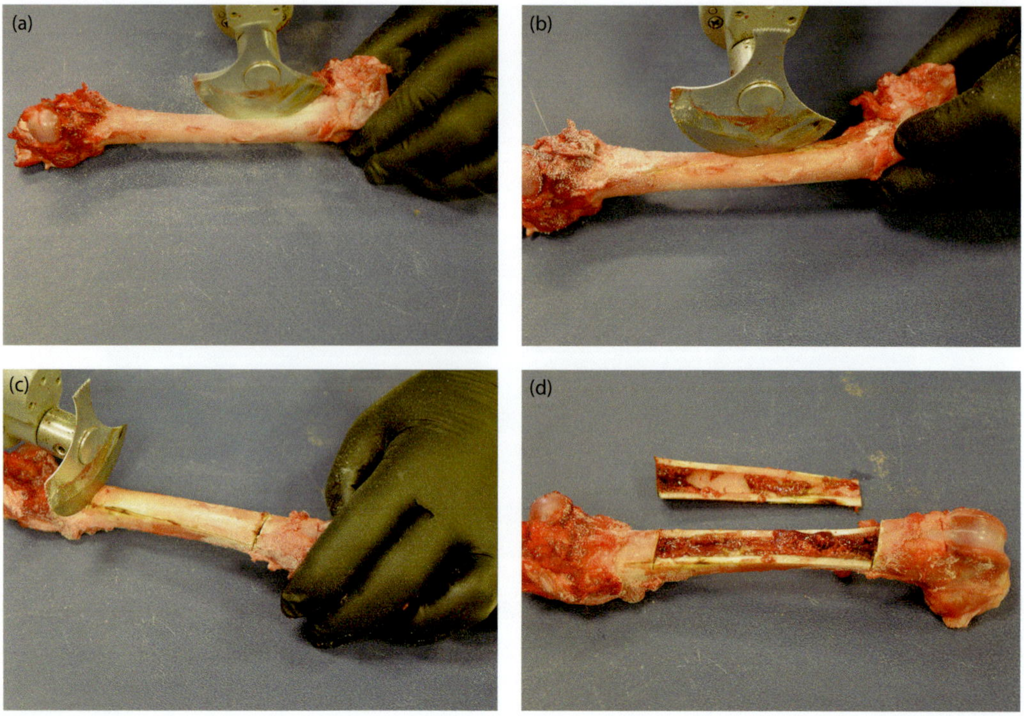

Figure 10.9 Marrow removal from the femur of a dog showing a four-sided cut in the cortical bone to expose the central marrow.

is bone marrow fat analysis (Meyerholtz et al., 2011). This chemical analysis of the bone marrow will calculate the percentage of marrow that is composed of lipid. The sample should consist of a portion of femur or humerus that contains approximately 2 grams of marrow. For larger bones, the bone can be sawn with an oscillating saw to expose the marrow, and the marrow can be removed for analysis (Figure 10.9). Marrow samples should be refrigerated if immediately submitted for analysis, otherwise they may be frozen for future analysis.

Microbiology

A very large number of diagnostic assays are available for veterinary microbial pathogens such as bacteria, viruses, and fungi. The examiner should consider submitting samples for microbiological testing if warranted. The reader is directed to other clinical resources for more information on infectious disease testing (McDonough & Southard, 2017).

Entomology

Just as the examiner must be diligent in the collection of the previously described forms of evidence at necropsy, great care must also be taken in the collection of insect evidence (Anderson, 2013). Insect life stages on, around, and within the body may offer some of the most concrete evidence of the postmortem interval as well as other features such as geographic location. In order for this evidence to be useful, however, it must be properly collected and preserved and then it must be evaluated by a trained professional. This topic is covered in great detail elsewhere in this text, so no further description will be included here. It is essential that the veterinary examiner is familiar with the proper techniques for collection and preservation of insects and how to submit them to a forensic entomologist for interpretation.

Other Analyses

While the previous items may represent many of the most commonly requested ancillary techniques in veterinary forensic necropsy, there are certainly many others that are useful in certain circumstances. The investigator and veterinary examiner may elect to request other supporting procedures such as trace evidence analysis, DNA analysis, ballistic analysis, and others as needed. Many of these analyses may be offered by crime labs; however, some crime labs will not accept samples of animal origin. The investigator and veterinary examiner are responsible for locating a laboratory capable of not only performing the desired analysis but also of interpreting the test results.

Collection of Evidence

The principles of evidence collection at necropsy are identical to those used in the collection of any other type of evidence and are described in other sections of this text, therefore they will not be specifically covered in this section. However, the reader is reminded of a few key points. The examiner should properly collect, package, label, secure, and preserve all items intended to be retained as evidence (Touroo & Fitch, 2018). Metal objects should be handled with plastic or rubber-tipped tools in order to preserve class characteristics by avoiding the creation of artifactual scratches and tool marks. An evidence log should be created to itemize and describe each piece of evidence collected; this should be coupled with a chain of custody form for each item to document its movement and transfer of custody over time. Following the necropsy, photographs and radiographs taken during the postmortem examination often become the only remaining evidence and should be retained securely. Some law enforcement agencies or veterinary examiners may prefer to transfer custody of any radiographs or photographs to the investigating agency. If this is not done, then the veterinary examiner is responsible for producing these documents in the future if requested by the court. This concept also applies to other physical evidence collected at necropsy, as described in the following section.

Disposition of the Body and Evidence

Upon completing the necropsy and collection of evidence, the examiner will be faced with the task of storing or discarding any items submitted or generated during the postmortem exam. It is critical that this process is not based on random decisions by the examiner, but rather that it is based entirely on a written agreement made with the submitter in advance. The ultimate fate of each item, known as its disposition, must be indicated by the submitter for the bodily remains, the biological samples collected and stored for ancillary testing, and any evidentiary items collected at necropsy. Options for disposition include storage of the item by the examiner, return of the item to the submitter or third party, or destruction of the item.

In the author's experience, if storage of items is offered to law enforcement agencies, they will likely choose this option. Therefore, the examiner should use diligence when offering storage for carcasses or evidence, especially for those samples requiring freezer space, because freezer space is likely limited. Items stored in a freezer should be bagged in plastic bags and sealed with some form of tamper-evident seal (Figure 10.10). The freezer should be locked, and access restricted to essential personnel. Even for items that can be stored at room temperature, great care is required to maintain an organized and secure storage cabinet that does not permit access to unauthorized parties (Figure 10.11). Thus, it is generally recommended to severely restrict the time of storage offered to agencies in order to prevent exceeding the capacity of the available laboratory space. The storage of any item should be recorded and tracked in an evidence log and/or chain of custody document. If items are to be returned to the submitter or to a third party, this also should be requested in writing by the submitter and then documented in the evidence log and/or chain of custody document.

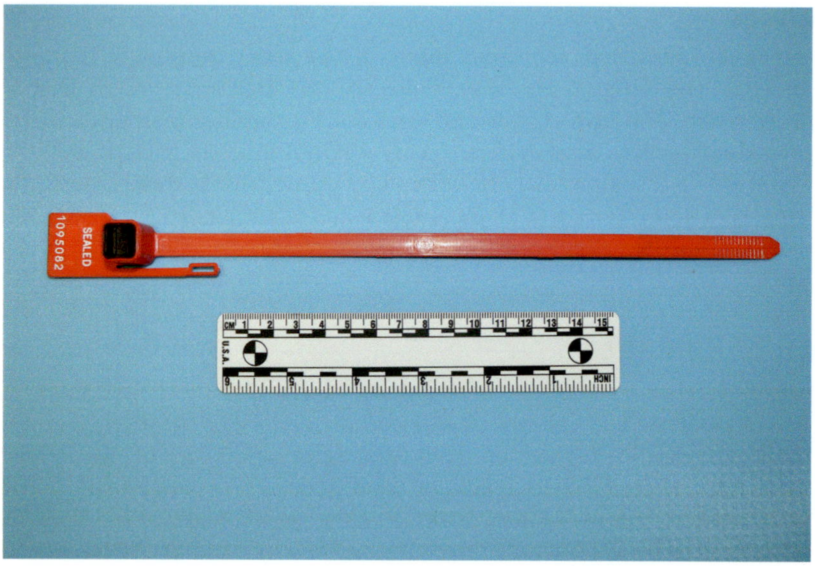

Figure 10.10 Example of tamper-resistant freezer seal showing a unique identifier.

If items are to be destroyed, this request by the submitter should be documented in writing, with care taken to specify which items are to be destroyed. It is not uncommon for agencies to request that the bodily remains be destroyed but that any evidentiary items be retained. Thus, caution must be used to address the submitter's intentions for the disposition of each item individually. The actual destruction of any item requested to be destroyed should be witnessed, documented, and signed by the examiner and/or responsible staff, indicating the date, time, and the method of destruction.

Figure 10.11 Example of evidence locker with storage boxes permitting airflow to allow samples to remain dry.

REPORTING NECROPSY RESULTS

The ultimate purpose for performing a forensic necropsy is for the submission of a written necropsy report by the medical examiner or veterinary examiner for use in court (Adams, 2008). Therefore, the pathologist should consider the written report to be the pinnacle of the veterinary medical death investigation, with all laboratory efforts culminating in the production of a single summary document. The format of this document is at the discretion of the examiner; however, several key components will be described here. Some pathologists or other veterinarians may be required to issue a report generated using a specific software such as a laboratory information management system. Many such systems, however, are designed for the production of clinical or diagnostic reports and do not lend themselves to the production of a cleanly formatted summary report for use in court. In this case, the pathologist is encouraged, if permitted by the employer, to write a stand-alone forensic necropsy report which may either be attached to the software-generated report or submitted separately. Regardless, the veterinary examiner should clarify with the submitter at the time of submission which parties are to receive reports at the conclusion of the examination. It is advised that all correspondence be conducted only through the investigating officer and that no communication with the owner occurs.

The necropsy report should contain a concise summary of the evidence known to the veterinary examiner at the time the report was written, a thorough objective summary of the necropsy findings, and an interpretive statement that should aid the court in understanding the necropsy findings in the context of the evidence available (Davis & McDonough, 2018). Specifically, the following outline is recommended for the necropsy report, although its content and format are at the discretion of the examiner.

1. *General information*: Objective information to identify the subject of the examination should be placed in either a header or footer or at the beginning of the report. This should include at a minimum the investigating agency and/or officer; the law enforcement agency case number and/or animal identification number or name if known; the species, breed, and sex of the animal; the date of the report; the date of the necropsy; the name, title, and affiliation of the veterinary examiner; and the case number assigned by the veterinary examiner if applicable.
2. *History*: The report should contain a concise but complete summary of the historical information including witness accounts, scene findings, and veterinary medical records that have been made available to the investigating officer at the time of the necropsy. This is an appropriate section in which to describe the way the body was delivered to the examiner, including the date, time, and method of delivery. It is also appropriate to state the questions that were asked of the examiner by law enforcement to be answered by the necropsy. If the submitter declined radiography of the body prior to examination or placed any other restrictions on the examination, that should be stated here.
3. *Necropsy results*: This section should include the objective findings of the gross examination and the microscopic examination. Brief interpretive phrases are appropriate, but this section should primarily consist of unfiltered objective findings and measurements observed or recorded during the examination. This should begin with a description of the container or packaging in which the body was submitted and the presence or absence of any cooling devices such as ice packs. The preservation status (frozen, thawed, refrigerated, unrefrigerated, etc.) and postmortem condition of the body should be described (Brooks, 2016). The identifying features of the body including weight, measurements, hair coat color and length, and sex should be described. The features of the external and internal examination should be described. Results of the microscopic examination should be included, stating all tissues that were examined. The results of any ancillary test procedures should be included if applicable, along with the name of the laboratory at which

those analyses were conducted. The examiner may choose to summarize the gross and microscopic findings for clarity under a heading such as Pathologic Anatomic Findings.

4. *Cause and manner of death*: The examiner's professional opinion regarding the cause of death, and the subsequent opinion section that expands upon this cause, are arguably the most important items contained within the necropsy report. Up to this point, the report contains entirely objective information provided either by the investigating officer or by the examiner through the course of the gross and microscopic examination. Only at this point in the report does the language change to that of opinion. The examiner is typically expected to provide the court with the cause of death of the victim examined. Cause of death is defined as the initiating event that resulted in the death of the victim. This may be further subdivided into immediate, also known as proximate, cause of death and underlying cause of death. The immediate or proximate cause of death is the final disease, injury, or condition that resulted in death. The underlying cause of death is the initial disease, injury, or condition that began the chain of events that ultimately led to death. Another term that is sometimes used, contributory cause of death, is a condition found in the victim that affected the progression of physiologic changes resulting in death but did not cause that sequence of events to begin. Some pathologists also prefer to include a mechanism of death, which is defined as the physiological process that resulted from the previously stated cause of death. For complex situations, the mechanism of death may add clarity to the sequence of events described in the report; otherwise, it often is unnecessary and does not need to be considered essential.

   The manner of death is defined as the legal classification of a death as having resulted from a natural cause, an accidental injury, or an intentional injury (Figure 10.12). Assigning a manner of death to a victim is a complex process that must include consideration of both the necropsy findings and the investigative findings, such as the known or reported event history and scene findings. The manner of death assignment in human death investigations typically is one of five classifications: natural, accidental, suicide, homicide,

Manner of death in human and animal death investigations

Human

- Natural
- Accidental
- Suicide
- Homicide
- Undetermined

Animal

- Natural
- Accidental*
- Nonaccidental*
    - Includes both nonaccidental injuries and neglect
- Undetermined

(*Accidental and nonaccidental manners of death may by collectively considered as unnatural.)

Figure 10.12 Classifications for the manner of death used in human death certificates and proposed classifications for the manner of death for use in animal death investigations.

or undetermined. Because suicide is not applicable to animal victims, this classification is removed for veterinary forensic investigations. Because the term homicide is not directly applicable to a nonhuman victim, this term is replaced by nonaccidental injury. Thus, the four classifications for manner of death in veterinary medicine are: natural, accidental injury, nonaccidental injury, or undetermined (Figure 10.12). The distinction between accidental and nonaccidental injury may be difficult and often relies heavily on the consideration of the synthesis of all of the case findings. Alternatively, accidental and nonaccidental manners of death may by collectively considered as unnatural. If the examiner is not able to determine the manner of death to a reasonable degree of certainty, then this classification should be listed as undetermined. Ideally the examiner will discuss the case with the investigator and/or the prosecutor in order to determine whether or not it is preferred to include manner of death in the report.

5. *Opinion*: The opinion section is simply the verbalization of the summary of the necropsy findings and the overall interpretation of the cause and manner of death. Beyond the cause and manner of death, this is the most valuable portion of the necropsy report for the court. It is critical that the opinion is written in plain language that is understandable to the court, including all members of the jury, and that all statements and interpretations made by the examiner are carefully presented to avoid bias or speculation. In the opinion statement, the examiner is expected to verbally address the questions asked by the submitter at the time of submission.

It is generally expected that the necropsy report will be submitted to the investigating law enforcement agency in a timely manner and by the route requested at the time of submission. Turnaround times are affected by caseload and complexity and by the extent of ancillary testing; however, this should be discussed with the submitter at the time of submission so that the investigator has realistic expectations. The parties should also discuss practices for future communications on this case and the expectations of the examiner in the subsequent legal proceedings.

As stated previously, at the completion of the necropsy all that remain of the permanent record are often the photographs and radiographs as well as the necropsy report. It is absolutely essential that these items are retained securely and filed in a manner that allows for their ready retrieval if records are requested by law enforcement or subpoena by an agent of the court.

References

Adams, V. I. 2008. *Guidelines for Reports by Autopsy Pathologists*. Totowa, NJ: Humana Press.

Anderson, G. 2013. Forensic entomology: The use of insects in animal cruelty cases. In *Veterinary Forensics: Animal Cruelty Investigations*, edited by M. Merck, 273–286. Ames, IA: John Wiley & Sons, Inc.

Brooks, J. and Sutton L. 2018. Postmortem changes and estimating the postmortem interval. In *Veterinary Forensic Pathology*, edited by J. W. Brooks, 43–63. Cham, Switzerland: Springer.

Brooks, J. W. 2016. Postmortem changes in animal carcasses and estimation of the postmortem interval. *Veterinary Pathology*. 53(5):929–40.

Brooks, J. W. 2018a. *Veterinary Forensic Pathology*, 1st ed. Vol. 1, edited by J. W. Brooks. Cham, Switzerland: Springer.

Brooks, J. W. 2018b. *Veterinary Forensic Pathology*, 1st ed. Vol. 2, edited by J. W. Brooks. Cham, Switzerland: Springer.

Brownlie, H. W. and Munro, R. 2016. The veterinary forensic necropsy: A review of procedures and protocols. *Veterinary Pathology*. 53(5):919–928.

CDC, Centers for Disease Control and Prevention. 2015. Public Health Law Program: Coroner/Medical Examiner Laws by State. Available from www.cdc.gov/publications/coroner.

Davis, G. and McDonough, S. P. 2018. Writing the necropsy report. In *Veterinary Forensic Pathology*, edited by J. W. Brooks, 139–149. Cham, Switzerland: Springer.

Dettmeyer, R.B. 2011. *Forensic Histopathology: Fundamentals and Perspectives*. New York: Springer.

Gerdin, J. A. and McDonough, S. P. 2013. Forensic pathology of companion animal abuse and neglect. *Veterinary Pathology*. 50(6):994–1006.

Institute of Medicine (U.S.). Committee for the Workshop on the Medicolegal Death Investigation System. 2003. *Medicolegal Death Investigation System: Workshop Summary.* Washington, DC: National Academies Press.

Kagan, R. and Brooks, J. 2018. Performing the forensic necropsy. In *Veterinary Forensic Pathology*, edited by J. W. Brooks, 27–42. Cham, Switzerland: Springer.

Lew, E. O. and Matshes, E. W. 2005. Death scene investigation. In *Forensic Pathology: Principles and Practice*, edited by D. Dolinak, E. W. Matshes and E. O. Lew, 9–64. New York: Elsevier/Academic Press.

Maloney, M. S. and Housman, D. 2014. *Crime Scene Investigation Procedural Guide*, edited by R. M. Gardner. Boca Raton: CRC Press.

McDonough, S. P., Gerdin, J., Wuenschmann, A., McEwen, B. J. and Brooks, J. W. 2015. Illuminating dark cases: Veterinary forensic pathology emerges. *Veterinary Pathology*. 52(1):5–6.

McDonough, S. P. and Southard, T.L. 2017. *The Necropsy Guide for Dogs, Cats, and Small Mammals.* Ames: IA: Wiley-Blackwell.

Merck, M., Miller, D. and Maiorka, P. C. 2013. CSI: Examination of the animal. In *Veterinary Forensics: Animal Cruelty Investigations*, edited by M. Merck, 37–68. Ames, IA: Wiley-Blackwell.

Meyerholtz, K. A., Wilson, C. R., Everson, R. J. and Hooser, S. B. 2011. Quantitative assessment of the percent fat in domestic animal bone marrow. *Journal of Forensic Sciences*. 56(3):775–777.

Munro, R. and Munro, H. 2011. Forensic veterinary medicine 2. Postmortem investigation. *In Practice*. 33(6):262–270.

Murphy, L. A. and Kagan, R. 2018. Poisoning. In *Veterinary Forensic Pathology*, edited by J. W. Brooks, 75–87. Cham, Switzerland: Springer.

Ottinger, T., Rasmusson, B., Segerstad, C. H., Merck, M., Goot, F. V., Olsen, L. and Gavier-Widen, D. 2014. Forensic veterinary pathology, today's situation and perspectives. *Veterinary Record*. 175(18):459.

Peterson, G. F. and Clark, S. C. 2006. Forensic autopsy—Performance standards. *American Journal of Forensic Medicine and Pathology*. 27(3):200–225.

Rogers, E. R. and Stern, A. W. 2018. *Veterinary Forensics: Investigation, Evidence Collection, and Expert Testimony*. New York: CRC Press.

Touroo, R., Brooks, J., Lockwood, R. and Reisman, R. 2018. Medicolegal investigation. In *Veterinary Forensic Pathology*, edited by J. W. Brooks, 1–8. Cham, Switzerland: Springer.

Touroo, R. and Fitch, A. 2018. Crime scene findings and the indentification, collection, and preservation of evidence. In *Veterinary Forensic Pathology*, edited by J. W. Brooks, 9–25. Cham, Switzerland: Springer.

CHAPTER 11

FORENSIC VETERINARY OSTEOLOGY

Maranda Kles and Lerah Sutton

INTRODUCTION

Osteology is the study of the structure and function of the skeleton and bony structures. Comparative osteology is the study of the similarities and differences in the osteology, or anatomy, of different species. From these fields comes forensic veterinary osteology, which is the application of veterinary, or comparative, osteology to questions of legal significance, often the identification of genus and species of animal remains, to then determine what legal statutes apply in animal cruelty or abuse cases (Figure 11.1). Why study bones?

Bone is dynamic; it is ideally structured to allow for growth and development, and it can be modified throughout life based on muscle use, health, diet, and trauma. In addition, bone is durable and survives long after soft tissue has decomposed, providing an enduring record that can be used for identification and analysis of both life history and cause of death. This fact has been known and utilized by forensic anthropologists for over 150 years to identify human skeletal remains and provide evidence in the determination of cause and manner of death. However, the field of forensic veterinary osteology is fairly young; most books on nonhuman osteology focus on simply identifying the bone based on comparative osteology, that is, does this bone look like this animal or that animal (e.g., Elbroch, 2006; France, 2009); or they are oriented toward zooarchaeology, which is the analysis of animal bones in the archaeological record, and typically focuses on prehistoric animals or domesticated animals, rarely mentioning dogs, cats, or other animals of forensic significance (Cornwall, 1968; Olsen, 1973; Gilbert, 1990; Hillson, 1999; Hulbert, 2001; Reitz and Wing, 2008; Beisaw, 2013). Those that do review modern animal identification rarely address variation with regard to age, sex, and breed, and those that do are not focused on the application of this knowledge

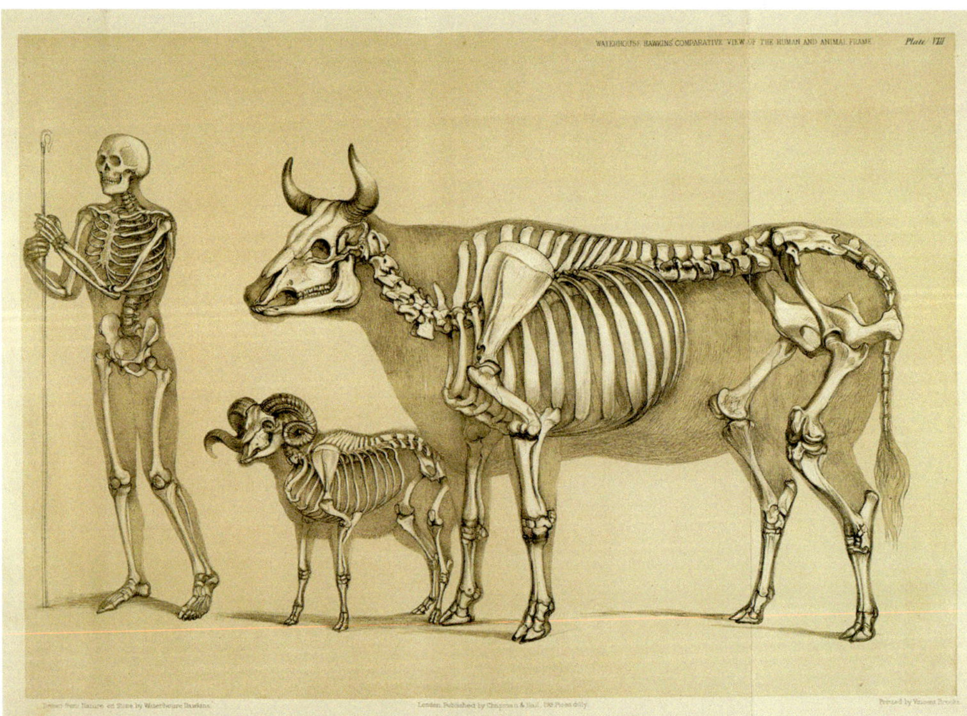

Figure 11.1 Comparative osteology: Man/cow/sheep. (From Hawkins, B.W. 1860. *A Comparative View of the Human and Animal Frame*. [Plate eight—Man, cow and sheep and explanatory text], pp. [unnumbered]-22. https://uwdc.library.wisc.edu/collections/ histscitech/companat/)

in forensic settings (e.g., Elbroch, 2006). Finally, there is very little literature that addresses trauma analysis from a skeletal perspective; most literature is focused on the analysis of trauma in soft tissues (e.g., Merck, 2013). Therefore, this is an exciting and rapidly growing field. This chapter seeks to open the door to this field through an introductory view of veterinary osteology focusing on mammalian osteology and touching on how this knowledge can then be used to address issues of abuse, cruelty, or neglect to demonstrate the utility of, and need for, veterinary osteology in forensic veterinary investigations.

BONE STRUCTURE AND GROWTH

Bone is made up of protein (collagen) and mineral (hydroxyapatite) portions. Collagen, the organic component, constitutes approximately 30% of a bone's content, while the mineral portion makes up approximately 65% of a bone's content, and the remaining 5% is water. Collagen gives bone the toughness and elasticity needed to flex and endure tension, while hydroxyapatite gives it the rigidity and hardness needed for stability (Romer & Parsons, 1977). Keratin is the hard tissue that comprises hooves, nails, and the "shell" of animals; keratin is made up of fibrous proteins (Reitz & Wing, 2008). These hard tissues may still be found in the forensic setting, and their analysis could assist in species identifications. The last tissue of osteological concern is cartilage, a dense connective tissue comprised mostly of collagen. This tissue decomposes faster than bone, but slower than soft tissues; therefore, it may still be present in forensic cases. However, due to elasticity of this tissue and the tendency for it to dry out, altering its appearance, the analysis of this tissue is limited, although there are sources available regarding this topic (see Bonte, 1975; Crowder et al., 2013).

Bone makes up approximately 20% of the total body weight of a mammal and is the rigid component of the musculoskeletal system. Bones give the body form and structure while acting as levers that are acted on by muscles. Bone is formed by osteoblasts, which are typically found underneath the periosteum of bone or the thin membrane on the outer surface of bone, while osteoclasts resorb or remove bone. Both of these cells are especially active during the growth and development phases of life but continue their activity throughout adulthood. These cells are what results in the growth and remodeling of bones throughout life. In growth, the body lays down immature bone, described as coarsely bundled or woven bone, rapidly, and it is high in osteocytes, or living bone cells. It is called woven bone due to the random pattern of collagen fibers when examined microscopically; macroscopically, the bone appears more porous and disorganized, or it does not have the smooth appearance of mature bone. Immature bone is also seen in fracture repairs and some bone tumors. Mature bone eventually replaces woven bone and is characterized by the organized structure of collagen. Being able to identify these types of bone and understanding the process and timeframe over which growth and maturation occur is the foundation of identifying and interpreting trauma. For example, evaluating the timing of fracture repair allows for the development of a timeline of trauma, which can then be used to build a case for systemic nonaccidental injury, i.e., abuse.

Compact bone (dense/spongy/cortical bone) is often found in the outer shaft of long bones or the joints of long bones and contains haversian canals to allow for nutrients to flow to the bone. Subchondral bone is found on the joint surfaces and is covered by cartilage; it has a smoother and shinier appearance than regular compact bone (Figure 11.2). Trabecular bone (cancellous bone), on the other hand, is fed by blood vessels and is found within the marrow cavity; it has a porous or honeycomb structure and is typically tightly packed at the joint ends of bone (Figure 11.3). Trabecular bone acts as a strut system giving support to bones without drastically increasing their weight. This is particularly obvious when viewing avian (bird) bone (Figure 11.4).

Bones are shaped by the surrounding soft tissues, muscles, veins, tendons, and organs; they are shaped by the activities of an individual, running, bending, squatting, lifting, chewing; they are shaped by their sex, age, and stature. This information helps identifying the bones that are present

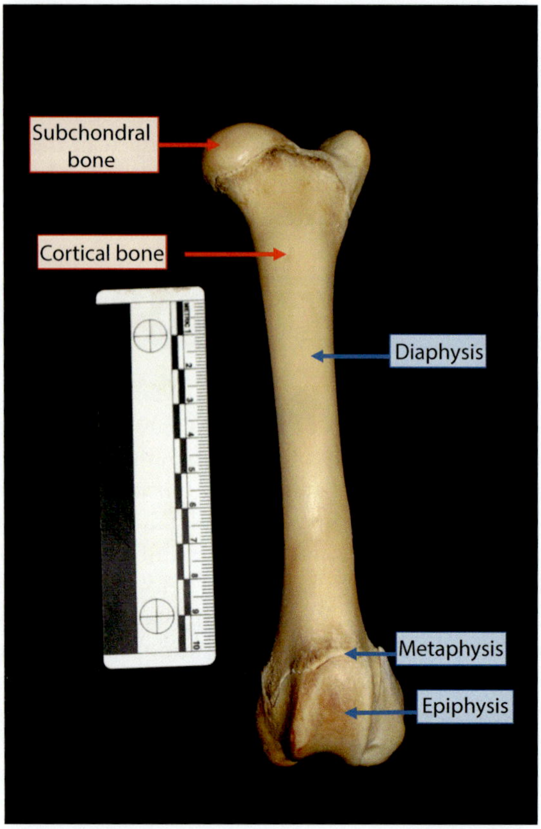

Figure 11.2 Parts of the bone and denoting compact versus subchondral bone.

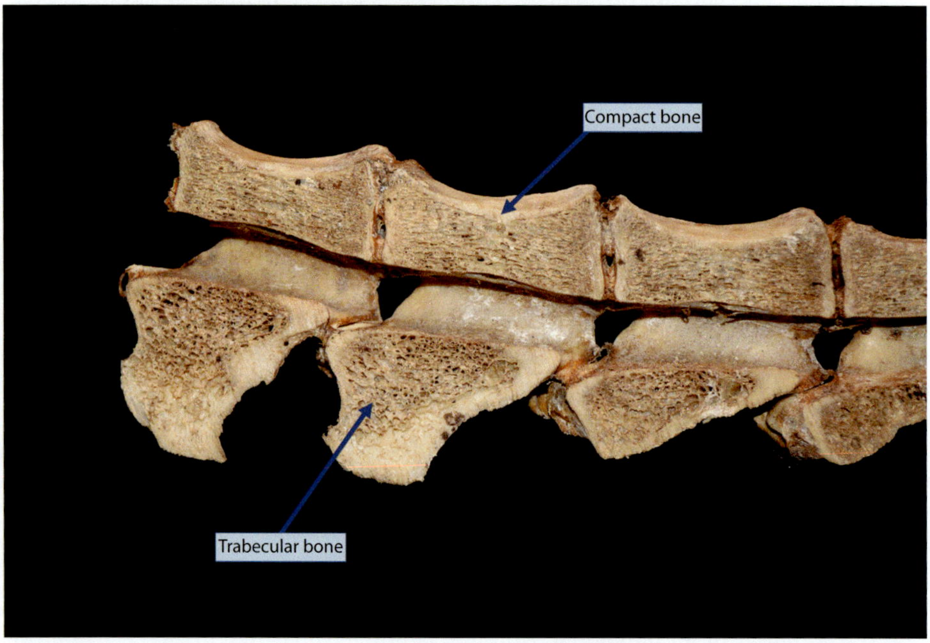

Figure 11.3 Compact bone versus trabecular bone. Image of deer vertebra.

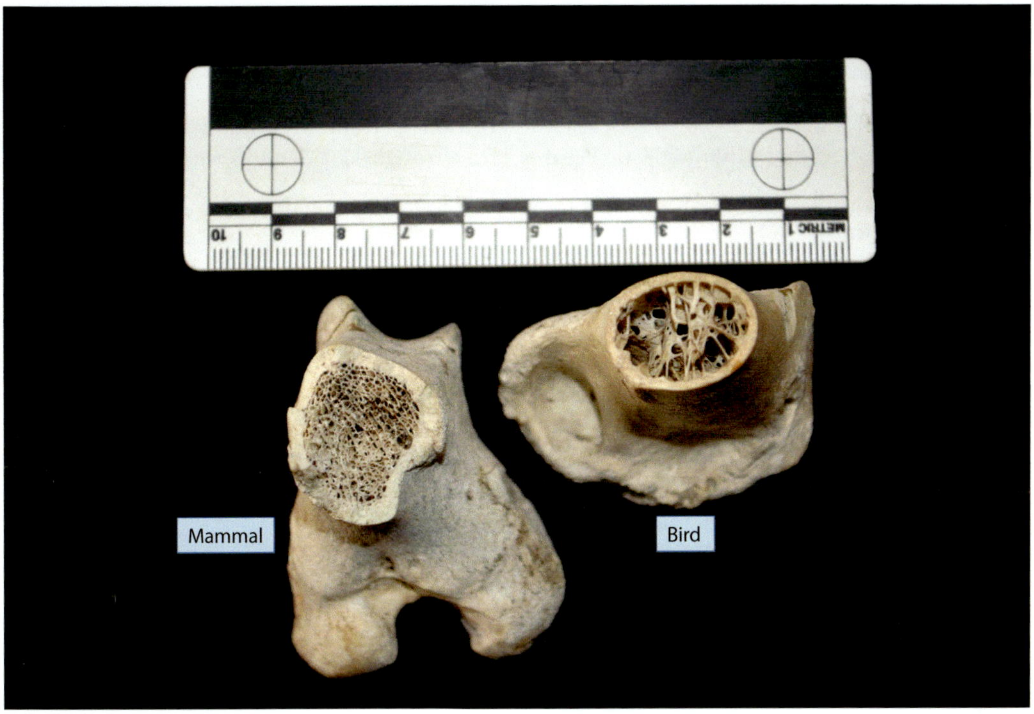

Figure 11.4 Mammal bone (deer) versus bird bone (turkey). Note the differences in the cortical bone thickness and the arrangement of the trabecular bone.

and then the species that are present. It also helps us understand the life histories of the individuals. Bone is built and modified according to Wolff's law, which was outlined by an orthopedic surgeon, Julius Wolff (1892), and simply states that bone is laid down where it is needed and resorbed where it is not.

Wolff's law is the foundation of the concept that form follows function; the skeleton of each class of animal (mammal, bird, reptile, and fish) has a generalized body plan with modifications that are grouped in class, genus, and species levels. These modifications are primarily based on locomotion (function) differences, that is, quadrupedal walking/running, slithering, flying, climbing, swinging, and so on, and dietary differences (i.e., herbivore, omnivore, carnivore).

Bones come in five basic forms, which help with initial identification. These are the long bones (limb bones; predominately compact bone), short bones (wrist and ankle bones; predominately spongy bone), flat bones (skull bones; plates of compact bone enclosing spongy bone), irregular bones (vertebrae; variable in composition), and sesamoid bones (patellae; bony structures that develop within tendons or ligaments).

Long bones are composed of three parts: the diaphysis (shaft), the epiphysis (end or joint surfaces), and the metaphysis (at the proximal and distal ends of the diaphysis) where bone growth occurs. During growth, a physis (growth plate) is present until the full length of the shaft is reached, at which point the diaphysis has met the epiphysis and fusion of the two begins. This process is tightly controlled by genetics and occurs in a highly predictable fashion, so as you can imagine, understanding the process could be useful for age determination (Figure 11.3).

Bones are not just straight tubes; they have bumps, ridges, and valleys, all of which have a name (see France, 2009 and White et al., 2012 for lists of features). These features are instrumental in determining the bones that are present, the side of the body from which the bone comes (i.e., right or left), and ultimately their class, genus, or species level association.

ANATOMICAL TERMS

Standardized anatomical terms allow for easier descriptions of trauma, pathology, or other variation between practitioners and other experts. Figures 11.5 through 11.7 demonstrate these terms.

Cranial: Toward the head
Caudal: Toward the tail
Rostral: Toward the nose when referencing the skull
Ventral: Toward the belly or the ground; down; it is not used when referencing the limbs
Dorsal: Toward the back or the sky; up; can be used to reference the superior surface of the fore and hind paws or feet
Medial: Toward the midline
Lateral: Away from the midline
Proximal: Nearer the trunk or axial skeleton or main mass, primarily used for limbs and tail
Distal: Farther from the trunk or axial skeleton or main mass, primarily used for limbs and tail
Palmar: Inferior surface of the fore paw or foot
Plantar: Inferior surface of hind paw or foot
Axial: Skeleton of the head, vertebra, and ribs
Appendicular: Skeleton of appendages; arms, legs, and their sockets

Dental Terms

Mesial: Toward the midline, or central incisors
Distal: Away from the midline, or toward the molars
Lingual: Toward the tongue
Labial: Toward the lips, typically referring to the anterior teeth or incisors
Buccal: Toward the cheeks, typically referring to the posterior teeth or molars
Interproximal: Between two teeth
Occlusal: Chewing surface, called incisal surface on incisors

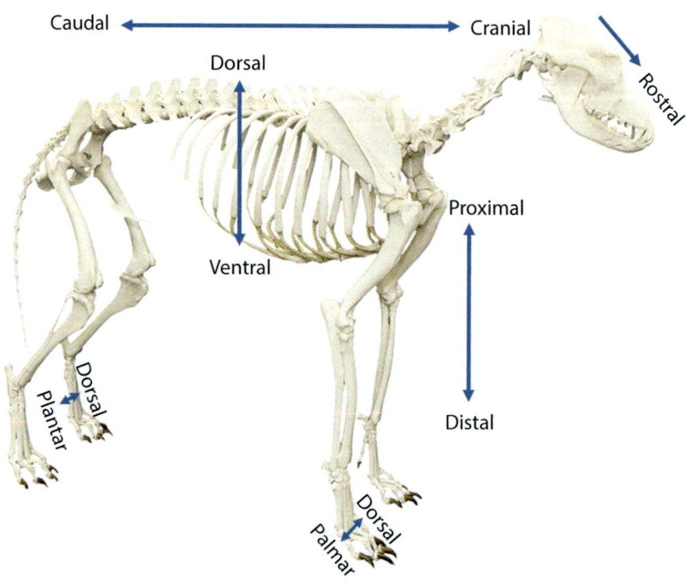

Figure 11.5 Direction terms indicated on *Canis* skeleton.

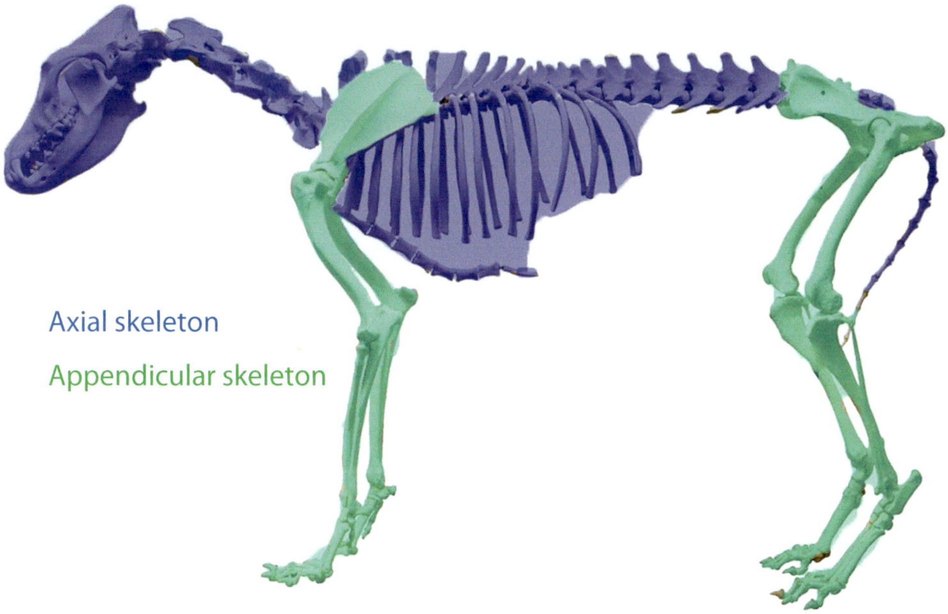

Figure 11.6 Axial versus appendicular skeleton indicated on *Canis* skeleton.

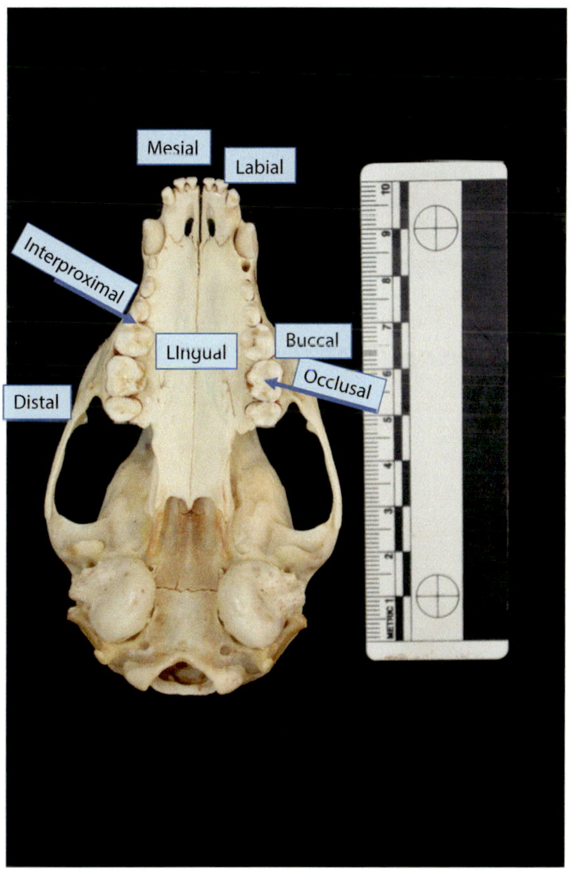

Figure 11.7 Dental direction terms indicated on inferior view of raccoon skull.

SKELETAL ELEMENTS

A detailed discussion of the skeletal elements is beyond the scope of this chapter. Therefore, a brief overview of the elements is provided (Figure 11.8). When examining various mammals, one will notice that *form follows function*; in the skull, vision, scent, and diet are the particularly influential functions, while in the distal limbs, locomotion is the primary influential function. Some elements are more diagnostic of species than other, with the skull being the most diagnostic, therefore it will be discussed in a little more detail to highlight some of the features that are examined.

Cranium

The cranium encompasses four of the five senses: sight, sound, smell, and taste (diet). The shape of the cranium and mandible can provide a great deal of information about the importance of these senses to the animal which can help quickly narrow the range of species under consideration.

Sight

The eye orbits are made up of a number of bones and are delineated by the zygomatic processes, also called the postorbital process, on the lateral aspect of the orbit. The size, orientation, and bony completeness of the orbits and the process can provide insight into an animal's reliance on vision for hunting/survival. The large and semi-complete orbits of felines (Figure 11.9) attest to their visual acuity in hunting. Similarly, owls have very large and well protected orbits to allow for nocturnal vision. In both species, anterior orbits create visual field overlap and stereoscopic vision or depth perception. Rodents have smaller, less protected orbits and less reliance on vision. Likewise, the armadillo (Figure 11.10) has minimal orbital protection; they rely on other senses to navigate the world or to protect themselves from predators. Ungulates, such as horses, deer, and cow, have large and laterally placed orbits which allow them to see nearly 360°, essential for watching for predators, but they see the world through monocular vision and they have no depth perception; as prey they need to know where their predators are, but not necessarily how close (Figure 11.11).

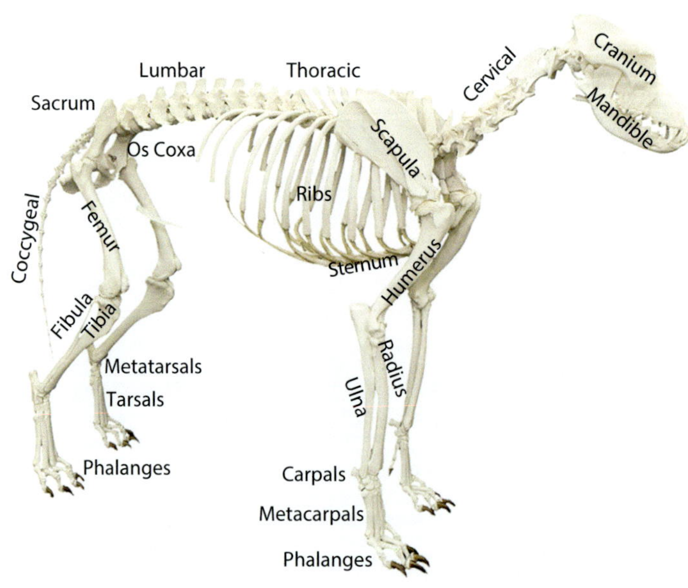

Figure 11.8 Bones identified on *Canis* skeleton.

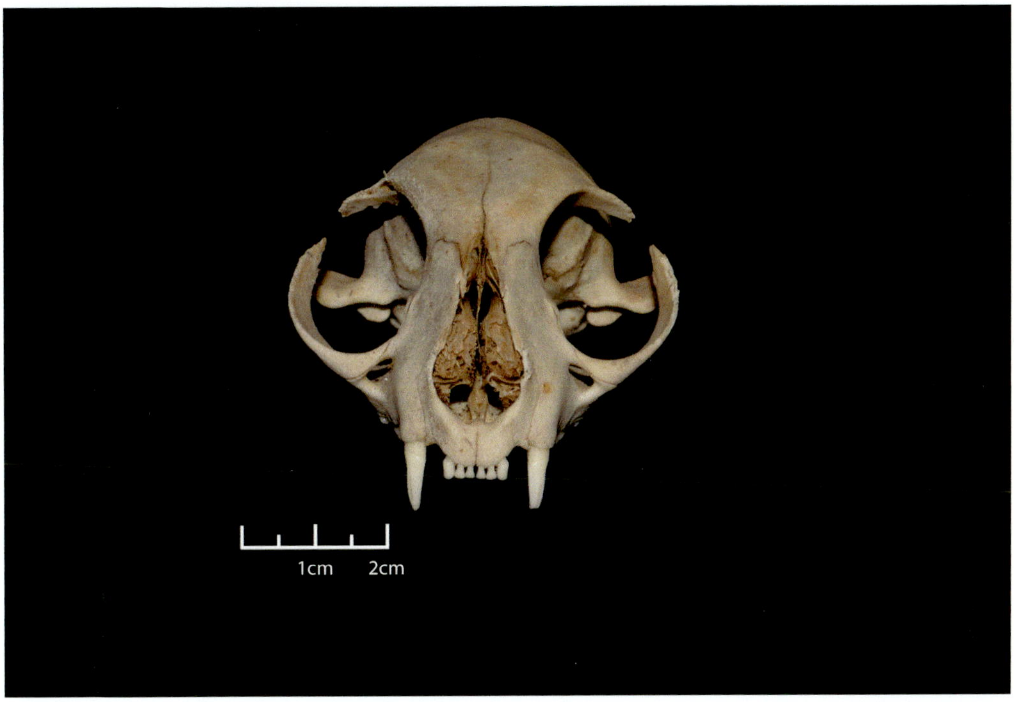

Figure 11.9 Anterior view of common house cat skull.

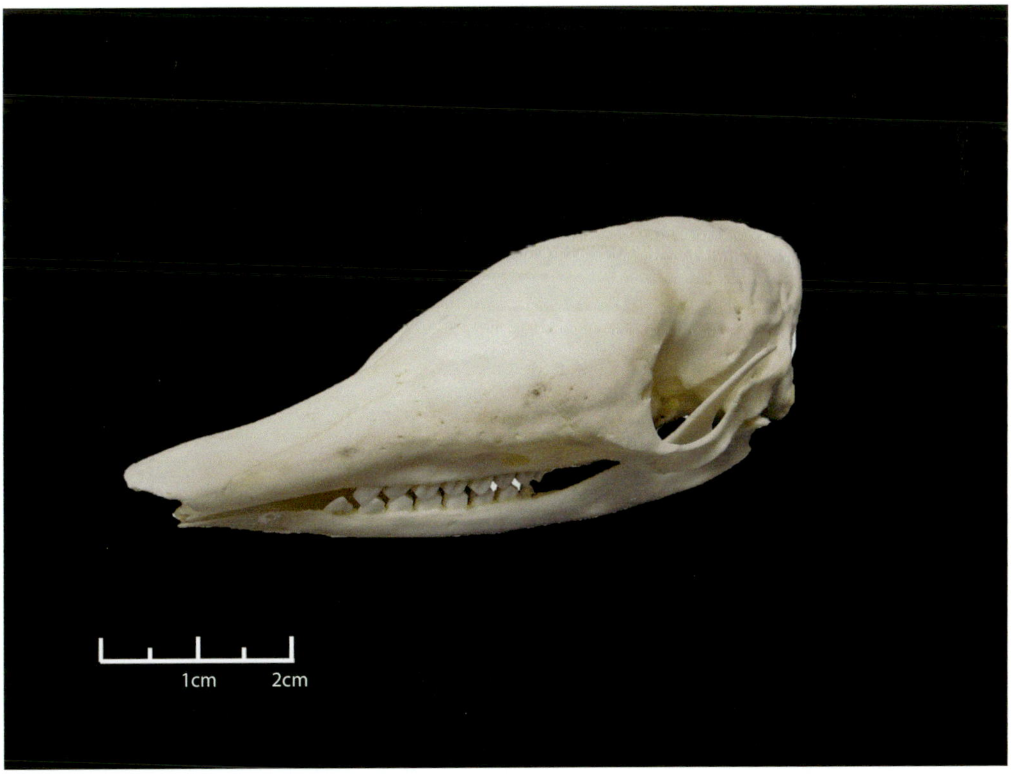

Figure 11.10 Lateral view of armadillo skull.

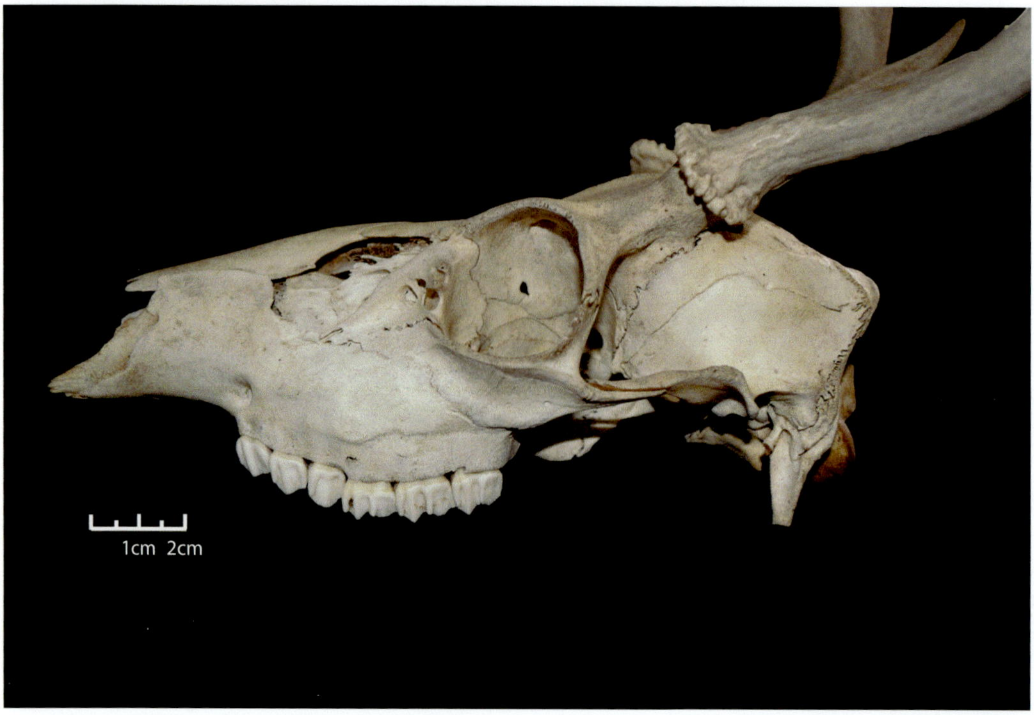

Figure 11.11 Lateral view of whitetail deer skull.

Sound

The temporal bones, on the sides of the skull, house the auditory structures, the auditory bulla and in some mammals the external auditory meatus, or ear hole. The auditory bulla is an inflated, thin-walled structure located just inferior to the external auditory meatus. It is enlarged in canids and felines, is moderate in deer, and is smaller in bears, opossum, and cattle. Again, this is based on the functional significance of hearing to each species in hunting and survival (Figures 11.12 and 11.13).

Smell

The nose is defined by the maxilla and the nasal bones. Within the nose are the nasal conchae, which are snail-like in their appearance, and act as turbines in the sense of smell. The nasal conchae are larger and more complicated in animals that rely more heavily on their sense of smell (Figure 11.14). The overall length of an animal's nose also reflects its reliance on smell for hunting/survival. The armadillo, which is heavily reliant on smell, has a very long nasal region and no orbital protection, while primates have reduced nasal regions and significant orbital protection (Figure 11.15).

Taste

Dietary habits dictate the size and shape of the maxilla and mandible and the articulation of the mandible with the skull via the temporomandibular joint, found on the temporal bone. Looser articulations with the cranium allow for more lateral movement of the mandible in grazing animals, while tighter articulations allow for exact tooth alignment and shearing of meat from carcasses. Also, the height of the mandibular condyle, the part that attaches to the cranium near the ear, in relation to the tooth row can inform diet. A condyle in line with the tooth row allows the teeth to meet more effectively, which is better for slicing, shearing, and grinding food or meat (carnivores and omnivores; e.g., the bobcat), while a condyle that is well above the tooth row is better for rolling food or milling vegetation (herbivores; e.g., the horse).

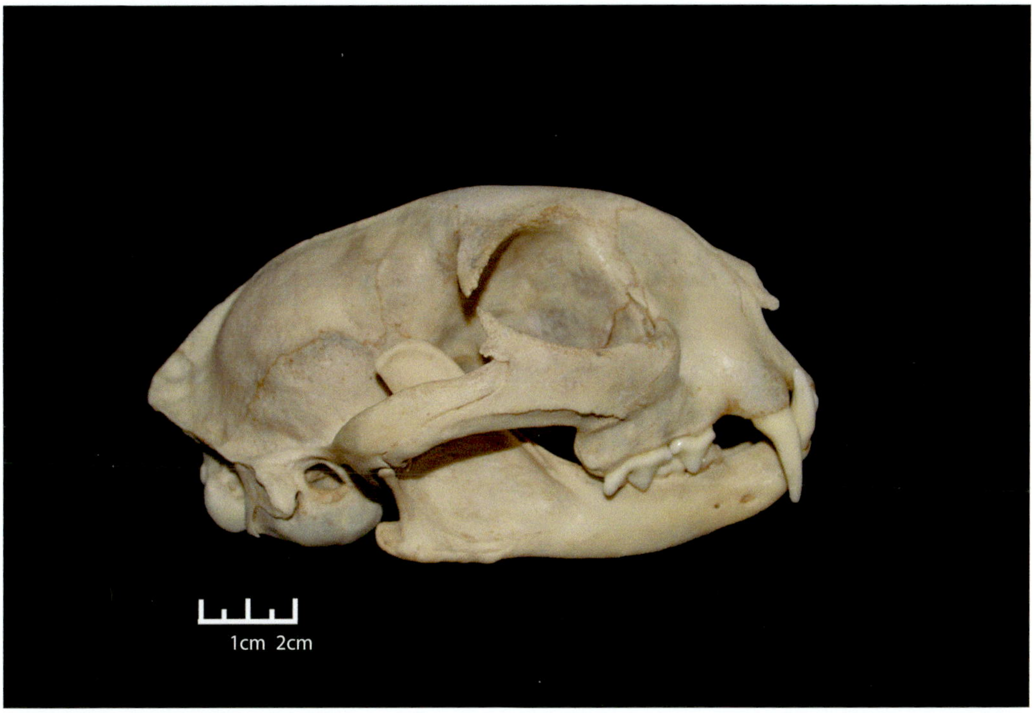

Figure 11.12 Lateral view of bobcat skull.

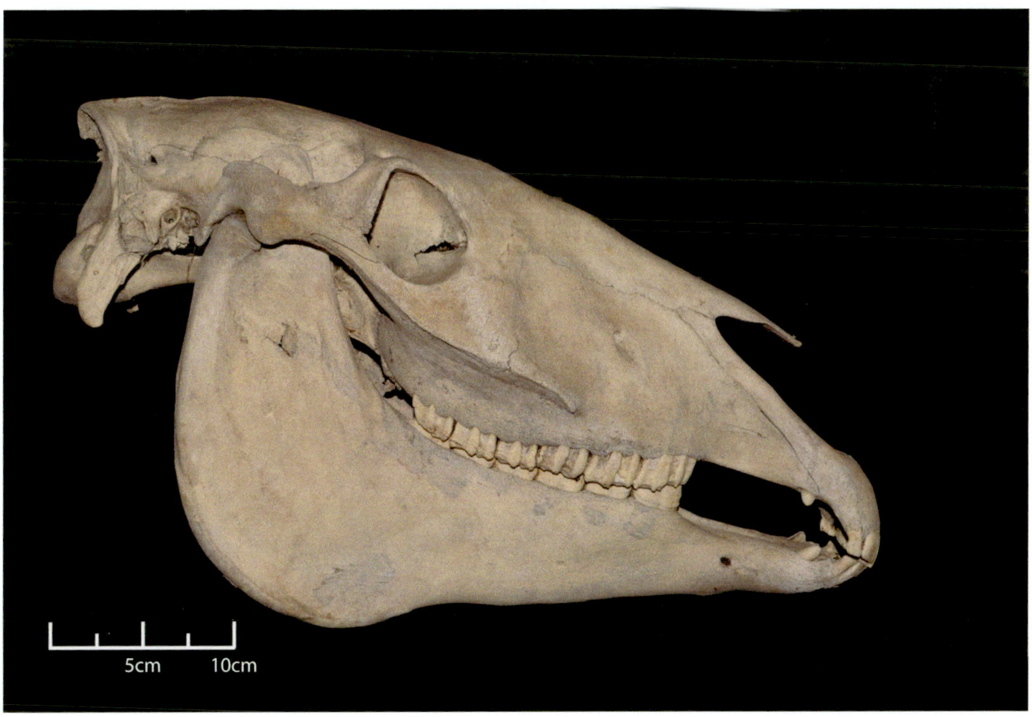

Figure 11.13 Lateral view of horse skull.

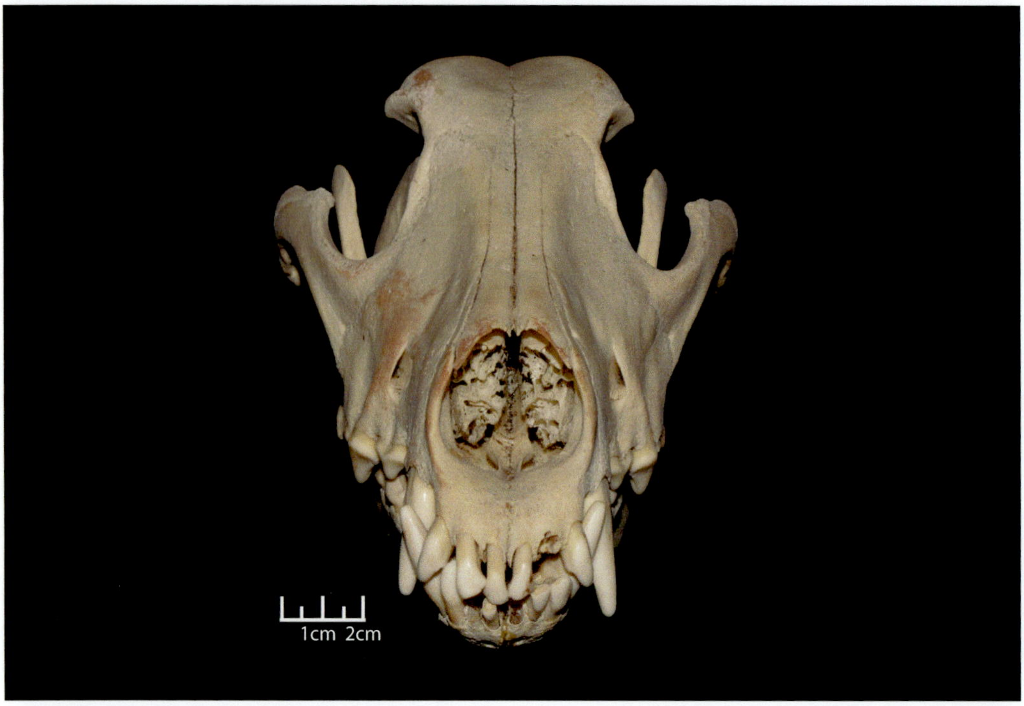

Figure 11.14 Rostral view of dog.

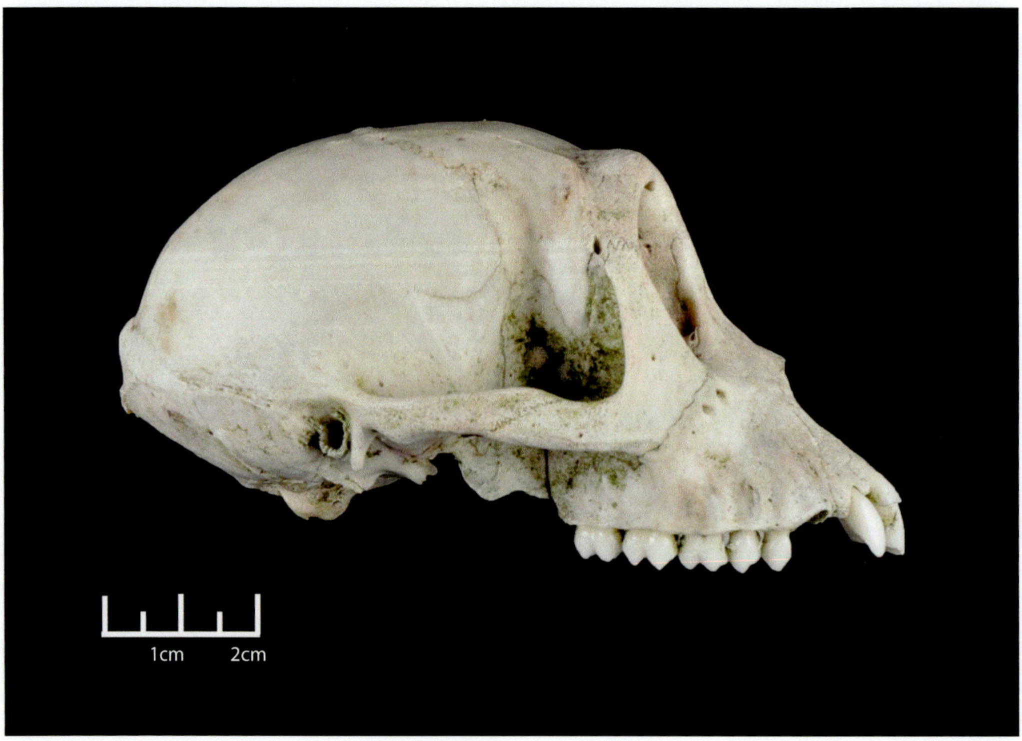

Figure 11.15 Lateral view of Old World monkey skull.

There are many other features found on the skull that can assist in distinguishing species, too many to detail in this chapter. Hopefully, this discussion of the senses has helped lay the foundation of what types of features are examined to evaluate class, genus, and species.

Dentition

Most mammals are diphyodont, meaning they have two sets of teeth during the course of their life—deciduous (baby teeth) and adult teeth. Some animals, called polyphyodonts, have teeth that are continuously replaced in life, including sharks and alligators. There are four types of teeth: incisors, canines, premolars, and molars (Figure 11.16). Animals that have two or more types of teeth are referred to as heterodonts, while those with a single type of tooth, like various reptiles and fish, are called homodonts.

Incisors (I) tend to be small, chisel-shaped teeth with a single cusp and a single root. Artiodactyls, or even-toed ungulates (i.e., cattle, deer), do not have any maxillary incisors (except pig). Other species, particularly rodents, have modified or enlarged incisors. These teeth are often used for nipping, scraping, and tearing.

Canines (C) tend to be conical and single-cusped with a single root. In horses and other ungulates, they have become rudimentary and incisor-like in appearance, while in large carnivores they can become quite large and distinctive. These teeth are often used to puncture, hold, and tear.

Premolars (P) and molars (M) are used for chewing or grinding food. Premolars are single or double rooted, and molars tend to have two or more roots. Molars are at the rear of the mouth and tend to be larger than premolars, but in some species, such as rodents, rabbits, and ungulates, they are very similar in size and appearance.

The numbers of types of teeth present can be useful in genus determination. A dental formula is used to describe how many of each type of tooth is present in one half of the maxilla and mandible. A dental formula is always given in the same order, from front to back I:C:P:M. The number of teeth

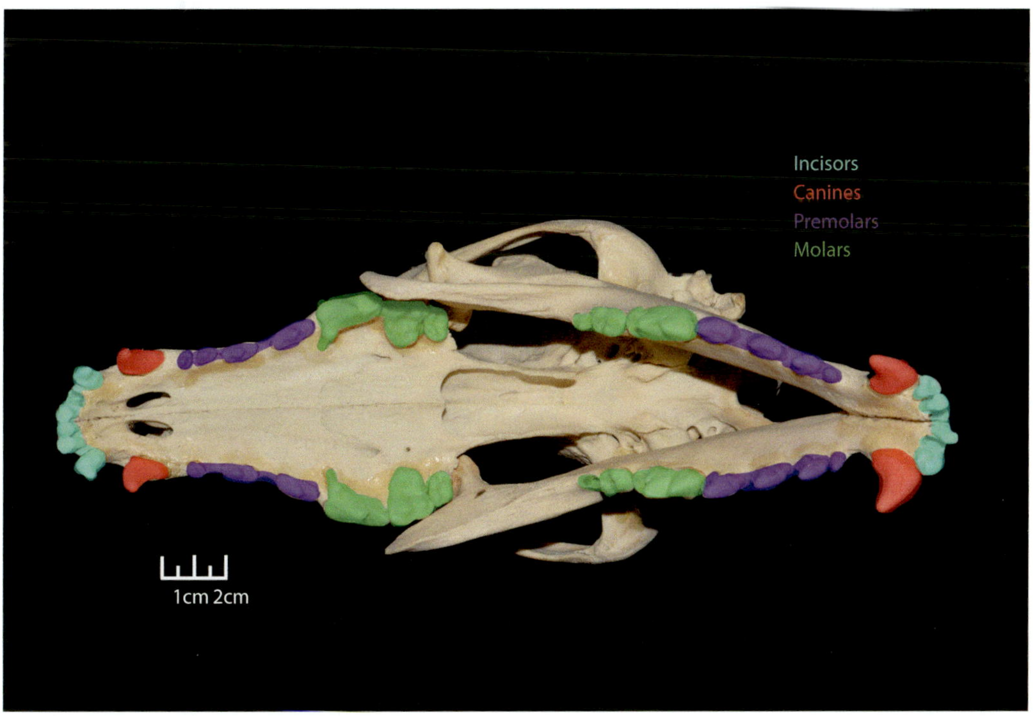

Figure 11.16 Tooth types indicated on inferior view of a dog skull.

can vary between the maxilla and mandible, so it is important to report both in the formula. For example, the dental formula for all dogs, coyotes, and wolves is 3/3:1/1:4/4:2/3, meaning they have three incisors in both the maxilla and mandible (3/3), one canine in each (1/1), four premolars in each (4/4), two molars in the maxilla and three molars in the mandible (2/3) (Figure 11.17). This is very different from a white-tail deer, which has a dental formula of 0/3:0/1:3/3:3/3, indicating they have no incisors or canines in the maxilla. When looking at closely related species, the domestic cat has a dental formula of 3/3:1/1:3/2:1/1, while the bobcat has a dental formula of 3/3:1/1:2/2:1/1 (Figure 11.18).

Occasionally, the dentition found will vary from the expected dental formula, and this is important to document. For example, the humans the dental formula is 2:1:2:3 (we have the same number of teeth in the mandible and maxilla); however, many people do not have third molars, often they are removed through surgery, which is noticeable by the space present or indications on radiographs. However, an increasing number of people never developed third molars, which tends to be evident from the very small retromolar space, and radiographs often confirm their congenital absence. At this time, the dental formula is still 2:1:2:3, and it is important to document the absence of the third molar and explain why. Eventually, the human dental formula may change to 2:1:2:2. Returning to animals, the same is found in some breeds; teeth are being lost due to dental crowding or other genetic modifications. Therefore, checking the literature on the expected dental formula and variations seen is important so one can then determine which teeth are missing and why, if possible (e.g., lost premortem due to trauma or disease, lost postmortem, juvenile so unerupted or not developed, or individual anomaly). For example, a right second maxillary premolar and a right mandibular third molar are absent on the dog dentition example (Figure 11.17); the premolar appears to be due to individual anomaly, it just never developed, while the molar was lost postmortem.

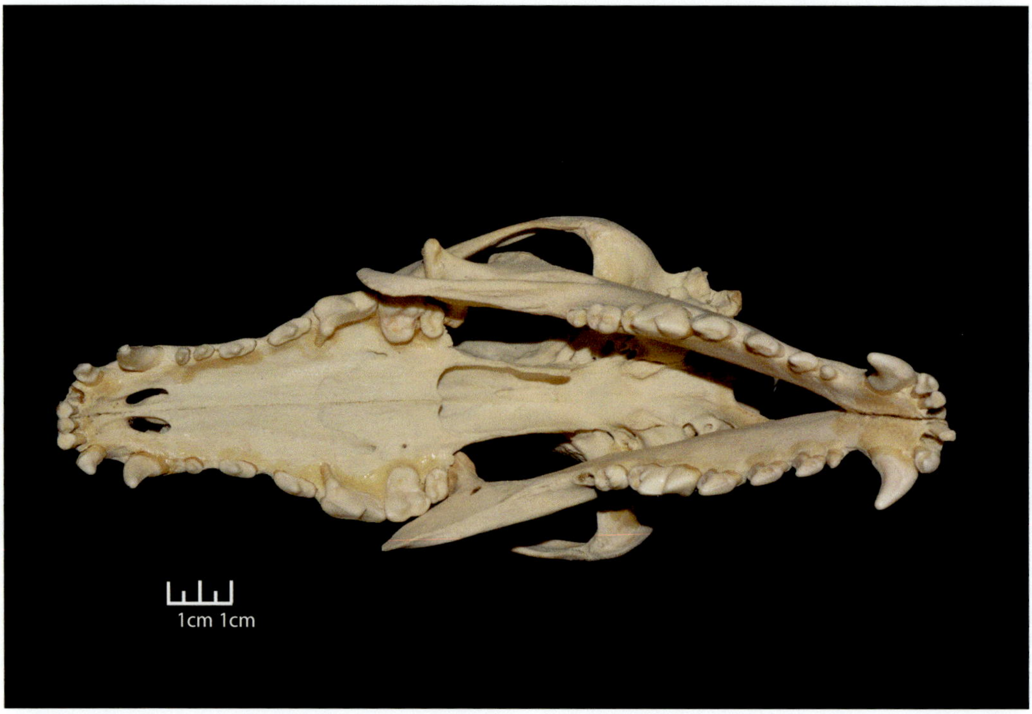

Figure 11.17 View of dentition: Dog skull.

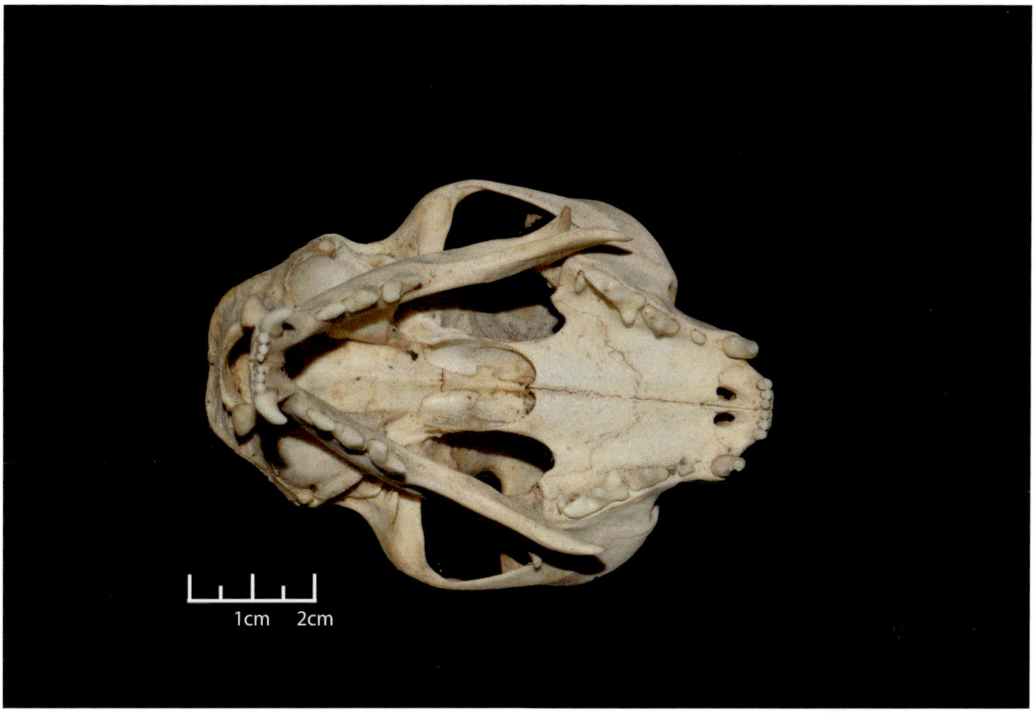

Figure 11.18 View of dentition: Cat skull.

Postcranial

The postcranial skeleton also contains a variety of modifications that are valuable in family, class, genus, and species identification. Form follows function, and this is especially true regarding locomotion; therefore, the lower portion of the limbs tends to be more modified in some species than in others, including the reduction in numbers of carpals and metacarpals, or the conversion of phalanges into hooves or claws.

Forelimb

Scapula

The scapula is typically located on the dorsolateral surface of most mammals. It is elongated to allow for muscle attachments. It is more elongated in some species, while more D-shaped or triangular in others.

Humerus

The humerus is the upper bone of the forelimb. The humeral head articulates with the scapula. It is a rounded structure that allows for rotation at the shoulder joint. The head tends to be more ovoid in species that require less rotation and more rounded in species that use their forelimbs for activities other than locomotion, such as digging, climbing, or swimming. The head tends to be oriented more posteriorly in quadrupeds for articulation with the downward-facing scapula, e.g., dog, while the head is more lateral in more upright animals, e.g., chimpanzee (Figure 11.19).

Radius and Ulna

The radius and ulna are the lower bones of the forelimb, and they tend to be of similar size. The radius is the more anterolateral bone, while the ulna is the more posteromedial bone. In a number of species, the ulna will fuse to the radius, becoming one bone, while in other species the ulna is vestigial and barely developed.

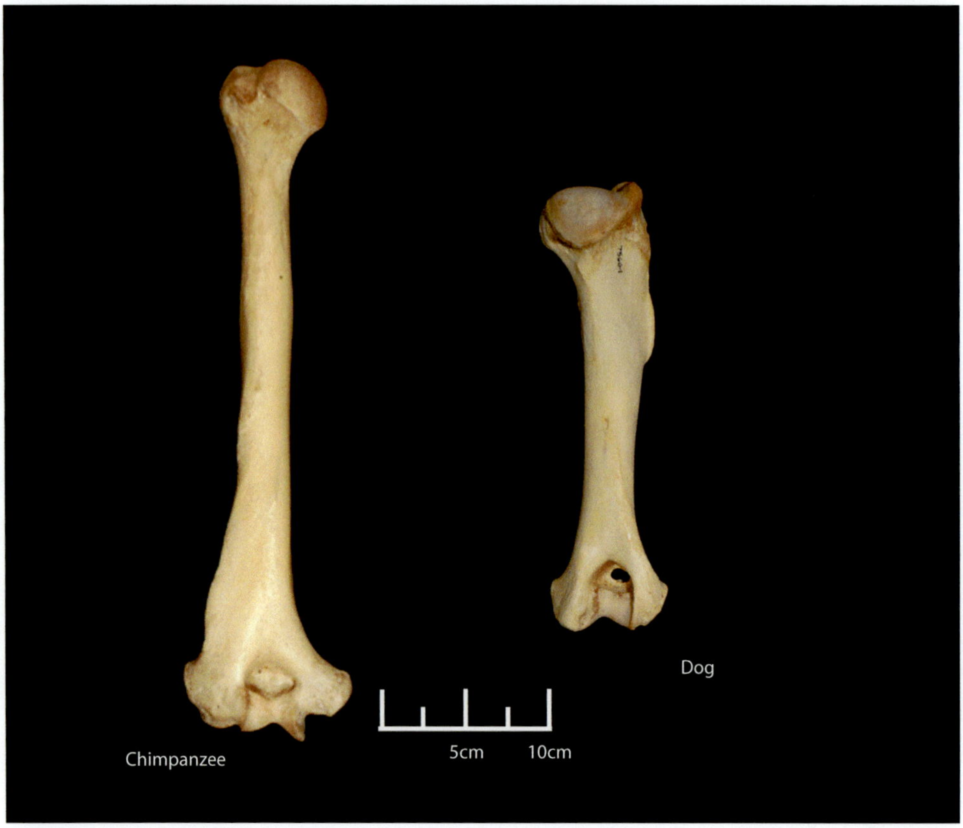

Figure 11.19 Chimpanzee and dog humeri.

Torso/Pelvis

Clavicle

This element is present in some mammals but is often vestigial or absent, so it is of limited use in species identification. Bony fish have clavicles; turtles incorporate them into the plastron, and they are found in birds in the form of the "wishbone."

Vertebrae

The vertebrae tend to be of similar length from neck to pelvis and are often cylindrical in overall shape. All vertebrae have similar structures with some modification to those structures that is indicative of each segment of the vertebral column.

Cervical

Typically, there are seven cervical vertebrae.

1. C-1 is called the atlas, and it articulates with the cranium.
2. C-2 is called the axis, and it allows the pivoting of atlas and rotation of the head. The overall shape of the dens, or the bony projection that the C-1 pivots around, can suggest the degree of rotation allowed.
3. *Thoracic*: There are usually between 11 and 16 thoracic vertebrae. The ribs articulate with these vertebrae on the body.
4. *Lumbar*: There are typically between four and seven lumbar vertebrae. These vertebrae tend to have longer bodies than the thoracic vertebra.

5. *Sacral*: The sacrum is typically composed of three to six fused vertebrae, but it can be as few as one. The first sacral element articulates with the most caudal lumbar vertebra. The wings of the sacrum are called alae and they articulate with the os coxa at the auricular surface. However, the sacrum often fuses to the os coxa forming one solid structure.
6. *Coccygeal*: The number of caudal or coccygeal vertebrae varies depending on the length of the tail.

Sternum

The sternum, when present, articulates with the clavicle, if present, and the ribs. It directly articulates with the more cranial ribs, often called the true ribs, via individual cartilaginous attachments, and indirectly, via common cartilage, with the lower ribs, or false ribs. The body of the sternum can present as several bodies, or sternabrae, joined by cartilage, or these can fuse into one element.

Ribs

Typically, there are twice as many ribs as thoracic vertebra, so if there are 12 thoracic vertebrae there should be 24 ribs; two ribs, one left and one right, articulate with each thoracic vertebra. Often the first 7 ribs articulate directly with the sternum (true ribs), ribs 8, 9, and 10 articulate via common cartilage (false ribs), and ribs 11 and 12+ do not articulate with the sternum (floating ribs). Some species may have cervical or lumbar rib, but these tend to be much smaller than the other ribs and typically do not develop all of the anatomical features of the thoracic ribs. Various publications provide lists of expected numbers of ribs per species. It should be noted that domesticated cattle and hogs tend to have variable numbers of ribs, based on breeding for meat or not.

Ribs tend to come in two forms: either very broad and flat, like those found in cattle, or very round, like those found in canines.

Os coxae

The pelvis in quadrupeds tends to be long and narrow, which allows for muscle attachment and maximizes muscle function. The pelvis is further modified in bipeds and in swimming mammals, becoming almost nonexistent in animals like manatees and dolphins.

The os coxa is actually made up of three bones: the ilium, the wing or blade-like portion; ischium, the more bulbous arched portion; and pubis, the thinner arched portion. These three structures fuse to form one structure called the os coxa or innominate; the acetabulum or acetabular fossa is where the three meet—this is the hip socket. The iliac crest is the protruding "hip" of an animal.

Hindlimb

Femur

The femur is the upper portion of the hindlimb. The femoral head, which is oriented medially, articulates with the acetabulum of the os coxa; the femoral head tends to be more ball-shaped than the humeral head, which allows more rotation at this joint. In the middle of the femoral head is the fovea capitis, which is a small depression for the insertion of the *ligamentum teres* from the acetabular notch of the os coxae. The humeral head does not have a depression, which allows for easy distinction between the two in fragmentary elements.

Patella

The patella, or the kneecap, is a large sesamoid bone and functions to increase the level arm of the quadriceps muscle in the leg.

Tibia and Fibula

The tibia is the larger of the two lower leg elements and is the more anteromedial bone, while the smaller fibula is the more posterolateral bone. In a number of species, the fibula will fuse to the tibia, becoming one bone, while in other species the fibula is vestigial and is barely developed or is absent.

Fore and Hind Paws

Carpals and Tarsals

There are up to eight carpals and seven tarsals.

Metacarpals and Metatarsals

In the ancestral mammalian form, there are five metacarpals (MCs) or metatarsals (MTs); however, this number is reduced in various species, and in some there is only a single long metacarpal or metatarsal. In dogs that have had the hind dew claw removed, the 1st metatarsal and the associated phalanges are absent. In dogs, and many other species, when this 1st metatarsal is present it may appear as a fully formed digit similar to that seen in the forepaw, or it may be vestigial in appearance, sometimes only having the distal phalanx.

The 1st MC or MT tends to be the shortest, and the 3rd and 4th tend to be the longest. The shaft of the metacarpals tends to be flatter or more D-shaped in cross-section, and they are shorter and thicker overall, while the metatarsals tend to be more ovoid or rounded in cross-section and longer and thinner in appearance.

Phalanges

There are typically 14 phalanges; the first digit (thumb) has two, a proximal and distal phalanx, while the other four digits contain a proximal, intermediate, and distal phalanx. The number of phalanges is reduced as the number of fingers/toes is reduced, so horses only have three phalanges per foot, one proximal, one intermediate, and one distal. The phalanges get smaller as you progress from proximal to distal. The forepaw phalanx tends to be larger than the comparable hindpaw phalanx.

The number and length of these elements and the presence of claws or hooves is useful in identification. For example, plantigrade (habitually walk with sole on the ground) animals have the full complement of toes, and the metacarpals and metatarsals tend to be shorter in relation to radius/ulna or tibia/fibula; digitigrade (toe-walker) animals have the full complement of toes or a slight reduction; however, the length of metacarpals and metatarsals has increased; unguligrade (hoof-walkers; essentially walking on the nails of the toes) have reduced numbers of toes, and the metacarpals and metatarsals have reached their peak length (Figure 11.20).

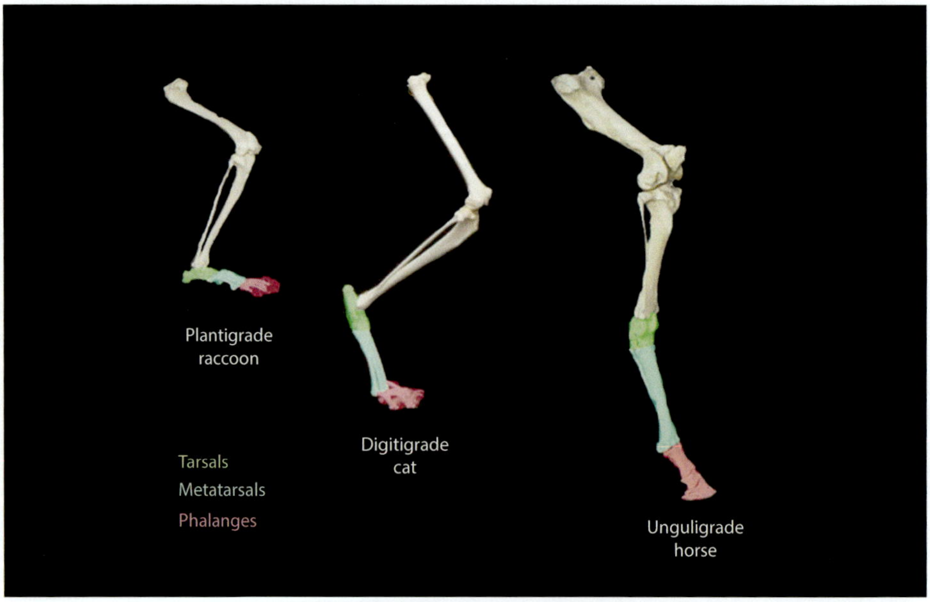

Figure 11.20 Posterior limbs of a raccoon, cat, and horse demonstrating the relationship of tarsals, metatarsals, and phalanges.

APPLICATION OF VETERINARY OSTEOLOGY

In forensic veterinary osteology, the ultimate purpose in the analysis of a set of skeletal remains is to develop a biological profile, or a set of characteristics that an individual possessed during life that can be used to identify them after death. In veterinary cases the biological profile would include class, order, family, genus, species, and breed, age, sex, stature/size, individualizing characteristics, health, pathology, and trauma. Practitioners utilize this information to develop an understanding of the life, and possibly the death, of the individual, or individuals, present in a case.

This last section will discuss how features of skeletal elements are used to evaluate class, order, family, genus, and species identifications. Only a select few animals are examined to highlight some of the distinct class features and species-specific features that can be used for identification. This is done as an example of how veterinary osteology can be utilized and is meant to be more illustrative than definitive. The list of differences is not absolute, and there are many more subtle distinctions that can be found with close inspection and additional research.

Identification Process

Bones vary in their appearance between species, because *form follows function*. These functions begin at the class level with variation in locomotion; moving down the classification system though order, family, and genus, functional changes appear due to specialized locomotion, diet, and/or environmental influences.

The identification process should proceed in four general steps that can be summarized as (1) elements present, (2) development and size, (3) form (order), and (4) variation (family, genus, and species). Cornwall (1968) gives a more detailed discussion of this process.

1. *Elements present*: When presented with a bone or a skeleton for identification, the first step should be to determine what bone or bones are present. Is it a cranial or postcranial element? Is it dental or a long bone? This step may help you rule out some classes or orders within a class; for example, if you are presented with a femur, you can easily rule out fish and snakes.
2. *Development and size*: Next, development and size should be evaluated to rule out additional animals. For example, if the femur measures 100 mm in length and is fully formed (indicating an adult), you can rule out larger animals, such as horse, cow, or deer.
3. *Form (orders)*: The third step is elimination of orders and families based on form. Deer (Artiodactyla) tend to have long slender elements, while cats and dogs (Carnivora) tend to have short squat elements. The 100 mm femur length would suggest short and squat, so we can rule out Artiodactyla.
4. *Variation (family, genus, and species)*: Other features of the femur would help distinguish Felidae from Canidae. This is elimination based on subtle variations. Species determination can be very difficult, particularly based on osteological evidence alone; some elements are highly diagnostic, while others are more generalized, providing very little support for a species or even a genus determination. This step is best accomplished through comparative analysis and it may not be possible if there are no distinguishing features on the elements present.

When presented with skeletal remains that were collected at a crime scene, a practitioner will typically want to initially remove the remains that are not of forensic concern. For example, if the case involved animal cruelty against dogs, the dog remains would be of forensic concern and the other remains would be less important (at least for now). With this in mind, the following section will work through the four steps of identification, highlighting some of the features used to remove the remains that are not dog in this case, first removing non-mammal remains and then removing some of the other animals that may be close in size and appearance to dog or found in the same environment, such as raccoon or cat.

Non-Mammal

There are a number of non-mammals that may be found during the course of a forensic investigation, including amphibians, reptiles, fish, and birds. The following is a brief discussion of some of the features used to distinguish these orders from mammals, which would roughly fall under steps 1 and 2 in the identification process.

One element that is easily recognizable and provides some class-specific identifying features are the vertebra. Mammals have acoelous vertebrae, which are flat on both the cranial and caudal surfaces. These are ideal for mammals, as these vertebrae are well suited for handling compressive forces. Procoelous are concave on the cranial surface and convex on the caudal surface, while opisthocoelous are the opposite, convex cranial and concave caudal. These types of vertebrae allow more flexibility of the spine without excessive stretching of the spinal cord. Frogs and most reptiles are procoelous, while most salamanders, gar fish, and some birds are opisthocoelous. Amphicoelous vertebra are concave on both surfaces, permitting a wide range of motion, and these vertebrae are found in most cartilaginous and bony fish and a few reptiles. Heterocoelous vertebrae are saddle-shaped and allow retraction of the neck and restrict twisting motion, reducing injury to the spinal cord. These are often found in the necks of birds and turtles (Figure 11.21).

The general appearance of the other bony elements can also be useful in identification. For example, the most noticeable feature of bird bone is the lightweight nature. Bird bones are highly pneumatized, or their bones contain many air cells. This is especially true of flight-birds, and although diving and terrestrial birds are less pneumatized, they are still more so than mammals. Bird bone typically has a thin cortical wall and very little bone in the medullary cavity. The cancellous bone is not compacted as in other mammals; instead, there are thin struts crossing throughout the

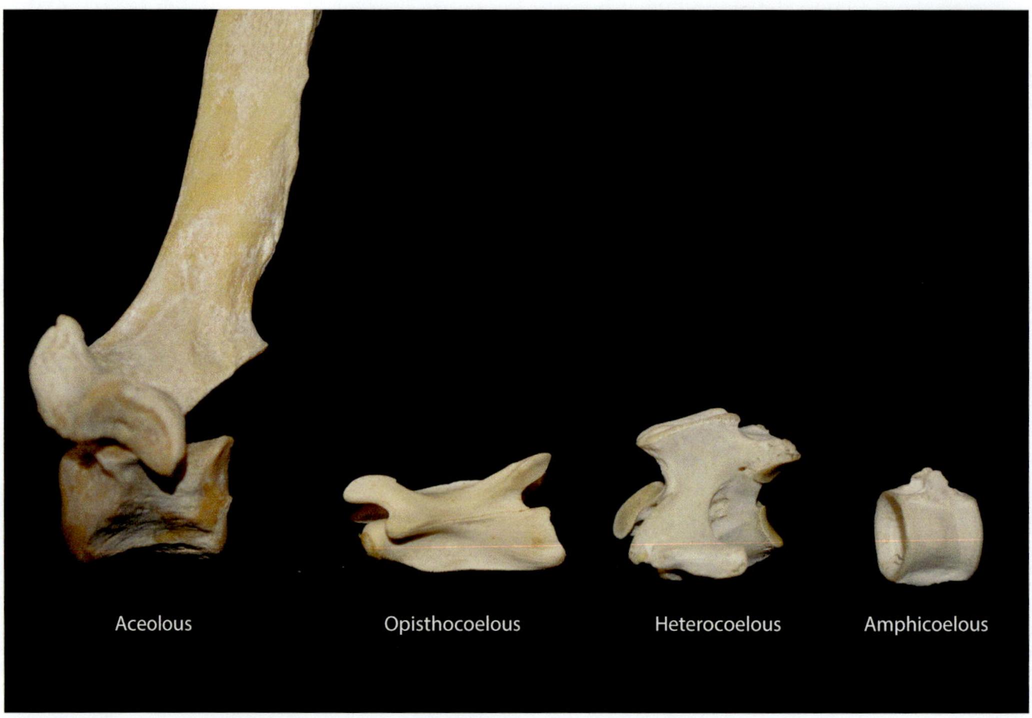

Figure 11.21 Differences in vertebra forms.

medullary cavity, giving the bone support but very little weight. On the other hand, reptiles tend to have very dense cortical bone with very little medullary cavity (Figure 11.22).

Turning to amphibians and reptiles, these animals have cartilaginous joints resulting in the ends of the bones being more rounded off, especially the long bones, and not sculpted as seen in mammals. Human infant bones are often mistaken for amphibian or reptile remains. However, with careful inspection, it will be noted that the amphibian or reptile bones will have a complete epiphysis with a smoothed end, whereas infant bones or juvenile mammal bones will still have growth occurring at the metaphysis, so the end will appear undulating or roughened (Figure 11.23).

Next, we will turn to examining mammal remains. We will focus on the classes carnivora, artiodactyl, and perissodactyla, as several species of forensic interest are found in these classes. The following would fall into the step 3 analysis of the identification process.

Carnivora versus Artiodactyla and Perissodactyla

Carnivora are meat-eating mammals, although many of them are omnivorous. All carnivores share a carnassial arrangement that includes the last upper premolar (P4) and the first lower molar (M1) that act together to shear meat and to sharpen each other. They also typically have enlarged canines, but the development of this complex varies in each group.

Artiodactyla are even-toed ungulates, hoofed animals, while Perissodactyla are odd-toed ungulates. They are both herbivores. Overall, these animals have teeth designed for milling and grinding food, but there is some variation in form (e.g., rounded cusps versus crescent-shaped cusps) that is indicative of different family or genus groups within each order.

Although few would confuse these two groups when presented with their skeletal remains, as carnivores (dog, coyote, cat, bobcat, etc.) tend to be much smaller than the artiodactyla (deer, cow, etc.) or perissodactyla (horse), discussing their overall differences can highlight the features that are examined in the identification process.

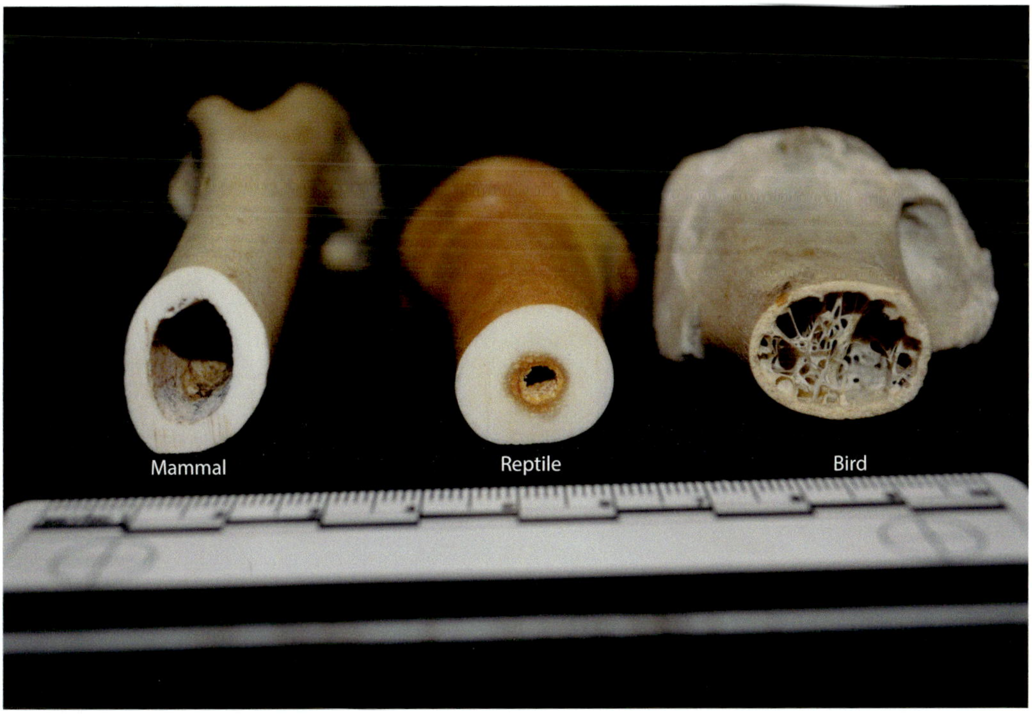

Figure 11.22 Mammal, reptile, and bird cross-sections demonstrating cortical thickness.

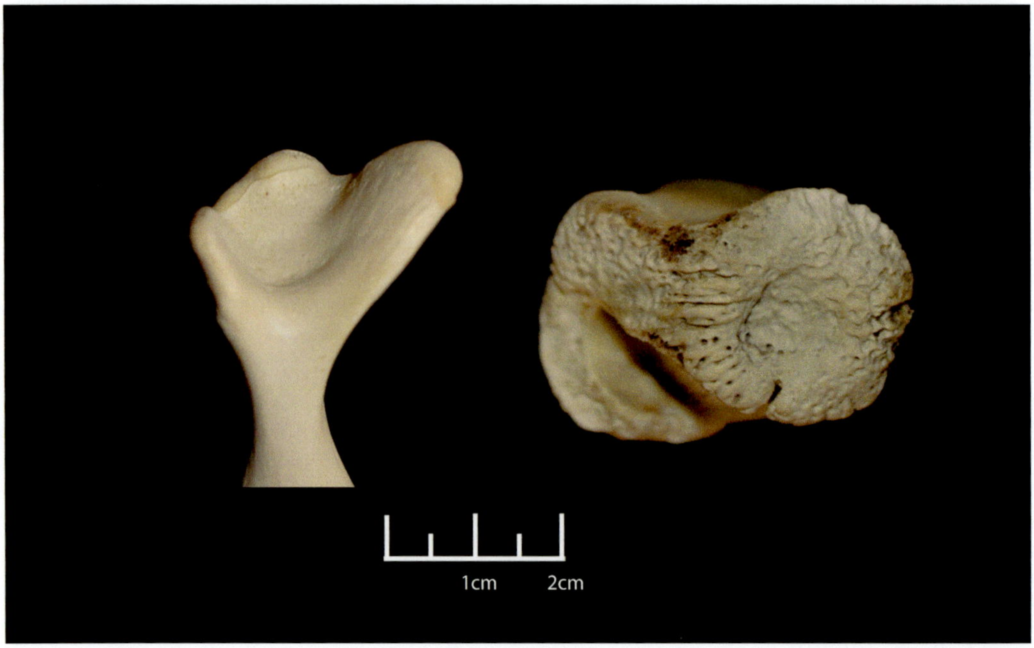

Figure 11.23 Turtle bone and an immature mammal bone. Note the smooth form of the reptile bone and the undulating surface on the mammal bone indicating it is incomplete.

In carnivores, the brain is larger overall, and the rostral region is reduced, particularly in some species (e.g., cat); various parts of the skull are modified to allow for the attachment of the large jaw muscles. The orbits tend to be more anteriorly focused. The auditory bullae are enlarged. Dentition is reduced in some species, while overall, canines are enlarged.

In ungulates, the brain is smaller, and the rostral region is large. Many ungulate groups have horns or antlers projecting from the skull. The orbits tend to be more laterally oriented. The auditory bullae are larger than some animal species, but not as inflated as the carnivora groups. Several orders lack incisors in the maxilla, canines are reduced or absent, and the premolars are often similar in shape and size to the molars.

In carnivores, the ribs tend to be more rounded in cross-section than the perissodactyla or artiodactyla. The scapula tends to be D-shaped in appearance. The humerus and radius/ulna tend to be similar in length. The humeral head is hemispherical and the tuberosities project above the head. The radius and ulna remain distinct. The os coxa is long and narrow with prominent ischial tuberosities. The femur is slender and straight in the digitigrades and short and stout in the plantigrades, though again the length relative to tibia and fibula is similar. The tibia and fibula remain distinct.

In perissodactyla or artiodactyla, the ribs tend to be flat in cross-section. The scapula is long and narrow, and there are a number of features on the scapula that can help distinguish between these two orders and between family groups as well. In perissodactyla, the ilia are long and broad but taper to a neck superior to the acetabulum. The opening on the acetabulum is wide and the ischium and pubis are short. In artiodactyla, the ilia are shorter, and the neck is thicker above the acetabulum. The opening on acetabulum is narrower, and the pubis and ischium are long and wide. The humerus is short in comparison to the radius and ulna in both groups; however, it is more lightly built in artiodactyla and more heavily built in perissodactyla. Artiodactyla have a full ulna, but it can fuse to the radius in some species. In contrast, perissodactyla have a significantly reduced ulna that is often fused to the radius. In perissodactyla, the femur is also short compared to the rest of the hindlimb, and the fibula is reduced to a splint and may be fused to the tibia. In artiodactyla, the femur and tibia are more similar in length than the forelimb elements, and the fibula is typically vestigial or fused. One notable exception is in pigs, which have a relatively large and distinct fibula.

For the fourth step in the identification process, the following will examine a few animals that are often found in similar environments, are similar is size and shape, and often occur in cases of animal identification.

Dog/Cat/Raccoon/Opossum

Cranially, some may confuse smaller dogs and larger cats, raccoons or opossums; however, there are several features that should help distinguish between these species. For example, the upper fourth premolar is molar-form in appearance (squared-off) in raccoons, while it is very elongated in dogs to form the carnassial. In the opossum, the first premolar is canine-like, while the third and fourth premolars are very blade-like. Raccoons also only have two lower molars, while dogs typically have three. Cats have reduced their dentition, only having three upper premolars, the third of which is the carnassial and one molar that is very small; they also only have two lower premolars and one molar that is comparable in size to the premolars.

Another feature that is easy observed is the palatine, or the posterior portion of the maxilla. In raccoons the palatine extends further caudally, nearly to the caudal aspect of pterygoid, whereas the palatine plate terminates much closer to the molars in dogs. In cats and opossum, the palate extends further than dogs, but not as far as raccoon; however, an opossum is easily identified by the numerous foramina in the caudal palate (Figure 11.24).

Postcranially on the humerus, cats, raccoons, and opossums have what is called an entepicondylar foramen, or a hole above the condyle on the distal end, and the size and shape of this varies between animals; dogs do not have this feature. Dogs often have what is called a supratrochlear foramen, or a hold in in the olecranon fossa above the trochlea. Although these very different animals share a similar feature, there are other differences between their humeri at both the proximal and distal ends that help distinguish them, some of which may be noticeable in the image (Figure 11.25).

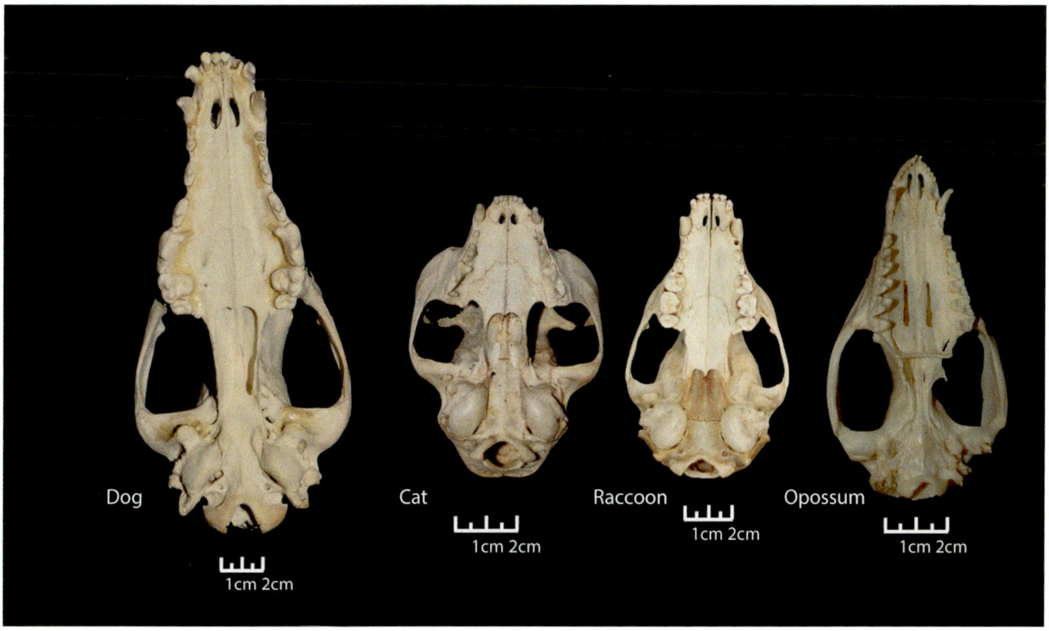

Figure 11.24 Inferior views of dog, cat, racoon, and opossum skulls demonstrating differences.

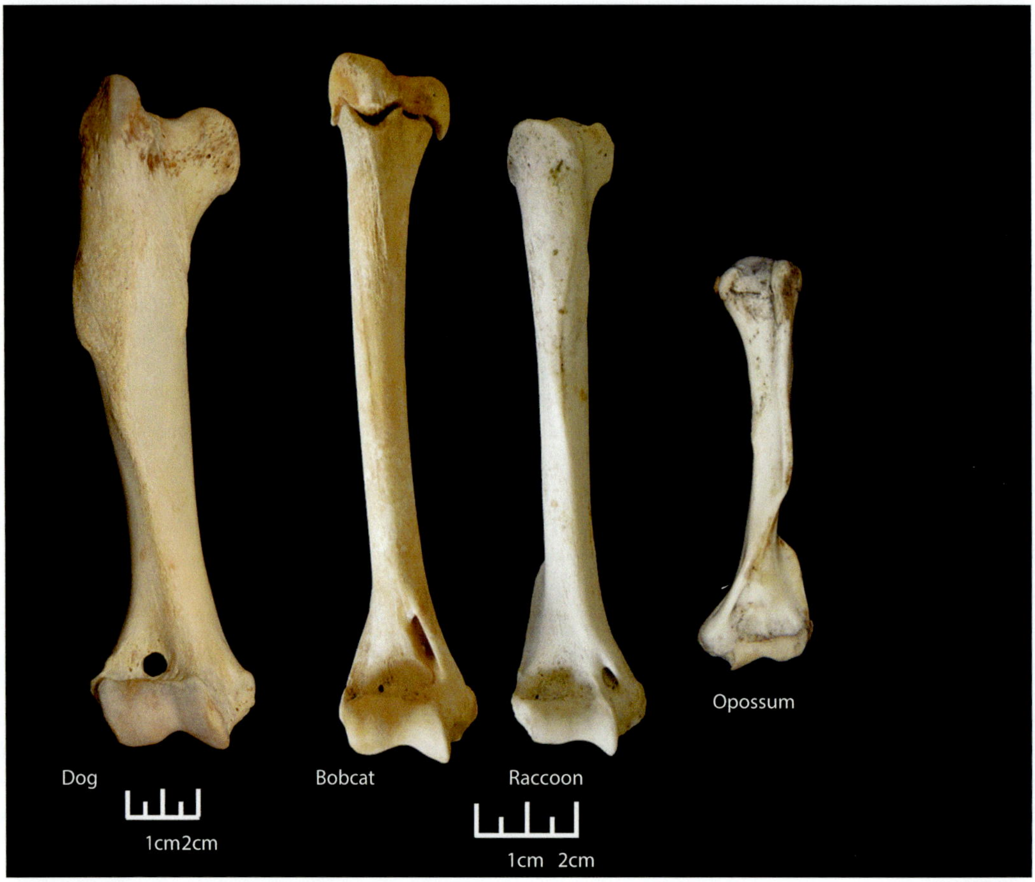

Figure 11.25 Dog, bobcat, raccoon, and opossum humeri.

Dog/Wolf/Coyote

These animals are similar in form and function and are all of the same genus. Distinguishing between species can be important, as dogs are our pets and are often the focus of abuse or neglect cases, while coyotes are often considered a nuisance animal, and wolves are protected in many areas so species determination could be important in cases of suspected poaching, or illegal killing, of protected species.

Comparison of the length and width of the palate can be informative of species. It has been found that if the length is approximately three times larger than the width, the animal is most likely a coyote, while in a domestic dog the length that is less than three times the width of the palate (Howard, 1949; Bekoff, 1977). Also, the reciprocal index, where the palate width is divided by the tooth row length and multiplied by 100, can help distinguish between these species, as values less than 33 are typically associated with coyotes, while dogs tend to value higher than 36 and it has been found that wolves typically fall in between (Howard, 1949; Gilbert, 1990; Elbroch, 2006). This index may also be useful for distinguishing some domestic dog breeds, as it has been found that police dogs (most likely German shepherds) averaged 38, greyhounds 39, and bulldogs 91 (Gilbert, 1990) (Figure 11.26).

In comparing dogs and wolves, it has been noted that the interorbital region of dogs is elongated in comparison to wolves; therefore, the ratio of the distance between the end of the tooth row and the anterior of the auditory bulla compared to the length of the tooth row provides a method of distinguishing between these animals. Domesticated dogs tend to have higher values, while wolves often have lower values (Olsen, 1973).

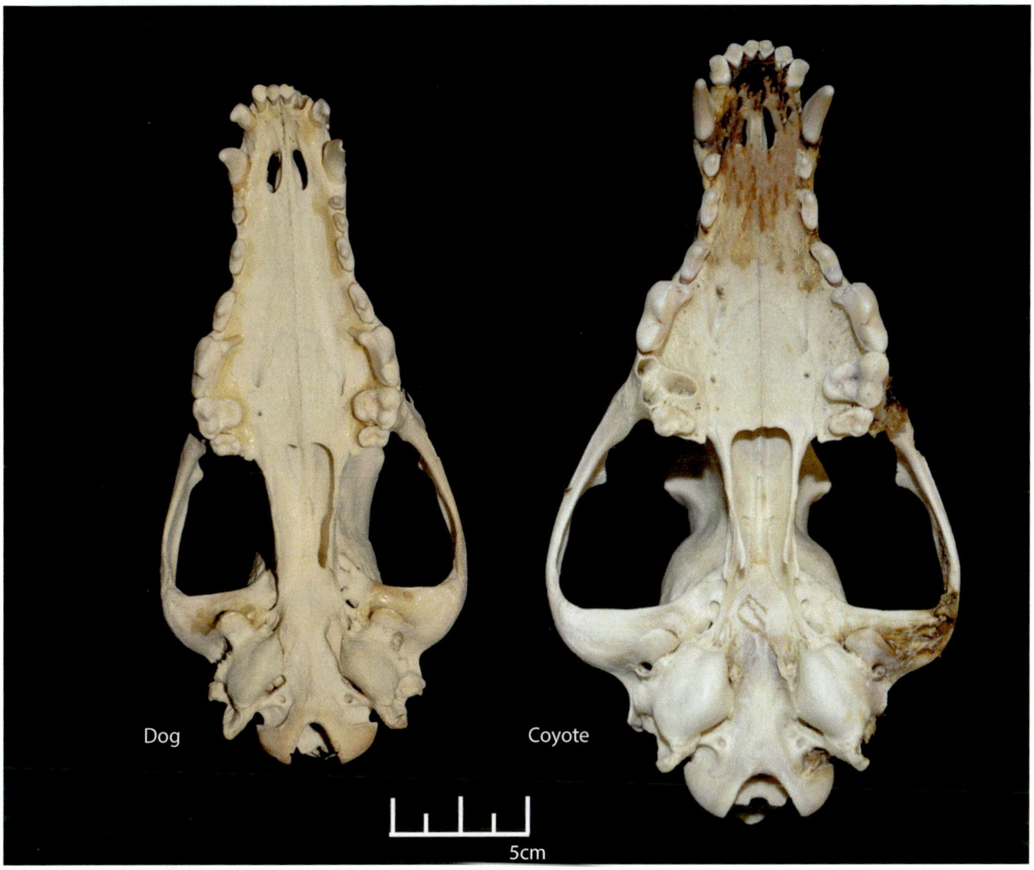

Figure 11.26 Inferior views of dog and coyote skulls.

CONCLUSION

The purpose of this chapter has been to provide the reader with a better understanding of veterinary osteology and to highlight some of the features that are examined in order to evaluate class, order, family, genus, and species. Evaluation of species present is essential to beginning a forensic veterinary investigation. From there, proper identification and siding of the elements present will allow the osteologists to evaluate the patterns of elements present in cases with multiple individuals or evaluate the patterns of pathology and trauma. In turn, this will allow the investigators to build a sound case for neglect or abuse, or possibly rule out these scenarios.

The value of forensic osteology goes beyond bone identification. Knowing the normal form of bones can be useful in trauma cases. For example, determining what bones have been modified, allowing for the assessment of type of trauma, patterns of trauma, and timing of trauma. Another example of a trauma case would be an animal that has been compensating for trauma to a leg, in which one leg may exhibit increased muscle markings and growth, while the other leg has lost mineral density from lack of use—the application of Wolff's law at the most minute level. Understanding how bones develop and change with age is valuable in puppy mill cases where an accurate assessment of the age of the puppies in each litter can help determine whether or not the female dogs were being given appropriate periods of time between litters. Knowledge of the features that distinguish male and female animals could also be valuable in certain cruelty cases where determining the sex of an animal could provide insight into the role each animal played in the criminal activity being investigated (e.g., dogfighting or breeding).

The potential applications of nonhuman osteology to veterinary forensic investigations are vast, but the value of these applications starts with an understanding of the bones themselves. The information contained in this chapter is designed to illustrate the importance of osteological investigation. Much more research needs to be done to bring the field of nonhuman osteology to the level of human forensic osteology studies, but even as it stands now, there is great significance to the types of analyses that can be performed and the information that can be gleaned from their results.

References

Beisaw, A.M. 2013. *Identifying and Interpreting Animal Bones*. Texas A&M Anthropology Series. Texas A&M University Press: College Station TX.

Bekoff, M. 1977. *Canis latrans* Mammalian Species No. 79, 9. American Society of Mammalogists: Lawrence, KS.

Bonte, W. 1975. Tool marks in bone and cartilage. *Journal of Forensic Sciences* 20:315–25.

Cornwall, I.W. 1968. *Bone for the Archaeologist*. Phoenix House: London.

Crowder, C., C. Rainwater, and J. Fridie. 2013. Microscopic analysis of sharp force trauma in bone and cartilage: A validation study. *Journal of Forensic Sciences* 58(5):1119–1126.

Elbroch, M. 2006. *Animal Skulls: A Guide to North American Species*. Stackpole Books: Mechanicsburg, PA.

France, D.L. 2009. *Human and Non-Human Bone Identification: A Color Atlas*. CRC Press: Boca Raton, FL.

Gilbert, B.M. 1990. *Mammalian Osteology*. Missouri Archaeological Society Inc: Columbia, MO.

Hawkins, B.W. 1860. *A Comparative View of the Human and Animal Frame*. [Plate eight—Man, cow and sheep and explanatory text], pp. [unnumbered]-22. https://uwdc.library.wisc.edu/collections/histscitech/companat/

Hillson, S. 1999. *Mammal Bones and Teeth: An Introductory Guide and Methods of Identification*. Henry Ling Ltd: London.

Howard, W. 1949. A means to distinguish skulls of coyotes and domestic dogs. *Journal of Mammalogy* 30(2):169–171.

Hulbert, R.C., ed. 2001. *The Fossil Vertebrates of Florida*. University Press of Florida: Gainesville, FL.

Merck, M. 2013. *Veterinary Forensics: Animal Cruelty Investigations*. Wiley-Blackwell: Ames, IA.

Olsen, S.J. 1973. *Mammal Remains from Archaeological Sites: Part 1*. Peabody Museum: Cambridge, MA.

Reitz, E.J., and E.S. Wing. 2008. *Zooarchaeology*, 2nd ed. Cambridge Manuals in Archaeology. Cambridge University Press: New York.

Romer, A.S., and T.S. Parsons. 1977. *The Vertebrate Body*, 5th ed. Saunders: Philadelphia, PA.

White, T.D., M.T. Black, and P.A. Folkens. 2012. *Human Osteology*, 3rd ed. Elsevier Academic Press: Boston, MA.

Wolff, J. 1892. *Das Gesetz der Transformation der Knochen (The Law of Bone Transformation)*. A Hirshwald: Berlin.

CHAPTER 12

ENVIRONMENTAL AND SITUATIONAL INJURIES/DEATH

Thermal, Chemical, Electrical, Hyperthermia, Hypothermia, and Drowning

Nancy Bradley-Siemens

INTRODUCTION

This chapter will explore causes that may result in environmental and situational injury or death encountered by companion animals in animal abuse scenarios. Situational injury or death may result from burns (thermal, chemical, or electrical in origin) or drowning from submersion in water. Environmental injury or death may result from hyperthermia or hypothermia caused by extremes in temperature through climate, confinement, and lack of shelter.

BURNS

Heat may be directed at the tissue in various forms; depending on the duration and intensity, necrotizing lesions may occur (Maxie, 2016). There are two types of heat: moist and dry. Dry heat uses hot air predominantly free from water vapor. Moist heat has moisture content in the form of liquid or vapor (Maxie, 2016). Dry heat causes desiccation and carbonization. Moist heat causes coagulation (boiling) (Maxie, 2016). Heat may affect the body internally via inhalation of steam, smoke, and chemicals. The lowest temperature that tissue can burn is 111°F (44°C) (Maxie, 2016).

At the University of Missouri Veterinary Teaching Hospital between 1990 and 1999, 18 patients were treated for burn-related injuries (Pope, 2003). In an 11-year period, in a report from a large metropolitan area, only 22 cats and 27 dogs were treated for smoke inhalation (Pope, 2003). Burns are relatively uncommon in veterinary medicine (Pope, 2003; Garzotto, 2015). When burns are encountered in companion animals, animal abuse as a differential should be ruled out, especially with the frequency that burns are encountered in veterinary medicine. The most common causes of burns in companion animals are electric heating pads, scalding water, fire exposure, heat lamps, vehicle engines, improperly grounded electric cautery units, and radiation therapy (Garzotto, 2015).

Burns are assessed using two major parameters: the degree of injury and the percentage of body surface area. A good place to start is a review of skin anatomy. The outer layer of the skin is the epidermis and the deeper layer is the dermis. The dermis consists of a superficial plexus and a middle plexus; this is where hair and glandular structures originate. Below the dermis resides the hypodermis containing the deep (subdermal) plexus and the panniculus muscle. This layer provides the blood supply to the above skin via the superficial and middle plexuses. There are capillary loops in the superficial plexus that supply the epidermis; these are poorly developed in companion animals compared to humans, resulting in less severe erythema and blistering than human burn victims (Garzotto, 2015).

Burn Classifications

Burns are classified by the cause or mechanism of the injury and by the depth and severity of the body tissue involved (Pope, 2003). Mechanisms of burns are categorized as thermal, radiation, electrical, and chemical (Pope, 2003; Wohlsein et al., 2016). Flames, hot liquids, semi-solids or semi-liquids such as hot metals, auto engines, or tar can cause thermal burns. In small animals, radiation burns are usually caused by therapeutic radiation sources. An electric burn may be caused by direct contact with an electric current or arcing of the current (Pope, 2003; Schulze et al., 2016). Chemical burns are caused by contact with strong acid or alkali substances resulting in tissue destruction by denaturing proteins or interfering with cell metabolism (Pope, 2003; Merck & Miller 2013).

Most of what is known about burn injuries to humans is from studies conducted on animal models. Veterinary medical texts have in-depth chapters detailing the evaluation and treatment of animals who have been burned or who have suffered from smoke inhalation. This material should be reviewed by any veterinarian investigating animal abuse cases involving burn injuries (Sinclair et al, 2006).

Burn wounds have been referred to as first-degree, second-degree, third-degree, and fourth-degree injuries. Terms that are more common now are superficial, partial thickness, and full thickness; these terms are considered more concise for animals (Garzotto, 2015; Pope, 2003). A first-degree burn is superficial and is localized in the external layer of the epidermis. The skin will be erythemic, dry, and painful to the touch. A second-degree burn is a partial-thickness injury that involves the epidermis and partial segments of the dermis. With only a superficial portion of the dermis involved, thrombosis of the blood vessels and leakage of plasma can occur. The hair follicles are usually not affected. Hair follicles can be destroyed in deeper partial-thickness wounds. The skin will appear yellow-white or brown, and sensation is usually minimal except with applied deep pressure (Garzotto, 2015; Sinclair et al., 2006). A third-degree burn wound is a full-thickness injury that obliterates the epidermis and the dermal layers. The skin lacks sensation and appears leathery and charred. A fourth-degree burn wound has similar characteristics to a third-degree burn, however it also involves deeper tissues such as muscle, tendon, and bone (Sinclair et al., 2006; Garzotto, 2015).

Companion animals with burns over 20% of their total body surface area (TBSA) may develop significant metabolic compromise (Garzotto, 2015). Animals with over 50% of their TBSA have a poor prognosis (Garzotto, 2015). TBSA can be calculated or estimated.

Total Body Surface Area

There are multiple methods to calculate or estimate TBSA. This is critical for the initial treatment and for documentation of burn wounds for medicolegal purposes. The extent of burn wounds must be determined and documented. The following discussion will consist of actual calculations and various estimations: the rule of nines (Sinclair et al., 2006; Garzotto, 2015) and the palm method. The TBSA can be calculated:

$$\text{TBSA (cm}^2\text{)} = K \times W^{2/3}$$

where K is a constant (10.1 for dogs and 10.0 for cats) and W is the weight of the animal in kilograms (Sinclair et al., 2006).

There are conversion tables of the body weight to surface area for dogs and cats to expedite the calculation process and avoid this lengthy calculation. One such conversion table can be obtained at petcancervet.co.uk/ (Sinclair et al., 2006). Once the patient's TBSA is established, the distribution of the burn injury is calculated by measuring the area of the burn wound with a metric ruler, dividing the area by the TBSA of the animal and multiplying by 100. As an example, the extent of a burn injury to a 14-kg dog (whose TBSA is calculated to be 5860 square centimeters) with a burn area of 7 cm × 6 cm (42 square centimeters) is 1% (42/5860 × 100) (Sinclair et al., 2006).

Rule of Nines

The rule of nines is used in humans to estimate the extent of a burn injury (Rodes et al., 2013). It is presented in the human medical text and is widely used as a method of estimation of burn wound body surface area in humans. Using the rule, the head and each arm accounts for 9% TBSA, the front and back torso are each 18%, and so on (Sinclair et al., 2006). The rule of nines has been used by veterinary authors to estimate burn injury distribution (Sinclair et al., 2006; Merck & Miller 2013). TBSA may be estimated in companion animals using percentages proportioned to a body area using the rule of nines (Garzotto, 2015). The head, neck, and each forelimb will account for 9% of body surface area. Each rear limb, dorsal trunk, and ventral trunk will count for 18% of body surface area (Garzotto, 2015) (Figure 12.1).

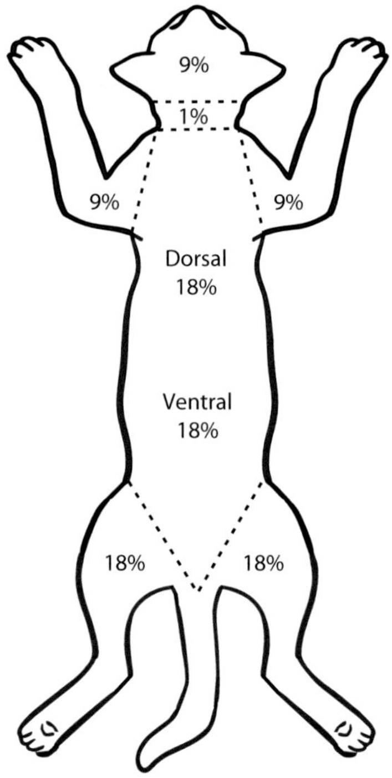

Figure 12.1 Rule of Nines TBSA burn percentage estimations. (Courtesy Les Siemens.)

Palm Method

Another possibility for future application is the determination of the palm area (Rodes et al., 2013). This is where the victim's palm surface area is applied over a burn wound injury to estimate the percentage extent of the injury. The palm of a human victim will represent 1% TBSA. This came to the author's attention after a tour of the Maricopa County Burn Unit, in Phoenix, Arizona. This has the potential to be replicated in companion animals using the palmar surface area of the front paw. The author is pursuing research for future application of this as an estimation of TBSA.

Actual measurement of burn wounds and calculation of TBSA is the most reliable and defensible approach for representation in written medical records and for court testimony (Sinclair et al., 2006).

Determining the depth of the burn injury is more difficult, especially in the initial stages of the injury. In the physiological process previously described, an injury of partial-thickness injury can progress to a full-thickness injury, depending on the type of treatment or lack thereof. The hair coat can be an effective insulator, and hairless skin is more vulnerable to injury (Pope, 2003). Partial-thickness burns may be painful, and the hair does not epilate easily. A full-thickness burn is usually not painful, and the hair epilates easily (Pope, 2003).

A staining technique can help differentiate the depth of injury (Pope, 2003). A modified van Gieson stain causes normal skin to stain red. In situations of tissue abnormality, areas of minor necrosis turn pale yellow and deep injuries a bright yellow (Pope, 2003). This will be beneficial for treatment determination (Pope, 2003) but may also have application for earlier determination of the full extent of a burn injury for medicolegal purposes.

Thermal

Thermal burns can be produced by contact or near-contact to a heat source. Factors that affect the extent of the injury include the temperature of the heat source, duration of contact, and the conductance of the tissue. Initially the appearance of the contact thermal burn may be delayed.

Initial findings may only consist of matted or moist fur, with eventual loss of hair and skin (Hedlund, 2002; Merck & Miller, 2013).

The animal's skin does not disseminate heat as human skin does, due to the lack of abundant superficial vascular plexuses. In a direct-contact burn wound there is coagulation, cellular protein denaturation, and blood vessel coagulation with plasma loss and tissue edema (Hedlund, 2002). Local tissue ischemia may be observed within 3 to 5 days (Merck & Miller, 2013). A transitional area develops between the devitalized and healthy tissue, which has possible reversible tissue injury, decreased blood flow, and intravascular sludging (Merck & Miller, 2013). There is continued release of vasoactive substances causing dermal ischemia, tissue edema, desiccation, and secondary bacterial invasion (Merck & Miller, 2013). This zone of transition is surrounded by hyperemic tissue. Eventually, eschar may form. This is a residue of coagulated skin particles made up of tough, denatured collagen fibers as a protective wound covering. When the eschar is raised or bent, separating from the underlying tissue, it will split in first- and second-degree burns. The eschar in a third-degree burn may or may not split, and the split may progress down to the subcutaneous tissue layers. Bacterial invasion beneath the eschar will occur within 4 to 5 days (Hedlund, 2002; Merck & Miller, 2013). Burns to the perineum, feet, eyes, ears, and face are considered severe due to potential loss of function and severity of pain (Saxon & Kirby, 1992).

Scalding

These types of burns are caused by contact with a hot liquid, and there is no singeing of the hair. Scaldings are caused by spills, splashing, immersion, or superheated steam. In animals, scalding may occur when fluid temperatures reach 120° Fahrenheit (48.8°C) (Sinclair et al., 2006; Merck & Miller, 2013).

In splash or spill burn injuries, the fluid cools as it flows down the side of the body. A burn is more severe where the liquid (fluid) had initial contact with the tissue surface, becoming more superficial as the fluid flows from the initial point of contact. Super-heated steam may cause severe scalding wounds. If the steam is inhaled, airway injury may result to the upper, lower, and deeper airways (DiMaio & DiMaio, 2001; Merck & Miller, 2013). This may cause edema in the larynx, resulting in occlusion of the airway and asphyxia. Intentional immersion burns are characterized by a straight line from the water level (Platt et al., 2006). This is dependent on the body part involved and the struggle or level of resistance from the animal victim. In the limbs this may develop in a stocking or glove distribution with a defined upper margin. A scald may be limited to the feet and the pads depending on the depth of foot immersion. In cats, the toes will retract with contact, protecting the areas between the pads (Merck & Miller, 2013). Gross findings of scald burns to the feet include loss of epithelium from the ventral pad surfaces with progressing drainage and darkening, normal non-erythematous areas between pads and toes, and erythematous skin with loss of hair and epidermis on the dorsal and lateral aspects of the toes or foot (Munro & Munro, 2008; Merck & Miller, 2013) (Figure 12.2).

Scalding burns over the dorsum may develop when water from an outdoor hose in hot climates is sprayed on an animal (Quist et al., 2011). In many instances, this is accidental. However, if the burn is not recognized or addressed this may be grounds for animal abuse charges.

Cigarette Burns

Cigarette burn wounds, although not as well documented as in child abuse cases, do occur in animals (Munro & Thrushfield, 2001). An acute burn is red and circular, approximately, 0.5–1.0 cm in diameter. The burn may be wedge shaped if the cigarette was used at an oblique angle. A deliberate wound may be full thickness, creating a crater-like wound. An older burn wound can be circular and sunken, with thinly developed scar tissue on the surface. Accidental burns tend to be superficial and eccentric due to the brief contact with the hot ash (Munro & Thrushfield, 2001; Merck & Miller, 2013).

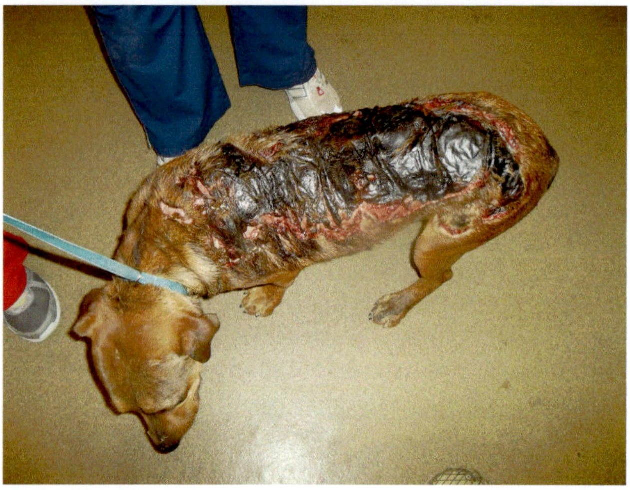

Figure 12.2 Scalding wounds: From hot water. (Photo courtesy R. Jesus.)

Solar Dermatitis

Solar injury or sunburns in conjunction with ultraviolet rays has been well documented in animals (Merck & Miller, 2013) in regions of diminished fur and light pigmentation. Thermal injury may also develop in dark pigmented areas from solar radiation. Darkened (black) skin can absorb 45% more solar radiation than light-colored areas of skin. Visible radiation penetrates the skin several millimeters and disseminates into thermal energy, further increasing the thermal burden (Merck & Miller, 2013). Histological findings demonstrate a full-thickness burn: epidermal adnexal necrosis, vascular necrosis, and subepidermal vesiculation (Merck & Miller, 2013). These types of cases present with burn lesions along the dorsum and may contain plaques and eschars. These wounds are often mistaken for animal cruelty in the form of a caustic agent applied to the animal's back (Merck & Miller, 2013). Solar thermal necrosis is due to exposure to the direct sunlight. It usually occurs when an animal cannot obtain shelter (escape) from direct sunlight, specifically environmental circumstances or physical limitations (Merck & Miller, 2013). Animal abuse charges may result in instances where an animal is tied outside without adequate shade or shelter. Burn lesions from this type of circumstances (sun exposure) may not appear for days or up to 2 weeks.

Radiant Heat Burns

These are near-contact burns caused by heat waves generated by a hot surface such as a flame, fire, heat lamp, heater, or radiator. Depending on the temperature, burns may occur in seconds. Radiant heat can cause substantial injury to the outside of the animal's body. In the early stages right after the injury, the hair is intact and the skin is erythemic and may be blistered (although not as common in animals) (Pope, 2003) with possible skin sloughing. After prolonged exposure the skin may develop a leathery consistency with eventual charring (DiMaio & DiMaio, 2001; Merck & Miller, 2013).

Chemical Burns

These types of burns result from chemical agents that are strong acids and alkalis causing damage by disrupting cell metabolism or denaturing proteins (Merck & Miller, 2013). These types of burns may be external, internal, or a combination of both types of burns. Burns must be examined carefully to determine the cause due to the similarity of injuries produced by chemical and thermal burns (Merck & Miller, 2013).

Damage to tissue may occur via multiple mechanisms of action with chemical burns. Chemicals that are dehydrating desiccate the tissues, oxidizing agents cause injury by coagulation of proteins, corrosive agents denature proteins causing erosion and ulceration, denaturing chemicals will fix or stabilize tissue through salt formation, and vesicants may cause the release of tissue histamine and serotonin resulting in blisters (Hedlund, 2002; Merck & Miller, 2013; Saukko & Knight, 2016).

Chemical contact with eyes can cause corneal damage, such as full-thickness perforation and necrosis of the cornea. A secondary effect of chemical burns can be heat resulting from a chemical reaction on the tissue causing injury (Hedlund, 2002; Merck & Miller, 2013). Ingestion of chemicals may result from an environmental exposure, either intentional or accidental. Additional methods are intentional feeding or applications to the body that are further complicated by grooming (i.e., licking). Wounds resulting from ingested chemical substances may be found on the muzzle, tongue, hard palate, gums, oropharynx, esophagus, stomach, and small intestine, depending on the amount of chemical and its properties. Some chemical agents may cause systemic poisoning as well as tissue burns (Merck & Miller, 2013).

A wide variety of chemicals have been associated with animal abuse to intentionally cause burns. There are chemicals that produce burns or irritation through prolonged exposure, such as an animal's presence in a residence used for illegal methamphetamine manufacturing. In the author's personal experience, hamburger meat or pancake batter has been used to facilitate ingestion of multiple types of chemical poisons.

The degree of injury is dependent on various factors such as the type of chemical, its action, volume of the chemical contacting the body, chemical strength, length of contact, chemical penetration, and if the chemical was ingested or absorbed. Chemical injuries can be superficial or result in third-degree burns (Merck & Miller, 2013) (Figure 12.3a–c).

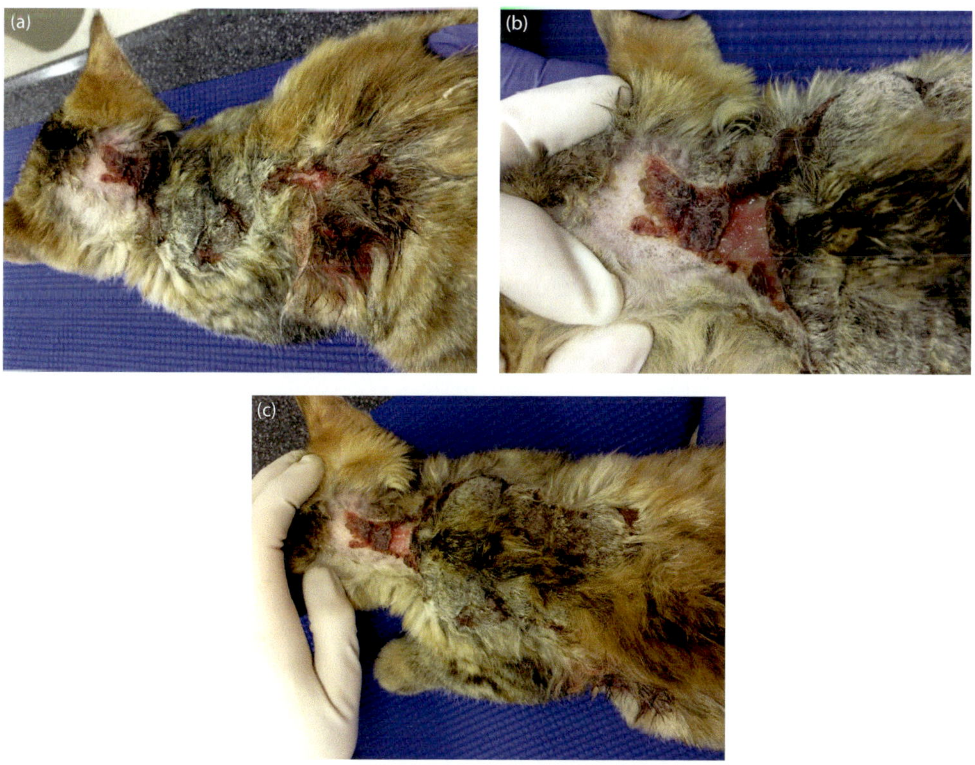

Figures 12.3 (a–c) Chemical burns: Kitten with necrotizing dermatitis from thermal glue. (Photos courtesy Dr. B.J. McEwen.)

Microwave

Microwaves produce heat through molecular agitation primarily through water. The common kitchen microwave has a frequency of 2450 Hertz. This means the microwave electric field reverses 2450 million times per second, causing water molecules in the tissue to be highly agitated (movement) and result in molecular friction thereby producing heat. The result is tissue burning (cooking) (Surrell et al., 1987; Merck & Miller, 2013). The amount of damage is dependent on the length of time in the microwave oven and the strength of the microwaves produced (Merck & Miller, 2013). Injuries are subject to water distribution within the tissues, with the greatest injury occurring internally. Microscopically, there is a sparing effect of tissues, resulting in relative layered (sandwich) tissue appearance in microwave burn biopsy specimens (Tans, 1989; Merck & Miller, 2013). Microwave burns can be distinguished from other types of wounds. Scald wounds (animal placed in container of hot water) will have a well demarcated burn consistent with the water line. An unrestrained animal may exhibit splash burns from flailing in a hot liquid. Direct-contact burn wounds from a metal object or cigarette may leave a characteristic pattern (Surrell et al., 1987).

Postmortem signs consistent with a microwave burn injury can include skin frailty leading to splitting of the tissue with defined edges and epilation of the hair, flexion of the forelimb near the carpus with or without extension of the claws, folding and erythema of the distal ear pinnae, and without burning or singeing of the hair. There may be congestion of the lung lobes possibly involving alveolar fluid accumulation and perivascular hemorrhage microscopically. There may be a cooked appearance to internal organs with tissue disintegration and a cooked chicken odor (Munro & Munro, 2008; Merck & Miller, 2013).

If animal abuse is suspected, the microwave oven in question should first be evaluated for any evidence of malfunction and determine if the animal body or body region affected would fit into the microwave oven. Microwave burns can be well demarcated and located on those parts of the body closest to the microwave-emitting device, usually in the top of the microwave device (Surrell et al., 1987). A full-thickness biopsy at the junction between normal and burned skin should be obtained (Surrell et al., 1987; DiMaio & DiMaio, 2001). These types of burns both grossly and histologically will illustrate a relative layered tissue sparing not observed from other burns such as flame, contact, electric, or chemical burns. Other deep structures within the abdomen and thorax may have acute visceral damage as well, resulting in bowel obstructions (Surrell et al., 1987).

Electric Burns

There are two types of electric currents: a direct current and an alternating current. Alternating currents are found in businesses and residential structures, and direct currents are more common in batteries. A direct current travels in one direction, whereas an alternating current frequently changes direction away from and toward its origin. In the United States most structural wall sockets are 110 volts unless for appliances and larger devices, which are usually 220 volts. A direct current (DC) is less dangerous than an alternating current (AC). A current of 50–80 mA (AC) can be fatal within seconds, in comparison to 250 mA DC for a similar time period, which is often survived in humans. In humans, an AC is more likely to cause cardiac arrhythmias (Saukko & Knight, 2016).

An electric current pulsing through tissue can cause skin lesions, organ damage, and death; this is referred to as electrocution (Saukko & Knight, 2016). The degree of damage is dependent on the current, voltage, generation of heat, and the time the animal victim is in contact with the electrical source (Merck & Miller, 2013; Schulze et al., 2016). The current is the quantity of electricity traveling through a wire and is measured in milliamps (mA). The damage to tissue is proportional to the amount of electricity flowing through it. Voltage is another factor; the higher the amount, the more electricity that passes through the tissue. The longer a current passes through a body, the higher the degree of damage produced. A low current exposed to the body for a long period of time can cause more damage than exposure to a higher current for a short period of time. Heat is generated from the electric current, causing thermal injury (Saukko & Knight, 2016). Due to the deep extension of generated heat, tissue damage can be severe. Death may result from respiratory paralysis or ventricular fibrillation (Hedlund, 2002) (Figure 12.4a–c).

When an electrical current enters a body, it will travel the shortest route from the origin of contact to a point of grounding or exit (Saukko & Knight, 2016). Tissue resistance to an electric current from greatest to least is bone, fat, tendon, skin, muscle, blood, and nerves. A current's flow along a path of minimal resistance includes blood vessels, nerves, and wet tissue (Hedlund, 2002; Merck & Miller, 2013; Saukko & Knight, 2016). A current will concentrate in tissue of greater resistance such as bone, causing the generation of increased thermal energy (Hedlund, 2002).

Animal victims of electricity may be found still in contact with an electrical source that caused the injury. The majority of electrical injuries in animals are accidental (Merck & Miller, 2013). In animal abuse cases electricity can be used as a form of torture or to kill an animal (Merck & Miller 2013). According to Chris Schindler, Animal Cruelty and Fighting Director, for the Humane Society of the United States, pit bulls are routinely culled by their owners using electricity after losing an event or if the owner just wants to get rid of them. A method known as "plugging" is used. This makes use of an electric extension cord that can be plugged into a wall socket or a portable jump box (for charging a car battery) (Figure 12.5). There are two electrode devices usually with alligator clips and a cord to be plugged into an outlet. The animal has a clip applied to an ear and the tail or anus and then then the device is plugged in, killing the dog (Schindler, personal communication, 2018). A similar method has been used in show and racehorses to kill them for insurance fraud (Schindler, personal communication, 2018). According to Detective Mike Duffey, Animal Cruelty Investigator for the Humane Society of Southern Arizona, another method of electrocution used in these dogs is using a metal roofing sheet and a hand-operated toy electric train "transformer" with wires attached to the piece of metal. The dog's feet are made wet and

Figures 12.4 (a–c) Magpie electrocution. (Photo courtesy Dr. J.D. Struthers.)

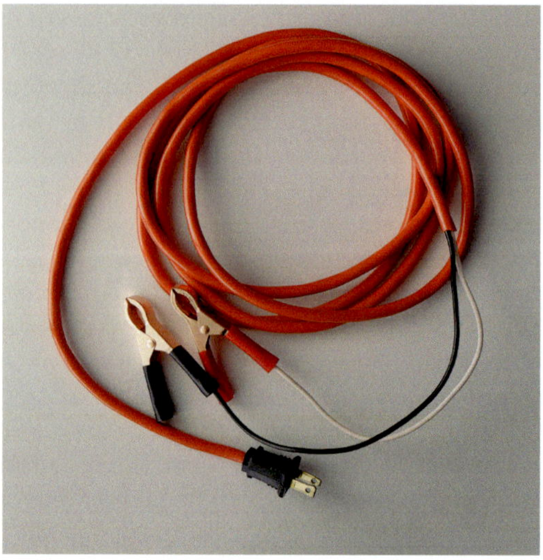

Figure 12.5 Simulated photo of the "clip" device used to electrocute fighting dogs; the device is attached to the lip and flank areas and plugged into a wall socket. Can be mistaken for utility cord at the scene. (Photo courtesy L. Siemens.)

the dog is placed on the metal sheet. The current is applied, killing the dog (Duffey, personal communication, 2018).

Electrocution by these methods may show external burns, such as pad injuries; however, the use of the alligator clips, especially in the anus region, may leave subtle if any electric marks and will need to be looked for during the necropsy on these animals. An animal injured from electricity might be found in a tonic state from prolonged contraction of striated muscles. There may also be evidence of vomiting or diarrhea (Merck & Miller, 2013). In humans this can lead to bone fractures (DiMaio & DiMaio, 2001). Lower amperage electrocution will cause muscle tremors, painful muscle contractions, and loss of consciousness. The animal may develop ventricular fibrillation or respiratory paralysis, causing damage. There may be decreased thermal damage to aqueous internal tissue, with evidence of pulmonary edema. If an animal survives when an electric source is removed, there will be generalized weakness and ataxia followed by secondary pulmonary edema. Electric burns can cause the release of vasoactive substances and vasoactive thrombosis, causing tissue necrosis. The tissue may appear charred, tan, or pale gray. Tissue edema may be observed in 1–2 days post injury. Local tissue ischemia can develop in 3–5 days. The full extent of the injury may take 2–3 weeks to be recognized (Hedlund, 2002; Merck & Miller, 2013).

Low-voltage electrical burns are called electrical marks and can be found in the area of electrical contact. These types of burns are generally small or appear as a chalky white lesion with an indented crater with raised borders or erythema (blistering) (Merck & Miller, 2013; Saukko & Knight, 2016). Some lesions have hyperemic borders surrounding a pale area or reddening within the zone. Burns may have yellow or black discoloration caused by heat (Saukko & Knight, 2016). Histologically, there may be disruption of the epidermal surface. There may be particles of metal deposits if a metal device such as a clip was used as a conduction surface. A pattern of calcification of collagen fibers both superficially and deeply in the skin within a zone of viable tissue in close proximity to necrotic tissue may be consistent with an electrically induced lesion. In experiments with pig skin using alternating currents and direct currents, these have been observed (Danielson et al., 1991).

High-voltage electric burns can result in charring of body tissue resulting in third-degree burns at the contact site. Multiple small burn wounds caused by arcing of the current can cause a crocodile-skin effect observed in humans (Saukko & Knight, 2016). If the electric current is obtained through a tertiary object, the resulting electrical burns can be large and irregular. The actual burns consist of a chalky white crater with raised borders, with the heat producing a yellow or black discoloration at the burn sites. In humans, massive tissue destruction from high voltage along with loss of extremities and organ rupture have been noted (DiMaio & DiMaio, 2001). Death usually results from cardiac arrest. There may be high voltage thermal damage to the respiratory center of the brainstem resulting in respiratory arrest (DiMaio & DiMaio, 2001).

Tasers

The Taser is an electric control device (conducted energy weapon) using high voltage to the body to incapacitate people via neuromuscular disruption causing the incapacitation. Two darts or probes are discharged from the weapon, penetrating the skin of the target. There are wires attached to the darts extending out over 35 feet depending on the weapon. There is a pulsed current output delivered with the pressing of the weapon's trigger. Skin lesions can be observed at the penetration site of the dart, and there are usually local burns at the contact sites. In studies done with Taser devices on canines, no cardiac arrhythmias were noted (Merck & Miller, 2013). In the author's personal experience, usually one or both of the barbed darts are still in place when the animal is found, with focal areas of irritation or reddening.

Histology

Electric burns versus thermal burns can be differentiated. Electric burns have sharp borders with an abrupt transition from normal to injured tissue. There is a honeycomb vacuolization in the stratum corneum. There are subepidermal bullae due to the detachment of the epidermis from the dermis, denaturing of the dermal collagen and vaporized metal on the surface of the skin with high voltage. Computed tomography and light microscopy can assist with differentiating electric, flame burn, or abrasion type skin injuries (Merck & Miller, 2013).

Elevated creatinine kinase levels may be used as marker for cellular damage in humans, another indicator consistent with electrocution (Teodoreanu et al., 2014).

Smoke Inhalation

Acute pulmonary injury is caused by smoke inhalation. If asphyxia is not immediate, the combined chemical and heat effects cause widespread epithelial necrosis and exudation, and may result in death within a few days (Maxie, 2016; Wohlsein et al., 2016).

Smoke inhalation and internal thermal injury can result from a companion animal exposure to fire in either a structure or direct contact (set on fire). The cause of death when an animal is caught in a fire environment is carbon monoxide poisoning, smoke toxicity, thermal injury to the airways or the body, or any combination (Merck & Miller, 2013).

The oral cavity, nostrils, and upper and lower airways may contain soot in the event of smoke inhalation (Figure 12.6). The soot can be swallowed, resulting in the presence of flakes in the esophageal and stomach lining (Spitz, 2006). To avoid oral or laryngeal soot particles from descending into the lower airways and causing potential contamination, a ball of absorbent cotton can be used to obstruct (block) the upper airway and trachea while the pluck is removed for examination during a necropsy. Soot may be present in mucus and can be removed by using a scalpel or spatula and spread onto a clean white paper towel for documentation (Spitz, 2006). The absence of soot is not definitive for death prior to a fire related event (Maxie, 2016).

Microscopic findings in the lung parenchyma can assist in determining if the animal was alive or dead before and during a fire (Figure 12.7a–c). Histological signs in humans consist of bronchial dilation, ductal over-insufflation, alveolar insufflation, and alveolar hemorrhage (Merck & Miller, 2013). Additional thermal damage may be the result of an animal breathing in hot gases causing edema and/or burns discussed earlier. This results in destruction of tissue in the oral mucosa, nasopharynx, and generalized damage to the remaining respiratory tract (Merck & Miller, 2013).

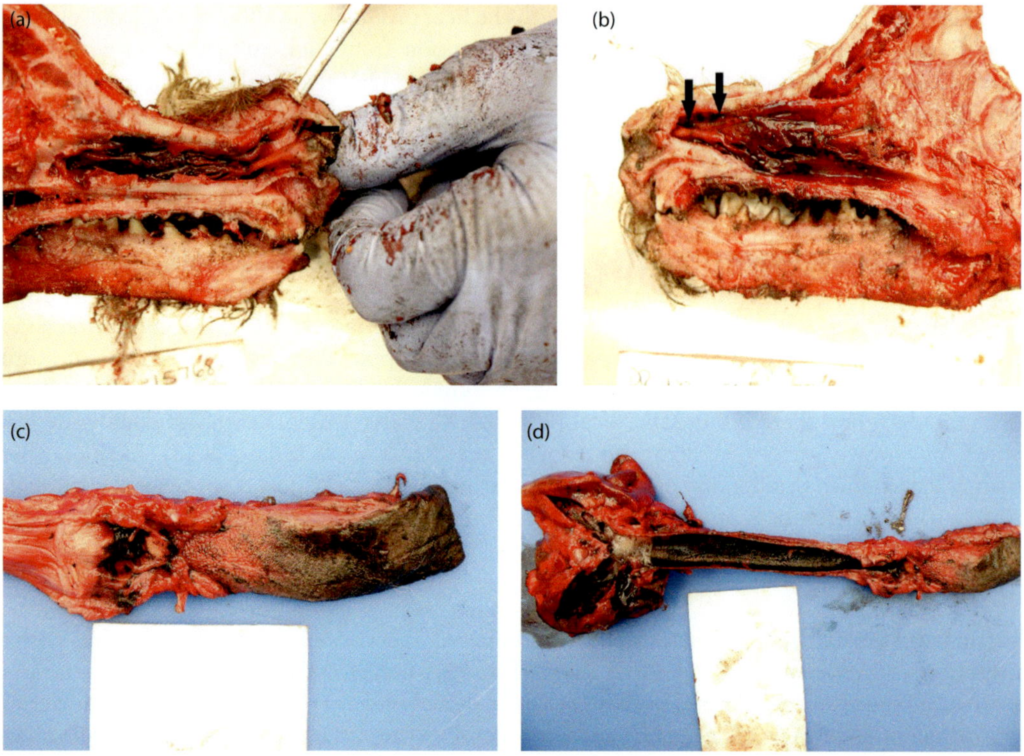

Figures 12.6 (a) Mucosal lining of the vestibule (arrows) is multifocally discolored by deposited black pigmented material (soot). (b) The nasal turbinates are congested. (c) The dorsal tongue and entrance to the larynx is discolored with black pigmented material (soot). (d) Nearly diffusely, mucosal lining of the larynx, trachea, and bronchi are discolored by deposited black pigmented material (soot). Mild amounts of foam within the carina and the lungs, trachea, and laryngeal muscles are dark red. ([b-d] Photos courtesy Dr. J.D. Struthers.)

The resulting thermal injuries may cause laryngeal edema resulting in obstruction and suffocation (Saxon & Kirby, 1992; Wang et al., 2014). During the initial 24 hours post-injury, damage to the upper airway passages may cause an obstruction in this region (Tans, 1989). Severe laryngeal burns manifest as severe edema or atrophy, either or both of which may result in obstruction (Wang et al., 2014). The mucosal lining of the airways may slough into the lumen, potentiating more airway obstruction within 2–6 days of the initial injury (Saxon & Kirby, 1992) and hinder surfactant production (Juthowitz, 2005). The resulting luminal burn wounds may cause systemic inflammation or result in sepsis that can cause acute lung injury or acute respiratory distress syndrome (ARDS) (Juthowitz, 2005).

Smoke inhalation injury can occur alone or in combination with thermal or chemical injury. This can be most severe when the animal is discovered in an enclosed space or unconscious within a fire (Saxon & Kirby, 1992). Thermal injury is usually restricted to upper airways due to poor heat-carrying capacity of dry air and efficient heat dissipating capacity of an airway (Pope, 2003). Steam has exponentially higher heat carrying capacity of dry air and can cause severe destruction in the lower airways. Thermal damage in lower airways occurs in less than 5% of cases of inhalation injury (Pope, 2003).

Carbon Monoxide

Carbon monoxide (CO) is a poisonous, colorless, odorless gas that is lighter than air, arising from incomplete combustion of hydrogen carbon fuels (Carson, 1986). Due to its significant binding affinity for hemoglobin (210–240 times that of oxygen), CO displaces oxygen from hemoglobin,

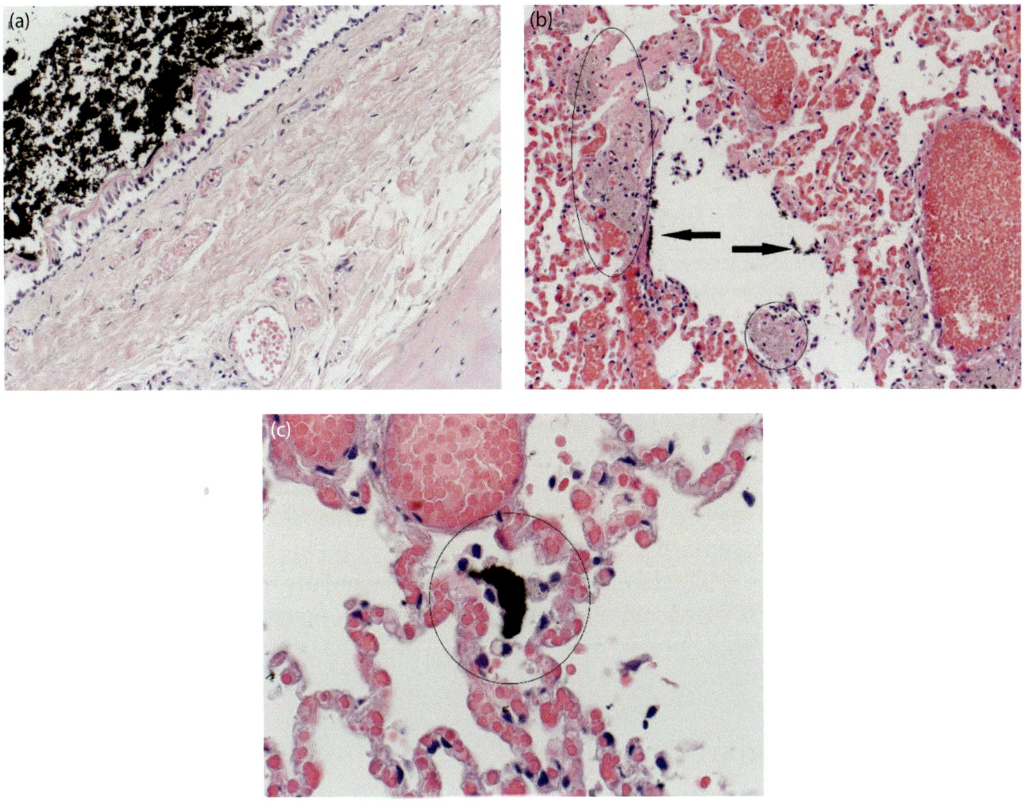

Figure 12.7 (a) Photomicrograph of the trachea, 40× objective. Surface epithelium is overlaid by deposited granular black pigmented material (soot). (b) Photomicrograph 20× objective. The surface epithelium of a respiratory bronchiole and spilling into alveolar ducts contains deposited granular black pigmented material (soot) (arrows). The airway interstitium and vessel adventitia contain nodules of macrophage-associated inhaled and retained inorganic dusts (circled). Pneumoconiosis = inhalation and retention of inorganic dusts + anthracosis = inhalation and retention of carbon. (c) Photomicrograph 60× objective. An alveolus contains deposited granular black pigmented material (soot) that is intimately surrounded by intra-alveolar macrophages, some of which have intracytoplasmic phagocytose material (circled). ([a-c] Photos and interpretation, courtesy Dr. J.D. Struthers.)

causing tissue hypoxia (Pope, 2003). The carbon monoxide binds to hemoglobin (carboxyhemoglobin [COHb]), inhibiting its ability to carry oxygen. This shifts the oxygen-hemoglobin dissociation curve to the left, additionally reducing oxygen delivery to the tissue (Pope, 2003) (Merck & Miller, 2013). Increased COHb levels cause cherry-red or pink discoloration to the skin or in areas of lividity (Merck & Miller, 2013). Carbon monoxide levels as high as 8% have been measured experimentally in controlled house fires (Pope, 2003). COHb levels greater than 40% can cause irreversible nervous system damage. COHb levels greater than 60% may be fatal (Pope, 2003). In addition, the direct effects of CO may cause pulmonary injury, reducing normal reflex decrease in breathing when heated air is inhaled (Pope, 2003). Death can occur rapidly with sudden high levels. This may result from cardiac arrest due to cardiac dysfunction occurring before CNS effects (Merck & Miller, 2013). With CO toxicity, the necropsy exam findings may consist of dilated bronchi and distension of the major blood vessels. The ventricles of the heart can be dilated, specifically the right ventricle resulting from a sudden increase in central venous pressure sometimes observed with CO toxicity (Carson, 1986; Merck & Miller, 2013). Brain changes are observed related to anoxia consisting of necrosis in white matter of the cerebral hemispheres, globus pallidus, brain stem, and cortex. Edema, demyelination, and hemorrhage in the brain and necrosis in the hippocampus may occur (Carson, 1986; Merck & Miller, 2013).

Testing for levels of CO is important in corroborating antemortem versus postmortem findings. Venous blood should be obtained and transported immediately on ice (Merck & Miller, 2013). The COHb levels will need to be run at a human laboratory. In the event the animal is alive, COHb levels will decrease over time, further increasing the importance of testing levels of COHb as soon as possible for documentation (Merck & Miller, 2013).

Cyanide Poisoning in Fires

The most common cause of death in fires is the inhalation of noxious gasses rather than thermal injury. Hydrogen cyanide gas, potentially the most toxic of combustion gasses, is seldom recognized as an important hazard in smoke inhalation (Jones et al., 1987). Sources of cyanide toxicity are the use of synthetic polymers in building materials and furnishings (Jones et al., 1987). Cyanide disrupts the ability of the cells to use oxygen by binding with and inhibiting cellular respiratory enzyme mitochondrial cytochrome oxidase (Merck & Miller, 2013). It primarily affects the heart and the brain. An animal's body may appear pink or cherry-red, corresponding to CO poisoning, caused by fully oxygenated blood due to the tissues' inability to extract oxygen from the blood (Merck & Miller, 2013). The victim may become cyanotic. Diagnostic testing for cyanide gas poisoning may be difficult. Decomposition of the body causes cyanide production in the blood, falsely increasing the levels. Other substances in blood such as sulfides can react similarly to cyanide, falsely elevating levels (DiMaio & DiMaio, 2001; Merck & Miller, 2013). Consideration for cyanide levels should be given; however, there have been human cases where death occurred before COHb could be formed (Gerling et al., 2001).

Examining the Animal Fire Victim

Before examination of the patient, considerations should be given to the crime scene and what occurred there. The animal body should be photographed and examined in place if possible, to define the circumstances of the body as it relates to the crime scene. Evidence as to the origin of the fire may be found on the animal's body, i.e., odors from an accelerant and the accelerant used. Evidence from the body should be collected. Consider discussing these considerations with a law enforcement crime scene analyst or local forensic laboratories. For example, samples of fur with an accelerant would need to be placed in an airtight paint can to be sent to a laboratory for analysis (Merck & Miller, 2013). Use whole-body radiographs to rule out antemortem trauma including fractures or projectiles. Extreme heat from a fire may cause fracturing of the bone (Merck & Miller, 2013).

A surviving animal victim's fur will smell like smoke. In addition to any external thermal burns that may be observed, there may be burns within the oral cavity and the upper and lower airways. Evaluate the patient for laryngeal spasms. Injury to the airways can consist of edema, mucosal erythema, ulceration, hemorrhage, and soot particle accumulation (Merck & Miller, 2013). Carbon monoxide poisoning may be demonstrated as cherry-red skin and mucous membranes. Eye injuries, including corneal abrasions and conjunctivitis, may be observed. Tracheal aspirate cytological exams in moderate to severe cases can reveal burned ciliated cells, strands of mucus, and soot particles (Carson, 1986).

Deceased Animal Fire Victim

It must be determined if the animal was alive or dead prior to the fire or if there is evidence of antemortem injury. There may or may not be evidence of external injury. Those bodies with minimal or no external injury may have succumbed to smoke inhalation. Some bodies may have external signs of searing damage causing the skin to be light brown and have a stiff leathery appearance (DiMaio & DiMaio, 2001) (Figure 12.8a–b).

The animal's body may be charred and swollen from heat. Heat accumulation in the thorax can cause blood to infiltrate the alveoli, airway, mouth, and nostrils, simulating an antemortem injury.

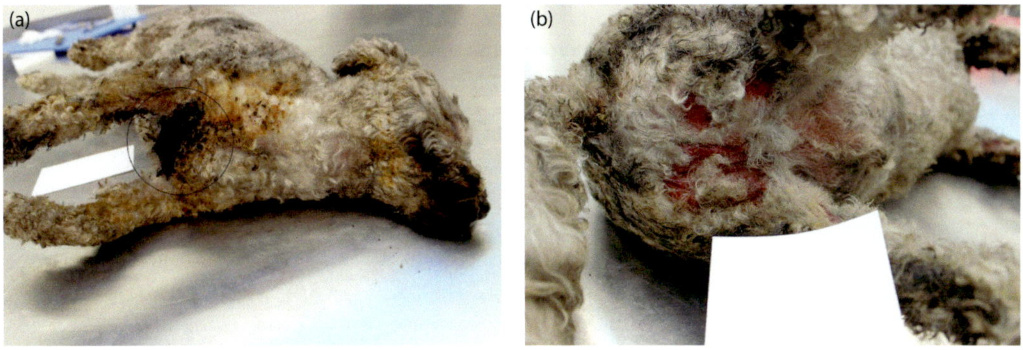

Figures 12.8 (a,b) Dog placed in BBQ; 40% of dog's exterior surface shows burning, scorching, and singeing of the fur and integument. (Photo courtesy Dr. J.D. Struthers.)

The presence of blood in the chest pleura (inner lining) can indicate antemortem trauma (Stern et al., 2014). The lung tissue may present with accelerant residue if the animal inhaled any of the vapors antemortem (Merck & Miller, 2013). In situations of a severely burned body, the skin may shrink, causing it to split. In other instances, with skin completely burnt away the underlying muscle may be exposed and can be ruptured due to the heat. Muscle will split parallel to the muscle fibers due to the heat traversing. Splits across the muscle may be due to trauma prior to death (Spitz, 2006; Merck & Miller, 2013). There may be areas of unaltered skin where the body was lying on a flat surface. The internal body wall may be removed from burning, exposing viscera which can be seared or charred (DiMaio & DiMaio, 2001; Merck & Miller, 2013).

It is very difficult to determine antemortem versus postmortem burns on gross examination. There may be microscopic evidence of vital response (inflammation); however, the lack of response is not indicative of postmortem injury. Thrombosis from heat in the dermal vessels may impede inflammatory cells from reaching a burn area (DiMaio & DiMaio, 2001; Merck & Miller, 2013).

Two dogs were found deceased in a house fire with a postmortem interval of approximately 24 hours. One of the two dogs had severe burns on over 50% of its body (majority on the dorsum and right body wall) with severe charring and splitting of the skin. No singe marks or soot deposit were observed on the eyelids. Internal examination of both dogs demonstrated deposition of soot (black pigmented material) mixed with mucous within the pharynx, larynx, trachea, and primary bronchi. The oral mucous membranes and musculature were red. The microscopic findings were limited to the respiratory system of both dogs. The was soot overlying the ciliated epithelium of the trachea and bronchi and the epithelium of the bronchioles. There was only minimal soot within the alveolar spaces (Stern et al., 2014).

In the deceased animal, blood collection and the determination of CO levels along with evidence of inspiratory activity (see above) are the best indicators an animal was alive before and during a fire. Whole blood can be obtained from the aorta, heart, or caudal vena cava. In conversations with Dr. Stern (Stern et al. 2014), blood samples for CO were collected in a green top heparin tube. These samples will need to be sent to a human laboratory or hospital for analysis. These samples should be obtained as soon as possible and sent for analysis (Stern et al., 2014).

In a fire, blood and marrow can be exuded from the skull and amass between the bone and dura mater, simulating a traumatic epidural hematoma present in the frontal, parietal, and temporal regions with possible involvement of the occipital region. The amassed material is a clot-like chocolate-brown color with a crumbly or honeycomb appearance (DiMaio & DiMaio, 2001; Merck & Miller, 2013). One indicator that an epidural hematoma is not antemortem is the presence of a skull fracture due to heat changes; this is absent antemortem. According to Spitz, subdural hemorrhage is an indicator of an antemortem injury (Spitz, 2006; Merck & Miller, 2013).

A burnt body may present with flexion of the limbs, causing a pugilistic posture. This is due to coagulation of the muscle tissue and contraction of muscle fibers from generation of heat when the body is burnt. The resulting muscle shrinkage may cause bone to fracture. The use of computed tomography can assist with differentiation of traumatic versus thermal changes (Merck & Miller, 2013).

Entomology

There may be evidence of live or deceased insects or larvae on burnt animal victims both internally and externally. After some time, insects present on the body can be the same first-wave insects as those found on fresh remains (Merck & Miller, 2013). These can assist with the postmortem interval. This can help assess when the fire occurred. Deceased entomology evidence (larvae) can be found internally, specifically in the skull or body cavities. This can indicate the animal was deceased before the fire (Merck & Miller, 2013).

HYPERTHERMIA

Heatstroke is the most severe of the heat-induced illnesses (Drobatz, 2015). It is classified as external (overheating from exercise) or non-external (classic heatstroke). Any body system may be involved; however, the major systems involved are the cardiovascular, central nervous, gastrointestinal, renal, and coagulation systems. There are three types of heat illness, presenting as a continuum from least to the most severe (Drobatz, 2015).

- *Heat cramping*: Muscle spasms from sodium and chloride loss
- *Heat exhaustion/prostration*: Fatigue, weakness, muscle tremors, vomiting, and diarrhea
- *Heatstroke*: Severe central nervous system disturbances and multi-organ dysfunction

A more recent definition of heatstroke is hyperthermia associated with a systemic inflammatory response leading to a syndrome of multi-organ failure in which encephalopathy predominates.

Heatstroke is the increase of core body temperature causing heat-induced illness (Drobatz, 2015). Heatstroke within domestic animals is more common in dogs and cats (Drobatz, 2015). A dog's body dissipates heat via multiple methods. One is the conduction of heat through cutaneous vasodilation ridding the body of heat by direct contact with a cooler surface. Convection occurs via postural changes and cutaneous vasodilation allowing air blowing over a body surface to remove the warmed air layer next to the animal's body. Radiation is the direct removal of radiation (infrared heat) into the environment, through cutaneous vasodilation. The final method and the most important when the environmental temperatures equal core body temperatures is evaporation. The first three methods discussed enact when environmental temperatures are at or below 89.6°F (32°C). (Merck & Miller, 2013). Dogs cannot sweat like humans and will dissipate heat by evaporation by panting. The oral cavity and nasal passages supply a large surface area for loss of water (evaporation) from the moist mucous membranes (Merck & Miller, 2013). Conditions that combine heat load and decreased heat dissipation can result in rapid and extreme body temperature elevation. Heatstroke occurs when the heat-disseminating mechanisms can no longer compensate for the rising body temperature, such as occurs with entrapment (in a hot vehicle) or exposure to extreme environmental temperatures without shelter or water (tying out) (Merck & Miller, 2013).

In animal abuse cases, hyperthermia is observed when animals are left inside a hot car or building or tethered outside without access to water or any protection from elevated environmental temperatures and direct sunlight (Merck & Miller, 2013). In addition, the environmental temperature is affected by the relative humidity. As the humidity increases, the heat index is higher than the recorded temperature (Merck & Miller, 2013).

Animals left in a hot vehicle commonly develop heatstroke. A dog may die in as little as 20 minutes in a parked car in direct sunlight even with the windows cracked slightly (Merck & Miller, 2013). There have been multiple studies conducted on the internal heating of vehicles in different conditions. In one study the average temperature rose 3.2°F (1.8°C) every 5 minutes with the windows closed and 3.1°F (1.7°C) with the window open several inches, the inside temperature eventually rising to its maximum level within 1 hour, with over 80% of the rise within the first 30 minutes regardless of the outside temperature. Even at low ambient temperatures, the internal temperature of a vehicle reached 117°F (47°C) with an average maximum increase of 41°F (5°C) (Merck & Miller, 2013). Even at 85°F (29°C) ambient temperature, the internal temperature even with the windows left open 1–2 inches can reach 102°F (39°C) within 10 minutes and 120°F (49°C) in 30 minutes (Merck & Miller, 2013). The temperature inside a car can rise 20°F in just 10 minutes. Even on a 70°F day it can become 110°F in a vehicle (AVMA, 2018), and cracking the windows makes no difference.

A dog's body maintains body temperature within a narrow range called the set point. When body temperature deviates from the set point, physiologic processes are initiated to elevate or decrease the body temperature. When a dog's body temperature reaches 106°F (41° C) the dog is in danger of a heat-caused illness. If the body temperature reaches above 110°F (43°C) there is a breakdown of the cellular processes and the dog can die in 5–15 minutes.

Heatstroke is not commonly reported in cats. This may be to the lack of detection (Merck & Miller, 2013). When it is discovered, it is usually caused by the cat being subjected to a sudden increase in temperature or confinement in high temperatures without an escape (Merck & Miller, 2013).

It is important to stress most state laws for animal abuse regarding animals in a hot car have verbiage concerning possible physical harm or actual physical harm. This stresses the importance of veterinary testimony to articulate what can happen even if fortunately, it did not.

Examination

Clinical signs that occur with heatstroke are not the same in all dogs due to physiological differences among dog breeds and different etiologies of heatstroke. The broad range of clinical signs in dogs with heatstroke may include rapid breathing, panting, respiratory distress, dehydration, vomiting and diarrhea (eventually becoming bloody), collapse, depression, and seizures. Depression and coma are more frequently observed than seizures (Merck & Miller, 2013).

The complex and severe pathological repercussions of heatstroke are caused by direct thermal injury to body tissues. Diagnosis of heatstroke is consistent with the temperature of the dog being above 10°F (41°C). The critical temperature believed to cause multi-organ damage is 109°F (43°C) (Merck & Miller, 2013).

The physical findings of dogs suffering from heatstroke vary with the intensity and duration of elevated body temperature and the individual pathophysiological response initiated (Drobatz, 2015). The rectal temperature may be elevated, normal, or decreased depending on the tissue perfusion and if cooling measures have been initiated. The pulse rate is usually elevated, and the respiratory rate is rapid in an attempt to increase heat dissipation (Drobatz, 2015). The mucous membranes are hyperemic, and the capillary refill time is short. The pulses become weak due to hypovolemic shock from evaporative fluid loss, vomiting, diarrhea, and vasodilation. Tachycardia is common. Central nervous system signs range from alert to comatose, with depression most commonly observed. If the dog remains ambulatory, it may be ataxic. The neuropathies can further consist of poor femoral perfusion, direct thermal damage, cerebral edema, CNS hemorrhage, or metabolism abnormalities (Drobatz, 2015). Acute renal injury may be a complication of heatstroke. Vomiting and diarrhea are observed with gastrointestinal involvement ranging from watery to hemorrhagic consistency (Figure 12.9). Gastric ulceration may occur as well. Disseminated intravascular coagulation (DIC) is a relatively common finding with heatstroke. This is illustrated through petechiae, ecchymosis, or blood in the urine and/or feces (Drobatz, 2015) (Figures 12.10a–b and 12.11).

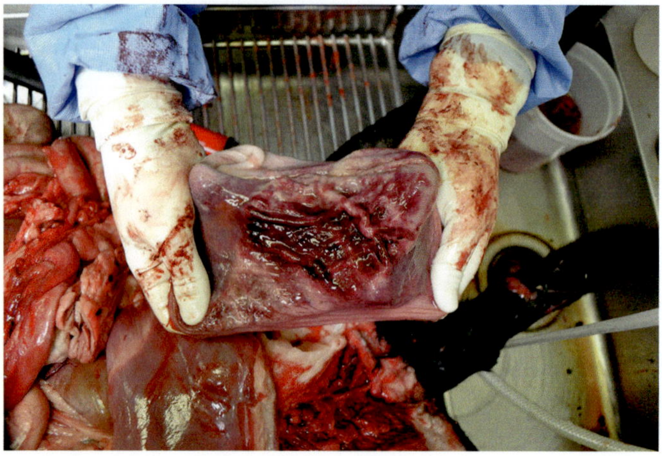

Figure 12.9 Hyperthermia: Extensive purpuric mucosal hemorrhage of stomach lining.

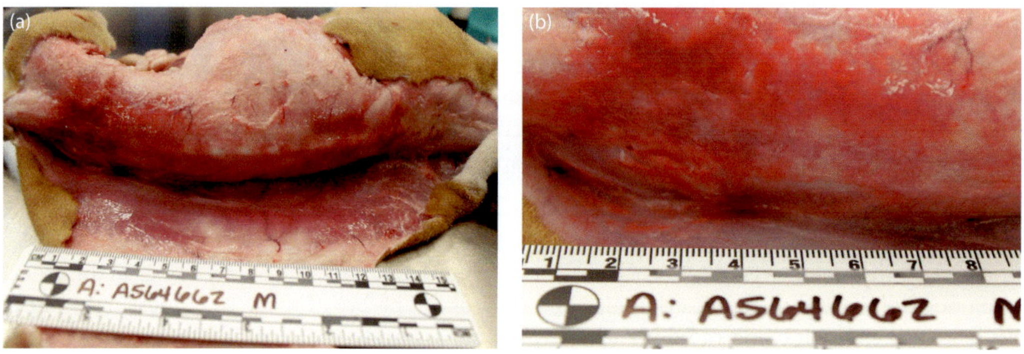

Figures 12.10 (a,b) Hyperthermia: Puppy; reflection of skin demonstrating hyperemia, congestion, and hemorrhage. (Photo courtesy Dr. J.K. Lee.)

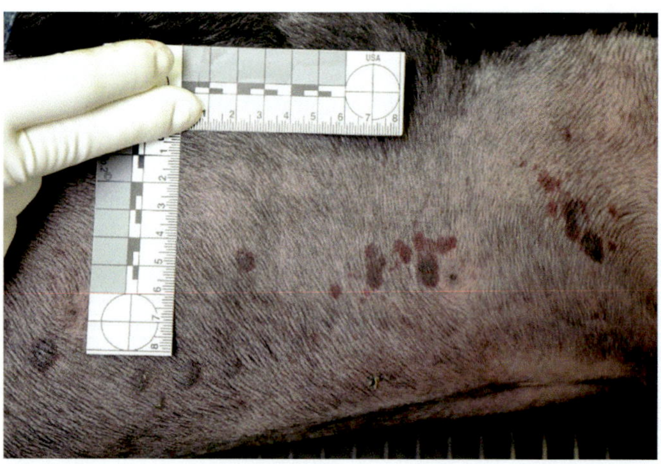

Figure 12.11 Hyperthermia: Multifocal areas of ecchymosis.

Gross/Histology Findings

The diagnosis of death from heatstroke is often a diagnosis of exclusion and is based on the circumstances surrounding the animal's death, specifically the crime scene findings (Merck & Miller, 2013). A full forensic necropsy including radiographs, histopathology, and clinical pathology should be done to rule out other causes or factors contributing to the death (Merck & Miller, 2013). In the author's personal experience with heatstroke cases in Arizona, I have found elevations in creatinine kinase with hyperthermia.

Heatstroke may cause rigidity of the body, especially in the limbs, and can be mistaken for rigor mortis (Figure 12.12). Rigor mortis is a temporary condition following postmortem. The rigidity incurred from heatstroke is permanent from coagulation of muscle proteins which are responsible for causing muscle shortening and rigidity (Merck & Miller, 2013). There may be generalized tissue autolysis within the internal body cavities. The autolysis observed is very similar to advanced or accelerated decomposition due to elevated environmental temperatures. A reliable indicator of heatstroke depending on the postmortem interval is advanced internal autolysis that is not consistent with a less advanced decomposition level observed in the external body. The level of autolysis may prevent microscopic analysis and additional testing. The heart may have gross evidence of myocardial ischemia, hemorrhage and necrosis (Merck & Miller, 2013) (Figure 12.13).

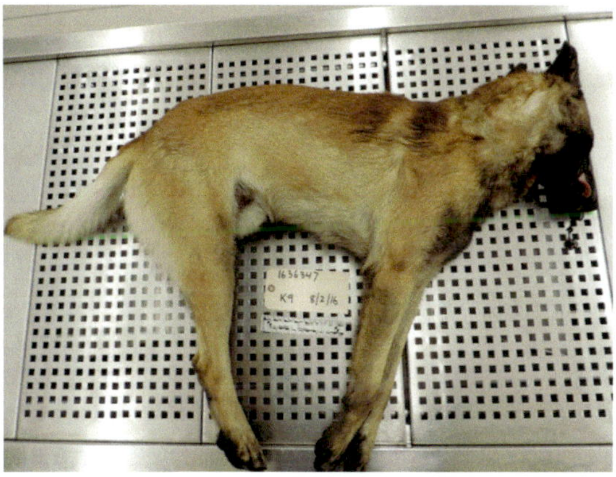

Figure 12.12 Hyperthermia: Hyper rigidity of the body after confinement in a hot car. (Photo courtesy Dr. A.W. Stern.)

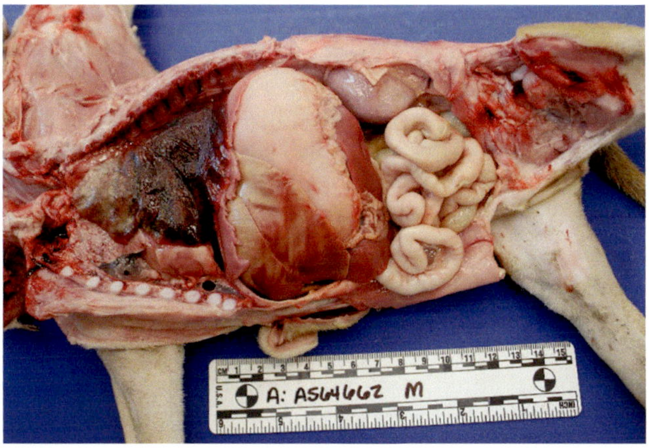

Figure 12.13 Hyperthermia: Pulmonary hemorrhage and petechial hemorrhage in the thymus. (Photo courtesy Dr. J.K. Lee.)

Histological signs seen in peripheral muscles heart, liver, and brain involve the striated muscles. These findings consist of rhabdomyosis (severe degeneration to necrosis) of muscle fibers, reactive proliferation of sarcolemmal nuclei and dystrophic calcification. The myocardial muscle can have focal degeneration and necrosis with "particular teased or motheaten appearance" (Merck & Miller, 2013).

Other histology findings may consist of liver focal degeneration and necrosis, centrilobular necrosis associated with shock. In the brain, focal neuronal shrinkage and necrosis may be observed. In the kidney, there may be pigment deposition from rhabdomyolysis. Tissue samples may show signs of endotoxemia.

It is important to document the ambient temperature in the location where the animals were found or died. Weather data for the United States is available from the National Weather Service www.nws.noaa.gov/climate (Merck & Miller, 2013).

DROWNING

Even though drowning is considered a form of asphyxia with death resulting from anoxia, the mechanism incorporated in drowning can have factors other than asphyxia and the physical characteristics differ from those found in other forms of asphyxia (Sinclair et al., 2006). The diagnosis of drowning is made from information dissimilar from typical asphyxia deaths (Sinclair et al., 2006). For these reasons, drowning is considered separately from other forms of asphyxia in this chapter.

A definition of drowning is death secondary to hypoxemia from asphyxia when immersed in a liquid (Merck & Miller, 2013). Submersion may be the whole body or enough to immerse just the external airway openings (Merck & Miller, 2013). A primary pathophysiologic abnormality observed in drowning is hypoxic tissue damage due to the inability to maintain adequate pulmonary gas exchange (Powell, 2015). Drowning appears to be an uncommon reason for the veterinary evaluation of companion animals (Heffner et al., 2008). This fact alone should raise suspicions about events and circumstances if drowning is suspected as a cause of injury or death. According to Pet-Abuse.com U.S. Animal Abuse Classifications as of September 2017, drowning encompassed less than 1% of animal abuse cases nationally (PetAbuse.com).

Intentional drowning as a form of animal abuse consists of several forms (Sinclair et al., 2006). A primary form of drowning is "nuisance animals": wildlife or unwanted offspring are drowned in a misdirected attempt at euthanasia or "disposal drowning" (Sinclair et al., 2006). A secondary form is an act of punishment or attack, meant to frighten, intimidate or abuse an animal victim or a human victim associated with an animal. This is known as "furious drowning" (Sinclair et al., 2006). A third form is "faux drowning" in which an animal is killed by some noninvasive means, for example strangulation or blunt force trauma to the head, and then the animal's body is saturated with water or immersed it in a container or body of water to simulate drowning. This type of drowning may be used as a means of intimidation of another person (as in domestic violence) or an attempt to cover up another form of animal abuse (Sinclair et al., 2006). According to the AVMA report on euthanasia, drowning is not an acceptable means of euthanasia and is inhumane. Investigation of a drowning case may demonstrate the cause of death may have been slow, stressful, and painful, consistent with the legal definition of torture, which can result in a felony charge (Sinclair et al., 2006).

In 2002, the World Health Organization (WHO) defined drowning and its possible outcomes by an international expert committee: "Drowning is the process of experiencing respiratory impairment from submersion/immersion in liquid" and "outcomes are death, morbidity, or no morbidity" (McEwen & Gerdin, 2016). The findings were that adoption of these new terms should be considered by veterinary pathologists and forensic veterinarians (McEwen & Gerdin, 2016). Submersion occurs when the entire body is under water, and immersion signifies the body being partially covered with water; it is necessary for the airway to be immersed as well for drowning to occur.

Establishing drowning as a cause of death in animals is challenging. When an animal is found in a body of water or completely wet, drowning must be a differential. A key question is whether the animal was alive at the time it entered the water or was exposed to water (McEwen & Gerdin, 2016). A diagnosis of drowning is often one of exclusion, requiring additional information from the crime scene, the medical history (if available), or witness statements (McEwen & Gerdin, 2016).

Mechanism of Drowning

The primary mechanism of drowning is the rapid and persistent onset of hypoxemia after the entrance of liquids into the airways (McEwen & Gerdin, 2016). The drowning process is multifaceted, involving cardiorespiratory reflexes and electrolyte and blood gas abnormalities. It results in the aspiration and swallowing of liquid (water) and vomit. Struggling ensues with involuntary movement, physical exertion/exhaustion, and breathlessness resulting in death (McEwen & Gerdin, 2016).

The overall effect is an immediate decrease in arterial oxygenation with concurrent acidosis and hypercarbia. The arterial levels of carbon dioxide are usually below the 95 mm of mercury for carbon dioxide–induced necrosis that was thought to cause unconsciousness in drowning animal victims (McEwen & Gerdin, 2016). This is a primary reason drowning is considered inhumane (McEwen & Gerdin, 2016).

Phases of Drowning

In the past, the drowning process was reviewed in the literature through experimentation on dogs, demonstrating behavioral and biological drowning responses (McEwen & Gerdin, 2016). These have been generalized in the five phases of drowning (McEwen & Gerdin, 2016). In phases 1 and 2 escape attempts, violent struggling, and breath holding are observed. The third phase has deep respiratory movements of the chest, swallowing, and convulsions. Phase 4 results in diminished corneal reflexes and dilated pupils. The final fifth phase has diminished respiratory movements, head and jaw muscle fasciculations, and death (McEwen & Gerdin, 2016).

A dog can struggle violently for up to 1.5 minutes; the glottis is usually closed and thoracic inspiratory movements continue to be attempted, resulting in liquid being swallowed (McEwen & Gerdin, 2016). If unconsciousness results due to hypoxemia, the larynx can relax, and liquid is aspirated, or if the animal does remain conscious water is aspirated and swallowed from inspiratory gasping (McEwen & Gerdin, 2016). After 3 minutes, spasmodic convulsions and seizures can occur, and resulting overinflation of the stomach with liquid causes vomiting (McEwen & Gerdin, 2016). Cardiac asystole or death can occur in 5 minutes but may take up to 10 minutes after submersion (McEwen & Gerdin, 2016). Initial hypoxemia is complicated by pulmonary edema, catecholamine release, vasoconstriction, cardiac arrhythmias, pulmonary hypertension, and right-to-left intrapulmonary shunting (McEwen & Gerdin, 2016).

Electrolyte and intravascular changes from drowning are due to the salinity and/or volume of water aspirated into the lungs. These biochemical effects of water are osmotic (McEwen & Gerdin, 2016). Differentiating saltwater and freshwater drowning is forensically important. In fresh water, animals may demonstrate hemodilution, hypervolemia, decreased serum chloride, sodium, osmolality, hematocrit, and hyperkalemia. These changes may be temporary via redistribution of fluids in the animal's body but can persist with larger volumes of water aspirated 22 mL/kg or above. In dogs, aspirated fresh water infiltrates the circulation within 3 minutes and approximately 10% of body weight can be absorbed in the lungs during a fresh-water drowning (McEwen & Gerdin, 2016).

Saltwater aspiration may be more deadly than freshwater, only requiring half the aspirated volume of fresh water to cause drowning. Drowning in saltwater causes hemoconcentration with increased serum sodium, osmolality, and potassium. The hypertonicity of saltwater pulls fluid from the circulation into the alveoli, altering the basement membrane, causing washout of surfactant and diminished lung capacity resulting in pulmonary edema (McEwen & Gerdin, 2016).

Drowning causes progressive cerebral hypoxia and death. Injury occurs in selective regions of the brain within 4–10 minutes and maybe irreversible. In addition, persistent coma may develop within minutes after this time period (McEwen & Gerdin, 2016).

Cold Water

After 2 minutes of submersion in cold water, an animal's core body temperature decreases more rapidly than just immersion, caused by the aspiration of larger quantities of liquid and contact with additional surface area within the pulmonary tissue. Hypothermia due to submersion is fatal when rectal temperatures drop to 68°F (20°C) or below (McEwen & Gerdin, 2016).

Complications in Surviving Animals

Complications in companion animals that survive drowning consist of decreased mentation or neurologic deficits, non-cardiogenic pulmonary edema, pneumonia, and ARDS (McEwen & Gerdin, 2016).

Gross and Microscopic Lesions

Lungs grossly appear heavy, edematous, and fail to collapse, and will sink in formalin (Figure 12.14a–b). Froth may be present in the mouth, nasal passages, or trachea (Figure 12.15a–b). The above listed signs are consistent with drowning but are not specific, and may be due to other causes. Externally the hair coat is wet, damp, or the fur if dried may be clumped in spikes (Figure 12.16a–b). A lack of water aspiration can be attributed to laryngeal spasm or failure to gasp. In

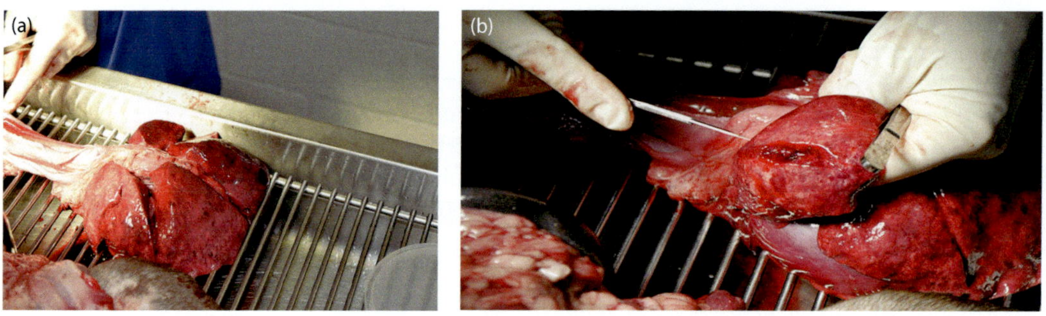

Figure 12.14 (a) Drowning: Edematous lungs. (b) Drowning: Incised lung tissue emitting fluid.

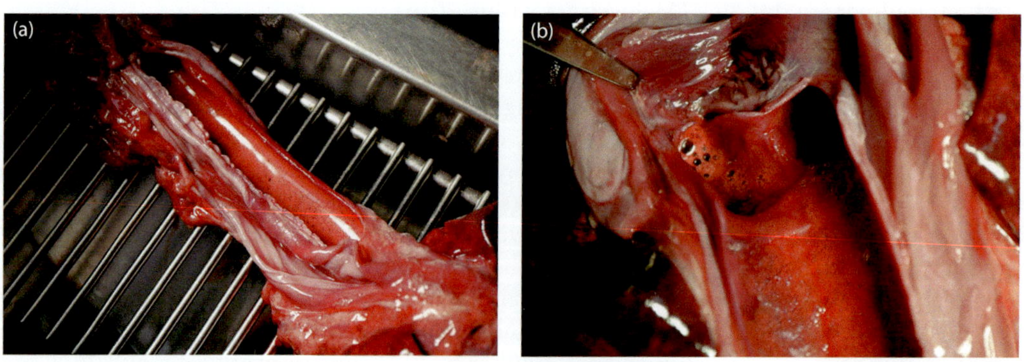

Figure 12.15 (a) Drowning: Red-tinged froth in trachea. (b) Drowning: Froth in the trachea progressing to the main stem bronchi.

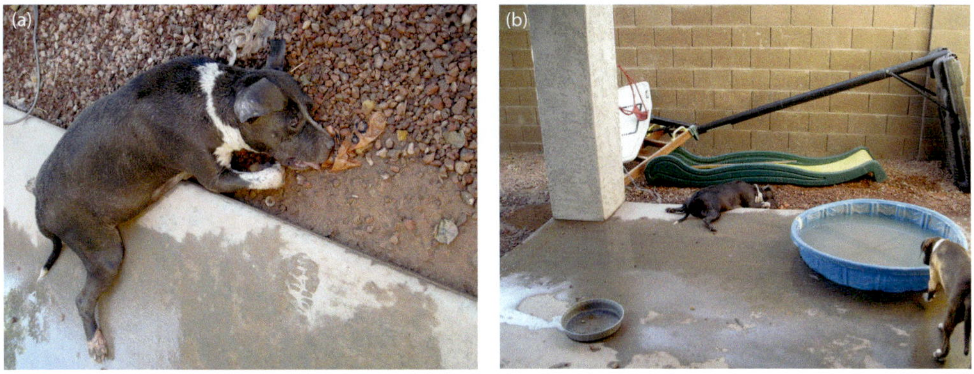

Figures 12.16 (a,b) Drowning: Importance of crime scene pictures and reports in documenting the incident to support necropsy findings. Pictures document dog is wet, and some kind of struggle ensued. (Photo courtesy Phoenix PD.)

studies of animal drowning lacking evidence of aspiration of fluid into the lungs demonstrated a mucous plug in the trachea. In humans, additional findings that may support drowning are pleural effusion, subdural discoloration of petrous temporal bone from congestion/hemorrhage in the mastoid process and middle ear, neck muscle hemorrhage, and a contracted spleen (McEwen & Gerdin, 2016).

Gastric content appearance and volume should be documented due to swallowing of water during drowning and if vomit is aspirated. Overdistension of the stomach with water causing gastric mucosal lacerations has been observed in human drowning victims (McEwen & Gerdin, 2016).

Postmortem Changes

Postmortem submersion interval and changes occurring while in the water and following the retrieval may hinder or complicate necropsy findings. Early alterations may be skin maceration, lividity, rigor mortis, and algor mortis. Late changes are initial putrefaction, advanced putrefaction including adipocere formation, and skeletonization. Adipocere is a waxy material generated on submerged bodies in water from the breakdown of adipose tissue by bacterial enzymes. Postmortem changes in water are similar to land in that they are time and temperature dependent. Decomposition in water is usually slower, but once removed from water the process will accelerate. An animal body will initially sink and eventually surface once putrefactive gases increase buoyancy. If water is cold enough this may not occur, and the animal body will never surface. Duration and conditions of submersion if extended may cause hair slippage from skin and waterlogging of the entire body. In addition, aquatic animal scavenging and other environmental factors, natural or manmade, can alter antemortem lesions or create postmortem lesions (McEwen & Gerdin, 2016).

A thorough forensic necropsy will rule out if other disease processes were present. Additional medical history may help identify any issues such as neuropathies hindering the animal from exiting itself from a body of water. Hyponatremic encephalopathy from excessive intake of fresh water (water intoxication) should be considered, especially in animals that play or train in fresh water (McEwen & Gerdin, 2016).

Weights, including blocks, tires, or chains secured to an animal indicate intentional submersion of the body, but if present should not be used to determine if the animal was alive or dead when entering the body of water. However, contusions, subcutaneous hemorrhages, and other injuries from blunt force trauma to the head, neck, or limbs may be present in animals forcibly immersed or submerged in water (McEwen & Gerdin, 2016) (Figure 12.17).

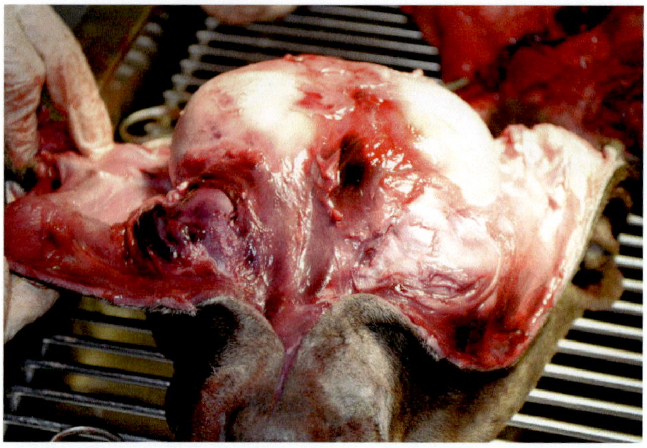

Figure 12.17 Skin reflected illustrating degree of force used to hold dog's head under water.

HYPOTHERMIA

Hypothermia or decreased body temperature in domestic animals is a condition caused by deep cooling from external cold, drugs, or failure of temperature regulating mechanisms. Local hypothermia can occur in the extremities without undue risk of damage unless freezing initiates. Systemic hypothermia occurs when an animal's core body temperature falls below the normal physiologic core temperature. Any scenario that causes increased heat loss, decreased heat production, or interruption of normal thermoregulatory function can result in hypothermia (Merck & Miller, 2013). An animal's body temperature may fluctuate throughout the day, so they are expressed as a range: dogs (100°F–103°F) 37.8°C–39.5°C, and for cats (99.5°F–102.5°F) 37.5°C–39.2°C (Merck & Miller, 2013). Individual or combined effects of heat loss, decreased heat production, and discontinuance of normal thermoregulatory function cause core (vital organ) body temperature to drop below species-specific physiologic parameters (Todd, 2015).

Hypothermia can be classified as primary or secondary (Todd, 2015). Primary hypothermia is present when the body has normal heat-producing capability and is exposed to low environmental temperatures. Secondary hypothermia exists when thermoregulation and heat production are altered from injury, illness, or drugs (Merck & Miller, 2013; Todd, 2015).

Hypothermia in the past has been classified as mild, moderate, or severe based on core body temperature. These classifications are simple; however, they do not address the functional changes that distinguish the different levels of symptoms not directly related to a specific core body temperature. The new philosophy is to classify hypothermia based on clinical consequences at each stage not just core body temperature (Todd, 2015). In mild hypothermia, the thermoregulatory mechanisms including shivering and heat seeking behavior are present, but ataxia may be observed. Moderate hypothermia causes the progressive loss of the body's thermoregulatory system, coinciding with decreased levels of consciousness and early cardiovascular instability. As hypothermia progresses into the severe form there is a complete loss of the animal's thermoregulatory system; the animal cannot shiver, and comatose states and ventricular fibrillation may occur (Todd, 2015).

Heat loss occurs through convection, conduction, radiation heat transfer, and evaporation heat transfer (Merck & Miller, 2013; Wang et al., 2014). Cutaneous heat loss is a product of the exposed body surface area. Immersion in cold water will cause a more rapid loss of body temperature then exposure to cold air temperatures. Metabolic production of heat is a function of body mass. Small dogs, cats, neonates, and cachectic animals can have a high body surface area to body mass ratio, are less able to generate heat, and are more disposed to rapid heat loss (Merck & Miller, 2013).

Lack of body insulation with decreased body fat results in heat loss. A companion animal will have increased heat loss if it is unable to escape environmental temperature extremes or if it is unable to handle a cold environment such as geriatric animals, neonates, and animals with untreated injuries or debilitating diseases (Merck & Miller, 2013).

Animals not acclimated are more sensitive to cold environments. Cats are more sensitive to drastic change in temperature than dogs. Hypothermia is not well documented in felines probably due to the lack of reporting or detection (Merck & Miller, 2013).

Hypothermia will cause cardiovascular, respiratory, electrolyte, central nervous system, acid–base, and coagulation abnormalities (Todd, 2015).

Animals may exhibit pain from cold stress. Muscle stiffness and increased viscosity of joint fluid may cause body and limb stiffness (Merck & Miller, 2013). Muscle rigidity in severe cases can affect breathing. If an animal is ill, they are more sensitive to extreme cold and may be at a greater risk of death. Hypothermic stress can result in weight loss and compromise the immune system. In the situation of starvation and cold stress, the body has conflicting requirements for energy use (Merck & Miller, 2013).

The body's defense against the cold is to initiate vasoconstriction of blood vessels in the skin and muscle to conserve body heat (Merck & Miller, 2013). There is increased heat production via behavioral responses, including huddling and curling, and reflex physiologic changes, including piloerection, peripheral vasoconstriction, and shivering (Todd, 2015). When the animal's body temperature falls below 94°F (34°C), it will discontinue shivering and seeking heat (Merck & Miller, 2013). Peripheral vasoconstriction progresses to vasodilation, allowing loss of core body temperature. Cellular metabolism is increased to effect chemical thermogenesis via shivering, eventually becoming overwhelmed; as the metabolic rate decreases, chemical heat production in cells is decreased, causing reduced heat production. This results in the depression of the CNS causing the hypothalamus to become less responsive to hypothermia. Once the core body temperature decreases below 88°F (31°C) thermoregulation will cease (Merck & Miller, 2013). As hypothermia continues, there is a reduction in heart and respiratory rates. Body temperatures below 77°F (28°C) may result in respiratory depression (Merck & Miller, 2013). Ventricular fibrillation and decreased myocardial contractility have been observed in temperatures (74–68°F) 23.5–20°C. This is further complicated by metabolic acidosis and increased blood viscosity, with hypothermia causing diminished myocardial function. Additional complications that can occur are hypoxia, respiratory distress syndrome, pneumonia, and pulmonary edema (Merck & Miller, 2013).

COLD INJURY

Frostbite is a relatively uncommon condition in healthy animals that have been properly acclimatized to cold temperatures. Animals that have recently moved from a warm climate to a cold one or those that are ill are more likely to succumb to frostbite. This may be due to prolonged exposure to freezing temperatures or contact with a frozen metal object. If an animal has a previous vascular condition or other abnormalities, external temperatures do not have to be very low to cause tissue necrosis (Maxie, 2016). Improper shelter, exposure to blowing wind, and wetness of the animal decrease the exposure time required for frostbite to develop (Maxie, 2016).

Frostbite usually affects the tips of the ears, scrotum, digits, mammary glands, skin folds in the flanks, and tip of the tail due to insufficient insulation by hair and blood vessels that are not as well protected in these locations (Merck & Miller, 2013; Maxie, 2016). When the skin is frozen it appears pale and is cool to the touch with decreased or impaired tactile senses (Merck & Miller, 2013; Maxie, 2016). There may be dark or bluish areas with diffuse subcutaneous edema and hemorrhage (Merck & Miller, 2013). After thawing, mild erythema, edema, scaling of margins, and eventual pain is observed. In mild cases, the hair in affected areas may turn white. The tips and pinnae of ears may curl. In severe cases the skin can become necrotic and slough. The lesions appear similar to burns (Maxie, 2016). Cell damage and death develop from ice crystal formation in the intracellular and extracellular spaces. Progression to ischemic necrosis may be observed followed by tissue sloughing. Full demarcation of the tissue damage may take 4–15 days (Munro & Munro, 2008).

Gross and Microscopic

Most macroscopic findings are nonspecific, and determination of hypothermia as a cause of death is based on the circumstances surrounding the death, exclusion of other causes, and physical examination findings (Merck & Miller, 2013). Microscopic findings can include intrapulmonary hemorrhage, acute hemorrhagic pancreatitis, focal pancreatitis with fat necrosis, and myocardial degenerative foci, and other complications such as frostbite may be observed. Histology of frostbite may illicit edema and hyperemia of the dermis with sporadic foci of inflammatory cell infiltrates (Merck & Miller, 2013).

CONCLUSION

This chapter explores multiple causes of environmental and situational injury or death encountered in companion animals. More research is required in many of the areas discussed. Consideration should always be given as to how such environmental and situation circumstances may affect companion animals to differentiate accidental versus nonaccidental etiologies.

References

AVMA Website (Temperature Scales). 2018. www.avma.org/public/Petcare/Pages/pets-in-vehicles.aspx.

Carson, T.L. 1986. Toxic Gases. In Kirk, R.W., ed. *Kirk's Current Veterinary Therapy X Small Animal Practice*. Philadelphia: WB Saunders: 203–205.

Danielson, L., Karlsmark, T., Thomsen, H.K., Thomsen, J.L., and Balding, L.E. 1991. Diagnosis of electrical skin injuries: A review and a description of a case. *American Journal of Forensic Medicine and Pathology*. 12(3): 222–226.

DiMaio, V.J., and DiMaio, D. 2001. *Forensic Pathology*, 2nd ed. Boca Raton, FL: CRC Press.

Drobatz, K.J. 2015. Heatstroke. In: Silverstein, D.C., and Hopper, K., eds. *Small Animal Critical Care Medicine*, 2nd ed. St Louis, MI: Elsevier Saunders: 795–799.

Duffey, M. 2018. Animal Cruelty Investigator, Humane Society of Southern Arizona. Personal Interview.

Garzotto, C.K. 2015. Thermal burn injury. In: Silverstein, D.C., and Hopper, K., eds. *Small Animal Critical Care Medicine*, 2nd ed. St Louis, MI: Elsevier Saunders: 743–747.

Gerling, I., Meissner, C., Reiter, A., and Oehmichen, M. 2001. Death from thermal effects and burns. *Forensic Science International*. 115: 33–41.

Hedlund, C.S. 2002. Surgery of the Integumentary System. In: Fossum, T.W., ed. *Small Animal Surgery*, 2nd ed. St Louis, MI: Mosby: 134–228.

Heffner, G.G., Rozanski, E.A., Beal, M.W., Boysen, S., Powell, L., and Adamantos, S., 2008. Evaluation of freshwater immersion in small animals: 28 cases (1996–2006). *Journal of the American Veterinary Medical Association*. 232: 244–248.

Jones, J., Mc Mullen, M.J., and Dougherty, J. 1987. Toxic smoke inhalation: Cyanide poisoning in fire victims. *American Journal of Emergency Medicine*. 5: 318–321.

Juthowitz, L.A. 2005. Care of the Burned Patient. In: *Proceedings of the Eleventh International Veterinary Emergency and Critical Care Symposium*. Atlanta, GA, September 7–11: 243–249.

Maxie, M.G. 2016. *Jubb, Kennedy, and Palmer's: Pathology of Domestic Animals* Volume 2, 6th ed. St Louis, MI: Elsevier Inc.

McEwen, B.J., Gerdin, J. 2016. Veterinary forensic pathology: Drowning and bodies recovered from water. *Veterinary Pathology*. 53(5): 1049–1056.

Merck, M.D. and Miller, D.M. 2013. Burn-, electric-, and fire-related injuries. In: Merck, M.D., ed. *Veterinary Forensics: Animal Cruelty Investigations*, 2nd ed. Ames, IA: Wiley-Blackwell: 139–150.

Munro, H.M., and Thrushfield, M.V. 2001. Battered pets: Non-accidental physical injuries found in dogs and cats. *Journal of Small Animal Practice*. 42: 279–290.

Munro, R., and Munro, H. 2008. *Animal Abuse and Unlawful Killing: Forensic Veterinary Pathology*. Edinburgh: Elsevier.

National Weather Service, Online Weather Data, www.nws.noaa.gov/climate

PetAbuse.com

Platt, M.S., Spitz, D.J., and Spitz, W.U. 2006. Investigation of deaths in childhood. Part 2: The abused child and adolescent. In: Spitz, W.U., and Spitz, D.J., eds. *Spitz and Fisher's Medicolegal Investigation of Death: Guidelines for the Application of Pathology to Crime Investigation*, 4th ed. Springfield, IL: Charles C Thomas: 357–416.

Pope, E.R. 2003. Thermal, electrical, and chemical burns and cold injuries. In: Slatter, D.H., ed. *Textbook of Small Animal Surgery*, Volume 1, 3rd ed. Elsevier–Health Sciences Division: 356–372.

Powell, L.L. 2015. Drowning and Submersion Injury. In: Silverstein, D.C., and Hopper, K., eds. *Small Animal Critical Care Medicine*, 2nd ed. St Louis, MI: Elsevier Saunders: 803–806.

Quist, E.M., Tanabe, M., Mansell, J.E.K.L., and Edwards, J.L. 2011. A case series of thermal scald injuries in dogs exposed to hot water from garden hoses (garden hose scalding syndrome). *Veterinary Dermatology*. 23: 162–166, e33.

Rodes, J., Clay, C., and Phillips, M. 2013. The surface area of the hand and the palm for estimating percentage of total body surface area: Results of a meta-analysis. *British Journal of Dermatology*. 169(1): 76–84.

Saukko, P., and Knight, B. (eds.). 2016. Electric fatalities. In: *Knight's Forensic Pathology*, 4th ed. Boca Raton, FL: CRC Press: 325–338.

Saxon, W.D., and Kirby, R. 1992. Treatment of acute burn injury and smoke inhalation. In: Kirk, R.W., and Bonagura, J.D., eds. *Kirk's Current Veterinary Therapy XI Small Animal Practice*. Philadelphia: WB Saunders: 146–154.

Schindler, C. 2018. Animal Cruelty and Fighting Director, HSUS. Personal Interview.

Schulze, C., Peters, M., Baumgartner, W., and Wohlsein, P. 2016. Electric injuries in animals: Causes, pathogenesis, and morphologic findings. *Veterinary Pathology*. 53(5): 1018–1029.

Sinclair, L., Merck, M., and Lockwood, R. 2006. *Forensic Investigation of Animal Cruelty: A Guide for Veterinary and Law Enforcement Professionals*. Humane Society of the United States.

Spitz, W.U. 2006. Thermal Injuries. In: Spitz WU., and Spitz DJ., eds. *Spitz and Fisher's Medicolegal Investigation of Death: Guidelines for the Application of Pathology to Crime Investigation*, 4th ed. Springfield, IL: Charles C Thomas: 747–782.

Stern, A.W., Lewis, R.J., and Thompson, K.S. 2014. Toxic smoke inhalation in fire victim dogs. *Veterinary Pathology*. 51(6): 1165–1167.

Surrell, J.A., Alexander, R.C., Cohle, S.D., Lovell, F.R., and Wehrenberg, R.A. 1987. Effects of microwave radiation on living tissues. *Journal of Trauma*. 27(8): 935–939.

Tans, T.R. 1989. Pneumonia. In: Kirk, R.W., and Bonagura, J.D., eds. *Kirk's Current Veterinary Therapy XI Small Animal Practice*. Philadelphia: WB Saunders: 376–384.

Teodoreanu, R., Popescu, S.A., and Lascer, I. 2014. Electrical injuries: Biological value measurements as a prediction factor of local evaluation in electrocution lesions. *Journal of Medical and Life*. 7(2): 226–236.

Todd, J.M. 2015. Hypothermia. In: Silverstein, D.C., and Hopper, K., eds. *Small Animal Critical Care Medicine*, 2nd ed. St Louis, MI: Elsevier Saunders: 789–793.

Wang, C., Zhao, R., Liu, W., La-na, D., Zhao, X., Rawg, Y., Ning, F., and Zhang. G., 2014. Pathological changes of the three clinical types of laryngeal burns based on a canine model. *Burns*. 40: 257–267.

Wohlsein, P., Peters, M., Schulze, C., and Baumgartner, W. 2016. Thermal injuries in veterinary forensic pathology. *Veterinary Pathology*. 53(5): 1001–1017.

CHAPTER 13

ANIMAL FIGHTING AND HOARDING

Nancy Bradley-Siemens and Barbara Sheppard

INTRODUCTION

Animal fighting and hoarding have the common elements of cruelty and neglect by an owner and secrecy. Animal fighting is defined as organized animal abuse, and hoarding is defined as severe animal neglect. A key distinction is that animal fighting is a money-generating business or enterprise carried out by owners as one of many of their personal criminal activities. This linkage of animal fighting to other criminal behavior prompted the creation of federal animal fighting laws used by law enforcement and prosecutors as tools to reduce other organized crime such as drug trafficking. These federal laws result in a consistent legal approach by states to animal fighting and provide a powerful set of legal tools. In contrast, hoarding is generally not linked to other knowingly criminal activities so there are no overarching federal laws. However, animal hoarding may be linked to child and elder abuse. States do not have a uniform legal set of standards for dealing with animal hoarding. Many states apply cruelty and neglect laws that were not originally intended to address hoarding.

The characteristics of hoarders are less predictable than those of people involved in animal fighting. Unlike the rather predictable criminal profit motive of an owner engaging in an animal fighting business, individuals who end up hoarding animals do not all fit into one mold and may not believe that they are at fault. Animal hoarders may be affected by mental illness, denial, the desperation of financial overextension, or their inability to provide care due to their own failing health, and well-intentioned concerns about euthanasia at animal shelters. Whereas most animal fighting businesses avoid contact with veterinarians to hide their criminal activity, some animal hoarders may seek veterinary care, thereby possibly raising the suspicions of a veterinarian, or neighbors may report odors or observe inadequate outdoor housing and care. Another important distinction is that animal fighting involves spectators and is associated with specific tools and paraphernalia; therefore, the federal dogfighting laws have made knowingly being a spectator at a dogfight and the possession of these tools illegal. In contrast, hoarding does not lend itself to similar laws. In addition, people, including hoarders, disagree about the level of acceptable husbandry for dogs and cats. It is more difficult to identify specific standards for hoarding that do not infringe on pet ownership by individuals and legal pet businesses.

ANIMAL FIGHTING LAWS

Some federal legal strategy has been to utilize anti-dogfighting laws as broader crime-fighting tools. Among these laws are the Animal Welfare Act (AWA), the Animal Fighting Prohibition Enforcement Act (AFPEA), and the Animal Spectator Act. Understanding the location of key federal statutes such as the AWA helps one gain perspective on the federal laws prohibiting animal fighting. This allows the informed reader to look up the laws themselves and follow potential subsequent revisions. It also provides perspective on what type of activity dogfighting is considered and where the federal government places the laws prohibiting it.

Laws passed by Congress are organized into "Titles" which are assigned a number and dedicated to a broad topic. Title 7 of the United States Code (7 U.S.C.) is assigned the broad designation "Agriculture." The 7 U.S.C. contains "Chapters" 1–115, each of which has a topic designation and contains either a single statute (§ X) or a range of numbered statutes (§§ X–XXX).

The relevant portions of 7 U.S.C. § 2131 and § 2156 are as follows:

- U.S.C. Title 7—Agriculture
  - Chapter 54: TRANSPORTATION, SALE, AND HANDLING OF CERTAIN ANIMALS (§§ 2131–2139).
    - Statute § 2131—Congressional statement of policy
    - Statute § 2156—Animal fighting venture prohibition

In 7 U.S.C. § 2131, Congress explains that this chapter is about commercial animal activities that cross state lines (interstate) or involve foreign commerce. Animal fighting belongs in this chapter because it is a commercial activity, albeit prohibited, using animals for an exhibition purpose. Chapter 24 regulates animals and activities "either in interstate or foreign commerce or substantially affect[ed] [by] such commerce or the free flow thereof" and the regulation is "necessary to prevent and eliminate burdens upon such commerce and to effectively regulate such commerce" to insure humane care and treatment of animals. These federal regulations "supersede or otherwise invalidate any such State, local or municipal legislation or ordinance relating to animal fighting ventures" only if there is "a direct and irreconcilable conflict between" the federal law and the other authority. (7 U.S.C. § 2156 (i)(1)).

ANIMAL WELFARE ACT (7 U.S.C. § 2156)

The Animal Fighting Prohibition Enforcement Act of 2007 (AFPEA) amended the Animal Welfare Act, Chapter 3 of Title 18 United States Code, with the intent to "strengthen prohibitions against animal fighting, and for other purposes." The AFPEA introductory section provided that "whoever violates subsection (a), (b), (c), or (e) of section 26 of the Animal Welfare Act shall be fined under this title, imprisoned for not more than 3 years, or both, for each violation." The main point of this act is that it made it a felony to organize a dogfight and allowed for penalties to include up to 3 years of imprisonment and up to $250,000 fine for each offense of interstate or foreign transport of animals for fighting purposes. The Office of the Inspector General of the U.S. Department of Agriculture has the power to enforce this act. ("H.R. 137—110th Congress: Animal Fighting Prohibition Enforcement Act of 2007." www.GovTrack.us. 2007. May 23, 2018 https://www.govtrack.us/congress/bills/110/hr137).

The AFPEA made the following changes to the AWA:

- Subsection (c)— insert "instrumentality of interstate commerce for commercial speech" to replace "interstate instrumentality";
- Subsection (d) & (e)—striking and inserting "[i]t shall be unlawful for any person to knowingly sell, buy, transport, or deliver in interstate or foreign commerce a knife, a gaff, or any other sharp instrument attached, or designed or intended to be attached, to the leg of a bird for use in an animal fighting venture."
- Subsection (i)—addition of this new subsection which read "The criminal penalties for violations of subsection (a), (b), (c), or (e) are provided in section 49 of title 18, United States Code."

ANIMAL FIGHTING

Animal fighting is organized animal abuse. The most common forms of animal-on-animal fighting to be discussed in this chapter are dogfighting, cockfighting, and hog-dogging. Other forms of organized animal fighting can include fish, small birds, and horses (Merck, 2013; National Humane Education Society, 2018).

COCKFIGHTING

Cockfighting dates back over 3000 years in Persia, India, China, and other Eastern countries. It was introduced in Greece near 400 BC and extended into Asia Minor and Sicily (Sakach & Parascandola,

2016). Greek writings from this period describe the use of gaffs (artificial spurs). Romans are credited with the introduction of cockfighting to Britain. Ancient writings describe artificial spurs made of iron, copper, and silver (Dinnage et al., 2004). Cockfighting spread throughout Europe and eventually made it to the American colonies, where it became popular along with dogfighting (Lockwood, 2013).

Cockfighting is now illegal in all 50 states in the United States. However, it is still legal in U.S. territories of Puerto Rico, the Virgin Islands, Northern Mariana Islands, and Guam. The AFPEA (2007) has made it a federal violation to transfer cockfighting implements across state or national borders. It increased the penalties for violations of the federal animal fighting laws. Cockfighting is legal throughout Southeast Asia and Latin America (Lockwood, 2013).

Many breeds of fowl have been developed from the red jungle fowl for fighting and showing. The two main fighting gamecocks originate from Spanish and Yankee gamecocks (Dinnage et al., 2004). Many gamecocks are hybrids of these birds bred to harness their aggressive characteristics (Merck, 2013). A gamecock will usually have its comb, wattles, and earlobes (dubbed) cut off. These are the red tissues above the head and below the beak. This is done to decrease the bird's weight and reduce potential injury during a fight, specifically bleeding. The feathers of the tail may be cut as well, as feathers that may hinder ambulation during a fight. In addition, fighting gamecocks have their natural spurs on the legs removed to facilitate attachment of gaffs and knives (Lockwood, 2013).

Types of Cockfights

The most common methods of staging cockfights involve the Main, Battle Royal, and Welsh Main. In the Main, two matched cocks fight an odd number of battles, with the majority of acquired victories deciding the winner. The Battle Royal involves any number of birds fighting at the same time and allowing them to kill each other until only one remains. The Welsh Main has eight pairs of cockfights; the eight victors fight one another until the last remaining pair fights one another. The most popular organized cockfight in the United States is the derby. This involves 10–30 cockers (owners/handlers) entering 4–12 gamecocks each. The cocks are fought round robin. The cocker who has the highest number of winning gamecocks is the winner (Sakach & Parascandola, 2016).

Cockfighting Participants

Promoter

This is the owner or controller of the fight location and is responsible for all arrangements necessary to facilitate the meet. These responsibilities entail scheduling, determining and collecting entry fees, providing an arena(s) or any other pit supplies, and selecting event staff including matchmakers, timekeepers, referees, and security personnel. In addition, the promoter may rent onsite facilities (cock houses)—small buildings with work benches and stalls to house fighting cocks—to cockfighters (Sakach & Parascandola, 2016).

Handler

May also be referred to as a "pitter." This is an individual who will heel (tie the gaffs on the legs of the gamecocks) and handle the birds during the fight. A handler may be a bird owner or be paid a percentage of the winnings if the bird is victorious. Only two handlers and a referee may enter the pit during a fight event (Sakach & Parascandola, 2016).

Referee

This individual will officiate in the pit during the event. A referee is familiar with cockfighting rules and they are responsible for evaluating matched cocks for weights, band numbers, and inspecting any implements placed on the birds for the fight. Depending on the event size, each pit will have an individual referee (Sakach & Parascandola, 2016).

Spectator

An individual attending a cockfight. Most spectators are male; however, any sex, age, or ethnicity may be a cockfighting enthusiast. (Sakach & Parascandola, 2016).

Other key personnel in the facilitation of cockfighting venues are matchmakers, timekeepers, scorekeepers, and security personnel (Sakach & Parascandola, 2016).

Cockfighting Profiles

There are three levels of cockfighters: the serious (professional cockfighter), hobbyist, and novice. The professional takes immense pride in breeding, training, and fighting their gamecocks. They may operate on a national and/or international level. Their homes or facilities may have hundreds or thousands of game fowl consisting of breeding stock and gamecocks for fighting. A hobbyist might own 50–100 game fowl in their yards. These individuals tend to participate in local derbies. A novice usually has fewer than 50 birds and will compete in local brush fights (smaller, less organized fights) in remote areas (Sakach & Parascandola, 2016) (Figure 13.1).

Training

Cockfighters will put their birds through an intensive training and conditioning program referred to as a "keep" before a scheduled fight. A keep can last 2–4 weeks prior to a fight. During the keep, the fighting cock undergoes a strict training regime and is given a special diet, and vitamins or other enhancement drugs. Training and conditioning involve running, flirting, flying, leg pulls, and sparring. Running builds endurance by forcing the bird to run the distance of an arm span by pushing it from behind with one hand on a level surface such as a carpeted bench. "Flirting" involves tossing the bird about 2 feet in the air from one hand to the other in a continuous rhythm requiring the bird to flap its wings. This exercise strengthens the wings. To "fly" entails a bird being held 5 feet above another bird on the ground. The bird on the ground flies toward the elevated bird.

Figure 13.1 Individual birds in cages, some with hens for breeding in a backyard operation.

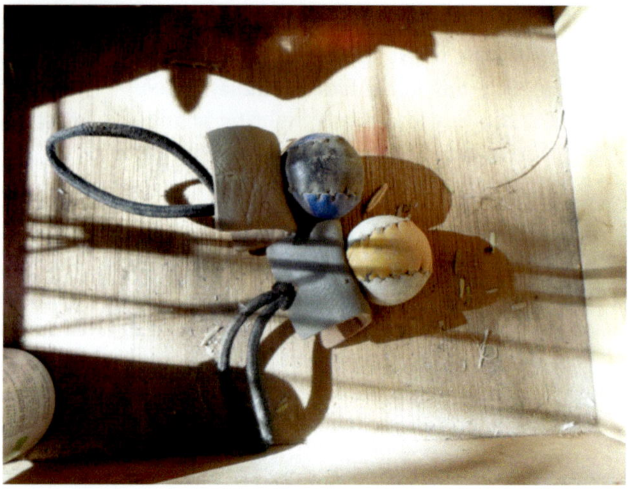

Figure 13.2 Sparring muffs used for training gamecocks.

"Leg pulls" simulate resistance pulling. The cock is supported under the belly and placed within reach of some type of surface. The bird will reach out with its legs, building endurance of the leg muscles. Sparring is conducted with sparring muffs (miniature boxing gloves) placed on the spurs. Sparring matches assess a gamecock's fighting style and training progress (Sakach & Parascandola, 2016) (Figure 13.2).

The Cockfight

Cockfighting is a blood sport comprising two or more specially bred and trained birds, known as gamecocks, that are placed in some type of enclosure to fight. The cockfight will usually end one of three ways. One of the birds will die, one of the bird's handlers will concede the fight, or a cock quits (fails to fight) for more than three counts of 10 seconds and one count of 20 seconds. A fight may last several minutes to over 30 minutes (Sakach & Parascandola, 2016).

CASE 1: Multiple Law Enforcement Agencies (NBS)

History: Local law enforcement in conjunction with a federal agency was concerned about an individual in possession of explosives. The individual also was involved in organized cockfighting. A search warrant to enter the property was obtained based on the presence of the birds.

Physical Findings: Upon entry to the property, suspects were removing combs and wattles on several gamecocks with scissors. There were several other birds with recently cut and bleeding combs and wattles. Over 100 gamecocks were on scene as well as hens. The front of the property consisted of breeding and training facilities for the birds. There was a shed containing medical supplies to treat birds on scene. Additional dwellings had cockfighting paraphernalia. The federal agency confiscated firearms and pornographic materials. Forensic exams were performed on all cockfighting roosters. Combs and wattles were cut along with one or both spurs. Many birds had wounds to the head and face. There were cuts and lacerations to the breast region, legs, and underlying wings. Many were stitched with cloth thread or had a purple powder substance present over the injuries (Figure 13.3).

Outcome: All birds were confiscated and eventually humanely euthanized. Hens were placed in rescue. Many were tested by the state avian veterinarian for exotic Newcastle disease (END) and avian influenza. While processing the scene, veterinary and law enforcement personnel were forced to evacuate the scene due to the presence of explosives found at the scene. A bomb disposal squad was called and rendered the explosives safe and the investigative process resumed. All suspects found at the scene plead guilty to felony cockfighting.

Figure 13.3 Purple powder commonly used on bird wounds during fighting. Obtained at local feed stores.

CASE 2: Derby (NBS)

History. Local law enforcement received information about a cockfighting derby. All resources were contacted and put into place ready to raid the event. Three weekends went by and all entities were finally mobilized.

Physical Findings: Law enforcement raided the event (derby) in a remote area outside the city. A cockfighting ring was found near the center of the makeshift event encampment. Discarded cock/rooster remains were in a large pile outside this ring. Many of the birds had deep cuts and appeared to have died of exsanguination; many had broken necks. After the raid, and when suspects had been placed in custody, individual birds were examined. There were puncture wounds to the heads and eyes. The birds had gaffs and knives attached to their legs. Many of the bids had cuts to their ventral chests and wings, and air sac punctures were present from sharp force injuries.

Outcome: There were over 80 arrests made for felony cockfighting and presence at a cockfight. Additional activities were discovered, and criminal charges were pursued for drug possession and distribution, illegal gambling, illegal sales of alcohol, illegal possession of firearms, and others.

Medications/Paraphernalia

Drugs and veterinary supplies are used extensively in cockfighting beyond just vitamins during the keep. There is a list in the humane society of the United States (HSUS) Final Round publication on cockfighting. The birds may be given injections of heart stimulants such as digitalis, vitamin K to help with blood clotting, hormones such as testosterone, and other anabolic steroids. Many cockers (owners) have their own "secret formula" that is injected into the bird and can consist of almost anything (Sakach & Parascandola, 2016) (Figure 13.4).

The birds are often given different types of drugs to enhance performance. These usually consist of hormones, stimulants, and blood clotting agents. Strychnine is a commonly used stimulant to increase the bird's level of agitation and aggression (Dinnage et al., 2004). Other drugs may consist of antibiotics, caffeine, methamphetamines, and vitamins (Merck, 2013).

The presence of these types of drugs helps solidify the documentation that gamecocks are being raised, trained, and fought at a given location. Veterinarians can help with the identification of these drugs and their applications. In addition, veterinarians can indicate to law enforcement any drugs that may be illegally possessed (i.e., anabolic steroids). A prescription may be required to possess the drug, or the drug may be illegal to possess, depending on the type of drug. These may lead to additional charges. Although not routinely done, blood can be drawn for toxicology purposes. A blood sample for toxicology should be in an EDTA or heparinized tube. A purple- top tube used for dogs and cats can be utilized. Blood can be drawn from the ulnar vein in the wing. Discuss this with law enforcement, especially if drugs such as methamphetamines (speed), PCP, cocaine, and so on, are suspected to have been given to the birds to enhance fighting.

The birds will have gaffs, long knives (Filipino slashers), or short knives (Mexican slashers) attached to their altered spurs on one or both legs. The attachment of these devices is called heeling (Christiansen et al. 2015). The birds are fought in a pit usually 15–20 feet. The pit may be rectangular or circular with walls to a height of 3 feet. Construction materials vary greatly. (Merck, 2013) (Figures 13.5 through 13.7).

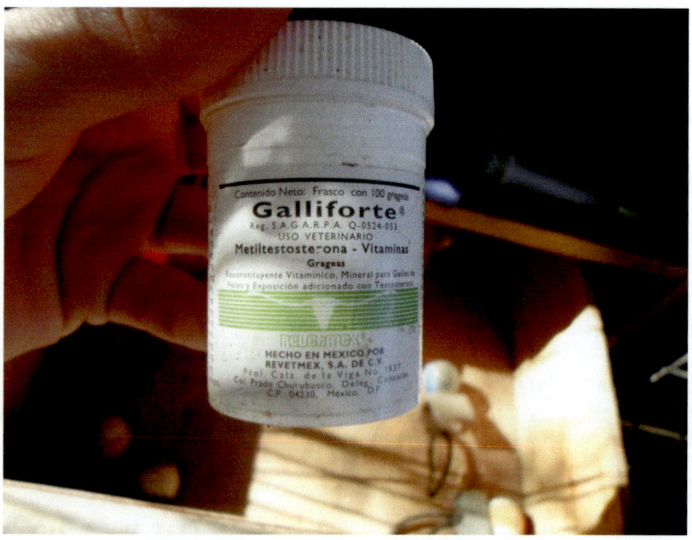

Figure 13.4 Hormones used in cockfighting. Many bottles will state specifically for a keep or cockfighting in English or Spanish. (Courtesy Ruthie Jesus.)

Figure 13.5 Gaffs laid out on a tarp. These are attached to the bird's leg in a process called heeling. (Courtesy Ruthie Jesus.)

Figure 13.6 Heeling accoutrements for gaff placement on the legs. (Courtesy Ruthie Jesus.)

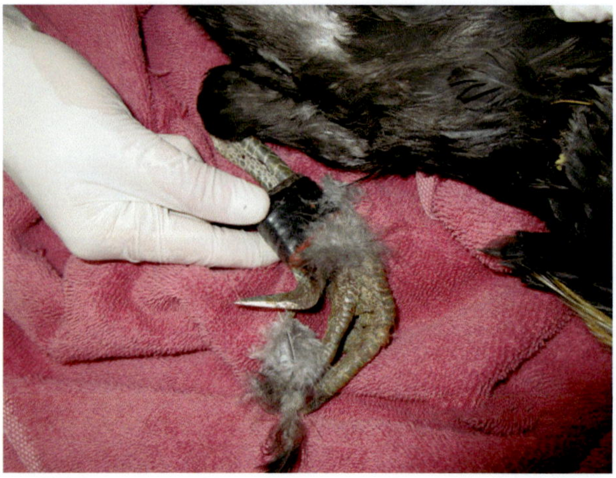

Figure 13.7 Leg with gaff attached. (Courtesy Ruthie Jesus.)

CASE 3: Loud Music Call (NBS)

History: A complaint of a loud music call was received by police; this is the predominant cockfighting call. Police responded and found a backyard (underground) cockfighting event. This usually involves as few as 20 birds up to as many as 100. Police received a call of loud music and a large body of people gathered behind an apartment complex. The scene was surrounded, and the suspects were detained.

Physical Findings: A makeshift ring of carpet and wood was present soiled with blood. Deceased fighting gamecocks were piled near the ring/pit. Many of these had lacerations and cut wounds. Death appeared to have resulted from exsanguination or broken necks with observable injuries affecting the fighting ability of the bird. Injuries were documented similar to previously mentioned cases. Gaffs and knives were present on the confiscated birds.

Outcome: Felony charges were filed for organizing, participating in, and acting as spectators for cockfighting.

Bird Processing

The conditions of the birds seized in a cockfight raid are not usually as significant as for the prosecution of dogfighting (Lockwood, 2013). Charges are usually based on possession of the birds and fighting paraphernalia. Detailed written and photographic documentation of bird conditions can add strength to other evidence. The bird should be photographed with case information, date, and so on. The gamecock should be held in a manner allowing the veterinarian to do a thorough gross exam. The head, body, wings, legs, and tail should be examined for any type of scars, injuries, or evidence of injury repair by the handler (i.e., stitches with thread or dental floss). Any of the aforementioned should be photographed with and without measurements. Each bird is assigned an identification number which all exam findings and photographs will be referred to for each individual gamecock (Figure 13.8).

In addition to the forensic exam, the veterinarian needs to document any bands (plastic or metal) that may be found on the bird's legs or wings. These may match up with keep cards or some form of fighting event schedule linking that bird to the day's proceedings. These types of bands may also assist in establishing where the bird originated (Figure 13.9).

Figure 13.8 Using marker board to photograph bird with case information.

Figure 13.9 Bird with band on leg. Used in fighting matches, will usually match up with event keep cards.

Types of Injuries

Gamecocks used for cockfighting usually have evidence of multiple injuries in different stages of healing. These injuries (scars and wounds) can be documented using a diagram of some sort (Merck, 2013, see Appendix 34). Wounds seen in surviving birds are usually to the head and eyes. The faces may be swollen, specifically around the eyes. The globe of the eye may be pierced, which may go undetected due to the tissue swelling. The nostrils may be obstructed with dried (clotted) blood causing respiratory compromise. These injuries may be from the adversary's beak or gaffs. Birds may sustain punctures or sharp force injuries to the air sacs, chest region, and wings (Merck, 2013). Bone injuries are observed in relation to the knives and gaffs used. There may be evidence of sharp force injury trauma and fractures. Additional injuries may be linked to the method of dispatching a gamecock, involving cervical dislocation (Merck, 2013). There may be injuries that were treated by a non-veterinarian. These usually involve cuts or lacerations being sutured with some type of thread. Wounds at various stages of healing with different colors of applied powdered over-the-counter medications are commonly found (Figures 13.10 through 13.12).

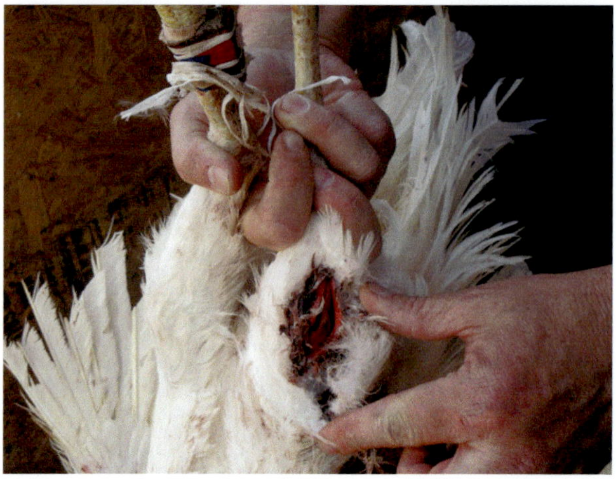

Figure 13.10 Laceration to the leg from a gaff.

Figure 13.11 Wounds to face and head. Notice combs and wattles have been removed. (Courtesy Ruthie Jesus.)

Figure 13.12 Laceration to breast muscle area sustained during a fight. (Courtesy Ruthie Jesus.)

Additional forensic evidence of cockfighting may be found in discarded (sometimes burned) skeletal remains. Consider taphonomic effects on bone for additional evidence, especially when sharp force injury is suspected.

Necropsy

Routinely in cockfighting cases, a gross exam observing for injuries either antemortem or postmortem is usually adequate. If additional animal cruelty charges are sought by law enforcement, a necropsy may be necessary. If this is anticipated, the bird should be cooled down immediately after death. Water can be sprayed under the feathers to cool the body quickly to minimize rapid deterioration of tissues. The body should be refrigerated, and the necropsy performed within 24 hours. To perform a poultry necropsy, proper personal protective equipment (PPE) consisting of gloves, apron/coveralls, and an M-99 mask or better is required to prevent spread of zoonotic diseases (Greenacre, 2014; Touroo & Reisman, 2018).

Housing

The circumstances of the seizure will dictate handling of the birds. If they are owner surrendered, which is rare, they can be euthanized after a forensic examination. If the birds need to be housed for a seizure period, they will need to be caged individually. Visual barriers are required to prevent them from seeing one another. If seized during an active cockfighting event, care must be taken when handling, as gaffs or knives may still be present on the legs and are very dangerous with an already aggressive bird.

Disease Testing

There are state and federal regulations for international, interstate, and intrastate transport of birds. Specific disease testing requirements vary depending on the applicable regulations (Merck, 2013). Cockfighting often involves illegal transportation of birds, especially in the southwestern United States. Outbreaks of END in Mexico and the United States have been linked to the illegal transportation of gamecocks for the purpose of cockfighting. (Merck, 2013). Many states require testing for avian influenza, Salmonella, and END when gamecocks are confiscated for cockfighting (Lockwood, 2013). These tests are usually performed by the state-designated avian veterinarian. The author (NBS) recommends contacting the state veterinarian in these types of cases for direction and possible assistance.

Outcomes/Euthanasia

Due to the aggressive nature of cockfighting birds, zoonotic disease potential, and concerns with reportable disease transmission to other birds, placement in a home or sanctuary may not be viable (Lockwood, 2013). In many cases where the birds are owner surrendered, the seizure is not being contested, or there is a conviction the only option is that the birds be humanely euthanized. The author (NBS) prefers intraperitoneal injection of sodium pentobarbital for euthanasia of these birds.

DOGFIGHTING

Dogs have been used against lions, wild boars, bulls, and humans for over 3000 years. In the thirteenth century in England, bull-baiting and bear baiting were fashionable forms of entertainment and consisted of dogs attacking a confined or tethered bull or bear (Lockwood, 2013). Popular dogfighting began in the 1830s after the banning of bull/bear-baiting events and became a popular alternative. In the United States, dogfighting became popular in the 1860s, with many of the dogs originating in Ireland and England (Lockwood, 2013).

In the United States, fighting dogs are usually American pit bull terriers. Other breeds of dogs have been used for fighting in Europe, South America, and Asia. These breeds include Neapolitan Mastiff, Akita, and Tosa from Japan; the Argentinean Dogo; Dogue de Bordeaux in France; and Chinese Sharpei. There are indications that dogfighters in the United States are exporting American pit bull terriers to Canada, Mexico, England, Europe, Australia, and the Far East (Christiansen et al., 2004).

Types of Dogfights

Dogfights may be held whenever and wherever fighters will assemble. Dogfights occur when two dogs specifically bred and trained to fight are placed in a pit. Events are called a match, show, or convention (series of matches) depending on the size and number of participants. The actual fight will occur in a makeshift or permanent pit or arena. The pit or arena is generally an area enclosed by plywood walls (Christiansen et al., 2004; Sakach & Parascandola, 2016). Matches may be staged in rural areas on the weekends in the evening or larger events near holidays that encompass 3-day weekends. Outdoor or indoor fighting pits may be utilized. A typical dogfighting area measures from 14 to 20 square feet with wooden walls approximately 24–36 inches high. The surface of the pit is usually carpet or canvas to enhance traction. A pit may be portable or made with makeshift items such as hay bales (Christiansen et al., 2004; Sakach & Parascandola, 2016) (Figure 13.13).

Dogfighting Participants

Personnel involved in dogfighting are similar to those in cockfighting events. The promoter is the individual making all the arrangements to conduct the match, show, or convention. They own or control the location, are responsible for selecting event staff, constructing or providing the pit or arena, and collecting entry and admission fees. In dogfighting, promoters give more scrutiny to security by hiring guards, using police scanners, and having outside peripheral lookouts that will blow a car horn if law enforcement is observed approaching. The handler (sometimes the owner) is responsible for handling the dog during the fight. A referee is the person officiating the event in the pit. In a national convention a referee is usually an established name in the dogfighting community. The referee will be paid for the event as well as compensated for travel, food, and lodging expenses. The fees can vary from $200 to $500 per day depending on the number of matches scheduled. Spectators are individuals who attend the events. These individuals come for

Figure 13.13 Outdoor fighting pit used in dogfighting. (Courtesy Mike Duffey.)

entertainment, gambling, or entering an animal. Spectators as well as handlers, promoters, referees, and fighters may be any age, sex, race, occupation, or financial status (Christiansen et al., 2004; Sakach & Parascandola, 2016).

Dogfighting Profiles

There are three levels of dogfighters: the serious (professional), hobbyist, and street fighter. The professional takes great pride in breeding, training, and fighting their own dogs. They may operate at a national and/or international level and may be known in underground publications. The fights they are involved with are high-stakes matches using experienced dogs with established bloodlines (Christiansen et al., 2004; Sakach & Parascandola, 2016). Hobbyists are individuals living short distances from one another. These individuals have a greater interest in gambling than the quality of their fighting dogs. They may purchase dogs of average ability and may consistently use the same fight location. Street fighters tend to be gang members or juveniles using pit bulls and pit bull crosses. Street fighters usually compete in impromptu matches in public parks, playgrounds, or back alleys. This group is generally amateur participants (Christiansen et al., 2004; Sakach & Parascandola, 2016).

Training

"Organized fighters" may own dozens of dogs and breed their own pups from proven bloodline stock. A common dogfight motto is "breed the best and bury the rest" (Christiansen et al., 2004). A quality desired in fighting dogs is "gameness"—the animal that is ready and willing to fight and will not yield. Puppies bred in these breeding programs are subjected to an intensive culling process. Only those puppies that exhibit aggressive behavior toward other dogs are kept. A dog that survives the first 16–18 months may become a prospect and be schooled. At this stage, the prospect dog is placed up against other dogs in a series of "short rolls" and "combats" to build confidence and expose them to different fighting styles (Christiansen et al., 2004). The opponents at this stage are not overly rough. Next a "game" test is facilitated. The young dog is usually pitted against a larger, rougher dog until they are thoroughly exhausted. The prospect dog is then expected to rush or scratch at another fresh dog. If the animal passes, it becomes a match dog (Christiansen et al., 2004; Sakach & Parascandola, 2016) (Figures 13.14 through 13.16).

Before a fight, the match dog will enter a keep. This is 4–6 weeks of intense conditioning. The keep is designed to build endurance, strength, and cardiovascular fitness. It consists of strenuous physical activity, much like a boxer. This may occur with treadmills (slat or carpet mills) or modified commercial treadmills. Other devices include cat mill or jenny for endurance and spring pole for strength building. A cat mill or jenny is similar to a horse walker where the dog is harnessed to a spoke projecting from a rotating central shaft; the dog will chase a small bait animal that is caged or tied to a leading spoke just ahead of the dog. A spring pole uses a hide, inner tube, or dog grip toy suspended from a heavy spring sapling pole that the dog can bite or hold onto (Christiansen et al., 2004; Sakach & Parascandola, 2016) (Figure 13.17).

These pieces of training equipment are key evidence in the investigation and should be confiscated for case evidence and to end the continued use for training.

CASE 4: Dogfighting Breeding and Training Operation (NBS)

History: Local law enforcement with a search warrant conducted a search of a residence for illegal drugs but came up empty. They photographed the residence and the backyard. In the yard were multiple American pit bull terriers tethered with heavy chains. There was a treadmill and string pole in the yard as well. This police agency presented scene pictures to another agency's animal crimes unit and were able to obtain another search warrant for the dogs and another look for illegal drugs.

Physical Findings: Upon entry to the house and property the dogs and the above listed paraphernalia were identified and confiscated. Additional medications, vitamins, and medical supplies consistent with dogfighting were confiscated. Six kilos of cocaine were found in the home. All of the dogs had healing wounds and scars to the neck and front legs.

Outcome: All the dogs (six) and equipment were confiscated. The dogs were given both physical and behavioral examinations and were either placed for adoption or humanely euthanized. The suspect was charged with drug possession with intent to distribute and multiple felony animal abuse charges.

The Fight

Before entering the pit, the dogs are washed and examined by the opponent's handler. This is done to prevent cheating, for example, applying something poisonous to the dog's coat. After washing, the animals are returned to their handler wrapped in a towel or blanket and placed in their pit corner to await the start of the fight. The dogs will face one another when commanded by the referee. On the command, both handlers will release their dogs. The dogs will collide in the pit in a chaotic mix of biting. A fight may last from one to several hours (Christiansen et al., 2004; Sakach & Parascandola, 2016).

Medications/Paraphernalia

The conditioning devices were discussed earlier in the training section of the chapter. Drugs and veterinary supplies are used extensively in dogfighting. The drugs may be vitamins, oral or injectable amphetamines, anabolic steroids, hormones, painkillers, and so on. The presence of these types

Figure 13.14 Basic sheltering using a barrel while toed out. (Courtesy Chris West.)

Figure 13.15 Tethered fighting dogs with heavy chains. (Courtesy Chris West.)

Figure 13.16 Bricks assembled and tied to the neck of the dog supposedly to build strength. (Courtesy Chris West.)

Figure 13.17 Slatted treadmill used in dogfight training. (Courtesy Chris West.)

of drugs, medical supplies, and paraphernalia help solidify the documentation that dogs are being raised, trained, and fought at a given location. As stated in the cockfighting section, veterinarians can be invaluable assisting with identifying and collecting this type of evidence and consideration for toxicology screening (Sakach & Parascandola, 2016) (Figure 13.18).

Dog Processing/Types of Injuries

Each dog will need to be assigned an identification number and photographed with the date and case information. Safety is a paramount concern with these animals. Staff (technicians) experienced with handling aggressive dogs are essential. These dogs are not bred for human aggression at the professional level; however, many backyard hobbyist animals can be extremely dangerous in the author's (NBS) experience.

Figure 13.18 Powdered protein mix used during a keep for dogfighting. (Courtesy Chris West.)

Each dog should have a complete physical examination, body condition scoring, diagnostic workup (including heartworm and fecal analysis), and whole-body radiographs if possible. All wounds will need to be documented (diagramed and photographed) with and without measurement and again after treatment. Scar charts documenting injuries complement photographs. Dr. Merck recommends using a blue pen for scars and healed wounds and a red pen for fresh and healing wounds (Merck, 2013).

Heartworm, intestinal parasites, and anemia are commonly found (Merck, 2013). *Babesia gibsoni* is a common parasite in fighting dogs (Merck, 2013). Pit bulls are highly susceptible to parvovirus, demodectic mange, and dermatophytosis. Fighting dogs may or may not have their ears and tails cropped. This is usually done, in the case of the ears, crudely with scissors. Fighting dogs grab, hold, and shake opponents, creating deep tissue punctures, lacerations, and fractures. Wounds consistent with dogfighting are usually found on the head, neck, and front legs. Many of these wounds are scars or at various stages of healing. The oral region should be examined for injuries sustained in the buccal and gingival tissue from the use of a break stick (used to disengage a bite) (Christiansen et al., 2004; Merck, 2013; Sakach & Parascandola, 2016). The hard palate may have puncture wounds as well, so consider dental radiographs. Consider obtaining additional blood and urine testing for performance-enhancing drugs. Many of these drugs are metabolized within several hours, increasing the importance of timely diagnostic testing.

Necropsy

If dogs are found deceased at the scene, it is crucial that a forensic necropsy be performed. This will include whole-body radiographs and toxicology screening (if warranted). Many of these dogs have died of shock or exsanguination resulting from their fight wounds; however, losers may be killed by their handlers/owners. The usual way dogfighters destroy their dogs is electrocution (see Chapter 12), strangulation, or drowning. These may lead to additional animal abuse charges (Touroo & Reisman, 2018).

Outcomes

Depending on the resources of the animal welfare organization and the health and behavior conditions of fighting dogs, euthanasia may be necessary. However, routine euthanasia is not necessarily common practice anymore when these animals are confiscated. It has been demonstrated that many of these dogs can go on to live normal lives in a loving home. The ASPCA Behavior Teams actively work with these types of dogs rescued from fighting and have had good success.

HOG-DOGFIGHTING

Hog-dogfighting is a form of staged animal fighting in the same category as dogfighting and cockfighting, which are both illegal. Hog-dogfighting originates from hog hunting, a legal endeavor in which hunters use dogs to find, chase, and catch feral hogs. Feral hogs are considered a nuisance in rural areas and hunting without a permit is common in many states. Dog breeds common to hog-dogging are American pit bull terriers and Catahoulas. In a hog-dog event, a hog with its board teeth removed is placed in a pen. Dogs are placed in the pen with the hog and encouraged to maul it. If the pig will not come out of the pen corner, a cattle prod is used on it. The hog will scream in agony as the dogs are allowed to viciously attack. Admission fees and bets are placed on the event. The owner of the fastest attacking dog is rewarded with cash prizes. A single pig may have to endure multiple events. Hog-dogging is legal in most states.

WORKING WITH LAW ENFORCEMENT

A veterinarian may have cockfighting birds or dogs from dogfighting events brought to the clinic or shelter for examination. They may be asked to come to the scene to conduct examinations and to evaluate overall conditions. The veterinarian can be instrumental in discussing animal abuse statutes and other statute offenses involving these animals. Veterinarians are invaluable to law enforcement to identify paraphernalia or other equipment associated with dog- and cockfighting.

Animal abuse and a multitude of other offenses are committed at cockfighting and dogfighting events (Sakach & Parascandola, 2016), including

- Cockfighting-specific offenses
- State anticruelty statutes
- Gambling
- Racketeering
- Unreported income tax or tax evasion
- Conspiracy
- Concealed weapons
- Disorderly conduct
- Animal Welfare Act or Animal Fighting Prohibition Enforcement Act (federal)
- Narcotics and controlled substances
- Illegal sales of alcoholic beverages
- Contributing to the delinquency of a minor

Animal Hoarding Laws

Animal Neglect and Cruelty with No Federal Strategy

Each state has its own laws that prohibit cruelty by owners and require a minimum level of care. Although the minimum level of care varies among states, they have several elements in common:

- The animal must be able to maintain a normal body weight by receiving sufficient quantities of food and clean drinkable water.
- The animal must be able to maintain a normal body temperature and be protected from getting wet by having adequate housing or shelter.
- The animal must have a clean, hygienic living space adequate to prevent soiling with feces and urine or trash.
- There is some degree of effort to relieve suffering, secondary to injury or illness, possibly by access to veterinary care.

Neighbors, delivery persons, and caregivers or other professionals including law enforcement are most likely to identify an animal neglect and cruelty by a hoarder based on violations of these living and care requirements. The only two states in the country with state-level animal hoarding laws are Illinois and Hawaii.

If the person involved is a competent adult, it may not be a violation for a competent adult to live in those same unclean conditions. A competent adult human may choose to live in squalid conditions as long as the characteristics of their housing do not violate housing codes or public safety regulations. In this scenario, the authorities tasked with investigating and potentially bringing charges against a hoarder might decide not to commit the resources necessary to pursue the case if their limited resources are needed for other law enforcement activities.

In contrast, if there is a minor or an incompetent adult in the home, the living conditions might attract the attention of child or adult protective services. The immediate priority of these protective service professionals is to address the needs of the person. Their responses might not include removing and providing care to the animals if that removal would be stressful to the person.

It is not always clear who has legal authority to investigate a hoarder, to take possession of the animals, and to leverage the threat to bring charges against the hoarder. The local animal warden, if there is one, sheriff's or police department, and state police have the authority to enforce local and state laws within their jurisdictions. Although police have the authority to enforce the law and intervene to investigate a hoarder and remove animals, they are more likely to prioritize use of their limited resources to protect the public by preventing and investigating burglaries, assaults, and other violent crimes. Some states allow specifically trained representatives from humane organizations to enforce animal cruelty statutes by explicitly granting enforcement power. All stakeholders should beware of humane organization representatives who attempt to intervene without having been granted this law enforcement authority. All parties exercising enforcement power must adhere to the rules of criminal procedure and evidence to assure that their efforts yield admissible evidence.

Types of Animal Hoarders

Unlike animal fighting, which is a criminal, commercial enterprise by persons generally involved in other criminal activities, people become hoarders for many different reasons. As a result, there is not one specific interventional approach that is successful with all types of hoarders. The Hoarding of Animals Research Consortium (HARC) divided hoarders into three groups, based on the motivations and circumstances of the hoarder, which include the overwhelmed caregiver, rescuer hoarder, and exploiter hoarder. These designations are descriptive of how the person became a hoarder and their level of receptivity or resistance to different types of intervention. Interventions can range from assistance with the care of and rehoming of animals for individuals who accept that there is a problem to threats of or actual legal prosecution as a last resort for individuals who aggressively reject all legal authority.

Overwhelmed Caregiver

The overwhelmed caregiver (Patronek et al., 2006) is personally devoted to the care of their animals, which they consider to be family members, but has experienced a decline in the ability or capacity to provide suitable care. This decline might be precipitated by one or more factors. One factor is an economic change, such as the loss of income, medical bills and other expenses, or loss of a spouse or other persons providing assistance. Another factor could be a reduction in the physical ability to maintain the standard of care, such as might occur due to personal illness, decline with age, or loss of assistance by a spouse or other person.

Although they may not initially acknowledge the severity of the problem, they have some degree of awareness that the level of animal care has declined and has probably made unsuccessful efforts to solve the problem before becoming completely overwhelmed. They are concerned about the animals, to whom they are very attached, and bases their self-esteem on their caregiver role for the animals, which they gradually passively acquired rather than having actively sought to rescue or acquire. While they may tend to be an isolated personality with possible Axis I psychological disorders, they are not purposely secretive and are not driven by a strong desire to control the situation.

They are the most likely of the hoarder types to be receptive to entry by an intervener and to be respectful of and compliant with authoritative recommendations. However, they will find it very emotionally difficult to be separated from their animals; they are the most likely to qualify for assistance or intervention by social services.

Rescuer Hoarder

The rescuer hoarder (Patronek et al., 2006) is a socially integrated person who has a personal mission or compulsion to prevent the euthanasia of animals by actively acquiring progressively increasing numbers of animals from a network of enablers. Because they are distrustful of authority and animal shelters, they see themselves as the only one capable of saving the animal. They find it difficult to refuse additional animals and keeps them permanently, although they may initially engage in rescues followed by adoption. As the animal number balloons, they gradually become unable to provide adequate care but stubbornly continue to believe that they are their only hope, based on a deep-seated fear that the animals would be euthanized elsewhere.

They are unlikely to acknowledge that there is a problem and are compulsively driven to collect more animals. Based on this mind-set, they will not be receptive to entry by an intervener, and it will be difficult to get them to comply with authoritative recommendations. They will be secretive and will fight to avoid losing control of their animals; they are unlikely to qualify for assistance or intervention by social services. The threat of prosecution may be necessary, and might not be enough in some cases.

Exploiter Hoarder

The exploiter hoarder (Patronek et al., 2006) is a highly manipulative, narcissistic, charming, and articulate person who actively collects animals for the sole purpose of serving their own needs. Unlike the other two groups, they are not motivated by empathy for animals, or people, and do not respond to animals' suffering or the harm they are doing to them.

Because they arrogantly believe that they are the ultimate expert, they seek to exert unchallenged control and are likely to completely deny that there is a problem and to reject any suggestion that there is a care issue. Based on this mind-set, they will employ manipulative and deceptive strategies including creating articulate excuses, lies, and plans to deceive and evade authorities including law enforcement, such as temporarily moving animals. They lack any sense of remorse and it is pointless to appeal to their nonexistent conscience regarding the animal issues. This is the most difficult type of hoarder to work with due to this manipulative nature, and prosecution may be necessary.

This individual will not be receptive to entry by an intervener, and it will be difficult to get them to comply with authoritative recommendations. They will be secretive and will fight to avoid losing control of their animals; they are unlikely to qualify for assistance or intervention by social services.

ANIMAL HOARDING

Hoarding is one of the most egregious forms of animal neglect, affecting an estimated 250,000 animals annually (Christiansen et al., 2004). Animal hoarders commit animal neglect by actions or omission of actions that are attributed to complex and often misunderstood mental conditions (Bradley-Siemens et al., 2018). Hoarding and rescuing behaviors can be manifestations of complex neuropsychiatric disorders. Compulsive hoarding is identified in the *Diagnostic and Statistical Manual of Mental Disorders* (DSM-5) under obsessive compulsive disorder (OCD). However in 2013, the American Psychiatric Association identified it as a distinct form of mental illness and it is generally viewed as a related OCD disorder by mental health experts (Bradley-Siemens et al., 2018). Animal hoarding is the compulsive need to collect and control animals without concern for any negative consequences to the animals or individuals.

Mental health conditions and personality disorders amid animal hoarders determine the form of neglect the animals may experience and cause barriers to constructive intervention. The stereotypical animal hoarder is the neighborhood "crazy cat lady," but this syndrome is much broader and complicated. Over 70% of animal hoarders are women; however, animal hoarding spans most socioeconomic and demographic boundaries (Merck et al., 2013). The average age of women who hoard is 53, and 49 for men (Patronek et al., 2006; Bradley-Siemens et al., 2018). Hoarding can involve any species of animal (Merck et al., 2013). The rate of recidivism is almost 100%, primarily because mental health issues regarding the hoarder are not addressed (Patronek et al. 2006; Merck et al., 2013).

Figure 13.19 Wire kennel in central part of a hoarder house, everything was covered in a deep layer of feces, especially in the kennel.

Hoarding is defined by the presence of three key features: clutter and disorganization, unrestrained accumulation of animals, and the inability to discard or relinquish animals. Hoarding usually begins as selfish acts of concern to save animals (Bradley-Siemens et al., 2018). The compulsive caregiving behavior is increased in an attempt to satiate unfulfilled human needs, while disregarding or ignoring the requirements of the animals in their care (Patronek et al., 2006; Bradley-Siemens et al., 2018) (Figures 13.19 and 13.20).

Figure 13.20 Bathtub used as communal litterbox by cats in a hoarder home. Feces measure almost 12 inches deep.

Hoarding can take place in the individual's home or in another facility; either may be misrepresented as a rescue or animal sanctuary. These may have legal nonprofit status with a 501.c.3 (Merck et al., 2013).

CASE 5: Animal Hoarding Felony (NBS)

History: A large-scale hoarding operation at two homes in a large municipality with over 200 dogs. This was brought to the attention of law enforcement due to noise, smell, and one of the caregiver's volunteers reporting her because of the animal conditions. This caregiver was a 501.c.3 (collecting donations) and at times adopting out animals for a fee.

Physical Findings: Both locations were simultaneously raided. Many animals were sick or deceased. There were feces and urine everywhere in the homes and yard areas. Many dogs were running around loose on the properties; however, many were confined in kennels full of feces and urine without food or water. Expired and inappropriate medications were being used on animals.

Outcome: Many of the sick and deceased dogs had a zoonotic disease. The case proceeded to state superior court and lasted several days. The hoarder was convicted on hoarding-related charges at both misdemeanor and felony levels due to the zoonotic components in the case. In addition, board complaints were brought against veterinarians for providing medications via prescription without examining the animals and failing to report animal abuse.

Animal hoarders are usually known to animal welfare organizations in a given community. In many instances, the local humane society investigator or animal control officer has a longstanding case history with an individual hoarder. In addition, if intervention or prosecution has been pursued, law enforcement will have information about the individual.

In a 2006 presentation by R.L. Lockwood on "Hoarding: Psychology and Punishment," typical animal hoarding behaviors consist of:

- No admittance of visitors to the home.
- Will not identify how many animals are in the residence.
- Continued acquisition of new animals in the presence of declining health of resident animals.
- Desire to care for animals who have contagious diseases or are paralyzed.
- The number of staff/volunteers assisting the caregiver, if any, are not sufficient for the number of animals present.

Warning signs that a veterinarian may observe, which may indicate hoarding include a client who brings in multiple animals that may have only been seen once, lack of preventative care for the animals, and/or the animals are presented with extreme illness or injury. The hoarder may go to multiple veterinarians in the community. There may be a foul odor from the animal, animal carrier, or owner/caregiver (Merck et al., 2013; Bradley-Siemens et al., 2018).

One major problem with animal hoarders is they do not believe they are doing anything wrong. They will not acknowledge the deteriorating conditions of the animals or living environment (Merck et al., 2013). Hoarding is a form of severe neglect constituting animal abuse, and is often associated with child and elder abuse (Merck et al., 2013).

As discussed earlier, many animal hoarders are often known to animal welfare organizations or humane investigators in a community. These organizations have been contacted by veterinarians, law enforcement agencies, or other service (gas, water, power) agencies that have had contact with the hoarder or the residence/facility. In the author's experience (NBS), the two primary things that alert outsiders to a hoarding environment are loud noises and/or foul odors from the animals. In these types of cases, animal welfare organizations and humane investigators first try to work with the hoarder through voluntary relinquishment or sterilization of their existing animals. In addition, the humane investigator will contact social services in an attempt to provide assistance for the human victim/abuser. This may or may not be successful.

There are multiple routes to deal with an animal hoarder depending on local laws and resources. Ideally, enough evidence is amassed through multiple humane investigator site visits to obtain a search warrant and seize the animals. If access to a facility or residence cannot be obtained, homeowner associations, building code enforcement, public health inspectors, or animal control officers may be able to assist. There may be limits on the number of animals allowed in a dwelling, public health/safety concerns about odors or sanitation from animal urine and feces, noise levels from animals, or structural damage to a building. If the hoarder is registered as a nonprofit and the state regulates these nonprofit animal shelters/rescues, then the regulatory agency which enforces the statutes may be able to assist with the investigation and prosecution of these cases. These can all provide access into the home and can lead to an eventual search warrant or force the hoarder to move and find other lodgings, making the number of animals public as they attempt to move.

In the event authorities do seize the animals in a hoarding situation, it is a multidisciplinary endeavor usually involving animal welfare personnel, law enforcement, fire department HAZMAT teams, code enforcement personnel, social services, and many other entities (Patronek et al., 2006). Hoarders are a severe drain on local animal welfare organizations, quickly taking up limited kennel space in local shelters and raising potential public health/safety concerns due to the presence of urine and feces, rodents, and zoonotic diseases. The author (NBS) was involved in a large-scale hoarding case at two different houses with over 200 dogs. Many dogs, alive and deceased, had *Leptospirosis*.

Hoarding Crime Scenes

Usually when the residence or facility is entered, PPE is required. Readings of ammonia and hydrogen sulfide levels are obtained by handheld devices initially (humane investigator), or a HAZMAT unit from the fire department will evaluate the levels and determine safety protocols and parameters. These levels are critical and should be documented or reports from the HAZMAT unit acquired for the case. Ammonia levels greater than 50 ppm are considered extreme irritants. Ammonia gasses at levels under 100 ppm can act as chronic stressors to animals. Anything above 300 ppm may cause threats to both health and life (Merck et al., 2013) (Figures 13.21 and 13.22).

A hoarding situation is treated much like a disaster response with an incident command structure depending on how many structures and animals are involved. The importance of multi-agency involvement cannot be understated. Each agency has a purpose and an area of expertise.

It is crucial that a veterinarian be present during a seizure operation. The entire environment and animals in it need to be treated as a crime scene (see Chapter 1). The veterinarian will need to walk through the scene evaluating the environment, access to food and water, storage of food, if any, and any medications used on the animals. In the case of medications, many are usually expired or not stored in the correct manner. The veterinarian can assist with the collection of evidence and processing the crime scene, that is, look in the refrigerator or freezer for deceased animals that the hoarder will not part with, or what to photographically document. These will be critical for the case to establish the mental status of the individual or if prosecution is sought (Figures 13.23a,b and 13.24a,b).

The veterinarian will need to be on scene to triage the animals as they exit the environment. Each animal will be assigned an identification number and photographed with all case information. The veterinarian will need to perform a thorough physical exam on each animal. A diagnostic workup including blood work and radiographs will be performed for each individual animal as dictated by the animal's condition, the number of animals involved, and the resources of the animal welfare organization. The veterinarian may have to perform diagnostics sparingly and

Figure 13.21 Fire department HAZMAT team at a hoarder home before entrance.

determined case by case. At minimum, a hands-on physical examination with body condition score, weight, temperatures, pulse, respiration, findings and any treatments performed must be documented. In the event that there are deceased animals present, a forensic necropsy should be performed. It is important to ascertain if the cause of death was due to disease, starvation, or other causes. In addition, it should be determined if the deceased animal was cannibalized by the

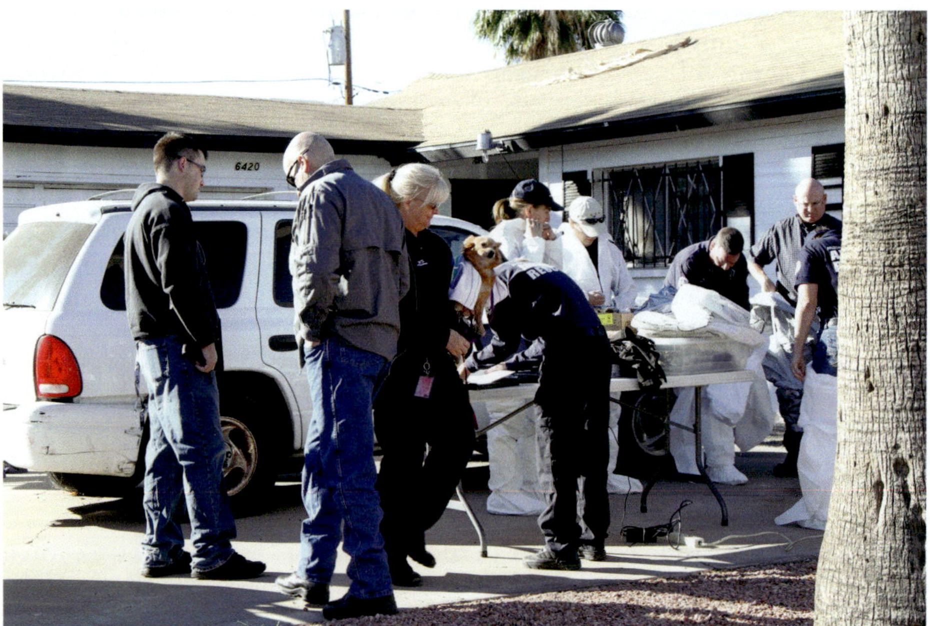

Figure 13.22 Personnel donning personal protective equipment to enter a hoarder residence under guidance of the fire department HAZMAT team.

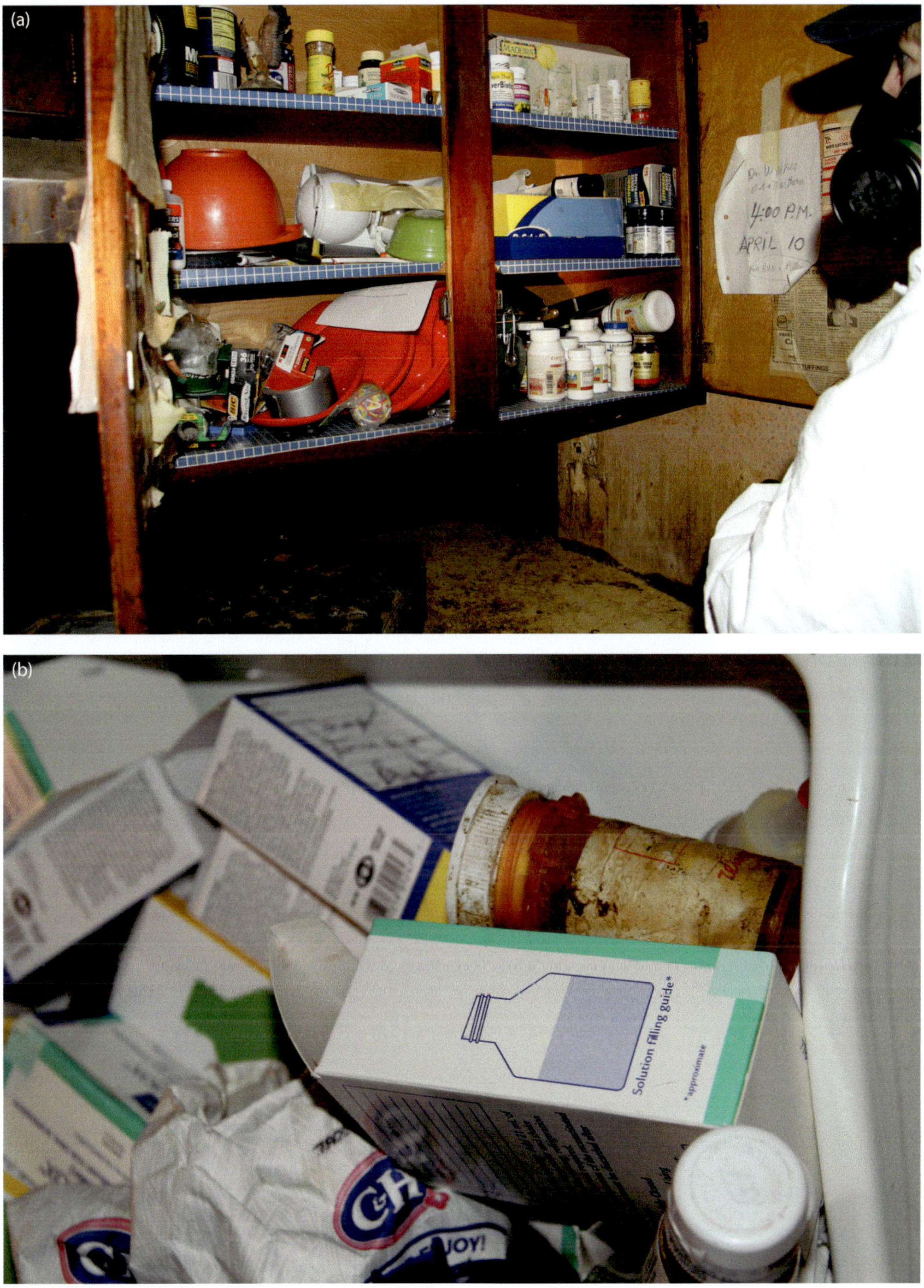

Figure 13.23 (a) Medications in cabinets at a hoarder house. (b) Medications in a refrigerator at a hoarder house haphazardly stored together.

Figure 13.24 (a) Feces in food and putrid water. (b) Beetles in food and bowls.

other animals, illustrating the degradation, resource-restricted conditions in which the animals existed (Figure 13.25).

The examination and/or necropsy findings will document the level of neglect. Neglect in a hoarding incident is defined as being subjected to stress from overcrowding, insufficient food and water, and unsanitary living conditions (Merck et al., 2013). In addition, these animals are usually suffering from prolonged malnutrition, starvation, and dehydration. Hoarded animals usually show signs of respiratory disease (especially in cats), gastrointestinal disease, infestations of external and internal parasites, and dermatophytosis. Other issues observed are severe hair matting, overgrown toenails, and bite wounds from fighting with one another due to space and limited resources (Merck et al., 2013).

CASE 6: Cat Hoarder (NBS)

History: This hoarding case involved over 40 cats housed in a backyard in wire cages without shelter, litter boxes, or adequate food or water. Humane investigators and law enforcement seized the cats under exigent circumstances since several cats appeared agonal.

Physical Findings: The cats were brought to an animal shelter were several had to be immediately humanely euthanized. The cats were later diagnosed with feline infectious peritonitis (FIP). Many of the other cats had titers for FIP.

Outcome: The animal hoarder was elderly and without financial resources. She was provided and subsequently fired multiple public defenders. She continued to contest the initial seizure, now without legal counsel, eventually going all the way to the state supreme court where the seizure was upheld after 3 years. The cats did well and were maintained by the shelter at a cost of over $400,000. The remaining cats were eventually adopted. No charges were brought against the defendant.

The importance here is identifying what the caregiver should have been able to observe as a health or husbandry concern regardless of medical training and that was not addressed or was addressed in an incorrect manner, such as using expired medications (Figure 13.26). A common question to consider concerning the standard of care is: "What would a reasonable person see and/or do?"

The Hoarding Cases

These cases in the author's (NBS) opinion are the most frustrating due to their complexity. They usually involve large numbers of animals. The prosecutors and the courts often don't understand the necessity of upholding and finalizing seizures (in the absence of relinquishment) so that animals don't languish in an animal shelter for years (crippling these organizations) or animal hoarders without legal counsel keeping the court system moving in circles with endless seizure appeals.

As discussed earlier in the chapter, there are only two states that have animal hoarding statutes: Illinois and Hawaii. Some municipalities have hoarding statutes, usually misdemeanor offenses as discussed below; however, some of these laws have mandated psychiatric evaluation for the hoarding defendant.

In most instances, hoarders are charged with multiple misdemeanor offenses consisting of failure to provide veterinary care or food, water, and shelter. In the former and even the latter, the importance of veterinary involvement cannot be overstated (Patronek & Nathanson, 2016).

Figure 13.25 Cannibalized cat leg. When a cat died, the other animals began to eat it because there was no food and they were unable to exit the home.

Figure 13.26 Cat in a hoarder house with severe ocular discharge from an upper respiratory infection and high levels of ammonia in the home.

CONCLUSION

Animal fighting and animal hoarding are ongoing issues that need veterinary involvement to effect continued change and resolution. There are now 35 states that have some form of mandatory or encouraged reporting of animal abuse. Veterinarians must actively participate in the reporting and prosecution of these cases and endorse/support national and state level legislation for stricter penalties and more resources directed at these types of animal abuse crimes that have a significant effect on human welfare and safety as well as animal welfare.

References

Bradley-Siemens, N., A.I. Brower, and R. Reisman. 2018. Neglect. In: Brooks, J., ed. *Veterinary Forensic Pathology*, Vol 2. Cham, Switzerland: Springer, pp. 37–65.

Christiansen, S., F. Dantzler, K. Johnson, R. Lockwood, P. Paulhus, and E. Sakach. 2004. *The Final Round: A Law Enforcement Primer for the Investigation of Cockfighting and Dogfighting.* Humane Society of the United States.

Christiansen, S., Dantzler, F., Goodwin, J., Reever, J., Schindler, C., Johnson, K., Paulhus, M., and Sakach, E. 2015. *The Final Round: Law enforcement Primer for the Investigation of Cockfighting and Dogfighting.* The Humane Society of the United States.

Dinnage, J., K. Bollen, and S. Giacoppo. 2004. Animal fighting. In: Miller, L., and S. Zawistowski, eds. *Shelter Medicine for Veterinarians and Staff.* Ames, IA: Blackwell Publishing, pp. 511–521.

Greenacre, C.B. 2014. Poultry Necropsy Laboratory. In *Proceedings; Pre-laboratory lecture Notes.* Knoxville, TN: American Board of Veterinary Practitioners (ABVP).

Lockwood, R.L. 2006. Hoarding: Psychology and Punishment. In *Proceedings.* Atlanta, GA: Animal Cruelty Cases: Investigation and Prosecutions and Animal Law.

Lockwood, L.R. 2013. Animal fighting. In: Miller, L., and S. Zawistowski, eds. *Shelter Medicine for Veterinarians and Staff*, 2nd ed. Ames, IA: Blackwell Publishing, pp. 441–452.

Merck, M. 2013. Animal fighting. In: Merck, M., ed. *Veterinary Forensics; Animal Cruelty Investigations*, 2nd ed. Ames, IA: Blackwell Publishing, pp. 243–253.

Merck, M., D.M. Miller, and R. Reisman. 2013. Neglect. In: Merck, M., ed. *Veterinary Forensics; Animal Cruelty Investigations*, 2nd ed. Ames, IA: Blackwell Publishing, pp. 207–232.

National Humane Education Society. 2018. Animal Fighting. nehs.org/animal-fighting/

Patronek, G., L. Loar, and J.N. Nathanson. 2006. *Animal Hoarding: Structure Interdisciplinary Responses to Help People, Animals, and Communities at Risk.* Hoarding Animals Research Consortium.

Patronek, G. and J.N. Nathanson. 2016. Understanding animal neglect and hoarding. In: Levit, L., G. Patronek, and T. Grisso, eds. *Animal Maltreatment: Forensic Mental Health Issues and Evaluators.* Oxford, NY: Oxford University Press, pp. 159–193.

Sakach, E. and A. Parascandola. 2016. *Investigating Animal Cruelty: A Field Guide for Law Enforcement Officers.* Humane Society of the United States.

Touroo, R. and R. Reisman. 2018. Animal fighting. In: Brooks, J., ed. *Veterinary Forensic Pathology*, Vol 2. Cham, Switzerland: Springer, pp. 97–119.

CHAPTER 14

VETERINARY FORENSIC TOXICOLOGY

Sharon Gwaltney-Brant

WHAT IS VETERINARY FORENSIC TOXICOLOGY?

Forensic toxicology is defined as the application of toxicology to matters of the law. Human forensic toxicology encompasses three subfields: postmortem forensic toxicology, human performance toxicology, and forensic drug testing (Levine, 2010). Postmortem toxicology aids in the determination of cause and manner of death through identification of foreign substances within the body. Performance toxicology is focused on the identification and interpretation of the presence of substances that may impair or enhance an individual's ability to perform a task. Forensic drug testing is the screening of body fluids or tissues from individuals to determine the presence or absence of illicit substances, such as would be conducted with workplace drug testing or court-ordered drug testing for parolees. The scope of human forensic toxicology is large enough for toxicologists to specialize in one or more of these fields. In comparison, veterinary forensic toxicology is a broader and less specialized discipline (Murphy, 2012). In addition to postmortem and performance toxicology, veterinary forensic toxicology encompasses other areas, including regulatory toxicology, insurance investigations, and wildlife toxicology (Ensley, 1995; Stroud & Kuncir, 2005). Historically, the majority of veterinary forensic toxicology focus has been regulatory toxicology, which is largely focused on policing of hazardous residues in food animals or their products (e.g., milk, eggs) that will enter the human food chain. Performance toxicology testing in the veterinary field is focused primarily on animal athletes, predominantly racing animals; this branch of veterinary forensic toxicology has been slowly declining as have the racing industries it serves. Toxicology testing for insurance purposes generally involves either the loss of large numbers of animals of significant monetary value (e.g., a herd of beef cattle) or loss of life or function of highly valuable animals (e.g., an elite racehorse). Postmortem investigations are most commonly done in situations involving loss of livestock for the purpose of identifying the source and preventing further losses. Postmortem forensic toxicology cases in companion animals most commonly relate to intentional and malicious poisonings and are less often performed, for reasons that will be discussed shortly; however, with more stringent enforcement of animal anticruelty laws, the frequency of investigations into malicious poisoning of companion animals appears to be increasing. The field of veterinary forensic toxicology is relatively small compared to human forensic toxicology, so most veterinary toxicologists tend to be "jacks-of-all-trades" and handle a variety of forensic toxicology cases as well as working in other areas of toxicology, such as research, teaching, and clinical toxicology (i.e., diagnosis and treatment of animal poisonings).

Veterinary forensic toxicology investigations are not performed as frequently as their human counterparts because of several factors unique to veterinary medicine (Gwaltney-Brant, 2016). First, suspicious animal injuries and deaths are not automatically investigated as they would be if a human were involved. While physicians are generally mandated to report suspected poisonings, there is no such mandate for veterinarians in many areas of the country; note, though, that some states do mandate that veterinarians report suspected animal abuse, which may include poisonings, depending on the statute. Unlike humans, where laws require investigation of malicious poisonings, it is generally up to the authorities whether they investigate animal poisonings, and historically many jurisdictions have chosen not to expend time and money to do so unless public health is involved, large numbers of animals are affected, or, occasionally, public outcry changes their minds. Unlike human forensic cases where governmental agencies cover the cost of the investigation and toxicology testing, in veterinary medicine those costs are usually passed on to animal owners, who may be unwilling or unable to pay for thorough forensic investigations. Often, the signs of poisonings are initially attributed to natural diseases, delaying the collection of appropriate samples for toxicological analysis; if the poisoning is finally recognized, the optimal time for collecting an appropriate and diagnostic sample may have passed.

Box 14.1 Veterinary Forensic Toxicology in the News: Selenium Toxicosis in Polo Ponies

On April 19, 2009, 20 Venezuelan polo horses attending the U.S. Polo Championships in Wellington, Florida, collapsed and died within a 6-hour time frame, with an additional horse dying several hours later. The cause of the deaths was determined to be acute heart failure due to damage to the heart muscle. Based on clinical signs and lesions found on necropsy, selenium toxicosis was suspected by veterinary toxicologists working on the case. Toxicological analysis confirmed the presence of toxic selenium concentrations in the tissues of all of the horses. The source of the selenium was found to be a vitamin and mineral supplement that had been administered by intramuscular injection to all but five horses in the Venezuelan polo horse stable. The fact that the five horses that had not been given the supplement were not affected led to the suspicion that the supplement may have been involved. It was determined that the supplement, which was formulated by a local pharmacy, contained 100 times more selenium than intended. In 2016, a jury awarded the owners of the horses $2.5 million in damages for the loss of the horses.

Since the focus of veterinary forensic toxicology is on the law, it is important to understand what those laws are. As of 2017, 12 U.S. states (Alabama, Arizona, Colorado, Delaware, Missouri, Montana, Nebraska, New Hampshire, North Dakota, Oregon, South Carolina, and Tennessee) and the District of Columbia did not specifically mention poisoning of an animal in their animal protection statutes (although one of these, South Carolina, did mention that it was illegal to poison a police dog or police horse). It could be argued that poisoning is implicitly covered by the terms "injury" or "harm" in many of these statutes; however, it could be argued that the omission of poisoning leaves a loophole in the laws. In some states, it is unlawful to poison an animal belonging to someone else; does this imply that it is legal to poison one's own animal? If the law states specifically that it is illegal to poison cats and dogs, does that make it legal to poison horses? Certainly, standardization of state laws would enable more consistent enforcement and better protection of animals from would-be poisoners.

Despite the laws, animal poisonings rarely meet the criteria for criminal cases unless they are part of a larger criminal prosecution, such as federal investigation of a dogfighting ring. Intentional poisoning of food animals with the intent to adulterate the food supply may result in prosecution under chemical terrorism statutes. However, the majority of animal poisoning cases are relegated to civil court, with one party seeking damages from a second party whom they hold responsible for the poisoning (Desta et al., 2011) (Box 14.1 and Figure 14.1). In many jurisdictions, the standards for evidence admissibility and burden of persuasion for civil cases are not as rigorous as in criminal court. Many civil cases are ultimately settled out of court and it is frequently the quality of evidence on one side or the other that can sway one side or the other to settle (Murphy, 2012).

PRINCIPLES OF VETERINARY TOXICOLOGY

Definitions

A **poison** is a physical or chemical substance that can cause adverse effects in living organisms (Eaton & Gilbert, 2008). A **toxin** is a poison of biologic origin, such as plants, animals, fungi and bacteria; the term toxin is often erroneously used to refer to any poison. **Toxicant** is a synonym for poison, so can refer to substances that are biologic or nonbiologic in origin. So, strychnine, derived from the plant *Strychnos nux-vomica*, can be referred to as either toxin or toxicant, while the metal

Figure 14.1 In 2009, forensic investigation of the deaths of 20 of 25 Venezuelan polo ponies determined that they died from selenium toxicosis from a misformulated vitamin/mineral supplement.

mercury is a toxicant but not a toxin. **Xenobiotic** is a term to refer to any compound that is foreign to the body. Xenobiotics can include foods, drugs, vitamins, minerals, and other compounds not endogenous to the organism. **Toxicity** refers to the relative potency or amount of a toxicant required to cause adverse effects, while **toxicosis** is the clinical syndrome that is caused by poison. So, the correct usage would be "The toxicity of nicotine was such that just a few milligrams produced a toxicosis in the dog," and we say that the dog experienced "nicotine toxicosis," not "nicotine toxicity." **Intoxication** is the state of being affected by a poison, so is similar to toxicosis; some toxicologists restrict the term "intoxication" to those toxicoses that result in central nervous system derangement (e.g., alcohol intoxication).

Concepts of Toxicology

The basic tenet of toxicology, as stated by Paracelsus (1493–1541), widely regarded as the father of toxicology, is: "All things are poison, and nothing is without poison; only the dose permits something not to be poisonous" (Eaton & Gilbert, 2008). This is an essential concept for understanding toxicology, because even the most toxic compound known will not have an adverse effect if it is not present at the appropriate dose in the body, and even the most apparently innocuous compound can be toxic at the appropriate dose. For instance, even water, which is essential for life, can cause intoxication and death if ingested in excess. Once the dose of a toxicant reaches a "threshold" dose, toxic effects begin to be seen, and they usually increase in severity as the dose increases. This pairing of dose to observed effects is known as the dose–response relationship, an important concept in both pharmacology (where the endpoint is a therapeutic effect) and toxicology (where the endpoint is a toxic effect) (Figure 14.2). The dose–response relationship makes some basic assumptions:

1. The exposure is related to known, observable effects
2. The effects are due to the interaction of the toxicant with some target site
3. The exposure dose is related to the concentration of the toxicant at the target site

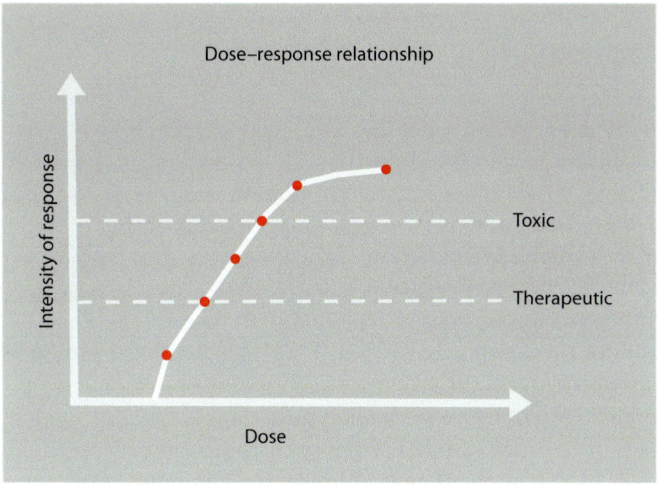

Figure 14.2 Dose–response relationship: the intensity of a response is dependent upon the dose of a given xenobiotic. For compounds that have medicinal effect, appropriate pharmacological response occurs when the dose meets or exceeds a therapeutic threshold. When the dose reaches the toxic threshold, adverse effects will occur.

In both pharmacology and toxicology, we expect that, at a given dose, the responses will be normally distributed with outliers at either end of the response spectrum (Figure 14.3). An individual animal's response may vary somewhat due to differences in age, state of health, nutritional status, and so on, so that, at a given dose, some individuals will show more severe toxic effects than the majority of the population (sensitive), while others will experience less severe effects than the population as a whole (resistant). However, once the toxic threshold has been breached for an individual, the progression of clinical signs caused by a toxicant is similar to the rest of the population (Dolder, 2013) (Box 14.2 and Figure 14.4).

The dose–response relationship also helps to distinguish a true toxicosis from other adverse events that may occur upon exposure to a xenobiotic substance (Tables 14.1 through 14.3) (Galey &

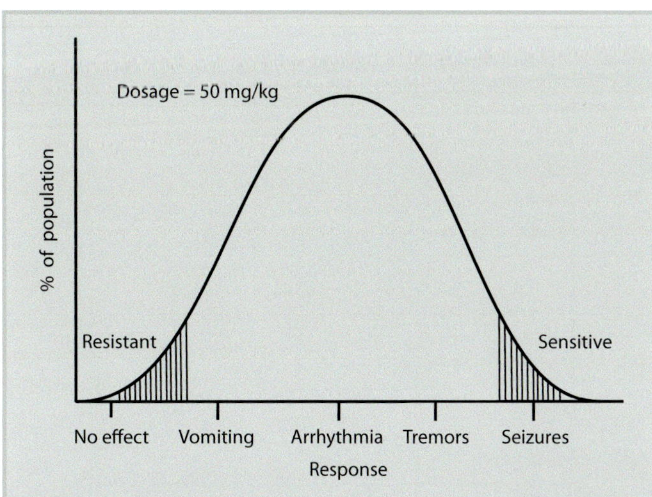

Figure 14.3 Spectrum of clinical effects that may be seen within a population exposed to the same dosage (50 mg/kg) of a toxicant. Individuals with responses at the left end of the curve are considered resistant, while those on the right end of the curve are considered sensitive to that toxicant.

Box 14.2 Dose–Response and the Individual

Caffeine is becoming a more common toxicant used to maliciously poison companion animals, particularly dogs. When a dog has ingested caffeine, how do we know if the dose was sufficient to cause a toxicosis? Unfortunately, individual patient information such as that is rarely available, so we must rely on population dose–response relationships. These relationships may have been derived through experimental dosing of animals, or they may have been obtained through the analysis of cases of exposures of patients reported by clinics or animal poison control centers. For instance, with caffeine toxicosis in dogs, on a population basis, the following spectrum of signs is expected with increasing dosage (Figure 14.4).

Of course, not all of these signs may occur in a single patient, but it is highly unlikely to see only seizures without some earlier signs such as vomiting, tachycardia, or agitation. We also know that some dogs will begin to develop mild signs (vomiting, etc.) at about 20 mg/kg of caffeine, whereas others may not show signs until dosages are closer to 30 mg/kg, and rare individuals may not show signs until around 40 mg/kg. Similar to humans where one cup of coffee barely gets one person going in the morning, but that same amount causes a different person to be jittery for hours, there will be individual variation in sensitivity to toxicants. However, once signs begin the progression in severity will be the same.

So how do we explain a dog that ate 80 mg/kg of caffeine, a dose where death has been reported in some dogs, but did not develop serious signs? Perhaps the dog vomited up enough of the caffeine to reduce the dose to a less toxic level (self-decontamination), or perhaps the caffeine was placed in some type of bait that prolonged absorption such that the dog was able to metabolize and eliminate some caffeine before full absorption occurred, or perhaps the dog had other food in the gastrointestinal tract to slow down the absorption of the caffeine.

Hall, 1990; Eaton & Gilbert, 2008; Millo et al., 2008; Dinis-Olivera et al., 2010; Gwaltney-Brant, 2016). Allergic responses are due to extreme over-response of the immune system to a xenobiotic (allergen); allergic responses can range from mild itching to life-threatening systemic reactions (anaphylaxis). Allergic responses require prior sensitization of the immune system to the allergen, they are not dose dependent, and the initial allergic response is not predictable. Idiosyncratic

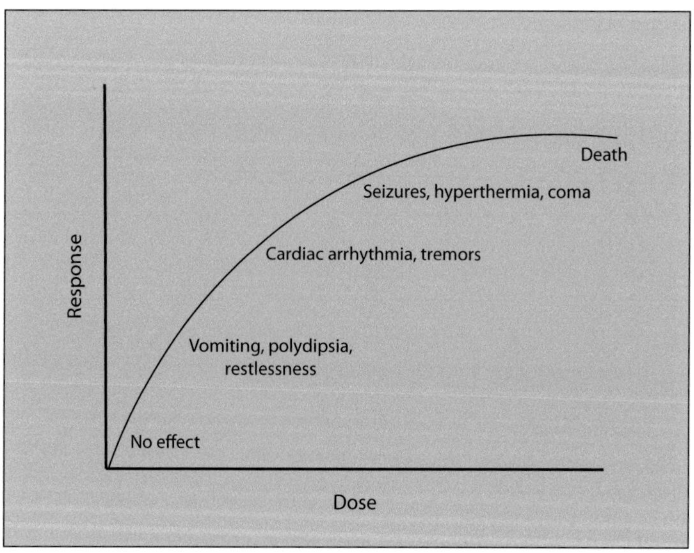

Figure 14.4 Spectrum of expected responses associated with increasing doses of caffeine.

Table 14.1 Features differentiating toxic, allergic, and idiosyncratic responses

Toxic	Allergic	Idiosyncratic
Dose-dependent	Not dose-dependent	+/− Dose-dependent
Predictable	Unpredictable	Unpredictable
	Requires prior sensitization	Extreme sensitivity or extreme insensitivity to standard doses

Source: Eaton and Gilbert (2008).

reactions are most commonly observed with pharmaceuticals; they are adverse reactions that are unpredictable, may or may not be dose-dependent for that individual, and they reflect extreme sensitivity or insensitivity to standard doses. Clinically, the signs of allergic and idiosyncratic reactions can resemble toxicoses, so sorting these out can be difficult.

We have seen that toxic responses are related to the amount of toxicant at a target site and that the responses to a given dose of a toxicant can vary between individuals. So, what factors are involved in determining an individual's response to a toxicant? We can separate out the intoxication process into three different phases: exposure, toxicokinetics, and toxicodynamics (Eaton & Gilbert, 2008). Discussing these phases separately allows one to consider them in a logical manner, but it is important to understand that these three phases are ongoing throughout an intoxication. For instance, a dog that ingests marijuana may continue to be exposed from the marijuana remaining in its stomach, while at the same time the drug is moving through his system (toxicokinetics) as well as exerting its narcotic effects (toxicodynamics). Exposure is the first essential step in development of a toxicosis. Major routes of toxicant exposure are the alimentary tract (ingestion), lungs (inhalation), and skin (topical), with ocular, intramammary, and parenteral injection being less common routes of entry in poisoned patients. Most toxic exposures are acute, single incidents with relatively short duration of exposure of less than 24 hours (e.g., a dog ingesting rodenticide placed in its yard); less commonly, toxic exposure may continue beyond 24 hours but last for several days up to a month (subacute exposure, e.g., cattle ingesting a batch of contaminated grain); in even rarer cases, exposure may occur for 1–3 months, termed subchronic exposure (e.g., cattle foraging on pastures with toxic plants); exposures exceeding 3 months' duration (e.g., pets living in households with cigarette smokers) are termed chronic exposures. Determination of the relationship between subacute, subchronic, and chronic exposures to xenobiotics and clinical signs that develop in animals can be difficult due to lack of knowledge of the chronic effects of many xenobiotics in many species as well as the need to account for other xenobiotics to which the animals may have been exposed during the same time frame.

Following exposure, the toxicokinetic phase describes the movement of toxicants through the body and encompasses four stages: absorption, distribution, metabolism, and elimination (Lehman-McKeeman, 2008). **Absorption** is the entry of a toxicant into the body. Toxicants pass through biological barriers by active (e.g., active transport, endocytosis) or passive (e.g., diffusion) processes that depend on the size, shape, and formulation of the toxicant as well as the physiological state of the biological barrier. For instance, a toxicant that is incapable of passing through the relatively thick epidermis of the skin may easily solubilize within the gastrointestinal tract and be readily absorbed. The pH of a toxicant can determine where that toxicant is best absorbed; for example, weak acids are more readily absorbed from the acidic stomach, while weak bases are more readily absorbed in the higher pH of the intestine. The term *bioavailability* is used to indicate what fraction of a xenobiotic dose is absorbed into the systemic circulation. **Distribution** of a toxicant within the body occurs via the circulatory and lymphatic systems. Water-soluble toxicants can dissolve in the circulation and tend to follow extracellular body water, whereas lipid-soluble toxicants may enter and concentrate in lipid-rich tissues such as the brain and adipose tissue. The degree of blood perfusion of an organ can determine how much toxicant that organ receives, with highly perfused organs such as liver and kidneys receiving a large share of absorbed toxicant.

Physiological barriers, such as the blood–brain barrier, blood–testis barrier, and placenta, restrict access of certain toxicants to select body compartments. Some toxicants are carried in the blood on plasma or serum proteins, which restricts their distribution since only unbound toxicant is available to reach its target site (Lehman-McKeeman, 2008). **Metabolism** (also called biotransformation) is the chemical alteration of a xenobiotic within the body. The liver is the major organ of biotransformation in the body, although significant xenobiotic metabolism also occurs in the kidney, lung, and intestine, with most tissues capable of some degree of metabolism. For toxicants, the desired outcome is for metabolism to detoxify a poison and promote its excretion from the body. For most metabolized toxicants, this entails rendering the toxicant molecule inactive, larger than parent toxicant, and more water soluble. Larger, water-soluble metabolites are less able to enter cells and are more easily processed and eliminated by the kidney. A smaller number of toxicants are biotransformed into more lipid-soluble metabolites that are eliminated through the bile; delivery of these metabolites into the intestinal lumen via the bile duct can result in reabsorption from the intestinal tract back into the systemic circulation, a process known as enterohepatic recirculation. Enterohepatic recirculation of a toxicant can prolong its presence in the body, resulting in longer duration of signs of toxicosis. Metabolism is largely accomplished by means of a variety of cellular enzymes; the relative number and amount of these enzymes is genetically determined, accounting for much of the variation in metabolic activity between species and individuals. **Elimination** is the final process for removal of a toxicant and their metabolites from the body. The kidney and gastrointestinal tract are the primary organs of excretion, although other organs such as the lungs, skin, and glandular organs also contribute to the elimination of toxicants. The length of time a toxicant stays in the body is dependent upon how widely it is distributed throughout the body, whether there is sequestration within specific body compartments (e.g., lead substitutes for calcium in bone, which serves as a long-term storage depot for lead), whether enterohepatic recirculation occurs, and whether the toxicant requires extensive metabolism prior to elimination. Some toxicants with minimal metabolism are eliminated quickly, and the amount of time it takes for the original concentration of the toxicant to reduce by one half (known as the half-life) may be a matter of minutes to hours. Other toxicants that require metabolism may be eliminated rapidly at low concentrations but more slowly at high concentrations as the metabolic pathways become saturated.

Toxicodynamics describes the interactions of the toxicant with its target site (Eaton & Gilbert, 2008). Many toxicants interact with and alter the function of specific target sites such as cellular receptors or enzymes in a reversible or irreversible fashion. For toxicants that have reversible effects on enzymes or receptors, removal of the toxicant by either administration of an agent to counter its effects or via metabolism and elimination may result in return to normal function with little to no residual damage. These types of reversible effects are most commonly seen with toxicants that affect the nervous system (neurotoxicants) and cellular ion channels (e.g., sodium-potassium ATPases). However, damage to tissues that occurs during the toxicosis (e.g., brain injury from lack of oxygen during seizure activity) may not be reversible. Toxicants may have a direct action on cells by disruption of cellular membranes, interference with cellular energy production, inhibition of protein or nucleic acid synthesis, or interference with transmembrane channels. Toxicants may also cause indirect damage through the formation of reactive oxygen species, resulting in oxidant-induced damage to organelles and cells. Cellular, tissue, and organ injuries caused by a toxicant may be reversible if the toxicant is removed and the tissue or organ has not been damaged beyond its ability to repair itself.

Target Organ Toxicity

The clinical effects of toxicants vary widely depending on the tissues or organs that are targeted, and there are several factors that determine which organs or tissues are affected (Eaton & Gilbert, 2008). First, the toxicant must get to the target in sufficient quantity to exert its effect, so the target must be well perfused with blood, and any physiological barriers (e.g., blood–brain barrier) must somehow be breached. Next, there must be some molecular target for which the toxicant has affinity within that tissue. The ability of a tissue to biotransform the toxicant also will influence whether the toxicant may exert its effect, either through detoxification or bioactivation. For instance, overdose of the drug acetaminophen most commonly causes liver injury because the liver has the highest levels of the enzymes that convert acetaminophen to its toxic metabolite. Note, however, that just because a toxicant can get to an organ or tissue and be stored there does not necessarily make that tissue a target. In veterinary toxicology, toxicants most commonly exert their effects in the liver, kidney, and nervous system. The liver is very well perfused, receiving blood from the systemic circulation via the hepatic artery and from the gastrointestinal tract via the portal system. A primary function of the liver is biotransformation, and it therefore has the highest concentrations and broadest ranges of biotransforming enzymes and cofactors. The liver has no barriers to limit the access of absorbed toxicants; in a sense, the liver itself functions as a protective barrier to the distribution of ingested toxicants through first-pass detoxification. The distribution of metabolic enzymes within the liver results in characteristic patterns of toxicant-induced injury. The kidney is the major organ of excretion and at any given time receives about 25% of cardiac output. The kidney is capable of a significant amount of biotransformation and, like the liver, the distribution of the biotransforming enzymes within the kidney can result in recognizable patterns of injury for different toxicants. The central nervous system has a blood–brain barrier and blood–neural barrier that exclude all but the smallest lipid-soluble toxicants from entry by diffusion from the blood. Molecules that are too large to pass through these barriers utilize special carrier proteins to cross the barriers. So, these physiological barriers largely protect the central nervous system from many toxicants. These barriers are prone to injury or dysfunction due to inflammation, trauma, immaturity, and genetic mutation; in these cases, toxicants (and some pharmaceuticals) that would normally be excluded may now pass into the central nervous system, resulting in toxicosis. The nervous system is highly susceptible to toxicants that interfere with energy production and nerve transmission.

VETERINARY FORENSIC TOXICOLOGY INVESTIGATIONS

Malicious Animal Poisonings

As noted earlier, the lack of a central agency for reporting animal poisonings makes determination of their frequency difficult. Add to that the fact that many toxicoses may be misidentified as natural disease, and the actual incidence of animal poisonings, both accidental and intentional, is not known. What little information is available on animal poisoning incidence generally comes from human and animal poison control centers (PCCs) who receive calls from animal owners and veterinarians regarding potential animal poisonings (Gwaltney-Brant, 2012). Assuming PCC data is a cross-section of all animal poisoning incidents, some generalities can be determined. Most reported animal poisonings are accidental in nature, with intentional or malicious poisonings making up less than 1/2 of 1% of all reported poisonings. Most single-animal poisonings involve companion animals, whereas most multiple-animal poisonings involve livestock. Dogs account for more than 75% of malicious poisoning cases, and cats are involved in ~15% of cases, with the remainder involving other species such as livestock and wildlife. Large breed (especially German shepherd dogs), intact male dogs of 2–4 years of age are at increased risk for malicious poisonings. More malicious poisonings are reported in the summer months, presumably because animals tend to be less closely confined and a variety of toxicants (e.g., rodenticides, pesticides) are readily available.

It is safe to say that the vast majority of malicious animal poisoners get away with their offenses. There are little data available regarding those who maliciously poison animals, and there are no good forensic profiles on animal poisoners (Gwaltney-Brant, 2016). Poisons make ideal weapons in that they are readily available, easily distributed, and difficult to trace to the source. One way to consider what type of person might be inclined to maliciously poison animals is to consider the various motives a person might have for doing so. Elimination of a perceived or real nuisance animal is likely at the top of the list of motives for malicious animal poisonings. Animals that make excessive noise, trespass, threaten humans and other animals, eliminate on or damage property of another, or injure livestock or other animals may become such an annoyance to trigger someone to take action. Indeed, it is not illegal to poison certain species universally accepted as threats to public health, such as mice and rats, so poisoning other species might be considered by some people to be a legitimate activity. Other malicious poisoners may act in order to retaliate against a particular animal and/or its caretaker; this has occurred in many livestock poisonings where the poisoners turned out to be disgruntled former employees. Would-be burglars might poison pets, watchdogs, or guard dogs in order to gain free access to protected property. Some people might poison an animal to gain some sort of control over its owner; this most commonly happens in situations involving domestic violence. Persons who are suicidal have poisoned their pets along with themselves. Some poisoners might derive a sort of pleasure over seeing an animal die from poison. Poisons have been involved in cases of Munchausen syndrome by proxy involving pets, whereby the pet caretaker (usually the owner) intentionally injures the pet in in order to gain sympathy and attention for themselves.

Forensic Investigations

Because the clinical syndrome produced by many poisons can mimic those caused by natural diseases, a toxicosis may not be initially suspected when dealing with ill or dead animals (Galey & Hall, 1990; Ensley, 1995). Conversely, when a toxicosis is suspected, it is important to consider whether other nontoxic diseases processes such as infectious disease, metabolic disease, neoplasia, and so on, may be involved instead. Determining the cause of an animal's illness or death requires an open mind and sound investigative work. Historical information is a vital component of the investigation, as it can help identify potential risk factors in the patient's background. When a poisoning is suspected, careful questioning of the animal's caretakers is essential to get an idea of the animal's husbandry, environment, and potential for exposure to toxicants. Questions about the patient should be asked such as basic signalment (species, breed, age, reproductive status, weight) and health history (e.g., vaccination status, prior health, current and past medications/supplements, etc.). For cases involving multiple animals, the number of animals at risk, number affected, and number of deaths should be determined. Time frames such as when the animal was last noted to be normal, gradual or sudden onset of clinical signs, and duration of signs should be documented. Also documented should be a list of signs that were noted (including any signs that have since resolved), the severity of signs, and any treatments administered by a caretaker or veterinarian (as well as response to treatment). The results of any diagnostic procedures (laboratory tests, diagnostic imaging, etc.) should also be obtained. If necessary, a trip to the animal's environment (home, farm, zoo, etc.) should be made to investigate potential hazards (e.g., toxic plants, questionable feeds) that might not have come up in the initial questioning (Galey & Hall, 1990). Physical examination of the affected animal(s) along with necropsy of any dead animals should be undertaken, with thorough documentation of both normal and abnormal findings.

Sample Collection and Handling

Proper sample collection, handling, and storage is essential for a successful veterinary forensic toxicology investigation (Millo et al., 2008; Gwaltney-Brant, 2016). For cases that end up in court, the most common reason for inadmissibility of toxicology results is mismanagement of samples (Galey & Hall, 1990). Consultation with a veterinary toxicologist at a veterinary diagnostic laboratory prior to sample collection can aid in determining which samples to collect, how to store them for shipping, and what analyses may be the most fruitful. Sample containers ideally should be glass or hard plastic, as soft plastics may leach compounds that may interfere with analysis; soft plastic baggies can be used for short-term transport if necessary but samples should be moved into more appropriate containers as soon as possible. Plants, mushrooms, and feed samples should be stored in paper or other breathable packaging to discourage mold formation. Liquids can be stored in glass bottles (Mason jars work well), and volatile compounds should be placed in airtight containers such as unused paint cans, or glass bottles with Teflon or metal foil-lined lids. Liquids can be collected via pipettes or syringes but should be transferred to a capped container to prevent spillage; samples should not be stored in capped syringes with needles due to potential for fluid loss and injury to personnel handling syringes (Gwaltney-Brant, 2016). Each container should be labeled with the patient's name, case number, date and time of collection, and type of sample (e.g., urine, heart), and a chain of custody log should be maintained for all samples. Each tissue sample should have its own container, and the sample collector should work with one tissue/organ at a time to avoid cross-contamination of tissues. Knives and other sectioning equipment should be cleaned, and gloves should be changed before working on a new type of tissue. Sufficient quantities of sample must be collected in order to perform multiple analyses. Each analysis will utilize sample, so it is possible to run out of sample before a diagnosis is obtained. In addition, for civil or criminal cases, the opposing party may wish to have samples provided to them so that they can have their own analysis performed (Levine, 2010; Murphy, 2012). So, it is always best to err on the side of collecting more than you need (it can be discarded later), because once thrown out, you cannot get it back. Table 14.2 lists samples and amounts to collect for analysis.

Types of Toxicology Analytical Methods

Once samples in a forensic toxicology case have been collected, they must be handled, secured, and stored as any other evidence, with chain of custody documentation maintained from the time of collection until delivery to the analytical laboratory (that will have their own internal protocols to maintain chain of custody) (Murphy, 2012; Gwaltney-Brant, 2016). Analytical testing of samples can be expensive, especially if the identity of the toxicant has not been determined and multiple tests are run without a rational plan. Therefore, the information obtained from the history, clinical signs, response to therapy, diagnostic testing, and necropsy findings should be evaluated to determine the toxicants that are the most likely candidates. Consultation with a veterinary toxicologist can be very helpful in whittling down the list of potential toxicants; the toxicologist should also be able to provide guidance as to which analytical methods are likely to be the most fruitful.

Unlike life in television land, where one machine is able to identify multiple poisons from a single sample in less than the hour it takes the television show to run, the real world of toxicology must utilize a variety of techniques in order to identify and quantitate toxicants in samples. There is no such thing as a "tox screen" that will pick up any poison—the screening test offered by diagnostic laboratories (e.g., heavy metal screen, convulsant screen) are actually just tests for each individual substance that are bundled together as a convenience to the person requesting the analysis. Each analysis that is performed ultimately destroys some of the collected sample, and running multiple tests can rapidly deplete the sample (as well as the client's wallet). The turnaround time for an analysis can be as short as a few hours or as long as several days or even weeks depending on the type of analysis performed. Samples being analyzed must be processed to isolate the fraction of the sample that contains the suspected toxicant. Tissue digestion, incubation, and the analysis itself can take hours or days, all of which add to the turnaround time.

Analysis of toxicology samples can be as simple as visualization of, say, a sample of feed for toxic plants or as elaborate as combining several sophisticated techniques as mass spectrometry and liquid chromatography (Levine, 2010). Physical inspection includes both visual and olfactory

Table 14.2 Sample collection for toxicology

Sample	Amount	Storage	Analysis
All major organs	Multiple small samples	10% buffered neutral formalin (or other fixative)	Histopathology
Liver	300 grams	Chilled, frozen	Heavy metals, pesticides, pharmaceuticals
Kidney	300 grams	Chilled, frozen	Heavy metals, ethylene glycol (Ca:P ratio), pharmaceuticals, plant toxins
Brain	½ (remainder for histopathology and infectious disease)	Chilled, frozen	Sodium, acetylcholinesterase activity, pesticides
Fat	300 grams	Chilled, frozen	Organochlorines, PCBs, bromethalin
Ocular fluid	Entire eye	Chilled	Potassium, nitrates, magnesium, ammonia
Retina	Entire eye	Chilled	Acetylcholinesterase activity
Lung/spleen	100 grams	Chilled, frozen	Paraquat, barbiturates
Lung	Entire lobe/lung with bronchi/trachea tied off	Chilled, placed in airtight container	Volatile agents
Injection site	100 grams	Chilled	Pharmaceuticals
Whole blood	5–10 mL	Chilled	Heavy metals, acetylcholinesterase activity, insecticides
Serum	5–10 mL	Chilled	Some metals, pharmaceuticals, alkaloids, electrolytes
Urine	5–100 mL	Chilled	Pharmaceuticals, heavy metals, alkaloids
Milk	30 mL	Chilled	Organochlorines, PCBs
Ingesta/feces	Up to 500 grams	Chilled	Metals, plants, mycotoxins, other organic toxicants
Hair	3–5 grams	Dry, store in paper	Pesticides, some heavy metals
Feed	1 kg composite	Dry: Store in paper Wet: Freeze	Ionophores, salt, pesticides, heavy metals, ionophores, mycotoxins, nutrients, botulism
Plant	Entire	Dry; press between sheets of newspaper	Alkaloids, glycosides, pesticides
Water	1–2 Liters	Glass containers	Pesticides, heavy metals, salt, nitrates, blue-green algae
Soil	500 grams	Glass containers	Pesticides, heavy metals
Insects, insect casings	3–5 grams (~100 maggots), include representatives from all life cycles present	Live: Place ½ in vial (no more than 1 maggot thick at bottom) with moist paper towel and raw meat; other ½ place in 75%–90% ethanol or 50% isopropyl in glass vials Dead, casings: Glass vials	Live: To forensic entomologist Dead: Toxicology testing depending on results of other testing; pharmaceuticals, heavy metals, other organic toxicants

Sources: Dinis-Olivera et al. (2010); Galey and Hall (1990); Millo et al. (2008).

evaluation of a sample, requiring little more than a pair of eyes +/− magnifying equipment. Visualization is used to identify toxic plants, toxic mushrooms, toxic algae, and gross contaminants in gastrointestinal contents, feeds, or other samples. Visualization is also used to determine some physical characteristics of samples or suspect materials, such as pH, dissolution in solvent, and density determination. Using olfaction to detect telltale odors from certain toxicants (e.g., the bitter almond odor to cyanide or the rotten fish odor to zinc phosphide) is another component of physical evaluation. Bioassays utilize living animals to aid in diagnosing poisoning cases, generally by exposing a normal animal to the suspect poison. Since they do not directly identify the poison, bioassays have little use in forensic toxicology, and they are rarely performed anymore except to detect the presence of botulinum toxin. Chemical reactions may be used as qualitative tests to indicate the presence of certain compounds, for example, the formation of Prussian blue indicates the presence of cyanide. However, these tests do not tell us how much of the toxicant is present, and further quantitative testing is required to determine whether toxic levels are present. Spectroscopy and spectrophotometry are used to detect compounds in liquid samples based on characteristic wavelength signatures. Immunoassays utilize antibodies to identify and quantitate compounds by means of a color change on a test strip or test well. Because they are relatively inexpensive, immunoassays are frequently used as screening tests, but any results would need to be confirmed by more robust techniques as they are prone to false positives. Mass spectrometry ionizes a compound down to its component atoms then separates the ions based on their mass-to-charge ratios. The mass spectra output gives the mass and relative amounts of the different ions, allowing determination of its chemical formula but not its chemical structure. Mass spectrometry is a rapid method that can be used alone to detect metals such as lead and arsenic, but it is when mass spectrometry is combined with chromatography techniques that its real power shines. Chromatography is commonly used to detect drugs, pesticides, and other organic compounds. Chromatography separates compounds based on their chemical properties, and the separated compounds can then be analyzed for their unique chemical properties. Chromatography may be performed on chemicals in liquids (high-performance liquid chromatography [HPLC]), solids (thin-layer chromatography [TLC]), and gas matrices (gas chromatography [GC]). GC followed by mass spectrometry is currently considered to be the gold standard of chemical analysis (Levine, 2010).

Interpretation of analytical results is an essential component of veterinary forensic toxicology (Ensley, 1995). With modern analytical equipment able to detect compounds down to the parts per trillion (ppt) level, it is now possible to detect the presence of compounds well below levels that are expected to be associated with toxicosis (Gwaltney-Brant, 2016). For instance, anticoagulant rodenticides such as brodifacoum are stored in the liver, so if a dog's liver is tested and shown to have detectable concentrations of brodifacoum, that does not necessarily mean that the dog died of brodifacoum toxicosis. It does tell us the dog was exposed to brodifacoum at some point before the sample was taken, but we would have to compare the amount found in the dog's liver with the amount that would be expected in a toxicosis. We would also have to determine if the clinical syndrome that the dog experienced was consistent with brodifacoum toxicosis, which causes uncontrollable bleeding. So, just because a poison is found in a tissue does not necessarily mean that a toxicosis occurred. Most veterinary diagnostic laboratories have developed nomograms of normal and toxic concentrations for common veterinary toxicants; assistance with interpretation of diagnostic laboratory results is another area where consultation with a veterinary toxicologist can be beneficial.

Toxicants Commonly Used in Intentional Animal Poisonings

Although there are literally thousands of potential poisons available for those who wish to maliciously poison animals, most poisoners aren't terribly knowledgeable about poisons, and they tend to use what they know (Merck, 2013; Gwaltney-Brant, 2016). So, it's not surprising that the most common poisons used in malicious animal poisonings are compounds that are fairly

Table 14.3 Toxicants associated with intentional poisoning of animals

Toxicant	Species Most Commonly Affected	Mechanism	Effects	Best Samples
Anticoagulant rodenticides (e.g., brodifacoum, bromadiolone, difethialone)	All	Interference with vitamin K recycling results in decreased formation of vitamin K-dependent coagulation factors	Uncontrolled hemorrhage, anemia	Liver (anticoagulant screen)
Acetaminophen	Dogs, cats	Toxic metabolites cause injury to liver and red blood cells	Vomiting, diarrhea, icterus, weakness, difficulty breathing, chocolate-colored gums	Plasma, serum, urine
Alcohols	Dogs	Cause central nervous system depression	Disorientation, vomiting, incoordination, coma, seizures	Blood, urine
Amphetamine, methamphetamine, pseudoephedrine	Dogs	Overstimulation of nervous and cardiovascular systems	Agitation, hyperactivity, heart arrhythmias, seizures	Blood, plasma, urine, stomach content
Arsenic	Livestock	Damages capillaries, causes kidney damage	Acute collapse, anemia, hemorrhagic vomiting and/or diarrhea, kidney failure	Gastrointestinal contents, urine, liver, kidney
Blister beetle (*Epicauta* spp.)	Horses	Vesicant action in gastrointestinal and urinary tracts	Acute death, hemorrhage of epithelium of gastrointestinal tract, urinary tract	Urine, intestinal content, examination of hay for insect
Bromethalin rodenticide	Dogs, cats	Interference with cellular pumps in nervous system causing edema	Ascending paresis, paralysis, weakness, seizures, coma	Brain, adipose tissue, liver, kidney
Caffeine	Dogs	Overstimulation of nervous and cardiovascular systems	Agitation, hyperactivity, heart arrhythmias, seizures	Stomach content, serum
Cardiac glycoside–containing plants Oleander (*Nerium oleander*) Foxglove (*Digitalis* spp.)	All	Alters cell membrane transport pumps, resulting in cell dysfunction	Vomiting, diarrhea, acute heart failure	Gastrointestinal contents
Cholecalciferol rodenticides	Dogs, cats	Causes elevated blood calcium levels, which result in mineralization of soft tissues	Increased thirst, increased urination, kidney failure	Kidney
Ethylene glycol	Dogs, cats	Initial alcohol effects, then kidney damage	Disorientation, vomiting, coma, seizures, kidney failure	Serum, kidney

(Continued)

Table 14.3 (*Continued*) Toxicants associated with intentional poisoning of animals

Toxicant	Species Most Commonly Affected	Mechanism	Effects	Best Samples
Ionophores	Horses, dogs, occasionally other livestock	Damages heart and/or skeletal muscle (species specific)	Acute heart failure in horses, other livestock; weakness, paresis, paralysis in dogs	Stomach content, feed samples
Metaldehyde	Dogs	May alter nerve conduction	Tremors, seizures, hyperthermia	Stomach content, serum, liver, urine
Nicotine	Dogs	Overstimulation of nicotinic nerves early, then neuromuscular blockade	Agitation, hypersalivation, vomiting, diarrhea, tremors, seizures followed by weakness, progressive paralysis	Stomach contents, blood, urine, kidney, liver
Organochlorine insecticides	All	Overstimulation of nerve conduction	Tremors, seizures	Adipose tissue
Organophosphate and carbamate insecticides	All	Overstimulation of muscarinic and nicotinic nerve receptors	Hypersalivation, vomiting, excessive bronchial secretions, diarrhea, lacrimation, tremors, weakness, seizures	Brain, retina
Paraquat	Dogs	Damages cells in lung, resulting in progressive lung injury and fibrosis; corrosive	Oral, esophageal or gastric ulcers; progressive respiratory failure (over days to weeks)	Urine, lung
Red maple (*Acer rubrum*)	Horses	Damages red blood cells	Weakness, collapse, anemia, death; secondary kidney injury	Gastric contents
Selenium	All	Depletes cell metabolic enzymes resulting in acute cardiovascular collapse	Weakness, tetanic spasms, respiratory depression, heart failure	Blood, liver, kidney
Strychnine	Dogs, cats	Loss of inhibitory function in spinal cord results in uncontrollable muscle activity	Convulsions, respiratory failure	Stomach contents, liver, bile, kidney
White snakeroot (*Ageratina altisimmia*, formerly *Eupatorium rugosum*)	Livestock	Damages heart and skeletal muscle	Acute heart failure, weakness, death	Urine
Yew (*Taxus* spp.)	Horses, dogs	Damages heart muscle cells in horses; causes central nervous stimulation in dogs	Horses: Acute heart failure Dogs: Seizures	Gastric contents
Zinc phosphide rodenticide	All	Converts to corrosive and toxic phosphine gas	Restlessness, agitation, abdominal pain, tremors, seizures, coma	Serum, liver, kidney, pancreas

Source: Gwaltney-Brant (2016)

widely known to be toxic, such as rodenticides and insecticides. More sophisticated poisoners might be aware of the toxicity of other compounds such as acetaminophen, caffeine, or nicotine. Most poisons used are compounds that are easily obtained and common in the environment; for companion animals, that might mean rodenticides, insecticides, snail killers, ethylene glycol, caffeine, nicotine, and human medications such as antidepressants or acetaminophen. Livestock poisonings commonly involve agricultural pesticides and fertilizers, rodenticides, and feed additives that are readily accessible in an agricultural setting. In attempts to collect on insurance, valuable horses have been intentionally poisoned with "natural" toxins such as blister beetles and yew plants in attempts to make the toxicosis appear accidental. There do seem to be some regional tendencies throughout the country, probably reflecting relative availability of the toxicants in these areas; for example, strychnine is a common malicious poison used in the U.S. Pacific Northwest, while aldicarb, a highly toxic carbamate insecticide, is often used in the southeastern United States (Gwaltney-Brant, 2012). A brief synopsis of some of the more commonly used toxicants to poison animals is listed in Table 14.3.

References

Desta, B., Maldonado, G., Reid, H., Puschner, B., Maxwell, J., Agasan, A., Humphreys, L., and Holt, T. 2011. Acute selenium toxicosis in polo ponies. *Journal of Veterinary Diagnostic Investigation*. 23(3):623–628.

Dinis-Olivera, R.J., Carvalho, F., Duarte, J.A., Remiao, F., Margues, A., Santos, A., and Magalhaes, T. 2010. Collection of biological samples in forensic toxicology. *Toxicology Mechimisms and Methods*. 20(7):363–414.

Dolder, L.K. 2013. Methylxanthines: Caffeine, theobromine, theophylline. In: Peterson, M.E., and Talcott, P.A., eds. *Small Animal Toxicology*. 3rd ed. St Louis, MO: Elsevier, pp. 647–652.

Eaton, D.L., and Gilbert, S.G. 2008. Principles of toxicology. In: Klaassen, C.D., ed. *Casarett and Doull's Toxicology, the Basic Science of Poisons*. 7th ed. New York, NY. McGraw-Hill. 11–43.

Ensley, F.D. 1995. Diagnostic and forensic toxicology. *Veterinary Clinics of North America: Equine*. 11(3):443–454.

Galey, F.D. and Hall, J.O. 1990. Field investigations in small animal toxicoses. *Veterinary Clinics of North America: Small Animal*. 20(2):283–291.

Gwaltney-Brant, S.M. 2012. Epidemiology of animal poisonings in the United States. In: Gupta, R.C., ed. *Veterinary Toxicology: Basic and Clinical Principles*. 2nd ed. San Diego, CA: Academic Press, pp. 80–87.

Gwaltney-Brant, S.M. 2016. Veterinary forensic toxicology. *Veterinary Pathology*. 53(5):1067–1077.

Lehman-McKeeman, L.D. 2008. Absorption, distribution and excretion of toxicants. In: Klaassen, C.D., ed. *Casarett and Doull's Toxicology, the Basic Science of Poisons*. 7th ed. New York, NY: McGraw-Hill, pp. 131–159.

Levine, B. 2010. *Principles of Forensic Toxicology*. 3rd ed. Washington, DC: AACC Press.

Merck, M.D. 2013. *Veterinary Forensics: Animal Cruelty Investigations*. 2nd ed. Ames, IA: Wiley-Blackwell.

Millo, T., Jaiswa, A.K., and Behera, C. 2008. Collection, preservation and forwarding of biological samples for toxicological analysis in medicolegal autopsy cases: A review. *Journal of Indian Academy of Forensic Medicine*. 30(2):96–100.

Murphy, M. 2012. Toxicology and the law. In: Gupta, R.C., ed. *Veterinary Toxicology:Basic and Clinical Principles*. 2nd ed. San Diego, CA: Academic Press, pp. 187–205.

Stroud, R.K. and Kuncir, F. 2005. Investigating wildlife poisonings cases. *International Game Warden Magazine*. Winter:8–13.

CHAPTER 15

ANIMAL ABUSE AND INTERPERSONAL VIOLENCE

Martha Smith-Blackmore

INTRODUCTION

Animal abuse has been found to be disproportionally present in situations of partner abuse, child physical abuse, child sexual abuse, and sibling abuse. In the domestic setting, pets can be used as weapons of terror and psychological abuse by an aggressive family member to exercise power and control over more vulnerable family members. However, animal abuse often occurs as part of a suite of antisocial behaviors, and animal abusers demonstrate an elevated risk of offending in both violent and nonviolent offenses, and not limited to the domestic setting (Walters, 2014).

The scope of this chapter is to explore the connection between crimes against animals and other forms of violent criminal behavior. It should be taken in the context of broad generalities and understandings of typical animal protection laws while acknowledging that there are localized differences.

DEFINING CRIME IN THE CONTEXT OF ANIMAL ABUSE

While veterinary forensic sciences may be applied in the context of civil litigation, the majority of veterinary forensic work is related to investigating and documenting suspected criminal harm to animals. In the study of animal abuse as a crime, what constitutes "crime" varies from one culture to another and what counts as crime in a single culture changes over time. Further, what constitutes criminal animal abuse depends on local statutory and case law, and the definition of "animal" within that context.

The discussion of defining crime emerged in the early 20th century. "The most precise and least ambiguous definition of crime is that which defines it as behavior which is prohibited by the criminal code. It follows that a criminal is a person who has behaved in some way prohibited by criminal law" (Michael, 1933). It may be further interpreted that crime is behavior or an act that is in violation of criminal law (statutory and case law), committed without defense or excuse, and penalized by the state as a felony or misdemeanor.

It can be agreed that crimes are a violation of conduct norms and they cause social injury. They often violate human rights and they may reflect forms of deviance. It may be most useful to consider crime as a sociological problem where patterns of crime arise from the interplay of political, economic, social, and ideological structures in society.

Considering that the concept of crime is difficult to define in a single context due to the wide variety of laws in various jurisdictions, crimes that impact animals are even more difficult to define. The formal purpose of criminal law is to protect individuals from the wrongdoing of others. Laws protecting animals against abuse exist in the moral code or chapters of law (reflecting that harming animals is an affront to our social sensibilities) and also in property crimes (reflecting that animals are property and we are to be protected from property losses). Animal abuse is often considered a form of interpersonal violence because animals are beings with distinct sentient experiences (Beirne, 2000).

HOW MUCH ANIMAL ABUSE IS OCCURRING IN OUR COMMUNITIES?

The measurement and tracking trends of crimes against animals is a difficult and a "not yet ready for prime time" task. There are scant but growing collections of official crime data, and there are also some measures of unofficial crime data. Official crime data are collected by the government and its official agencies such as the Federal Bureau of Investigation (FBI) and the Department of Justice (DOJ). Unofficial crime data are the nongovernmental data usually collected by private or independent agencies and researchers in a variety of methodologies.

Data Collection: It's Complicated

The Uniform Crime Report (UCR) is compiled each year from statistics collected by the FBI; one component of the UCR is the National Incident Based Reporting System (NIBRS). A much-heralded change in the collection of statistics related to animal abuse in NIBRS was the change of designation on animal cruelty from a Crime Against Property (Type B crime) to a Crime Against Society (Type A crime) in 2016. As a designated Crime Against Society, data related to an animal cruelty incident is collected when it is reported. In the property crimes category, data of an incident is only recorded when an arrest is made. The FBI's adoption of animal cruelty crime as a separate category in NIBRS acknowledges that animal maltreatment is associated with other offenses, and it is harmful to our society.

This change in reporting status to a Type A crime implies the FBI's adoption of the concept that nonhuman animals are in a category other than that of property and that animal cruelty crimes are important to investigate and to charge. NIBRS has four subcategories for incidents of animal cruelty: A, simple abuse or neglect; I, intentional abuse or torture; O, organized animal abuse or fighting; and S, animal sexual abuse.

Prior to 2016, animal abuse data was collected in an aggregated "other" category, so there is no national reference database on the incidence or prevalence of animal abuse. The preliminary data are only just being reported.

It is important to note that only law enforcement agencies with automated data submission through a records management software system (RMS) and an Originating Agency Identification (ORI) number supply data to NIBRS. An ORI is a unique nine-character identifier that the FBI's National Crime Information Center (NCIC) has assigned to each law enforcement agency. It is estimated that approximately half of animal control offices (ACOs) are located within the jurisdiction of a police department or a sheriff's office with an ORI. With the various placements of the animal control agencies, the training, investigatory, and arrest powers of animal service officers also vary widely within and across states.

ACOs are generally employed by municipalities, while humane law enforcement (HLE) departments are employed by private animal welfare organizations. HLE officers may have peace officer rights and responsibilities through a contract, memorandum of understanding (MOU) or other arrangement. In many cases, ACOs and HLE departments lack an RMS necessary to submit data directly to NIBRS and will in fact also require an MOU.

In communities where animal control is not within the public safety department or where animal cruelty investigations are delegated to HLE officers, the data are not automatically collected. Just 1126 incidents of animal cruelty were reported to NIBRS in 2016, and 40% of those were made in Delaware. This is because the HLE departments in Delaware are designated with an ORI number and have automated data submission. By 2021, NIBRS is scheduled to become the national standard for crime reporting in all states, and MOUs are encouraged to help non–ORI-based animal cruelty investigators submit data (DeSousa, 2017).

Who Investigates Allegations of Animal Abuse?

Animal abuse investigations are vital because animal maltreatment is a co-occurring and central aspect of interpersonal violence. However, a variety of agencies or authorities may respond to reports of animal cruelty in different communities, and there may be a failure to understand the roles among agencies. Law enforcement, animal control, town animal inspectors, the department of agriculture, and nonprofit organizations with police powers have a variety of rights and responsibilities with regard to allegations of animal maltreatment, depending on individual jurisdictions.

Because of a lack of clarity in reporting and response, animal victims sometimes do not benefit from an investigation, and their abusers may not be brought to justice. There is no uniform, reliable way to report animal cruelty and know that the case will be fully and appropriately investigated.

Reporting animal cruelty, abuse, and neglect is complicated. There are no national or statewide systems. Contrary to common understanding, local humane societies or societies for the prevention of cruelty to animals (SPCAs) are not branches or affiliates of any national organization. Each local animal welfare organization is independent, with its own board of directors, and law enforcement powers range from full to none. Many city or county animal control or animal services officers are empowered to enforce cruelty laws, but many are not—and many are limited in the scope of which laws or species they are allowed to assist. Individuals wishing to report allegations of animal cruelty are encouraged to call 911 and also to follow up with the local responsible agency. The National Link Coalition maintains a database of local responsible agencies organized by state and community (Arkow, 2018).

Not All Crime Is Reported, Not All Reported Crimes Are Solved

There is a prevailing "wisdom" that is often repeated, that police or prosecutors "don't care" about animal abuse. There are barriers to the investigation and prosecution of all types of crime, and animal abuse crimes are no different. In an annual survey, the Bureau of Justice Statistics (BJS) victims of crime are asked whether they reported that crime to police. In 2016, only 42% of the violent crime tracked by BJS was reported to police.

Most of the crimes that are reported to police are not solved, at least using an FBI measure known as the "clearance rate." That's the percentage of cases each year that are closed, or "cleared," through the arrest, charging, and referral of a suspect for prosecution. In 2016, police cleared 46% of violent crimes that were reported to them (Gramlich, 2018). In the future, more robust statistical analysis of crimes against animals will allow comparison of crimes against animals in the context of all crime.

Beyond Broken Windows

The "broken windows" theory of crime prevention stems from the work of two criminologists, George Kelling and James Wilson, who suggested that minor disorders, like vandalism and panhandling, acted as a gateway to more serious crime. By focusing on smaller offenses, often referred to as "quality of life" crimes, Kelling and Wilson proposed that violent crime and other undesirable activity would decrease.

The broken windows theory of policing has fallen out of favor, partially because of disproportionate enforcement. Later research found flaws in the broken windows theory of policing, finding that targeting minor crimes harms poor people, as well as minorities. The broken windows theory of policing led to a disproportionate number of drug arrests for blacks and Hispanics.

Selectively directing resources to crimes of violence, whether against people or animals, may have an interrupting effect that is more effective than a focus on petty or property crime. "It is definitely time for law enforcement to stop focusing on minor disorder and to target, instead, serious crimes involving guns and physical injury" (Harcourt, 2005). When animal abuse is approached as a crime of interpersonal violence it is a crime involving physical injury.

THE LINK VERSUS THE MESH

The association between animal abuse and interpersonal violence is commonly referred to as "The Link." Animal cruelty may precede, coincide with, or follow a broad range of antisocial behaviors, including domestic violence and elder and child abuse. Rather than the graduation or escalation hypothesis which proposes that animal cruelty precedes subsequent acts of human violence, a more accurate description of animal abuse may be one of generalized deviance. Although animal abuse and interpersonal violence are correlated with one another, it varies as to which is seen first in a setting where both are encountered.

Multiple forms of social deviance are potentially interrelated, at various ages; childhood animal abuse may relate to adult offending without those two variables being connected in a unique or distinctive way that can be identified with certainty in any given situation. Therefore, the nature of the relationship of animal cruelty and interpersonal violent offending is "general rather than specific" (Walters, 2014). It can be agreed that a "general mesh" of antisocial violence exists and is expressed in individual offenders to varying degrees (Levitt, 2016).

Animal Abuse and Its Relationship to Serial and Mass Murders

Sadistic serial killers appear to commit animal abuse commonly, at a rate approaching 90%, if all kinds of animal abuse, not just the sadistic hands-on variety, are considered (Levin, Arluke 2009). Perpetrators of mass shootings frequently have both domestic violence and animal abuse in their histories.

In school shootings, 43% of the perpetrators commit animal cruelty before massacres, and the cruelty is usually directed against anthropomorphized species (dogs and cats) in an up-close manner (Arluke & Madafis, 2014). In 1997, Luke Woodham, a sophomore at Pearl High School, in a suburb of Jackson, Michigan, opened fire on classmates with a hunting rifle, killing two girls and wounding seven other students. He also stabbed and bludgeoned his mother to death earlier that morning. Investigators later found Woodham's description of torture and killing of the family dog "Sparkle" with an accomplice in his journal. He wrote about beating her inside a plastic bag and setting it on fire. He referred to this incident as his "first kill"; he wrote "I will never forget the howl she made. It sounded almost human. We laughed and hit her hard" (Sack, 1997).

In 1998, 15 year old Kip Kinkel shot his parents to death before emptying three firearms at his classmates in Thurston High School, Springfield, Oregon, leaving 1 dead and 26 injured. His attacks on animals also illustrated the up close and personal variety of animal abuse; he allegedly decapitated cats, dissected live squirrels, blew up cows, set a live cat on fire, and put firecrackers in gophers and cats (Tallichet & Hensley, 2004). Albert DeSalvo (the "Boston strangler"), David Berkowitz (the "Son of Sam"), and Jeffrey Dahmer all reported animal torture as their first act of violence.

The desire to exercise power and control over the lives of others seems to be shared by sadistic serial killers and school shooters; both decide who lives and who dies. In so doing, they get to be the ones who regulate the degree of pain and suffering experienced by their victims. Some cases of animal cruelty and human-oriented violence are similarly motivated: compensating for the perpetrator's feelings of powerlessness and vulnerability, imparting a sense of strength and superiority (Kellert & Felthouse, 1985).

Animal Abuse and Its Relationship to Domestic Violence

The connection between violence to people and animals is not only found in extreme examples. Everyday domestic violence is also associated with violence to animals. Threats to pets, or their actual harm, are commonly used to control domestic violence victims (Walker, 1984). In one study of women in a domestic violence shelter, 71% of pet-owning women reported their partners had threatened to kill or actually killed their pets (Ascione, 1998).

Youth participation in animal cruelty is a significant marker for the development of aggressive behavior (Merz-Perez). Among juveniles who were referred to an arson intervention group, those who were cruel to animals were more likely to repeat fire setting (Slavkin, 2001).

Animal Abuse as a Marker of Antisocial Behavior

The association between crimes of violence against people and animals provides an avenue to identifying violent actors in our communities. Abusers exercising power and control over any vulnerable being through violence and intimidation are flagging themselves as threats. Violence is not limited to crimes against people, and it does not have any single socioeconomic niche. Animal abuse laws exist in every jurisdiction, and suspected violations of these laws deserve investigation in and of their own right.

When a person dies in questioned circumstances, their body will be thoroughly examined by a medical examiner whose services are supplied by the state or other governmental office. When it comes to investigating the death or harm to animals in questioned circumstances, there is no equivalent office to turn to for investigative support. Veterinarians contributing to the investigation of allegations of animal cruelty are helping to protect both animal welfare and human safety. Indeed, animal care professionals, animal control officers, and humane law enforcement officers all have roles to play in the prevention, identification, and treatment of interpersonal violence.

References

Arkow, P. 2018. How Do I Report Suspected Abuse? NationalLinkCoalition.org, National Link Coalition, March 19. nationallinkcoalition.org/how-do-i-report-suspected-abuse.

Arluke, A., Madfis, E. 2014. Animal abuse as a warning sign of school massacres. *Homicide Studies*. 18(1), 7–22.

Ascione, F.R. 1998. Battered women's responses of their partners' and their children's cruelty to animals. *Journal of Emotional Abuse*. 1(1).

Beirne, P. and Messerschmidt, J. eds. 2000. What Is Crime? *Criminology*. Westview Press.

DeSousa, D. 2017. *NIBRS User Manual for Animal Control Officers and Humane Law Enforcement*. NIBRS User Manual–National Animal Care & Control Association, Animal Welfare Institute, April 1. www.nacanet.org/?page=NIBRS_Manual

Gramlich, J. 2018. *5 Facts about Crime in the U.S.* Pew Research Center, January 30. www.pewresearch.org/fact-tank/2018/01/30/5-facts-about-crime-in-the-u-s/

Harcourt, B. 2005. Is broken windows policing broken? *Legal Affairs Magazine*. http://www.legalaffairs.org/webexclusive/debateclub_brokenwindows1005.msp

Kellert, S. R. and Felthous, A. R. 1985. Childhood cruelty toward animals among criminals and noncriminals. *Human Relations*. 38, 1113–1129.

Levin, J. and Arluke, A. 2009. Refining the link between animal abuse and subsequent violence. In A. Linzey (ed.), *The Link between Animal Abuse and Violence*. Eastbourne, UK: Sussex Academic Press.

Levitt, L., Patronek, G., and Grisso, T. 2016. *Animal Maltreatment: Forensic Mental Health Issues and Evaluations*. Oxford University Press.

Merz-Perez, L., Heide, K.J., and Silverman, I.J. 2001. Childhood cruelty to animals and subsequent violence against animals. *International Journal of Offender Therapy and Comparative Criminology*. 45, 556–573.

Michael, J. and Adler, M. 1933. *Crime, Law and Social Science*. New York: Harcourt, Brace & Co.

Sack, K. 1997. Grim Details Emerge in Teen-Age Slaying Case. *New York Times*, October 15.

Slavkin, M. 2001. Enuresis, firesetting, and cruelty to animals: Does the ego triad show predictive validity? *Adolescence*. 36(143), 461–466.

Tallichet, S. and Hensley, C. 2004. Exploring the link between recurrent acts of childhood and adolescent animal cruelty and subsequent violent crime. *Criminal Justice Review*. 2, 304–316.

Walker, L.E. 1984. *The Battered Woman Syndrome*. New York: Springer Publishing.

Walters, G. 2014. Testing the direct, indirect, and moderated effects of childhood animal cruelty on future aggressive and non-aggressive offending. *Aggressive Behavior*. 40(3), 238–249.

CHAPTER 16

ANIMAL NEGLECT AND ABUSE

Patricia Norris

DEFINITIONS OF ANIMAL NEGLECT AND ABUSE

Animal neglect and animal abuse are extensive and intertwined subjects. These two acts, or failures to act, often coexist and the line can blur in the application of the definition. Several definitions of animal neglect have been published. Most are variations of failure(s) of a caregiver to provide basic sustenance and care to an animal (Merck, 2013). The definition of basic sustenance can vary depending on local, state, or other governing body's ordinances, regulations and/or statutes. These regulations may include variations of the following: water; food appropriate for the life stage of the animal and/or their condition; environment that allows the animal to maintain a normal body temperature; sufficient space to engage in species-appropriate positions and activities; sanitation of living area(s), such as sufficient living space and sanitation so the animal is able to avoid contact with its waste; provision(s) of veterinary care appropriate for the medical condition of the animal; and grooming/farrier care appropriate for the hair coat/hooves of the animal.

Traditionally in industry literature, state statutes, and the media, the harming of an animal is labeled as "animal cruelty." The general concept is that an act inflicts pain and suffering onto the animal and that the act was intentional on the part of the perpetrator. The definition of animal cruelty used by the Uniform Crime Reporting System (UCRS) of the Federal Bureau of Investigation (FBI) in the National Incident Based Reporting System (NIBRS) is:

> Intentionally, knowingly or recklessly taking an action that mistreats or kills any animal without just cause, such as torturing, tormenting, mutilation, maiming, poisoning, or abandonment. (FBI)

When reporting animal crimes to the FBI, law enforcement agencies have four categories to choose from: simple/gross neglect, intentional abuse and torture, organized abuse (like dogfighting and cockfighting), and animal sexual abuse (FBI).

Some authors include the failure to provide for the emotional needs of animals (McMillan, 2005; Merck, 2013). The reasoning is that failure to provide for the emotional needs will cause stress and distress for the animal. Emotional needs would depend somewhat on the species. To date, emotional abuse has not been included in statutes as a criminal act in the United States, Canada, or the UK (Arkow et al., 2013).

While some definitions of animal cruelty focus on the effect of the act or failure to act on the animal or the actual act, Ascione focused on the behavior of the perpetrator. Ascione (1993) defined animal cruelty as, "Socially unacceptable behavior that intentionally causes unnecessary pain, suffering, or distress to and/or of an animal" (Brewster & Reyes, 2013). As the study of animal cruelty has evolved, there has been a movement for the terminology to mirror that of the child protection field. In the child protection field, abuse means maltreatment of the child regardless of the perpetrator's intention (Touroo, 2011). To that end, researchers are moving toward the use of the term "animal abuse." Ascione and Shapiro (2009) revised the terminology by defining "animal abuse" as "nonaccidental, socially unacceptable behavior that causes pain, suffering or distress to and/or death of an animal."

For the purposes of this chapter, the term "animal abuse" will be used instead of animal cruelty, as the word "abuse" can encompass all acts or failure(s) to act that causes discomfort, stress, distress, pain, and/or suffering on an animal regardless of the intent of the perpetrator.

ANIMAL NEGLECT

Animal neglect is the failure to provide for the basic needs of an animal. Which specific unmet need(s) constitute(s) a criminal act will depend on the applicable statutes and ordinances. This failure to act is often due to a person's or an animal owner's ignorance of the needs of the animal(s) or

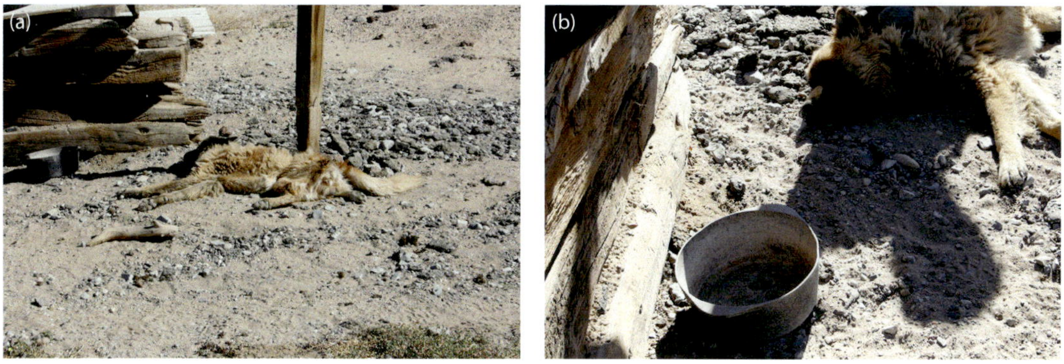

Figure 16.1 (a) Dog without water (b). Dry water bowl.

that person's lack of resources. Each case warrants careful examination of the intent and knowledge held by the person at the time of the incident. Often law enforcement, animal control officers, and/or veterinary personnel will approach an incidence of animal neglect more as a need to educate the person/owner than as a need to prosecute as a criminal act. Inherent to this assessment is the degree or extent of harm to the animal caused by the failure to provide appropriate care of the animal.

One common cause of animal neglect is the failure to provide sufficient food and/or water for the animal. Enforcement agencies commonly consider the failure to provide water and/or food to an animal to be willful neglect because most reasonable people understand that an animal will need sufficient food and water to maintain a reasonable degree of health (see Figure 16.1a,b). If the neglect is willful, malicious, and/or results in the animal suffering significant dehydration and/or starvation or the death of the animal, the case is often considered by the judicial system to reach the threshold of criminal abuse. In addition, a few localities recognize the concept of "malicious neglect," in which the argument is made that a reasonable person would know that the act, or the failure to act, would result in the suffering and/or death of the animal.

On the other hand, someone who has never owned a horse may not be knowledgeable about hoof care required by equines. Obviously, if the horse is assessed has having mildly to moderately overgrown hooves, education of the owner concerning the needs of the horse may be all that is appropriate for the case (see Figure 16.2a,b). Should this person continue to fail to provide proper hoof care or if the effect of the prolonged lack of hoof care results in severe lameness or inability to ambulate, then the case is more consistent with willful neglect.

In situations involving lack of access to resources, especially when due to transient or extraordinary circumstance, the regulatory authority will often assist the person in acquiring the necessary

Figure 16.2 (a) Overgrown horse hooves. (b) Overgrown horse hooves—second view.

resource(s) with the caveat that the owner is expected to provide for the animal in the future. Failure to continue to provide the necessary sustenance, once the person has been educated and/or provided access to the resource(s), may be considered deliberate neglect, crossing the line into abuse.

As with many animal crimes, discovering the intent of the owner (or responsible person) is more a responsibility for the enforcement agency than it is for the person providing the veterinary assessment of the animal. The veterinary assessment of the animal contributes in large part to determining the criminal aspect of a case of neglect, but it is not the sole deciding factor. Other contributors include the definition of animal cruelty/abuse for that locality and the findings of the remainder of the investigation. In other words, the "totality of the circumstance" decides whether an act or failure to act constitutes a criminal act.

A more complex variation of animal neglect is seen in hoarding cases. These animals may be provided with some food, some water (which may or may not be potable), and some veterinary care. However, the living conditions are such that the care of the individual animal is severely lacking. Hoarding as a specialized type of animal neglect/abuse is discussed in Chapter 13.

ANIMAL ABUSE

The prosecution of a case of animal abuse and/or neglect depends on the specific language of statutes that are under the jurisdiction of the enforcement/regulatory agency. These statutes vary tremendously depending on locality. These statutes commonly use the term "animal cruelty" instead of "animal abuse," reflecting the era in which they were adopted by states and provinces. These statutes commonly center on the prohibition of an act inflicted upon an animal which would cause the animal to suffer unnecessary harm. Language contained in many of the statutes may also consider the intentionality of the act. This language often appears to be an attempt to separate intentional abuse from inadvertent harm.

Legal definitions vary by state or locality and may list very specific acts such as burning, drowning, torturing, tormenting, and so on. The definition of animal cruelty or abuse may also include vague language such as "overdrive" or "overload." When the legal definition is vague, it is the prosecutor's decision, based on the findings of the investigation and examination of the animal, if a specific act or failure to act rises to the level of torment, torture, overload, and so on. The relevance of where the act, and the suffering it inflicts, falls on the spectrum of "torment" to "torture" is that, for many localities, "torment" is used to describe crimes classified as misdemeanors, whereas "torture" is often restricted to crimes charged as felonies.

Legal definitions often contain several exclusions. The most common exclusions are hunting, veterinary procedures, standard agricultural practices, and certain pest control actions. Depending on the locality (state, province, etc.), certain species may be excluded. For example, in New Mexico, insects and reptiles are excluded in the definition of animals (Animal Legal Defense Fund and the Michigan State Animal Legal and Historical Center). Therefore, if a person harms a collection of snakes, the crime of animal cruelty cannot be charged, but another crime such as destruction of property might be allowed as the snake collection was considered property of the owner. References such as Animal Protection Laws of the United States of America and Canada (Animal Legal Defense Fund and the Michigan State Animal Legal and Historical Center) provide updated information on statutes for the United States and Canada.

Again, the role of the person supplying the veterinary forensic services for these cases is to provide a complete, detailed, unbiased, fully documented evaluation of the animal, so the judicial system can determine the presence or absence of a crime. In the case of a live animal, this live evidence is subject to change. A very important piece of the evaluation and documentation may be, depending on the nature of the case, the change of the animal's condition over time. This will be discussed further in the section on Animal Assessment of Animal Neglect and Abuse Cases.

Society's Concern with Animal Abuse Cases

Animal abuse is of significant concern to most of today's societies. This concern is reflected in the attention that these cases receive from the public and the media. Particularly disturbing to society are acts of intentional abuse in which there is deliberate abuse, torture, or killing. Based on the reported association between animal abuse and interpersonal violence (commonly referred to as "The Link"), there is a legitimate fear that these perpetrators are a danger to society now and in the future.

Animal cruelty was added to the *Diagnostic and Statistical Manual of Mental Disorders* (DSM) in 1987 (DSM III-R). Animal cruelty was listed as diagnostic of conduct disorder in the list for "destruction of property." In later revisions, MDSM-IV (1994) and DSM-V (2013)—animal cruelty is listed as "associated with violence against others."

Researchers have noted the connection between serial killers and their prior acts of animal abuse. Also noted is the common history of previous acts of animal abuse and juveniles who commit school shootings. Animal abuse also occurs in the context of domestic violence, elder abuse, and child abuse as a method of the abuser to manipulate and control the victim. Domestic violence and its link with animal abuse are discussed in Chapter 15.

As a result of the recognition of the link between animal abuse and other crimes of violence, cross-training of animal control officers, child protective service workers, adult protective service workers, and others who may encounter victims of violence is becoming more common.

Types of Animal Abuse

There are several classifications of animal abuse. They include but not are limited to physical abuse, emotional abuse, sexual abuse, neglect, abandonment, organized abuse (animal fighting), and ritualistic abuse.

Physical abuse is what most people think of when they hear of incidents of animal abuse or animal cruelty. It is the act of causing direct harm to an animal by hitting or kicking an animal or inflicting other types of blunt force trauma, sharp force trauma such as the cutting or stabbing of an animal, shooting an animal with a gun or arrow, burning, drowning, suffocating, or other similar act. Typically, physical abuse results in the diagnosis of "nonaccidental injury."

Emotional abuse was introduced in the previous section of this chapter. Conditions that may be considered emotional abuse include:

1. Keeping a social animal (one that typically lives in a pack or herd) in isolation
2. Keeping an animal in a small space such that it cannot exhibit normal postures or activities
3. Housing an animal so that it cannot exercise or move about freely
4. Housing an animal in an environment devoid of mental stimulation appropriate for the age, sex, species, and traits of the animal
5. Maintaining an animal in an environment where it has no control or ability to avoid aversive conditions
6. Maintaining an animal in an environment in which it is repeatedly exposed to danger and has no escape from the unsafe conditions (McMillan, 2005; Merck, 2013)

Sexual abuse of animals is discussed in Chapter 6.

Abandonment is a legal definition that can vary by state or jurisdiction, but it typically means forsaking an animal without making any provisions for its care or needs. Abandonment can be considered as a type of animal abuse, or it may have its own criminal statute. For example: NC General Statute § 14–361.1 Abandonment of Animals states: "Any person being the owner or possessor, or having charge or custody of an animal, who willfully and without justifiable excuse abandons the animal is guilty of a Class 2 misdemeanor."

Organized abuse refers to arranged fighting of animals. This is typically dogfighting and cockfighting but there are other types of animal fights. This subject is discussed in Chapter 13.

Ritualistic abuse is a form of abuse in which animals are mutilated, tortured, and/or killed as part of a cultural or religious observance or practice. Some religions that may involve animal abuse include Brujeria, Palo Mayombe, Neopaganism, Satanism, Santeria, Voodoo, Vooduon, Wicca, and Witchcraft (Touroo, 2011).

ASSESSMENT OF AN ANIMAL(S) FOR A POTENTIAL ANIMAL ABUSE OR NEGLECT CASE

General Considerations

The general assessment of live animals as evidence is discussed in Chapter 2. These general principles apply to assessment of animals for a neglect and/or abuse case: (1) the animal(s) should be uniquely identified and that identification should follow the animal for the entire case; (2) the animal should be examined by a licensed veterinarian in good standing; (3) the chain of custody for the live evidence must be maintained as well as for any sample or test result that comes from that live evidence; (4) the animal should be reevaluated periodically, preferably by the same veterinarian; (5) the documentation of the examination should be compliant with the standard set by the veterinary regulatory authority; (6) the documentation should be consistent between the evaluations; and (7) live and non-live evidence is to be kept secure for the duration of the case.

Special Considerations for Neglect/Abuse

Ancillary Testing

The physical examination results in neglect/abuse cases are often very revealing and graphic. However, quite often, important information beneficial to the case can be obtained with ancillary testing (Ettinger & Feldman, 2000).

The advantages of ancillary testing include: (1) completeness and defensibility of the evaluation, and (2) more thorough understanding of the extent of the harm done to the animal by the neglect/abuse. The expense of ancillary testing can be prohibitive when the cost of a case is being borne by an agency with limited resources, especially in large-scale cases. However, even if just the basic tests can be performed, the results can be invaluable to the judicial system (author's personal experience).

Depending on the type of presentation, typical ancillary tests for an animal abuse and/or neglect case may include complete blood cell count (CBC), serum chemistry, heartworm test, fecal analysis, skin scraping, and radiographs (overviews of entire animal and specific views of affected areas) (see Figure 16.3a–c). Specific findings may warrant additional testing. Abnormalities in these tests should be monitored and followed during the animal's recovery.

As these animals are live evidence, all samples and test results are considered evidence. Therefore, the samples and results should be handled with an appropriate chain of custody and with the defense being allowed access to review. All test results and notes pertaining to such are discoverable for the court case.

Body Condition Scoring

Body condition scores (BCS) and scoring systems are detailed in Chapter 1. A BCS should be assessed and documented for every animal involved in a neglect or abuse case. This score should be reassessed at each subsequent evaluation. The initial BCS can indicate the effect the neglect or abuse had on the animal. Equally important to the judicial system is the change and/or return to normal BCS of the animal (see Figure 16.4a,b). Documentation of the time and intervention(s) necessary for the animal to return to normal assists the prosecuting authority and judge/jury in understanding the severity of the neglect and/or abuse.

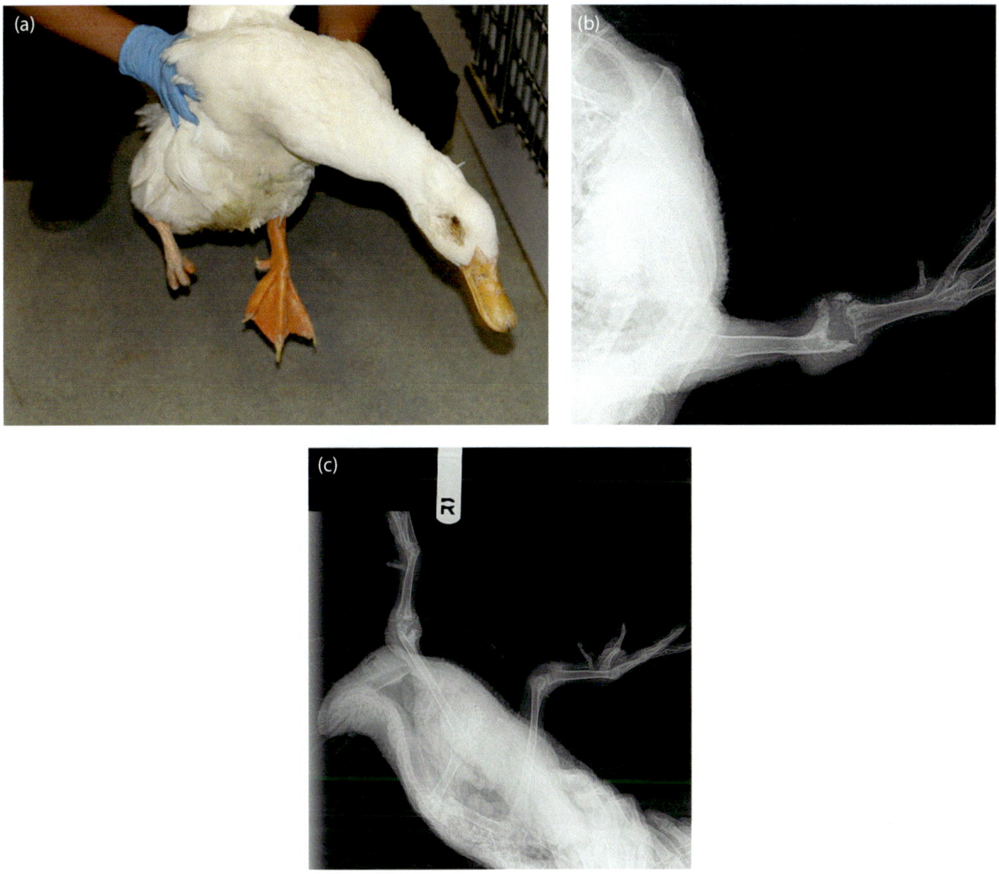

Figure 16.3 (a) Duck with chronic injury. (b,c) Radiographs of an injured duck.

Pain Scale Scoring

The veterinarian's ability to assess the pain the animal is experiencing, document the assessment in the case report, and articulate this information to the judicial agencies is critical to the neglect and/or abuse case. The veterinarian should be knowledgeable in the general indicators of pain in animals and for those specific to the species of animals involved in the case. The evaluation of the animal

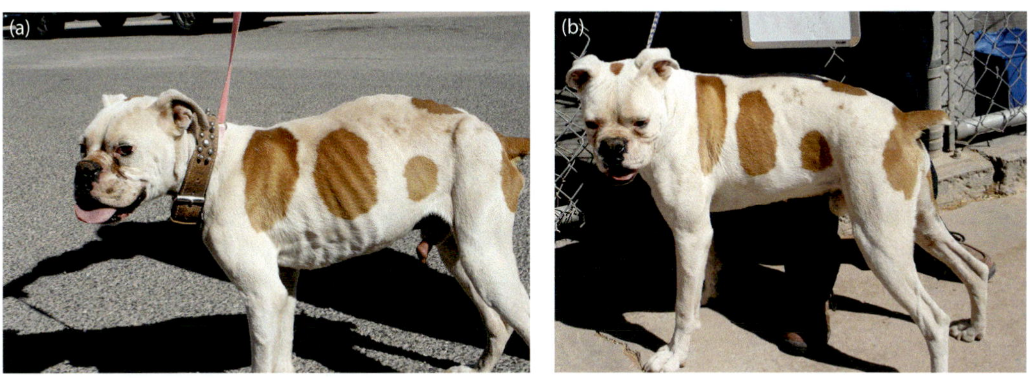

Figure 16.4 (a) Emaciated Boxer-type dog, initial examination photograph. (b) Emaciated Boxer-type dog, follow-up examination photograph.

within its environment and then during the physical examination should note pain indicators such as attitude, facial expressions, body posture, willingness to move, reluctance to move, sit, or lie down, restlessness, withdrawal or reluctance to interact with others of the same species and/or humans, aggression, bite attempts when touched, vocalization, under- or over-grooming, and/or self-mutilation. Several references that discuss pain assessment and management are listed at the end of this chapter.

Another valuable assessment tool that can be incorporated into the initial and subsequent physical examination of animals from a neglect or abuse case is pain scale scoring.

The extent of pain and suffering that an animal has endured due to the act of abuse, or failure to act, in animal neglect, is a core concern for the judicial system. While suffering and pain are not the same, pain is one component of suffering. Often, whether the judicial system considers an act to be "torment" (often charged as a misdemeanor) or "torture" (often charged as a felony) [NC General Statute § 14–360(a), (a1) and (b)] may rest on the veterinarian's ability to articulate the amount of pain inflicted on the animal by the act or failure to act. Although specific acts may, by their very nature, define the seriousness of the criminal charge, often it is a judgment call. Being able to refer to an objective assessment of pain is beneficial to making that judgment call.

Several pain scales for dogs and cats have been published. Colorado State University Veterinary Medical Center has published the CSU Acute Pain Scale for canines and felines and a Canine Chronic Pain Scale. These scales have pictures of typical body postures associated with pain levels as well as descriptive text (Colorado State Veterinary College Pain Scales 2006, 2006)

Another set of veterinary pain scales is the Glasgow Composite Pain Scale for Dogs, and a similar one for cats (Glasgow Composite Pain Scale (https://www.ava.eu.com/wp-content/uploads/2015/11/GlasgowPainScale.pdf).

Regardless of which pain scale is used for the initial assessment, as an animal is recovering from the neglect and/or abuse, the animal pain/comfort level should be evaluated at each subsequent examination using the same pain scale. Valuable information can be gleaned from the animal's return to a normal comfort level. Information to be included in the documentation of the case includes the animal's initial level of pain, what measures were required to relieve the animal's pain and for what duration, and the animal's new "normal" comfort level once it has recovered. In the event in which damage done by the neglect/abuse results in significant pain which cannot be relieved, this information should also be relayed to the judicial agencies in as objective a manner as possible, so the best decision can be made for the disposition of the animal.

Periodic Reevaluations

Although the initial physical examination and test results are vital to the assessment of the case, the case often does not end at this stage. How the animal and its medical conditions respond to reasonable veterinary care and normal husbandry practices can be critical information for the judicial system. For instance, if an emaciated dog returns to a normal body condition within a short time frame with just the provision of a medium-grade dog food that is easily available to most people, then this information may be clear and convincing evidence of the neglect of that animal by its owner. On the flip side, if the damage done to the animal is so severe that the animal cannot recover despite the provision of veterinary care, this too can speak volumes to the judicial system as to the criminality of the suspects act or failure to act.

Inherent to these cases is the periodic reevaluation of the animal victim. The frequency of such reevaluation in a neglect case will depend on the age and medical condition of the animal. In the author's experience, neonates, very young animals, and animals in critical condition may need to be reevaluated daily if not several times a day. An emaciated adult animal should be reassessed on at least a weekly basis until such time as the body condition has return to a stable, noncritical level. The medical record of neglected and victims of abuse should contain the medical plan of action, which includes the schedule for reevaluations. This schedule can be modified as appropriate to the animal's recovery.

Questions

Some common questions asked of veterinarians who assess animals for neglect and cruelty cases will be answered during the physical examination of the animals (author's personal experience). The examiner should consider questions typically asked in these cases: (1) Are the medical conditions/lesions acute or chronic in nature? (2) If chronic, in the judgment of the veterinarian, how long was the neglect/abuse occurring in order for the animal to present in its condition? (3) Is there evidence of chronic malnutrition? (4) Are there veterinary medical conditions present that resulted from failure to treat minor conditions? (5) Was this condition(s) preventable? (6) Could the suffering of this animal have been avoided or minimized if the owner or person responsible had acted earlier? (7) Did the environment in which the animal was housed contribute to the animal's suffering? (8) Was there an underlying medical condition present that may have caused or contributed to the animal's current condition? and (9) What would a reasonable person have done?

TYPICAL MEDICAL CONDITIONS FOUND IN ANIMAL ABUSE AND NEGLECT CASES

Although almost any veterinary medical condition is possible in animal abuse and neglect cases, some of the more common veterinary findings associated with abuse and neglect are as follows.

Embedded Collars or Tethering Chains/Ropes

Documentation of this condition can be quite telling. The details of the animal's initial presentation should be documented. Information such as the percentage of the neck circumference involved, the width and depth of the lesion, the extent of the treatment required to remove the collar/chain, and so on. Pictures should be taken of all aspects of the neck and collar/chain. The depth of the lesion once the collar/chain has been removed should also be recorded. The normal, resting circumference of the neck and the circumference of the collar should also be noted. Pictures should be taken throughout the removal process. If surgery is required, documentation of the procedure with photographs and videos would be beneficial. Postoperative photographs showing the sutured wound or the open wound, if the wound is left to heal by secondary intention, should be taken. Periodic photographs taken during the healing interval should also be taken (see Figure 16.5a–d). Periodic physical examinations during the healing process are appropriate. Consideration should be given to remeasuring the neck circumference once the healing process is complete. If this is done, documentation of any change in body weight and/or body score should be noted at the same time. Photographs of the lesions and stages of healing should be taken both with and without appropriate scales for measurements.

Overgrown Nails/Hooves

Each paw/hoof should be examined closely during the initial physical examination. If the paw is overgrown with matted hair such that the condition of the nails is not immediately visible, then documentation, including photographs, starts with the condition at initial presentation, removal of the matted hair, and the presenting condition of the nails under the mats. Photographs should be taken of the entire paw/hoof and then each nail. The use of a scale such as a ruler or calipers in photographs is appropriate to give perspective on the extent of the overgrowth (Figure 16.6a–c). When the nail is removed, documentation of the size of the excess amount removed with a ruler for scale is beneficial. If the nail was embedded into the paw, the lesion caused by the nail in the skin should also be photographed. If the overgrown/embedded nails are severe enough to affect the gait of the animal, a video of the animal walking may help demonstrate the discomfort/pain the animal was enduring due to this condition.

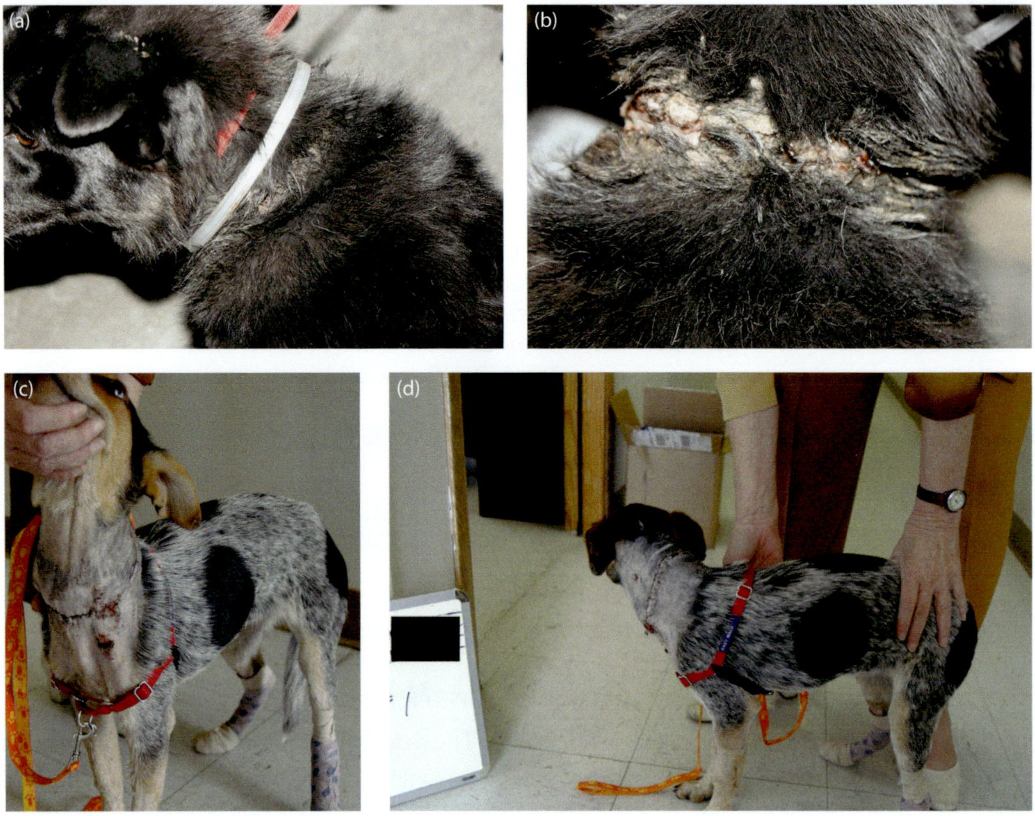

Figure 16.5 (a) Dog #1 with embedded collar. (b) Dog #1 with embedded collar, dorsal view. (c) Dog #2 postop photograph after surgery to remove embedded collar. (d) Dog #2 postop photograph after surgery to remove embedded collar.

If the overgrowth is of an equine hoof, radiographs may be beneficial, if not essential. Depending on the severity of the lameness caused by the overgrowth, the findings of the radiographs may determine the appropriate final disposition of the animal. Severe overgrowth of the hoof of an equine can be associated with severe deterioration of the hoof and possibly rotation of the coffin bone. This rotation results in severe, unrelenting pain for the animal without extensive veterinary and farrier intervention. Even with extraordinary measures, some of these animals cannot be made comfortable. Therefore, full assessment of this condition, including radiographs, should be done early in the case.

Developmental Abnormalities from Chronic Malnutrition

Young animals may show clinical signs related to chronic malnutrition or nutrition not suited to their life stage. Hoarding, overcrowded, underfunded rescues or shelters, and puppy mills often result in the animals enduring intense competition for limited resources. In these situations, the young animals may not be able to secure sufficient food. These animals may be stunted, have soft or brittle bones, and/or have sparse, abnormal hair coats due to insufficient or improper nutrition.

Although technically not a developmental abnormality, the neonate may not be afforded the opportunity to survive, as dams (female dogs) and queens (female cats) commonly cannibalize their young when in high-stress, low-resource housing situations. Under normal husbandry conditions, a queen or dam may neglect or even cannibalize a sickly neonate. However, in hoarding or other high-stress situations, cannibalism can reach the point of killing most (if not all) of the young animals.

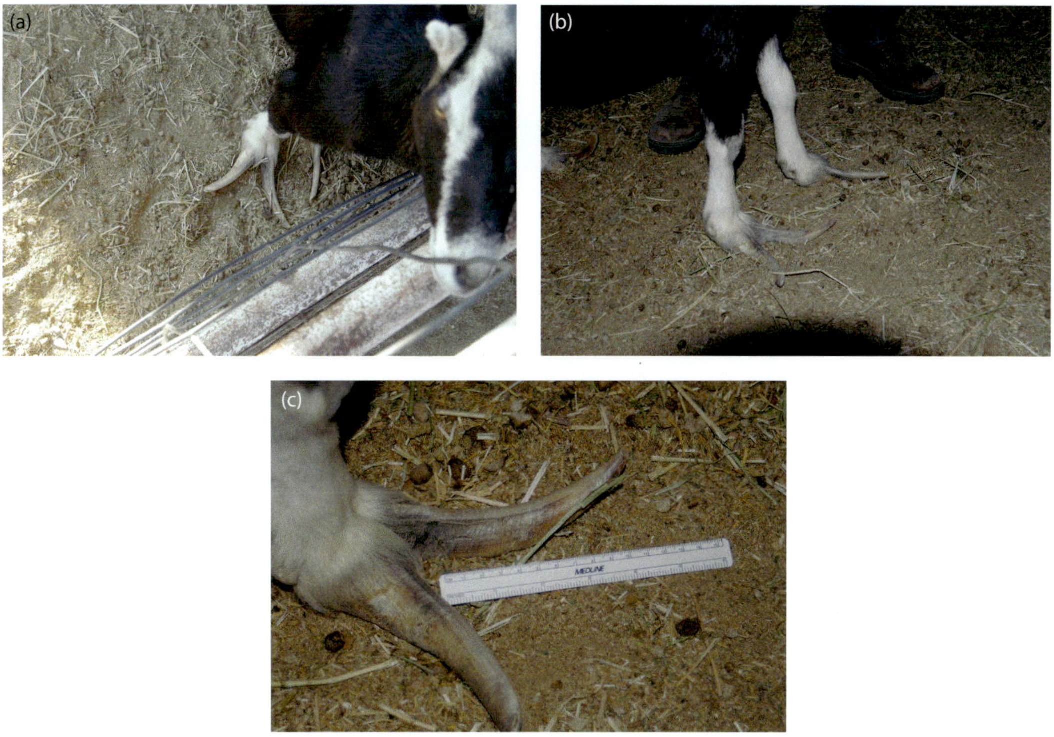

Figure 16.6 (a) Goat with overgrown hooves. (b) Mid-range photograph of goat with overgrown hooves. (c) Close-up of overgrown hooves with scale.

Congenital Deformities/Abnormalities from Inbreeding

Inbreeding of animals can result in a higher than normal appearance of congenital abnormalities, as it can concentrate the occurrence of recessive genes and the defects they cause. Reputable breeders carefully examine the pedigree of the potential breeding mates to avoid or minimize such defects. Breeding in hoarding situations, puppy mills, and disreputable rescues/shelters is usually indiscriminate. Often the dominant male will breed multiple generations and thereby concentrate the gene pool. In one hoarding case, in which the animal owner was convicted of animal cruelty, two litters of mixed-breed puppies were diagnosed with cerebellar abiotrophy (author's professional experience). This inherited disorder is a fairly rare degenerative cerebellar condition seen in breeds such as Kerry Blue terriers, Australian Kelpies, and rough-coated Collies (Chrisman, 1991; De LaHunta, 1977; Kahn, 2010).

Matted Coats

Some breeds of animals have naturally long and/or curly coats that require regular clipping and grooming. In neglect cases, some animals may present with their hair coat as one solid mat. The matting may extend from the top of their heads, across their face obscuring the animal's vision, and/or down to their paws (Figure 16.7). In these cases, consideration should be given to collecting the following data: photographs of initial presentation; weight of the animal prior to clipping; photographs during the clipping process; photographs of the animal after the fur has been removed to include all lesions; photographs of the paws, as often this severe matting can cause secondary pododermatitis (skin infection of the paw) lesions; weight of the removed hair; photographs through the holding period during the course of the case to document the appropriate routine grooming of the animal; and full documentation of all routine grooming required during the course of the

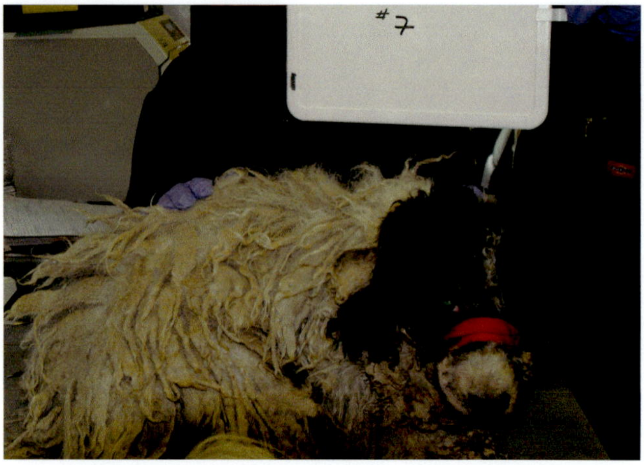

Figure 16.7 Dog with matted hair coat.

case and its associated costs. It may also be advisable to vacuum-pack the hair mat as evidence and document it photographically as well.

External Parasite Infestations

In neglect cases, either single-animal or large-scale cases, external parasite infestations are common. Full documentation of the extent of the infestation(s) is necessary for each case and for each animal involved in the case. The author has had the experience of having a large number of fleas jump on the personal protection equipment (PPE) to the point of discoloring the PPE upon entry into a hoarded residence. Since these parasites are easily visible on a white Tyvek suit, photographic documentation of this occurrence is recommended.

Tick infestations are fairly common, depending on the geographic location of a scene and the season. Whenever possible, documentation of the number of ticks on the animal is beneficial. In some cases, the infestations are such that actual counts are impractical. In this case, estimates with photographic documentation can be used (Figure 16.8a–e). If the notation of "TNTC" (too numerous to count) is used, then an explanation of the threshold for use of that designation is recommended. For example: "TNTC" is used whenever the number of parasites exceeds 1000. In the event of a tick infestation, ancillary testing for tick-borne diseases such as Anaplasmosis, Rocky Mountain Spotted Fever, and Lyme disease is warranted. Presence of one or more of these diseases is further evidence of the harm done to the animal by the neglect of the caretaker as tick infestations, and subsequent disease transmissions, are preventable with routine use of over-the-counter (OTC) medications.

Lice can be found in situations of crowding and/or poor husbandry. Avians with lice may show poor feather conditions, plucked areas, or areas of broken feathers. Mammals may show areas of alopecia (missing hair), excoriations (scratches), and/or raw spots (Kahn, 2010). Documentation of the overall condition of the animals and their environment, photographs of the parasites, identification of the parasites, documentation of the treatment of the animals and the subsequent improvement of the animals will substantiate the neglect and harm caused. As lice and other external parasites can be found in cages, kennels, and bedding, if any of these items are removed from the scene, precautions should be taken and the items sanitized before they can contaminate another area. The sanitation measures and justifications should also be documented in writing and with photographs.

In hoarding situations and disreputable dog/cat/rabbit rescues/shelters, ear mite infestations can be rampant and severe. Due to failure to treat this condition, the ears may develop polyps, scarring,

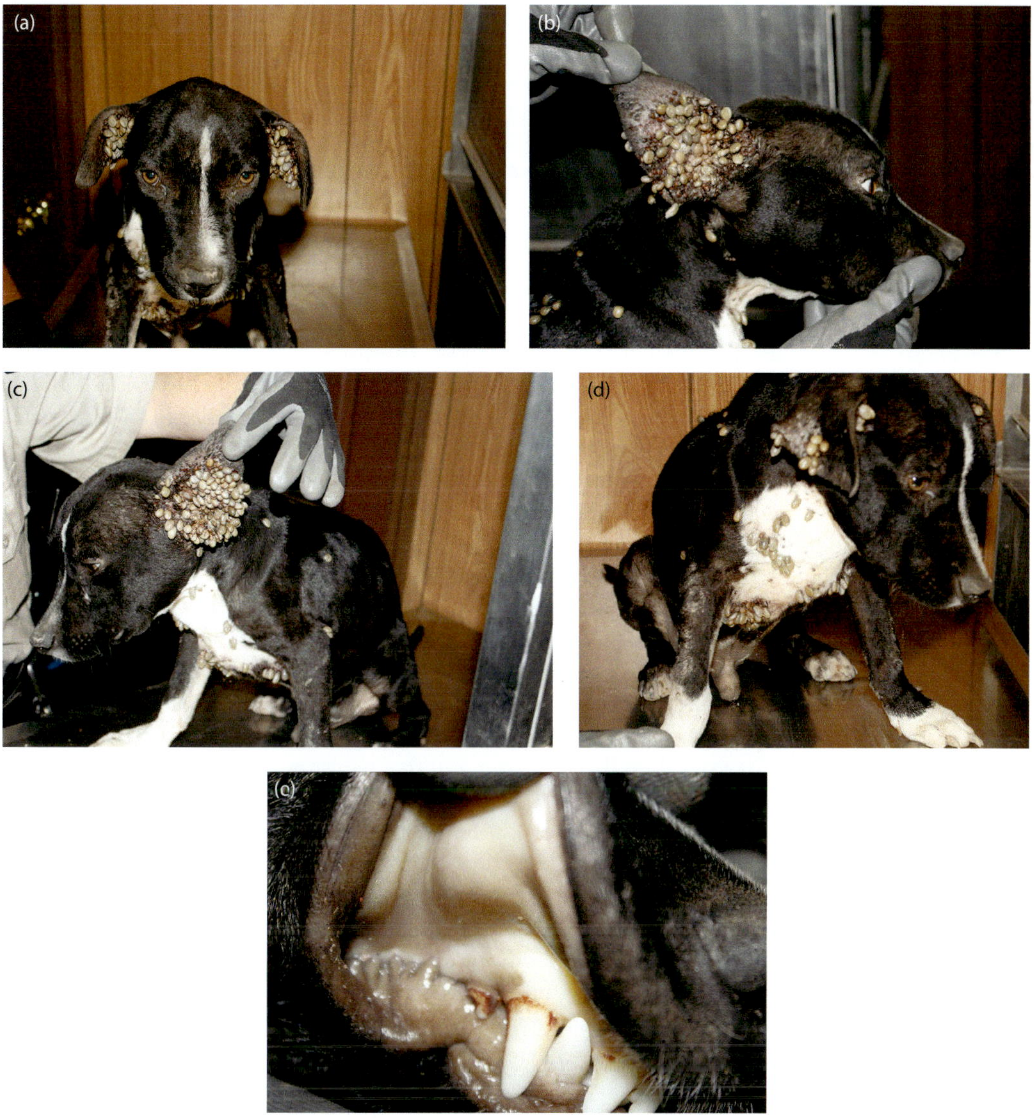

Figure 16.8 (a) Tick infestation, front view. (b) Tick infestation, right view. (c) Tick infestation, left view. (d) Tick infestation, chest view. (e) Pale mucus membranes of dog with tick infestation.

pinna (ear flap) alopecia (hair loss), and ulcerated, bleeding lesions within and on the ears. Cats with severe ear mite infestations are extremely resistant to handling or treatment of the ears due to the severe pain and discomfort from this condition. Quite often these cats require heavy sedation or anesthesia in order to clean and treat the ears. Ear mites can also be seen in dogs, especially puppies housed in unsanitary conditions (Kahn, 2010; Medleau & Hnilica, 2001).

Mange, both sarcoptic (scabies) and demodectic (demodex), is caused by external skin mites and are often seen in neglect cases. The lesions in scabies may initially present as alopecia around the pinnae margins and may have progressed to complete alopecia of the entire body with secondary changes such as lichenification (wrinkling) of the skin, hyperpigmentation (darkening of the skin), and ulcerated sores. Scabies causes intense pruritus (itchiness) and the dogs often scratch themselves endlessly. The scabies mite is zoonotic and has been known to cause similar lesions in humans. Therefore, care should be taken to mitigate transmission to humans and other animals when handling and housing these animals. Demodex is most commonly found in young and/or immunocompromised animals. Malnutrition can cause immune incompetency which could predispose and/or worsen the condition in a susceptible animal. Demodex mange can result in severe secondary bacterial infections, and in some cases progress to septicemia. Depending on the animal's capability to become immune-competent, the treatment for demodex may be prolonged and/or lifelong. Demodex mange is not zoonotic (Kahn, 2010; Medleau & Hnilica, 2001).

Birds housed in crowded and/or unsanitary conditions can also be infested with several different species of mites, some of which will feed on humans as well (Kahn, 2010).

Internal Parasite Infestations

Internal parasites are commonly found in neglected animals. Intestinal parasites, such as roundworms, hookworms, whipworms, tapeworms, and protozoa (such as coccidia and cryptosporidia), all have deleterious effects on animals. The severity and subsequent effects of intestinal infestations tend to be more significant in young animals. Young animals in neglect situations may already be suffering from anemia and hypoproteinemia due to malnutrition. Intestinal parasites will significantly exacerbate these conditions. Early detection and prompt treatment are essential during the initial phases of the animal intake and evaluation. Some of these parasites and protozoa are zoonotic (can be transmitted from animal to human and cause disease in humans), which is another reason why early detection and treatment are vital (Kahn, 2010; Miller & Zawistowski, 2013).

Most of these parasites and protozoa thrive in areas of poor sanitation, as their life cycle involves fecal-oral transmission or life-stage development in organic (often dirt or feces) material. This is another reason why the documentation of the environment is crucial for a neglect case.

Most "reasonable" animal caretakers will seek veterinary care for their young pets or in the event that the animal becomes too thin or develops diarrhea from internal parasites. Most caretakers are at least aware that puppies and kittens may have "worms" and either seek veterinary care or give them OTC dewormers, and then seek veterinary care if the condition continues (author's professional experience).

Depending on the geographic location of the alleged neglect case and the animal's age, dogs should be tested for heartworm infection. Dogs, and to a lesser extent cats, can be infected with heartworms from the bite of an infected mosquito. Heartworm preventative administration is considered routine veterinary care in endemic areas and failure to administer heartworm preventative medication may be considered failure to provide reasonable veterinary care. Left untreated, heartworm disease often results in death from emboli and/or heart failure (Ettinger & Feldman, 2000; Miller & Zawistowski, 2013) (Figure 16.9).

The type(s) of internal parasites and/or protozoa, the presenting condition of the animal, the treatment administered for the condition, and the improvement of the condition after the treatment

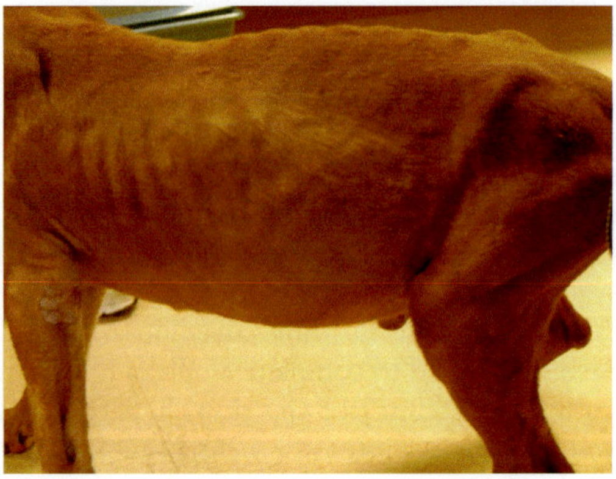

Figure 16.9 Side view of a dog suffering from advanced heartworm disease.

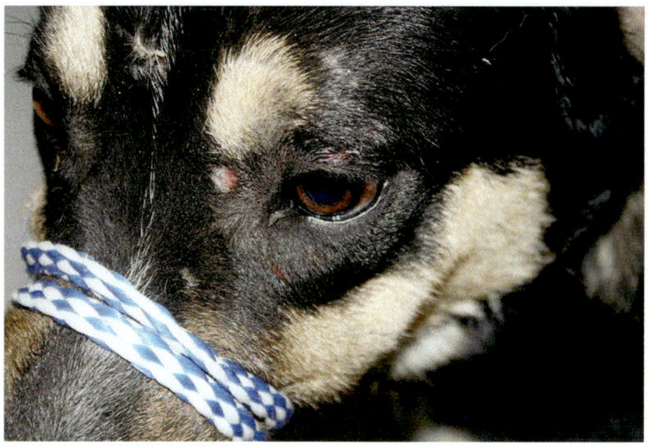

Figure 16.10 Fight wounds on the face of a dog seized from a hoarding site.

(if any) or failure to respond due to progression and severity of the disease is crucial for information for the judicial system.

Wounds from Fighting

In crowded, stressful, resource-limited environments, competition for resources such as water, food, space, and breeding often results in fights and fight wounds. Injuries are commonly found on the ears, face, and genitals (in the case of breeding animals) (Figure 16.10). Intact male cats may have one or more untreated abscess(es) from fighting and subsequent failure of the owner to provide veterinary care for the fight injuries.

Untreated Medical Conditions

Neglect cases often present with chronic conditions for which most reasonable caretakers would have sought veterinary care (Figures 16.11a,b, and 16.12a,b). Abscesses and tumors are commonly found to be large and/or ruptured with no record of veterinary care (see Figure 16.13a,b). Skin diseases from parasites, infections, and irritation from unsanitary environments may be fairly advanced at the time of the initial presentation (Figure 16.14a–c).

The author's experience is that cats in confined, unsanitary environments such as hoarding situations or disreputable rescues/shelters often have severe upper respiratory disease. These cats may present with the typical ocular and nasal discharge (Figure 16.15a,b). They may have moderate to severe gingivitis with missing teeth. Oral ulcers are common as well, depending on the virus(es) present. The URI may have progressed to the point that the ocular globe (eyeball) has corneal ulcers, has ruptured, or has ruptured and collapsed. Enucleation (removal of the eye) may be the

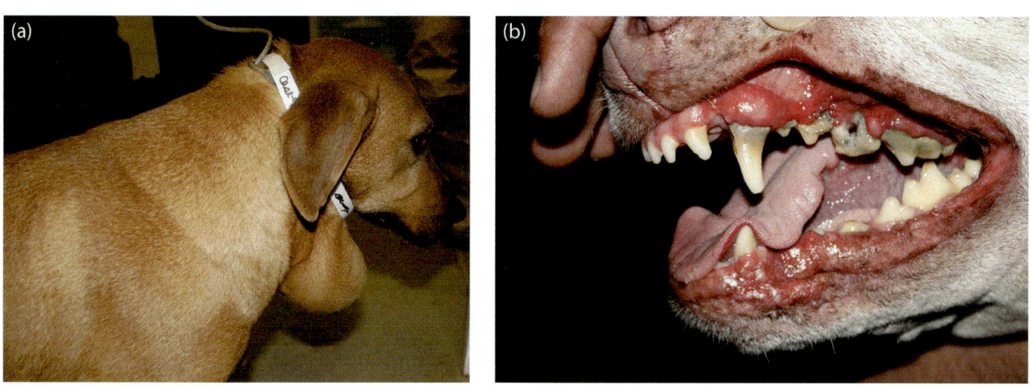

Figure 16.11 (a) Untreated salivary mucocele. (b) Untreated dental disease.

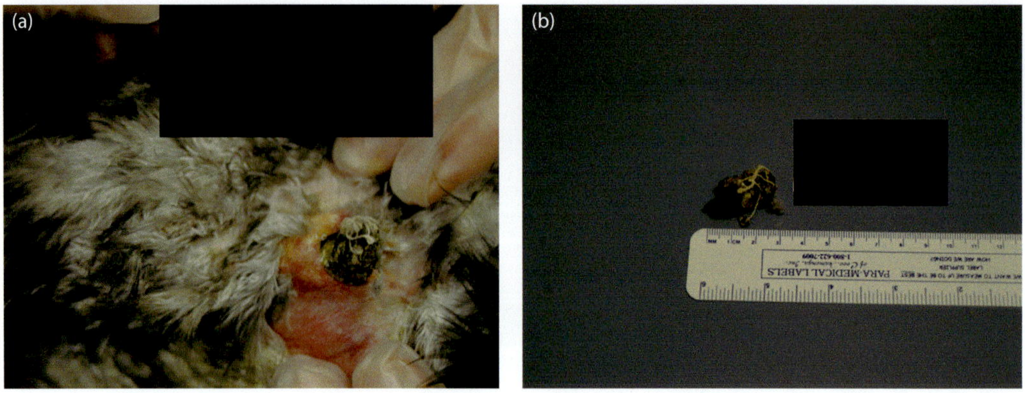

Figure 16.12 (a) Chicken with foreign-body reaction due to repair of sharp force injury with sewing thread. (b) Foreign body with scale.

only option left for these animals once they become well enough to withstand surgery. These cats tend to be chronic carriers of these URI viruses and this must be factored into the final disposition decisions for these animals (Miller & Zawistowski, 2013).

Complete diagnostic workup of these conditions is essential for the veterinarian to be able to fully relay to the judicial system the complete diagnosis, the extent of the disease/condition, the treatment options that could have been done early in the disease, the implications for the animal's long-term prognosis, the treatment options that remain, and the suffering caused by the disease and the caretaker's failure to provide treatment and/or prevention. If the disease/condition has progressed to the stage in which the only reasonable, humane option left is euthanasia, then a veterinary report containing this information is needed so that a court order authorizing the euthanasia can be obtained.

Conditions Related to the Environment

Animals confined to unsanitary environments can develop medical conditions that are directly related to the way in which they are housed. The documentation of these conditions in conjunction with an accurate, unbiased description of the environment and explanation of how the two are related is an invaluable aid to the judicial system in their assessment of the case. Animals confined to wire mesh cages may have swollen paws with ulcerations due to abrasions from the wire. The animals may have yeast infections and saliva staining of their toes and nail beds from incessantly licking due to the discomfort of chronic pododermatitis (inflammation of the paws/feet). Severe

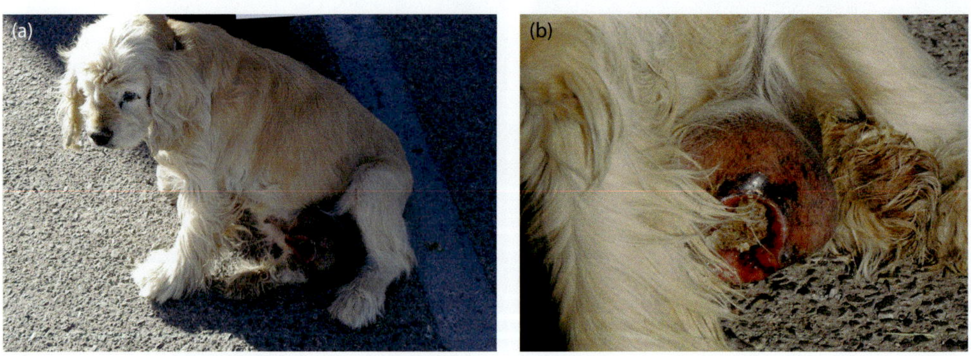

Figure 16.13 (a) Cocker Spaniel with untreated ruptured tumor. (b) Closer view of untreated ruptured tumor.

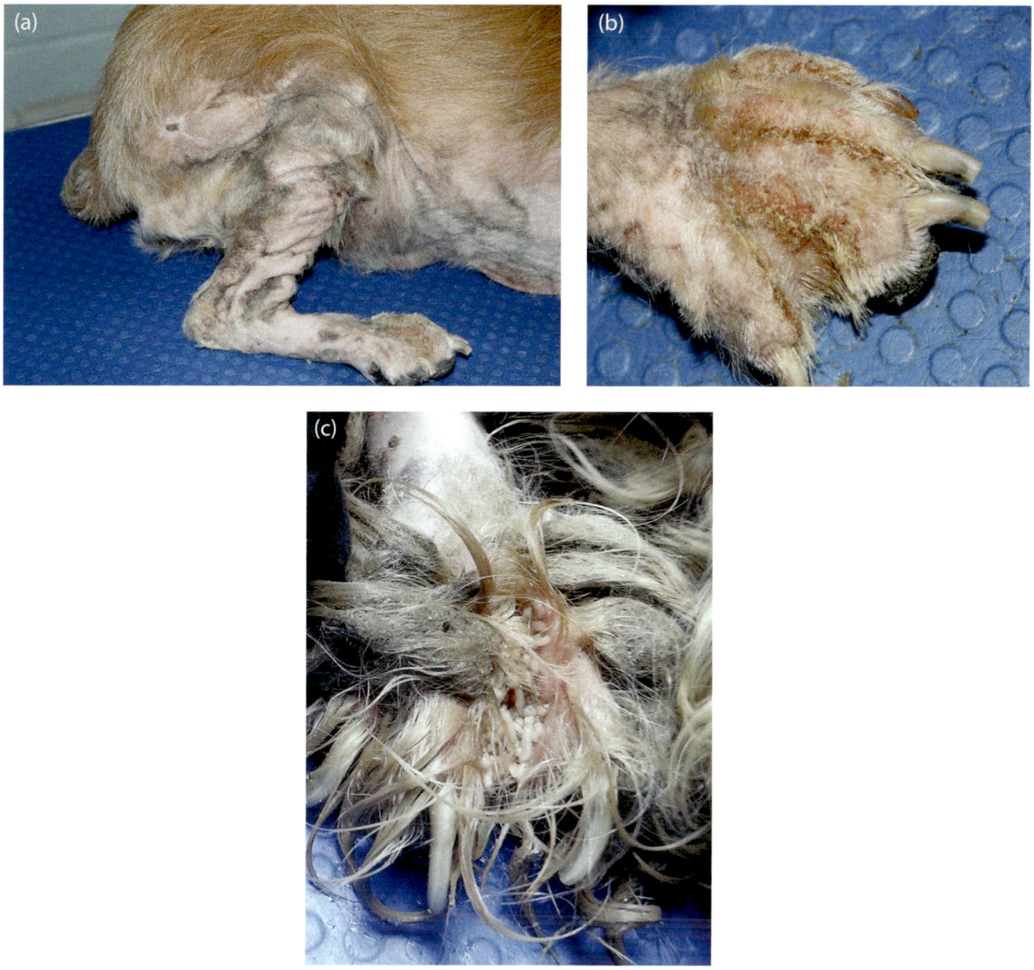

Figure 16.14 (a) Cocker Spaniel with untreated chronic skin disease. (b) Close-up view of paw of Cocker Spaniel with chronic pododermatitis. (c) Cocker Spaniel with untreated chronic skin disease with maggots.

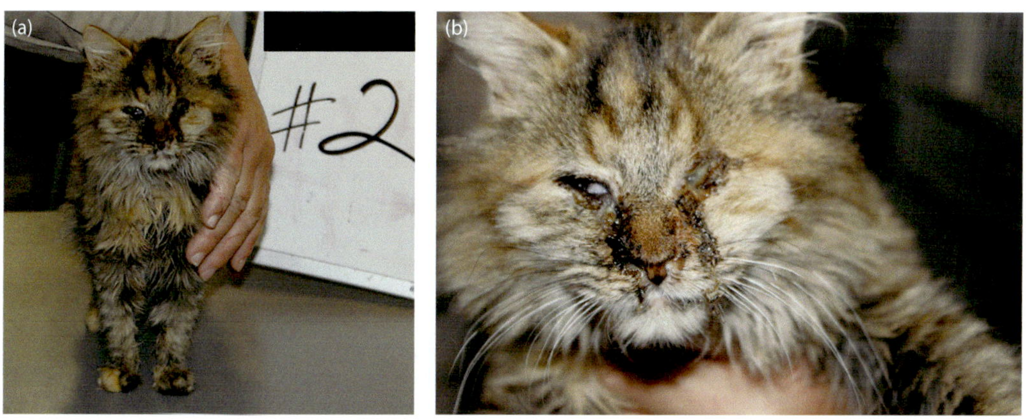

Figure 16.15 (a) Upper respiratory infection (URI) in cat seized from a hoarding site. (b) Closer view of cat with URI.

Figure 16.16 (a) Chained dog initial photograph. (b) Chain being weighed.

arthritis and degenerative changes often develop in animals housed under these conditions long term. Radiographs of these arthritic paws can be very revealing. These animals may not be able to walk well when placed on solid surfaces; videographic documentation of this difficulty should be considered.

Animals confined to small crates commonly seen in disreputable rescues and shelters may suffer from lesions due to urine and/or fecal scalding. Due to the small size of the cage and the subsequent excessive amount of time spent in contact with the urine and feces, the chemicals in the waste will burn the skin. Secondary infections and self-trauma of these lesions are common.

Chained or tethered animals may present with embedded collars and/or skin irritation from the collar or harness. These animals may also be restrained with chains that are too heavy for them and the chains may be secured with very large, heavy padlocks (Figure 16.16a,b). Helpful photographs in these situations include in situ photographs, photographs of the skin underneath the chain, and weight and/or length measurements of the chain. If entanglement of the chain prevented the animal from reaching food, water, or shelter, that should also be photographed (Figure 16.17a,b).

Deceased Animals

A deceased animal(s) in an animal crime case is evidence and must be treated as such. The animal should not be touched or moved until its position and surrounding environment are fully documented. The animal should receive a unique identification number that stays with it through processing and necropsy. The procedures for a veterinary forensic necropsy are discussed in Chapter 10.

Figure 16.17 (a) Overview of dog entangled in rope. (b) Dog entangled in rope.

BATTERED PET SYNDROME

Munro and Munro noted synonyms of physical abuse to be "nonaccidental injury" and "battered pet syndrome" (Munro & Munro, 2008). As inconceivable as a single act of animal abuse may be to some, the thought that an animal may be subjected to repeated injury is even more difficult to process. When assessing an animal that has been subjected to an act of abuse or neglect, the veterinarian should keep this possibility in mind as a possible rule out for the lesions seen during the animal's examination.

The presence of wounds in various stages of healing such as burns or fractures, and/or multiple, different types of wounds or injuries can be consistent with this diagnosis. Even if the age of the wounds cannot be specified, as can be the case in severely protein-deficient animals (protein is necessary for the normal healing process), the presence of multiple wounds of different stages of healing makes the defense of an accidental occurrence much less credible. Obviously, the veterinarian would need to rule out the rare, but possible, diseases that cause fragile or brittle bones, such as metabolic or neoplastic bone disease or osteogenesis imperfecta. If an animal presents with multiple abrasions, lacerations, and/or bruises, conditions causing spontaneous bleeding such as hemophilia or thrombocytopenia (decreased platelet counts) or easily torn skin (i.e., Ehler-Danlos) should be considered (Cote, 2007; Ettinger & Feldman, 2000).

Munro also detailed other potential indicators that an animal being presented to veterinarian may be the victim of abuse. These include (1) the history or description of the incident does not match the injuries, (2) the owner will not give an account of the incident, (3) the owner does not seem concerned about the animal and/or its injury, (4) the owner does not seek veterinary care in a timely manner, and (5) the animal seems overly quiet or intimidated in the presence of the owner and may be more outgoing when the owner leaves (Munro, 1999).

Pattern of Injury

Patterns of injury found in nonaccidental injury (NAI) cases have been compared to patterns found in trauma from vehicular accidents. In vehicular accidents, injuries commonly included abrasions, degloving injury, pelvic fractures, and injuries to the thorax such as pneumothorax, lung contusions, and rib fractures. The rib fractures tended to be found on the cranial ribs on one side. NAI trauma tended to include fractured teeth, vertebrae, and skulls. The rib fractures occurred bilaterally and were not concentrated cranially. Another finding of NAI was the occurrence of fractures in different stages of healing, indicating different times of occurrence (Intarapanich, 2016).

Pattern of injuries for other acts of animal abuse, such as "ring lesions" found in dogs that have been subjected to organized dogfighting (Figure 16.18), are discussed in the chapters specific to that act.

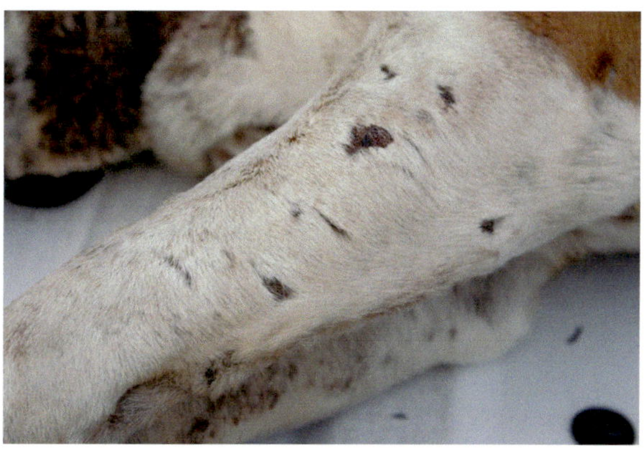

Figure 16.18 Typical wounds associated with organized dogfighting.

Appendix

Resources for Pain Assessment and Management

Epstein, M., I. Rodan, G. Griffenhagen, J. Kadrlik, M. Petty, S. Robertson and W. Simpson. 2015. 2015 AAHA/AAFP Pain Management Guidelines for Dogs and Cats. https://www.aaha.org/public_documents/professional/guidelines/2015_aaha_aafp_pain_management_guidelines_for_dogs_and_cats.pdf

Gaynor, J. S. and W. W. Muir III. 2015. *Handbook for Veterinary Pain Management*. St. Louis: MI.

Guidelines for the Use of the Glasgow Composite Pain Score. University of Glasgow. 2008. http://www.aprvt.com/uploads/5/3/0/5/5305564/cmps_eng.pdf

Hellyer, P. W., S. A. Robertson, and A. D. Fails 2007. Pain and Its Management. In: *Lumb & Jones' Veterinary Anesthesia and Analgesia*. eds. Tranquilli, W. J. J. C. Thurmon and K. A. Grimm. Ames, IA: Blackwell Publishing, p. 31.

Intarapanich, N. P., E. C. McCobb, R. W. Reisman, E. A. Rozanski, and P. P. Intarapanich. Characterization and Comparison of Injuries Caused by Accidental and Non-Accidental Blunt Force Trauma in Dogs and Cats. *Journal of Forensic Science*. 61(4). doi: 10.1111/1556-4 029.13074; onlinelibrary.wiley.com

Mathews, K., P. W. Kronen, D. Lascelles, A. Nolan, S. Robertson, P. V. M. Steagall, B. Wright, and K. Yamashita. 2014. Guidelines for the Recognition, Assessment and Treatment of Pain. *Journal of Small Animal Practice*. https://www.wsava.org/WSAVA/media/PDF_old/jsap_0.pdf

Matthews, N. S. and G. L. Carroll. 2007. Review of Equine Analgesics and Pain Management. *AAEP Proceedings*. 53. 240–244.

References

Animal Legal Defense Fund of the Michigan State Animal Legal and Historical Center. Animal Protection Laws of the United States of America and Canada. https://www.animallaw.info/

Arkow, P., P. Boyden, and E. Patterson-Kane. 2013. Practical Guidance for the Effective Response by Veterinarians to Suspected Animal Cruelty, Abuse and Neglect. AVMA. https://ebusiness.avma.org/Files/ProductDownloads/AVMASuspectedAnimalCruelty.pdf

Ascione, F. 1993. Children Who Are Cruel to Animals: A Review of Research and Implications for Developmental Psychopathology. *Anthrozoös*. 6(4): 2226–2247.

Ascione, F. and K. Shapiro. 2009. People and Animals, Kindness and Cruelty: Research Directions and Policy Implications. *Journal of Social Issues*. 65(3): 569–589.

Brewster, M. P. and C. L. Reyes. 2013. *Animal Cruelty: A Multidisciplinary Approach Understanding*. Durham, NC: Carolina Academic Press, p. 7.

Chrisman, C. 1991. *Problems in Small Animal Neurology*. 2nd ed. Philadelphia, PA: Lea & Febiger, pp. 28–38.

Colorado State Veterinary College Pain Scales. 2006. http://www.vasg.org/pdfs/CSU_Acute_Pain_Scale_Canine.pdf and http://www.vasg.org/pdfs/CSU_Acute_Pain_Scale_Kitten.pdf

Cote, E. ed. 2007. *Clinical Veterinary Advisor: Dogs and Cats*. Canada: Prince Edward Island, p. 1537.

De LaHunta, A. 1977. *Veterinary Neuroanatomy and Clinical Neurology*. Philadelphia, PA: W.B. Saunders Company, pp. 246–249.

Ettinger, S. and E. Feldman. 2000. *Textbook of Veterinary Internal Medicine: Diseases of the Dog and Cat*. 5th ed. Philadelphia, PA: W.B. Saunders Company, pp. 72–77; 931–967; 1981; 1995.

Federal Bureau of Investigation. U.S. Department of Justice. https://www.fbi.gov/news/stories/-tracking-animal-cruelty

Glasgow Composite Pain Scale. https://www.ava.eu.com/wp-content/uploads/2015/11/GlasgowPain Scale.pdf

Intarapanich, N., E. C. McCobb, R. W. Reisman, E. A. Rozanski, and P. P. Intarapanich. 2016. Characterization and Comparison of Injuries Caused by Accidental and Non-Accidental Blunt Force Trauma in Dogs and Cats. *Journal of Forensic Science*. 61(4). doi: 10.1111/1556-4 029.13074; onlinelibrary.wiley.com

Kahn, C. eds. 2010. *The Merck Veterinary Manual*. 10th ed. Whitehouse Station, NJ: Merck & Co., Inc, pp. 382–389; 840-841; 1121; 2475–2477.

McMillan, F. D. ed. 2005. Emotional Maltreatment of Animals. *Mental Health and Well-Being of Animals*. Ames, IA: Wiley-Blackwell, pp. 167–180.

Medleau, L. and K. Hnilica. 2001. *Small Animal Dermatology: A Color Atlas and Therapeutic Guide.* Philadelphia, PA: W.B. Saunders Company, pp. 66–70; 203–204.
Merck, M. 2013. *Veterinary Forensics.* 2nd ed. Ames, IA: Wiley-Blackwell Publishing, p. 89.
Miller, L. and S. Zawistowski. eds. 2013. *Shelter Medicine for Veterinarians and Staff.* 2nd ed. Ames, IA: Wiley-Blackwell, pp. 156–162; 311–314.
Munro, H. 1999. The Battered Pet: Signs and Symptoms. In: *Child Abuse, Domestic Violence, and Animal Abuse.* eds. F. R. Ascione and P. Arkow. West Lafayette, IN: Purdue University Press, pp. 199–208.
Munro, R. and H. M. C. Munro. 2008. *Animal Abuse and Unlawful Killing: Forensic Veterinary Pathology.* Philadelphia, PA: Saunders Elsevier, p. 3.
Touroo, R. 2011. (Lecture). Introduction to Veterinary Forensics Spring 2011. Course 6575, University of Florida: ASPCA.

CHAPTER 17

PROCESSING FORENSIC CASES INVOLVING AGRICULTURAL ANIMAL SPECIES

Ann Cavender

INTRODUCTION

Evaluation of agricultural animal welfare involves a working knowledge of breeds, basic husbandry, geographic and seasonal factors, accepted agricultural practices, management schemes, biosecurity, reportable diseases and federal, state, and local regulations regarding care, identification systems, transport, and approved drugs for use in each individual species. The presence of livestock species in cruelty, hoarding, and/or neglect cases changes the logistics of animal seizures with regard to identification, evidence collection, documentation, and transport for treatment or foster care.

ADDITIONAL CHALLENGES WHEN DEALING WITH LIVESTOCK CASES

Cases involving large numbers of dogs and cats are becoming increasingly common (Frost et al., 2015; Morton, 2017). Humane societies and animal control agencies generally have rescue groups and veterinarians available to process pets efficiently. Documentation and foster care proceed smoothly as animals are examined, triaged, and moved to appropriate levels of care. With few exceptions, the jurisdiction in these cases remains local.

Cases involving agricultural animal species must address several additional challenges. Federal and state departments of agriculture are tasked with maintaining a healthy, sustainable food supply. Programs requiring unique identification, disease surveillance, quarantine, trace back, movement restrictions, and monitoring carcasses at processing facilities for residues, illness, and/or injury fall under state and/or federal oversight. Category II United States Department of Agriculture (USDA) accredited veterinarians can execute health certificates and submit laboratory tests (Coggins, tuberculosis, brucellosis) in all species. Category I accreditation limits the veterinarian to dog, cats, laboratory animals, rabbits, ferrets, hedgehogs, and non-ruminant wildlife. The state veterinarian can assist in locating accredited veterinarians or provide personnel for necessary testing (Figure 17.1).

- Current restrictions on the movement of specific species
- Required identification (official tags, brands, tattoos) prior to movement
- Required disease testing prior to movement (Coggins, tuberculosis, bluetongue, brucellosis, pullorum)
- Any permit numbers or testing required for interstate transport
- Permits or requirements for transport of dead livestock
- Presence of reportable diseases in the area (emergency, regulated, or monitored)
- Limitations on medications that can be legally used in livestock species (United States Animal Medicinal Drug Use Clarification Act of 1994 [AMDUCA])
- Maintenance of records in the appropriate format when veterinary chemicals are used including withholding times for every animal or group of animals treated with a therapeutic or deworming medication
- Veterinary Feed Directive (VFD) requirements

Figure 17.1 Federal and/or state authorities may have to be contacted to verify current regulations and requirements.

Livestock tertiary care facilities may not be equipped to handle large numbers of critical cases. It is imperative to determine the location and capacity of these facilities prior to the seizure. Weak, debilitated, and down livestock may need hip lifts (cattle) or slings (equine, camelids). In addition, a building with beams or heavy equipment to support a thrashing large animal is necessary to prevent compartment syndrome and decubitus ulcers. Most facilities have a limited number of lift devices. Quarantine facilities also have limited space. Advanced planning prior to seizure will alert medical facilities to a potential influx of cases. The facility should be willing and able to perform a complete forensic necropsy in the event of death of any of the animals in their care.

HANDLING

Safety for the animals and personnel is a persistent concern (Sheldon et al., 2009; Forrester et al., 2018). Interactions with large animal livestock species can be dangerous. Knowledgeable stockmen with species-appropriate equipment and careful advanced planning will minimize risk (Grandin, 2000).

The optimum equipment for sorting and handling will depend on the size of the enclosure, the nature of the terrain, security of barriers (walls, gates, and fences), species, sex, and breeds involved. For example, Longhorn and Watusi cattle require specialized head gates to accommodate their excessive horn length. Properties of several acres will require large numbers of people, mounted stockmen, or handlers with dogs trained for that species. Swine can be moved with boards and flags if enclosures have secure barriers. Cattle are moved with holding pens and connected chutes/alleys and are restrained with head gates of an appropriate size. Sheep can be driven into holding pens and treated in chutes without the need for head gates. Camelids and horses can be driven or led with halters and lead ropes if previously trained. Goats are driven or led with collars. Poultry are herded with flags or caught as individuals after confining to a smaller area.

Handlers often have experience and equipment for only one or two species, with cattle and horses being a common example. Cattlemen will be most efficient when working beef cattle and have the experience to troubleshoot problems before they arise. They can often recognize disease or injury and remove the affected individual from the herd with a minimum of stress. Stockmen and veterinarians with experience in multiple species are rare. Large animal veterinarians commonly restrict their practice and continuing education to one species or agricultural activity (dairy cattle, beef cow-calf, feedlot, swine, or poultry). Veterinarians with practices limited to a single livestock discipline are invaluable during the initial examinations and can provide consultation services should future illness or injury arise. If the state has a veterinary school, the clinicians may be able to provide names of veterinarians with specialized training. State and national professional veterinary groups limited to a single species are another source (American Association of Bovine Practitioners, American Association of Equine Practitioners, and so on. See Resources for contact information).

Strict biosecurity measures must be maintained to prevent the spread of disease among the animals or to neighboring premises. Prompt recognition of contagious, reportable, and zoonotic diseases is important to control disease, protect personnel, and report to the appropriate government agencies. Disinfection of equipment and vehicles, rodent control, foot baths, and control of traffic into and out of the area may be necessary biosecurity precautions. USDA Animal and Plant Health Inspection Service (APHIS) has information on biosecurity procedures for poultry and livestock (https://www.aphis.usda.gov/aphis/ourfocus/animalhealth/emergency-management/ct_sop_biosecurity).

TRANSPORT

Transportation injuries are most common during loading and unloading. Safe conveyance is dependent upon the numbers, age, size, species, distance, health status, and weather conditions.

Open stock trailers in subzero weather are not appropriate for the movement of neonates or poultry because of the risk of hypothermia. Trailering during periods with a high heat index increases the risk of heat exhaustion and death in all species. Young foals and calves should not be placed in open stock trailers with adults as they can be crushed during movement. Transport with their dams or similar-sized members of the same species will decrease the risk of injury. Cattle and sheep may crowd during transport, injuring or killing the smaller, weaker animals. Sexually intact males should be segregated during transport either by solid barriers or in a separate conveyance to avoid injury or unintended pregnancies. Further considerations related to transport include stress of travel, disease transmission, ventilation, distance, and space allowance. Transport vehicles should be thoroughly disinfected between loads to prevent unnecessary exposure to pathogens (Grandin, 2000).

Table 17.1 Recommended space allowance during transport[a]

Species	Weight/Age	Space Requirement
Cattle		
	<250 pounds	1½ × 2½ feet
	250–500 pounds	2 × 3½ feet
	500–1000 pounds	3 × 5 feet
	1000–1500 pounds	3 × 6 feet
	>1500	4 × 10 feet
Horses		
Ponies and foals	<500 pounds	2½ × 5 feet
Horses and mules	500–1000 pounds	3 × 10 feet
Warmbloods and draft	1000–2000 pounds	3.3 × 12 feet
Swine		
Miniature pigs	<40 pounds	Comparable size dog kennel
Meat pigs	30 pounds	8 × 20 inches/1.1 ft^2
	80 pounds	12 × 24 inches/2 ft^2
	160 pounds	24 × 48 inches/3 ft^2
	550 pounds	48 × 84 inches/11 ft^2
Sheep		
Lambs	<50 pounds	1½ × 2½ feet
Adults	<100 pounds	2 × 3 feet
Adults	100–300 pounds	2½ × 4½ feet
Poultry		
Chicks		3.8 in^2
Chickens	<3.5 pounds	50 in^2/0.34 ft^2
	3.5–6.0 pounds	75 in^2/0.52 ft^2
	6.0–10 pounds	90 in^2/0.62 ft^2
Turkey Poults	Hatchling	4.2 in^2
Turkey	3.5–6.6 pounds	75 in^2/0.52 ft^2
	6.6–11 pounds	90 in^2/0.62 ft^2
	11–16.5 pounds	120 in^2/0.84 ft^2

Note: Load fewer animals when temperature and humidity are high. Adjustments must be made for climate and trailer configuration.

Sources: Grandin, 2014, Knowles et al., 1998, Miles, 2017, Parish et al., 2013, Schwartzkoph-Genswein et al., 2012, Warriss, 1998, Warriss et al., 2002, Whiting and Brandt, 2002.

[a] Trailer configuration and gross vehicle weight rating must not be exceeded.

The stress of transport can result in recrudescence of subclinical or inapparent disease states (shipping fever, salmonella). Young animals can be infected with many diseases when mixed with carrier adults shedding organisms (equine strangles, contagious ecthyma in small ruminants). In addition, commingling species can result in disease transmission. Swine can infect sheep with pseudorabies. Johnes disease can be passed between cattle and small ruminants. Sheep and goats can cross-infect with contagious keratoconjunctivitis ("pinkeye"). In general, animals that were housed together should be kept separate from unfamiliar groups of livestock during processing/transport to decrease stress, minimize the risk of injury and contagious disease transmission (Grandin, 2000; Smith & Sherman, 2009).

Overcrowding during transport increases the risk of injury and disease. Space allowances during transport must be modified according to the species, age, and climatic conditions. Increased heat indices will decrease recommended stocking densities to allow for increased air flow and cooling by convection. For cattle, too much space can be as detrimental as too little space (Petherick & Phillips, 2009; Schwartzkopf-Genswein et al., 2012; Parish et al., 2013). Table 17.1 lists recommended space allowance during transport for a variety of species. Remember, these calculations are based on normal, healthy animals. Space allowances for underweight livestock must maintain the length because the skeletal structure does not change, while the width may be less. Research has been conducted to determine best practices for commercial vehicles where airflow is generally limited compared to private conveyances (Petherick & Phillips, 2009). General considerations for trailering are listed in Figure 17.2.

- Loading and unloading are more stressful than road travel
- Curves and irregular road surface are more stressful that straight, smooth pavement
- Bedding is preferred for longer distances because of warmth, improved footing, and cleanliness
- Cattle will preferentially orient perpendicular or parallel to travel and will avoid standing diagonally during transport
- Horses tend to orient diagonal to the direction of travel
- Camelids, turkeys, and young (<1 month old) calves lay during transport—do not tie camelids on short leads prior to movement as they can hang themselves as the trailer begins to move
- Sheep and cattle tend to splay their legs and brace while in motion
- Stocking density appropriate for size, age, and species—animals with full fleece and those with horns require 5%–10% more space
- Crowded cattle may be unable to regain a standing position once fallen
- Microclimate including ventilation varies within the trailer depending on the species factors (age, body condition score [BCS], hair coat), travel speed, trailer design (slats/vents), and weather conditions outside the trailer
- Fractious animals (especially equids) may need to be sedated for safe transport
- Quick-release hardware or knots should be employed for animals who are tied during transport
- Trailers should be thoroughly disinfected between loads
- Species or groups that have not been housed together should not be comingled
- Trailer should be suitable for the species
- Distance, travel time, road conditions (pavement vs. unpaved), weather conditions, and the condition of the individuals should be taken into consideration (Parish et al., 2013; Grandin 2014)

Figure 17.2 Considerations when transporting livestock.

INJURED, DISEASED, OR DEAD ANIMALS

Necropsy of deceased animals should be performed by a veterinarian experienced with that species or by a veterinary pathologist. The size of carcasses may require special equipment for loading and transport. Local ordinance(s) may require watertight conveyance or permits. Chain of custody must be maintained. Field necropsy should *not* be performed if anthrax is suspected, to protect personnel and the environment (Muller et al., 2015). If transport to a diagnostic laboratory is not practical, then a field necropsy should be performed. The entire procedure should be photographed beginning with overall, multiple mid-range and close-up photographs where the animal died. Livestock field necropsy techniques are described in several references (Mason & Madden, 2007; Brown et al., 2008; Griffin, 2012; Frank et al., 2015).

ASSESSING WELFARE

There are no federal laws governing minimum welfare standards of farmed animal species. Animal cruelty and animal neglect are legal definitions that vary by jurisdiction. While all 50 states have anticruelty laws, each defines cruelty differently, and regulations may exempt some or all of the agricultural animal species. Nearly all of the statutes address the adequacy of food, water, shelter, and necessary veterinary care, while exempting "accepted agricultural practices." These minimum requirements vary regionally; therefore, utilizing guidelines available from the local extension offices has probative value as being relevant to the current case and utilizing information readily available to the general public. For example, ventilation and shade are vital in warm climates during summer, so an open-air covered shelter or natural shade is essential. In contrast, cold, winter conditions necessitate windbreaks and possibly supplemental heat for some species. The adequacy of minimum standards is assessed in relation to breed, husbandry system, geographic area, season, and production stage. Herd health is comparable to human public health in that management practices are designed to promote optimum health, welfare, and productivity in a population. Both systems monitor disease and death losses and adjust practices to minimize their incidence.

Availability of adequate amounts of quality forage, crop yields, and fluctuating market prices can all have an impact on management practices during difficult climatic and financial times. State extension services provide information on recommended nutrition and husbandry practices in their geographic area and modify their recommendations based on current local conditions (Hancock et al., 2017). Nontraditional feedstuff may be utilized during these times. For example, some producers utilize spent grains from local custom breweries or day-old bakery products and balance the ration accordingly (Saleh et al., 1996; Mavromichalis, 2013; Bernard, 2017).

ASSESSING AND DOCUMENTING THE ANIMALS AND PREMISES

Prior to the initial site inspection, determine if additional resources are required. Are there areas where the animals can be collected, assessed, and processed with minimum stress? Are there sufficient pens, chutes, head gates, flags, pig boards, or halters to expedite handling? Are there sufficient numbers of experienced individuals for all species involved? Are there knowledgeable stockmen with experience moving and restraining the species present? Do the veterinarians have experience with all species likely to be present?

On the Initial Walkthrough

Photograph or videotape *everything*. Overall photographs before the scene is altered by the authorities are critical. For example, the presence or absence of a group of trees in or near an enclosure may demonstrate or refute the adequacy of natural shelter. Be aware that unfamiliar personnel may put animals on alert, and they will appear more active and healthy as a defense mechanism. Critically ill animals may be beyond the "fight-or-flight" response. Animals that appear depressed on the initial walkthrough may appear more normal as additional commotion agitates the group.

Note the size of the facility, number of buildings, state of the fences/gates, condition and size of pastures, and potential holding/loading areas. A rough sketch of the property based on a plat map or Google Earth image prepared in advance is helpful to divide the property into regions or zones. Locate water sources, feeders, food and medication storage areas, pastures, pens, paddocks, cages, compost piles, shelter areas, and burial pits.

Note the overall appearance of the group(s). Take several photographs and videotape the group of animals. This will document the overall behavior and condition of the animals in the group as you arrived and prevent future claims of damage to the animals and premises by your agency's activities. The health and well-being of the group, not the individual animal, is the focus of herd health programs. As long as 80% or more of the animals are in good health, then the care is probably adequate. If one production or age group seems less healthy than another group, then efforts can be concentrated on these individuals. If the problem involves all age, species, and production stages, then a more in-depth investigation of all aspects of management will be required. For example, if the lactating goats are averaging a BCS of 3/9 while the young animals are well fleshed, then the nutrition, including water supply, shelter, and milking practices need to be documented in addition to testing for parasites and chronic diseases (Johnes, caprine arthritis encephalomyelitis, caseous lymphadenitis).

The conditions present in the group will guide the collection of evidence. Respiratory diseases may be an indication of substandard housing (elevated ammonia levels, increased stocking density, poor biosecurity). Diarrhea may indicate parasites (coccidia, *Cryptosporidia*), abrupt change in feed, Johnes, or other infectious disease (salmonellosis). Underweight animals may indicate a lack of calories, unbalanced ration, parasitism, disease, or an inability to access food and water. Neurologic signs are seen with dehydration, infectious disease (viral encephalitis, rabies), toxicosis (larkspur, locoweed, selenium, salt), parasites (meningeal worm), and hepatic encephalopathy secondary to acute or chronic liver disease. Skin diseases may be the result of unsanitary conditions, nutritional imbalances (vitamin A deficiency, calcium:zinc), contagious disease (dermatophytosis, papillomavirus), parasites (mange), or toxicosis (chronic *Lantana camara* exposure).

Determine if the sick animals are exhibiting any signs of reportable or zoonotic diseases. Contact the state veterinarian for guidance as "emergency," "reportable," and "monitored" diseases may differ from state to state. The area may be currently under quarantine for a disease, and movement of animals may be prohibited (highly pathogenic avian influenza, equine strangles, bovine tuberculosis, etc.). Personnel may be at risk or act as fomites and spread the disease to other premises. Federal or state funds and personnel may be available to diagnose or control disease.

Plan the scene assessment from the animals in poorest health to the animals in the best condition to facilitate triage, euthanasia decisions, or transport of critically ill individuals. If critically ill animals need to be transported to a hospital setting, and it is legal to do so, a veterinarian should determine if the animal is likely to survive the stress of transport. If hospital placement is limited, the veterinarian can assist in selecting those animals that are most likely to benefit from treatment. University veterinary hospitals are often the only choice for care in cases involving multiple livestock species, but they may have limited space in quarantine areas or other secure wards. Private equine facilities are an option for that species, space permitting. If survival is unlikely, then an acceptable method of euthanasia for that species should be utilized. American Veterinary Medical Association (AVMA) Guidelines for the Euthanasia of Animals lists acceptable techniques for a variety of agricultural species (https://www.avma.org/KB/Policies/Documents/euthanasia.pdf).

If transport is a viable option, be sure the facility is equipped to care for the animal in its present condition (lifts, slings, critical care, surgery, quarantine). Communicate the necessity of maintaining a forensically useful record of the condition and treatment of the animal and explain that the animal is living evidence. Some facilities are reluctant or unable to provide care for forensic cases and will not permit, for insurance reasons, outside veterinarians to provide care or assistance in their facility. Hospitalization of critically ill large animals is costly. Funding needs to be adequate to cover treatment of these animals. Humane euthanasia with a full forensic necropsy may be the best choice for animals in extremely poor health and provide more evidence for the prosecution. Verify that the veterinarian or veterinary pathologist understands the difference between a forensic and diagnostic necropsy and is willing to testify in court if necessary, before submitting the animal(s) for postmortem.

Before the animal is moved, photograph it in situ from all angles and in context with overall, mid-range, and close-up images. Assign a unique number based on the location on the premises (Field #) and individual number. For example, if two goats were in Field #1 and in Shed A, they would be assigned numbers 1-A-1 and 1-A-2. Any individual tags or tattoos must be recorded on the individual animal physical exam sheets (see Resources).

Documenting Adequate Nutrition Including Feed and Access to Feed

Access to adequate feed can be assessed, in part, by the BCS of the animals. Several BCS charts are available through extension offices, breed organizations, and agricultural university websites (see Resources). Every animal should be assessed for body condition based on a scoring system specific to that breed type, use, and production state. Selection of an appropriate scale depends on recognition of livestock use (meat vs. dairy), breed/type (light vs. draft horses; *Bos taurus* vs. *Bos indicus*, broilers vs. layers) and production stage (gestating, milking, open, in lay). Cite the scoring system used for the assessment of that species to avoid confusion. A BCS of 3 is "Ideal" in a 1–5 system, "Thin" if using a 1–9 scale, and "Fat" using 0–3. By tradition, BCS is recorded as: 3/5, 3/9, and 3/3, respectively. Some systems require visualization only while others require palpation of defined anatomical landmarks. Note that body condition scales with a range of 1–9 reserve the 1/9 score for animals that are demonstrably weak and/or ataxic. Videotape the animal in motion or attempting to rise if you report an individual as "emaciated." If weakness is not demonstrable, then 2/9 is the lowest score that can be assigned to that individual. Animals that drop quickly in condition will show a loss of strength and coordination at relatively heavier weights than individuals who have had time to acclimate to a lower ration over a longer period of time. Dehydration hastens death in both chronic and acute cases (Madea, 2005; Gerdin et al., 2015).

If possible, record an actual weight at intake. Determining the weight of livestock species can be accomplished in several ways. Small ruminants, miniature horses, calves, some swine, and camelids can be weighed while on the farm with a portable platform scale, providing there is a solid, flat spot for installation. Some of the models have rechargeable batteries if electricity is not available. Large animal scales used at livestock auctions are less common. Alternatively, trailers can be weighed at a certified scale while empty and animals loaded individually, transported to the scale and returned to the farm. This method is labor intensive, time consuming, and stressful for the animals. Alternatively, weight tapes can be used to approximate the weight of horses (Ellis & Hollands, 1998; Hoffman et al., 2013), cattle (Wangchuk et al., 2018), pigs (Groesbeck et al., 2002; Sungirai et al., 2014), goats (Perez et al., 2016), and sheep (Thomas et al., 1997). Having an accurate weight at the beginning and end of rehabilitation provides objective evidence of the number of pounds gained and can be expressed as a percentage of total body weight. For example:

Horse X weighed 750 pounds (BCS 2/9) at seizure and was 1150 pounds with a BCS of 5/9 when released for adoption. This represents a 34.8% loss of body weight.

$$(\text{Current Weight}) - (\text{Previous Weight}) \div \text{Current Weight} = \%\ \text{Body Weight Lost}$$

An estimated Ideal Weight can be used for Current Weight if the animal is still recovering when the case goes to court.

Accurate documentation of body condition can be a challenge because of hair coat and lighting conditions. Photographing the animal from a variety of angles and with indirect lighting can highlight ribs or spines that are otherwise invisible. Utilizing bendable wire to demonstrate the contour of spines, short ribs, and breastbones that are palpated during assessment provides visible proof for court in fiber and feathered breeds. The technique was first described in laying hens (Gregory & Robins, 1998) but can be adapted to any species to provide a visual record. With the bird laying on its back, the wire is placed under the feathers and over the keel (breastbone) midway along its length. Gregory used a plastic coated 3 mm diameter wire, but any bendable wire that will hold its shape will work. Wire can be purchased at craft stores that have jewelry departments, hardware stores, or feed mills selling electric fence wire (14 gauge works well). For small ruminants with fiber, the wire can be molded over the midpoint of the loin (Figure 17.3). Photograph the wire on the animal and after removal on a contrasting background. The wires can be labeled with a piece of tape or a peel-and-stick label. Mounting the wire(s) next to a chart showing the contours with the assigned BCS provides a graphic but non-inflammatory depiction of the condition of the animal. Subsequent wires can show the improvement over time as the animal regains condition (Figure 17.4a–c).

If more than 20% of the animals in the group are underweight to emaciated, then one or more husbandry or animal-related causes may be evident (Ferrucci et al., 2012; Odriozola et al., 2018; Oliver-Espinosa, 2018). Investigation and documentation of all potential contributing factors must be undertaken. See Figure 17.5.

Determining Quality and Quantity of Feed

If the animals are utilizing vegetation as part of their ration, the nutritional value is dependent on the plant species present, maturity of the plants, and growing conditions. Poorer quality feed must be fed in higher quantities to provide sufficient nutrients. It is possible to have rations so poor in nutrient content that it is impossible for the animals to consume sufficient quantity to meet their protein/energy requirement.

There are several places nationally that can analyze forage (see Resources). Members of the National Forage Testing Association can gain Certified Laboratory status by demonstrating proficiency. Use of a certified laboratory increases the chances of repeatability and decreases the likelihood of challenge in court. Contact the laboratory for their recommendations for best practices regarding sampling and shipment for your specific situation. In general, observe the plants the animals are consuming and collect 25–30 handfuls from each area of the pasture that has different varieties of grazed plants (ditches, under trees, along fence rows). Collect the plants at the level likely to be consumed by that species; cattle the top one-third of the plant, pigs and poultry the entire plant, and small ruminants, camelids, and horses within an inch of the soil. Sample packages should have identical labels on the inside and the outside of the container (case number, agency, location, time, date, contents, collector, and a unique sample number). Place the samples in a plastic bag, squeeze out the excess air, and label with the appropriate information after sealing with frangible tape. Freeze to prevent fermentation and ship overnight on ice via a courier service to maintain chain of custody.

Animals generally will not graze near manure piles or around water troughs or weed-filled areas unless there is no other forage available. These areas should be deducted from calculations

Figure 17.3 Documenting BCS in a fleeced animal. (a) Restrain the animal (a milking stand works well if the animal will tolerate it). (b) Part the fleece to expose the skin over the loin at the midpoint. (c) Bend malleable wire over the contour. (d) Trace the inside of the curved wire. Inclusion of the reference scale in the medical record facilitates clear communication during legal proceedings.

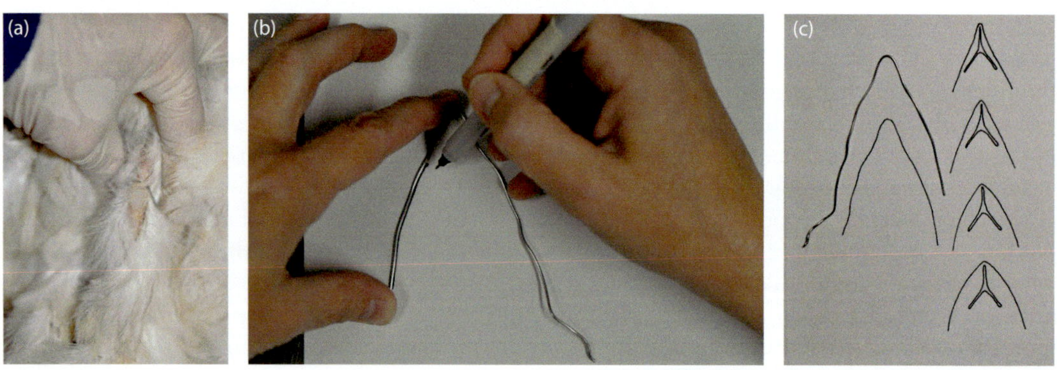

Figure 17.4 Documenting BCS of avian species using malleable wire. (a) Wire is pressed over the keel midway along the length. (b) Trace the inside contour of the bent wire. (c) Photograph the wire and the tracing with the individual's unique identification. The column of illustrations on the right represent BCS 0-3 (Gregory & Robbins, 1998).

Husbandry causes:

- Insufficient/inappropriate feedstuff for environmental conditions, species, or production stage (lactating animals require more calories to maintain condition; heat-stressed animals will not eat; more calories required in cold weather)
- Poor quality feed
- Insufficient bunk space
- Insufficient time to consume rations (social starvation or limited time in feeding area)
- Inability to prehend, masticate, swallow, or digest ration (dental or other maxillofacial disease; halter too tight)
- Exposure to environmental extremes (heat, humidity, cold)
- Toxins

Animal causes:

- Inability to access feed (lameness, weakness, feed barriers)
- Heavy internal or external parasite burden
- Acute or chronic disease (Johnes disease, neoplasia, heart disease, ovine progressive pneumonia, chronic pulmonary disease)
- Geriatric conditions
- Poor milk production of dam prior to utilization of solid food

Figure 17.5 Causes of poor body conditions.

of grazeable area. If a dirt lot has uneaten weeds and no other available forage, then the weeds should be collected or photographed, and the species identified. Nutritionists, toxicologists, and/or botanists can determine if the plants are toxic or have any nutritional value for the species present. Sparse pastures may be the result of chronic overgrazing or a reflection of a single incident of overstocking, because pastures overgrazed in the fall will take longer to regrow and produce fewer nutrients in the spring. Similar in appearance, the former situation would provide better nutrition than the latter. As a general rule, well-managed pastures are rotated when 50% of the useable forage has been consumed (Undersander et al., 2002; Sprinkle & Bailey, 2004; Bartlett, 2005). Remember that the nutrition provided by pasture forage is dependent on the plants present, growing conditions, maturity of the plant, and the portions consumed of leaves, stems, and flowers (Undersander et al., 2002; Bartlett, 2005; USDA Natural Resource Conservation Service, 2003).

Hay should be free from mold and excessive dust and be stored in a dry, well-ventilated area. In general, the greener and leafier the hay, the more nutrients are available. The subsequent harvests from a hay field have a lower yield per acre, but the hay is more nutrient dense. For example, the second cutting (harvest) from an alfalfa field has greener, more nutrient-dense plants than the first cutting (Balliette & Torell, 1998). Round bales that are stored outside on the ground will mold on the outside. Livestock species will strip away the outside layers to access the edible inner portion. Hay samples should be collected with a coring device or representative flakes should be placed in paper, a label inside and outside on the container, marked as evidence, and shipped to a laboratory for nutrient analysis via a courier service.

Document the weight of all types of concentrates and supplements. Collect labels from mineral blocks, grain bags, and additives to determine if a balanced ration was available. If the grain is custom mixed by a local feed mill, it should be analyzed for content. The mill is required to supply the list of ingredients and proportions for each batch of prepared custom mix feed. If the list of ingredients is not included on the invoice, a phone call or visit to the feed store will provide the necessary information.

In addition to the qualitative analysis, the amount of grain purchased (documented with invoices, check stubs, or farm account at the feed store), divided by the time interval (in days) and the number of animals fed will give a pound/head/day amount for an individual. For example:

Table 17.2 Minimum feeder space for meal fed animals

Species	Bunk Space Required/Head
Beef calves	18–22 inches
Finishing cattle >600 lbs	20–26 inches
Bred dairy cows	24–30 inches
Lactating cows	30 inches
Dairy calves 2–4 months old	18 inches
Dairy calves 5 months until breeding	20–24 inches
Pigs	1.1 times the shoulder width
Sheep	16–20 inches
Lambs	9–12 inches
Goats	16 inches
Laying hens and broilers	5 inches
Broiler chicks up to 4 weeks	1 inch
Broiler chicks 4–8 weeks	2 inches
Broiler chicks 8–16 weeks	3 inches

One ton of grain is purchased every 2 weeks for 50 head of cattle.

$$2000 \text{ lb grain} \div 14 \text{ days} = 142.86 \text{ lb/day fed to 50 cattle}$$

$$142.86 \text{ lb/day} \div 50 \text{ cattle} = 2.86 \text{ lb/head/day}$$

The amount of hay, silage, haylage, or other forage can be similarly calculated if the weights are known. Square hay bales can be weighed. Round bale weight can be estimated based on the diameter of the bale and the moisture content. Alternatively, a few representative bales can be loaded on a flatbed and the trailer weighed with and without cargo at a certified scale. Certified scales can be found at truck stops, grain elevators, and bulk landscape supply stores.

Forage purchases coupled with concentrate purchases are used to calculate the number of calories and nutrients provided to the animal(s). The National Research Council (NRC) series on nutrient requirements for the various species can be used as a minimum standard for adequate nutrition (https://www.nap.edu/collection/63/nutrient-requirements-of-animals).

If feed is being provided in adequate amounts but there is inadequate room at the feeders, then social starvation can occur when dominant herd members prevent the smaller, weaker animals from accessing the feed. Recommended space allowances are available from the state cooperative extension offices. If all animals are feeding simultaneously, minimum bunk space is required to accommodate all the individuals with extra space for the less aggressive feeders. Animals fed ad lib need less bunk space. Note if the feeders are appropriate for the species in size and configuration. Table 17.2 lists recommended feeder space.

Adequate Water

Water in liquid form is the most important nutrient. A total lack of water will result in death within a few days. Insufficient amounts of water cause prolonged suffering due to impaction, inappetence, decreased food digestibility, and increased susceptibility to disease from hyponutrition (Rübsamen & von Engelhardt, 1975). Minimum water requirements will vary by breed, environmental conditions, production stage, and diet. Recommended amounts for a variety of species, sizes, and production stage are provided by state extension offices, agricultural colleges, and numerous textbooks (Jurgens et al., 2012; Kellems & Church, 2010; Ward, 2007). See Table 17.3.

Water can be provided via natural sources (rivers, ponds, lakes, streams) as well as via troughs. Availability of natural water sources can be seasonal, with ice-over in the North during the winter

Table 17.3 Minimum water requirements

Species and Age/Production	Amount of Water or Drinker/Trough Space
Dairy cattle calves <4 months old	2.5 gallons
Dairy calves 5–24 months	6.5 gallons
Lactating dairy cattle	30 gallons
Non-lactating adult cattle	11 gallons
Beef cattle dry lot 400–800 pounds body weight	7 gallons
800–1400 pounds	11 gallons
Lactating beef cattle	14.5 gallons
Dry cows/bulls/bred heifers	10 gallons
Swine 15–50 pounds	½ gallon
50–150 pounds	1.25 gallons
150–250 pounds	2.4 gallons
Gestating sows and boars	4 gallons
Lactating sows	5.25 gallons
Horses	1 gallon/100 pounds body weight
Lactating mares	2 gallons/100 pounds body weight
Sheep: Lambs 50–125 pounds	1 gallon
Adults	1.5 gallons
Lactating ewes	2.75 gallons
Goats: Adults	1–3 gallons/day
Lactating does	Maintenance plus 1 quart/pint of milk produced
Adult chickens	1 pint–1 quart/bird/day
Ducks	Free choice 8–12 hours a day unless temperature is ≥90°F, then unlimited water
Turkeys 0–4 weeks	½ inch drinker space/bird
5–16 weeks	1 inch drinker space/bird
16–29 weeks	1 inch drinker space/bird
Adults	1 inch drinker space/bird

Note: Amounts are averages. Consumption increases with exercise and increases in temperature/humidity above thermal comfort.

and summer droughts causing evaporation and diminished tributary supply. Note if the collection pond appears to be spring fed or otherwise in constant supply. Vernal ponds are seasonal during wet seasons and may provide inconsistent quality as well as quantity. Pollutants will be concentrated during droughts, rendering the water seasonally undrinkable. Water testing services are available at several commercial and university laboratories.

Troughs must be accessible to all individuals as the water level drops (Figure 17.6). Safeguards against drowning should be in place. Troughs and tanks need to refill at a reasonable rate in light of the number of animals accessing them. A single cow can consume 2–6 gallons of water a minute in warm weather. Check automatic waterers for refill rates and cleanliness.

Distance to water can have an impact on welfare. Recommended distance to water in confined, rotationally grazed pastures is 800 feet. Open-range recommended maximum distance to water is 2 miles over flat terrain and 1 mile if the topography is rugged (Smith et al., 1986). It is acceptable agricultural practice for cattle to utilize snow as a sole water source providing there is an abundance of untrampled snow and they have been acclimated to its use.

Water must be potable. In coastal areas, salinity might be a problem, especially after storm surges. Total dissolved solids (TDS), a measure of salinity, >5000 ppm will decrease consumption and weight gain. Water containing >10 000 ppm should not be used as a water source (Dyer,

Figure 17.6 Troughs must be accessible to all individuals as the water level drops.

2012; Gadberry, 2016). Surface water sources may be contaminated with runoff, algal blooms, or botulism. Well water may contain heavy metals (lead, mercury, cadmium, arsenic, chromium), nitrites, elements (zinc, boron, selenium, fluoride), or coliform bacteria (Sallenave, 2016).

If the water supply and drinking space appear to be adequate, check for stray voltage that would discourage utilization of the tank (Fisher, 2008). Water flavor may be off due to the presence of noxious smells, mold in the tanks, or chemicals. Water can be analyzed for mineral content, toxins, bacterial contamination, pH, algae, and mold. If particulate matter is a concern, photographing water bottles filled with samples prior to laboratory analysis will be provide graphic evidence of the water quality (Figure 17.7).

Adequate Shelter

Shelter is adequate if it provides protection from the elements and a place to rest. The animals should be reasonably clean and dry. Cleanliness scores are available for a variety of breeds and are generated according to the body parts affected and the severity. See Resources for a list of useable scoring charts. Lack of cleanliness in dairy cattle has been linked to an increase in somatic cell counts, lameness, hock lesions, and claw problems (Reneau et al., 2005; Sadig et al., 2017). Low cleanliness scores in beef cattle have been linked to increased lameness and culling due to disease (Gottardo et al., 2008).

Evidence of thermal stress includes signs of both heat and cold intolerance. Thermal comfort zones vary by species and breed. See Table 17.4 for a partial list. Signs of heat stress/heat exhaustion include excessive sweating (horses, cattle), excessive panting, postural changes, (poultry, cattle, pigs), inappetence, open mouth breathing, salivation/ptyalism, staggering, elevated rectal temperature, and/or collapse. Heat index charts are available for a variety of species to determine the relative risk of heat exhaustion (Kerr, 2015). Avoid moving, handling, or stressing livestock when the temperature and humidity are high and 10% of the group is exhibiting signs of moderate heat stress. Panting scores are used to assess the current level of heat stress in individuals (Table 17.5). Animals that score $\geq$3.5 are in danger of dying. Heat stress is cumulative, especially in sheep and South American camelids. Recording temperature and humidity at the animal level inside the pen or stall will provide an accurate reflection of the true conditions experienced by the livestock.

Figure 17.7 Photograph water samples before laboratory submission to document color and turbidity.

Table 17.4 Thermoneutral zones

Species	Weight	Thermoneutral Zone
Bovine		
Calves	<500 pounds	50–68°F
Adult cattle	>500 pounds	41–68°F
Goats		50–68°F Fiber goats lower
Horses		41–77°F
Pigs		
	4–12 pounds	85–96°F
	12–25 pounds	70–79°F
	25–35 pounds	65–73°F
	35–65 pounds	60–69°F
	65–130 pounds	58–65°F
	130–280 pounds	55–62°F
Sows and boars	>500 pounds	53–65°F
Poultry		Depends on housing and stocking density
Broiler adults		73.5–84.5°F
Layer adults		68–77°F
Turkey		68–78°F
Ducks		47–74°F
Sheep		70–77°F depending on age, fleece and humidity

Sources: Adapted from Arieli et al. (2007), Cherry & Morris (2008), Gaughan et al. (2008), Ghassemi Nejad & Sung (2017), Global Animal Partnership (n/d), Gottardo et al. (2008), Kerr (2015), Lammers et al. (2007), Meat and Livestock Australia (2006), Meltzer (1983), Morgan (1998), Watkins et al. (2008), Whay et al. (2003).

Note: Humidity will narrow the range.

Table 17.5 Panting scores

Species	Panting Score	Respiratory Rate bpm	Chest Movement	Saliva/Drool	Mouth	Tongue	Posture
Cattle							
	0	<40	Barely visible	None	Closed	Not seen	Normal
	1	40–70	Easily seen	None	Closed	Not seen	Normal
	2	70–120	Fast pant	Visible	Closed	Not seen	Normal
	2.5	70–120	Fast pant	Visible	Occasionally open	Not seen	Normal
	3	120–160	Fast pant	Visible	Open	Not seen	Head and neck extended level with back
	3.5	120–160	Fast pant	Excessive drool	Open	Out at times	Head and neck extended
	4.0	>160	Fast pant	Ropes of drool	Open	Extended	Head and neck extended
	4.5	May slow to <160	Deeper excursions	May cease	Open	Extended	Lowered head and neck
Sheep							
	0	30	Barely seen	None	Closed	Not seen	Normal
	1	40–60	Slight pant	None	Closed	Not seen	Normal
	2	60–80	Fast pant	None	Occasionally open	Not seen	Normal
	3	80–120	Fast pant	Present	Open	Not seen	Head and neck extended
	4	>200	Fast pant	Present	Open	Extended	Lowered head and neck
Poultry							
	0		Normal breathing				Normal posture
	1		Episodes of panting				Normal posture
	2		Prolonged panting				Wings outstretched
	3		Prolonged panting				Wings outstretched and sitting
	4		Panting				Prostration

Sources: Adapted from Arieli et al. (2007), Bird et al. (1988), Global Animal Partnership, Welfare Quality Protocol for Poultry, Mack et al. (2013), Gaughan et al. (2008).

Stocking density is defined as "the concentration of animals in a given space." Stocking rate is a reflection of the number of animals that can be grazed on a piece of land with a limited amount of forage for a grazing season, (Example: 2 head/acre). Minimum stocking density has been suggested in a variety of references by species (AssureWel®, Global Animal Partnership®, Welfare Quality®).

Animals living in confinement have minimum requirements for ventilation and air exchange that are affected by housing type and weather conditions. A higher rate of air exchange is required during hot, humid conditions to maintain air quality. During colder weather, too high a rate will create drafts. Inadequate ventilation is reflected in elevated ammonia levels.

Adequacy of bedding is dependent on bedding type, quantity, and flooring. If the animals are clean and dry and the ammonia levels are acceptable, then bedding is probably adequate. Inadequate bedding is reflected in an increase in lameness (pododermatitis in poultry, digital dermatitis in ruminants, thrush in equine), abscesses (ruminants, swine, poultry), and hock lesions (cattle and swine raised in confinement). Bedding that is compacted, saturated, or moldy causes poor air quality by increasing particulates and ammonia. Research information on the adverse effects of ammonia is available for cattle: decreased function of respiratory protective functions and consequent increase in respiratory disease (Marschang, 1973); swine: increased neonatal loss, arthritis, abscesses (Donham, 1991); poultry and humans: rhinitis, cough, dyspnea, death (Carlile, 1984; Issley, 2015). The animals will exhibit one or more of the following clinical signs if the ammonia levels rise:

- Epiphora (watery eyes/tearing) all species
- Decrease weight gain in growing pigs at >50 ppm
- Respiratory lesions in pigs at >100 ppm (Drummond et al., 1978, 1980, 1981a,b)
- Respiratory lesions in cattle at >80 ppm (Lillie & Thompson, 1972)
- Ocular and respiratory signs in poultry at >40 ppm (Carlile, 1984)
- Pododermatitis, breast and hock burn in poultry (Global Animal Partnership; Kaukonen et al., 2016)

Commercial devices can be used to measure ammonia levels before personnel enter the premises and open the doors. Local fire departments, police stations, or environmental protection agencies can be contacted to assess air quality prior to exposure. If levels are high, use of Tyvek suits will limit contact dermatitis.

Further assessment of air quality is documented by measuring airborne particulate matter. A sheet of black paper is placed on a level surface in each enclosure housing livestock for 30 minutes. After collecting the dust, cover the sheet with acetate and label with the location, case, date and time, and collector. A black sheet of paper serves as a control. Photograph the sheets next to each other and retain them as evidence, if needed, for court.

Poultry litter quality is measured by the quality and cleanliness of the feathers and a lack of lesions on the foot pads, hocks, and breasts. If a large number of birds are present, a random sampling of birds can be used to document the cleanliness of the birds. If 50 or fewer birds are present, then individual birds should be assessed utilizing a body region technique (Campe et al., 2018). Presence and cleanliness of feathers should be noted on the head, neck, tail, wings, back, breast, and vent separately (LayWel, 2006). Wounds should be recorded in the same areas. Utilization of photographs and individual scar charts (see Resources) will aid documentation. While establishment of a pecking order is a normal expression of avian behavior, feather pecking refers to the damage or removal of feathers by a dominant bird. Feather loss can also be a result of normal thinning of feathers during a laying period. Molting during laying periods and seasonal molts are normal events. A characteristic pattern of broken feathers along the dorsal neck will be seen as a result of males grasping the neck of the females during the mating process. In extreme cases, generally flocks with a high male to female ratio, the skin may be damaged. Feathers damaged along the cranial surface of the wings are an indication the bird is using its wings to ambulate. Feather pecking can lead to cannibalism, which is a multifactorial problem involving genetics and husbandry practices. The

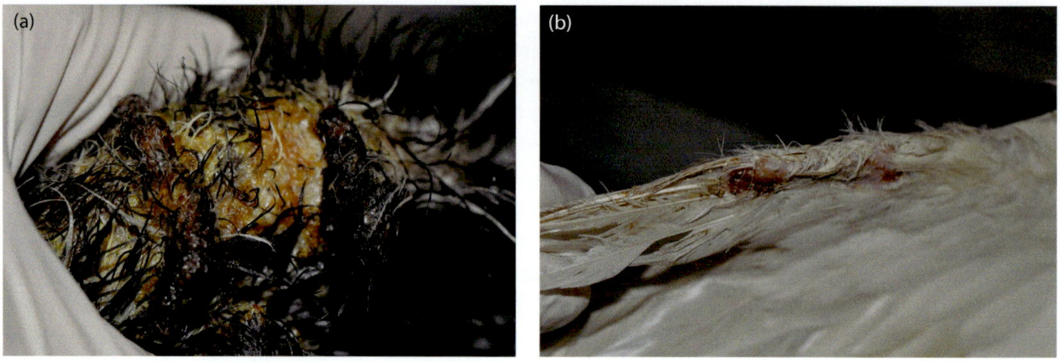

Figure 17.8 (a) Broken feathers and damaged skin on the dorsal neck of a female duck. (b) Abraded skin and damaged feathers on the cranial surface of the wing. This bird had severe, bilateral, tibiotarsal osteomyelitis and used her wings as crutches to ambulate.

victim birds should be segregated and treated (Clauer 2009, Jacob 2015). Note the extent and depth of the injury and presence of topical medications (Figure 17.8a,b).

Pododermatitis is an inflammation of the skin on the plantar surface of the avian foot that varies in appearance from small areas of discoloration to large erosions with crusts. Wet and sticky litter is a contributing factor in the development of the lesions (de Jong & van Harn, 2012). Bacteria can enter the disrupted skin causing septicemia or infectious arthritis. Lesions can be described as "no lesions," "mild lesions," and "severe lesions" or be graded according to one of the established welfare assessment protocols (Global Animal Partnership, LayWel, Welfare Assure). The scale chosen should be referenced in the report. The number and severity of lesions should be tallied and expressed as a percentage of the group affected (Figure 17.9a,b). Hock lesions may be documented with pododermatitis or be listed as a separate defect.

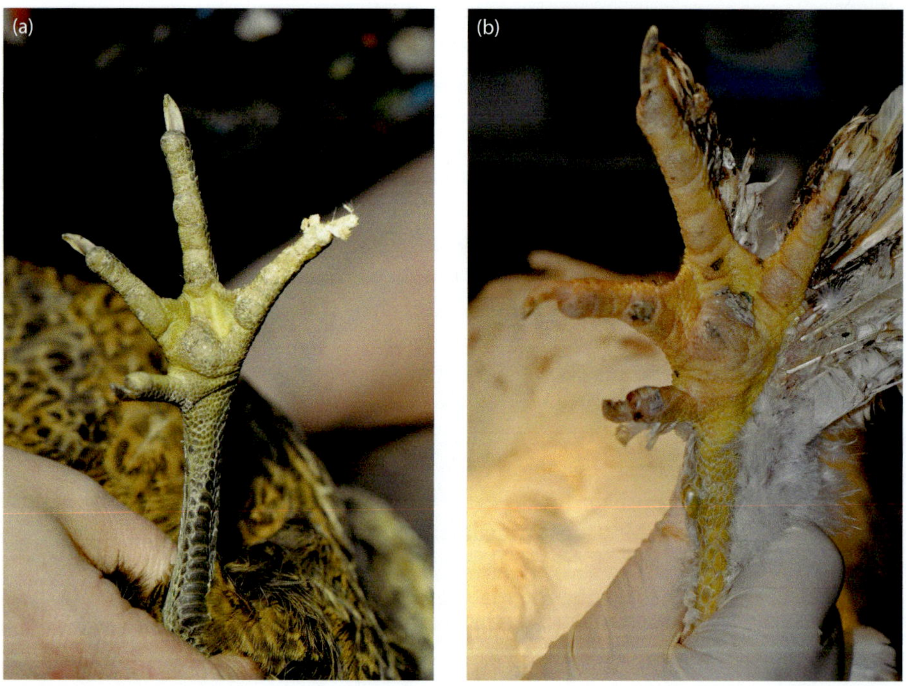

Figure 17.9 Plantar surface of chicken feet. (a) Normal/no lesions. (b) Mild lesions/score 2/3 LayWel® system.

Hock and carpal lesions in dairy cattle are considered a welfare issue related to abrasive lying surfaces, inadequate bedding materials, and rubbing against the cubicle fittings. These lesions can become infected and cause lameness (Kester and Frankena, 2014). Lesions should be documented photographically and drawn on the individual's scar chart. Potterton et al. (2011) used four-point scale: "none" is a normal hock with no evidence of damaged hair, "mild" indicates the hair is worn, "moderate" reflected a loss of skin integrity, and "severe" lesions included swelling as well as a break in the skin (Whay et al., 2003). The presence and grade of lameness is also noted.

Adequate Medical Care

Welfare evaluation protocols developed for commercial production units (Global Animal Partnership, Welfare Quality, Red Tractor Assurance, Royal Society for the Prevention of Cruelty to Animals) can be modified for smaller, multiple species scenarios. Guidelines for choosing techniques to evaluate representative samples and parameters to consider can be adapted effectively. Untreated wounds, lameness, and evidence of preventive medicine are documented.

Vaccination and parasite control programs are evidenced by low fecal egg counts, veterinary receipts, and vaccination records appropriate for the species and region. To assess the adequacy of parasite control, the condition of the animals must be considered. If the BCS is adequate, then the parasite burden is not detrimental to that individual. Animals with low BCS, diarrhea, or ill thrift should have a fecal egg count (FEC) performed. The modified McMaster technique is the current gold standard for FECs in ruminant species. The results are reported in eggs per gram (epg) of feces. The acceptable epg is dependent on the species, the season, and the production stage. Horses are generally dewormed at >200 epg. Recommended levels for small ruminants during warm weather when the barber pole worm (*Haemonchus contortus*) is most problematic are non-pregnant adults at 2000 epg, bred females and young stock at 1000 epg, and lactating does at 750 epg. During the colder months, other species of worms (brown stomach worm [*Ostertagia ostertagi*] and bankrupt worm [*Trichostrongylus columbriformis*]) predominate that produce fewer eggs per female, so deworming should occur at one-half of the summer numbers (nonpregnant adults at 1000 epg, etc.) (Fernandez, 2012). References and videos demonstrating the technique are available online (https://www.wormx.info/fecal-egg-counting). Submission to a veterinary clinic or laboratory is also an option. If you suspect *Cryptosporidium parvuum*, submission to a laboratory is preferred as these organisms can be challenging to document without special staining and a trained observer. After deworming, a reduction in the egg count should be documented to demonstrate that a resistant strain of parasite is not present in the herd (Sanders, 2015). In most livestock species, internal parasites are never eliminated. If FECs are low, then the ill-thrift of the animals is likely due to another cause.

External parasites impact welfare by causing weight loss, anemia, pruritus, and alopecia. Some external parasites are USDA/APHIS reportable diseases. These include Old World screwworm (*Chrysomya bezziana*) and New World screwworm (*Cochliomyia hominivorax*) in all livestock species, and mange in sheep and goats. Some external parasites can be visualized with the naked eye or with the aid of a hand lens, while others require skin scraping or tape prep for a definitive diagnosis. Lice tend to be species specific and spend their life cycle on the host, surviving for about a week in the environment. Transmission can be direct from animal to animal or indirect via shared grooming tools, or contaminated bedding or equipment. Lice are more numerous in the winter because they stop reproducing or die at higher temperatures. Cattle and goats are commonly infested with lice while horses, unless debilitated, are less susceptible. Affected cattle will lick themselves, leaving saliva-matted hair, while goats, horses, and pigs will rub against objects. Lice will avoid light and move into another sheltered location as the hair shafts are parted. Nits will be found attached to the hair/feathers. Nits can be collected in a glass vial with or without alcohol. Lice can be photographed on the animal with a macrolens and/or images taken from a microscope slide to demonstrate the biting or sucking mouthparts that aid in identification

Figure 17.10 Pig with scabies and lice. Note red, thickened skin, hyperplastic gray areas on snout, regions of alopecia, and evidence of self-trauma.

of the species. Nits on the hair will demonstrate that lice have had sufficient time to reproduce (20–40 days). Poultry can be infested with several species of lice simultaneously—40 species have been identified to date including, most commonly, the body louse (*Menacanthus stramineus*), head louse (*Culclotogaster heterographa*), and the shaft louse (*Menopon gallinae*), which deposits nits on the base of the feather shaft. Light burdens are common and not detrimental. Heavy burdens can cause anemia, feather loss, and ill-thrift. The northern fowl mite/feather mite (*Ornithonyssus sylvarium*) will cause soiled feathers on the ventrum of the bird (vent, tail, legs). Red mites (*Dermanysus galllinae*) feed on the birds at night and then seclude themselves in the hen house during the day. Heavily infested birds will lose weight. Providing the birds with a dust bath containing diatomaceous earth, wettable sulfur powder, or sand will control the external parasite load (Martin and Mullens, 2012). Pigs with scabies (*Sarcoptes scabei* var *suis*) will rub against objects, lose hair, and develop thickened skin (Figure 17.10 and Table 17.6).

Regionally, the Cooperative Extension Service, the state veterinarian, or local livestock veterinarians can offer guidance regarding minimum vaccination requirements for that area. Receipts from online veterinary supply and local feed stores may document vaccine purchases. The farm veterinarian may have administered or dispensed vaccine. Biologicals should be stored in the refrigerator at a controlled temperature. The presence of a preventable disease in the flock/herd should be documented in conjunction with the amount of vaccine purchased and evidence of timely administration.

Lameness Scores

Lameness can be the result of an acute injury or a chronic problem. A small percentage of mild lameness in a group is normal, but large numbers of lame animals or severely lame animals without evidence of treatment is cause for concern. Each livestock species has its own protocol for scoring lameness (Desrochers et al., 2001; Penev, 2011; Olechnowicz & Jaskowski, 2013; Sadiq et al., 2017; Sprecher et al., 1997). In general, individual animals should be observed as they are moved slowly across a smooth, flat surface with good traction. Horses, if halter broken, can be walked and jogged on a slack lead and observed from the front, back, and side at both gaits. Poultry are moved in a group. Table 17.7 lists lameness scoring protocols by species.

Table 17.6 Parasites and their preferred location on the body

Species	Parasite	Location on Body
Bovine		
Lice—sucking	*Hematopinus eurysternus*	Poll, nose, eye, neck, brisket
	Lignathus vituli	Withers, tail, axillae, groin
	Solenopotes capillatus	Head, especially the face, and jaw
Lice—biting	*Bovicola bovis,* formerly (*Damalina bovis*)	Neck, withers, tail head
Ticks—Hard ticks	*Amblyomma americanum* Lone Star Tick	Perianal region, udder, dewlap, flank fold, axillary fold
	Dermacentor sp. American Dog or Wood Tick; Rocky Mountain Wood Tick	Around the ears, udders, tailhead
	Dermacentor nitens Tropical Horse Tick	Ears
	Rhipicephalus sp. Cattle or Blue Tick	Around the face
Soft ticks	*Otobius megnini* Spinose Ear Tick	Medial pinnae
Mites	*Sarcoptes scabiei* var *bovis*	Face, neck, shoulders, rump
	Psoroptes ovis	Tailhead, base of horns, around the neck—may cover entire body
	Chorioptes sp. Leg Mites or Barn Itch	Lower legs, hooves, between legs, tail
	Demodex bovis Follicle Mite	Neck, shoulders, axillae, udder
	Raillietia auris Cattle Ear Mite	Ears
Flies Muscidae Biting flies	*Stomoxys* Stable Fly	Legs, ventral abdomen, flanks
	Siphona irritans Horn Fly	Backs, withers, sides (ventral abdomen in hot weather)
	Musca autumnalis Face Fly	Eyes, nose, lips
Ox Warble	*Hypoderma bovis* Warble Fly	Lay eggs on legs—adults do not feed
Goat		
Lice—sucking	*Linognathus africanus* African Blue Louse or African Goat Louse	Body, head, neck
	Linognathus stenopsis Goat Sucking Louse	Entire body
	Linognathus pedalis (Sheep) Foot Louse	Feet, legs
Lice—biting	*Bovicola caprae* Goat Biting Louse	Entire body
	Bovicola crassipes Angora Goat Biting Louse/ Hairy Goat Louse	Entire body

(Continued)

Table 17.6 (*Continued*) Parasites and their preferred location on the body

Species	Parasite	Location on Body
	Bovicola limbata Fringed Goat Louse/ Angora Goat Louse	Entire body
Ticks—Hard ticks	*Amblyomma maculatum* Gulf Coast Tick	Base of the horns, in ears
	Amblyomma americanum Lone Star Tick	Withers and neck, less commonly head and axillae
	Dermacentor variabilis American Dog Tick	
Soft ticks	*Otobius megnini* Spinose Ear Tick	Medial pinnae, ear canal, ear margins
Mites	*Demodex caprae* Goat Follicle Mite	Face, neck, axillae, udder (Saanen breed more severely affected)
	Sarcoptes scabiei Scabies Mite	Muzzle, eyes, ear margins, inner thighs to hocks, scrotum, ventrum
	Psoroptes cuniculi Psoroptic Ear Mite	Medial surface of pinnae
	Chorioptes bovis Chorioptic Scab Mite	Legs and feet
Fleas	*Ctenocephalides felis* Cat Flea	Entire body especially head, neck, ventrum
	Echidnophaga gallinacea Sticktight Flea	Face and ears
Flies—Keds	*Melophagus ovinus* Sheep Ked/Sheep Tick (Wingless Fly)	Neck, sides, rump, abdomen
Diptera	*Oestrus ovis* Nasal (Nose) Bot Fly	Larva deposited on muzzle, develop in sinuses
Muscidae Biting flies	*Haematobia irritans* Horn Fly	Back, sides, ventrum, legs
	Stomoxys calcitrans Stable Fly	Legs and feet
	Tabanus sp. Horse Fly	Legs and back
	Chrysops sp. Deer Fly	Head, back, legs
Horse		
Lice—sucking	*Hematopinus asini* Horse Sucking Louse	Mane, head, neck, back, inner thigh
Lice—biting	*Werneckiella* (*Damalina, Bovicola*) *equi* Horse Biting Louse	Head, mane, tail base, shoulders
Ticks—Hard ticks	*Ixodes scapularis* Black-Legged or Deer Tick	
	Ixodes pacificus Western Black-Legged Tick	
	Dermacentor variabilis American Dog Tick	
	Dermacentor albipictus Winter Tick	

(Continued)

Table 17.6 (*Continued*) Parasites and their preferred location on the body

Species	Parasite	Location on Body
	Dermacentor andersoni Rocky Mountain Wood Tick	
	Amblyomma americanum Lone Star Tick	
	Amblyomma maculatum Gulf Coast Tick	
	Amblyomma cajennense Cayenne Tick	
	Rhipicephalus sanguineus Brown Dog Tick	
Tick—Soft ticks	*Otobius megnini* Spinous Ear Tick	External ear canal, pinnae
Mites	*Chorioptes (equi) bovis* Leg Mange Mite	Legs, feathered area of fetlock in draft horses
	Psoroptes (equi) ovis	Mane, base of tail, axillae, between hind legs (rare in USA)
	Psoroptes (cuniculi) ovis	Ears
	Sarcoptes scabiei Sarcoptic Mange, Scabies	Sides, back, shoulders
	Demodex equi	Body
	Demodex caballi	Muzzle, around eyes
	Pymotes sp. Forage or Straw Itch Mites	Face, neck (hay rack or net) Muzzle, legs (fed off ground)
Flies—Diptera Muscidae	*Stomoxys calcitrans* Stable Fly	Legs
	Haematobia irritans Horn Fly	Neck, withers, back cool times of day Ventral midline during times of full sun
	Musca autumnalis Face Fly	Face, eyes, nasal discharge
	Musca domestica House Fly	Entire body
Tabanidae	*Tabanus* sp. Horse fly	Head, dorsum
	Chrysops sp. Deer Fly	Head, neck, shoulders
Oestridae	*Gasterophilus intestinalis* Horse Bot Fly/Stomach Bot Fly	Eggs deposited on legs
	Gasterophilus nasalis Nose Bot Fly	Eggs deposited intermandibular space
	Gasterophilus haemorrhoidalis Throat Bot Fly	Eggs deposited on muzzle
Pigs		
Lice—sucking	*Haematopinus suis*	Ears, neck folds, axillae, groin
Ticks—Hard ticks	*Dermacentor variabilis* American Dog Tick	
	Dermacentor andersoni Rocky Mountain Wood Tick	

(Continued)

Table 17.6 (*Continued*) Parasites and their preferred location on the body

Species	Parasite	Location on Body
	Amblyomma maculatum Gulf Coast Tick	
	Amblyomma auricularium	
	Ixodes scapularis	
Ticks—Soft ticks	*Otobius megnini* Spinose Ear Tick	Ear canal
Mites	*Sarcoptes scabiei* var *suis*	Ears initially, then whole body
	Demodex phylloides	
Fleas	*Echidnophaga gallinacean* Sticktight Flea	Ears
Flies—Diptera Muscidae	*Stomoxys calcitrans* Stable Fly	
Poultry		
Lice—Biting lice (40 identified species)	*Menacanthus stramineus* Chicken Body Louse	
	Menopon gallinae Shaft Louse	Nits at base of feather shaft
	Culclogaster heterographa Head Louse	
Ticks—Soft ticks	*Argas persicus* Fowl Tick/Blue Bugs	Feed on birds at night especially in the coop
Mites	*Ornithonyssus sylvarium* Northern Fowl Mite/ Feather Mite	Vent, tail, rear legs, on eggs
	Dermanyssus gallinae Chicken Mite/Red Mite/ Roost Mite	Feeds on poultry at night and lives in coop during the day
	Knemidocoptes mutans Scaly Leg Mite/Face and Leg Mite	Proliferative lesions on scaled portion of legs
Fleas	*Echidnophaga gallinae* Sticktight Flea	Featherless areas—around eyes, combs, wattles, turkey head and neck
Sheep		
Lice—sucking lice	*Linognathus stenopsis* Sheep Sucking Louse	Whole body infested
	Linognathus africanus Blue Louse	Body, head, neck
	Linognathus pedalis Foot Louse	Feet, lower legs
Lice—Chewing lice	*Damalinia* (*Bovicola*) *ovis* Biting Louse	Dorsum
Ticks—Hard ticks	*Dermacentor variabalis* American Dog Tick	
	Dermacentor andersonii Rocky Mountain Wood Tick	
	Amblyomma americanum Lone Star Tick	

(Continued)

Table 17.6 (*Continued*) Parasites and their preferred location on the body

Species	Parasite	Location on Body
	Amblyomma maculatum Gulf Coast Tick	
Ticks—Soft ticks	*Otobius megnini* Spinose Ear Tick	Ear canal
Mites	*Sarcoptes scabiei* var. *ovis* Mange Mite	Head, sides, back, legs
	Psorobia ovis Sheep Itch Mite	Entire body
	Psoroptes ovis Sheep Scab Mite	Areas with dense wool
	Chorioptes sp. Chorioptic Scab Mite	Feet, legs
	Psoroptes cuniculi Psoroptic Ear Mite	Ear margins, ear canal
Flies—Keds	*Melophagus ovinus*	Neck, sides, rump, abdomen
Bot Fly	*Oestrus ovis* Sheep Nasal Bot Fly	Larvae in nasal sinuses

Sources: Foreyt (2001), French et al. (2016), Greenacre & Morishita (2015), Kahn & Line (2010), Kaufman et al. (2015a), Kaufman et al. (2015b), Koehler et al. (2015), Loftin (2008), Martin & Mullens (2012), McClendon & Kaufman (2007), Merrill et al. (2018), Mertins et al. (2017), Scott (1988), Smith & Sherman (2009), Talley (2015), Teders (2008), Watson & Luginbuhl (2015).

Table 17.7 Lameness scoring by species

Species/Author	Lameness Grade	Description
Cattle		
Desrochers et al. (2001) Beef	0–Normal	Walks easily, readily bears weight evenly on all four legs.
	1–Mild	Walks easily, bears full weight on limb, but stride is shortened or altered. Back level.
	2–Moderate	Reluctant to walk and bear weight, but still uses the limb to ambulate with a shortened stride. Back may be arched.
	3–Severe	Reluctant to stand. Recumbent most of the time. Refuses to walk without stimulation. Hops over limb to prevent weight-bearing. Nonweight-bearing when standing. Back is arched. Pelvis is tipped.
	4–Catastrophic	Recumbent and unable to rise. Humane euthanasia is indicated.
Berry (Zinpro Dairy)	1–Normal	Walks normally. Level back. Long strides.
	2–Mildly lame	Gait slightly abnormal. Back level when standing, but arches when walking.
	3–Moderately lame	Shortened strides on one or more legs. Back arched when standing and walking. Dewclaws sink on leg opposite of affected leg.
	4–Lame	Lame on one or more limbs. Still partially weight-bearing. Back arched when standing or walking. Sinking of dewclaws obvious.
	5–Severely lame	Reluctant to move with almost complete weight transfer off the affected limb. Pronounced arching of back.

(Continued)

Table 17.7 (*Continued*) Lameness scoring by species

Species/Author	Lameness Grade	Description
Beef/Zinpro	0–Normal	Walks normally with no change in gait. Hind feet land close to hoof print of forefeet.
	1–Mild lameness	Short strides when walking. Drops head slightly. Limp not observed at walk.
	2–Moderate lameness	Obvious limp, but still weight-bearing. Slight head bob when walking.
	3–Severe lameness	Little or no weight-bearing. Reluctant or unable to move. Back is arched with dropped head and tipped pelvis. Head bob when moving. Recumbent most of the time.
	4–Catastrophic	Reluctant or unable to rise. Humane euthanasia recommended.
AHDB–United Kingdom Dairy	0–Good mobility	Flat back. Walks with even weight-bearing and rhythm on all four legs. Long, fluid strides.
	1–Imperfect mobility	Steps uneven (rhythm or weight-bearing) or a shortened stride. Affected limb or limbs not immediately identifiable.
	2–Impaired mobility	Uneven weight-bearing on a limb that is immediately identifiable and/or a shortened stride. Usually an arch in the center of the back.
	3–Severely impaired mobility	Unable to keep up with the herd (walk at a brisk human pace). Lame leg easy to identify-limping, may barely stand on leg. Back arched when standing or walking.
Equine AAEP Lameness Scale		
Industry Standard	0	Lameness not perceptible under any circumstances.
	1	Lameness is difficult to observe and is not consistently apparent regardless of circumstances (under saddle, hard surfaces, on incline, circling).
	2	Lameness difficult to observe at a walk or when trotting in a straight line, but becomes apparent under certain circumstances (under saddle, circling, incline, hard surfaces)
	3	Consistently observable at a trot under all circumstances.
	4	Obvious at a walk.
	5	Minimal weight bearing at a walk or at rest. Reluctant to move.
Pigs		
Zinpro—Sows	0	Moves easily. Comfortable on all four feet.
	1	Moves relatively easily—visible signs of lameness are apparent in at least one leg. Reluctant to bear weight but moves easily from site to site in barn.
	2	Lame in one or more limbs. Compensatory behavior evidenced by head bobbing or arched back.
	3	Reluctant to walk or weight bear. Difficult to move from place to place.
Main et al. (2004) Finishing pigs; this system includes behavioral assessment as well	0	Even strides. Caudal body sways slightly when walking. Pig is able to accelerate and change direction rapidly.

(Continued)

Table 17.7 (*Continued*) Lameness scoring by species

Species/Author	Lameness Grade	Description
	1	Abnormal stride length (not easily identified). Movements no longer fluid (pig appears stiff). Still able to accelerate and change direction.
	2	Shortened stride. Lameness detected. Swagger of caudal body when walking. No hindrance in pig's agility.
	3	Shortened stride. Minimum weight-bearing on affected limb. Swagger of caudal body while walking. Will still trot and gallop.
	4	Pig may not place affected limb on floor when moving.
	5	Pig does not move.
Welfare Quality Protocol	0	Normal gait or difficulty in walking but using all four legs. Swagger of caudal body when walking. Shortened strides.
	1	Severely lame. Minimal weight-bearing on affected limb(s).
	2	No weight-bearing on the affected limb(s). Unable to walk.
AssureWel	0–Not lame	Not lame. No apparent lameness, stiffness or uneven gait.
	1–Lame	Standing without full weight-bearing; standing on toes; walking with shortened stride; swagger in hindquarters, but still able to keep up at a trot or gallop.
	2–Severely lame	Nonweight-bearing
Poultry		
Chickens–Broilers		
Kestin et al. (1992)	0–"Gait Score 0"	Walks normally with no detectable abnormality. Dexterous and agile. Toes partially furled when the foot was in the air. No sway when walking. Can balance on one foot and walk backwards easily. Can easily deviate course to avoid other birds.
	1–"Gait Score 1"	Slight defect in the gait which is difficult to identify but would have precluded the bird's use as a breeding animal if gait were the sole selection criteria used. Uneven gait.
	2–"Gait Score 2"	Definite and identifiable gait defect, but not severe enough to prevent it from accessing resources.
	3–"Gait Score 3"	Obvious gait defect that hinders its ability to move about with maneuverability, acceleration and speed affected. Prefers squatting to moving.
	4–"Gait Score 4"	Severe gait defect. Still capable of walking, but with difficulty and only when strongly motivated. Squats down at the first available opportunity.
	5–"Gait Score 5"	Bird is incapable of sustained walking on its feet. May still be able to stand but can only move using wings or crawling in shanks.
Welfare Quality Broilers/ Laying Hens	0	Normal, agile, dexterous.
	1	Slightly abnormal, but difficult to define.
	2	Definite and identifiable abnormality.
	3	Obvious abnormality, affects ability to move.
	4	Severe abnormality, only takes a few steps.
	5	Incapable of walking.

(Continued)

Table 17.7 (*Continued*) Lameness scoring by species

Species/Author	Lameness Grade	Description
Webster et al. (2008) Broilers	0	No impairment of walking ability.
	1	Obvious impairment, but still ambulatory.
	2	Severe impairment, not able to walk without great difficulty.
Global Animal Partnership Turkeys 2018	0	Smooth gait with even steps that may be uneven at times. Well balanced. Foot may or may not curl when foot is lifted by the turkey. Able to walk quickly and/or run. Difficult to identify any abnormality when walking or running.
	1	Uneven gait. Irregular, short strides. Poor balance. Foot does not curl when lifted by the bird. May use wings to help with balance while walking. Squats within 15 seconds of standing or being forced to move with a gentle nudge. May lie down after several steps.
	2	Reluctant or unable to move. Shuffles or uses wings to help with movement. Takes few, if any, steps.
Sheep		
Kaler (2009)	0	Bears weight evenly on all four legs.
	1	Uneven posture, but no clear shortening of stride. Short stride one leg.
	2	Visible nodding of head with shortened, uneven stride.
	3	Excessive flicking of the head, more than nodding, in time with each stride.
	4	Nonweight-bearing when moving.
	5	Extreme difficulty rising, reluctant to move when stands. More than one limb affected.
	6	Will not stand or move.
Global Animal Partnership	0–Sound	Walks normally on all four legs. Easy, fluid strides.
	1–Moderately lame	Limp, head bob and shortened strides, but is able to keep up with the flock. May be hesitant to stride out. When standing, may be frequently weight-shifting onto toes or heels.
	2–Severely lame	Obvious limp. No longer able to keep up with the flock. Prominent head bob. Takes deliberate, choppy strides. May not put any weight on affected leg. May graze by resting on knees.
Responsible Wool Standard	0–Not lame	Movement smooth with weight borne evenly on all four feet with no shortened strides. Some minor head bobbing is acceptable if walking on uneven ground.
	1–Minor lameness	Clear shortening of stride with obvious head nodding or flicking as affected limb touches the ground.
	2–Lame	Very obvious head nodding and nonweight-bearing on affected limb when moving. Foot may be held up while stands. May be grazing on knees with front leg lameness. Steps shortened or uneven.
	3–Severe lameness	Recumbency or reluctance to stand or move. Affected limb is easily identifiable and may be held off the ground when walking or standing.

Sources: AssureWel, Cramer et al. (2018), De Jong & van Harn (2012), Desrochers et al. (2001), Greenough et al. (2003), Global Animal Partnership (2017), Gottardo et al. (2008), Kaler et al. (2009), Kestin et al. (1992), Main et al. (2000), Olechnowicz & Jaskowski (2013), Penev (2011), Responsible Wool Standard (2016), Sadiq et al. (2017), Sprecher et al. (1997), Webster et al. (2008), Whay et al. (2003).

DOCUMENTING LIVESTOCK SPECIES

Documenting the Individual

Established protocols that have been evaluated for repeatability between and among evaluators include:

- AssureWel at www.assurewel.org (laying hens, dairy cattle, broilers, pigs, beef cattle, sheep)
- Global Animal Partnership at www.globalanimalpartnership.org (beef cattle, broiler chickens, turkeys, sheep, goats, pigs, laying hens, bison)
- Welfare Quality at www.welfarequality.net or https://ec.europa.eu/food/sites/food/files/animals/docs/aw_arch_pres_092011_winckler_cattle_en.pdf (dairy cattle, pigs, poultry)
- Red Tractor certification at https://assurance.redtractor.org.uk/standards/search (dairy cattle, pigs, poultry)

Photographs

Each individual should be photographed in its enclosure, stall, field, or paddock. Photograph the enclosure from all four corners across the area with sufficient overlap to be able to reconstruct a 360° view if possible. Photograph the individual with its unique identification and case number with the agency, location, date, and photographer in at least the first photograph of the series. The individual should be photographed from the front, back, both sides, and a dorsal and/or a ventral view. Consider taking three additional views of the head to better document face markings, cowlicks, ear tags, ear notches, or tattoos. Placement of an LED or bright light behind the ear may increase the visualization of faded tattoos. Mid-range and close-up photographs with and without an ABFO 2 scale or ruler will document lesions. Wounds or scars that encircle the limb may require several images taken perpendicular to the lesion for accurate documentation. Individuals who are aged by tooth eruption pattern should have the relevant teeth photographed if possible.

Description

Breed and use matter, but unless there are registration papers with photographs, tattoos or microchips that match the individual, the animal should be described as a "type" to avoid challenge in court. For example: Individual 2-B-6-b is an approximately 4-year-old chestnut Arabian type mare with an elongated star and no natural leg markings. Use the color descriptions employed by the breed association the individual most closely resembles or define the color description in the report.

Bovine

Beef cattle breeds are grouped by geographic region of origin. The European breeds (*Bos taurus*) include Hereford, Aberdeen Angus, Charolais, Limousin, Simmental, Shorthorn, and their crosses. These breeds are characterized by their beef type, production longevity, and rapid growth. The South Asia breeds (*Bos indicus*) are also referred to as zebu or "humped" cattle. Characterized by their large dewlaps, droopy ears, and humped backs, they are tolerant of heat and humidity, resistant to internal and external parasites, and can efficiently use poorer quality (high-fiber) forages. They are slower to mature and carry less fat than the *Bos taurus* breeds. BCS charts have been developed for both types of beef cattle. Crosses of the two species are seen, and assessment of BCS will depend on "type" evidenced by the individual.

Dairy cattle (*Bos taurus)* may be single or dual purpose. When utilizing BCS charts, specify the chart that was used and include the reasons for assigning that score to that individual. For example, cow B-1-a-16, tag number left ear 206, a red and white Holstein type, 2-year-old female. BCS 2.5/5 using Edmonson et al. (1989) scale. Sharp, prominent ridge on dorsal spinous processes, depression visible from the dorsal to transverse spinous process, one half of the transverse spinous process visible, hooks and pins obvious with slight padding on the pins, pelvic line v-shaped, hooks rounded, definite depression between the hooks, tailhead to pins prominent with a "U"-shaped depression under the tail.

Physical exam will include vital signs (temperature, heart rate, respiratory rate and effort, mucous membrane color and capillary refill time, rumen motility), attitude and behavior (bright, quiet, responsive, somnolent, stuporous, fearful, fractious), and a full assessment of all body systems. Examination of the udder of females may indicate production status and evidence of mastitis. The use of a California Mastitis Test will document cases of subclinical mastitis (see Resources). Lameness score and evidence of the cause is generally included in the examination notes of the musculoskeletal system. Careful examination of the bovine hoof requires special restraint equipment for all but the gentlest family or 4-H cow that has been taught to submit to foot handling and treatment. Photography of the hoof from the front, sides, back, and ventral surface will demonstrate the presence of abscesses, dermatitis, hairy heel wart, overgrown claws, and foot rot (Relun et al., 2011).

Lameness should be scored and documented with video if possible. There are several protocols proposed for this species (Table 17.7). Be sure to cite the protocol used in your report and utilize the same protocol with each subsequent evaluation. Finding an optimal surface and conditions for gait analysis can be challenging (smooth, flat, non-slip footing with observer perpendicular to the animal's direction of movement). Sequential evaluation of locomotion will document response to treatment.

Equine

Identification photographs of all four sides should be accompanied by photographs of whorls and all four chestnuts (on the medial surface of the upper legs). A horse's chestnuts are considered to be as individual as fingerprints. Whorl patterns are documented with close-up images of the face and, if present, on the neck (Figure 17.11a,b).

Horses involved in cruelty/neglect cases are often underweight (BCS $\leq 3/9$), are heavily parasitized, have mild to moderate lameness, and/or have dental problems (Stull & Holcomb, 2014). In addition to routine identification photographs, images of the incisor teeth will document age estimation (see Resources). Sedation, mouth speculum, physical and/or chemical restraint, and auxiliary lighting are required for good intraoral photography to document pathology. Radiographs are useful in documenting tooth root abscesses and fractured or missing teeth. Photographs of the hoof should include front, back, sides, and ventral surface to document the health of the hoof capsule and

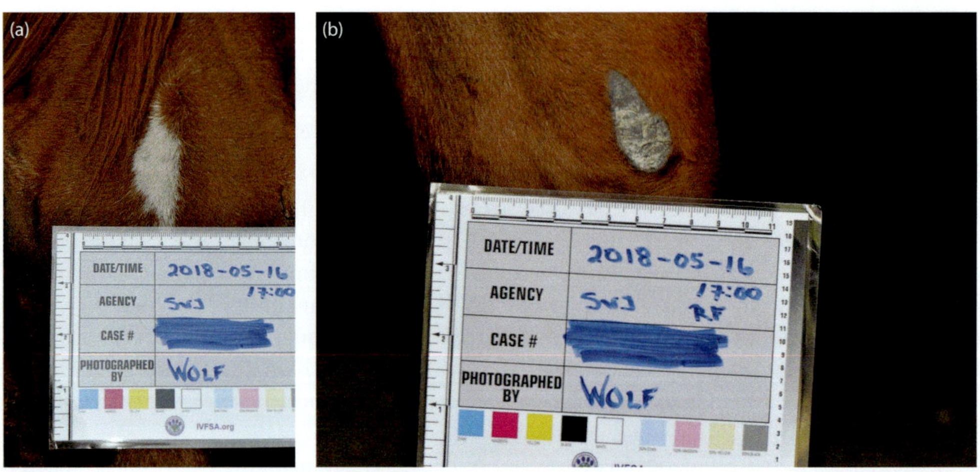

Figure 17.11 In addition to standard photographs for identification (front, back, sides, top, and belly), close-up photographs of (a) facial markings and whorls, and (b) chestnuts with the case placard indicating the leg (RF) insure positive identification of the individual.

evidence appropriate farrier care. Horseshoe wear patterns can indicate abnormal foot load, long-term lameness, or inappropriate shoeing. Lesions should be drawn on a species-appropriate scar chart with measurements, descriptions, estimated duration (fresh, healing, chronic), and any evidence of treatment. Receipts from the farrier will indicate frequency of hoof care unless the owner claims to have provided the necessary care. Examination of the caretaker's farrier tools will indicate recent use (or lack thereof). Lameness scoring protocols are well established in this species (Table 17.7).

Pigs

Depending on the individual and previous handling, most of the exam will be visual from a distance. Behavior, respiratory rate and effort, lameness, appetite, skin lesions, BCS, and joint swelling(s) can be documented without handling. Videotape can be used to document behavior, lameness, and respiratory patterns, while photography will reflect BCS and external lesions. Pigs will need to have some form of identification applied if not already in place. USDA APHIS requires all swine, except those shipped for slaughter, to have an official ear tag or tattoo based on the premise of origin prior to movement (see Resources). Lameness in this species is most often associated with claw lesions and joint swelling (Boyle et al., 2003). Photographic documentation of the affected areas will complement lameness scoring (Table 17.7).

Sheep and Goats

Goat descriptions should include the length and carriage of the ears. Nubians and Boer goats have pendulous ears, LaMancha goats have elf or gopher ears, while most of the other breeds have erect ears. The presence of horns, evidence of dehorning, and number and location of wattles should also be included in the description (Figure 17.12). The breed associations commonly have examples of accepted color descriptions (see Resources). Age can be approximated by examining the incisors, and is documented photographically.

Hair sheep are similar to non-fiber goats to document BCS and calculating a body weight based on measurements: $\text{Girth}^2 \times \text{Length} \div 300 = \text{Body Weight} +/- 2$ pounds (Teders, 1998). Animals in full fleece/fiber must have the wool parted to obtain an accurate girth circumference. Length measurement requires palpation of the point of the shoulder and point of the hip (Figure 17.13). BCS

Figure 17.12 Photo of goat with gopher ears, wattles, and evidence of dehorning.

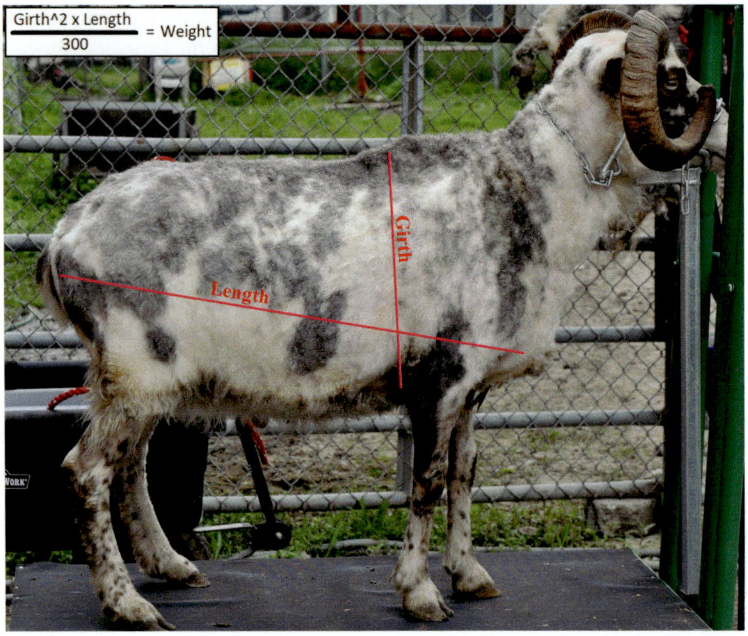

Figure 17.13 Body weight in small ruminants can be calculated using the following formula: Girth^2 × Length (point of the shoulder to the point of the hip) ÷ 300 = Body Weight +/− 2 pounds (Teders, 1998).

requires palpation of the lumbar vertebrae. A written description in concert with a photograph of a wire bent to the contour of the vertebrae will verify the accuracy of the assessment in the absence of standard photographic documentation (sides, front and back, dorsal) of BCS. Lameness should be documented with videotape, and any associated lesions should be documented photographically or radiographically. The presence or absence of internal and external parasites is documented by visual inspection, skin scraping (if indicated), and fecal exam. Mammary tissue is visually inspected for lesions (warts, wounds, abscesses) and palpated for heat, pain, firmness, or nodules.

Poultry

Small flocks allow assessment of individual animals. In addition to photographing the birds from four sides with a unique identification number, the dorsum and ventrum should be photographed with outstretched wings. A close-up of both sides of the head including the wattles and comb will further help to identify the bird, document respiratory signs, and delineate the extent and severity of any head wounds. Poultry fanciers recognize several types of combs, ear lobes, and wattles that should be included in the description of the bird. The comb and wattle can be sketched on the physical exam chart in addition to photographic documentation (see Resources). The report should include the weight, BCS, cleanliness score, plumage score, pododermatitis score, lameness score, and an assessment of the bird's body systems. All lesions should be described with the extent, depth, and evidence of treatment noted.

REPORT WRITING

The final report should include the investigator's name(s), the investigator's agency, the agency requesting the report, the case number, the location of the exam, the personnel present, and the time and date(s) of the assessment. It is useful to note when the report writing process began and when the final report was drafted and signed.

Many authors place a summary near the beginning of the report to make it easier to find. All the areas of investigation must be mentioned in the summary (food, water, shelter, medical care).

The report should follow a logical progression and be easily understood by the court. Jargon should be avoided to prevent confusion. An unbiased, fair, and accurate account of all conditions, both good and substandard, needs to be communicated. A glossary of terms should be included for technical terms.

The description of the site should include the date and time of arrival as well as a description of the weather, including temperature, humidity, precipitation, and wind speed. Changes in conditions during the scene assessment should also be recorded. The number and dimensions of any structures should be included on a scene sketch with the disclaimer "not to scale," case number, date, time, location, and the name and agency of the person making the sketch. The sketch should include fences, gates, burial pits, compost piles, water hydrants, electrical sources, and food and water troughs as well as natural features such as shade trees, creeks, streams, and ponds. A written description of the condition of the buildings, troughs, fences, pastures, pens, and stalls will include the security of the barriers, usable space, and evidence of maintenance.

The management scheme needs to be defined to provide a framework for the assessment. Total confinement systems have different incidences of injury, illness, and death than free-range/pastoral situations. Organic facilities lose higher numbers of chicks than conventional systems. The cooperative extension service can provide statistics on expected losses for each type of management system in the region. Information is available on management strategies to mitigate those losses. Local or state veterinarians will supply information on recent disease outbreaks. If a higher-than-expected particular malady is present, management's response, or lack thereof, is described and the outcomes are documented.

Adequacy of food and water supply is documented by the amount of forage and concentrate on the premises and the delivery systems. Receipts documenting the dates, type, and amount of feed purchased can be used to calculate the amount of feed available to the group over a given period of time. The technique used to gather forage and concentrate as well as the laboratory used for feed analysis is included. The BCS of the individuals can be expressed as the number of individuals of each species at each score and then expressed as a percentage. These percentages can be converted to graphs and used in court to visually represent the data in the report. For example: "Of the 55 beef cattle of *Bos taurus* type, 20 were BCS 2.5/5, 25 were BCS 2.0/5, 5 were BCS 1.5/5, and 5 were BCS 1.0/5 (Vermont Cooperative Extension Service). All of the animals scored 2.5 or less. Animals scoring 2.0 or less comprised 63.6% of the herd. All of the animals were steers and should have scored 3.0 or higher."

Individuals are assessed and the illnesses or lesions are catalogued and expressed as a percentage. A spreadsheet can be generated to compile the data, and pie charts or graphs can be used to visually represent the incidence of each problem.

The conclusion should include a summary of the areas investigated and your assessment of the condition of the animals, the (in)adequacy of the care provided, and how that care has impacted the health and well-being of the livestock.

The statement, "I reserve the right to alter or amend this report as additional information becomes available" should be included with the author's signature and date. Amended reports with your assessment should be forwarded to the appropriate agency as soon as they are available.

CONCLUSION

Forensic cases involving agricultural animals offer challenges beyond those encountered when dealing with companion animals such as dogs and cats. Federal, state, and local laws may dictate identification, testing, treatment, and transport restrictions to limit the spread of reportable and zoonotic diseases thereby protecting the human food supply. Available personnel may have equipment and handling expertise in only one or two species requiring recruitment of multiple teams to assist at a scene involving several livestock species. Nutrition, management, and accepted agricultural practices vary by geographic region and must be considered when assessing these animals and the available resources. Herd health, the welfare of the majority of the group, carries more evidentiary value than the condition of a few outliers.

Meticulous documentation of all husbandry practices, physical conditions, available nutrients, shelter, and medical care coupled with a precise and unbiased report will provide the prosecution and the court with the necessary information for optimal case management.

RESOURCES

Body Condition Score Charts

Beef Cow External Examination

Case No. ______________	**Weight**: ______________ g/kg
Animal No. ______________	**Color:** ______________
Live / Deceased	**Estimated Age**: ______________
Veterinarian/Pathologist: ______________	**Breed**: ______________
Technician: ______________	**Sex**: ______________
Date: ______________	**Stage of Production**: ______________
	BCS: ______________

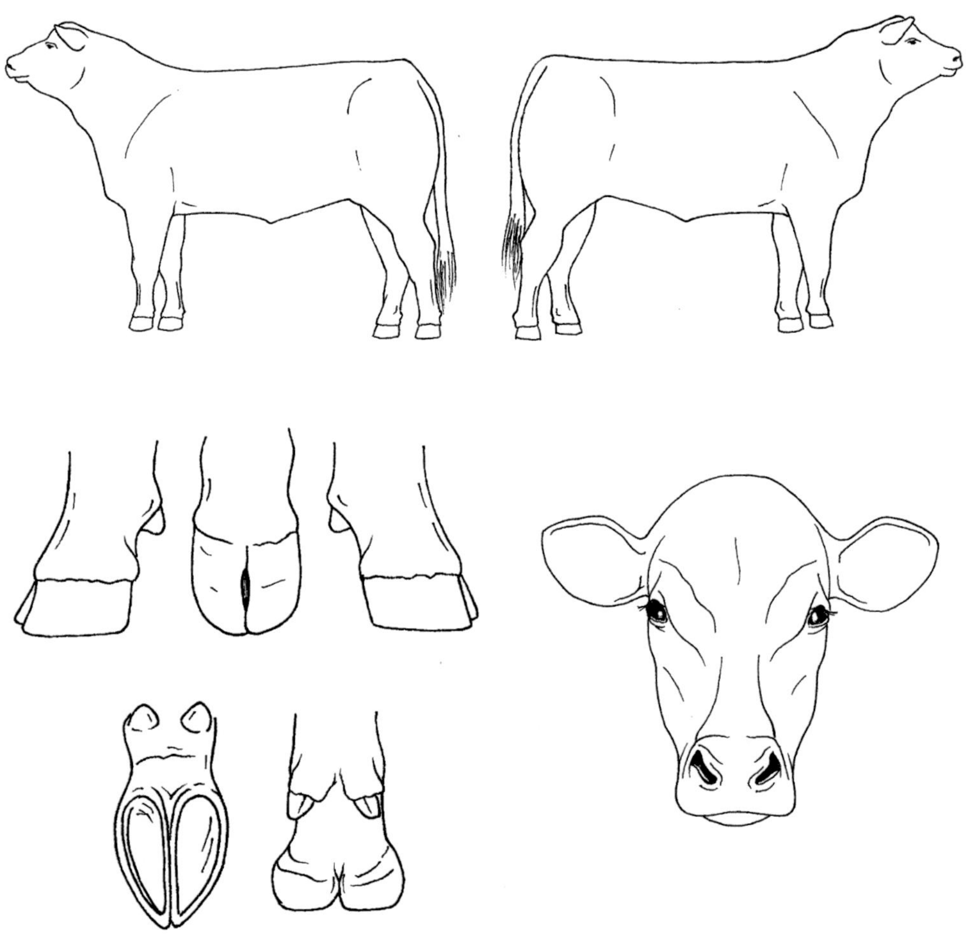

Canine External Examination

Case No. ______________________________ Weight: ______________________________ g/kg
Animal No. ______________________________ Color: ______________________________
Live / Deceased Estimated Age: ______________________________
Veterinarian/Pathologist: ______________________________ Breed: ______________________________
Technician: ______________________________ Sex: ______________________________
Date: ______________________________ Microchip: ______________________________

Chicken External Examination

Case No. ____________________________
Animal No. ____________________________
Live / Deceased
Veterinarian/Pathologist: ____________________________
Technician: ____________________________
Date: ____________________________

Weight: ____________________________ g/kg
Color: ____________________________
Estimated Age: ____________________________
Species/Breed: ____________________________
Sex: M F Unk
BCS: ____________________________

Case No. ______________________________

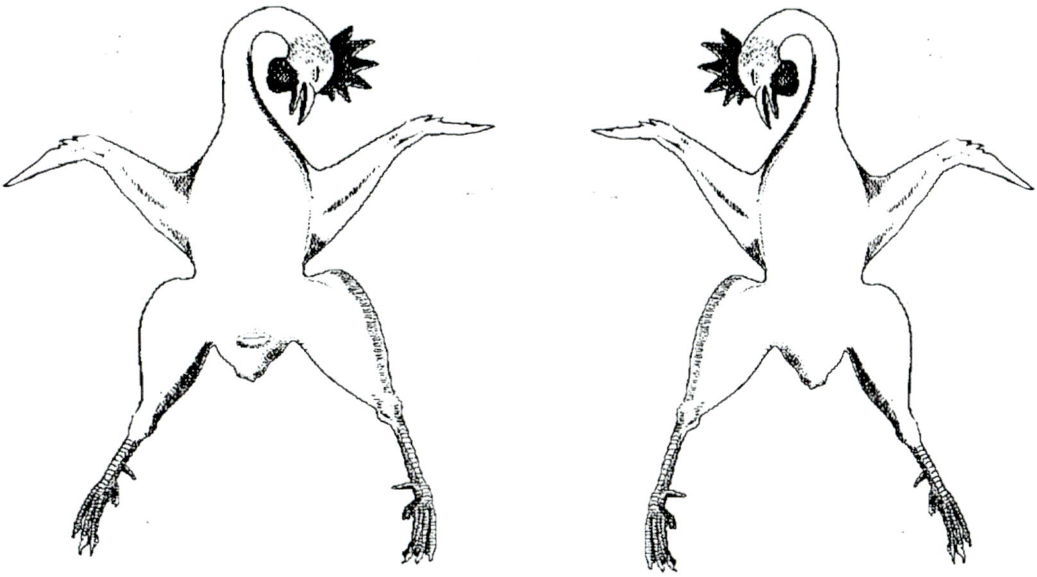

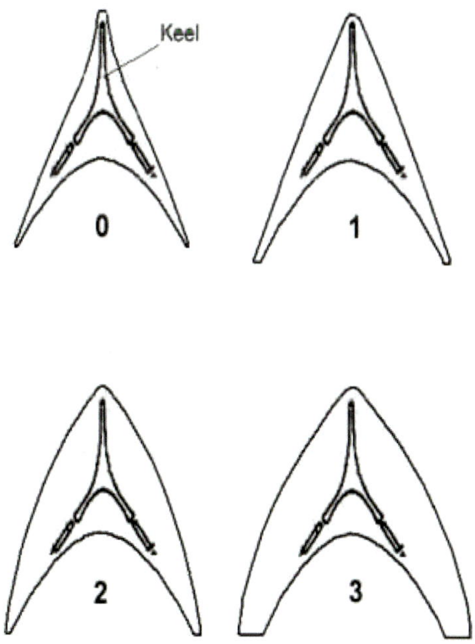

Score	Characteristics
0	Prominent ridge on the keel with limited overall breast muscle and a concavity of the breast muscle alongside the keel
1	Greater development of breast muscle which is not concave and feels more or less flat. Keel still prominent.
2	Moderately developed convex breast muscle. Keel less prominent.
3	Well developed relatively plump breast. Smooth over the keel.

Case No. ______________________________

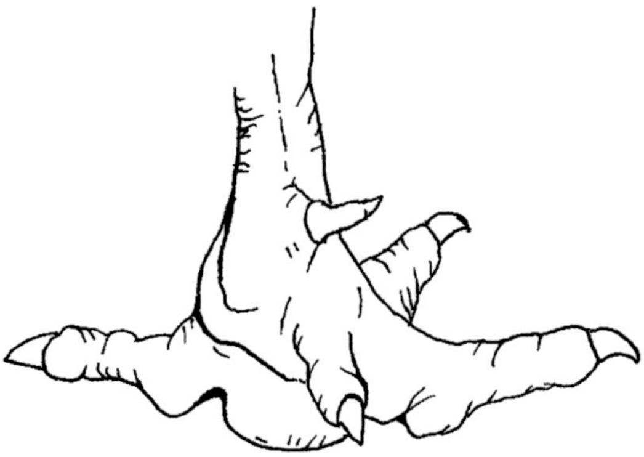

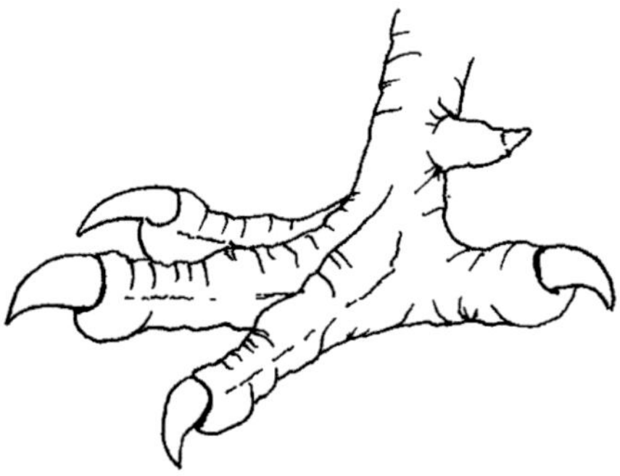

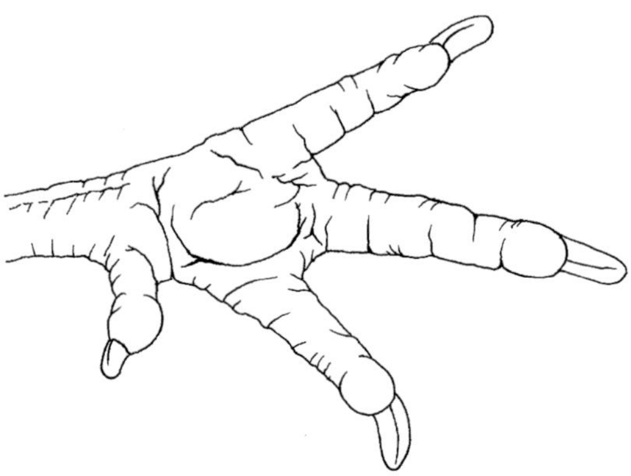

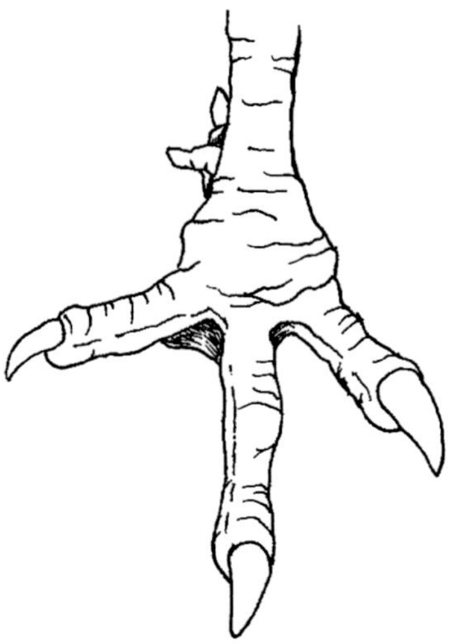

Dairy Cow External Examination

Case No. ______________________________

Animal No. ______________________________

Live / Deceased

Veterinarian/Pathologist: ______________________________

Technician: ______________________________

Date: ______________________________

Weight: ______________________________ g/kg

Color: ______________________________

Estimated Age: ______________________________

Breed: ______________________________

Sex: ______________________________

Stage of Production: ______________________________

BCS: ______________________________

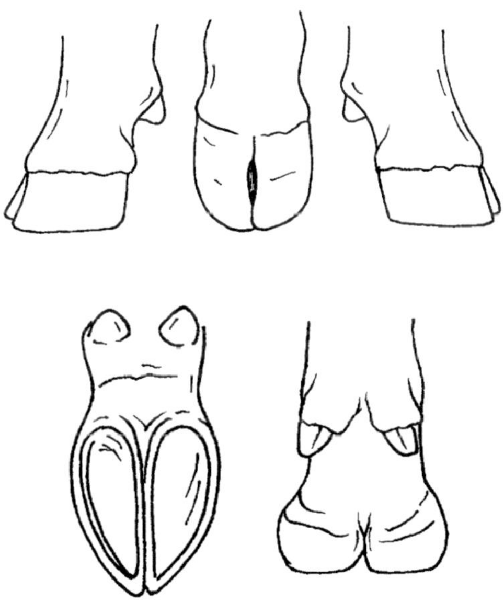

Donkey External Examination

Case No. ______________________________
Animal No. ______________________________
Live / Deceased
Veterinarian/Pathologist: ______________________________
Technician: ______________________________
Date: ______________________________

Weight: ______________________________ g/kg
Color: ______________________________
Estimated Age: ______________________________
Breed: ______________________________
Sex: ______________________________

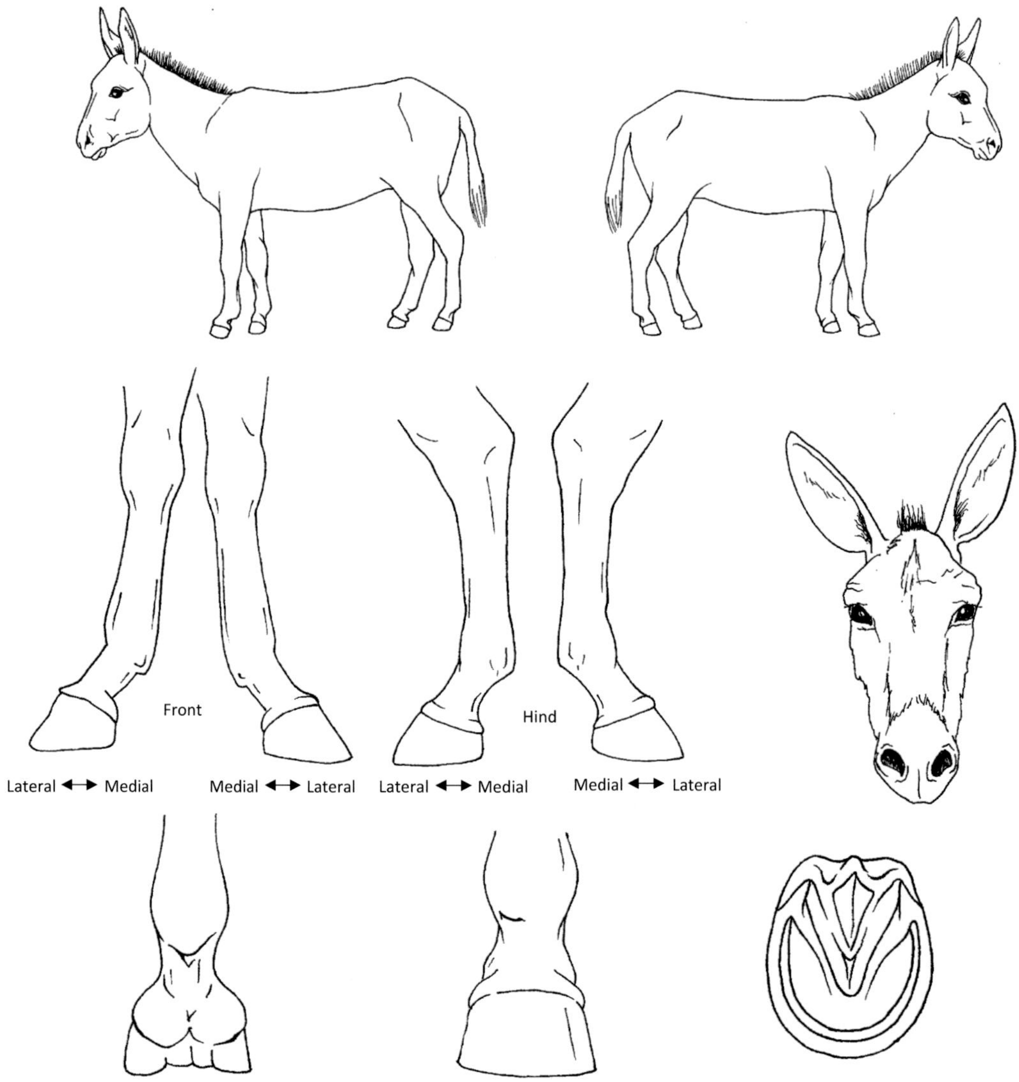

Equine External Examination

Case No. ______________________

Animal No. ______________________

Live / Deceased

Veterinarian/Pathologist: ______________________

Technician: ______________________

Date: ______________________

Weight: ______________________ g/kg

Color: ______________________

Estimated Age: ______________________

Breed: ______________________

Sex: ______________________

Tattoo: ______________________

Microchip: ______________________

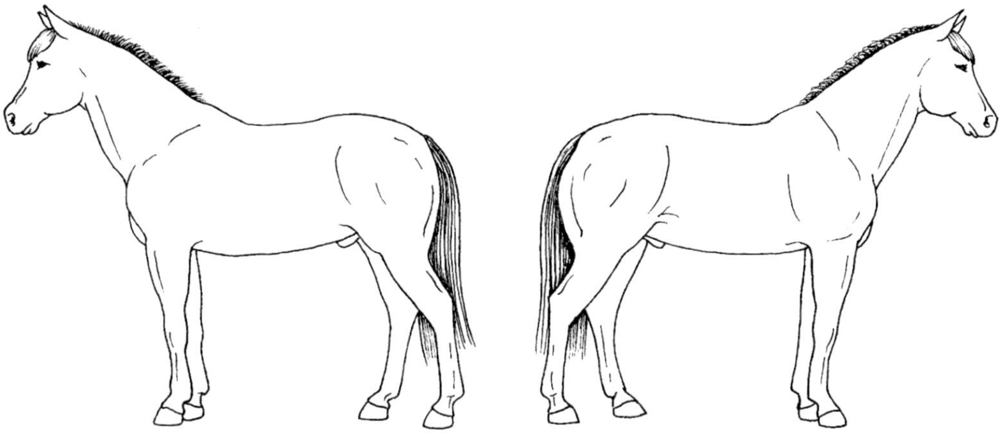

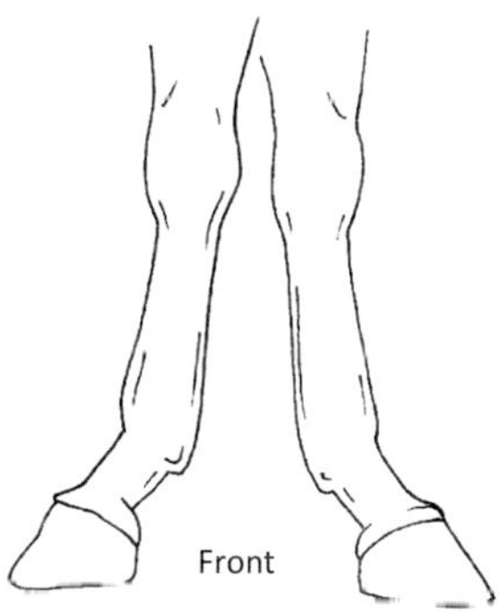

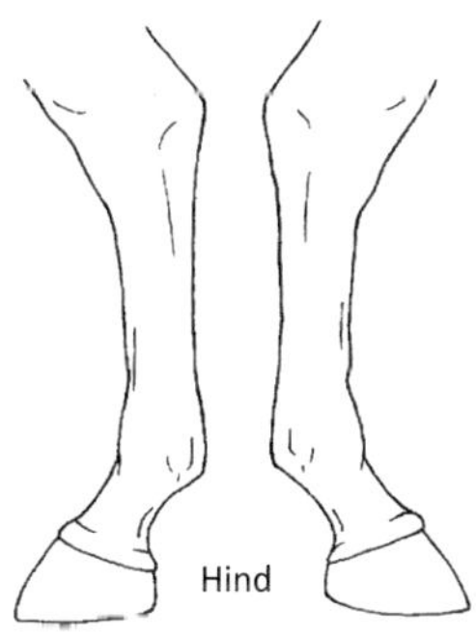

Lateral ↔ Medial   Medial ↔ Lateral   Lateral ↔ Medial   Medial ↔ Lateral

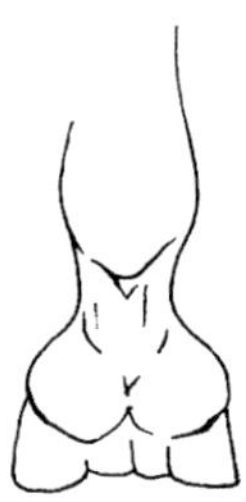

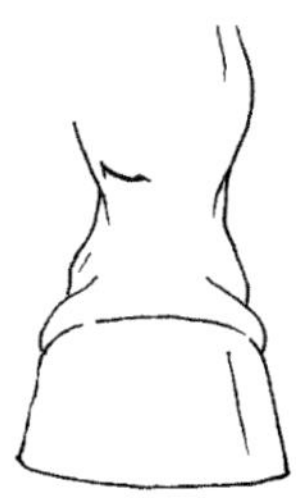

Feline External Examination

Case No. ______________________

Animal No. ______________________

Live / Deceased

Veterinarian/Pathologist: ______________________

Technician: ______________________

Date: ______________________

Weight: ______________________ g/kg

Color: ______________________

Estimated Age: ______________________

Breed: ______________________

Sex: ______________________

Microchip: ______________________

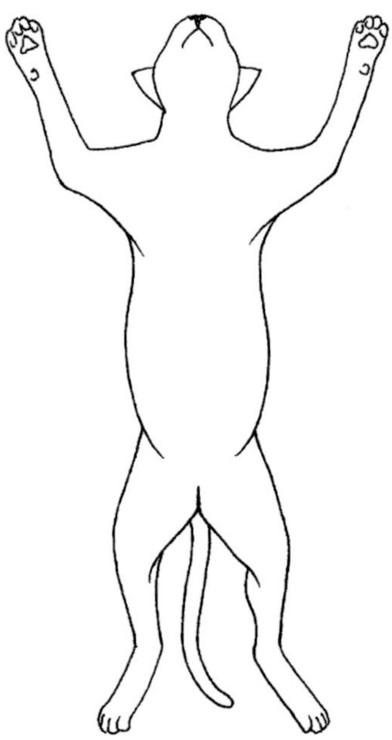

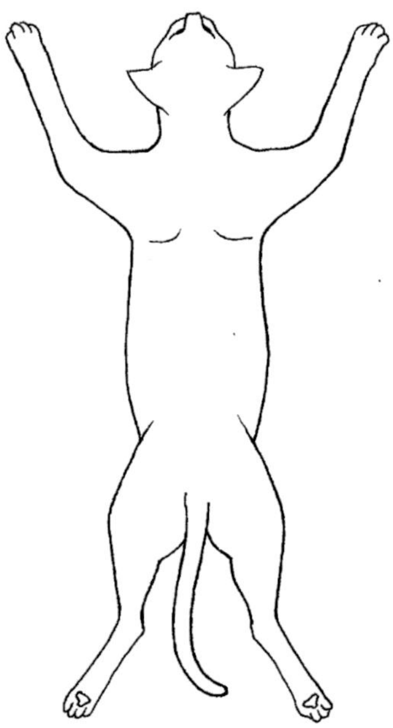

Goat External Examination

Case No. ______________________________

Animal No. ______________________________

Live / Deceased

Veterinarian/Pathologist: ______________________

Technician: ______________________________

Date: ______________________________

Weight: ____________________________ g/kg

Color: ______________________________

Estimated Age: __________________________

Breed: ______________________________

Sex: ______________________________

Stage of Production: ______________________

BCS: ______________________________

Tag/Tattoo: ___________________________

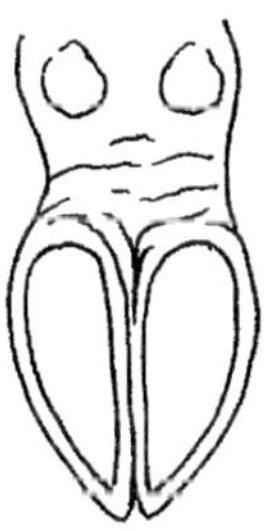

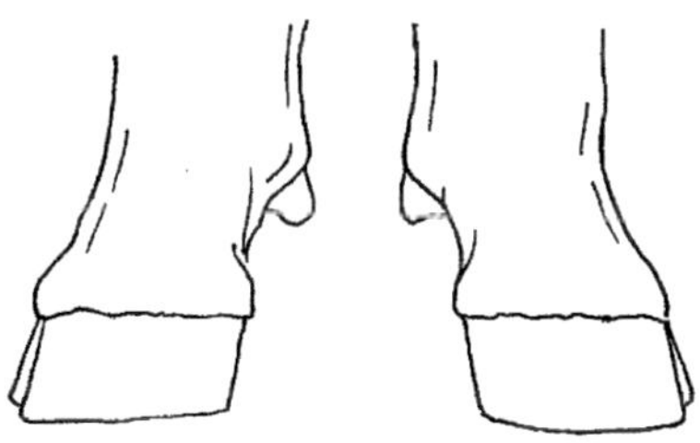

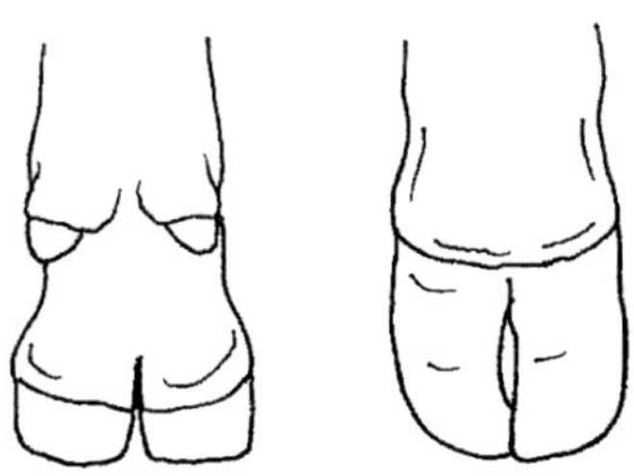

Body Condition of Goat	Score	Dorsal Spines of Backbone	Ribs	Short Ribs
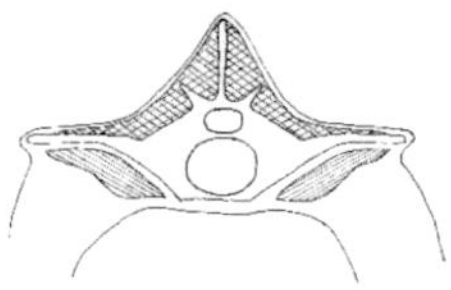	**1** Very Thin	Sharp, easy to see and feel	Easy to feel. Can feel under	No covering
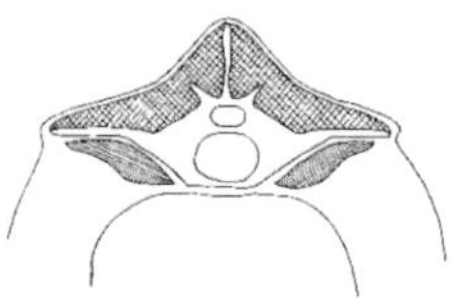	**2** Thin	Easy to feel, but smooth	Smooth, slightly rounded. Felt with slight pressure	Smooth cover
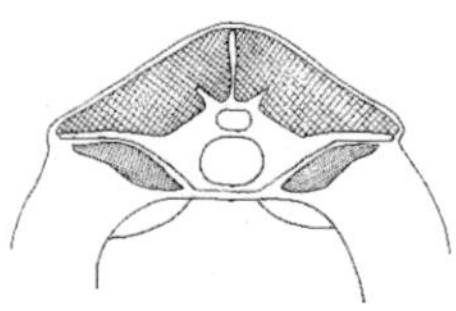	**3** Ideal	Smooth covering	Felt with slight pressure	Even fat cover
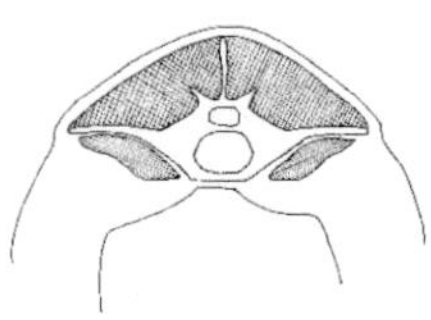	**4** Fat	Palpable only with pressure	Cannot feel ribs, barely palpable indent between ribs	Thick fat
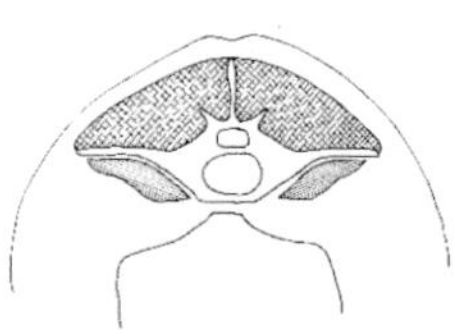	**5** Obese	Not palpable	Cannot feel ribs or indent between ribs	Very thick fat

Goose External Examination

Case No. ______________________________
Animal No. ______________________________
Live / Deceased
Veterinarian/Pathologist: ______________________
Technician: ______________________________
Date: ______________________________

Weight: ______________________________ g/kg
Color: ______________________________
Estimated Age: __________________________
Species/Breed: __________________________
Sex: M F Unk
BCS: ______________________________

Case No. ______________________________

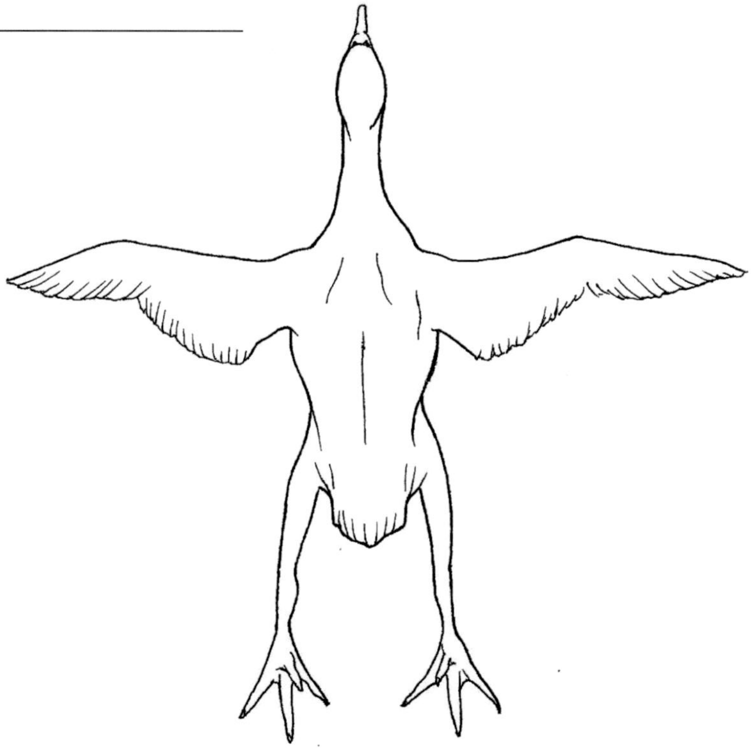

Case No. ______________________________

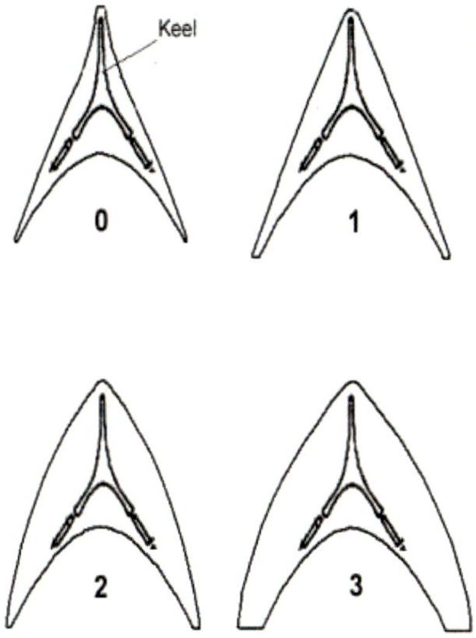

Score	Characteristics
0	Prominent ridge on the keel with limited overall breast muscle and a concavity of the breast muscle alongside the keel
1	Greater development of breast muscle which is not concave and feels more or less flat. Keel still prominent.
2	Moderately developed convex breast muscle. Keel less prominent.
3	Well developed relatively plump breast. Smooth over the keel.

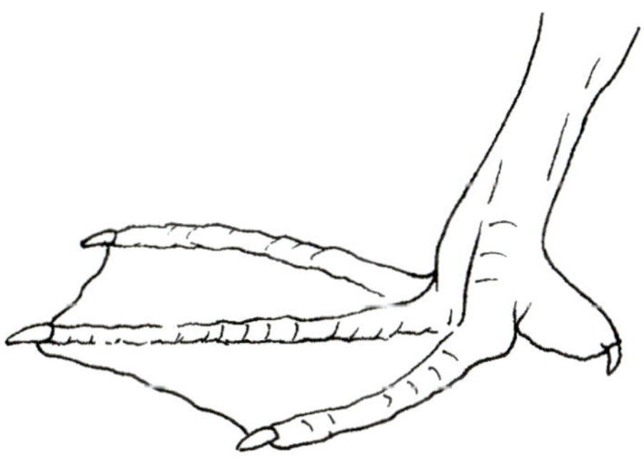

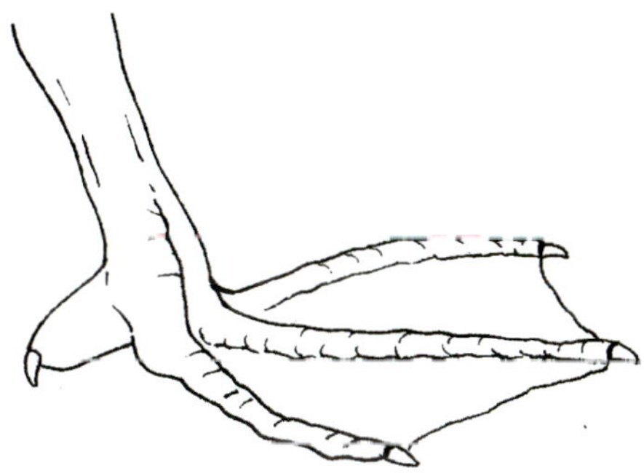

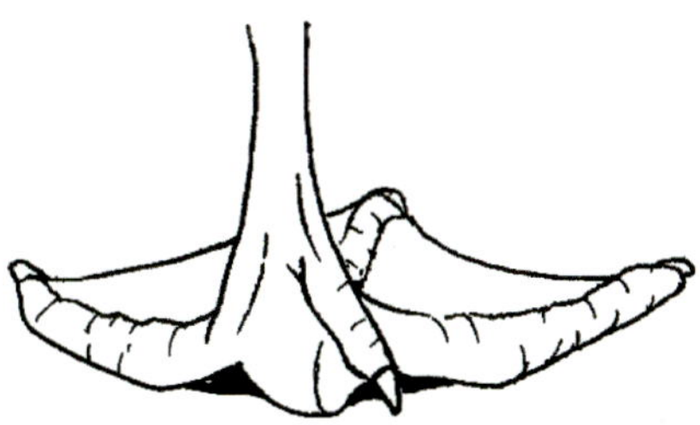

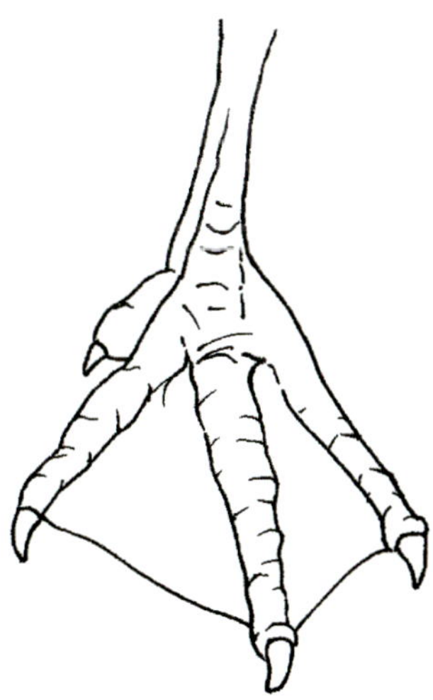

Case No. ______________________________

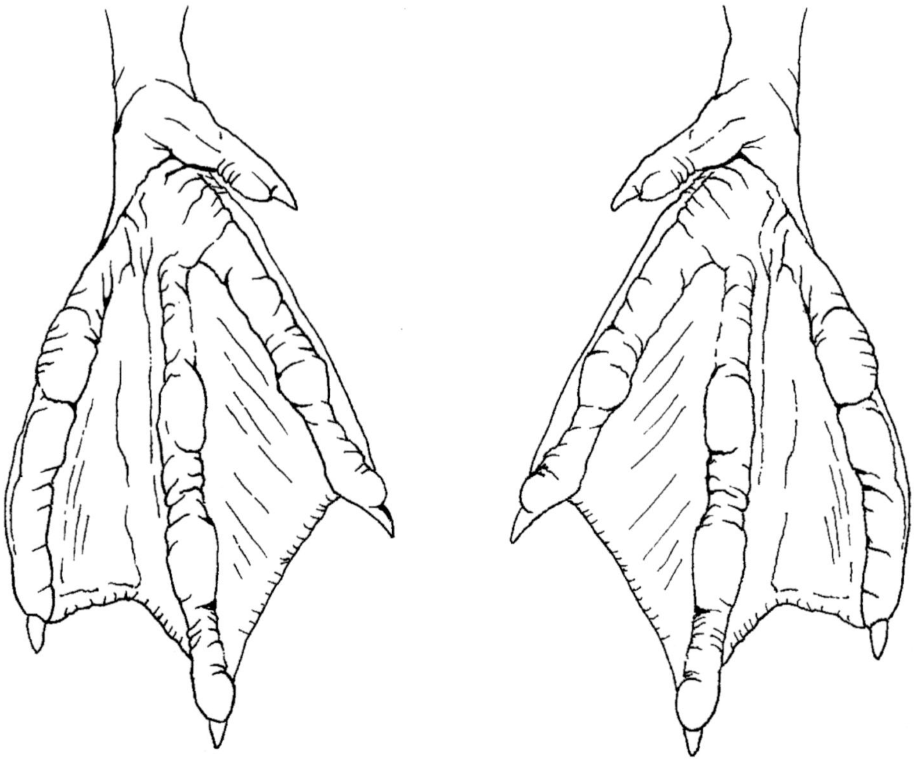

Llama External Examination

Case No. ______________________________

Animal No. ______________________________

Live / Deceased

Veterinarian/Pathologist: ______________________________

Technician: ______________________________

Date: ______________________________

Weight: ______________________________ g/kg

Color: ______________________________

Estimated Age: ______________________________

Breed: ______________________________

Sex: ______________________________

Microchip: ______________________________

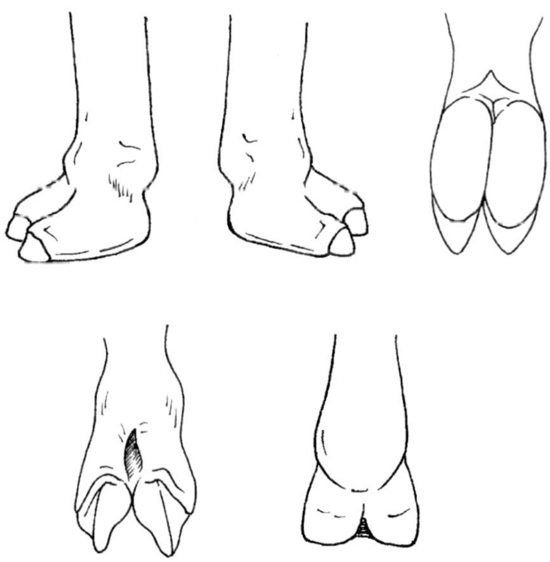

Body Condition of Camelid	Score	Dorsal Spines of Backbone
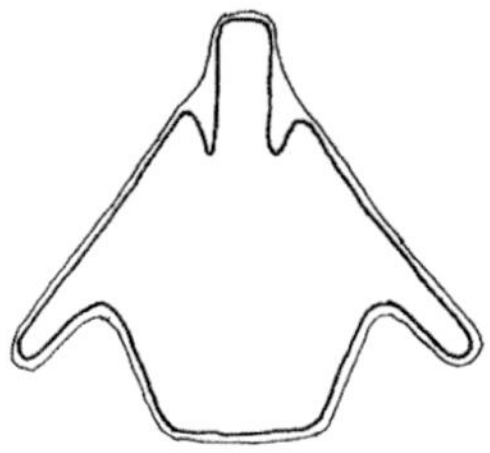	**1** Emaciated	Steep angle from spine to ribs curves inward Ribs and rib spaces easily felt Minimal muscle and no fat
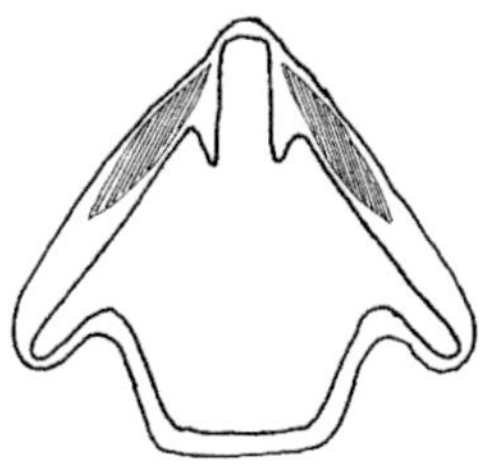	**2** Thin	Slope from spine to ribs >45 degrees Ribs easily felt
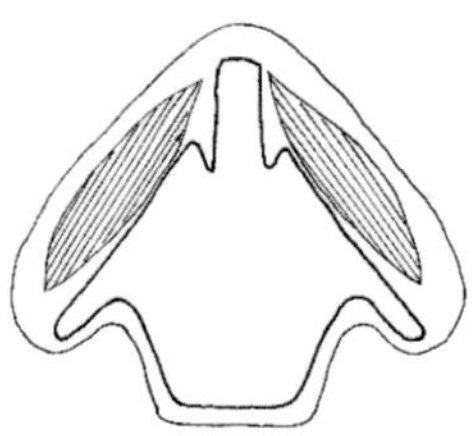	**3** Ideal	Slope from spine to ribs >45 degrees Ribs palpable with slight pressure
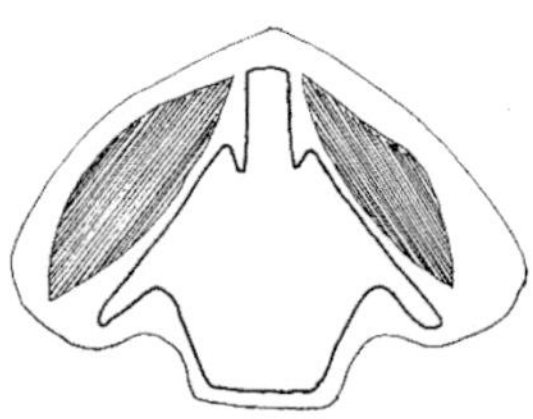	**4** Overweight	Slope from spine to ribs convex Ribs palpable with firm pressure
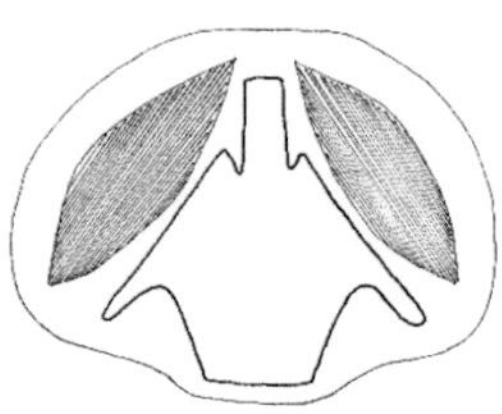	**5** Obese	Broad, flat, or concave along spine Ribs not palpable

Pig External Examination

Case No. ____________________

Animal No. ____________________

Live / Deceased

Veterinarian/Pathologist: ____________________

Technician: ____________________

Date: ____________________

Weight: ____________________ g/kg

Color: ____________________

Estimated Age: ____________________

Breed: ____________________

Sex: ____________________

Stage of Production: ____________________

BCS: ____________________

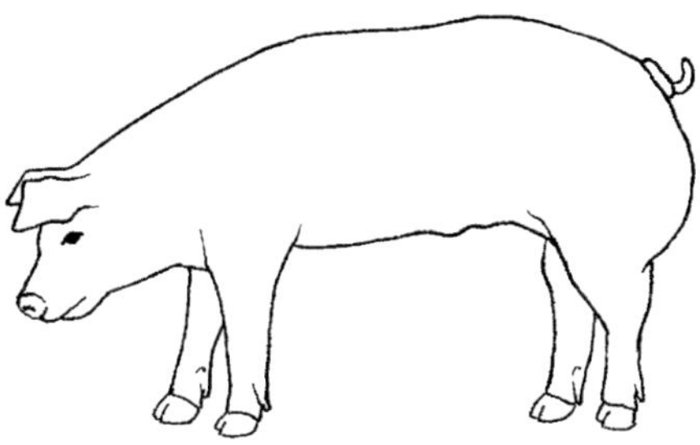

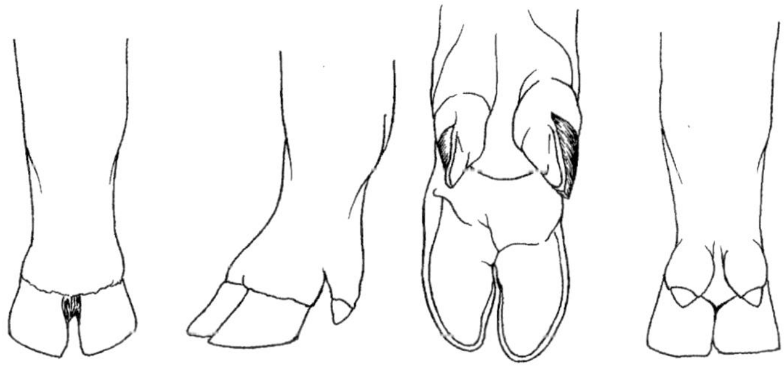

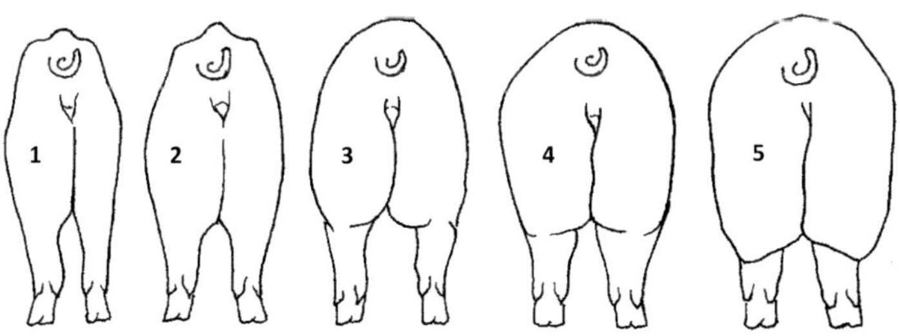

Body Condition Scoring

1 = **Emaciated**: hips, spine visible to the eye

2 = **Thin**: hips, spine easily felt with no pressure

3 = **Ideal**: hips, spine felt with firm pressure

4 = **Fat**: hips, spine cannot be felt with the palm

5 = **Obese**: hips, spine cannot be felt even by pressing down with a single finger

Sheep External Examination

Case No. ______________________________

Animal No. ______________________________

Live / Deceased

Veterinarian/Pathologist: ______________________

Technician: ______________________________

Date: ______________________________

Weight: ______________________________ g/kg

Color: ______________________________

Estimated Age: ______________________________

Breed: ______________________________

Sex: ______________________________

Stage of Production: ______________________

BCS: ______________________________

Tag/Tattoo: ______________________________

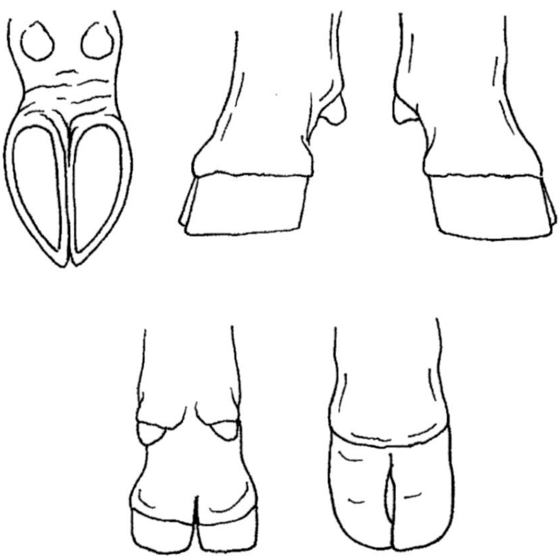

Body Condition of Sheep	Score	Dorsal Spines of Backbone	Short Ribs
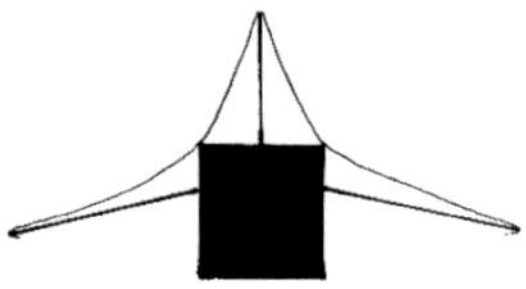	**1** Very Thin	Sharp, spaces between, easily felt	Square ends and spaces easily felt
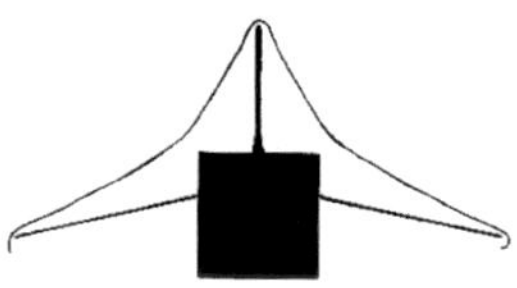	**2** Thin	Covered, but palpable	Ends cover, spaces between palpable, fingers pass underneath
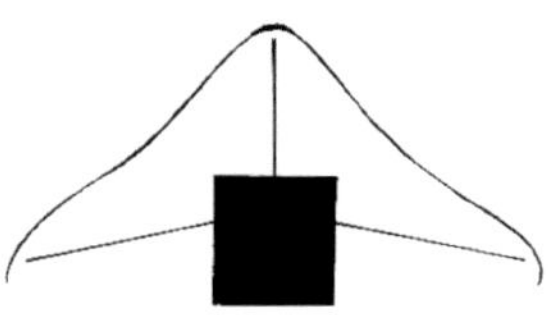	**3** Ideal	Palpable with covering	Ends palpable, fingers do not pass underneath
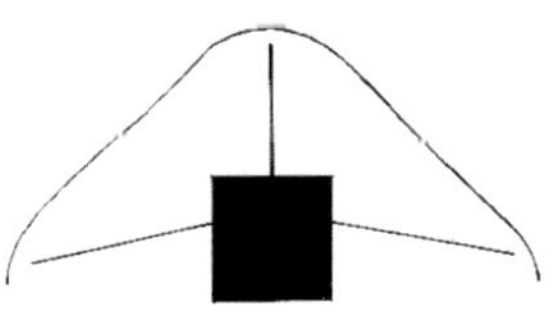	**4** Fat	Back rounded. Dorsal spines felt only with firm pressure	Feels like the side of the palm of the hand
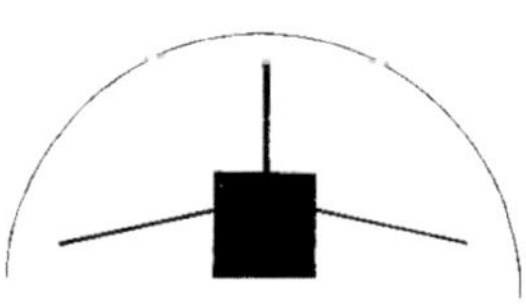	**5** Obese	Difficult or impossible to palpate	Not palpable; fat over tailhead

Bovine

Bos taurus: https://pubs.ext.vt.edu/content/dam/pubs_ext_vt_edu/400/400-795/400-795_pdf.pdf, https://beef.unl.edu/a-practical-guide-to-body-condition-scoring

Eversole DE, Browne MF, Hall JB, Dietz RE. 2009. *Body Conditioning Beef Cows*. Blacksburg, VA: Virginia Cooperative Extension, 400–795.

Bos indicus: https://pdf.usaid.gov/pdf_docs/PNAAV664.pdf, http://www.fao.org/Wairdocs/ILRI/x5496E/x5496e01.htm#TopOfPage, https://beef.unl.edu/a-practical-guide-to-body-condition-scoring

Dairy Breeds: https://www.uaex.edu/publications/pdf/FSA-4008.pdf, http://extensionpublications.unl.edu/assets/pdf/g1583.pdf, https://assurance.redtractor.org.uk/contentfiles/Farmers-5476.pdf?_=635912156462522175, http://people.vetmed.wsu.edu/jmgay/courses/documents/363engl.pdf, https://dairy.ahdb.org.uk/resources-library/technical-information/health-welfare/body-condition-scoring/#.Wypxx1Una1 s, https://ahdc.vet.cornell.edu/programs/NYSCHAP/docs/Rumensin_Heifer_BCS_Guide.pdf

https://www.researchgate.net/profile/Ian_Lean/publication/312456989_A_body_condition_scoring_chart_for_Holstein_dairy_cows/links/58a6cceda6fdcc0e0788c47a/A-body-condition-scoring-chart-for-Holstein-dairy-cows.pdf

Camelids

Alpaca: https://nagonline.net/wp-content/uploads/2016/08/AlpacaBCS.jpg

Alpaca and llama: https://nagonline.net/wp-content/uploads/2016/08/Camelids-Penn-State-2009.pdf

Camel: https://nagonline.net/wp-content/uploads/2016/08/Camel-BCS.pdf, https://nagonline.net/wp-content/uploads/2016/08/Faye-et-al.-2001-Body-condition-score-in-dromedary-camel-A-tool-fo.pdf

Equine

Light horses: https://www.purinamills.com/horse-feed/education/detail/body-condition-scoring-your-horse, https://ker.com/published/body-condition-score-chart/, http://animal.ifas.ufl.edu/youth/horse/documents/BCS/Body%20Condition%20Score_Fluke.pdf, https://www1.agric.gov.ab.ca/$department/deptdocs.nsf/all/agdex9622/$FILE/bcs-horse.pdf, https://www.aht.org.uk/skins/Default/pdfs/cal_bcs.pdf, www.bhs.org.uk/~/media/bhs/files/pdf-documents/condition-scoring-leaflet.ashx, https://www.baileyshorsefeeds.co.uk/body-condition-scoring, http://www.vetfolio.com/husbandry/equine-body-condition-scoring

Donkey: http://www.gov.scot/Publications/2007/10/16091227/4, http://www.nfacc.ca/pdfs/codes/equine_code_of_practice.pdf

Goats, Dairy: https://adga.org/wp-content/uploads/2017/11/adga-dairy-goat-body-condition-scoring.pdf, http://articles.extension.org/pages/21636/goat-body-condition-score-introduction

Meat Breeds

https://extension.psu.edu/courses/meat-goat/reproduction/body-condition-scoring/body-condition-scoring-table, http://www.sa-boergoats.com/asp/4H/Goat-Facts/Body-Condition-Meat-Goats.asp, https://content.ces.ncsu.edu/monitoring-the-body-condition-of-meat-goats-a-key-to-successful-management, https://www.researchgate.net/publication/264889567_Body_Condition_Scores_in_Goats

Poultry

Chickens: Layers: https://nagonline.net/wp-content/uploads/2016/08/Layer-Chicken-BCS.jpg

Chickens: Broilers: https://assurance.redtractor.org.uk/contentfiles/Farmers-5616.pdf

Ducks: RSPCA standard: https://science.rspca.org.uk/sciencegroup/farmanimals/standards/ducks

Goose: https://nagonline.net/wp-content/uploads/2017/03/Owen_1981_JWildlManag_conditionindexgeese.pdfn

Sheep

https://www.uaex.edu/publications/pdf/FSA-9610.pdf, https://www.agric.wa.gov.au/management-reproduction/condition-scoring-sheep, https://www1.agric.gov.ab.ca/$department/deptdocs.nsf/all/agdex9622/$FILE/bcs-sheep.pdf, https://beefandlamb.ahdb.org.uk/wp-content/

uploads/2013/06/brp_l_Sheep_BCS_190713.pdf, https://ir.library.oregonstate.edu/downloads/9p290956v, http://www.ablamb.ca/images/documents/resources/health/Ewe-body-condition-scoring-handbook.pdf, https://beeflambnz.com/knowledge-hub/module/body-condition-scoring-sheep#block-1339

Swine

Farm (meat) Pigs: http://www.thepigsite.com/stockstds/23/body-condition-scoring/, https://extension.psu.edu/courses/swine/reproduction/body-condition-scoring, https://research.unc.edu/files/2012/11/Body-Condition-Scoring-Swine.pdf, http://www.cpc-ccp.com/uploads/userfiles/files/ACA-Appendix-10.pdf

Pet Pigs: http://www.petpigeducation.com/body-condition.html, https://www.minipiginfo.com/mini-pig-body-scoring.html, http://www.carrsconsulting.com/thepig/petpig/petpignotes/weightproblems.htm

Estimation of Body Weight Using a Measuring Tape

Pater S. 2007. *How Much Does Your Animal Weigh?* Cochise County: University of Arizona Cooperative Extension. Backyards and Beyond. Winter 2007 Newsletter 11–12. https://cals.arizona.edu/backyards/sites/cals.arizona.edu.backyards/files/p11-12.pdf. Retrieved April 16, 2018.

Age Estimation Using Dentition

Cattle

https://futurebeef.com.au/knowledge-centre/aging-cattle-by-their-teeth/
https://www.fsis.usda.gov/OFO/TSC/bse_information.htm
https://extension.msstate.edu/sites/default/files/publications/publications/p2779.pdf
https://www.youtube.com/watch?v=0JdgnCDU0k1

Horses

https://extension2.missouri.edu/g2842
http://www.vivo.colostate.edu/hbooks/pathphys/digestion/pregastric/aginghorses.html
https://www.uaex.edu/publications/pdf/FSA-3123.pdf
https://www.aphis.usda.gov/aphis/ourfocus/animalhealth/nvap/NVAP-Reference-Guide/Appendix/Equine-Teeth-and-Aging

Goats and Sheep

https://www.dpi.nsw.gov.au/__data/assets/pdf_file/0004/179797/aging-sheep.pdf
https://www.blackbellysheep.org/about-the-sheep/articles/telling-how-old-a-sheep-is/
https://pdfs.semanticscholar.org/presentation/8c63/90ed86449f8cf1c1bfef509d19af647469ae.pdf
https://aglearn.usda.gov/customcontent/FSIS/FSIS-CombinedBSE-02/Module4/media/documents/sheep-dentition.pdf

Greenfield HJ, Arnold ER. 2008. Absolute age and tooth eruption and wear sequences in sheep and goat: Determining age-at-death in zooarchaeology using a modern control sample. *Journal of Archaeological Science* 35(4):836–849. https://doi.org/10.1016/j.jas.2007.06.003

https://www.youtube.com/watch?v=gwpXzdE7h1I
https://www.youtube.com/watch?v=VW2R12OXjZM

Animal Identification Charts for Lesions

Assessment Protocols

Dairy Cattle

http://www.welfarequalitynetwork.net/media/1088/cattle_protocol_without_veal_calves.pdf
https://www.vetmed.wisc.edu/dms/fapm/fapmtools/4hygiene/hygiene.pdf
http://www.assurewel.org/dairycows

Beef Cattle

http://www.welfarequalitynetwork.net/media/1088/cattle_protocol_without_veal_calves.pdf
http://www.assurewel.org/beefcattle

Laying Hens

http://www.welfarequalitynetwork.net/media/1019/poultry_protocol.pdf All Poultry
http://www.assurewel.org/layinghens

Broilers

http://www.assurewel.org/broilers

Sheep

http://www.assurewel.org/sheep
http://uni-sz.bg/truni11/wp-content/uploads/biblioteka/file/TUNI10015667(1).pdf

Goats

https://www.researchgate.net/publication/275341689_AWIN_welfare_assessment_protocol_for_goats

Pigs

http://www.welfarequalitynetwork.net/media/1018/pig_protocol.pdf

Horses

https://www.researchgate.net/publication/309712791_Welfare_assessment_of_horses_The_AWIN_approach
http://www.vetmed.ucdavis.edu/vetext/local_resources/pdfs/pdfs_animal_welfare/CAStandards-Feb2014.pdf
https://aaep.org/sites/default/files/Guidelines/AAEPCareGuidelinesRR2012.pdf
https://c.ymcdn.com/sites/www.kvma.org/resource/resmgr/files/ky_minimum_standards_care_hr.pdf
https://extension.tennessee.edu/publications/Documents/PB1741.pdf
http://www.mdhorsecouncil.org/files/2011-MinimumStandardsofCareforEquines-1page.pdf
https://air.unimi.it/retrieve/handle/2434/269097/384836/AWINProtocolHorses.pdf
https://spca.bc.ca/wp-content/uploads/fact-sheets-equine-code-merged.pdf
https://www.mpi.govt.nz/dmsdocument/11003/loggedIn

Donkeys

https://air.unimi.it/retrieve/handle/2434/269100/384805/AWINProtocolDonkeys.pdf
http://www.gov.scot/Publications/2007/10/16091227/4
http://www.nfacc.ca/pdfs/codes/equine_code_of_practice.pdf

Lameness Score Charts

Beef Cattle

https://www.drovers.com/article/cattle-lameness-grading-systems
https://www.zinpro.com/lameness/beef/locomotion-scoring

Dairy Cattle

https://www.zinpro.com/lameness/dairy
https://www.merckvetmanual.com/musculoskeletal-system/lameness-in-cattle/locomotion-scoring-in-cattle
Agriculture and Horticulture Development Board (United Kingdom). Dairy Cattle. https://dairy.ahdb.org.uk/resources-library/technical-information/health-welfare/mobility-score-instructions/#.Wz1tO1Una1s

Horses

American Association of Equine Practitioners
https://aaep.org/horsehealth/lameness-exams-evaluating-lame-horse

Pigs

Sows: https://www.zinpro.com/lameness/swine/locomotion-scoring
Finishing Pigs:
Main DCJ, Clegg J, Spatz A, Green LE. 2000. Repeatability of a lameness scoring system for finishing pigs. *Veterinary Record* 147:574–576.

Sheep

Kaler J, Wassink GJ, Green LE. 2009. The inter- and intra-observer reliability of a locomotion scoring scale for sheep. *Veterinary Journal* 180(2):189–194. doi: 10.1016/j.tvjl.2007.12.028

Performing Fecal Egg Counts

https://www.wormx.info/fecal-egg-counting

Performing a California Mastitis Test

https://milkquality.wisc.edu/wp-content/uploads/sites/212/2011/09/california-mastitis-test-fact-sheet.pdf
https://www.youtube.com/watch?v=7WtMTV-rjlQ

National Forage Testing Association

http://www.foragetesting.org/
http://animalrangeextension.montana.edu/forage/documents/2016_Certified_Labs.pdf

National Professional Veterinary Associations

American Association of Bovine Practitioners http://www.aabp.org/
American Association of Equine Practitioners https://aaep.org/
American College of Poultry Veterinarians https://aaap.memberclicks.net/acpv-home
American Association of Small Ruminant Practitioners (sheep, goats, camelids, captive cervids) http://www.aasrp.org/
American Association of Swine Veterinarians https://www.aasv.org/

USDA APHIS Animal Identification Requirements

https://www.aphis.usda.gov/aphis/ourfocus/animalhealth/nvap/NVAP-Reference-Guide/Animal-Identification

References

Arieli A, Meltzer A, Berman A. 2007. The thermoneutral temperature zone and seasonal acclimatization in the hen. *British Poultry Science* 21(6):471–478
AssureWel® (www.assurewel.org).
Balliette J, Torell R. 1998. *Alfalfa for Beef Cows*. Cooperative Extension Fact Sheet 93–23. University of Nevada.
Bartlett B. 2005. *The ABC's of Pasture Grazing*. Ames, Iowa: MidWest Plan Service, Iowa State University.
Bernard JK. 2017. *Considerations for Using By-Product Feeds. Bulletin 862*. UGA Extension Office. University of Georgia.
Bird NA, Hunton P, Morrison WD, Weber LJ. 1988. *Poultry: Heat stress in caged layers.451/20*. ISSN 1198-712X. Queen's printer for Ontario. Ontario Ministry of Agriculture, Food and Rural Affairs. http://www.omafra.gov.on.ca/english/livestock/poultry/facts/88-111.htm Accessed June 20, 2018.
Boyle L, Quinn A, Diaz JC. 2013. *Proceedings Teagasc Pig Farmers Conference*. County Cork, Ireland: Moorepark Teagasc Food Research Center.
Brown C, Rech R, Rissi D, Costa T. 2008. *Poultry Necropsy Manual: The Basics*. Athens, Georgia: Department of Pathology, University of Georgia. http://web.uconn.edu/poultry/poultrypages/Poultry%20necropsy%20manual%20%2002008.pdf.

Campe A, Hoes C, Koesters S, Froemke C, Bougeard S, Staack M, Bessei W et al. 2018. Analysis of the influences on plumage condition in laying hens: How suitable is a whole body plumage score as an outcome? *Poultry Science* 97(2):358–367. https://doi.org/10.3382/ps/pex321.

Carlile FS. 1984. Ammonia in poultry houses: A literature review. *World Poultry Science* 40:99–113.

Cherry P, Morris TR. 2008. *Domestic Duck Production: Science and Practice.* Cambridge, MA: CABI. doi: 10.1079/9780851990545.0000.

Clauer PJ. 2009. *Cannibalism: Prevention and Treatment.* Virginia Cooperative Extension.

Cramer G, Winders T, Solano L, Kleinschmit D. 2018. Research: Evaluation of agreement among digital dermatitis scoring methods in the milking parlor, pen, and hoof trimming chute. *Journal of Dairy Science* 101(3):2406–2414.

De Jong I, van Harn J. 2012. Management tools to reduce footpad dermatitis in broilers. *Avigen.* http://en.staging.aviagen.com/assets/Tech_Center/Broiler_Breeder_Tech_Articles/English/AviaTech-FoodpadDermatitisSept2012.pdf.

Desrochers A, Anderson DE, St-Jean G. 2001. Lameness examination in cattle. *Veterinary Clinics: Food Animal Practice* 17(1):39–51.

Donham KJ. 1991. Association of environmental air contaminants with disease and productivity in swine. *American Journal of Veterinary Research* 52:1723–1730.

Drummond JG, Curtis SE, Simon J. 1978. Effects of atmospheric ammonia on pulmonary bacterial clearance in the young pig. *American Journal of Veterinary Research* 39:211–212.

Drummond JG, Curtis SE, Simon J, Norton HW. 1980. Effects of aerial ammonia on growth and health of young pigs. *Journal of Animal Science* 50(6):1085–1091.

Drummond JG, Curtis SE, Meyer RC, Simon J, Norton HW. 1981a. Effects of atmospheric ammonia on young pigs experimentally infected with *Bordetella bronchiseptica. American Journal of Veterinary Research* 42(6):963–968.

Drummond JG, Curtis SE, Simon J, Norton HW. 1981b. Effects of atmospheric ammonia on young pigs experimentally infected with *Ascaris suum. American Journal of Veterinary Research* 42(6):969–974.

Dyer TG. 2012. *Water Requirements and Quality Issues for Cattle. The University of Georgia Cooperative Extension. Special Bulletin* 56. https://secure.caes.uga.edu/extension/publications/files/pdf/SB%20 56_4.PDF.

Edmonson AJ, Lean IJ, Weaver LD, Farver T, Webster G. 1989. A body condition scoring chart for Holstein dairy cows. *Journal of Dairy Science* 72:68–78.

Ellis JM, Hollands T. 1998. Accuracy of different methods of estimating the weight of horses. *Veterinary Record* 143:335–336.

Fernandez D. 2012. *Fecal Egg Counting for Sheep and Goat Producers.* University of Arkansas at Pine Bluff Cooperative Extension Program. Bulletin FSA 9608.

Ferrucci F, Vischi A, Zucca E, Stancari G, Boccardo A, Rondena M, Ferro E. 2012. Multicentric hemangiosarcoma in the horse: A case report. *Journal of Equine Veterinary Science* 32(2):65.

Fisher M. 2008. Stray voltage may impact your livestock before you know it. *High Plains/Midwest Ag Journal.* http://www.hpj.com/archives/stray-voltage-may-impact-your-livestock-before-you-know-it/article_45cad071-61cd-5484-b122-dfc77c5fadf5.html.

Foreyt WJ. 2001. *Veterinary Parasitology: Reference Manual,* 5th ed. Ames, IA: Iowa State Press.

Forrester JA, Weiser TG, Forrester JD. 2018. Original research: An update on fatalities due to venomous and nonvenomous animals in the United States (2008–2015). *Wilderness & Environmental Medicine,* 29(1):36–44. doi: 10.1016/j.wem.2017.10.004.

Frank C, Madden DJ, Duncan C. 2015 Field Necropsy of the horse. *Veterinary Clinics of North America: Equine Practice* 31(2):233–245.

French D, Craig T, Hogsette J, Pelzel-McCluskey A, Mittel L, Morgan K, Pugh D, Vaala W. 2016. *AAEP External Parasite and Vector Control Guidelines.* AAEP External Parasite Control Task Force. Lexington, KY: AAEP. https://aaep.org/sites/default/files/Guidelines/AAEP-ExternalParasites071316Final.pdf.

Frost RO, Patronek G, Arluke A, Steketee G. 2015. The hoarding of animals: An update. *Psychiatric Times* 32(4):1.

Gadberry S. 2016. *Water for Beef Cattle.* University of Arkansas Division of Agriculture, Research and Extension, Agriculture and Natural Resources. FSA 3021. https://www.uaex.edu/publications/PDF/FSA-3021.pdf.

Gaughan JB, Mader TL, Holt SM, Lisle A. 2008. A new heat load index for feedlot cattle1. *Journal of Animal Science* 86(1):226–234. Retrieved from https://login.lp.hscl.ufl.edu/login?URL=http://search.proquest.com/accountid=10920?url=https://search.proquest.com/docview/218137123?accountid=10920.

Gerdin J, McDonough S, Reisman R, Scarlet J. 2015. Circumstances, descriptive characteristics, and pathologic findings in dogs suspected of starving. *Veterinary Pathology* 53(5):1087–1094.

Ghassemi Nejad J, Sung K. 2017. Behavioral and physiological changes during heat stress in Corriedale ewes exposed to water deprivation. *Journal of Animal Science and Technology* 59(13). http://doi.org/10.1186/s40781-017-0140-x.

Greenough RR, Weaver AD, Broom DM, Esselmont RJ, Galindo FA. 2003. *Basic concepts of bovine lameness. Lameness in Cattle*, 3rd ed. Amsterdam: Elsevier Science.

Global Animal Partnership. Austin, Texas. https://globalanimalpartnership.org/5-step-animal-welfare-rating-program/chicken-standards-application/.

Gottardo F, Brscic M, Contiero B, Cozzi G, Andrighetto I. 2008 Towards the creation of a welfare assessment system in intensive beef cattle farms. *Italian Journal of Animal Science* 8:325–342.

Grandin T. 2000. *Livestock Handling and Transport*. Wallingford, Oxon, UK: CABI Publishing.

Grandin T. 2014. *Livestock Handling and Transport*, CABI, ProQuest Ebook Central, https://ebookcentral.proquest.com/lib/ufl/detail.action?docID=1794188.

Greenacre CB, Morishita TY. 2015. *Backyard Poultry Medicine and Surgery*. Ames, IA: Wiley Blackwell.

Gregory NG, Robins JK. 1998. A body condition scoring system for layer hens. *New Zealand Journal of Agricultural Research* 41(4):555–559. https://doi.org/10.1080/00288233.1998.9513338.

Griffin D. 2012. Field necropsy of cattle and diagnostic sample submission. *Veterinary Clinics of North America: Food Animal Practice*, 23(3):391–405.

Groesbeck CN, Goodband RD, DeRouchey JM, Tokach MD, Dritz SS, Nelssen JL, Lawrence KR, Young MG. 2002. Using heart girth to determine weight in finishing pigs. *Swine Day 2002 proceedings*. Kansas State University. https://www.asi.k-state.edu/doc/swine-day-2002/heartgirthpg166.pdf.

Hall JB. 2004. *The Cow-Calf Manager*. Virginia Cooperative Extension, Virginia Tech and Virginia State University.

Hancock D, Rossi J, Lacy RC. 2017. *Forage Use and Grazing Herd Management during a Drought. Circular 914*. University of Georgia Extension.

Hoffmann G, Bentke A, Rose-Meierhöfer S, Ammon C, Mazetti P, Hardarson GH. 2013. Original research: Estimation of the body weight of Icelandic Horses. *Journal of Equine Veterinary Science* 33(11):893–895.

Issley S. 2015. Ammonia toxicity. Medscape. https://emedicine.medscape.com/article/820298-overview.

Jacob J. 2015. *Feather Pecking and Cannibalism in Small and Backyard Poultry Flocks*. University of Kentucky Cooperative Extension Service. http://articles.extension.org/pages/66088/feather-pecking-and-cannibalism-in-small-and-backyard-poultry-flocks.

Jurgens MH, Hansen SL, Coverdale J, Bregendahl K. 2012. *Animal Feeding and Nutrition*. Iowa: Kendall Hunt Publishing.

Kahn CM, Line S. 2010. *The Merck Veterinary Manual*. Whitehouse Station, NJ: Merck & Co., 2010.

Kaler J, Wassink GJ, Green LE. 2009. The inter- and intra-observer reliability of a locomotion scoring scale for sheep. *Veterinary Journal* 180(2):189–194.

Kaufman PE, Koehler PG, Butler JF. 2015a. *External Parasites of Sheep and Goats. Publication #ENY-273*. University of Florida IFAS Extension. http://edis.ifas.ufl.edu/ig129.

Kaufman PE, Koehler PG, Butler JF. 2015b. *External Parasites of Swine. Publication #ENY – 287*. University of Florida IFAS Extension. http://edis.ifas.ufl.edu/ig138.

Kaukonen E, Norring N, Valros A. 2016. Effect of litter quality on foot pad dermatitis, hock burns and breast blisters in broiler breeders during the production period. *Avian Pathology* 45(6):667–673.

Kellems RO, Church DC. 2010. *Livestock Feeds and Feeding*. Boston: Prentice Hall.

Kerr SB. 2015. *Livestock heat stress: Recognition, response and prevention*. FS157E. Washington State University Extension.

Kester E, Frankena K. 2014. A descriptive review of the prevalence and risk factors of hock lesions in dairy cows. *Veterinary Journal* 202(2):222–228.

Kestin SC, Knowles TG, Tinch AE, Gregory NG. 1992. Prevalence of leg weakness in broiler chickens and its relationship with genotype. *Veterinary Record* 131:190–194.

Knowles TG, Warriss PD, Brown SN, Edwards GE. 1998. Effects of stocking density on lambs being transported by road. *Veterinary Record* 142(19):503–509.

Koehler PG, Pereira RM, Kaufman PE. 2015. *Sticktight Flea, Echidnophaga gallinae. Bulletin #ENY-244.* University of Florida IFAS Extension. http://edis.ifas.ufl.edu/mg236 Accessed February 23, 2018.

Lammers PJ, Stender DR, Honeyman MS. 2007. Niche pork production: Environmental needs of the pig. IPIC NPP210 2007. https://www.ipic.iastate.edu/publications/210.environmentalpigneeds.pdf.

LayWel. 2006. LAYWEL. Welfare implications of changes in production systems for laying hens. http://www.laywel.eu/web/xmlappservlet11da.html?action=Process.

Loftin KM. 2008. *Protect Swine from External Parasites. Bulletin FSA-7034.* University of Arkansas Cooperative Extension Service. https://www.uaex.edu/publications/PDF/FSA-7034.pdf.

Lillie LE, Thompson RG. 1972. The pulmonary clearance of bacteria by calves and mice. *Canadian Journal of Comparative Medicine* 36:121–128.

Mack LA, Felver-Gant JN, Dennis RL, Cheng HW. 2013. Genetic variation alter production and behavioral responses following heat stress in 2 strains of laying hens. *Poultry Science* 92(2):285–294.

Madea B. 2005. Death as a result of starvation. Diagnostic criteria. In: Tsokos M (ed.) *Forensic Pathology Reviews, Volume 2.* Totowa, NJ: Humana Press, Inc.

Main DCJ, Clegg J, Spatz A, Green LE. 2000. Repeatability of a lameness scoring system for finishing pigs. *Veterinary Record* 147:574–576.

Marschang F. 1973. Ammonia, loss and production in large cattle stables. *Deutsche Tierärztliche Wochenschriff* 80(5):112–115.

Martin CD, Mullens BA. 2012. Housing and dustbathing effects on northern fowl mites (*Ornithonyssus sylvarium*) and chicken body lice (*Menacanthus stramineus*) on hens. *Medical and Veterinary Entomology* 26(3):323–333.

Mason GL, Madden DJ. 2007. Performing the field necropsy examination. *Veterinary Clinics of North America: Food Animal Practice* 23(3):503–526.

Mavromichalis I. 2013. Formulating poultry and pig diets with bakery meal. https://www.wattagnet.com/articles/17816-formulating-poultry-and-pig-diets-with-bakery-meal.

McClendon M, Kaufman PE. 2007. Horse Bot Fly. Featured Creatures Publication EENY- 406, University of Florida IFAS. http://entnemdept.ufl.edu/creatures/livestock/horse_bot_fly.htm.

Meat and Livestock Australia. 2006. Tips and tools: Heat load in feedlot cattle. https://futurebeef.com.au/wp-content/uploads/Heat-load-in-feedlot-cattle.pdf.

Meltzer A. 1983. Thermoneutral zone and resting metabolic rate of broilers. *British Poultry Science* 24(4):471–476.

Merrill MM, Boughton RK, Lord CC, Sayler KA, Wight B, Anderson WM, Wisely WM. 2018. Wild pigs as sentinels for hard ticks: A case study from south-central Florida. *International Journal for Parasitology: Parasites and Wildlife* 7(2):161–170. https://doi.org/10.1016/j.ijppaw.2018.04.003.

Mertins JW, Vigil SL, Corn JL. 2017. *Amblyomma auricularium* (Ixodida:Ixodidea) in Florida: New hosts and distribution records. *Journal of Medical Entomology* 54(1):134–141. https://doi.org/10.1093/jme/tjw159.

Miles A. 2017. From the driver's seat. *Ag News & Views* 35(10):1–3.

Morgan K. 1998. Thermoneutral zone and critical temperatures of horses. *Journal of Thermal Biology* 23(1):59–61.

Morton GR. 2017. Animal hoarding in Florida: Addressing the ongoing animal, human, and public health crisis. *Florida Bar Journal* 91(4):30–35.

Muller J, Gwozdz J, Hodgeman R, Ainsworth C, Kluver P, Czarnecki J, Warner S, Fegan M. 2015. Diagnostic performance characteristics of a rapid field test for anthrax in cattle. *Preventive Veterinary Medicine* 120(3–4):277–282.

Odriozola ER, Rodríguez AM, Micheloud JF, Cantón GJ, Caffarena RD, Gimeno EJ, Giannitti F. 2018. Enzootic calcinosis in horses grazing *Solanum glaucophyllum* in Argentina. *Journal of Veterinary Diagnostic Investigation* 30(2):286.

Olechnowicz J, Jaskowski JM. 2013. Lameness in small ruminants. *Medycyna Weterynaryjna* 67(11):715–719. https://www.researchgate.net/publication/257993409_Lameness_in_small_ruminants.

Oliver-Espinosa O. 2018. Diagnostics and treatments in chronic diarrhea and weight loss in horses. *Veterinary Clinics of North America-Equine Practice* 34(1):69–80.

Parish JA, Karisch BB, Vann RC. 2013. *Transporting Beef Cattle by Road.* Publication 2797. Mississippi State University Extension Service.

Penev T. 2011. Lameness scoring systems for cattle in dairy farms. *Agricultural Science and Technology* 3(4):291–298. https://www.researchgate.net/publication/259970699_Lameness_scoring_systems_for_cattle_in_dairy_farms.

Perez ZO, Ybanez A, Ybanez RHD, Sandoval J. 2016. Body weight estimation using body measurements in goats (*Capra hircus*) under field condition. *Philippine Journal of Veterinary Animal Science*42(1):1–7.

Petherick JC, Phillips CJC. 2009. Space allowances for confined livestock and their determination from allometric principles. *Applied Animal Behaviour Science* 117(1–2):1–12. https://doi.org/10.1016/j.applanim.2008.09.008.

Potterton SL, Green MJ, Millar KM, Brignell CJ, Harris J, Whay HR, Huxley JN. 2011. Prevalence and characteristics of, and producer's attitudes towards, hock lesions in UK dairy cattle. *Veterinary Record* 169(24):634–644.

Rübsamen K, von Engelhardt V. 1975. Water metabolism in the llama. *Comparative Biochemistry and Physiology Part A: Physiology* 52(4):595–598.

Relun A, Guatteo R, Roussel P, Bareille N. 2011. A simple method to score digital dermatitis in dairy cows in the milking parlor. *Journal of Dairy Science* 94(11):5424–5434.

Reneau JK, Seykora AJ, Heins B, Bey R. 2005. Association between hygiene scores and somatic cell scores in dairy cattle. *Journal of the American Veterinary Medical Association* 227(8):1297–1301.

Responsible Wool Standard. 2016. Lameness Scoring Guidance. http://responsiblewool.org/wp-content/uploads/2016/07/Lameness-Scoring-Guidance.pdf.

Sadiq MB, Ramanoon SZ, Shaik Mossadeq WM, Mansor R, Syed-Hussain SS. 2017. Association between lameness and indicators of dairy cow welfare based on locomotion scoring, body and hock condition, leg hygiene and lying behavior. *Animals: An Open Access Journal from MDPI* 7(11):79. http://doi.org/10.3390/ani7110079.

Saleh EA, Watkins SE, Waldroup PW. 1996. High-level usage of dried bakery product in broiler diets. *Journal of Applied Poultry Research* 5:33–38.

Sallenave R. 2016. *Water Quality for Livestock and Poultry*. Bulletin Guide M-122. New Mexico State University Cooperative Extension Service. College of Agricultural, Consumer and Environmental Services.

Sanders C. 2015. Barber pole worms in sheep, goats, a hazard after wet spring. *High Plains/Midwest Ag Journal*. http://www.hpj.com/livestock/barber-pole-worms-in-sheep-goats-a-hazard-after-wet/article_23cfd4cf-5a76-5463-a3fb-8493b806bb6a.html.

Schwartzkopf-Genswein KS, Faucitano L, Dadgar S, Shand P, González LA, Crowe TG. 2012. Road transport of cattle, swine and poultry in North America and its impact on animal welfare, carcass and meat quality: A review. *Meat Science* 92(3):227–243.

Scott DW. 1988. *Large Animal Dermatology*. Philadelphia, PA: W.B. Saunders Company.

Sheldon KJ, Deboy G, Field WE, Albright JL. 2009. Bull-related incidents: their prevalence and nature. *Journal of Agromedicine* 14:357–369

Smith B, Pingsun L, Love G. 1986. *Intensive Grazing Management: Forage, Animals, Men, Profits*. Hawaii: The Graziers Hui.

Smith M, Sherman D. 2009. *Goat Medicine*, 2nd ed. Ames, IA: Wiley-Blackwell.

Sprecher DJ, Kaneene JB, Hostetler D. 1997. A lameness scoring system that use posture and gait to predict dairy cattle reproductive performance. *Theriogeneology* 47(6):1179–1187.

Sprinkle J, Bailey D. 2004. How Many Animals Can I Graze on My Pasture? Determining Carrying Capacity on Small Land Tracts. University of Arizona College of Agriculture and Life Sciences Publication AZ-1352.

Stull CL, Holcomb KE. 2014. Role of U.S. animal control agencies in equine neglect, cruelty, and abandonment investigations. *Journal of Animal Science* 92(5):2342–2349, https://doi.org/10.2527/jas.2013-7303.

Sungirai M, Masaka L, Benhura BL. 2014. Validity of weight estimation models in pigs reared under different management conditions. *Veterinary Medicine International* 530469. http://doi.org/10.1155/2014/530469.

Talley J. 2015. External Parasites of Goats. Oklahoma Cooperative Extension Service EPP-7019.

Teders K. 2008. *How to Identify Lice on Swine*. Purdue University Cooperative Extension Service. https://www.extension.purdue.edu/pork/health/lice.html.

Thomas G, Proverbs G, Patterson H. 1997. *Weight tape for sheep*. Factsheet. Caribbean Agricultural Research and Development Institute. http://www.cardi.org/wp-content/uploads/downloads/2012/11/PRODN-HUS_Weight-tape-for-sheep.pdf.

Undersander D, Albert B, Cosgrove D, Johnson D, Peterson P. 2002. *Pastures for Profit: A Guide for Rotational Grazing (A3529)*. Cooperative Extension Publishing, University of Wisconsin-Extension.
USDA Natural Resource Conservation Service National Range and Pasture Handbook 2003.
Wangchuk K, Wangdi J, Mindu M. 2018. Comparison and reliability of techniques to estimate live cattle body weight. *Journal of Applied Animal Research* 46(1):349–352.
Ward D. 2007. *Water Requirements of Livestock*. Ontario Ministry of Agriculture, Food and Rural Affairs Factsheet ISSN1198-712X Agdex # 176/400. http://www.omafra.gov.on.ca/english/engineer/facts/07-023.htm#1.
Warriss PD. 1998. Choosing appropriate space allowances for slaughter pigs transported by a road: A review. *Veterinary Record* 142(17):449–454.
Warriss PD, Edwards JE, Brown SN, Knowles TG. 2002. Survey of the stocking densities at which sheep are transported commercially in the United Kingdom. *Veterinary Record* 150(8):233–236.
Watkins SE, Jones FT, Clark FD, Wooley JL. 2008. Raising broilers and turkeys for competition. FSA8004. University of Arkansas, Division of Agriculture Cooperative extension Service.
Watson W, Luginbuhl JW. 2015. *Lice: What They Are and How to Control Them*. North Carolina State Extension Publications.
Webster AB, Fairchild BD, Cummings TS, Stayer PA. 2008. Validation of a three-point-gait scoring system for field assessment of walking ability of commercial broilers. *Journal of Applied Poultry Research* 17(4):529–539.
Whay HR, Main DCJ, Green LE, Webster AJF. 2003. Assessment of the welfare of dairy cattle using animal-based measurements: Direct observations and investigation of farm records. *Veterinary Record* 153:197–202.
Whiting TL, Brandt S. 2002. Minimum space allowance for transportation of swine by road. *Canadian Veterinary Journal* 43(3):207–212.

CHAPTER 18

VETERINARY FORENSIC RADIOLOGY AND IMAGING

Elizabeth Watson

INTRODUCTION, SCOPE, AND DEFINITIONS

Veterinary forensic radiology and imaging is a discipline of veterinary forensic medicine involved in the noninvasive acquisition and interpretation of radiographs and other imaging studies for legal documentation and use by the courts. The application of veterinary radiology and imaging to the law may include documentation of the health of an insured animal, determination of the appropriateness of veterinary medical treatment, cause of death determinations, and the investigation of animal abuse and neglect. In addition, forensic radiology and imaging may be contributory in the evaluation and identification of unknown dissociated body parts, the assessment of mummified animal bodies (McKnight et al., 2015), in inspection of forensically important inanimate objects, in investigations of animal deaths due to poaching (Thali et al., 2007), or occasionally in evaluation of animals used to smuggle illicit drugs (Baker & Rashbaum 2006; Maurer et al., 2011).

Like clinical radiology, forensic radiology encompasses multiple imaging modalities in addition to radiography; primarily, computed tomography (CT), magnetic resonance (MR), and ultrasound (US). It may seem intuitive that since the nomenclature "diagnostic imaging" has largely replaced the designation "radiology" in clinical medicine, forensic radiology would evolve to "forensic imaging"; however, the terminology forensic radiology and imaging is preferred to avoid confusion with the historical use of forensic imaging to denote an exact copy of an electronic device.

MEDICAL IMAGES AS EVIDENCE AND REPORTING

In contrast to veterinary clinical diagnostic imaging, which attempts to identify and characterize animal disease processes to guide treatment options, veterinary forensic radiology and imaging seeks to answer questions related to the law, such as the timing of injuries, the standard of care, the features and duration of the perimortem period, and cause of death determinations. In contrast to the external forensic physical examination of the live animal and the forensic autopsy, forensic radiology and imaging provides a noninvasive method to evaluate internal structure and physiology for the courts. In addition to the noninvasive acquisition of evidence and documentation of the condition of the live and deceased animal, forensic radiology and imaging allows for temporal review throughout a forensic investigation without any degradation of the imaging evidence.

Within only a year after Professor Wilhelm Conrad Roentgen's discovery of x-rays in 1895, the radiograph was admitted as evidence in legal proceedings (Scott, 1946). Today all medical imaging modalities are similarly admitted as evidence. Unlike photographic evidence, which may stand alone, a radiograph or other imaging study must be accompanied by an expert interpretation or report. Should a digital or analog imaging study be unavailable or lost, the report alone may be admitted as evidence. The forensic radiology report is dated and includes the credentials of the reporting expert, the animal identification, the requesting individual or agency, and a summary of the available historical information. A forensic radiology report may follow the standard format of the diagnostic imaging report, consisting of a description of pertinent imaging abnormalities or normalities, usually under the subheading "Findings," and an interpretation of those findings, usually under a subheading "Impression" or "Conclusion." The report may include a "Recommendations" section if the expert determines a need for additional imaging studies. Similar to a diagnostic imaging report, the forensic radiology report is a method of communication with a specific reader. Unlike the diagnostic imaging report that communicates with a referring clinician who possess medical knowledge, the forensic radiology report must also answer questions for the courts and inform a reader who may not have a broad medical background. The veterinary forensic radiology and imaging report will often include a "Summary" section, which answers specific questions for the court, clarifies medical terminology, or provides references.

PRODUCTION OF THE RADIOGRAPHIC IMAGE AND RADIATION PROTECTION

Recent advances in medical imaging have facilitated the use of radiography and imaging in the forensic sciences. Digital radiography has largely replaced analog imaging in diagnostic imaging and forensic radiology. X-rays used in both digital and analog systems are created in a sealed glass tube by directing high-speed electrons, released at the cathode, toward a tungsten target at the anode. The radiographic image is produced by differential absorption of the x-rays as they pass through the animal to a digital image detector (digital radiography [DR], direct digital radiography [DDR], computed radiography [CR]) or the analog film/screen system. The positive and negative features of the various digital imaging systems and the artifacts they produce are thoroughly described in many radiology references (Drost et al., 2008; Armbrust, 2009). The utilization of digital radiography in veterinary forensic radiology has decreased throughput time and greatly facilitated field radiography, archiving, image sharing, and chain of custody. The digital image is saved and shared between computers by a file exchange protocol called Digital Imaging and Communications in Medicine (DICOM). Patient information and equipment information are stored in a DICOM header which cannot be separated from the image. In the field of veterinary forensic radiology and imaging the ability to permanently store all modifications to the image within the DICOM protocol is a great advantage. The DICOM protocol is used in radiography, US, CT, and MR. The software and hardware, which control the retrieval, distribution, and display of images, the archiving of DICOM studies, and the integration of the DICOM heading with the report or medical record, are referred to as a picture archiving and communication system (PACS).

The exposure factors used in both digital and analog imaging systems are similar, and attention to radiation safety protocol is equally important in forensic radiography and clinical imaging. An effort to limit personnel exposure to as low as reasonably achievable (ALARA) during live animal radiography is a regulatory requirement and a basic tenet of radiation safety. Using the shortest exposure time possible, increasing personnel distance from the source of radiation (the tube and the animal) and wearing appropriate protective lead are the basic pillars of radiation protection known as time, distance, and shielding.

Interpretation of an imaging study requires attention to patient positioning, technical parameters, and labeling. Failure to obtain an adequate number of views, nonstandard positioning of the animal, absent or incorrect identifying data and markers of laterality, incorrect exposure factors, and technical artifacts degrade the quality of the image and diminish the amount of information available to the expert and the court. Any quality factor that limits the expert's ability to interpret the images will be disclosed and can diminish the value placed on the imaging evidence. A minimum of two orthogonal views and additional tangential or oblique views for complex anatomy are standard procedure in diagnostic imaging and forensic radiology. To reduce scatter radiation, which is caused by the interaction of the x-ray beam with the patient, and to optimize image quality, images are centered on and collimated to the area of interest. Standard positioning and collimation performed in clinical diagnostic imaging is also utilized in forensic radiography. It should be recognized that improper or nonstandard centering of the x-ray beam or inadequate collimation may have a detrimental effect on the digital system's production of the image.

Forensic radiography can differ from diagnostic imaging in the total number of images routinely obtained. Radiography of the entire body is indicated in cases of suspected nonaccidental injury (NAI). To reduce the number of required images needed in forensic evaluations, protocols for whole-body imaging are available (Table 18.1). If abnormalities are noted on standard views, additional detail images are performed. Although digital imaging has eliminated the need to apply an identifying or date label in the path of the x-ray beam, the identifying information must be electronically entered at the time of radiography. The identifying patient information and acquisition

Table 18.1 Recommended guidelines[a] for small animal whole-body imaging in NAI

Anatomical Region	Views	Number of Images
Thorax	Lateral, VD	2
Abdomen	Lateral, VD	2
Skull	Lateral, VD, rostrocaudal	3
C Spine	Lateral, VD	2
Pelvis	Lateral, VD	2
R forelimb[b]	Lateral, CrCd	2
L forelimb[b]	Lateral, CrCd	2
R hindlimb[b]	Lateral, CrCd	2
L hindlimb[b]	Lateral, CrCd	2
		19 Total

Abbreviations: NAI, nonaccidental injury; CrCd, craniocaudal; VD, ventrodorsal.

[a] Guidelines are not intended as legal standards of care and may be modified in individual cases or based on available resources.

[b] For larger animals, two lateral and two CrCd views are needed to image each limb.

date and time are available in the DICOM header, and this identifying information cannot be separated from the images. Application of right- and left-side markers are an essential part of the production of the x-ray image. To help reduce the potential human error of mislabeling and provide a secondary verification of laterality, right or left markers are placed within the path of the x-ray beam. Placing a left- or right-side marker in the primary x-ray beam at the time of radiography is preferred to computer-generated side labels. Single-marker techniques for labeling oblique views of the thorax and skull often produce confusion in interpretation. If the animal is in right lateral recumbency, the skull can be rotated ventrally or dorsally. Placing a single right marker indicating that the patient is in right lateral recumbency provides no benefit in differentiating the right and left skull. With the animal in right lateral recumbency and the dorsal skull rotated rightward, the right side of the patient is projected ventrally on the image and the left side of the patient is projected dorsally on the image. A right marker is placed on the ventral surface of the skull and a left marker is placed on the dorsal skull surface. Alternately, with the animal in right lateral recumbency and the dorsal skull rotated to the left, the image would be marked with a ventral "L" and a dorsal "R."

Some variation in protocol is required for radiography of deceased animals. Decomposition and rigor mortis prevent standard positioning, increase the overall size of the animal body, and increase the distribution of gas and soft tissue in the body. An approximation of standard positioning may be needed, and collimation to larger areas of interest may be acceptable in postmortem radiography. Whole animal images, like whole baby images in the medical field, are not acceptable practice (Dwek, 2011), and the acquisition of orthogonal views is always required. Like all diagnostic images, forensic radiographic images will optimize conspicuity of the soft tissues and the osseous structures. Large volumes of intracavitary and subcutaneous gas associated with decomposition will adversely affect image quality and may require modification in the typical imaging algorithm or radiographic technique. Overexposure and underexposure are technical errors rarely acknowledged in digital imaging due to the digital post-processing capabilities and the broad exposure latitude of the digital system; however, image degradation in the digital system, more commonly recognized as diminished image contrast and increased quantum noise or mottle, can be caused by inappropriate exposure settings or post-processing settings. Postmortem increases in intracavitary and subcutaneous gas enlarge the body, which can result in an overestimation of body size, overexposure, and loss of image dynamic range or latitude, which refers to the digital imaging system's ability to record a wide range of densities. Diminished soft tissues and increased gas in a body will decrease attenuation of the x-ray beam. Failure to recognize the increased gas to soft tissue ratio in body composition can result in an overestimation of the exposure factors and inappropriate post processing. Saturation of the detector in a digital system, resulting in loss of visualization of anatomical structure, is the most severe consequence of overexposure. Exposure factors in clinical imaging and live animal forensic radiography are optimized to produce a quality image, reduce exposure to personnel by scatter radiation, and minimize patient motion artifact. The digital detector may optimize image quality with increased radiation exposure. With no concern for motion and no need for personnel to be in the room during radiography of the deceased animal, postmortem images can be optimized for image quality.

FORENSIC APPLICATIONS OF COMPUTED TOMOGRAPHY, MAGNETIC RESONANCE, AND ULTRASOUND

CT, MR, and US are used to supplement radiographic examination of the live and deceased animal in veterinary forensic evaluations. CT, MR, or US imaging of the live animal in a forensic examination is similar to clinical imaging and is most often performed following routine radiography. Data to form the CT image is collected by a series of detectors which measure the attenuation of ionizing radiation passing in multiple angles through the animal. The data collected in a volume of tissue is reconstructed to form an image. The image can be reformatted in multiplanar cross-sectional images or three-dimensional (3D) images. Where available postmortem CT (PMCT) may replace whole-body radiography and is of particular value in instances of multiple osseous injuries, severe decomposition (Figure 18.1), charring of the body, or any other friable conditions of the body (Figure 18.2). PMCT imaging can identify pneumothorax, pneumomediastinum, and intravascular accumulations of gas which may not be readily identified during a forensic autopsy, document

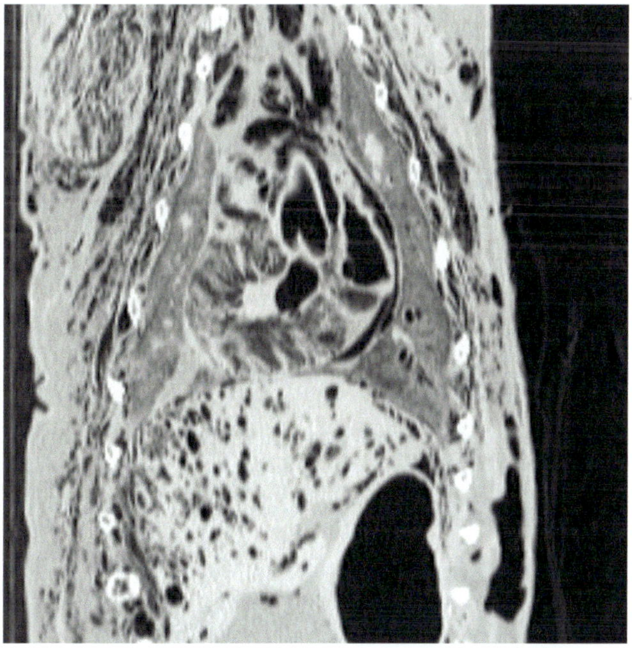

Figure 18.1 Dorsal multiplanar reconstruction PMCT of a dog. Gas and hyperattenuating clotted blood are visible in the cardiac chambers. Large amounts of gas are present in the subcutaneous soft tissues, the musculature including the myocardium, and in the great vessels.

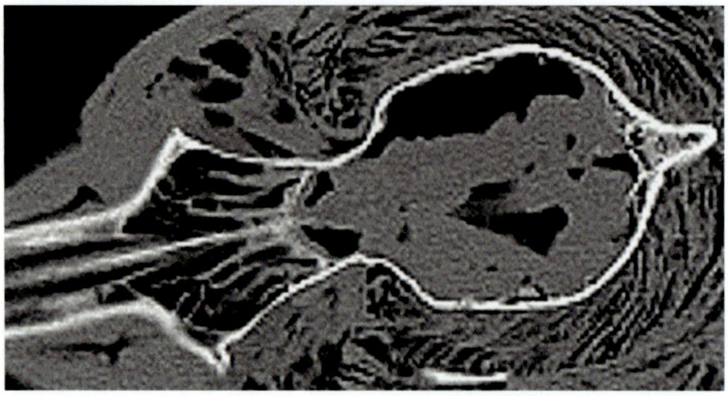

Figure 18.2 A PMCT of the skull of a dog demonstrating partial liquefaction of the brain.

nondisplaced rib fractures, and localize foreign material or projectiles. The ability to reformat the images in 3D can be helpful (Figure 18.3) to confirm projectile tracts or to describe abnormalities for the courts. A PMCT examination of the whole body can be accomplished within minutes and is a more rapid procedure than whole-body radiography. The animal body remains in the body bag and is minimally manipulated or positioned for the examination. As with postmortem radiography, the CT technical parameters can be altered to increase image quality without concern for patient or personnel exposure or motion artifact. In live animal CT examinations, breath-hold techniques and intravenous contrast administration are routine practice. Methods for delivery of intravenous contrast agents and techniques to aerate the lung are available in PMCT of humans and are under investigation in animals (Watson & Heng, 2017). The ability to evaluate the body in cross-section, the superior soft tissue resolution of CT when compared to radiographs, and the decreased time needed to complete a study are reasons PMCT, when available, is preferred to postmortem radiography.

Postmortem magnetic resonance (PMMR), which utilizes a strong magnetic field for imaging rather than ionizing radiation, may follow forensic radiography as a supplemental examination. MR offers even greater soft tissue resolution than CT (Figure 18.4a,b); however, PMMR is not typically employed as a whole-body imaging technique in veterinary forensic studies. In contrast to PMCT, PMMR is time consuming and the equipment is less readily available. Most often the PMMR will

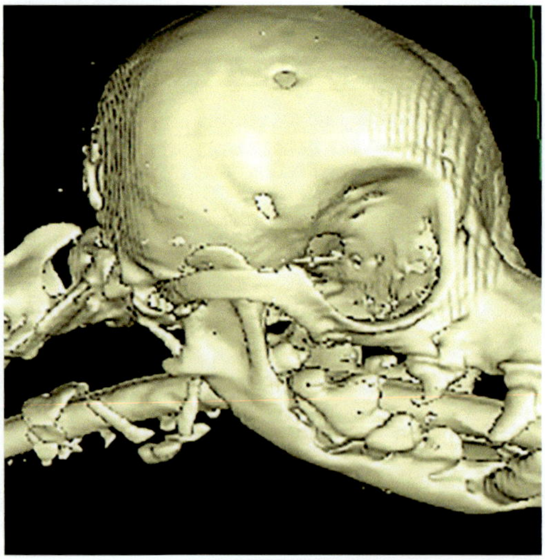

Figure 18.3 3D surface rendering CT of a dog presenting with head trauma and soft tissue wounds to the skull. Round defects in the right parietal bone are consistent with bite wounds.

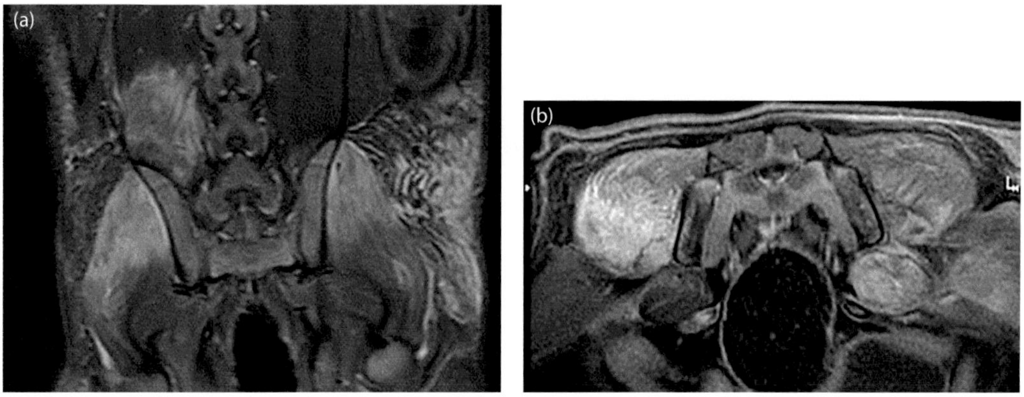

Figure 18.4 MR STIR image in dorsal plane (a) and transverse plane (b) and post-gadolinium-based contrast administration transverse T1-weighted image of a dog presenting with trauma to the hind end. Hyperintense signal and contrast enhancement are present in multiple muscle bellies including the right gluteal muscle.

be a targeted study, usually of the brain, particularly in the late stages of decomposition when the brain may be partially liquefied and difficult to handle on autopsy. In the musculoskeletal system, MR can be contributory to document a vital reaction, assisting in the differentiation of perimortem and postmortem trauma (Ruder et al., 2011). In addition, PMMR has been used to document serous atrophy of fat in emaciated horses (Sherlock et al., 2010) and may be useful in forensic cases of suspected starvation.

Two characteristics of MR need to be recognized prior to undertaking a PMMR study: temperature dependence and the interaction of the MR magnet with metals. Although PMMR typically possess high contrast resolution, MR is temperature dependent and the image quality will be diminished as the body cools. Below 20°C (68°F) the contrast between fat and soft tissue is degraded, resulting in poor quality images from frozen or cold bodies (Ruder et al., 2014). The strong magnetic field used in MR imaging presents a potential danger to personnel and to equipment from the pull of environmental ferromagnetic objects into the magnet. Similarly, ferromagnetic structure within a body can move and heat when placed in the strong magnetic field. Although radiographs to detect metal are obtained prior to PMMR, not all metals are a contraindication for PMMR. Non-ferromagnetic materials are not moved by the magnet, show no significant heating, and produce a small signal void. Steel-containing metals are ferromagnetic and can move during PMMR. Heating of steel-containing ballistics is not significant at 1.5 to 7 Tesla (Dedini et al., 2013). Steel-containing materials will produce a larger signal void artifact, reducing the quality of the PMMR images.

US may supplement imaging studies in live animal forensic investigations (Figure 18.5) and provide valuable limited information in postmortem examinations. US equipment is portable, widely available in the veterinary field, does not involve ionizing radiation, and is inexpensive to acquire and operate relative to other imaging modalities. Animal preparation and operator skill and training are perhaps the greatest challenges to the use of US in the forensic sciences. Animal preparation involves obtaining an air-free contact point on the skin, which can be accomplished by thoroughly wetting the hair, parting the hair or shaving the hair, and applying a coupling gel. The US unit can be taken directly to the animal, making it appropriate for field investigations involving small or large animals. Rapid identification of intracavitary effusions or pleural and peritoneal free air, confirmation of fractures, assessment of soft tissue swellings, and confirmation of pregnancy are some potential uses of US in the forensic investigation. Postmortem US (PMUS) is limited by the presence of subcutaneous, bowel, and intracavitary gas associated with decomposition and postmortem increased body wall echogenicity (Charlier et al., 2013). Every gas–tissue interface within the body reflects sound waves back toward the transducer and reduces visualization of deeper structure. US, like MR, is temperature dependent. The image is further degraded by diminished

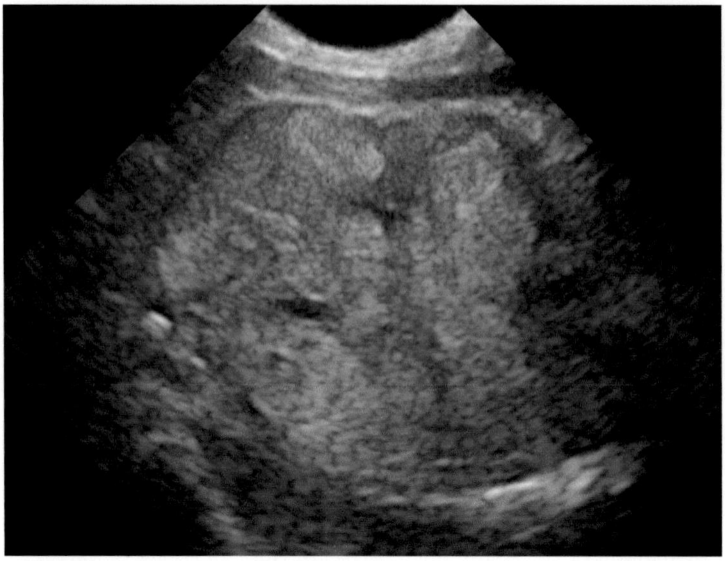

Figure 18.5 Sagittal ultrasound image of an enlarged prostate due to benign prostatic hypertrophy in an intact male dog with blood dripping from the penis.

returning signal in low-temperature bodies (Charlier et al., 2013). PMUS has the greatest benefit in guiding tissue samples or in localization of known projectiles or foreign objects.

RADIOLOGY AND IMAGING IN IDENTIFICATION AND AGE DETERMINATION

Postmortem individual animal identification is not commonly performed in veterinary forensic radiology and imaging. Some skeletal features of the skull, spine, long bones, or thoracic cavity can indicate a general breed or body type, such as brachycephalic and chondrodystrophic dogs and brachycephalic cats. When previous clinical images are available for comparison, matching trabecular patterns in long bones, evaluating nasal conchae patterns or anomalous bone malformations and injuries, and comparing previous surgical or dental procedures can facilitate individual animal identification. Regression formulas have been used to estimate the shoulder height of dogs from long bone measurements and from the internal dimensions of the cranial cavity (Chrószcz et al., 2007). Although these formulas are described on skeletal specimens in dogs, the use of anthropometric measurements obtained from CT and radiographic images is well documented to estimate stature in humans (Hishmat et al., 2015).

The appearance time of centers of ossification and the time of growth plate closure are used in age determination when other indications of age are inconclusive or absent (Figure 18.6). Physeal closure does not occur uniformly and is variable in different species. Physeal closure can vary among dog breeds and by sex and reproductive status. Physeal closure determined by radiography will differ from physeal closure determined by US or histological examination; however, the charts found in most reference texts are based on radiographic closure and can be used to estimate age. Most physeal closure in dogs ranges from approximately 4 to 12 months. Most physes in the cat close slightly later, primarily from 4 to 19 months. The general health and nutritional status of the animal and the load-bearing status will affect physeal closure. Knowledge of the location of primary and secondary centers of ossification and familiarity with the location and closure times of growth plates in various species is important to prevent mistaking these normal structures for trauma.

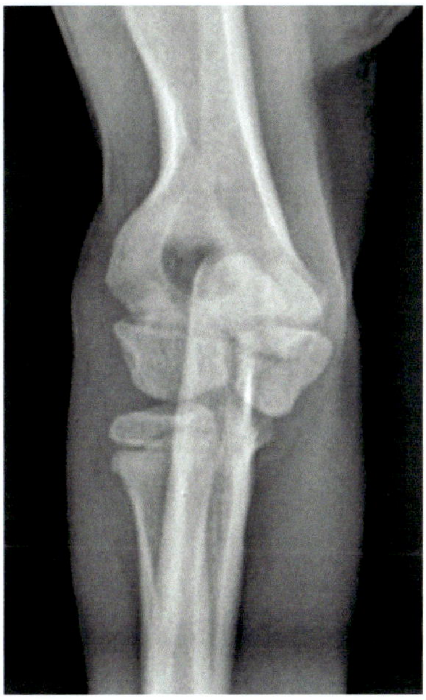

Figure 18.6 Craniocaudal elbow radiograph of a 10-week-old pit bull–type dog. The physis of the medial and lateral humeral condyle is open and typically fuses between 8–12 weeks of age.

The radiographic determination of the pulp cavity to tooth width or tooth volume ratio is another method described for estimating the chronological age of domestic cats, foxes, coyotes, wild dogs, and in human remains (Park et al., 2014). With age, the volume of the pulp cavity decreases in size owing to the deposition of dentin. Measurement of this ratio on radiographs can be performed in the live or deceased animal or in incomplete skeletal remains which include some teeth. The canine teeth are primarily used for measurement of the pulp cavity to tooth width ratio at the cemento–enamel junction. A bisecting angle technique is applied to prevent radiographic distortion, which occurs if the imaging receptor is not parallel to the long axis of the tooth.

RADIOLOGY AND IMAGING OF THE OSSEOUS RESPONSE TO TRAUMA

In forensic evaluations, radiographs are often utilized to estimate the chronicity of a fracture. The presence or absence of an osseous reaction to trauma predicts whether a skeletal injury occurred before death or postmortem. Identifying mild periosteal reaction associated with a fracture confirms that the fracture did not occur immediately prior to death and is not due to postmortem trauma. In the live animal, the radiographic changes identified in bone following trauma are variable based on the animal's age, nutritional status or health, location of the injury, and degree of immobilization or weight-bearing status. In addition, most knowledge regarding the radiographic appearance of healing bone is based on clinical experience and on the study of fractures that have been stabilized or have undergone direct healing. With knowledge and understanding of these confounding factors, the radiographic progression of change in injured bone over time can be used as a general guideline to the timing of injuries (Figure 18.7a,b).

Bone is dynamic and changes during growth, following injury, and throughout life by a process of resorption and new bone production called remodeling. The radiographic identification of skeletal injury and the remodeling which follows injury are used in forensic evaluations. Radiographs can

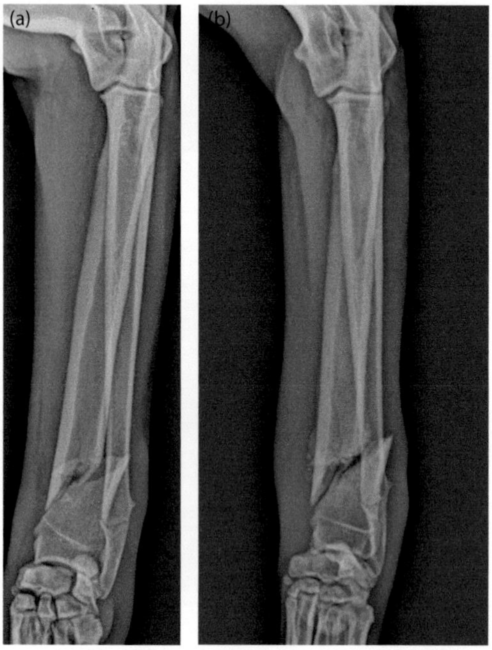

Figure 18.7 Craniocaudal projections of the antebrachium in a dog. (a) The sharp margins of the mildly comminuted distal antebrachial fracture are consistent with an acute fracture. (b) At 3 weeks following injury periosteal callus and resorption at the fracture margins are visible.

indicate the type of skeletal injury and potentially the mechanism of injury. Radiography and imaging can be useful in assessing the healing process and estimating when the injury occurred. Radiography and imaging studies may help distinguish antemortem and postmortem trauma and in some cases differentiate perimortem and postmortem injury.

Bone can be anatomically divided into regions of the periosteum or periosteal membrane, cortex, medullary cavity, nutrient foramen, endosteum, and articular surfaces. The periosteum can provide important evidence in medicolegal cases, such as how the trauma occurred, when it occurred, and if the injury is healing. The periosteum, which covers the entire bone with the exception of articular cartilage, can provide important components needed in bone healing and in bone growth of the immature animal. In the immature animal the periosteum is tightly attached to the underlying bone at the level of the physis and very loosely attached throughout the remainder of the bone. This configuration explains the appearance of the Salter-Harris II fracture, which cannot propagate completely across the physis due to the tight periosteal attachment, and deviates through the metaphysis (Figure 18.8). In the area of loose periosteal attachment, subperiosteal hemorrhage can occur secondary to trauma. The inner cambium layer of the periosteum is thick and cell-rich in the immature animal and gradually decreases in cellularity and thickness with age. This change in the structure of the periosteum explains why periosteal mineralization or periosteal reaction will occur earlier and will be more pronounced with trauma to immature bone compared to mature bone. Periosteal reactions are described as continuous or interrupted and by various descriptive terms such as solid, lamellated, palisading, spiculated, sunburst, and Codman triangle. Stable healing fractures show a smooth periosteal pattern. An onion skin or lamellated periosteal reaction may occur with waxing and waning disease or secondary to repeated trauma. Palisading periostitis can be seen with chronic soft tissue inflammation or with hypertrophic osteopathy. Spiculated new bone occurs with rapidly changing disease such as neoplasia. Sunburst patterns and Codman triangle are often associated with rapidly growing aggressive processes where the underlying disrupted periosteum has not had time to mineralize.

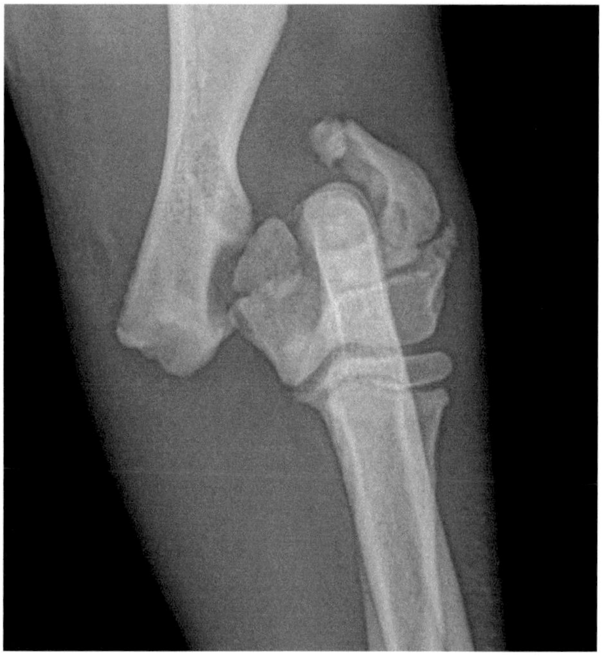

Figure 18.8 Craniocaudal view of the elbow in a young dog. The fracture has propagated through the medial distal humeral physis and exited through the lateral condyle. Note that the medial humeral epicondyle, which typically fuses to the remainder of the humerus between 6 and 8 months of age, is unfused. The medial and lateral condyles are fused.

Periostitis may be the first sign of accidental or nonaccidental trauma and may be present without a fracture and without outward signs of trauma. Torsional force may tear the periosteum in an immature animal and the secondary periosteal mineralization will be radiographically apparent days after injury. Periosteal mineralization can first be seen as early as 5 days or as late as 10 days following injury. Cases of suspected nonaccidental trauma with no abnormalities on the initial radiographic study can be radiographed in 10 days to look for early periosteal mineralization. Nondisplaced fractures that are occult on an initial radiographic examination may become conspicuous on follow-up imaging performed between 5 and 10 days, when the periosteal reaction is visible. The amount of periosteal reaction will progress with increased displacement or motion at a fracture site.

In addition to evaluation of the periosteum, assessment of the cortex, endosteum, medullary cavity, callus, and soft tissues at a fracture site may provide estimates as to the duration of fracture and trauma. In the 5 to 10 days following a fracture, the margins of fracture fragments will become less sharp and may decrease in opacity. In clinical imaging, when comparison images are available, an increased fracture gap may be initially identified due to this loss of opacity. In the 10 to 20 days following a fracture, endosteal callus may be visualized. Callus is initially hazy and less opaque than the cortex. Callus will become progressively more opaque 20 to 30 days after fracture. Identification of trabecular bone within a callus and remodeling generally take at least 30 days to occur.

Evaluation of the soft tissues at a fracture site may also provide some indication of the age of a fracture. Radiographically identified soft tissue swelling associated with a fracture will be pronounced in the first few days following injury and will diminish during the weeks after the trauma. The loss of soft tissues or soft tissue atrophy can be noted as early as 2 weeks following injury of the appendicular skeleton. When the contralateral limb is available for comparison, detecting marked muscle atrophy more likely indicates an injury of several weeks' duration. Decreased bone opacity distal to a fracture site or osteopenia is further support of disuse and chronicity of a lesion.

Although radiography is primarily used for evaluating osseous trauma and is readily available in the veterinary field, other imaging modalities can assist in the forensic evaluation of osseous trauma. US by an experienced operator can detect cortical defects, callus, and hemorrhage. Removal of the air interface between the US probe and skin surface would require shaving the area of interest, and due to pain associated with the direct pressure of the transducer, sedation of the animal would likely be necessary. When available, CT and MR imaging are excellent adjunctive studies in the forensic evaluation of the bone's response to trauma due to their superior contrast resolution and cross-sectional imaging capabilities and the ability of MR to detect areas of increased vascularity or bone marrow lesions (previously referred to as bone marrow edema). The potential of PMMR to provide evidence of a vital reaction could be useful in cause of death determinations.

RADIOLOGY AND IMAGING OF FIREARM INJURY

Radiography and imaging are an important part of the live and postmortem forensic examination of animals with suspected firearm, air gun, or other projectile injury. Orthogonal radiographic images are obtained in cases of known gunshot injury to localize the projectile, determine the number of projectiles, assist in evaluation of the trajectory, gain some idea of the type of weapon used, and evaluate damage to vital structure. Routine radiography in forensic evaluations may identify a projectile in an animal with a previously unknown cause of trauma.

Firearm and air gun injuries may be penetrating, meaning the projectile remains in the body (Figure 18.9), or perforating, indicating that the projectile has exited the body. In general, the projectile that remains in the body has a greater wounding potential. Radiographically identified deformed or mushroomed projectiles in the body may possess sharp edges, necessitating a cautious approach at autopsy (Figure 18.10). Radiographically identified small metallic fragments, intracavitary or subcutaneous gas, or osseous injury with no projectile can be evidence of a perforating firearm injury.

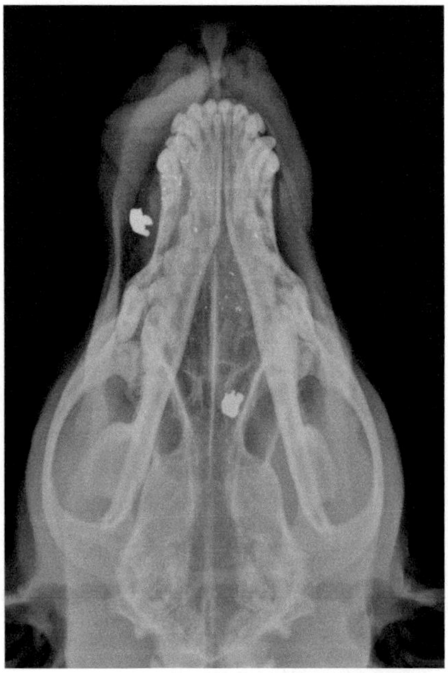

Figure 18.9 Ventrodorsal skull of a dog shot with a 22-gauge rifle. The orthogonal view confirmed the more caudally located projectile to be within the nasal cavity.

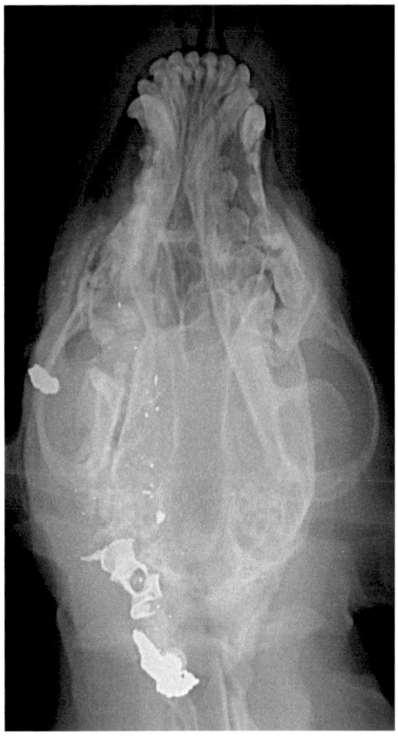

Figure 18.10 Ventrodorsal skull of a dog shot with a 9-mm projectile. Notice the less opaque jacket material adjacent to the right bulla.

In some forensic evaluations it will be important to determine the direction of projectile travel. Since a bullet will tumble or flip end-to-end on impact, the orientation of a bullet on imaging studies may not indicate the direction of travel. Evaluating trajectory on imaging studies can also be confounded by fragmentation of the bullet or a change in direction of the bullet once it impacts bone. Gas may not be useful in evaluating trajectory as it does not typically remain in a wound tract, but extravasates along fascial planes. Imaging findings which may assist in the determination of projectile trajectory include bone beveling, propagation of projectile and bone fragments, and hemorrhage. Internal beveling of bone is usually indicative of an entrance wound, and external beveling of bone is more often an exit wound. With CT imaging, projectile trajectory may be indicated by an array of small bone fragments, projectile fragments, and a tract of attenuation representing hemorrhage. Smaller projectile fragments than those detected on radiographs may be identified on CT images.

Bullet caliber and the exact size of a projectile cannot be conclusively determined from imaging studies due to deformation of the projectile and imaging magnification; however, radiographically identifying the general type of projectile, such as slug, shot, or air gun pellet (Figure 18.11), and locating additional cartridge components are useful in medicolegal investigations. Sometimes other cartridge components such as wadding or jacket will be present in a wound, and imaging studies are valuable in determining the location of such forensically important material. These materials are typically soft tissue opaque or less opaque than the bullet, and can be identified on routine radiographs and CT imaging studies. Differentiating steel and lead shot is important, as lead shot is banned in waterfowl hunting and in certain jurisdictions. If MR imaging is considered, distinguishing the ferromagnetic lead shot from the non-ferromagnetic steel shot is important from a safety and image quality perspective. Steel shot and lead shot can be differentiated by their shape on routine radiographs. Lead shot, which is softer, will deform with impact, and the harder steel shot will maintain a round

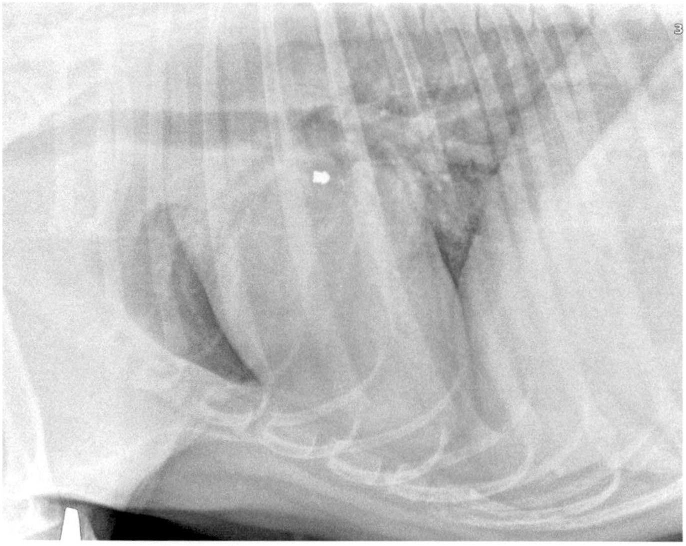

Figure 18.11 A lateral thoracic view of a dog presented for coughing. An orthogonal view confirmed the air gun projectile to be outside the heart and within the lung. The common diablo air gun projectile has a characteristic shape.

shape. The most common type of air gun pellets is the diablo type with a characteristic hourglass shape, making an air gun projectile easily distinguishable from other projectile types. In cases of multiple projectiles resulting in skull fractures, the priority rule, also called Puppe's rule, can predict the sequence of trauma. A fracture will not propagate beyond a previous fracture.

RADIOLOGY AND IMAGING OF SOFT TISSUE INJURY

Good quality radiographs can evaluate the subcutaneous soft tissues for swelling, gas, or foreign material; however, CT and MR offer higher-contrast resolution compared to radiography, and CT can rapidly survey the entire body. Ultrasonographic evaluation of the soft tissues can detect small amounts of subcutaneous fluid or bruising in targeted areas of the body. Radiographs and CT imaging are appropriate modalities to evaluate the thorax and abdomen for internal injury. CT can rapidly survey the thorax and abdomen, although anesthesia may be required. Radiographic evaluation of the emergent live animal is usually preferred due to availability and lack of need for anesthesia.

Two radiographic projections of the thorax are standard: lateral and ventrodorsal views. Two oblique projections from the ventrodorsal and two from the lateral position are beneficial for evaluation of the chest wall and ribs. Lung contusions, which may be present adjacent to rib fractures or in absence of rib fracture, are recognized as patchy interstitial or alveolar infiltrate, with normal lung volume. Younger animals have greater chest wall elasticity, which may explain why contusions without rib fractures are more common in the immature animal. Serial thoracic radiographs at intervals of 24 hours are recommended when chest wall trauma is present. Radiographic visualization of a pulmonary contusion may not be present on images obtained immediately following injury and may progress in opacity over a short time. Lung contusions without laceration would be expected to resolve within 72 hours (Figure 18.12a,b).

Traumatic pneumothorax secondary to blunt force trauma and free peritoneal air, secondary to a ruptured viscus, are most often identified on radiographs. Intracavitary air can be identified on US by an experienced sonographer. Cross-sectional imaging is rarely needed for diagnosis of intracavitary air. Radiographs are also the most appropriate modality for identification of pneumomediastinum,

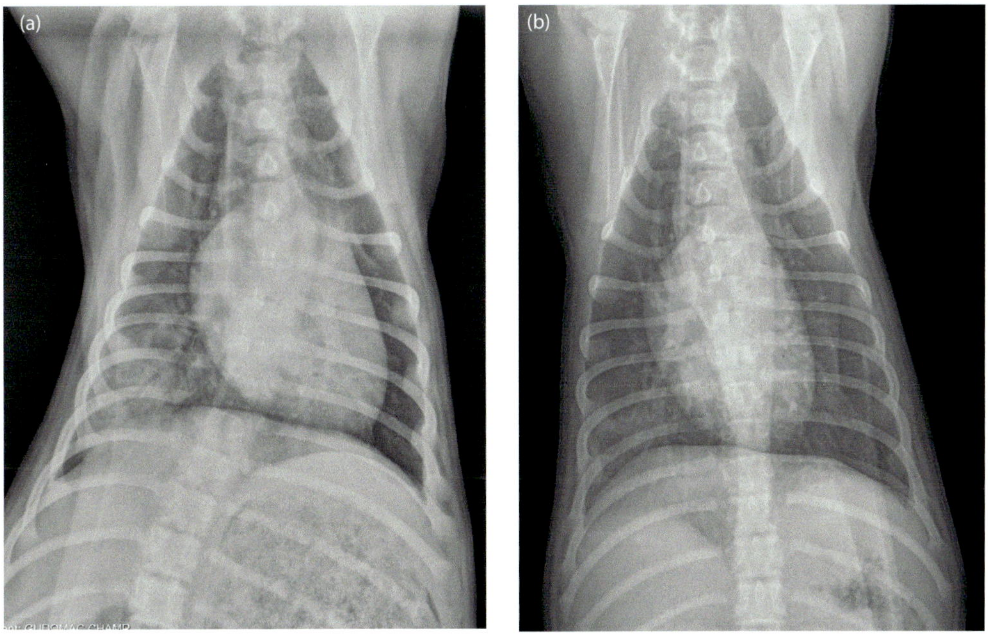

Figure 18.12 Ventrodorsal views of an immature dog following NAI. (a) Contusion is present in the right caudal lung lobe hours following injury. (b) Forty-eight hours later the contusion is almost completely resolved.

which can occur secondary to blunt force trauma and rupture of alveoli, dissection from cervical soft tissue wounds, and esophageal or tracheal tears. Fluid collections in the peritoneal cavity, the retroperitoneal space, and the pleural space can be identified with radiographs, US, or cross-sectional studies. Most often, US is used to evaluate structures obscured by intracavitary fluids and guide sampling of the fluid. Lacerations in the spleen or liver can be detected with US or CT. Trauma to the urinary tract requires positive-contrast radiography or contrast-enhanced CT imaging.

Although radiography is of value in identifying skull fractures, intracranial hemorrhage, which can occur without skull fractures, cannot be radiographically detected. US cannot penetrate bone and is only of value in skull trauma if fractures or an open fontanel have provided an acoustic window. Both MR and CT are appropriate for assessment of skull trauma in live animal forensic examination and in postmortem imaging. MR provides the greatest soft tissue resolution; however, CT is often favored in the emergent live animal due to the more rapid acquisition time. The appearance of hemorrhage on cross-sectional imaging changes over time. Hemorrhage on CT is initially hyperattenuating or bright relative to normal brain. Over time, hemorrhage will become isoattenuating and then hypoattenuating to the brain parenchyma.

RADIOGRAPHY AND IMAGING SIGNS OF NEGLECT

Radiographs and additional imaging studies can benefit medicolegal investigations of animal neglect such as imaging evidence of failure to provide a minimum standard of veterinary care, imaging signs which support starvation, and imaging evidence supporting clinical findings of diminished body condition.

Subcutaneous fat and diminished intra-abdominal fat can be evaluated on radiographs. The measurement of subcutaneous fat surrounding the ventrodorsal thorax has been shown to correlate with the nine-point body condition score (BCS) in live animals (Linder et al., 2013).

The subcutaneous fat measurement is compared to the T4 vertebral body length and the T8 vertebral body width in a regression formula. With this method the body condition score could be radiographically determined when a body condition score was not performed or when the animal is no longer available.

Although radiographs may distinguish cortical and medullary bone and detect changes within the medullary cavity, MR is more sensitive for the identification of fat in the bone marrow. Serous atrophy of fat has been histologically identified in the bone marrow of emaciated animals and humans (Whiting et al., 2012). Increased fluid content of the bone marrow fat, consistent with serous atrophy, is identified on MR as a low signal on T1-weighted images and a high bone marrow signal on short tau inversion recovery (STIR).

RADIOLOGY AND IMAGING MIMICS OF ABUSE

Delayed presentation fractures, fractures in various stages of healing, bilateral fractures (Figure 18.13), and fractures inconsistent with the clinical history can be indicative of abuse in animals (Figure 18.14). No individual fracture location or fracture type is considered highly specific for nonaccidental injury in animals. Several disease processes can produce radiographic changes which could be mistaken for nonaccidental injury in animals. Endocrine disease, metabolic disease, and genetic disorders can produce multiple fractures in various stages of healing. Variations in ossification, normal growth plates, secondary centers of ossification, multipartite sesamoid bones, or skeletal anomalies must be distinguished from nonaccidental trauma. Periosteal new bone can occur secondary to disease processes unrelated to subperiosteal hemorrhage and trauma.

Increased radiolucency of bone is described as osteopenia and may be due to a variety of mechanisms (Figure 18.15). Osteoporosis, meaning increased porosity of bone associated with an imbalance in the normal homeostasis of bone and osteomalacia, indicating abnormal mineralization of bone matrix, is occasionally used interchangeably with osteopenia. Although most cases of

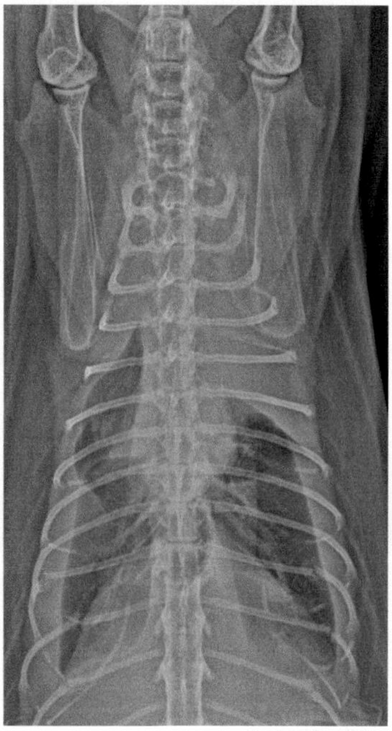

Figure 18.13 Ventrodorsal view of the thorax in a cat with multiple bilateral rib fractures and hemothorax. Mild periosteal new bone surrounds the rib fractures, indicating healing.

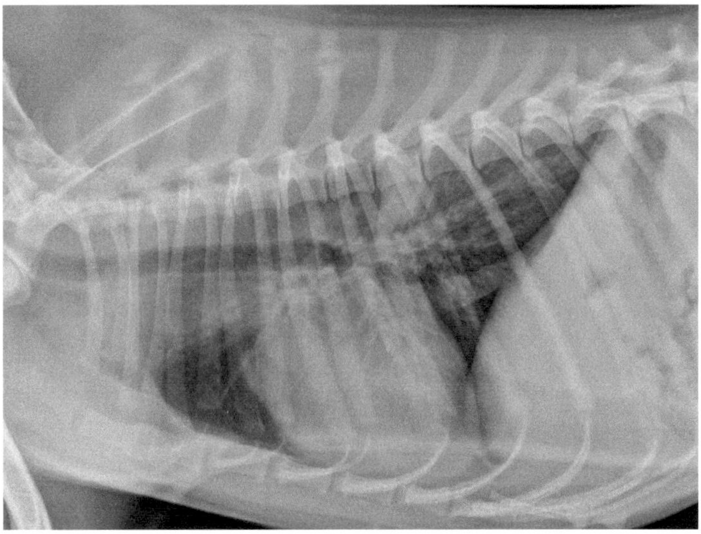

Figure 18.14 Lateral thoracic view of a rescue dog with unknown history. Multiple healing spinous process fractures and a pulmonary hematoma are present.

osteopenia are due to osteoporosis, causes of decreased bone opacity cannot be determined from radiographic evaluation and in such cases the term osteopenia would be preferable. Osteopenia is recognized on radiographs as a decreased medullary opacity in bone and cortical thinning. The diminished visualization of number and size of trabeculae in the ends of the long bones may be the earliest finding of decreased bone opacity. The identification of cortical thinning in osteopenia

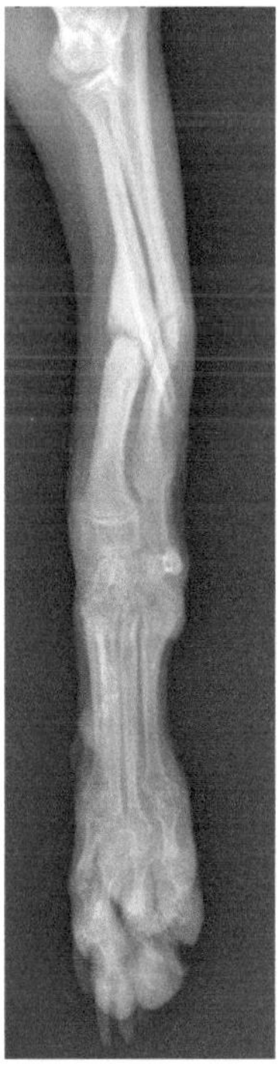

Figure 18.15 A lateral projection of the antebrachium in a dog with a chronic malaligned nonunion fracture. There is generalized osteopenia in the manus consistent with disuse.

generally occurs later than the medullary changes. In addition, radiographs are not very sensitive for identification of bone mineral loss, and at least 30% bone mass loss is required before radiographic detection is possible. Without comparison to normal bone and without densitometry, generalized osteopenia is difficult to radiographically confirm and can be an artifact of overexposure. CT is superior to radiographs for detection of bone mineral density. Hounsfield unit values in regions of interest (ROI) are converted to bone mineral opacity by comparison to a bone density phantom through linear regression analysis. Quantitative CT has been validated in poultry and dogs to determine bone mineral density (Korver et al., 2004).

Endocrine disease, metabolic disease, reproductive status, and aging may contribute to an increased porosity of bone, predisposing an animal to fracture. Without bone densitometry, bone loss can be present prior to the radiographic identification of osteopenia. Endocrine diseases such hyperadrenocorticism, hypothyroidism, hyperthyroidism, and primary hyperparathyroidism can be associated with osteopenia. The radiographic identification of osteopenia on radiographs of patients with hyperadrenocorticism has been questioned; however, bone loss secondary to exogenous steroids is known to occur in animals with Cushing disease and can also be expected in any animal on chronic steroid therapy. Imbalances of parathyroid hormone, thyroid hormone, and estrogen may also result in osteoporosis.

Any disease process or diet that results in a change in circulating PTH, calcium, phosphorous, or vitamin D can result in fibrous osteodystrophy, which is increased osteoclastic or resorptive activity of bone replaced by fibrous connective tissue. Radiographically, the medullary cavity will enlarge and the cortices will appear thinner. The earliest changes are seen in the skull, where increased lucency is present in the bone surrounding numerous teeth and moth-eaten lysis can be visible in the calvarium. Joint subluxation may be apparent on imaging studies. As the disease progresses, thin cortices and medullary lucency will be observed in the long bones and multiple bone fractures may be recognized. Because of the softening of the bones, the fractures are often described as folding fractures. In young animals with fibrous osteodystrophy, the physes remain normal.

In immature animals presenting with multiple fractures without history of trauma and without evidence of nutritional or renal hyperparathyroidism or endocrine disease, an underlying genetic disease may need to be ruled out (Figure 18.16a,b). Osteogenesis imperfecta is a hereditary disorder resulting from defects in the genes responsible for the development of collagen. Animals and humans with this disease can present with multiple pathologic fractures, including fractures of the teeth. An overall diminished bone opacity and thin cortices may be appreciated on radiographs. Osteogenesis imperfecta has been reported in several dog breeds, including the dachshund, beagle, golden retriever, poodle, Bedlington terrier, collie, and Norwegian elkhound, and in cats. Reports in other animals, some of which are used as research models for osteogenesis imperfecta in humans, include mice, zebra fish, sheep, tigers, and cows. Genetic testing is available in certain dog breeds to determine carrier or affected status of osteogenesis imperfecta. Fibroblast cultures from a skin biopsy can be used for confirmation in other animals.

A silicate-associated osteoporosis or equine bone fragility disorder has been identified in horses in California. Affected horses without a history of trauma can present with acute fractures and fractures in various stages of healing and lysis of multiple bones.

Rickets is a metabolic disease which can occur in immature and mature animals. The radiographic findings may be similar to the findings of osteoporosis; however, the disease is due to a failure of the bone matrix to mineralize or osteomalacia, rather than an increased bone resorption. Rickets is primarily caused by a dietary deficiency of vitamin D or phosphorus. Inherited forms of rickets have also been reported in cats, dogs, pigs, and sheep. Llamas and alpacas outside of the Andes are prone to develop rickets, most likely due to a dietary deficiency of vitamin D and decreased exposure to sunlight during the winter months. Radiographic signs of rickets may include widened physes, flared metaphyses, thin cortices, decreased bone opacity, and pathologic fractures. Changes

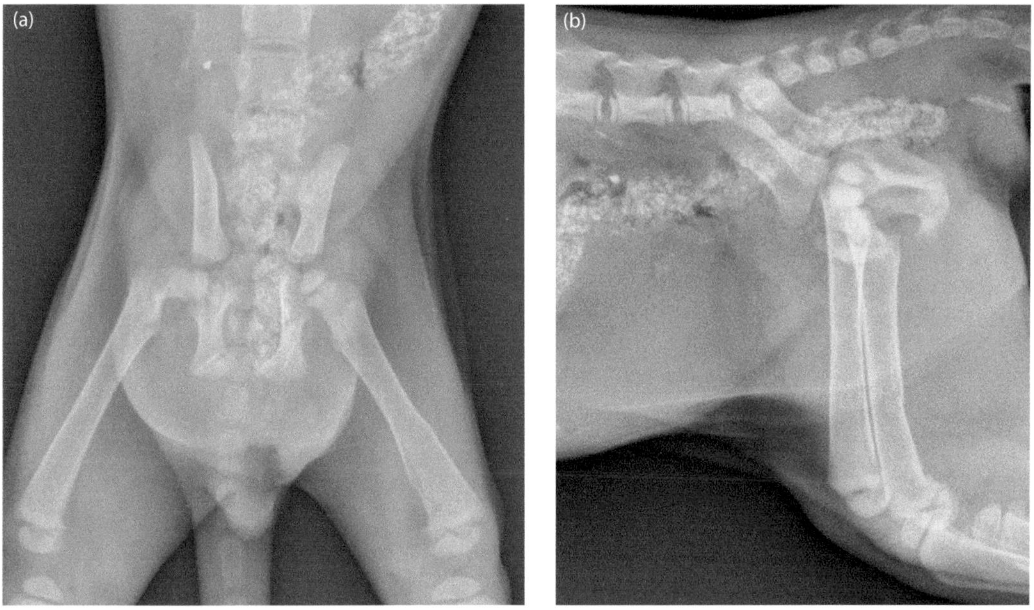

Figure 18.16 Ventrodorsal (a) and lateral (b) pelvic views of a kitten with suspected osteogenesis imperfecta after ruling out metabolic disease. Note the folding fracture in the left femur and the right femoral neck fracture.

are most pronounced in the tibiae, radii, metacarpal bones, and metatarsal bones. Costochondral enlargements are also described and should be differentiated from normal costochondral remodeling.

When evaluating animals with multiple fractures and little evidence of trauma, three additional conditions or mimics of nonaccidental injury are considered: (1) small-breed dogs presenting with single or bilateral antebrachial fractures and a history of a jumping down or minor falling down event; (2) multiple dog breeds, particularly cocker spaniels, Brittany spaniels, Labrador retrievers, and Rottweilers, presenting with single or bilateral elbow fractures after minor trauma; and (3) young cats presenting with bilateral femoral fractures and no history of a traumatic event.

Distal antebrachial fractures are reported to be the third most common fracture in dogs, and small breed dogs have a tendency to sustain distal antebrachial fractures with minor falls or jumping. These fractures, usually transverse, tend to be located in the distal one-third of the antebrachial diaphysis and can be confirmed on physical examination and radiographs. Bone density and geometric properties such as cross-sectional area, cortical thickness, and properties of shape that determine deflection are potential reasons for the propensity of small-breed dogs to sustain antebrachial fractures with minimal bending or torsion (Brianza, Delise, Ferraris, Amelio, & Botti 2006).

The canine humeral condyle develops from three ossification centers: one for the medial humeral condyle, one for the lateral humeral condyle, and one smaller center for the medial humeral epicondyle. The physis between the medial and lateral condyles will fuse by 12 weeks of age. In some spaniel breeds, Labrador retrievers, and Rottweilers, a predisposition to fracture at the physis has been observed either due to incomplete or delayed closure or a tendency for stress fracture at this site. Radiographs are sufficient to confirm a condylar fracture and may detect incomplete ossification; however, CT is more sensitive for evaluation of the physis and any adjacent sclerosis.

Cats greater than 1 year of age may present with bilateral femoral capital physeal fractures and no history of trauma. Although the femoral head physes typically close between 6 to 9 months in the cat, spontaneous unilateral or bilateral femoral head physeal fractures may be observed in cats greater than 1 year of age. The femoral head physeal fractures are diagnosed by routine pelvic radiographs, including a lateral and extended-leg or frog-leg ventrodorsal views.

CONCLUSION

Radiography, CT, MR, and US provide visual evidence of the condition and health status of the live animal in medicolegal investigations and assist in cause of death determinations as part of the postmortem examination. Compared to other types of evidence, imaging studies are noninvasive, perpetual, and require the interpretation of an expert. Although a lesion on a live animal will change over time and the complete deceased animal body is no longer available after forensic autopsy, the imaging studies persist and can be reviewed and re-reviewed as a case progresses. Forensic radiology and imaging studies provide visual descriptions of complex injuries or conditions for the court. With knowledge of the most efficient use of the various imaging modalities to document nonaccidental injury, body condition, and an understanding of imaging mimics of nonaccidental trauma, radiology and imaging can be an informing presentation for the court and a valuable part of a veterinary forensic investigation.

References

Armbrust, L.J. 2009. Comparing types of digital capture. *Veterinary Clinics of North America: Small Animal Practice*. 39(4), 677–688.

Baker, A. and Rashbaum, W.K. 2006. *New York Times*. February 6. http://www.nytimes.com/2006/02/02/nyregion/heroin- implants-turned-puppies-into-drug-mules-us-says.html

Brianza, S.Z., Delise, M., Ferraris, M.M., D'Amelio, P., and Botti, P. 2006. Cross-sectional geometrical properties of distal radius and ulna in large, medium and toy breed dogs. *Journal of Biomechanics*. 39(2), 302–311.

Charlier, P., Watier, L., Carlier, R., Cavard, S., Herve, C., de la Grandmaison, G.L., Huynh-Charlier, I. 2013. Is post-mortem ultrasonography a useful tool for forensic purposes? *Medicine. Science and the Law*. 53(4), 227–234.

Chrószcz, A., Janeczek, M., Onar, V., Staniorowsk, P., and Pospieszny, N. 2007. The shoulder height estimation in dogs based on the internal dimension of cranial cavity using mathematical formula. *Anatomia, Histologia, Embryologia*. 36, 269–271.

Dedini, R.D., Karracozoff, A.M., Shellock, F.G., Xu, D., McClellan, R.T., and Pekmezci, M. 2013. MRI issues for ballistic objects: Information obtained at 1.5, 3-, and 7-Tesla. *Spine Journal*. 13(7), 815–822.

Drost W.T., Reese D.J., and Hornof W.J. 2008. Digital radiography artifacts. *Veterinary Radiology & Ultrasound*. 49(S1), S48–S56.

Dwek, J.R. 2011. The Radiographic Approach to Child Abuse. *Clinical Orthopaedics and Related Research*. 469(3), 776–789.

Hishmat, A.M., Michiue, T., Sogawa, N., Oritani, S., Ishikawa, T., Fawazy, I.A., Hashem, M., and Hitoshi, M. 2015. Virtual CT morphometry of lower limb long bones for estimation of the sex and stature using postmortem Japanese adult data in forensic identification. *International Journal of Legal Medicine*. 129(5), 1437–1596.

Korver, D.R., Saunders-Blades, J.L., and Nadeau, K.L. 2004. Assessing bone mineral density in vivo: Quantitative computed tomography. *Poultry Science*. 83(2), 222–229.

Lee, D., Lee, Y., Choi, W., Chang, J., Kang, J.-H., Na, K.-J., and Chang, D.-W. 2015. Quantitative CT assessment of bone mineral density in dogs with hyperadrenocorticism. *Journal of Veterinary Science*. 16(4), 531–542.

Linder, D.E., Freeman, L.M., and Sutherland-Smith, J. 2013. Association between subcutaneous fat measured on thoracic radiographs and body condition score in dogs. *Journal of the American Veterinary Medical Association*. 74(11), 1400–1403.

Maurer, M.H., Niehues, S.M., Schnapauff, D., Grieser, C., Rothe, J.H., Waldmuller, D., Chopra, S.S., Hamm, B., and Denecke, T. 2011. Low-dose computed tomography to detect body-packing in an animal model. *European Journal of Radiology*. 78(2), 302–306.

Mcknight, L.M., Atherton-Woolham, S.D., and Adams, J.E. 2015. Imaging of ancient Egyptian animal mummies. *RadioGraphics*. 35(7), 2108–2120.

Park, K., Ahn, J., Kang, S., Lee, E., Kim, S., Park, S., and Seo, K., 2014. Determining the age of cats by pulp cavity/tooth width ratio using dental radiography. *Journal of Veterinary Science.* 15(4), 557–561.

Ruder, T.D., Germerott, T., Thali, M.J., and Hatch, G.M. 2011. Differentiation of ante-mortem and post-mortem fractures with MRI: a case report. *British Journal of Radiology.* 84(1000), e75–e78.

Ruder, T.D., Thali, M.J., and Hatch, G.M. 2014. Essentials of forensic post-mortem MR imaging in adults. *British Journal of Radiology.* 87(1036), 20130567. http://doi.org/10.1259/bjr.20130567

Scott, C.C. 1946. X-ray pictures as evidence. *Michigan Law Review.* 44(5), 773–796.

Sherlock, C.E., Mair, T.S., Murray, R.C., and Blunden, T.S. 2010. Magnetic resonance imaging features of serous atrophy of bone marrow fat in the distal limb of three horses. *Veterinary Radiology & Ultrasound.* 51(6), 607–613.

Thali, M.J., Kneubuehl, B.P., Bolliger, S.A., Christe, A., Koenigsdorfer, U., Ozdoba, C., Spielvogel, E., and Dirnhofer, R. 2007. Forensic veterinary radiology: Ballistic-radiological 3D computertomographic reconstruction of an illegal lynx shooting in Switzerland. *Forensic Science International.* 171(1), 63–66.

Watson, E. and Heng, H.G. 2017. Forensic radiology and imaging for veterinary radiologists. *Veterinary Radiology & Ultrasound.* 58(3), 245–258.

Whiting, T.L., Postey, R.C., Chestley, S.T., and Wruck, G.C. 2012. Explanatory model of cattle death by starvation in Manitoba: Forensic evaluation. *Canadian Veterinary Journal.* 53(11), 1173–1180.

CHAPTER 19

LEGAL INVESTIGATIONS IN SHELTER MEDICINE

Mary Manspeaker

INTRODUCTION

Animal shelters frequently encounter victims of animal cruelty ranging from misdemeanor-level negligence to intentional felony level abuse. Members of the shelter staff, including veterinarians, animal intake personnel, and animal control officers, are responsible for recognizing, documenting, and reporting evidence of animal cruelty. Animal control officers are often the first to respond when animal cruelty is reported. Likewise, animal intake personnel are the first to witness victims when citizens surrender their pet or deliver a stray animal to the shelter. Personnel must be trained on how to recognize signs of animal abuse, document findings, and collect evidence. In addition, shelter personnel must recognize situations necessitating the input of the shelter veterinarian, who must in turn be familiar with how to recognize animal abuse, collect and process evidence, perform a forensic examination, and process remains for a postmortem examination.

ANIMAL WELFARE LAWS

Animal welfare laws vary by jurisdiction (ALDF, 2017). Fundamentally, most animal welfare laws state that it is unlawful for any person to perform harmful activities toward any animal. Commonly used words include "overload," "torment," "torture," and "deprive of necessary sustenance" (ALDF, 2017). Definition of these terms is not always detailed within the written law so it is imperative that shelter personnel understand appropriate animal husbandry. A helpful resource regarding acceptable animal care is the decades-old doctrine of the Five Freedoms (FAWC, 2009). These five statements were originally developed as guidelines for appropriate care for livestock, but they have been widely used as guidelines for animal welfare, regardless of species (Table 19.1).

In addition to varying state laws, shelter personnel have differing levels of authority. It is important that all personnel responsible for the investigation of animal cruelty understand their legal responsibilities and restrictions. For example, an officer employed by a municipal shelter may be restricted to issuing summons for city ordinance violations, where in the same jurisdiction, an officer for a private humane society may have enforcement power similar to that of a police officer. Because of the varying authority, it is usually necessary for police officials and animal control officers to collaborate during an investigation for animal cruelty.

Some states mandate veterinary reporting of suspected animal abuse. This is due to increased awareness, stricter laws regarding animal cruelty, and the association between violence toward animals with that of violence toward humans, particularly child and elderly abuse, and domestic violence, as described in works such as those by Ascione and Arkow (1999) and Linzey (2009). The American Veterinary Medical Association has an available list of reporting requirements by state (AVMA, 2018). Shelter veterinarians frequently encounter victims of animal cruelty and should be familiar with the legal obligations regarding reporting, not only for the welfare of the animal involved but also for potential human victims. Communication between shelter personnel,

Table 19.1 The Five Freedoms provide guidance for the basics of acceptable animal care

Five Freedoms	
1.	Freedom from hunger and thirst
2.	Freedom from discomfort
3.	Freedom from pain, injury, or disease
4.	Freedom to express normal behavior
5.	Freedom from fear and distress

the police department, child and adult protective services, and domestic violence services should be established and utilized whenever necessary.

RECOGNITION OF ANIMAL CRUELTY

Many animals entering the shelter system show physical evidence of neglect. Some of the obvious physical symptoms frequently observed include:

- Low body weight
- Poor body condition
- Starvation
- Unkempt hair coat
- Matting of hair coat
- Overgrown toenails
- Parasites including fleas, ticks, heartworms, ear mites, intestinal parasites
- Scars
- Untreated wounds or fractures
- Untreated medical conditions such as KCS, otitis, periodontal disease, and dermatitis
- Fecal/urine scald
- Dehydration
- Ravenous appetite and excessive thirst upon intake
- Exhaustion
- Embedded collar; ligature wounds from tether/restraint
- Hypothermia
- Hyperthermia
- Anemia

In addition, nonaccidental injuries may be seen including:

- Gunshot wounds
- Stab wounds
- Burns
- Ligature wounds (e.g., rubber bands on testicles, tails, extremities)
- Strangulation
- Evidence of nonprofessional surgery (e.g., ear/tail cropping, dubbing of fighting birds)
- Scars and wounds consistent with organized dogfighting

A large percentage of shelter animals are strays and must be placed on a stray hold for a period of time, allowing the owner time to reclaim their pet. It is common for stray pets to show evidence of abuse, particularly in the form of neglect. Since seeking the owner of every stray pet requires manpower that is beyond the capabilities of most shelters, a process should be established in the event that the responsible owner attempts to reclaim an abused pet. Although the rate of reclaimed pets is typically low and forensic examinations require time that is scarce in most shelters, protecting stray animals from returning to an abusive home is a fundamental duty of an animal shelter. Basic exam findings and concerns should be documented in the medical record, recommending the issuance of a citation should the pet owner attempt to reclaim the pet. Thorough documentation is especially worthwhile when a microchip or other identifier is found on a stray pet with evidence of abuse, since this type of identification increases the likelihood of locating the responsible party.

If an owner appears to reclaim, a citation is issued with requirements for improved care, and a follow-up visit is scheduled to monitor compliance. At times the pet's condition is severe enough to justify refusal if the owner attempts to reclaim. The veterinarian and investigator in charge usually make this decision collectively. Under these circumstances it is not uncommon for the owner to surrender the pet to the shelter. This is ideal, as it allows the shelter to find suitable placement without waiting for the stray hold to expire. Surrendering an abused pet does not mean the owner will not be held accountable. Pursuance of legal action, including a citation and further investigation such as inspection of the home to determine if other victims are involved, is sometimes warranted and is usually based on information gained during the consultation with the owner. This information could include veterinary records, financial restrictions that prevent appropriate care, and reveal true ignorance and remorse for a pet's condition. Sometimes the information provided by the owner will alleviate fears of abuse and the reclaim is allowed.

COLLECTION OF EVIDENCE

In order to ensure that cases are managed appropriately, it is imperative to have standard operating procedures readily available any time evidence of animal cruelty is encountered.

The case file for every animal should include the following:

- Document describing scene findings (Figure 19.1)
- Photographs of scene (when applicable)
- Photograph log of scene photos
- Animal control officer/intake personnel report
- Forensic photographs of animal
- Photograph log of animal photos
- Forensic examination
- Follow-up examinations
- Evidence log and chain of custody form
- Veterinary forensic report

When an animal is part of a cruelty investigation, the animal, environmental findings from where the animal was seized, and items removed from the animal are all considered evidence. Collecting evidence of abuse involves many steps, including investigation of the animal's environment and physical examination through both photographic and written documentation. Environmental findings frequently reveal as much or more compelling evidence of cruelty than the physical exam findings. It is imperative that photographs and written documentation of the environment in which an animal was found is gathered at the time of seizure. This should include photographs and a description of available shelter, water, and food. Photographs should show both an overview and close-up views of the animal's surroundings, both before and after the animal has been removed. The series of photos should begin with a dry erase board with the date, location, case number, and photographer (Figure 19.2). This starting photograph should be followed by overall photographs of the scene (Figure 19.3), mid-range photographs showing the item of evidence in question (Figure 19.4), a close-up, full-frame photograph showing the detail of the item of evidence (Figure 19.5), and finally a close-up photograph showing the area once the item of evidence has been removed (Figure 19.6).

In addition to scene photographs, a standardized form should be created for the shelter personnel to use on scene. This form should allow room for a description of available water and food (e.g., none, clean, dirty, frozen, etc.) as well as available shelter and bedding (e.g., doghouse with straw, no shelter, muddy ground, etc.) and include additional information as indicated (see Figure 19.1).

Every shelter should have a forensic kit that holds all the items necessary to conduct an investigation. In order to reduce loss of items, this kit should be kept secure in a designated location

CRUELTY INVESTIGATIONS SCENE FINDINGS

Date	
Officer Name	
Activity Number	
Address	

Animal ID	
Description	

Environmental Conditions

Water: ☐ None ☐ Clean ☐ Dirty ☐ Frozen ☐ Accessible Description:	Food: ☐ None ☐ Edible ☐ Dirty ☐ Soggy ☐ Frozen ☐ Accessible Description:
Shelter: ☐ None ☐ Type ____________________ ☐ Clean ☐ Dry ☐ Dirty ☐ Wet ☐ Adequate ☐ Accessible Description:	

Additional Findings:

Figure 19.1 Example form to document environmental findings.

and only used by authorized personnel. For shelters with numerous animal control officers it is ideal to assign a kit for each animal control vehicle to use in the field.

The forensic kit should include the following:

- Good-quality SLR camera
- Backup camera batteries
- Small dry erase board
- Dry erase markers
- Forensic scales
- Extra data storage cards
- Crime scene findings document
- Physical exam form

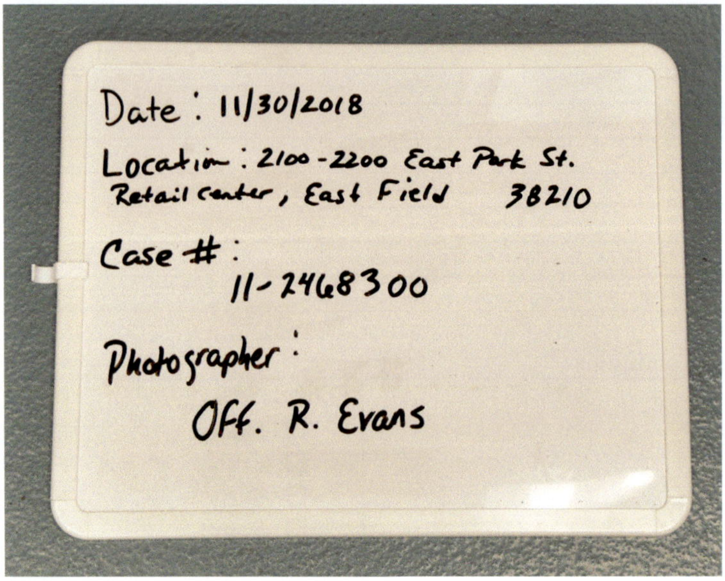

Figure 19.2 Dry erase board with case information.

Figure 19.3 Overview of scene where dog was found abandoned in a plastic bin.

- Ink pens
- Photo log
- Evidence log
- Evidence markers
- Evidence bags
- Evidence tape

Photographs are critical for documenting evidence of abuse. Since evidence changes quickly once appropriate care and medical treatment is provided, obtaining photographs as soon as possible is important not only to preserve the initial findings but also to reduce any delay in providing medical care.

Figure 19.4 Midway view of same scene.

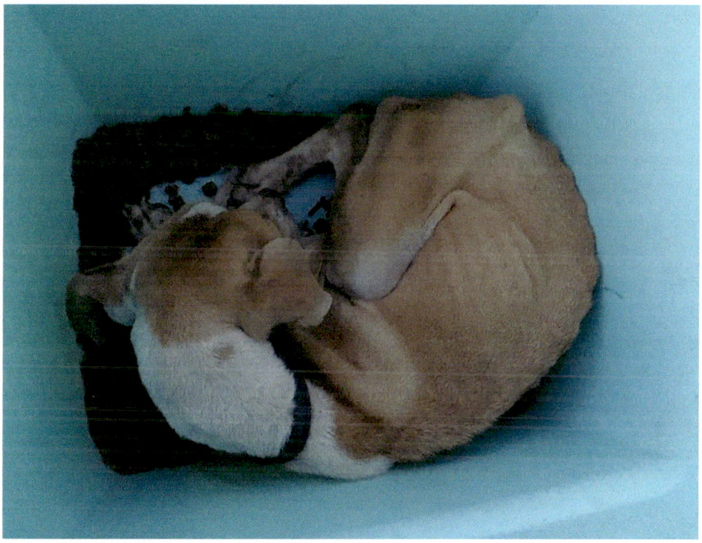

Figure 19.5 Close-up of dog in bin.

There should be a minimum of eight photographs obtained for each animal. These include:

1. Dry erase board only with date, case number, animal ID, location, and photographer's name (Figure 19.7)
2. Dry erase board with cranial view of pet (Figure 19.8)
3. Cranial view of pet without dry erase board (Figure 19.9)
4. Left lateral view (Figure 19.10)
5. Caudal view (Figure 19.11)
6. Right lateral view (Figure 19.12)
7. Dorsal view (Figure 19.13)
8. Ventral view (Figure 19.14)

Figure 19.6 Close-up of bin after dog is removed, revealing dog food.

Figure 19.7 Dry erase board only with date, case number, animal ID, location, and photographer's name.

Additional photos should be obtained to capture any abnormalities. A representative photograph should accompany all abnormalities listed in the physical examination. Photographs of physical exam findings should always be taken both with and without a measurement scale (Figure 19.15a, b). Photos should be of high quality and the background should be clear of any debris or irrelevant

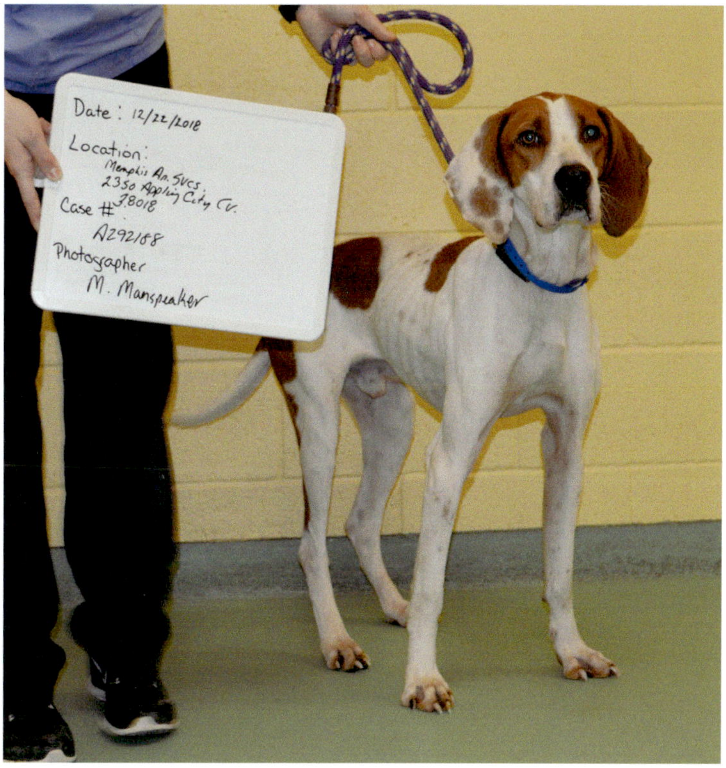

Figure 19.8 Dry erase board with cranial view of pet.

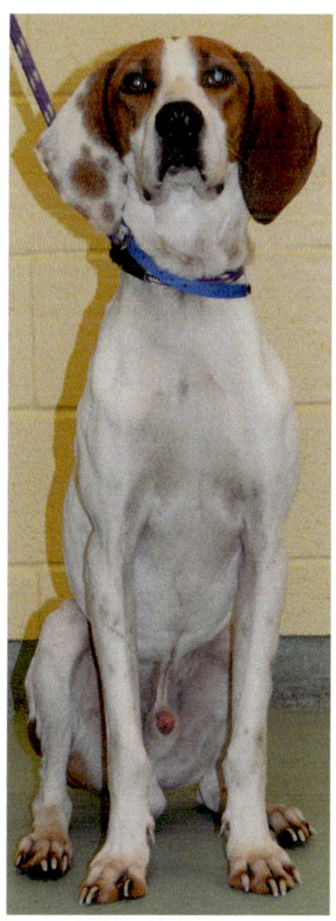

Figure 19.9 Cranial view of pet without dry erase board.

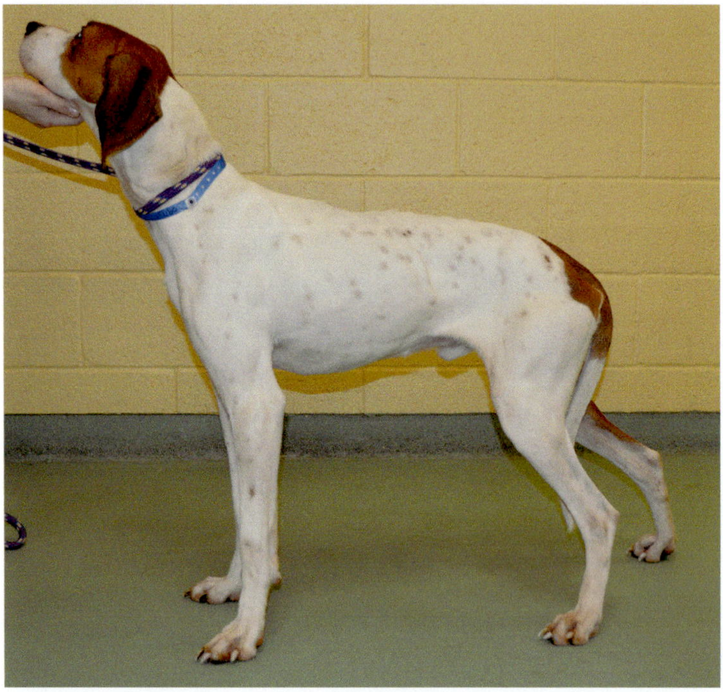

Figure 19.10 Left lateral view.

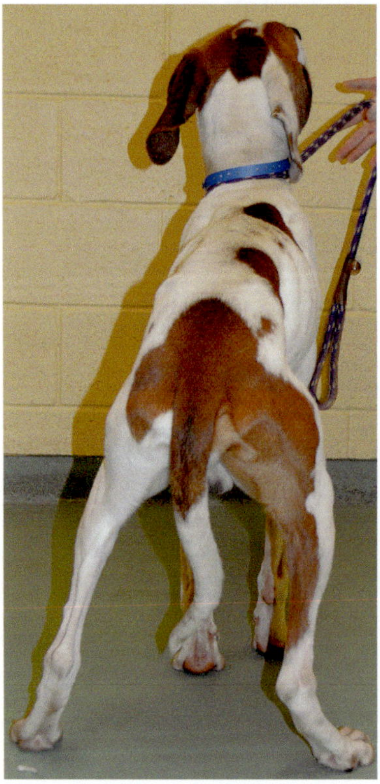

Figure 19.11 Caudal view.

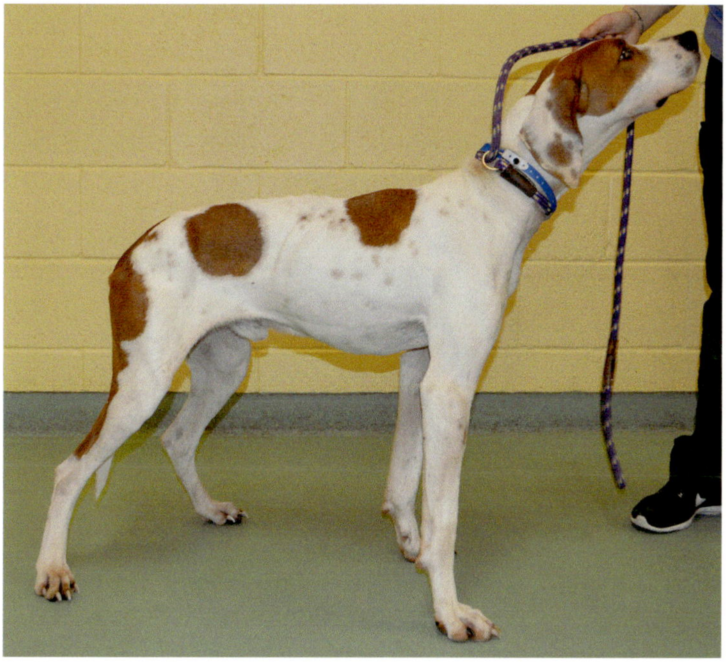

Figure 19.12 Right lateral view.

Figure 19.13 Dorsal view.

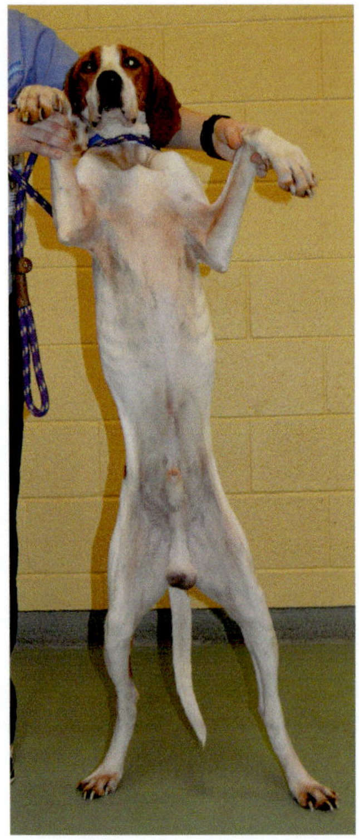

Figure 19.14 Ventral view.

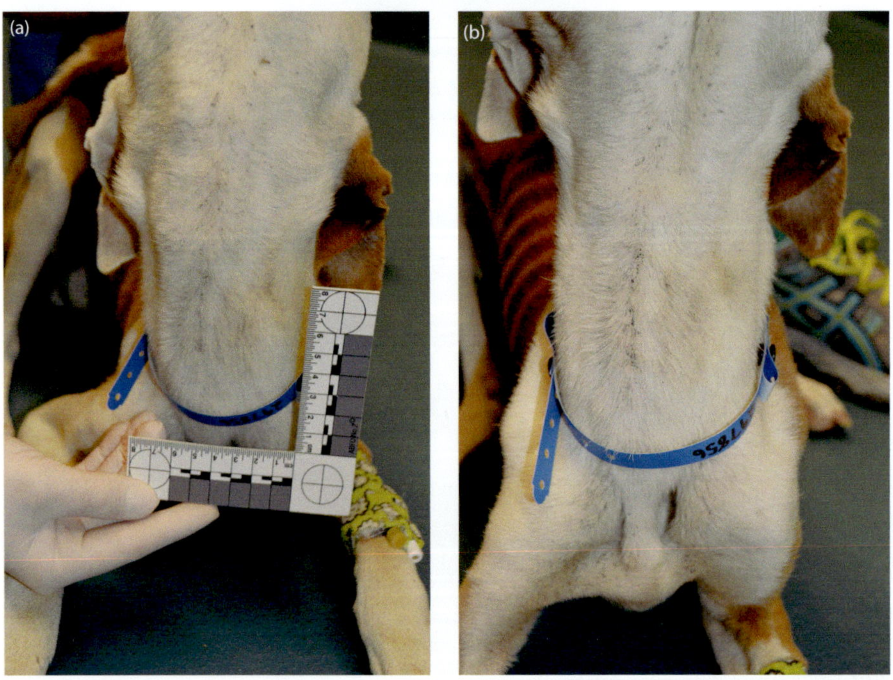

Figure 19.15 (a,b) Ventral cervical view of a dog both with and without a forensic scale depicting evidence of a flea infestation. All close-up (macro) photographs should be made to show the area of interest with and without measurement scales. The ABFO number 2 scale is common and preferred for three-dimensional surfaces.

FORENSIC EXAMINATION PAGE 3/3

Date		Animal ID	
Case #		Location	
Veterinarian		Assistant	

Photograph Log

Date Taken	Taken By	Location	Description	Digital Image #	Data Storage Card #

Notes:

Figure 19.16 Example log for forensic examination photographs.

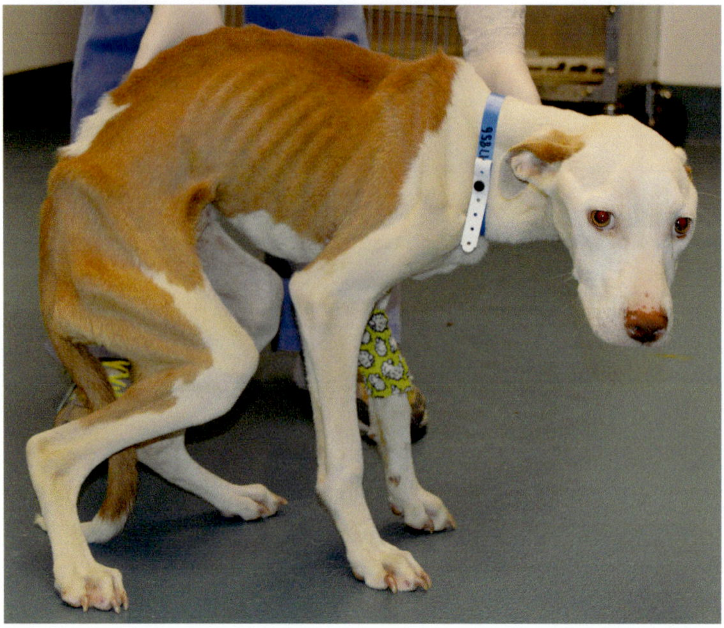

Figure 19.17 Right lateral body of starvation victim. A clear outline of the markings on the hair coat is shown as well as the low body condition score [1/9 on the Purina scale (Laflamme, 1997)]. Body weight at the time of intake was 18.80 pounds.

items. Avoid capturing any identifying features of the personnel holding the pet. Photos should never be deleted. Photos may be cropped for the purposes of the forensic report if the original photo remains intact and unaltered.

In addition to photographs, video footage may be obtained in order to document evidence that might be lost with photographs alone, such as appetite, thirst, mobility, and behavior.

A photograph log should be kept for each pet that lists the date, case number, animal ID, photographer, location, description of each photo, and digital image number (e.g., JPEG number). The photographs should be kept on the original data storage disk but also backed up to a hard drive in digital file folders for preservation and easy retrieval (Figure 19.16).

Follow-up photographs and physical examination of medical progress are sometimes indicated, especially when they will capture significant changes. One of the benefits of photographs at the time of intake is that as the animal's physical state changes, the photographs should provide details that show it is the same animal in the pre- and post-treatment photos. Figures 19.17 and 19.18 show an example of this in a starvation case. Although the animal appears significantly different in the before- (Figure 19.17) and after- (Figure 19.18) treatment photos, the markings on the hair coat are clearly identical.

FORENSIC EXAMINATION

Prior to performing the forensic examination, the veterinarian should be briefed on the case by the officer in charge. For the examining veterinarian to fully understand the legal implications and accurately interpret physical examination findings, the briefing should include access to the initial report and photographs.

The forensic examination must be conducted as soon as possible to document the initial physical condition of the victim and expedite the medical treatment. For example, evidence of severe flea

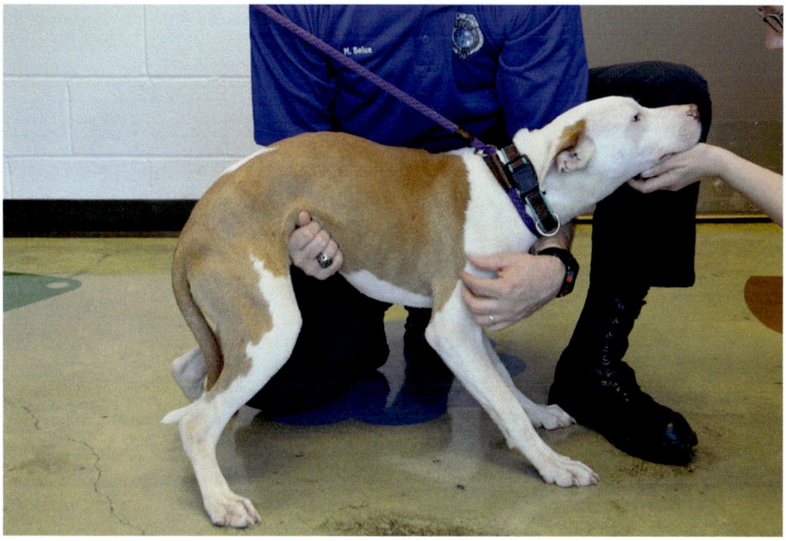

Figure 19.18 This photo, taken 1 month after Figure 19.17, shows the same view, and with a normal body condition score [4/9 on the Purina scale (Laflamme, 1997)]. The body weight was 37.40 pounds.

infestation should be documented and photographed prior to flea treatment. If critical medical care is needed and photographic documentation must be postponed until the patient has been stabilized, the forensic report should include an explanation for any missing items.

Except for photographs, forensic examinations are no different from any other physical examination. Veterinarians are trained to produce a thorough medical exam for every patient, documenting all findings, both normal and abnormal. The enormous workload of most shelter veterinarians often necessitates brief physical examinations and documentation of only the abnormal findings. This is unacceptable for a forensic examination, for this could suggest an incomplete or biased assessment. In addition, the physical exam findings will be used to help the court make important decisions regarding the fate of both the abused animal and alleged abuser.

Having a forensic examination form is a good way to ensure that physical findings are thoroughly documented. If the shelter has an electronic medical record system, then the information may be recorded directly into the system. If the data entry will be performed by someone other than the examining veterinarian, it is recommended that the veterinarian proofread the medical notes to correct misspelled words and inappropriate entries before they are finalized. If examination findings will be written and later entered into an electronic record, a paper exam form should be created that mimics the electronic medical form. This will help to reduce discrepancies and errors in the record and will streamline the data entry process. If possible, all paper documents should be scanned and attached to the electronic medical record. Writing must be legible. All documents will be considered part of the legal case and may be reviewed in the discovery process, so in order to reduce inconsistencies it is ideal to keep the duplication of information to a minimum. To reduce the number of physical pages and loss of documents, pages should be numbered and have the same identifying information at the top of each page (Figures 19.19 and 19.20). To avoid writing redundant information, double-sided pages can be used.

Physical examination should list signalment including species, breed, age, gender with spay/neuter status, weight, colors (primary, secondary, tertiary, special markings), and long or shorthaired if not obvious by the breed listed. All pets should be scanned for a microchip, document whether one was found, and list the microchip number when applicable. Subjective findings that describe the animal's overall attitude should be listed (e.g., bright, alert, responsive, etc.) Objective findings include all physical exam findings. Vital signs including body temperature (list route, i.e., rectal,

FORENSIC EXAMINATION PAGE 1/4

Date		Animal ID	
Case #		Location	
Veterinarian		Assistant	

Signalment

Species		Breed	
Sex		Primary Color	
Secondary Color		Special Markings	
Microchip type#		Weight	

Physical Examination

Subjective/Behavior (description)

Objective

Temperature		Pulse/HR	
Respiratory Rate		MM/CRT	

Body System	NE	NSF	Description of abnormalities
Eyes			
Ears			
Oral			
Heart			
Lungs			
Abdomen			
Urogenital			
GI			
Neuro			
MS			
Dermatological			
Lymph Nodes			
BCS (1-9 Purina)			
Pain			

(NSF= No significant findings; NE= not examined)

Notes:

Figure 19.19 Example page 1 of a forensic examination form. This form should include a heading containing the same information as the other pages of the physical exam and include signalment and all physical examination findings. This form follows the subjective, objective, assessment, and plan (SOAP) format commonly taught to veterinarians.

FORENSIC EXAMINATION PAGE 2/4

Date		Animal ID	
Case #		Location	
Veterinarian		Assistant	

Assessment/Differential Diagnosis

Plan

Diagnostics

Test Name	Sample Type	Results	Comments
Heartworm (Include type)	Whole blood	Negative	
Intestinal parasite screen	Feces	Pending	

Preventative Care/Treatments

Type	Amount	Route/Location
Rabies vaccine	1cc	SQ/RR
Pyrantel pamoate	4cc	PO

Recommendations/Additional Medical Notes

Figure 19.20 Example page 2 of a forensic examination form. This form should include a heading containing the same information as the other pages of the physical exam form. This page is a continuation of the SOAP format from page 1, and also includes information regarding initial diagnostics, treatments, and recommendations.

otic, etc.), heart and pulse rate, respiratory rate, mucous membrane color, and capillary refill time should be obtained. Body condition score (BCS) should be determined by both visual appearance and palpation (Laflamme, 1997). If palpation is not possible then it should be documented that the BCS is an estimate only. The BCS system used should be referenced and should be predetermined and consistent for all animals involved. All body systems should be evaluated including the eyes, ears, nose, throat, oral cavity, skin, hair, heart, lungs, musculoskeletal, neurological, peripheral lymph nodes, and urogenital. Oral examination should describe all abnormalities and include a dental chart when indicated. If there are testicles present, they should be described. Estrus or possible pregnancy should be noted. Evidence of previous surgery and any tattoos should be described. All lesions including scars, fresh wounds, and tumors should be described and drawn on an anatomical chart. This is particularly important in cases of suspected animal fighting. Any pain detected or suspected should be listed with an explanation and given a score using a referenced pain scale. Following the physical examination is the overall assessment, where findings are concluded and a differential diagnosis is listed. Finally, a plan is documented. This plan should include recommended testing, treatments, and rechecks.

When indicated, a definitive diagnosis should be avoided without supporting documentation. For example, "yeast otitis" should not be a definitive diagnosis without an ear cytology result consistent with yeast overgrowth and supporting clinical signs. If obtaining an ear cytology is not possible, then "yeast otitis" should be listed as a differential diagnosis in the assessment, with the supportive findings such as odor, erythema, stenosis, and so on, placed in the objective findings, and ear cytology should be in the plan section as a recommended diagnostic. If cytology will not be possible, treatment can be initiated based on a presumptive diagnosis based on clinical signs, but this should be explained in the plan section. A similar situation is pain assessment. If you suspect a pet is in pain, for example from dental disease, but there are no overt symptoms to support this suspicion such as a thin body condition, flinching upon oral exam, food avoidance, and so on, then a definite declaration of pain should be used cautiously. In such instances an appropriate description would be "suspect pain due to periodontal disease" with recommendations for pain management, antimicrobials as indicated, and dental care as soon as possible.

It is not uncommon for animal victims to be fearful or aggressive, sometimes to the degree that precludes hands-on examination without sedation. Since sedation can alter vital signs and appearance in photographs, the reason for the sedation and possible effects should be included in the medical record. If an examination is not performed, then the reason should be listed with the best physical description possible.

DIAGNOSTICS

Diagnostic testing is often indicated in order to help assess the animal's overall health. Financial restrictions often prevent animal shelters from performing diagnostic testing, but diagnostic recommendations should be documented even if the tests will not be performed at the shelter.

As indicated based on the physical examination, recommended diagnostics include:

- Heartworm test
- FELV/FIV test
- Intestinal parasite screen
- Tick panel
- Ear cytology
- Skin scrape
- Skin cytology
- Skin culture
- Wood's lamp

- Radiographs
- PCV/TP
- Complete blood count
- Blood chemistry
- Urinalysis
- Urine culture
- Electrolyte panel
- Histopathology

Sometimes referral is necessary, such as when the medical needs exceed the capabilities of the shelter, or if a victim is seized when a shelter is closed. It is important that the receiving veterinarian is made aware of the legal situation and prompted to thoroughly document all findings and treatments. If properly equipped shelter personnel will not be able to accompany the animal to a referral facility, photographs should be requested with necessary instructions. It should also be requested that case details be kept confidential.

TREATMENT AND PREVENTATIVE CARE

When a cruelty victim is seized and enters the shelter system, the pet is not automatically the property of the shelter. At times the owner of the pet has not been located, or the owner is disputing the allegations and will attempt to reclaim possession of the animal. During the time that the shelter is acting as the custodian, it is the shelter's responsibility to provide appropriate care. Daily assessments of the animal's health should be documented. At times, treatments or preventative measures may be contraindicated. For example, if a pregnant dog is seized from a commercial breeder and taken to the shelter, the shelter veterinarian will have to decide whether a vaccination against common shelter pathogens or other needed medical treatment outweighs the risk to the unborn puppies. In this situation, documentation of the reasoning behind the treatment choice is recommended.

EVIDENCE PRESERVATION

Just as the animal is considered evidence, all biological samples and items removed from the animal are also considered evidence. It is important that every item of evidence is logged and accounted for until it is released by the court. An evidence log, evidence bags, tape, and chain of custody forms should be used in order to appropriately process evidence. A designated evidence area should be available and should be used to securely store all items until they are approved for disposal. When samples are collected from an animal, such as blood, feces, urine, ear swabs, collar, hair, etc., these items should be listed on an evidence log and given an evidence number. For example, the evidence number may be the animal's ID followed by a subsequent letter for each item of evidence. (Figure 19.21) There should be a date for the collection, a description of the item, and the disposition of the item. If the sample is sent to an outside laboratory for processing, then a chain of custody form should accompany the sample. The outside lab should be informed that evidence will be sent, and documentation of receipt should be requested and saved as part of the case file.

At times the animals are under a court order to remain in the custody of the shelter. This usually occurs when the owner is disputing the charges. This can be a difficult situation for the shelter and the animals involved. Shelters are frequently at full capacity, so pets on a court-ordered hold are occupying space that is needed for other animals. This can cause otherwise healthy, adoptable animals to be euthanized. In addition, since shelter animals are stressed and exposed to infectious

FORENSIC EXAMINATION PAGE 4/4

Date		Animal ID	
Case #	A210120	Location	
Veterinarian		Assistant	

Evidence Log (Additional biological samples and physical items)

Evidence #	Date Taken	Location Collected	Description	Location Test Run	Disposition
A210120A	4/4/2017	On scene	Metal chain and ground spike, weight 15 pounds, 6 feet x 2 inches	N/A	Evidence storage
A210120B	4/4/2017	Shelter	Collar, metal chain with bolt snap, 1 pound, 12 inches x 1 inch	N/A	Evidence storage
A210120C	4/4/2017	Shelter	Blood	In house lab	Discarded in house
A210120D	4/4/2017	Shelter	Feces	Offsite lab (list name of lab)	Offsite lab

Figure 19.21 Example of an evidence log. This form should include a heading containing the same information as the other pages of the physical exam. This page is the evidence log, where any biological sample or item collected from the animal is logged. This information should contain the date and location the evidence was collected, description of the evidence, where the evidence was sent for testing, and disposition of the evidence.

disease, prolonged shelter stays can have serious detrimental consequences on the health of an animal. It is for this reason that animals on a court hold should have a record of daily observations, preventative care, and appropriate treatment for illness. Needless to say, a shelter that attempts to hold a perpetrator accountable for animal cruelty and then neglects the needs of the victim in its care is exercising inappropriate and possibly criminal behavior. In addition, in order to help reduce deleterious effects of a shelter stay, it is imperative that a plea be made to the court to place the pet in a suitable foster home until an outcome decision has been made. At times a compelling argument can be made and will be approved by the judge.

If an animal shelter becomes overwhelmed by a large cruelty case, aid from a larger animal rescue organization can sometimes be obtained. This can include additional funding, staff, and even relocation of the animals involved to a temporary holding facility. This is a resource that should be sought in order to reduce the impact on the normal sheltering operation that includes euthanasia of healthy animals due to lack of space.

POSTMORTEM EXAMINATION

It is not uncommon for animal investigators and control officers to find the remains of deceased animals when responding to reports of animal abuse. Shelter personnel should be trained on appropriate handling of remains in order to maintain integrity of the evidence. Photographs of the remains as they are found should be taken prior to any movement. The remains must be carefully packaged in order to reduce loss of evidence, and then transported to the shelter. This process, including the shelter personnel responsible for transporting and shipping remains, should be predetermined.

The veterinarian who performs a forensic postmortem examination needs to be very comfortable with the process and have a firm understanding of both normal and abnormal postmortem findings. In addition, forensic postmortem examinations, when performed correctly, are extremely time consuming, so the veterinarian needs to be able to dedicate a large amount of time to this task. If the shelter veterinarian does not have the required time or knowledge, the remains should be transferred to a veterinary pathologist who routinely performs postmortem examinations for legal cases.

Appropriate preservation of animal remains is critical to accurately determine the cause of death. Since freezing and thawing creates artifacts, determination of whether to refrigerate or freeze the remains will depend in part on how quickly the postmortem examination will be performed. If remains will be sent to an outside lab for processing, shipment date and time will be a determining factor. Instructions should be obtained from the receiving lab regarding the best time to ship as well as storage of the remains before and during shipment.

VETERINARY FORENSIC REPORT

Once evidence has been collected, the information must be clearly presented in a veterinary forensic report. This report should be concise, factual, nonbiased, and easily understood by members of the court. This document, in addition to being one of the most important factors in determining the fate of those involved in the legal case, also reflects the competency of the authoring veterinarian. It should be free of typos and should accurately reflect physical exam findings and diagnostic test results, include a differential diagnosis, and explain the significance of all listed abnormalities. The report should begin with an overview of the case, including all personnel and animals involved and a description of the scene. In order to clearly demonstrate findings, photographs should be included with a description and the digital image numbers. In addition, pathology reports, normal values, relevant laws, and other reference materials, such as BCS charts, should be included. The report should include a statement indicating honesty and accuracy of the contents, signed by the authoring veterinarian.

CONCLUSION

Animal shelters, being among the leading institutions to encounter evidence of cruelty, have a responsibility to educate their personnel on the recognition, legal rights, and protection of victims. Through the development and execution of a thorough investigation process, shelter personnel exhibit intent toward upholding animal welfare laws. It is only through this type of dedication that the laws protecting animals and associated human victims will continue to evolve and strengthen.

References

American Veterinary Medical Association (AVMA). 2018. Abuse Reporting Requirements by State. Retrieved on July 22, 2018 from https://www.avma.org/KB/Resources/Reference/AnimalWelfare/Pages/Abuse-Reporting-requirements-by-State.aspx

Animal Legal Defense Fund (ADLF). 2017. Animal Protection Laws of the United States of America. Retrieved on July 22, 2018 from https://aldf.org/article/animal-protection-laws-of-the-united-states-of-america/

Ascione, F., Arkow, P. 1999. *Child Abuse, Domestic Violence, and Animal Abuse: Linking the Circles of Compassion for Prevention and Intervention*. West Lafayette, IN: Purdue University Press.

Farm Animal Welfare Council (FAWC). April 16, 2009. Five Freedoms. Retrieved on July 22, 2018 from http://webarchive.nationalarchives.gov.uk/20121010012427/http://www.fawc.org.uk/freedoms.htm

Laflamme, D. 1997. Nutritional Management. *Vet. Clin. North Am. Small Anim. Pract.* 27(6): 1561–1577.

Linzey, A. 2009. *Link between Animal Abuse and Human Violence*. Portland, OR: Sussex Academic Press.

CHAPTER 20

ANIMAL LAW

Michelle Welch

The practice of animal law has grown in the last 20 years from near nonexistence to a thriving field.[1] Both the American Association of Law Schools and the American Bar Association have animal law sections today, and more than 160 U.S. law schools offer courses in animal law.[2] Part of the newfound societal interest in animal welfare is the developing evidence of a strong correlation between violence against animals and violence against people.[3] Even those who are indifferent to animals have cause to be concerned about the presence of animal abusers in our society. Animal abusers are often involved in domestic violence, child abuse, sexual abuse, elder abuse, assault, mass shootings, and murder. Some types of animal abuse are also associated with other criminal activities that society has an interest in eliminating.[4]

Most codified animal law is criminal, whether in the areas of protection from abuse, agricultural and hunting regulation, wildlife preservation and conservation, or public health and safety. Because animals are considered to be personal property in every state, standard civil laws typically govern, and specialized civil laws are largely unnecessary.[5] There are contract disputes, ownership disputes, and personal injury, family law, veterinary malpractice cases, to name a few.[6] Some companion animals can be very expensive, which likely contributes to the number of civil cases that are brought. Many people consider their pets to be family members, giving them great emotional value. Over 144 million households have companion animals in the United States, making it a $393 million dollar industry.[7] This chapter will describe the laws that protect companion animals and the link between animal crimes and crimes against humans.

CIVIL LEGAL ISSUES

As personal property, animals have no rights. We have developed protections as we have for children. Because animals are personal property, money that can be recovered as damages in a civil suit is limited to the value of the animal. Although there are exceptions, the average companion animal is of relatively minimal monetary value. In many states, one cannot recover for emotional distress in the absence of harm to a person, which leaves little recourse when a person's pet is stolen, injured, or killed. There are also laws governing dangerous and vicious dogs, which fall into the civil arena. Veterinary malpractice cases are more likely to involve high-dollar animals like horses than common house pets. Animal ownership is often disputed, especially in divorce cases. Some states have codified the ability to create a trust for the care of an animal after the death of the owner. Contract disputes might arise in breeding and adoption situations, or between landlords and tenants. These are just a few examples of civil legal animal issues that arise. This chapter will focus largely on criminal laws regarding companion animals, as those are the most likely to be encountered by veterinarians.

CRIMINAL LEGAL ISSUES

Across the nation, animal protection laws are strengthening and being enforced more strictly each year. In the near future, reliable statistics regarding the frequency with which crimes are perpetrated against animals will be available, and will no doubt show how prevalent neglect and abuse have become. In 2017, the Federal Bureau of Investigation (FBI) added animal abuse to its crime reporting system, the National Incident Based Reporting System.[8] It categorized animal cruelty into four types: simple/gross neglect, intentional abuse/torture, organized abuse (animal fighting), and animal sexual abuse. Every state has enacted some type of prohibition against the crimes in each of the FBI's categories. Laws regarding animal welfare vary from state to state, and locality to locality. Typically, state laws categorize and differentiate these crimes based on severity. A state will often codify neglect laws, which punish the failure to provide care, and cruelty laws, which largely punish intentional acts. Some states have laws prohibiting specific acts, such as animal fighting. Some states specify the penalties and sentences associated with a violation of each. The sections below discuss the general types of criminal laws, based on Virginia law, where the author practices, and provide a fundamental overview of laws that are common across the country, with several laws from individual states outlined in the Endnotes.

Animal Neglect

Animal neglect laws are sometimes referred to as "adequate care"[9] laws, and by either name, they carry the lowest penalties.[10] Neglect can be either simple or gross.[11] Simple neglect is a lesser crime and carries less severe penalties. Depending on the facts, gross neglect can rise to the level of cruelty. Almost every state has laws prohibiting neglect that provide protections only for *companion animals*, or domestic pets.[12] Dogs and cats are always protected, and in some states other small mammals, birds, and reptiles, including exotic species, are also protected.[13] Definitions of companion animals typically exclude all agricultural animals and research animals.

Neglect laws usually prescribe the minimum conditions the animal owner must provide in the way of care. Therefore, neglect can be most easily proven based on an owner's *failure to provide* a required item—typically food or water, though neglect can be based on inadequate living conditions and other factors discussed below.[14] The standards are often similar to what guardians are required to provide children—the fundamental provisions needed to survive in a healthy condition. Simple neglect, or the failure to provide adequate care, is usually punished by fine only, while the penalty for gross neglect can include jail time. However, in some states, multiple offenses of simple negligence may result in minimal jail time. Also, some laws allow the court to ban abusers from owning or harboring animals in the future.

Neglect laws usually specify what an owner has to provide for the animal and include definitions of those requirements. For instance, adequate food is generally considered to be that which is of sufficient quantity and nutritional value to maintain the animal in good health.[15] Many states take into account the animal's age, species, condition, and size in establishing the requirements.[16] For instance, feeding hard kibble to a senior dog with deteriorated teeth may not be adequate. Food must also be provided in a clean and sanitary manner, meaning free of dirt, pests, excrement, and the like. Finally, most states require food to be given at least once per day.[17]

In one Virginia case, a dog starved to death because its food was on top of a cage where the dog could not reach it.[18] The owner went out of town for weeks and had no one check on the dog. In a notable case from Richmond, Virginia, a dog starved because it was only fed table scraps. In another case, a dog was starved because only moldy bread was available for food. The dog measured a three on the body condition score (BCS) scale used by veterinarians of one through nine, which showed that the dog was not eating the bread.[19]

Like adequate food, adequate water is usually defined in the code. Adequate water is typically defined as water that is present, accessible, and potable. Potable water is considered to be that fit for human consumption.[20] Water must be provided in sufficient volume at suitable intervals appropriate for the weather and temperature. For instance, in the winter the water cannot be in the form of ice or snow. The water must be available in liquid form. Adequate water must maintain normal hydration for the age, species, condition, size, and type of animal. It must be provided in clean, durable receptacles that are placed so as to minimize contamination of the water by excrement and pests. The specific conditions should be considered when assessing an animal's water. For example, an animal that is chained outside all the time needs more water than one living in an air-conditioned home.

Many neglect laws also include requirements around appropriate space and shelter.[21] In fact, many states combine adequate space and shelter definitions into one requirement or definition. In part, because companion animals are often kept outside, clear definitions of adequate space and shelter are imperative to ensuring the provision of adequate care.[22] Adequate space can be defined as an area sufficient to allow the animal to comfortably stand, sit, lie, turn around, and make all other normal body movements.[23] The space must also be safe and protect the animal from injury, inclement weather, direct sunlight, physical suffering, and any impairment of health.[24] The code may also contain requirements with respect to appropriate lighting.[25] Under many adequate shelter definitions, shelters with grid, wire, or slat floors (i) permit the animals' feet to pass through the openings, (ii) sag under the animals' weight, or (iii) otherwise do not protect the animals' feet or toes from injury are not allowed.[26] The shelter may not be ramshackle or decrepit, and must be properly cleaned, and allow the animal to remain clean and dry. In addition, adequate space means that the animal is able to interact safely with other animals present in the enclosure. In hoarding cases, for example, animals maintained in overly cramped quarters will fight each other for resources.

In a very recent case, animal control seized seven pigs and twenty hunting dogs which were living in a literal soup of feces and mud. The conditions were some of the worst that seasoned officers had seen. In another instance, Chihuahuas were left out on an extremely cold night with a large doghouse that did not provide insulation or allow them to benefit from body heat. Ultimately, the dogs were seized because the owner refused to relocate them to appropriate shelter. In one case, a black Labrador Retriever puppy was left outside on a particularly hot day. The puppy had an igloo doghouse which was located in full sun, and not protecting the dog from the heat. Rather than seizing the animal, local animal control officers helped the owner erect a tarp above the house to bring the temperature down. Animal control officers educated the owner about adequate care laws, and the requirements related specifically to adequate shelter, and explained that the law prohibits leaving the dog outside when the weather is not appropriate.

What is considered to be adequate shelter varies depending on the animal. For example, a black dog with a thick coat will become overheated more quickly than many other breeds. In another case, a puppy was kept in a metal crate inside a thin child size tent with no insulation or bedding when the temperature was in the teens. Luckily, a rescue group was able to convince the owners to let them take the puppy to safety. Animal control should, and often does, take proactive steps to ensure proper shelter and protection from the elements. Recently, in advance of a deep freeze, officers educated owners of outdoor animals about adequate shelter laws in advance of a deep freeze and assisted in moving the animals to safety. If, after being made aware of the requirements, an owner is reluctant or obstinate, the law requires action on the part of the officer.

In many jurisdictions, especially in rural areas, dogs may be lawfully chained outside, and there are no restrictions with respect to location, length, or composition of the tether. A person can lawfully keep a dog outside at all times, dragging a short, heavy chain, and the dog can become entangled with surrounding objects. Tethering requirements, when present, are often codified at the city or county level. In the absence of a tethering ordinance, animal control officers and prosecutors can often rely on the adequate space requirement to pursue an inhumane tethering situation. In addition, some laws require the tether to be applied to a collar, halter, or harness to ensure safety. In Lunenburg, Virginia, a man had chained his dog without any collar or harness, and the dog choked himself nearly to death by pulling on the tether. Because tethers and chains can injure an animal, most definitions require the owner to ensure that the tether does not become entangled with objects or other animals or extend over an object or edge that could lead to strangulation. In addition, the tether must, in some states, be configured so as to protect the animal from injury. Tethering can also lead to boredom in an animal, which may lead it to injure itself in the absence of requirements like these. Some definitions also regulate the length of the tether, which is frequently specified in relation to the length of the animal as measured from the tip of its nose to the base of its tail. Some laws limit the amount of time the animal can be tethered. Across the country, there is a growing trend among localities to enact ordinances that are more restrictive than state law.[27] Many of the ordinances require a time limit for the dog to be on a tether/chain. For instance, in the City of Richmond, Virginia, you can only chain a dog for 1 hour in a 24-hour period.[28]

Adequate veterinary care is also a requirement under some state laws, and the failure to provide it is frequently a violation of both animal neglect and animal cruelty laws.[29] To be prosecuted, the owner must fail to provide veterinary care when needed to prevent suffering or disease transmission. To defend against such a charge on this basis, the owner must be able to provide documentation that the animal received appropriate medical care. Owners often claim financial hardship as rationale for failure to provide veterinary care, which is not a defense under the law.

State laws may also require an owner to provide adequate exercise.[30] Whether or not an animal is receiving adequate exercise is not determined by the weight of the animal, but rather the manner in which it is housed. Adequate exercise usually means that the animal has the opportunity to move sufficiently to maintain normal muscle tone and mass for the age, species, size, and condition of the animal.

Inadequate exercise is frequently seen in animal hoarding cases. In a recent hoarding case, a pit bull had been kept in a small crate with feces and urine at all times. When animal control officers freed him, he ran in circles repeatedly for at least 20 minutes, clearly evidencing inadequate exercise. In another hoarding case at the home of a breeder, Standard Poodles were drenched in feces and urine, and were housed in cages at all times. From a medical exam, a veterinarian documented the lack of normal muscle mass on the dogs.

Dogs kept at commercial breeding facilities and puppy mills do not typically receive adequate exercise. While the puppies are sold quickly, the breeding sire and dam typically remain in cages with painful mesh floors (which allow the excrement to fall to the ground) for their entire lives.

In addition to the requirements and prohibitions set forth in most state laws, neglect cases often rely on the statutory *definition* of "adequate care" itself. Adequate care has been defined as the responsible practice of good animal husbandry, handling, production, management, confinement, feeding, watering, protection, shelter, transportation, treatment, and, when necessary, appropriate for the age, species, condition, size, and type of the animal.[31] Definitions of adequate care will often also require euthanasia when it is necessary to prevent suffering.[32]

Many states have also codified the meaning of "owner" by statute. Typically, the definition states that the person has a right of property in the animal or is acting as the custodian, caretaker, or harborer.[33] A well-drafted definition is expansive enough that a neglector cannot claim, for example, to be a custodian rather than an owner in an effort to avoid prosecution for failing to provide care. If an animal were not provided with appropriate veterinary care, under a limited definition of "owner," only the person who has a property right in the animal would be responsible for the violation.

Veterinarians often evaluate the presence of abuse based on whether or not good "animal husbandry" is being practiced. While originally a concept applied to agricultural animals, its meaning is sometimes codified in companion animal welfare laws.[34] An evaluation of animal husbandry includes consideration of the animal's general health, housing, breeding, and sustenance. In one example of poor animal husbandry, a zebra and donkey were housed with cows, and the cows killed the donkey. In roadside zoos, species that should be kept a significant distance apart are often caged next to each other. This can not only cause the animals distress, but also lead to the spread of disease. In another example, two dogs were tethered to the same chain, and became entangled with each other. Poor animal husbandry is often practiced in commercial breeding operations where several dogs are often kept in one crate. Often, abusers attempt to rely on the defense that their actions complied with standard animal husbandry practices, but expert testimony often refutes this claim.

Animal Cruelty

Neglect charges can be brought when an animal is not provided basic care; cruelty charges usually lie when a person proactively causes harm to an animal. Animal cruelty falls under one of two categories: gross neglect and intentional cruelty. Gross neglect is simply neglect to the extent that it cannot be seen as unintentional, while intentional cruelty is a crime of commission, and is usually codified as an act of brutality. Across the United States, neglect provisions, whether simple or gross neglect, are subsumed in cruelty provisions.

Gross neglect is an utter disregard of prudence that would shock the conscience of fair-minded people.[35] To be guilty of neglect, the owner must fail to make available *adequate* provisions, like food and water. To be guilty of gross neglect, the person must fail to make available even *necessary* provisions, and must deprive the animal of food, water, shelter, or emergency medical care necessary for life and good body condition.[36] Only a veterinarian is qualified to testify regarding an animal's body condition, and how long the animal had been suffering prior to seizure. A veterinarian can also testify to the fact that providing an insufficient amount of food, but enough to keep the animal alive, only prolongs suffering. For these reasons, veterinarians are critical to cruelty prosecutions. They can explain the process of metabolizing body muscle and fat and describe medical conditions that may not be apparent on visual inspection. They can also explain common symptoms of starvation, such as eating rocks, which would be discovered by necropsy. The prosecutor can and should emphasize that the abuser could have surrendered the animal to a shelter instead of letting it starve.

Many intentional cruelty statutes require that the person "cruelly" committed the act.[37] Most cruelty codes include some form of "cruelly treat" or "cruel treatment" in the language of the statute.[38] However, some statutes require the killing of an animal to have been done "unnecessarily."[39] In one recent instance, a farmer was angered by the presence of hunting dogs on his property, so he instructed a friend who was hunting on a close-by deer blind to shoot the dogs. In another instance, a man shot multiple dogs to death in the back of a pickup truck. He was angry because he believed the dogs had previously been in his chicken coop. Yet another example involved a man shooting a dog and claimed that he did so because the dog was dangerous and was charging him. The necropsy proved that the dog was running away from the shooter, not toward him as he claimed. Other than self-defense, it is difficult to contemplate circumstances under which it would be "necessary" to abuse an animal.

Like neglect laws, the provision of food and water is required under cruelty laws.[40] In one example where the lack of water rose beyond neglect, and the owner was charged with cruelty, the abuser provided his hunting dogs no food or water at all, and the dogs were severely dehydrated. The dogs were kept outside with only thin, uninsulated, plastic houses with no insulation or bedding. There was also nothing to break the wind. The totality of the circumstances supported a cruelty charge.

Cruelty laws often require the provision of *emergency* veterinary treatment, which is usually an increased form of veterinary treatment.[41] Emergency veterinary treatment is often statutorily defined, and is not necessarily limited to the situation in which the animal needs to be rushed to a veterinary clinic.[42] In Virginia "emergency veterinary treatment" is defined as the treatment necessary to stabilize a life-threatening condition, alleviate suffering, prevent disease transmission, or prevent disease progression.[43] Failure to comply with *only one* of these elements is necessary in order to establish cruelty. In one case, an owner outright stated that he planned to let his sick horse die in the field instead of seeking care. Luckily an animal control officer was able to convince the owner to seek treatment. The owner could have been charged with animal cruelty for allowing the animal to suffer. Virginia's cruelty laws require custodians, caretakers, and owners to act, as do many cruelty laws across the United States. If the animal is not facing a life-threatening condition, but is in distress, a prosecutor can rely on the requirement to obtain medical care to alleviate suffering. Frequently, the owner has failed to comply with multiple components of the applicable neglect or cruelty laws.

In an extreme instance of cruelty, a dog was discovered with maggots covering its underside. After it was seized, the owner called animal control and requested euthanasia, saying that she could not bring the dog into the house because it was "leaking." The officer euthanized the dog humanely and a necropsy was performed. The veterinarian was able to testify in court that the dog had been sick with an underlying medical condition for multiple weeks, and the maggots were between 3 and 4 days old. The defendant testified that the dog had eaten that morning and was acting normal, but the veterinarian's testimony disproved her defense. The necropsy uncovered rocks in the dog's stomach, and he had the lowest body condition score possible—a one. In another case, an owner was convicted of cruelty for the failure to provide veterinary care to a dog that had been hit by a car.[44] The owner was offered assistance but refused, and the dog suffered with a broken leg for over 7 weeks. Animal control seized the dog, and the owner was subsequently convicted of cruelty. He appealed his conviction but the Court of Appeals of Virginia upheld it, making it clear that the failure to treat a broken bone is cruelty.[45] The court was struck by the fact that the owner knew that the dog needed treatment; multiple people told him the dog's condition was severe or urgent, and the owner failed seek medical treatment for the dog for more than 7 weeks.[46] The circuit court stated that it "could reasonably infer...that [the owner] would have continued to let [the dog] lay at home indefinitely in a painful, paralyzed state," and that only the intervention of the animal control officers ended the dog's ongoing suffering.[47] This case established precedent, meaning that lower courts should follow the ruling going forward unless the court can find a way to distinguish the facts of a subsequent case.

Emergency veterinary care in Virginia includes that care which would prevent further disease transmission and progression. Veterinary testimony is typically necessary to establish that a condition would be transmitted or would progress. In one case, a hunter moved out of his rental house, and his landlord later discovered that he had left dogs behind. Some were alive, and some were dead. Animal control retained a highly experienced veterinarian to perform a necropsy and testify that the owner should have obtained medical care based on the presence of all four sets of circumstances that care is required under the code. Each dog had the life-threatening condition of starvation and they were all suffering. The dogs were also infested with worms, which would only multiply, progressing disease over time, and the dogs were transmitting the worms among themselves.

Abusive hunters often claim that thin dogs are better hunters, and veterinary testimony can rebut such assertions. Animal hoarders are frequently charged with animal cruelty. Animals confined in unsanitary conditions, surrounded by a large number of other animals, can develop and transmit a multitude of health conditions. Cats frequently develop upper respiratory problems. Expert testimony from a veterinarian would be necessary to explain at trial the correlation between the quality of living conditions and medical conditions.

Animal abandonment is a form of cruelty commonly encountered by law enforcement and veterinarians and is specifically set forth as a crime in most intentional cruelty statutes.[48] Animals have been left tied outside of shelters, on remote roads, parking lots, and similar locations. Abandonment is the deserting, forsaking, or giving up an animal without first securing another owner or custodian. Failing to provide the elements of basic care as set forth in the code for a specified number of days is also considered abandonment in some states. Natural disasters present a quandary with respect to abandonment, because it is difficult to know when an animal was intentionally left behind, or if the situation was too dangerous for then owner to retrieve the pet.

Veterinarians often encounter animal abandonment. Sometimes owners have good intentions in seeking veterinary care, but are not able to pay for it, and therefore leave the animal behind. In that instance, it may be difficult to prosecute the person as having abandoned the animal, as it could be argued that the individual did, in fact, secure a new custodian—the veterinarian. In other cases, owners have opted for euthanasia for lack of finances. These are difficult situations for veterinarians. One can provide the necessary care at no charge, or ask the owner to transfer ownership, in which case it should be documented in signed writing. The worst-case scenario is for a suffering animal to leave with the owner. Leaving an animal outside a veterinary clinic after hours would clearly be considered abandonment. In such a situation, any video or photographic evidence obtained should be provided to law enforcement.

Many intentional cruelty statutes include language prohibiting the willful infliction of inhumane injury or pain that is not connected with scientific or medical experimentation. Medical experimentation is exempted from all cruelty statutes.[49] Certain acts are specifically enumerated in some cruelty codes as inflicting inhumane injury, such as starving, skinning, burning, throwing, and bludgeoning. In a Virginia case, the judge articulated that starving an animal to death is equivalent to inflicting of inhumane injury, or gross neglect/cruelty. The owner was convicted and sentenced to 12 months in jail for starving a mother dog and her puppies, one of which died.[50] The owner appealed the conviction, but the appellate court upheld the trial court's ruling, and provided a detailed analysis of what it means to willfully inflict injury. The court stated that the owner voluntarily acted with a consciousness that "inhumane injury or pain" would result because he watched the dog starve over the course of weeks, the dog was infected with parasites, and the owner admitted that he knew that the dog needed veterinary care. In these types of cases, veterinarians are often called to court to testify about whether an intentional act inflicted inhumane injury on the subject animal(s).

The most egregious cases involve torture.[51] In one case, a man made five attempts to kill three German shepherd puppies—he fed them prescription drugs and firecrackers, he burned them, he glued their mouths shut, and finally, he disemboweled them. In another torture case, a cat was set on fire, and in another, a cat was skinned alive. In addition, a cat torture case, the cat experienced massive trauma to the neck which the vet suspected was because of strangulation. Unfortunately, a lot of torture occurs around Halloween, often involving black cats.

One distinction between neglect and cruelty is the breadth of applicability. Neglect laws often apply to companion animals alone, while cruelty laws typically apply to animals of all kinds. The definition of the term "animal" varies state by state.[52] Generally, it means any nonhuman vertebrate species except fish. Some statutes include every dumb animal or any animal except humans. Another distinction is that prohibitions against neglect apply only to the animal's owner, while any person can commit and be prosecuted for cruelty. The law cannot require someone to provide care to an animal it has no affiliation with, and abusers often have no relationship to the animals they abuse.

Another important and practical distinction between neglect and cruelty is the way in which the two crimes can be lessened. Neglect can often result from a lack of education and knowledge, misinformation, a lack of resources, or a variety of other factors. People who neglect animals do not always have bad intentions, and therefore charging criminal activity is not always the best solution. In some cases, people simply need assistance, which can be provided by animal control, nonprofit organizations, and sometimes veterinarians. Animal control officers can work with the owner and gain compliance through education.

Animal cruelty is different in that the perpetrator has a fundamental disregard for the animal's health, comfort, and safety, and in many instances, is acting with bad intentions. Someone intentionally harming an animal is not likely to be stopped through education or assistance, and criminal prosecution, fines, and jail time may be the only inhibiting measure. It is common—if not the norm—to see violations of several neglect and cruelty laws in one case. Typically, an owner who does not provide an animal with adequate food also fails to comply with other requirements, like the provision of water and veterinary care. Each violation can, and should, be the basis for a separate criminal charge.

Animal welfare laws can be broad, which can lead to more protections. For example, some intentional cruelty codes include terms like "ill-treat," which is synonymous with cruel treatment or maltreatment.[53] This language is frequently relied upon in the prosecution of animal fighting cases, but it is applicable to a variety of types of cruelty because of its breadth. Cruelty exists in many forms. In a poultry abuse case at a commercial breeder farm, the defendants stepped on the animals' heads to dispose of them. They also kicked and threw the birds into transport cages. An agriculture veterinarian was able discredit their defense that they were following standard animal husbandry practice.

Animal Fighting

Dogfighting and cockfighting are illegal in every state.[54] Dogfighting is a felony in all states, but cockfighting is only a misdemeanor in some.[55] In a criminal case, both direct and circumstantial evidence may be introduced. The testimony of a witness or of an officer who raided a fighting ring is an example of direct evidence. Animal fighters are often convicted based on circumstantial evidence, because the act of fighting is intentionally hidden from public view. In addition, because gangs and drugs are frequently involved, individuals do not often turn others in. Obtaining direct evidence would, in large part, require a raid during a fight, which is extremely difficult.[56] Fighting paraphernalia found on an individual or in his house is an example of circumstantial evidence. Essentially, circumstantial evidence does not prove something standing alone, but relies on an inference to reach the conclusion of criminal activity.[57] Despite a common misconception, circumstantial evidence can be sufficient to lead to conviction. Often fighters are found with pits where the fights take place, treadmills, cat-mill jennies, spring poles, and bite sticks. Cock fighters are often found with gaffes, and short and long knives. [58] Either type of animal fighter might possess medications, steroids, wound dressing supplies, trophies, pedigrees, and other suggestive evidence.[59] The presence of one piece or type of paraphernalia is not usually enough to lead to a conviction, but the presence of multiple items can be sufficient. Finally, fighters often maintain documents evidencing their activities.[60] These documents may contain the blood lines of the animals, past wins and losses, information on the dates and locations of fights, and even information on other fighters and their animals. The pedigree of a fighting animal determines its value, and the value of a defeat against it.

The strongest laws ban not only fighting but possessing fighting paraphernalia.[61] A ban on owning paraphernalia gives law enforcement additional bases on which to arrest and charge a perpetrator. Many state laws prohibit the possession of steroids and other performance-enhancing drugs and any implements to enhance the animal's ability to fight, including gaffes, and short and long knives.[62] Fighters use both prescription and illegal drugs to improve the endurance, stamina, and aggressiveness in their animals. In some cases, roosters have been given methamphetamine or other controlled substances which are regulated under drug laws. Strong laws prohibit attending a fight as a spectator, which discourages the most organized fighting establishments. Some states also prohibit the possession, ownership, training, transportation, and sale of an animal with the intent that the animal will engage in an exhibition of fighting with another animal.[63] This means that a person does not have to be caught in the act of fighting, but can be charged by simply possessing a fighting animal. In the states with the most comprehensive laws, one arrest can lead to multiple charges including a charge for possessing the animal, possessing paraphernalia, fighting the animal, attending a fight, and participating in a fight.

Illegal gambling is commonly involved in animal fighting. Fighters gamble not only on which animal will win, but also on how fast the losing bird will die, as well as various games played in conjunction with the fighting. The stakes can be high, with fighters walking away with hundreds to many thousands of dollars. In one cockfighting case, an undercover officer received over $3600 from a single fight. With gambling comes tax evasion and IRS violations, as the income cannot easily be reported. Most states have outlawed gambling at and paying admission fees to attend fighting events.[64] While dogfighting seems to attract the most media coverage, cockfighting events garner larger amounts of money because, unlike in dogfighting, multiple animals are usually fought by each participant in a derby. In the investigation of a very large fighting operation in Kentucky, the Big Blue Sportsman's Club, law enforcement discovered that the affiliated gambling involved millions of dollars. Once convicted, the pit manager was required to forfeit approximately one million dollars to the United States government.

Many states also expressly forbid involving minors in animal fighting as either participants or spectators.[65] Children are frequently exposed to fighting by their parents. In the Big Blue case, one of the fighters encouraged his teenage son to fight the rooster himself. The mere exposure to animals being fought is psychologically damaging to children. Animal fighters often intentionally involve their children to initiate the next generation into the culture, thereby perpetuating the crimes.

Family members and friends of the individual who operate fighting rings often provide assistance in a variety of ways, including housing and caring for the animals.[66] For example, the person might spar roosters or roll pit bull–type dogs. Sparring means fighting two birds that have "muffs" over the spurs. The muffs allow the birds to practice fighting without causing injury. Rolling is a form of training for fighting dogs. The most comprehensive laws ban individuals from allowing animal fighting to occur on their premises, and outlaw any form of aiding or abetting animal fighting. The most stringent laws outlaw spectator animal fighting, thus even going to and being at a fight is illegal and can be charged as a felony.[67]

Veterinarians are often called to examine animals recovered from fighting raids. While the examinations are in part to ascertain the necessary medical care, they are also very important to evidence collection and prosecution. There are several physical signs of animal fighting. In fighting roosters, the combs and wattles are typically removed, and their natural spurs are often cut to make it easier to securely attach knives and gaffes. Alternatively, the spurs may be filed to sharp points. Dogs will often have wounds and scarring in the head, neck, chest, and forearm areas—a clear sign that the injuries were caused by intentional fighting rather than a normal dog altercation over food, for example. The examining veterinarian must meticulously evaluate and document each animal's general health and physical condition, noting all abnormalities, and evaluate and document the general health and body condition of each dog, and chart the scene so that each animal can later be identified. The veterinarian often opines as to whether or not an animal should be euthanized and conducts necropsies when appropriate. The veterinarian also documents any signs of disease and reports any condition that might present a public health concern. In addition, they will identify and document the presence of any drugs, steroids, and medical supplies that appear to be used on the fighting animals. The veterinarian will later be called to testify as a witness at trial, at which time the medical evidence must be presented in a way that a judge and jury can easily understand. The involvement and testimony of the veterinarian is critical to the prosecution of animal fighting cases.

Animal fighting is essentially organized animal cruelty, and it is almost always linked to other criminal activity. In addition to gambling, animal fighting is often linked to illegal drugs and weapons, as well as gang activity. Dogfighting, in particular, is frequently associated with gangs and crimes that gang members are often involved in. Dogfighting is a form of entertainment for gang members, and gang surveillance often leads law enforcement officers to dogfighting operations.[68] Animal fighting is also frequently discovered through drug investigation. In one case, police officers who were serving a warrant for drugs suspected that the drugs were hidden under doghouses and discovered a fighting operation as a result. The defendant was ultimately convicted and received a 2-year jail sentence for animal fighting. Upon release, he returned to dogfighting, was discovered again, and was ultimately convicted of a felony carrying a 10-year prison sentence. In the Big Blue cockfighting case discussed earlier, every drug imaginable could be purchased in the parking lot of the fighting ring. In addition, there have been rapes, assaults, and murders at animal fights. Because animal fighting and animal fighters are violent, human violence occurs at animal fights as well. Also, illegally obtained veterinary medications are often dispensed at the fights.

Animal Sexual Abuse

Animal sexual abuse is outlawed in many states but the manner in which it is defined is inconsistent, which leads to different types of acts being banned in different parts of the country. Forty-four states have passed laws prohibiting sexual abuse of animals and 21 states treat bestiality as a felony-level offense.[69] Animal sex crimes may be called bestiality, crimes of moral turpitude, or crimes against nature, among other titles.[70] Many states have outlawed any sexual intercourse with any animal (or "brute animal," which means a nonhuman animal).[71] Some states have outlawed carnal knowledge of an animal and may define what that means. Some states have more inclusive laws, prohibiting oral sodomy, cunnilingus, fellatio, and any other overt sexual act with an animal.[72] There have been cases of a perpetrator performing sexual acts on the animal using inanimate objects. Perpetrators have also trained animals to perform sexual acts on themselves. This type of abuse is evidence of serious human sexual deviance and is often perpetrated by persons who are capable of or involved in other types of illegal activities, like child sexual abuse and pornography. Animals frequently perish as a result of sexual abuse or have to be euthanized. A veterinarian can be in the position of witnessing statements made by offenders in the rare cases where the animal is taken for treatment. In the heat of passion, people sometimes make damaging statements, which can later assist in law enforcement investigations if documented and retained.

WHY SHOULD WE CARE ABOUT ANIMAL CRIMES?

The Link to Violence against Humans

Why should we care about crimes against animals? There are multiple reasons, but perhaps the most fundamental is that we are judged as a society based on how we treat the most vulnerable in our society. Mahatma Gandhi said "The greatness of a nation can be judged by the way its animals are treated."[73] Only adult humans have legal "rights" by law. Animals and children do not have rights, so society has created legal protections.[74] There is a link or correlation between violence against animals and violence against people—both physical and sexual.[75] An individual who is capable of abusing an animal has the same moral deficit that allows for the abuse of others—often the vulnerable, such as children and the elderly.

In domestic violence situations, animals are often used to gain control over or punish the victim. A victim may choose not to leave the abuser because the pet would have to be left behind.[76] In Loudoun County, Virginia, an abuser videotaped himself wrapping his girlfriend's cat in duct tape and her reaction on his phone. The woman can be heard crying while her cat is meowing pitifully, while the perpetrator is laughing at the distress of both. The video also shows that soon after, he strikes her in the face, breaking her nose. In another recent example, a man recorded himself kicking and strangling his girlfriend's kitten and sent the video to her via text message. He also threw her ferrets out the window. Animal control was dispatched and was able to retrieve the cat, one ferret, and a fish tank. Twenty-four hours later, he killed his girlfriend in the presence of two other people. In Georgia, a man axed his wife's puppy to death and threatened to decapitate her with the same weapon in front of three children. He was subsequently charged with cruelty to animals, child cruelty, and aggravated assault. A Pennsylvania man shot his family dog and ordered his four children to clean up the scene under threat of death.

In another domestic violence case, the victim gathered enough courage to leave, but left her small dog behind with her abuser. He locked the dog in the basement and starved it to death as punishment for her leaving. In another example, a woman told her husband to leave the home, which he did. However, he returned the next day when no one was home, and beat their pet Beagle with a blunt object until its eye came out of its head. The Beagle could not be treated and had to be euthanized. Someone in such a fit of rage would likely have assaulted the wife had she come home during the beating. While not an incident of domestic violence, children were seen setting a cat on fire. A witness was nearby. The children threatened the woman's physical safety, and she refused to testify against them for fear of being harmed.

Animal abuse has also been linked to sexual abuse of children. Frequently, the abuser harms the animal to instill fear in or to silence the child. In a Richmond case, a child came forward after 10 years of abuse at the hands of her stepfather. He had killed her kitten with a bow and arrow to scare her into silence—a clear message that she might suffer the same fate if she disobeyed him. In another instance, a father blamed the family dog for waking his daughter up in the night. He then forced her to watch him beat the dog to death, light it on fire, and bury it. He told the child that it was okay because the dog was in heaven. He was also sexually abusing this child. In another sexual abuse example, the child's kitten was meowing, and the father strangled it in front of the child because he had not given permission for the child to get the kitten. Studies have shown that that witnessing animal abuse is extremely detrimental to children. Abusers use the power of the human-animal bond to manipulate their victims into doing things against their will, and to scare them into silence.

Elderly citizens are often vulnerable and are taken advantage of by animal abusers. In an animal hoarding situation, a senior citizen was relegated to the second floor of a house where she had to defecate in a bucket. Her relatives, who were taking her social security checks, lived downstairs with over 10 dogs. They blamed her for the smell in the house, though it was actually a result of the dog feces rather than the abused woman. In another example, a very obese woman who also had to defecate in a bucket because she was immobile thought she was causing a stench in her home. In actuality, her husband had been hoarding dogs, and the house was full of animal urine and feces.

In recent years, school shootings have almost become commonplace in the United States. Between 1988 and 2012, there were 23 school shootings.[77] In each instance, the shooter had previously abused or tortured animals. Nikolas Cruz, in Parkland, Florida, and Luke Woodham, in Pearl Mississippi, tortured animals prior to their mass shootings.[78] The Columbine High School shooters, Eric Harris and Dylan Klebold, killed neighborhood dogs, and both told classmates that they had mutilated animals in the past.[79] Kip Kinkel, who murdered his parents and injured 25 classmates in an Oregon high school, previously mutilated a cow and stuffed fire crackers in cats' mouths as a child.[80] Often young people who are violent toward animals or humans are experiencing violence in their homes. Reporting a young animal abuser may lead to the discovery of evidence of child abuse or other domestic violence.

Serial killers frequently abuse and torture animals. Perhaps the most well-known of them, Jeffery Dahmer, had a history of carving animals in his garage and posting their heads on sticks. His father thought his son was going to be a doctor, so he encouraged the behavior. Dennis Rader (the BTK killer) wrote that he hanged a dog and a cat during his childhood. Lee Boyd Malvo, who shot and killed 10 people as a teenager, previously killed numerous cats with a slingshot and marbles.[81] Albert DeSalvo (the Boston Strangler), who killed 13 women, had a history of trapping dogs and cats in boxes and shooting arrows at them as a child.[82] David Berkowitz (Son of Sam) killed and tortured multiple animals, including his mother's parakeet. The bird was tortured by being fed small doses of cleaning fluid over a 3-week period. He also killed thousands of bugs with rubber cement and burning.[83] John Wayne Gacy set turkeys on fire with gasoline-filled balloons.[84] Ted Bundy, who killed at least 30 women, mutilated dogs and cats as a child.[85]

PROSECUTING ANIMAL CRIMES

Animal Control and Law Enforcement

The structure and management of animal control units varies from locality to locality within a state, and from state to state across the country. Animal control may be housed under the local police chief, the sheriff's department, another administrative governmental unit, or it may be a stand-alone agency. Unfortunately, in some localities—usually the most rural—animal control officers are viewed as no more than old-time dog catchers, are given little to no training or education, and are not provided adequate resources or equipment. Animal control departments and shelters are often understaffed, in part because of low salaries. In other localities, animal control officers are well-respected professionals, provided with regular continuing education and the equipment needed to perform effectively. Officers may also be given the special designation of animal protection police. Some officers carry firearms and have full or partial law enforcement powers. Others must rely on law enforcement to execute search warrants and make arrests. These animal control officers are often unarmed in very dangerous situations.

Prosecution

To understand the practical implementation of criminal animal laws, one must have a basic understanding of the prosecution process. Because they are personal property, the unauthorized seizure of an animal is a constitutional violation. Therefore, whether or not an officer obtains a search warrant before seizing the animal, the process becomes twofold. The first step is a hearing to determine whether the seizure was lawful. The second step is the criminal trial. In most states, the seizure hearing is a civil proceeding, with a lower burden of proof than the criminal trial. In the criminal case, the prosecutor must prove to the judge or jury that the defendant is guilty beyond a reasonable doubt. The burden of proof in a civil seizure hearing can be lower than that of a criminal trial. The prosecutor must establish that there is either probable cause to believe,[86] or a civil standard of proof that the act in question was committed. However, some states apply a criminal standard to the seizure hearing. In a criminal case, the prosecutor must prove that the criminal act was committed beyond a reasonable doubt.[87] Probable cause is a reasonable basis that the crime has been committed and is the lowest burden of proof in any proceedings. Reasonable doubt means sufficient doubt for an acquittal. However, the prosecutor is not required to prove it beyond all doubt or a shadow of a doubt.

The seizure hearing is very important in that the fate of the animal is often determined at this stage, regardless of the subsequent outcome of the prosecution for the criminal wrongdoing. If the seizure hearing is not successful, the animal(s) can be returned to the accused abuser pending the criminal trial. A veterinarian is typically called to present expert testimony and evidence of neglect or abuse at both a seizure hearing and the criminal prosecution. It is crucial that the veterinarian is fully educated on both the facts and the law, though the veterinarian is not asked to opine upon the application of the law—only those facts related to the condition of the animal. The knowledge and preparedness of the veterinarian is particularly important at the seizure hearing because the same or similar testimony will typically be elicited at the criminal prosecution stage. A veterinarian with inconsistent testimony can damage the overall credibility of the prosecution. It is critical for the veterinarian to prepare a written report and review all notes and the report prior to testifying. Many court cases will not take place for several months after examination of the animals, so preparation is critical to a successful outcome in court.

In several states, the penalties and punishments for neglect and cruelty are set forth within the neglect and cruelty laws themselves. Prosecutors pursue misdemeanor level charges for simple neglect. Because prosecutors have discretion, many gross neglect and cruelty cases are also tried as misdemeanors rather than felonies. An individual convicted of a misdemeanor is usually punished with a fine or short jail sentences, often less than a year. However, each state has some form of a felony cruelty statute. When animal cruelty can be punished as a felony it is almost always at the lower level of the felony scale, with relatively short jail sentences of 5 years or less. Felony provisions of cruelty statutes usually mirror the misdemeanor language but are used for more egregious acts. In some states, a felony conviction requires the prosecutor to prove specific elements in addition to those required for a misdemeanor. In many states, the abused animal must die or be euthanized in order for the prosecutor to charge a felony. This means that the prosecutor can initially charge a misdemeanor and increase it to a felony if the animal dies. However, there is a nationwide trend toward enacting laws that make intentional cruelty a felony regardless of whether or not the animal dies or is euthanized. An owner can be convicted of a felony, if, as a direct result of his actions, the animal suffers "serious bodily injury."[88] In fact, Virginia recently enacted this type of law, which came into effect July 1, 2019.[89]

VETERINARY EXAMINATION AND TREATMENT OF ABUSED ANIMALS

Because abusers and cruelty perpetrators do not typically seek medical care for their animals, veterinarians are not likely to treat abused animals on a regular basis. However, it does occur, so it is important for veterinarians to recognize the signs of potential abuse. Veterinarians may also encounter evidence of neglect. It may be that, as previously mentioned, the owner has good intentions, and is either overwhelmed or cannot afford veterinary care, but will bring the animal to the veterinarian in a critical situation. In one instance, a man brought dead kittens to his veterinarian on more than one occasion, and he smelled of urine. The veterinarian did not call anyone for assistance or report the situation for fear of angering the client. A veterinary assistant, however, called the attorney general's animal law unit because she suspected that something was wrong. Animal control was asked to investigate and discovered that the man had unaltered cats that had bred to the point that the dead kittens were the result of inbreeding. He lacked adequate resources, and the situation had become overwhelming for him. Animal control ultimately provided assistance with altering the cats rather than seizing the animals.

Some animal fighters will seek veterinary care, often for their most prized fighting animals. They may claim that the animal was in an unintentional fight. There have been instances in which, unfortunately, the veterinarian turns a blind eye to the signs, opting for the profit from treating the animals. Some have actually formed unwritten partnerships with the fighters, and care for the animals' fighting injuries on an ongoing basis. One veterinarian was found freezing the semen of a fighting dog bloodline for future use in the breeding of fighting dogs. In most states, it is a crime to aid or abet animal fighting. Veterinarians are often asked to assist law enforcement in the investigation of suspected animal abuse and fighting. In a fighting seizure, the condition of the animals at the time of seizure is critical, and only a veterinarian can opine on that topic. Typically, the veterinarian will travel to the scene and physically examine and photograph each animal, taking detailed notes of anything that could be helpful in prosecuting the case.

Because of the known link between animal abuse and domestic violence, a veterinarian may see evidence of harm to an abused animal's owner. Though it seems far-fetched, abused people will sometimes volunteer information about abuse—human or animal—in unusual circumstances. In some instances, the person has very few opportunities to talk to someone outside the presence of the abuser. In this type of situation, it could be argued that informing authorities is not only the appropriate thing to do but is a veterinarian's responsibility. The Veterinarian's Oath contains an obligation to not only promote animal health, but to promote public and human health. In many states, veterinarians are legally required to report animal abuse.[90] These laws usually protect not only against civil liability but also criminal prosecution for good faith reporting. Some states require the veterinarian to have direct knowledge of abuse, while others only require a reasonable suspicion. When any type of abuse is suspected, it is imperative that the veterinarian document all observations and statements in order to assist with any future prosecution.

Veterinarians are often asked to produce records in pending civil and criminal proceedings. Unlike humans, animals are not protected under the Health Insurance Portability and Accountability Act (HIPAA), or doctor/patient privilege because they are considered personal property. However, most state laws prohibit the release of records to anyone except the client, unless the vet is issued a subpoena or court order (which includes search warrants). Veterinarians often have no notice before receipt of a subpoena or search warrant and are given a very short timeframe in which to respond. Therefore, it is very important to be familiar with the relevant state laws regarding record production.

COURTROOM TESTIMONY

As briefly mentioned, veterinarians are almost always called to testify as expert witnesses in neglect, abuse, and fighting cases. This is usually the veterinarian who treated the animal, if there was one. If not, an independent veterinarian will be selected and educated on the facts of the case. An expert is typically more educated, experienced, and knowledgeable on the pertinent issues than the judge and the jury. An expert witness is required to testify to a reasonable degree of certainty with respect to opinions rendered. An expert witness is also the only person in court who is expected to offer opinions in addition to testifying to the facts. Because of this, the veterinarian's opinions have the potential to win or lose a case.

At the start of testimony, the expert is asked a series of questions about their education, experience, and qualifications, before the court is asked to certify the person as an expert. In a criminal case, the prosecuting attorney will then elicit information supporting the presence of neglect, abuse, or fighting evidence. The veterinarian will also be asked to testify to the severity and age of the animal's injuries, as well as the extent to which the animal suffered or was in pain. At the close of the prosecutor's questioning, the defendant's attorney has the opportunity to cross-examine the witness and will attempt to point out flaws in the expert's conclusions. The defendant may also call an expert witness to challenge the evidence. The veterinarian's role is to explain medical evidence in terms that are understandable to the lay person. Typically, the expert's goal is to establish why injuries were medically impossible, or unlikely to have been caused in the manner claimed by the defendant. For instance, in a cat torture case, the perpetrator claimed that the cat fell down a set of stairs. However, the veterinarian's necropsy showed massive neck trauma. The veterinarian, having examined and treated hundreds of cats with neck injuries, was able to explain that neck trauma does not typically result from a fall, and that the cat had likely been hung or strangled. The expert veterinarian does not have to rule out every possible explanation but must establish the cause of injury that is most likely, and why that is the case. In the same case, the owner returned a cat to the shelter it came from, in poor health. It was suffering from a respiratory condition, was very lethargic, and had superglue on its teeth. When questioned, the owner said the cat had chewed on a superglue tube. The expert veterinarian was able to opine that, based on cat's symptoms, the super glue was more likely to have been intentionally applied—possibly in an effort to poison the kitten. A third kitten from the same residence died and the owner had disposed of it, making necropsy impossible. Three cats died in this abuser's care. A veterinarian is the only witness who can testify to why the defendant's explanation is unreasonable, or even impossible.

The courtroom, jury, judge, and attorneys can be intimidating. A good lawyer thoroughly prepares their witnesses, and a good expert ensures that the attorney knows both the favorable and the unfavorable evidence to avoid surprises and opportunities to be discredited at trial. A well-prepared expert with the proper education and experience is unlikely to be swayed or unnerved on the witness stand by an attorney who has learned the medical information in a highly condensed time frame. A veterinarian who treated the animal will likely be summoned to court, which means attendance is not optional.

CONCLUSION

Civil and criminal animal cases are becoming more common in the United States. Laws are also being strengthened and enforced more strictly, and law schools across the country are accepting animal law as a standard practice area. At the same time, animals continue to be neglected, abused, and tortured at an alarming rate. The link between animal mistreatment and violence against humans is undisputable. Veterinarians play a key role in identifying and prosecuting animal crimes, which are likely to become more common as neglect and abuse are being taken more seriously every year. It is important to recognize and report the signs of neglect and abuse in animals, as it is often indicative of abuse in the home, and veterinarians have a duty to support both animal and human health, as well as public safety.

ACKNOWLEDGMENTS

I want to thank Robin McVoy, Assistant Attorney General, Virginia Attorney General's Office, for her considerable writing and editing skills. I also thank Paul Kugelman, Senior Assistant Attorney General and the Chief of the Environmental Section for lending his editing talent to this chapter and for his unwavering support of our Animal Law Unit. A special thank you goes to our Deputy Attorney General, Don Anderson, who has supported me in editing this chapter and has provided incredible support and his optimistic outlook for our Animal Law Unit for several years. Finally, I want to express gratitude and a heartfelt "thank you" to the Attorney General of the Commonwealth of Virginia, Mark R. Herring, for creating our Animal Law Unit and for supporting it wholeheartedly for more than 5 years. The animals of Virginia have been safer because of you.

Endnotes

1. https://www.animallaw.info/article/charting-growth-animal-law-education; https://www.superlawyers.com/colorado/article/rights-and-bites-the-growing-field-of-animal-law/e11610aa-7607-4a00-a098-054903cc1d1f.html.
2. https://aldf.org/article/animal-law-courses/; https://www.aals.org/; https://www.americanbar.org/groups/tort_trial_insurance_practice/publications/the_brief/2018-19/fall/animal-law-committee-raising-bar-nonhuman-animals/.
3. https://www.humanesociety.org/resources/animal-cruelty-and-human-violence-faq; https://aldf.org/article/the-link-between-cruelty-to-animals-and-violence-toward-humans-2/; Ascione, F.R., McDonald, S.E., Tedeschi, P., & Williams, J. 2018. The relations among animal abuse, psychological disorders, and crime: Implications for assessment; *Behavioral Sciences and the Law*, https://doi.org/10.1001/bsl.2370; Ascione, F.R. 1998. Battered women's responses of their partners' and their children's cruelty to animals. *Journal of Emotional Abuse*, 1(1), 119–133; Ascione, F.R. Weber, C.V., Thompson, T.M., Heath, J., Maruyama, M., & Hayashi, K. 2007. Battered pets and domestic violence: Animal abuse reported by women experiencing initiate violence and by non-abused women. *Violence Against Women*, 13, 354–373; and Barrett, B.J., Fitzgerald, A, Stevenson, R., & Cheung, C.H. 2017. Animal maltreatment as a risk marker of more frequent and severe forms of intimate partner violence. *Journal of Interpersonal Violence*, doi: 10.1177/0886260517719542.
4. https://www.animallaw.info/article/detailed-discussion-dog-fighting; McDonald, S.E., Collins, E.A., Nictera, N., Hageman, T.O., Ascione, F.R., Williams, J.H., & Graham-Bermann, S.A. 2015. Children's experiences of companion animal maltreatement in households characterized

by intimate partner violence. *Child Abuse & Neglect*, 50, 116–127; Simmons, C.A. & Lehmann, P. 2007. Exploring the link between pet abuse and controlling behaviors in violent relationships. *Journal of Interpersonal Violence*, 22, 1211–1222; Newberry, M. 2017. Pets in danger: Exploring the link between domestic violence and animal abuse. *Aggression and Violence Behavior*, 34, 273–281; Upadhya, V. 2014. The abuse of animals as a method of domestic violence: the need for criminalization. *Emory Law Journal*, 63, 1163–1209; Taylor, N. & Fitzgerald, A. 2018. Understanding animal abuse: Green criminological contributions, missed opportunities and a way forward. *Theoretical Criminology*, 22(3), 402–425; and Thompson, K.L. & Gullone, E. 2006. An investigation into the association between the witnessing of animal abuse and adolescents' behavior toward animals. *Society & Animals*, 14, 221–243.

5. https://supreme.findlaw.com/legal-commentary/pets-as-property.html; Waisman, S.S., Frasch, P.D., & Wagman, B.A. 2014. *Animal Law: Cases and Materials*, 5th ed., Carolina Free Press, p. 35.
6. http://www.animallaw.com/Case-Law.cfm; Waisman, S.S., Frasch, P.D., & Wagman, B.A. 2014. *Animal Law: Cases and Materials*, 5th ed., Carolina Free Press.
7. https://www.iii.org/fact-statistic/facts-statistics-pet-statistics.
8. https://www.fbi.gov/news/stories/-tracking-animal-cruelty; ASPCA Position Statement on Protection of Animal Cruelty Victims, 2019, https://www.aspca.org/about-us/aspca-policy-and-position-statements/position-statement-protection-animal-cruelty-victims.
9. For purposes of this chapter, neglect and inadequate care will be referred to collectively as "neglect."
10. "Adequate care" or "care" means the responsible practice of good animal husbandry, handling, production, management, confinement, feeding, watering, protection, shelter, transportation, treatment, and, when necessary, euthanasia, appropriate for the age, species, condition, size and type of the animal and the provision of veterinary care when needed to prevent suffering or impairment of health. *See, e.g.*, Va. § Code Ann. 3.2-6500; Animal Protection Laws of the United States (13th Edition), 2018 Animal Legal Defense Fund (https://aldf.org/project/us-state-rankings/): 8 MICH. COMP. LAWS § 750.50. Definitions; crimes against animals, cruel treatment, abandonment, failure to provide adequate care, etc.; penalties; multiple prosecutions; payment of costs; exceptions. Sec. 50. (1) As used in this section and section 50b: (a) "Adequate care" means the provision of sufficient food, water, shelter, sanitary conditions, exercise, and veterinary medical attention in order to maintain an animal in a state of good health. (b) "Animal" means any vertebrate other; and OR. REV. STAT. § 167.310. Definitions. As used in ORS 167.310 to 167.351: (9) "Minimum care" means care sufficient to preserve the health and well-being of an animal and, except for emergencies or circumstances beyond the reasonable control of the owner, includes, but is not limited to, the following requirements: (a) Food of sufficient quantity and quality to allow for normal growth or maintenance of body weight. (b) Open or adequate access to potable water in sufficient quantity to satisfy the animal's needs. Access to snow or ice is not adequate access to potable water. (c) For a domestic animal other than a dog engaged in herding or protecting livestock, access to adequate shelter. (d) Veterinary care deemed necessary by a reasonably prudent person to relieve distress from injury, neglect or disease. (e) For a domestic animal, continuous access to an area: (A) With adequate space for exercise necessary for the health of the animal; (B) With air temperature suitable for the animal; and (C) Kept reasonably clean and free from excess waste or other contaminants that could affect the animal's health.
11. Animal Neglect, U.S. Legal, https://definitions.uslegal.com/a/animal-neglect/.
12. Feral dogs and feral cats are included in most definitions. Companion animal is defined in Virginia Code § 3.2-6500 as "any domestic or feral dog, domestic or feral cat, nonhuman primate, guinea pig, hamster, rabbit not raised for human food or fiber, exotic or native animal, reptile, exotic or native bird, or any feral animal or any animal under the care, custody, or ownership of a person or any animal that is bought, sold, traded, or bartered by any person; Animal Protection Laws of the United States (13th Edition), 2018 Animal Legal Defense Fund (https://aldf.org/project/us-state-rankings/): KAN. STAT. ANN § 21-6411. Unlawful acts concerning animals; definitions. As used in K.S.A. 21-6412 through 21-6417, and amendments thereto: (e) "domestic pet" means any domesticated animal which is kept for pleasure rather than utility; MINN. STAT. § 343.20. Definitions. Subd. 6. Pet or companion animal. "Pet or companion animal" includes any animal owned, possessed by, cared for, or controlled by a person for the present or future enjoyment of that person or another as a pet or companion, or any stray pet or stray companion animal.

13. Animal Protection Laws of the United States (13th Edition), 2018 Animal Legal Defense Fund (https://aldf.org/project/us-state-rankings/): TENN. CODE ANN. § 39-14-201. Definitions for animal offenses. "Non-livestock animal" means a pet normally maintained in or near the household(s) of its owner(s), other domesticated animal, previously captured wildlife, an exotic animal, or any other pet, including but not limited to, pet rabbits, a pet chick, duck, or pot-bellied pig that is not classified as "livestock" pursuant to this part.
14. Most states have a food and water requirement. The top tier states also have adequate shelter definitions which may include adequate space. For a complete listing of all state laws, see Animal Protection Laws of the United States (13th Edition), 2018 Animal Legal Defense Fund (https://aldf.org/project/us-state-rankings/).
15. Animal Protection Laws of the United States (13th Edition), 2018 Animal Legal Defense Fund (https://aldf.org/project/us-state-rankings/): COLO. REV. STAT. § 18-9-202: or otherwise mistreats or neglects any animal, or causes or procures it to be done, or, having the charge or custody of any animal, fails to provide it with proper food, drink, or protection from the weather consistent with the species, breed, and type of animal involved; 510 ILL. COMP. STAT. 70/3.01. b). No owner may abandon any animal where it may become a public charge or may suffer injury, hunger or exposure.
16. Animal Protection Laws of the United States (13th Edition), 2018 Animal Legal Defense Fund (https://aldf.org/project/us-state-rankings/): COLO. REV. STAT. § 35-42-103. Definitions. As used in this article, unless the context otherwise requires: (4)"Neglect" means failure to provide food, water, protection from the elements, or other care generally considered to be normal, usual, and accepted for an animal's health and well-being consistent with the species, breed, and type of animal.
17. Virginia Code § 3.2-6500: "Adequate feed" means access to and the provision of food that is of sufficient quantity and nutritive value to maintain each animal in good health; is accessible to each animal; is prepared so as to permit ease of consumption for the age, species, condition, size and type of each animal; is provided in a clean and sanitary manner; is placed so as to minimize contamination by excrement and pests; and is provided at suitable intervals for the species, age, and condition of the animal, but at least once daily.
18. In a Lunenburg, Virginia case, the abuser left a dog in a wire crate in her house with a food bowl with food in it on top of crate and left the dog for 2 weeks. The dog died and the owner was charged with cruelty, not neglect. This example shows why "access" is crucial as a protection under neglect or adequate laws.
19. BCS tells you the story of whether the animal is eating. You don't have to rule out every possible reason. Giving the dog food after seizure and having the animal eating readily is good corroborative evidence. Purina Body Condition Chart is 1–9 (https://www.morrisanimalfoundation.org/sites/default/files/filesync/Purina-Body-Condition-System.pdf), BCS of a 1 is emaciated and BCS of 9 is overweight, BCS of 5 is an ideal BCS; and Tufts Body Condition Chart 1–5 (https://vet.tufts.edu/wp-content/uploads/tacc.pdf) (5 is emaciated on this chart and 1 is a good body condition scale).
20. Animal Protection Laws of the United States (13th Edition), 2018 Animal Legal Defense Fund (https://aldf.org/project/us-state-rankings/): WASH. REV. CODE § 16.52.011. Definitions—Principles of liability, (1) "Necessary water" means water that is in sufficient quantity and of appropriate quality for the species for which it is intended and that is accessible to the animal.; Indiana IND. CODE § 35-46-3-0.5(1),(4): (4) "Neglect" means: (A) endangering an animal's health by failing to provide or arrange to provide the animal with food or drink, if the animal is dependent upon the person for the provision of food or drink; Virginia Code 3.2-6500 and 3.2-6503: "Adequate water" means provision of and access to clean, fresh, potable water of a drinkable temperature that is provided in a suitable manner, in sufficient volume, and at suitable intervals appropriate for the weather and temperature, to maintain normal hydration for the age, species, condition, size and type of each animal, except as prescribed by a veterinarian or as dictated by naturally occurring states of hibernation or fasting normal for the species; and is provided in clean, durable receptacles that are accessible to each animal and are placed so as to minimize contamination of the water by excrement and pests or an alternative source of hydration consistent with generally accepted husbandry practices.
21. Adequate shelter law: (Adequate space is included within the standards of shelter for most states). Animal Protection Laws of the United States (13th Edition), 2018 Animal Legal Defense Fund (https://aldf.org/project/us-state-rankings/): ME. REV. STAT. ANN. tit. 17, § 1037 §1037. Proper shelter; protection from the weather and humanely clean conditions: No person owning or responsible for confining or impounding any animal may fail to provide the animal with proper shelter, protection

from the weather or humanely clean conditions as prescribed in this section. 1. Indoor standards. Minimum indoor standards of shelter shall be as follows. A. The ambient temperature shall be compatible with the health of the animal., B. Indoor housing facilities shall be adequately ventilated by natural or mechanical means to provide for the health of the animal at all times, 2. Outdoor standards. Minimum outdoor standards of shelter shall be as follows. A. When sunlight is likely to cause heat exhaustion of an animal tied or caged outside, sufficient shade by natural or artificial means shall be provided to protect the animal from direct sunlight. As used in this paragraph, "caged" does not include farm fencing used to confine farm animals. B. Except as provided in subsections 5, 5-A and 7, shelter from inclement weather must be provided according to this paragraph. (1) An artificial shelter, with a minimum of 3 sides and a waterproof roof, appropriate to the local climatic conditions for the species and breed of the animal must be provided as necessary for the health of the animal, (2) If a dog is tied or confined unattended outdoors under weather conditions that adversely affect the health of the dog, a shelter must be provided in accordance with subsection 7, paragraph A to accommodate the dog and protect it from the weather and, in particular, from severe cold. Inadequate shelter may be indicated by the shivering of the dog due to cold weather for a continuous period of 10 minutes or by symptoms of frostbite or hypothermia. A metal barrel is not adequate shelter for a dog. Space standards. Minimum space requirements for both indoor and outdoor enclosures shall include the following: A. The housing facilities shall be structurally sound and maintained in good repair to protect the animal from injury and to contain the animal. B. Enclosures shall be constructed and maintained to provide sufficient space to allow each animal adequate freedom of movement. Inadequate space may be indicated by evidence of overcrowding, debility, stress or abnormal behavior patterns, Humanely clean conditions. Minimum standards of sanitation necessary to provide humanely clean conditions for both indoor and outdoor enclosures shall include periodic cleanings to remove excretions and other waste materials, dirt and trash to minimize health hazards; R.I. GEN. LAWS § 4-13-1.2. (Adequate space or tethering laws may also be included under adequate care laws: R.I. GEN. LAWS § 4-13-1.2. Definitions. (1) "Adequate shelter" means the provision of and access to shelter that is suitable for the species, age, condition, size, and type of each dog; provides sufficient space for the dog to maintain comfortable rest, normal posture, and range of movement; and is safe to protect each dog from injury, rain, sleet, snow, hail, direct sunlight, the adverse effects of heat or cold, physical suffering, and impairment of health. Shelters with wire grid or slat floors that permit the dog's feet to pass through the openings, sag under the dog's weight, or otherwise do not protect the dog's feet from injury, are not considered adequate shelter; R.I. GEN. LAWS § 4-13-42. Care of dogs. (a) It shall be a violation of this section for an owner or keeper to: (1) Keep any dog on a permanent tether that restricts movement of the tethered dog to an area less than one hundred thirteen square feet (113 sq. ft.), or less than a six foot (6′) radius at ground level. (2) Tether a dog with a choke-type collar, head collar, or prong-type collar. The weight of any chain or tether shall not exceed one-eighth (⅛) of the dog's total body weight. (3) Keep any dog tethered for more than ten (10) hours during a twenty-four- hour (24) period or keep any dog confined in an area or primary enclosure for more than fourteen (14) hours during any twenty-four- hour (24) period, and more than ten (10) hours during a twenty-four-hour (24) period, if the area is not greater than that which is required under the most recently adopted version of the department of environmental management's rules and regulations governing animal care facilities. (4) Tether a dog anytime from the hours of ten o'clock p.m. (10:00 p.m.) to six o'clock a.m. (6:00 a.m.), except for a maximum of fifteen (15) minutes. (5) Keep any dog outside, either tethered or otherwise confined, when the ambient temperature is beyond the industry standard for the weather safety scale as set forth in the most recent adopted version of the Tufts Animal Care and Condition Weather Safety Scale (TACC). (b) It shall be a violation of this section for an owner or keeper to fail to provide a dog with adequate feed, adequate water, or adequate veterinary care as those terms are defined in § 4-19-2; provided, however, that adequate veterinary care may be provided by an owner using acceptable animal husbandry practices. (c) Exposing any dog to adverse weather conditions strictly for the purpose of conditioning shall be prohibited. (d) The provisions of this section, as they relate to the duration and timeframe of tethering or confinement, shall not apply: (1) If the tethering or confinement is authorized for medical reasons in writing by a veterinarian licensed in Rhode Island, the authorization is renewed annually, and shelter is provided; (2) If tethering or confinement is authorized in writing by an animal control officer, or duly sworn police officer assigned to the animal control division, for the purposes, including, but not limited to, hunting dogs, dogs protecting livestock, and sled dogs. Written authorization must be renewed annually; Virginia

Code § 3.2-6500: "Adequate shelter" means provision of and access to shelter that is suitable for the species, age, condition, size, and type of each animal; provides adequate space for each animal; is safe and protects each animal from injury, rain, sleet, snow, hail, direct sunlight, the adverse effects of heat or cold, physical suffering, and impairment of health; is properly lighted; is properly cleaned; enables each animal to be clean and dry, except when detrimental to the species; and, for dogs and cats, provides a solid surface, resting platform, pad, floor mat, or similar device that is large enough for the animal to lie on in a normal manner and can be maintained in a sanitary manner. Under this chapter, shelters whose wire, grid, or slat floors: (i) permit the animals' feet to pass through the openings; (ii) sag under the animals' weight; or (iii) otherwise do not protect the animals' feet or toes from injury are not adequate shelter; 510 ILL. COMP. STAT. 70/3.01, No owner of a dog or cat that is a companion animal may expose the dog or cat in a manner that places the dog or cat in a life-threatening situation for a prolonged period of time in extreme heat or cold conditions.

22. Virginia separates adequate space and shelter by definition. "Adequate space" means sufficient space to allow each animal to: (i) easily stand, sit, lie, turn about, and make all other normal body movements in a comfortable, normal position for the animal; and (ii) interact safely with other animals in the enclosure. When an animal is tethered, "adequate space" means a tether that permits the above actions and is appropriate to the age and size of the animal; is attached to the animal by a properly applied collar, halter, or harness configured so as to protect the animal from injury and prevent the animal or tether from becoming entangled with other objects or animals, or from extending over an object or edge that could result in the strangulation or injury of the animal; and is at least three times the length of the animal, as measured from the tip of its nose to the base of its tail, except when the animal is being walked on a leash or is attached by a tether to a lead line. When freedom of movement would endanger the animal, temporarily and appropriately restricting movement of the animal according to professionally accepted standards for the species is considered provision of adequate space Virginia Code § 3.2-6500; Adequate Space: Animal Protection Laws of the United States (13th Edition), 2018 Animal Legal Defense Fund (https://aldf.org/project/us-state-rankings/): 18 PA. CONS. STAT. ANN. § 5536. Tethering of unattended dog (a) Presumptions.-- (1) Tethering an unattended dog out of doors for less than nine hours within a 24-hour period when all of the following conditions are present shall create a rebuttable presumption that a dog has not been the subject of neglect within the meaning of section 5532 (relating to neglect of animal): (i) The tether is of a type commonly used for the size and breed of dog and is at least three times the length of the dog as measured from the tip of its nose to the base of its tail or 10 feet, whichever is longer. (ii) The tether is secured to a well-fitted collar or harness by means of a swivel anchor, swivel latch or other mechanism designed to prevent the dog from becoming entangled. (iii) The tethered dog has access to potable water and an area of shade that permits the dog to escape the direct rays of the sun. (iv) The dog has not been tethered for longer than 30 minutes in temperatures above 90 or below 32 degrees Fahrenheit. (2) The presence of any of the following conditions regarding tethering an unattended dog out of doors shall create a rebuttable presumption that a dog has been the subject of neglect within the meaning of section 5532: (i) Excessive waste or excrement in the area where the dog is tethered. (ii) Open sores or wounds on the dog's body. (iii) The use of a tow or log chain, or a choke, pinch, prong or chain collar.
23. *Id.*
24. *Id.*
25. *Id.*
26. Va. Code Ann. § 3.2-6500; adequate shelter definition.
27. Some examples of strong anti-tethering ordinances can be found here: http://www.humanesociety.org/sites/default/files/archive/assets/pdfs/pets/Passing-a-Tethering-Ordinance.pdf
28. Sec. 4–96. Cruelty to animals: (d) It shall be unlawful for any person to fail to provide any dog with adequate space. (1) As used in this section, the term "adequate space" has the meaning ascribed to that term by Code of Virginia, § 3.2-6500. (2) It shall be unlawful for any person to tether a dog for more than one hour cumulatively within any 24-hour period, whether or not the tethered dog has been provided adequate space. No dog shall be tethered for any amount of time while the owner or custodian thereof is physically absent from the property where the dog is tethered. No dog shall be tethered for any amount of time in inclement, adverse, or extreme weather conditions; Norfolk Sec. 6.1–77. Failure to perform duties of ownership; d) It shall be unlawful for any animal to be tethered unless the owner or custodian is outside with the animal and the animal is in sight view.

29. Veterinary care: Animal Protection Laws of the United States (13th Edition), 2018 Animal Legal Defense Fund (https://aldf.org/project/us-state-rankings/): OR. REV. STAT. § 167.310. (As used in ORS 167.310 to 167.351): (9) "Minimum care" means care sufficient to preserve the health and well-being of an animal and, except for emergencies or circumstances beyond the reasonable control of the owner, includes, but is not limited to, the following requirements: (a) Food of sufficient quantity and quality to allow for normal growth or maintenance of body weight. (b) Open or adequate access to potable water in sufficient quantity to satisfy the animal's needs. Access to snow or ice is not adequate access to potable water. (c) For a domestic animal other than a dog engaged in herding or protecting livestock, access to adequate shelter. (d) Veterinary care deemed necessary by a reasonably prudent person to relieve distress from injury, neglect or disease; CAL. PENAL CODE § 597.1. California's law goes even further regarding veterinary care: (h) If the animal requires veterinary care and the humane society or public agency is not assured, within 14 days of the seizure of the animal, that the owner will provide the necessary care, the animal shall not be returned to its owner and shall be deemed to have been abandoned and may be disposed of by the seizing agency. A veterinarian may humanely destroy an impounded animal without regard to the prescribed holding period when it has been determined that the animal has incurred severe injuries or is incurably crippled. A veterinarian also may immediately humanely destroy an impounded animal afflicted with a serious contagious disease unless the owner or his or her agent immediately authorizes treatment of the animal by a veterinarian at the expense of the owner or agent; Maine ME. REV. STAT. ANN. tit. 7, § 4014. Necessary medical attention. No person owning or responsible for confining or impounding any animal may fail to supply the animal with necessary medical attention when the animal is or has been suffering from illness, injury, disease, excessive parasitism or malformed or overgrown hoof.
30. Adequate exercise: Animal Protection Laws of the United States (13th Edition), 2018 Animal Legal Defense Fund (https://aldf.org/project/us-state-rankings/): FLA. STAT. ANN. § 828.13. Confinement of animals without sufficient food, water, or exercise; abandonment of animals. (1) As used in this section: (a) "Abandon" means to forsake an animal entirely or to neglect or refuse to provide or perform the legal obligations for care and support of an animal by its owner. (b) "Owner" includes any owner, custodian, or other person in charge of an animal. (2) Whoever: (a) Impounds or confines any animal in any place and fails to supply the animal during such confinement with a sufficient quantity of good and wholesome food and water, (b) Keeps any animals in any enclosure without wholesome exercise and change of air, or (c) Abandons to die any animal that is maimed, sick, infirm, or diseased, is guilty of a misdemeanor of the first degree, punishable as provided in s. 775.082 or by a fine of not more than $5,000, or by both imprisonment and a fine.; Virginia Code § 3.2-6503, 3.2-6500: "Adequate exercise" or "exercise" means the opportunity for the animal to move sufficiently to maintain normal muscle tone and mass for the age, species, size, and condition of the animal.
31. *See supra* definitions of adequate care, footnote 10.
32. *See, e.g.*, Va. Code Ann. § 3.2-6500.
33. Owner: Animal Protection Laws of the United States (13th Edition), 2018 Animal Legal Defense Fund (https://aldf.org/project/us-state-rankings/): 510 ILL. COMP. STAT. 70/2.06. Owner defined. "Owner" means any person who (a) has a right of property in an animal, (b) keeps or harbors an animal, (c) has an animal in his care, or (d) acts as custodian of an animal; .Virginia Code § 3.2-6500: Owner defined as "any person who: (i) has a right of property in an animal; (ii) keeps or harbors an animal; (iii) has an animal in his care; or (iv) acts as a custodian of an animal.
34. *See supra* definitions of adequate care, footnote 10.
35. *Ferguson v. Ferguson*, 212 Va. 86, 92, 181 S.E.2d 648, 653 (1971).
36. Gross neglect in a cruelty statute: Va. Code Ann. § 3.2-6570(A)(iii); Animal Protection Laws of the United States (13th Edition), 2018 Animal Legal Defense Fund (https://aldf.org/project/us-state-rankings/): TEX. PENAL CODE ANN. § 42.09. Cruelty to Livestock Animals. (a) A person commits an offense if the person intentionally or knowingly: (1) tortures a livestock animal; (2) fails unreasonably to provide necessary food, water, or care for a livestock animal in the person's custody.
37. Va. Code Ann. § 3.2-6570(A)(i).
38. Intentional cruelty: "illtreat" is defined as cruelty treat or maltreat: Some statutes use the actually words, cruelly treats: Animal Protection Laws of the United States (13th Edition), 2018 Animal Legal Defense Fund (https://aldf.org/project/us-state-rankings/): 510 ILL. COMP. STAT. 70/3.01. Cruel treatment. (a) No person or owner may beat, cruelly treat, torment, starve, overwork or

otherwise or otherwise abuse any animal; Va Code § 3.2-6570(A)(i) A. Any person who: (i) overrides, overdrives, overloads, tortures, **ill-treats**, abandons, willfully inflicts inhumane injury or pain not connected with bona fide scientific or medical experimentation, or cruelly or unnecessarily beats, maims, mutilates, or kills any animal, whether belonging to himself or another.

39. Va. Code Ann. § 3.2-6570(A)(i).
40. *See, supra,* footnote 35. (water).
41. Va. Code Ann. § 3.2-6570(A)(iii).
42. Va. Code Ann. § 3.2-6500; "Emergency veterinary treatment" means veterinary treatment to stabilize a life-threatening condition, alleviate suffering, prevent further disease transmission, or prevent further disease progression.
43. Va. Code Ann. § 3.2-6500.
44. *Baker v. Commonwealth,* 2016 Va. Unpub. LEXIS 24 No. 151120. (2016).
45. *Id.*
46. *Id.*
47. *Id.*
48. Animal Protection Laws of the United States (13th Edition), 2018 Animal Legal Defense Fund (https://aldf.org/project/us-state-rankings/); Abandonment: 510 ILL. COMP. STAT. 70/3.01. Cruel treatment. (a) No person or owner may beat, cruelly treat, torment, starve, overwork or otherwise abuse any animal. (b) No owner may abandon any animal where it may become a public charge or may suffer injury, hunger or exposure; CAL. PENAL CODE § 597f. Abandoned or neglected animals; Duties of public authorities; Euthanasia. (a) Every owner, driver, or possessor of any animal, who permits the animal to be in any building, enclosure, lane, street, square, or lot, of any city, city and county, or judicial district, without proper care and attention, shall, on conviction, be deemed guilty of a misdemeanor. And it shall be the duty of any peace officer, officer of the humane society, or officer of a pound or animal regulation department of a public agency, to take possession of the animal so abandoned or neglected and care for the animal until it is redeemed by the owner or claimant, and the cost of caring for the animal shall be a lien on the animal until the charges are paid. Every sick, disabled, infirm, or crippled animal, except a dog or cat, which shall be abandoned in any city, city and county, or judicial district, may, if after due search no owner can be found therefore, be killed by the officer; and it shall be the duty of all peace officers, an officer of such society, or officer of a pound or animal regulation department of a public agency to cause the animal to be killed on information of such abandonment. The officer may likewise take charge of any animal, including a dog or cat, that by reason of lameness, sickness, feebleness, or neglect, is unfit for the labor it is performing, or that in any other manner is being cruelly treated; and, if the animal is not then in the custody of its owner, the officer shall give notice thereof to the owner, if known, and may provide suitable care for the animal until it is deemed to be in a suitable condition to be delivered to the owner, and any necessary expenses which may be incurred for taking care of and keeping the animal shall be a lien thereon, to be paid before the animal can be lawfully recovered; MICH. COMP. LAWS § 750.50. Definitions; crimes against animals, cruel treatment, abandonment, failure to provide adequate care, etc.; penalties; multiple prosecutions; payment of costs; exceptions. Sec. 50. (2) An owner, possessor, or person having the charge or custody of an animal shall not do any of the following: (e) Abandon an animal or cause an animal to be abandoned, in any place, without making provisions for the animal's adequate care, unless premises are vacated for the protection of human life or the prevention of injury to a human. An animal that is lost by an owner or custodian while traveling, walking, hiking, or hunting is not abandoned under this section when the owner or custodian has made a reasonable effort to locate the animal.
49. Animal Protection Laws of the United States (13th Edition), 2018 Animal Legal Defense Fund (https://aldf.org/project/us-state-rankings/); Willfully inflicting (inhumane) injury or pain (intentional cruelty): WASH. REV. CODE § 16.52.205. Animal cruelty in the first degree. (1) A person is guilty of animal cruelty in the first degree when, except as authorized in law, he or she intentionally (a) inflicts substantial pain on, (b) causes physical injury to, or (c) kills an animal by a means causing undue suffering or while manifesting an extreme indifference to life, or forces a minor to inflict unnecessary pain, injury, or death on an animal; FLA. STAT. ANN. § 828.12. Cruelty to animals. (1) A person who unnecessarily overloads, overdrives, torments, deprives of necessary sustenance or shelter, or unnecessarily mutilates, or kills any animal, or causes the same to be done, or carries in or upon any vehicle, or otherwise, any animal in a cruel

or inhumane manner, commits animal cruelty, a misdemeanor of the first degree, punishable as provided in s. 775.082 or by a fine of not more than $ 5,000, or both. (2) A person who intentionally commits an act to any animal, or a person who owns or has the custody or control of any animal and fails to act, which results in the cruel death, or excessive or repeated infliction of unnecessary pain or suffering, or causes the same to be done, commits aggravated animal cruelty, a felony of the third degree, punishable as provided in s. 775.082 or by a fine of not more than $ 10,000, or both.

50. *Pelloni v. Commonwealth*, 65 Va. App. 733 (2016).
51. Animal Protection Laws of the United States (13th Edition), 2018 Animal Legal Defense Fund (https://aldf.org/project/us-state-rankings/): CAL. PENAL CODE § 597. Cruelty to animals. (a) Except as provided in subdivision (c) of this section or Section 599c, every person who maliciously and intentionally maims, mutilates, tortures, or wounds a living animal, or maliciously and intentionally kills an animal, is guilty of a crime punishable pursuant to subdivision (d). (b) Except as otherwise provided in subdivision (a) or (c), every person who overdrives, overloads, drives when overloaded, overworks, tortures, torments, deprives of necessary sustenance, drink, or shelter, cruelly beats, mutilates, or cruelly kills any animal, or causes or procures any animal to be so overdriven, overloaded, driven when overloaded, overworked, tortured, tormented, deprived of necessary sustenance, drink, shelter, or to be cruelly beaten, mutilated, or cruelly killed; and whoever, having the charge or custody of any animal, either as owner or otherwise, subjects any animal to needless suffering, or inflicts unnecessary cruelty upon the animal, or in any manner abuses any animal, or fails to provide the animal with proper food, drink, or shelter or protection from the weather, or who drives, rides, or otherwise uses the animal when unfit for labor, is, for each offense, guilty of a crime punishable pursuant to subdivision (d); MASS. GEN. LAWS ch. 272, § 77. Cruelty to Animals. Whoever overdrives, overloads, drives when overloaded, overworks, tortures, torments, deprives of necessary sustenance, cruelly beats, mutilates or kills an animal, or causes or procures an animal to be overdriven, overloaded, driven when overloaded, overworked, tortured, tormented, deprived of necessary sustenance, cruelly beaten, mutilated or killed; and whoever uses in a cruel or inhuman manner in a race, game, or contest, or in training therefor, as lure or bait a live animal, except an animal if used as lure or bait in fishing; and whoever, having the charge or custody of an animal, either as owner or otherwise, inflicts unnecessary cruelty upon it, or unnecessarily fails to provide it with proper food, drink, shelter, sanitary environment, or protection from the weather, and whoever, as owner, possessor, or person having the charge or custody of an animal, cruelly drives or works it when unfit for labor, or willfully abandons it, or carries it or causes it to be carried in or upon a vehicle, or otherwise, in an unnecessarily cruel or inhuman manner or in a way and manner which might endanger the animal carried thereon, or knowingly and willfully authorizes or permits it to be subjected to unnecessary torture, suffering or cruelty of any kind shall be punished by imprisonment in the state prison for not more than 7 years in state prison or imprisonment in the house of correction for not more than 2 1/2 years or by a fine of not more than $5,000 or by both fine and imprisonment; provided, however, that a second or subsequent offense shall be punished by imprisonment in the state prison for not more than 10 years or by a fine of not more than $10,000 or by both such fine and imprisonment. Notwithstanding section 26 of chapter 218 or any other general or special law to the contrary, the district courts and the divisions of the Boston municipal court department shall have original jurisdiction, concurrent with the superior court, of a violation of this section; IND. CODE § 35-46-3-12. Beating vertebrate (c) A person who knowingly or intentionally tortures or mutilates a vertebrate animal commits torturing or mutilating a vertebrate animal, a Level 6 felony.
52. Definition of animal: Animal Protection Laws of the United States (13th Edition), 2018 Animal Legal Defense Fund (https://aldf.org/project/us-state-rankings/): IND. CODE § 35-46-3-3. "Animal" defined. As used in this chapter, "animal" does not include a human being; ME. REV. STAT. ANN. tit. 7, § 3907. Definitions. 2. Animal. "Animal" means every living, sentient creature not a human being; CAL. PENAL CODE § 599b. Words and phrases; imputation of knowledge to corporation. In this title, the word "animal" includes every dumb creature.
53. Va. Code Ann.§ 3.2-6570(A)(i); https://law.justia.com/codes/virginia/2014/title-3.2/section-3.2-6570/.
54. https://www.aspca.org/animal-cruelty/dogfighting/closer-look-dogfighting; (Although it is a felony offense in all 50 states, organized dogfighting still takes place in many parts of the country. Historical accounts date as far back as the 1750s, with professional fighting pits proliferating in the 1860s.); https://www.humanesociety.org/resources/cockfighting-fact-sheet. (It is illegal in every

state, and most states specifically prohibit anyone from being a spectator at a cockfight. As of 2011, 39 states have passed felony cockfighting laws. In addition, the federal Animal Welfare Act prohibits the interstate transport of any animal that is to be used in an animal fighting venture).
55. *Id.*
56. https://www.law.cornell.edu/wex/direct_evidence.
57. https://www.law.cornell.edu/wex/circumstantial_evidence.
58. https://www.humanesociety.org/resources/cockfighting-fact-sheet.
59. https://www.aspca.org/animal-cruelty/dogfighting/closer-look-dogfighting.
60. *Id.*
61. Animal Fighting: Animal Protection Laws of the United States (13th Edition), 2018 Animal Legal Defense Fund (https://aldf.org/project/us-state-rankings/): 510 ILL. COMP. STAT. 70/4.01. Animals in entertainment.; No person shall own, possess, sell or offer for sale, ship, transport, or otherwise move any equipment or device which such person knows or should know is intended for use in connection with any show, exhibition, program, or activity featuring or otherwise involving a fight between 2 or more animals, or any animal and human, or the intentional killing of any animal for purposes of sport, wagering or entertainment: § 3.2-6571. Animal fighting; A. No person shall knowingly: 1. Promote, prepare for, engage in, or be employed in, the fighting of animals for amusement, sport or gain; (B) 5. When any animal is possessed, owned, trained, transported, or sold with the intent that the animal engage in an exhibition of fighting with another animal; CAL. PENAL CODE § 597j. Persons who own, possess or keep or train any bird or other animal with intent that it be used or engaged in fighting exhibition; penalties. (a) Any person who owns, possesses, keeps, or trains any bird or other animal with the intent that it be used or engaged by himself or herself, by his or her vendee, or by any other person in an exhibition of fighting as described in Section 597b is guilty of a misdemeanor punishable by imprisonment in a county jail for a period not to exceed one year, by a fine not to exceed ten thousand dollars ($10,000), or by both that imprisonment and fine; CAL. PENAL CODE § 597.5. Fighting dogs; felony; punishment; spectators; misdemeanor; exceptions. (a) Any person who does any of the following is guilty of a felony and is punishable by imprisonment pursuant to subdivision (h) of Section 1170 for 16 months, or two or three years, or by a fine not to exceed fifty thousand dollars ($50,000), or by both that fine and imprisonment: (1) Owns, possesses, keeps, or trains any dog, with the intent that the dog shall be engaged in an exhibition of fighting with another dog.
62. Animal Protection Laws of the United States (13th Edition), 2018 Animal Legal Defense Fund (https://aldf.org/project/us-state-rankings/): CAL. PENAL CODE § 597i. Cockfighting implements; prohibitions; penalties. (a) It shall be unlawful for anyone to manufacture, buy, sell, barter, exchange, or have in his or her possession any of the implements commonly known as gaffs or slashers, or any other sharp implement designed to be attached in place of the natural spur of a gamecock or other fighting bird; 510 ILL. COMP. STAT. 70/4.01. Animals in entertainment (d) No person shall manufacture for sale, shipment, transportation or delivery any device or equipment which that person knows or should know is intended for use in any show, exhibition, program, or other activity featuring or otherwise involving a fight between 2 or more animals, or any human and animal, or the intentional killing of any animal for purposes of sport, wagering or entertainment; Virginia Code § 3.2-6571. Animal fighting; penalty. A (1) (B)(2). When any device or substance intended to enhance an animal's ability to fight or to inflict injury upon another animal is used, or possessed with intent to use it for such purpose; NEV. REV. STAT. § 574.070. I (b) Manufacture, own, possess, purchase, sell, barter or exchange, or advertise for sale, barter or exchange, any gaff, spur or other sharp implement designed for attachment to a cock or other bird with the intent that the implement be used in fighting another cock or other bird. 4. Except as otherwise provided in subsection; COLO. REV. STAT. § 18-9-204. (1)(b)(VI) Knowingly possesses any animal used for such a fight or any device intended to enhance the animal's fighting ability.
63. Animal Protection Laws of the United States (13th Edition), 2018 Animal Legal Defense Fund (https://aldf.org/project/us-state-rankings/): NEV. REV. STAT. § 574.070. 2. A person shall not: (a) Own, possess, keep, train, promote or purchase an animal with the intent to use it to fight another animal; Any person who knowingly commits any of the following acts commits a felony of the third degree, punishable as provided in s. 775.082, s. 775.083, or s. 775.084; FLA. STAT. ANN. § 828.122. F (3) (a) Baiting, breeding, training, transporting, selling, owning, possessing, or using any wild or domestic animal for the purpose of animal fighting or baiting; R.I. GEN. LAWS § 4-1-10. Possession or training of fighting animals. Whoever owns, possesses, keeps or trains any bird, dog, or other animal, with the

intent that that bird, dog, or animal engages in an exhibition of fighting, shall be fined not exceeding one thousand dollars ($1,000) and/or be imprisoned not exceeding two (2) years for the first offense, and for any subsequent offense shall be fined not less than one thousand dollars ($1,000) nor more than five thousand dollars ($5,000) or be imprisoned not exceeding two (2) years, or both.

64. Animal Protection Laws of the United States (13th Edition), 2018 Animal Legal Defense Fund (https://aldf.org/project/us-state-rankings/): Virginia Code § 3.2-6571(A)(1)(B)(3) 3. When money or anything of value is wagered on the result of such fighting; COLO. REV. STAT. § 18-9-204. (1)(b)(I) Is knowingly present at or wagers on such a fight; A. REV. STAT. ANN. § 14:102.5.(A)(4) Sell a ticket of admission or receive money for the admission of any person to any place used, or about to be used, for any activity described in Paragraph (2).
65. Animal Protection Laws of the United States (13th Edition), 2018 Animal Legal Defense Fund (https://aldf.org/project/us-state-rankings/): 510 ILL. COMP. STAT. 70/4.01 (l) No person shall solicit a minor to violate this Section; Virginia Code § 3.2-6571(B) (6). When he permits or causes a minor to (i) attend an exhibition of the fighting of any animals or (ii) undertake or be involved in any act described in this subsection.
66. Virginia Code § 3.2-6571 A. No person shall knowingly: 1. Promote, prepare for, engage in, or be employed in, the fighting of animals for amusement, sport or gain, 3. Authorize or allow any person to undertake any act described in this section on any premises under his charge or control; or4. Aid or abet any such acts; ANIMAL PROTECTION LAWS OF THE USA (13TH EDITION), 2018 Animal Legal Defense Fund (https://aldf.org/project/us-state-rankings/): WASH. REV. CODE § 16.52.117. (1)(c) Keeps or uses any place for the purpose of animal fighting, or manages or accepts payment of admission to any place kept or used for the purpose of animal fighting; (d) Suffers or permits any place over which the person has possession or control to be occupied, kept, or used for the purpose of an exhibition of animal fighting.
67. Animal Protection Laws of the United States (13th Edition), 2018 Animal Legal Defense Fund (https://aldf.org/project/us-state-rankings/): WASH. REV. CODE § 16.52.117. (1) (b) Promotes, organizes, conducts, participates in, is a spectator of, advertises, prepares, or performs any service in the furtherance of, an exhibition of animal fighting, transports spectators to an animal fight, or provides or serves as a stakeholder for any money wagered on an animal fight; MASS. GEN. LAWS ch. 272, § 95. Penalty for Being Present at Exhibition, etc. Whoever is present at any place, building or tenement where preparations are being made for an exhibition of the fighting of birds, dogs or other animals, with intent to be present at such exhibition, or is present at, aids in or contributes to such exhibition, shall be punished by a fine of not more than $1,000 or by imprisonment in the state prison for not more than 5 years or imprisonment in the house of correction for not more than 2 ½ years or by both such fine and imprisonment.; IND. CODE § 35-46-3-9. Promotion, use of animals or attendance with animal at animal fighting contest. A person who knowingly or intentionally: (1) promotes or stages an animal fighting contest; (2) uses an animal in a fighting contest; or (3) attends an animal fighting contest having an animal in the person's possession; commits a Level 6 felony
68. https://www.justice.gov/opa/pr/new-mexico-man-sentenced-four-years-prison-role-multi-state-dog-fighting-conspiracy.
69. https://www.humanesociety.org/news/vermont-governor-signs-bill-banning-sexual-abuse-animals.
70. Animal Protection Laws of the United States (13th Edition), 2018 Animal Legal Defense Fund (https://aldf.org/project/us-state-rankings/): R.I. GEN. LAWS § 11-10-1. Abominable and detestable crime against nature. Every person who shall be convicted of the abominable and detestable crime against nature, with any beast, shall be imprisoned not exceeding twenty (20) years nor less than seven (7) years; MICH. COMP. LAWS § 750.158. Crime against nature or sodomy; penalty. Sec. 158. Any person who shall commit the abominable and detestable crime against nature either with mankind or with any animal shall be guilty of a felony, punishable by imprisonment in the state prison not more than 15 years, or if such person was at the time of the said offense a sexually delinquent person, may be punishable by imprisonment in the state prison for an indeterminate term, the minimum of which shall be 1 day and the maximum of which shall be life; CAL. PENAL CODE § 286.5. Sexually assaulting animal; misdemeanor. Any person who sexually assaults any animal protected by Section 597f for the purpose of arousing or gratifying the sexual desire of the person is guilty of a misdemeanor.

71. Animal Protection Laws of the United States (13th Edition), 2018 Animal Legal Defense Fund (https://aldf.org/project/us-state-rankings/): OR. REV. STAT. § 163A.005 (1)(s) Sexual assault of an animal; WASH. REV. CODE § 16.52.205. (3) A person is guilty of animal cruelty in the first degree when he or she: (a) Knowingly engages in any sexual conduct or sexual contact with an animal; (b) Knowingly causes, aids, or abets another person to engage in any sexual conduct or sexual contact with an animal; (c) Knowingly permits any sexual conduct or sexual contact with an animal to be conducted on any premises under his or her charge or control; (d) Knowingly engages in, organizes, promotes, conducts, advertises, aids, abets, participates in as an observer, or performs any service in the furtherance of an act involving any sexual conduct or sexual contact with an animal for a commercial or recreational purpose; or (e) Knowingly photographs or films, for purposes of sexual gratification, a person engaged in a sexual act or sexual contact with an animal; IND. CODE § 35-42-4-5. (b)(2) engage in sexual conduct with an animal other than a human being.
72. FLA. STAT. ANN. § 828.126. Sexual activities involving animals. (1) As used in this section, the term: (a) "Sexual conduct" means any touching or fondling by a person, either directly or through clothing, of the sex organs or anus of an animal or any transfer or transmission of semen by the person upon any part of the animal for the purpose of sexual gratification or arousal of the person. (b) "Sexual contact" means any contact, however slight, between the mouth, sex organ, or anus of a person and the sex organ or anus of an animal, or any penetration, however slight, of any part of the body of the person into the sex organ or anus of an animal, or any penetration of the sex organ or anus of the person into the mouth of the animal, for the purpose of sexual gratification or sexual arousal of the person. (2) A person may not: (a) Knowingly engage in any sexual conduct or sexual contact with an animal; (b) Knowingly cause, aid, or abet another person to engage in any sexual conduct or sexual contact with an animal; (c) Knowingly permit any sexual conduct or sexual contact with an animal to be conducted on any premises under his or her charge or control; or (d) Knowingly organize, promote, conduct, advertise, aid, abet, participate in as an observer, or perform any service in the furtherance of an act involving any sexual conduct or sexual contact with an animal for a commercial or recreational purpose.
73. https://www.brainyquote.com/quotes/mahatma_gandhi_150700.
74. Waisman, S.S., Frasch, P.D., & Wagman, B.A. 2014. *Animal Law: Cases and Materials*, 5th ed., Carolina Free Press, p. 35.
75. Baldry, A.C. 2005. Animal abuse among preadolescents directly and indirectly victimized at school and at home. *Criminal Behavior and Mental Health*, 15, 97–110; *Barrett, B.J., Fitzgerald, A, Stevenson, R., & Cheung, C.H. 2017. Animal maltreatment as a risk marker of more frequent and severe forms of intimate partner violence. *Journal of Interpersonal Violence*, doi: 10.1177/0886260517719542; Bright, M.A., Huq, M.S., Spencer, T, Applebaum, J.W., & Hardt, N. 2018. Animal cruelty as an indicator of family trauma: Using adverse childhood experiences to look beyond child abuse and domestic violence. *Child Abuse & Neglect*, 76, 287–296; Duncan, A., Thomas, J.C., & Miller, C. 2005. Significance of family risk factors in development of childhood animal cruelty in adolescent boys with conduct problems. *Journal of Family Violence*, 20, 235–239; Febres, J., Brasfield, H., Shorey, R.C., Elmquist, J., Ninnemann, A., Schonrum, Y.C., & Stuart, G. 2014. Adulthood animal abuse among men arrested for domestic violence. *Violence Against Women*, 20, 1059–1077; Hensley, C., Browne, J.A., & Trenthamm, C.E. 2018. Exploring the social and emotional context of childhood animal cruelty and its potential link to human violence. *Psychology, Crime and Law*, 24, 489–499.
76. Ascione, F.R. Weber, C.V., Thompson, T.M., Heath, J., Maruyama, M., & Hayashi, K. 2007. Battered pets and domestic violence: Animal abuse reported by women experiencing initiate violence and by non-abused women. *Violence Against Women*, 13, 354–373; Ascione, F.R., Weber, C.V., & Wood, D.S. 1997. The abuse of animals and domestic violence: A national survey of shelters for women who are battered. *Society & Animals*, 5, 205–218.
77. https://www.miamiherald.com/opinion/op-ed/article207997174.html.
78. https://www.washingtonpost.com/news/posteverything/wp/2018/02/21/how-reliably-does-animal-torture-predict-a-future-mass-shooter/?noredirect=on&utm_term=.9caf5e76496b.
79. Ascione, F.R. Weber, C.V., Thompson, T.M., Heath, J., Maruyama, M., & Hayashi, K. 2007. Battered pets and domestic violence: Animal abuse reported by women experiencing initiate violence and by non-abused women. *Violence Against Women*, 13, 354–373; Ascione, F.R., Weber, C.V., & Wood, D.S. 1997. The abuse of animals and domestic violence: A national survey of shelters for women who are battered. *Society & Animals*, 5, 205–218.
80. https://www.miamiherald.com/opinion/op-ed/article207997174.html.

81. https://www.miamiherald.com/opinion/op-ed/article207997174.html.
82. *Id.*
83. http://maamodt.asp.radford.edu/Psyc%20405/serial%20killers/Berkowitz,%20David.pdf.
84. https://www.miamiherald.com/opinion/op-ed/article207997174.html.
85. *Id.*
86. Probable cause standards are often used in search warrants or preliminary hearings. It means Courts usually find probable cause when there is a reasonable basis for believing that a crime may have been committed (for an arrest) or when evidence of the crime is present in the place to be searched (for a search). Cornell Law School. Legal Information Institute, 1992. https://www.law.cornell.edu/wex/probable_cause.
87. Reasonable doubt means sufficient doubt on the part of jurors for acquittal of a defendant based on a lack of evidence. Cornell Law School. Legal Information Institute, 1992. https://www.law.cornell.edu/wex/reasonable_doubt.
88. Serious bodily injury means bodily injury that involves substantial risk of death, extreme physical pain, protracted and obvious disfigurement, or protracted loss or impairment of the function of a bodily member, organ, or mental faculty. https://lis.virginia.gov/cgi-bin/legp604.exe?191+ful+CHAP0536.
89. https://lis.virginia.gov/cgi-bin/legp604.exe?191+ful+CHAP0536.
90. https://www.avma.org/KB/Resources/Reference/AnimalWelfare/Pages/Abuse-Reporting-requirements-by-State.aspx.

INDEX

A

C

G

H

I

K

L

N

O

P

Q

R

U

V

W

X

Y

Z

For Product Safety Concerns and Information please contact our EU representative GPSR@taylorandfrancis.com Taylor & Francis Verlag GmbH, Kaufingerstraße 24, 80331 München, Germany

Batch number: 10777152

Printed by Printforce, the Netherlands